BETTINA

BETTINA

Photographs and works by Bettina Grossman
Texts by Yto Barrada, Ruba Katrib, and Antonia Pocock
Edited by Yto Barrada and Gregor Huber

aperture

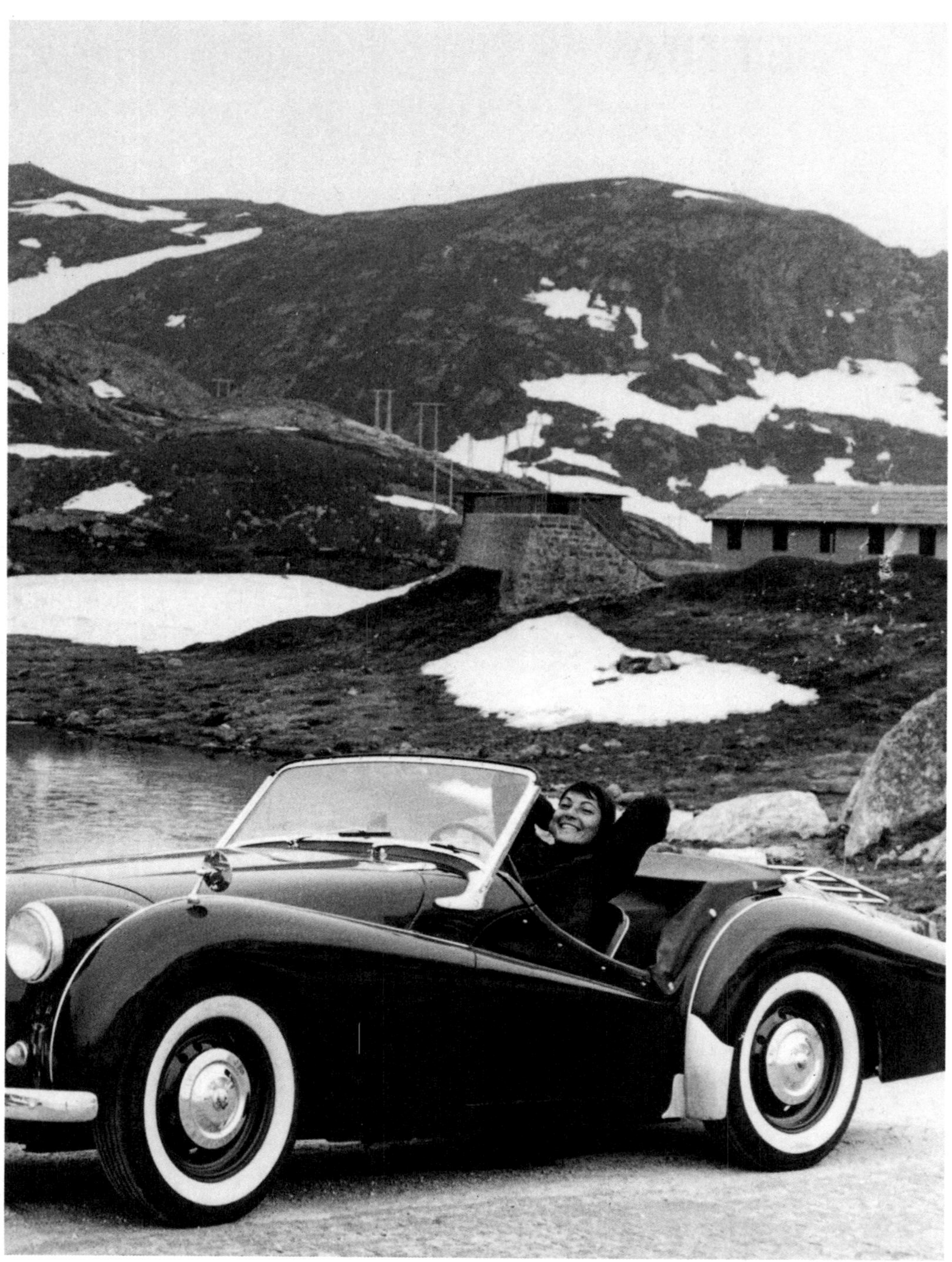

Bettina, Switzerland, 1960s

For a series of works on paper created in the 1970s, Bettina Grossman xeroxed strands of her hair, transforming them into abstracted, twisted, and bundled lines. As a viewer looks at them today, sinuous strands start to take their own form, each one unique. These intimate works are key examples of Bettina's working methodology—a system of reduction that reveals new qualities—but they may also operate as metaphors for the arc of Bettina's own life, and more broadly the twists and turns that each journey takes. In these abstract line drawings that center on the reduction of one thing, another thing emerges. In some sketches, three-dimensional shapes appear out of the two-dimensional strands of hair, bringing forth new qualities of depth and potential. What was previously unseen can become visible, or at least imagined. This process of one thing leading to another can be seen throughout Bettina's biography. Key events deeply impacted her and affected her trajectory as an artist, notably the devastating fire she suffered in her Brooklyn studio in 1966. This was the destructive and traumatic event that dogged her, even as it gave her renewed purpose to keep going and a mission to build back what she lost. However, the precariousness of being a woman artist in the 1960s couldn't withstand a setback of that caliber—the wholesale loss of her work to date. Bettina was burdened with the feeling that she had to start over, that whatever headway she had made was lost. It was a sensation that took her years to shake.

The fire wasn't the only event that charted the course of Bettina's life and work. As this publication makes evident, an artist is part of the world; they touch it and it touches them. Even when an artist is described as a "recluse," as Bettina was at times, during her last decades, it is a community that supports and sustains artists. Later in her life, it was younger artists who became the stewards of her work. As often happens, new generations are ready to receive artists who were ahead of their time. For Bettina, these encounters with younger artists, importantly with Yto Barrada, whom Bettina engaged in her artistic legacy, marked a new turn for her and signaled a renewed interest in her work prior to her death in 2021. During the years she worked in relative obscurity, Bettina was here, charting her path and creating a body of work that ultimately surpassed what was lost in the blaze.

Bettina's oeuvre reveals her resilience, intelligence, and inventiveness. Her work is a contribution to Conceptual art, as well as a document of, and portal into, a unique artistic practice. Living in the Chelsea Hotel from 1972 until her death, she took her immediate surroundings—her room, the hotel, the neighborhood, the city—as much of her subject matter. She used straightforward and humble methods for creating complex works. After the fire, some of her first pieces were a series of black-and-white sculptures made in marble—hardy objects that played with line and form. But she used her neighborhood and the city as a source of inspiration and deep looking. Her location on the fifth floor on Twenty-Third Street became a key nexus of her artistic activity, always nourished by her refined sense of abstraction. Bettina was drawn to the everyday, whether the strands of hair found in her apartment to her views from her window, zeroing in on a Conceptual art practice that took biography and even anthropology as organizing principles. Bettina's lens-based works tracked the patterns, as well as their distortions, on her block. She took photographs from her balcony recording the behaviors and commonalities between New Yorkers strolling down the street; people walking while reading, people carrying umbrellas, people wearing red, and other recurring commonplace activities that speak to the qualities of life in the city. Even some of those aerial views of pedestrians were transformed by Bettina's copying, distilled until they became shape and form, figures merging with shadow. She photographed and filmed distortions on the glass and steel of buildings, creating surreal portals into a familiar yet warped city. She catalogued newspaper headlines and created lists tracking her observations, which in turn generated new categories for her artistic inquiries.

The trove of Bettina's work speaks to a legacy that will continue to be unpacked and sorted, much as she sorted the world around her. This publication offers many important entry points into a rich and complex practice. In this work, we meet an artist who understands the importance of looking and recording, as well as touching on and working through the loss that is an inevitable part of life.

Ruba Katrib

Contents

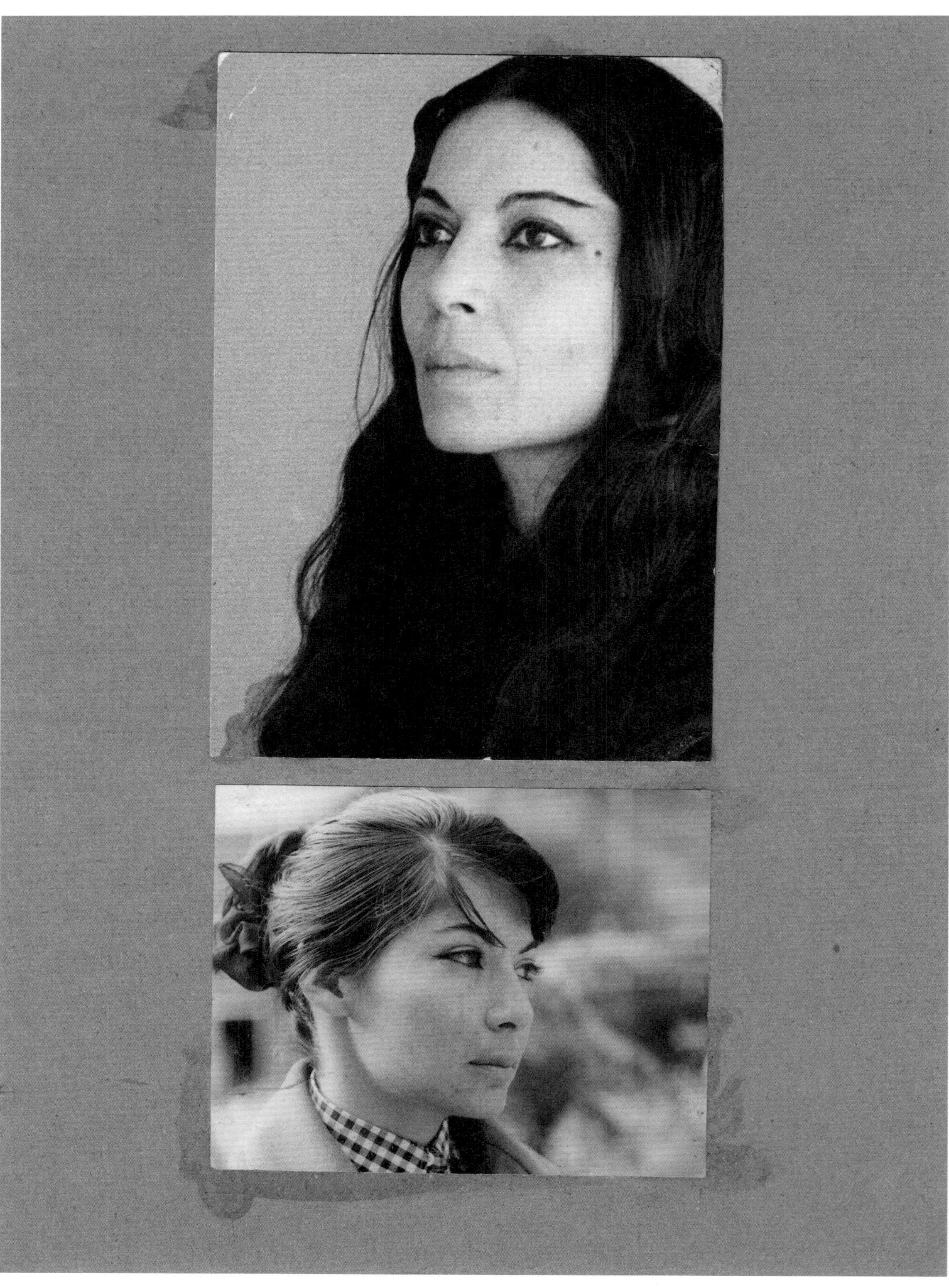

Portraits of Bettina from her scrapbooks, ca. 1970s (top); 1960s (bottom)

"When I get really angry—like, when I think, *This work is Stolen*—instead of screaming bloody murder, I make a word work: *Contribution*. My contribution. *Attribution*. My tribute ... *Retribution*. And *Institution* ... and *Substitution* ... they substituted a dupe for an original. And then there's ... *Constitution*. And then there's *Destitution*. And then there's *Restitution*."

EXPRESSION
REPRESSION
DIGRESSION
SUPPRESSION
DEPRESSION
OPPRESSION
REGRESSION
AGGRESSION

SANCTUARY
protect the magic

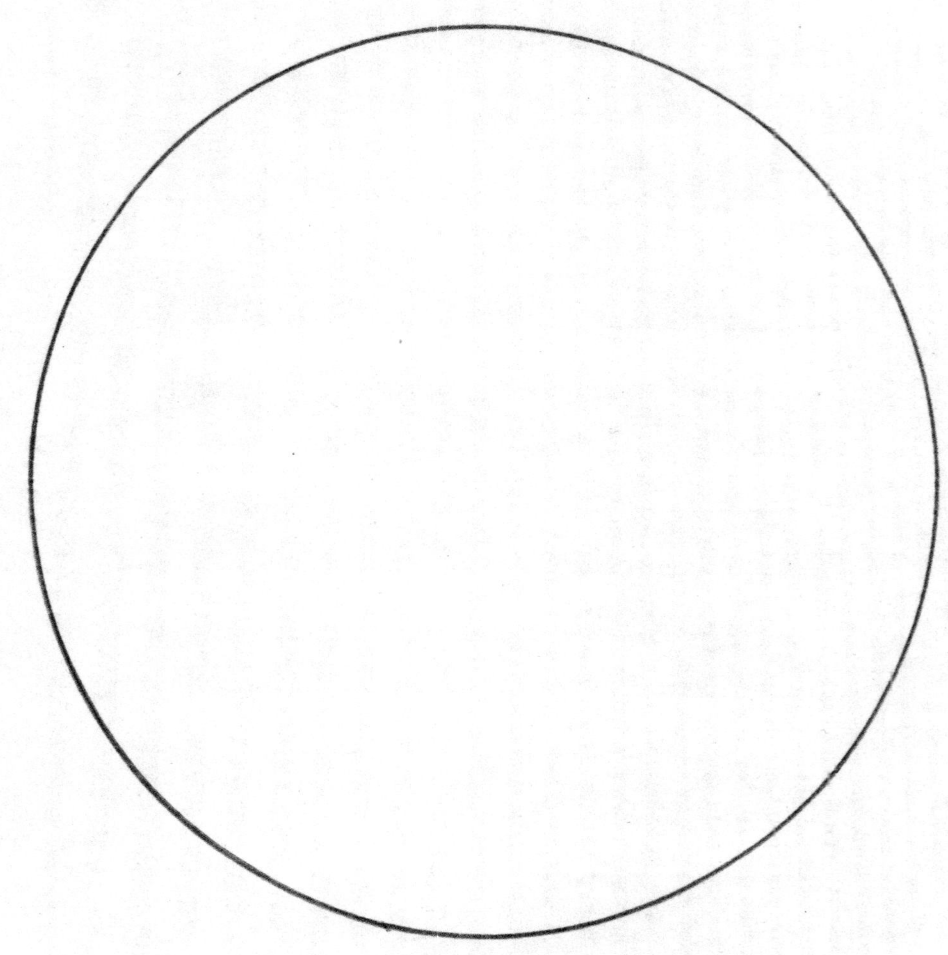

WORLD TRADE CENTER / 1975

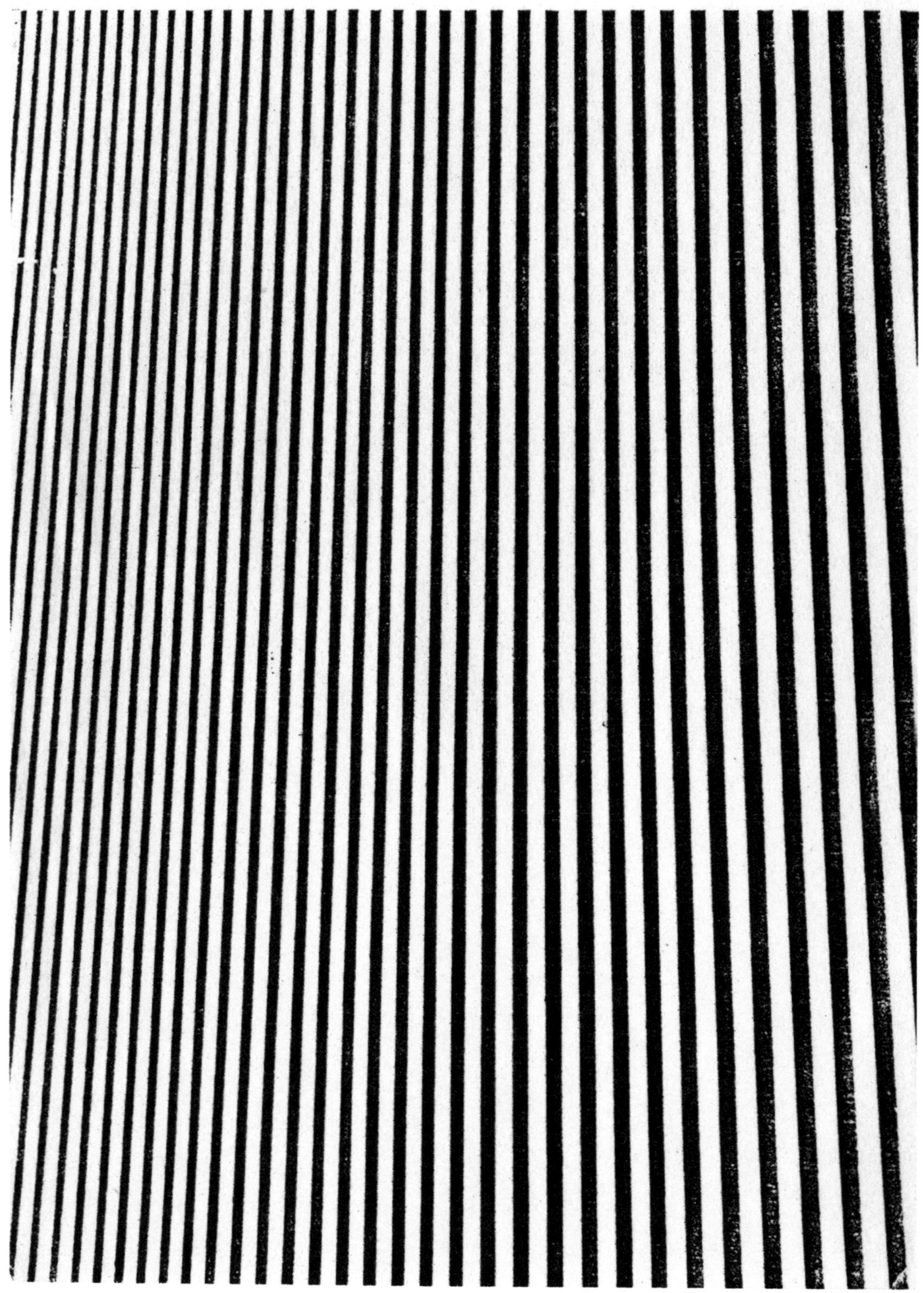

N.Y. BANKERS STEPS 1975

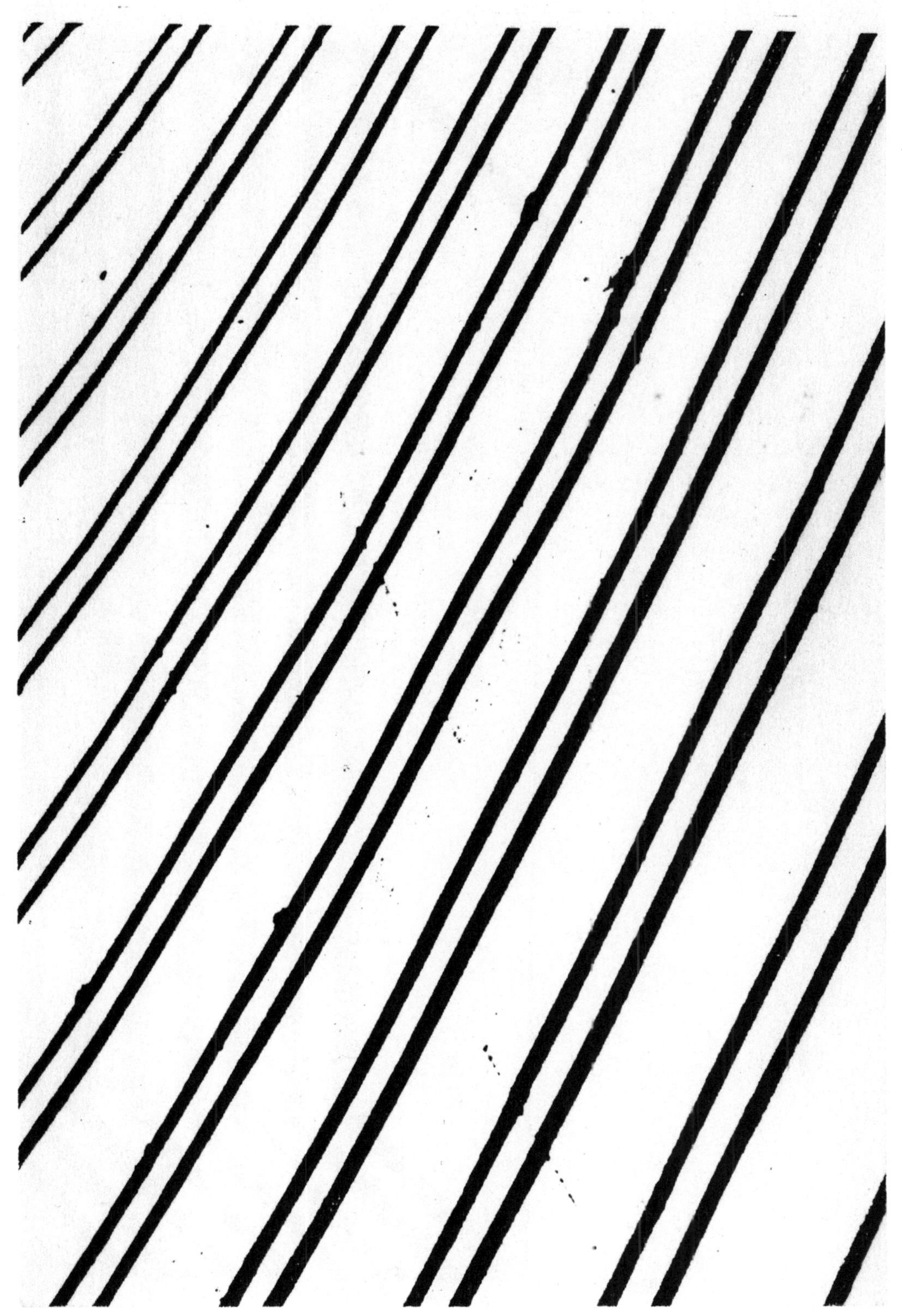

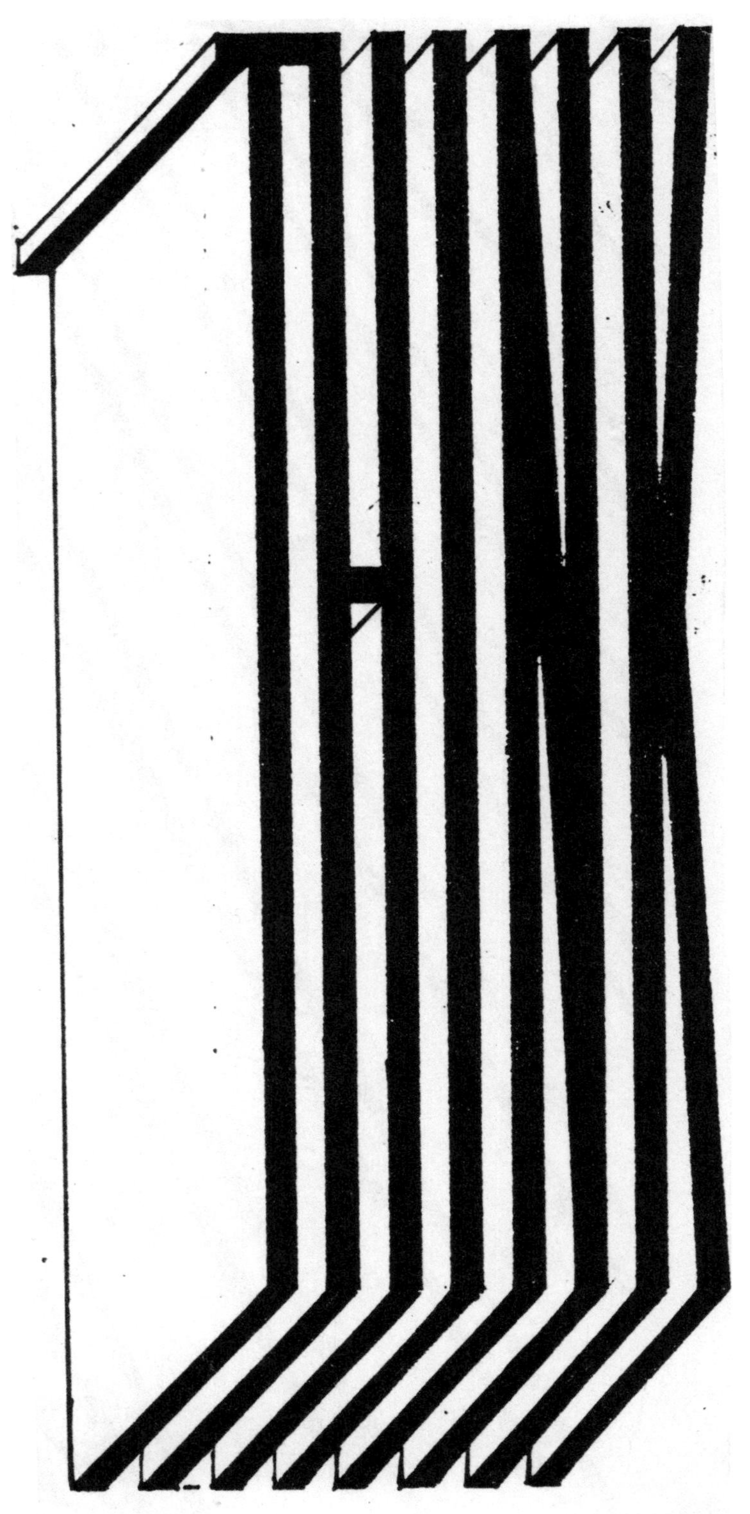
THINK

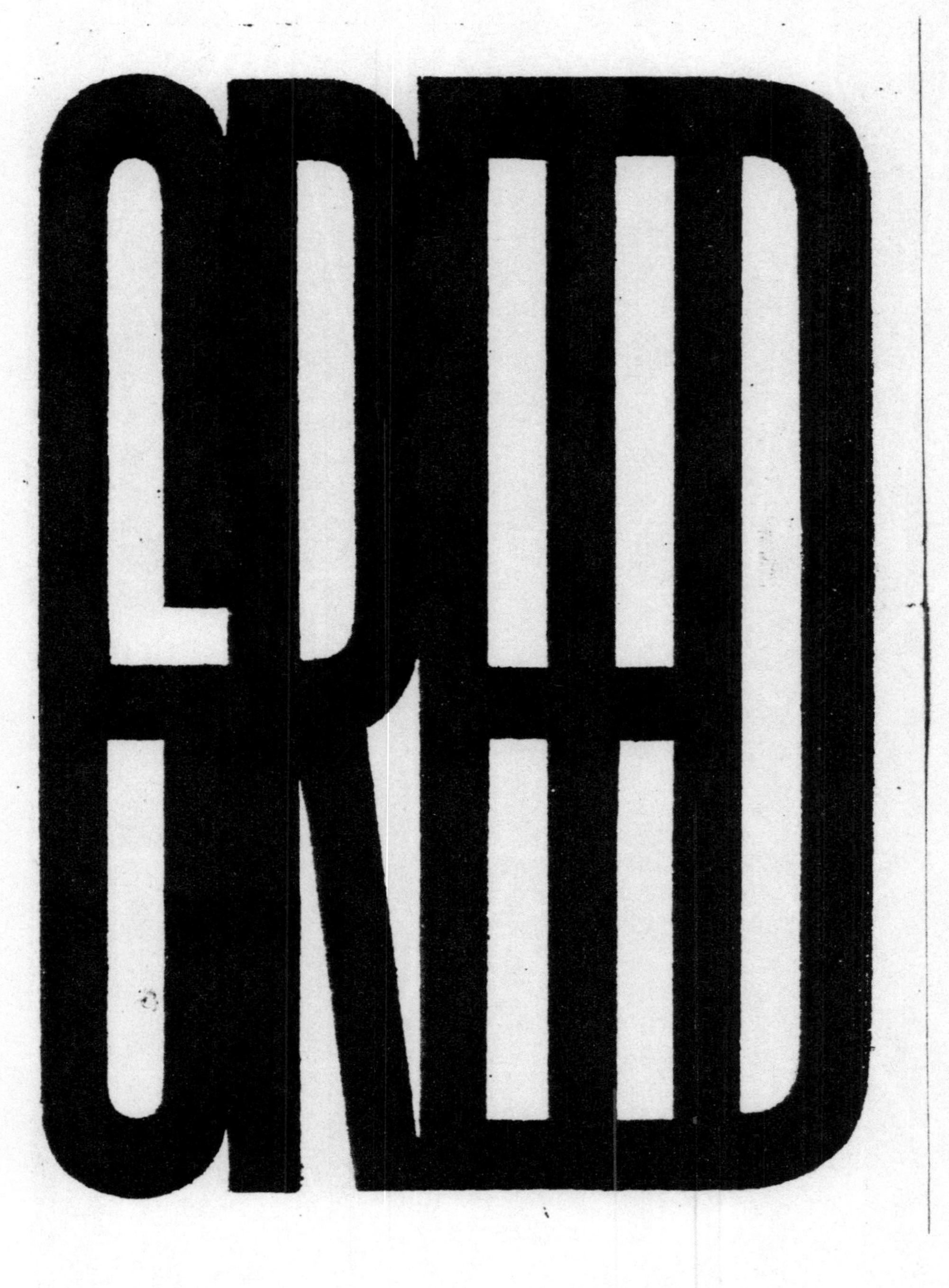

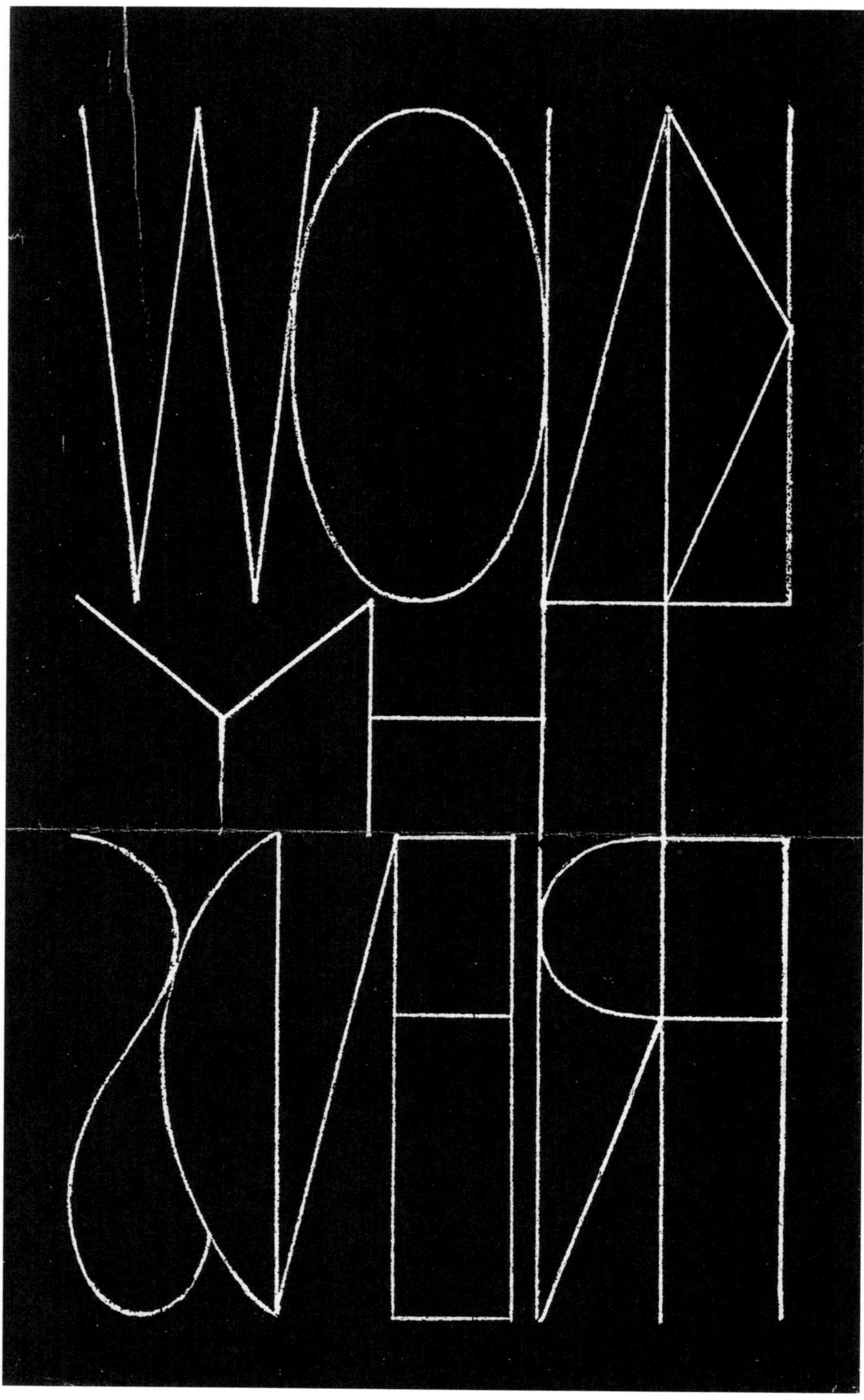

NEW YORK PATTERN BOOK
four-dimensional studies in random constant
from phenomenological new york / urban energy strategies 1972-86
film/video/serial-image

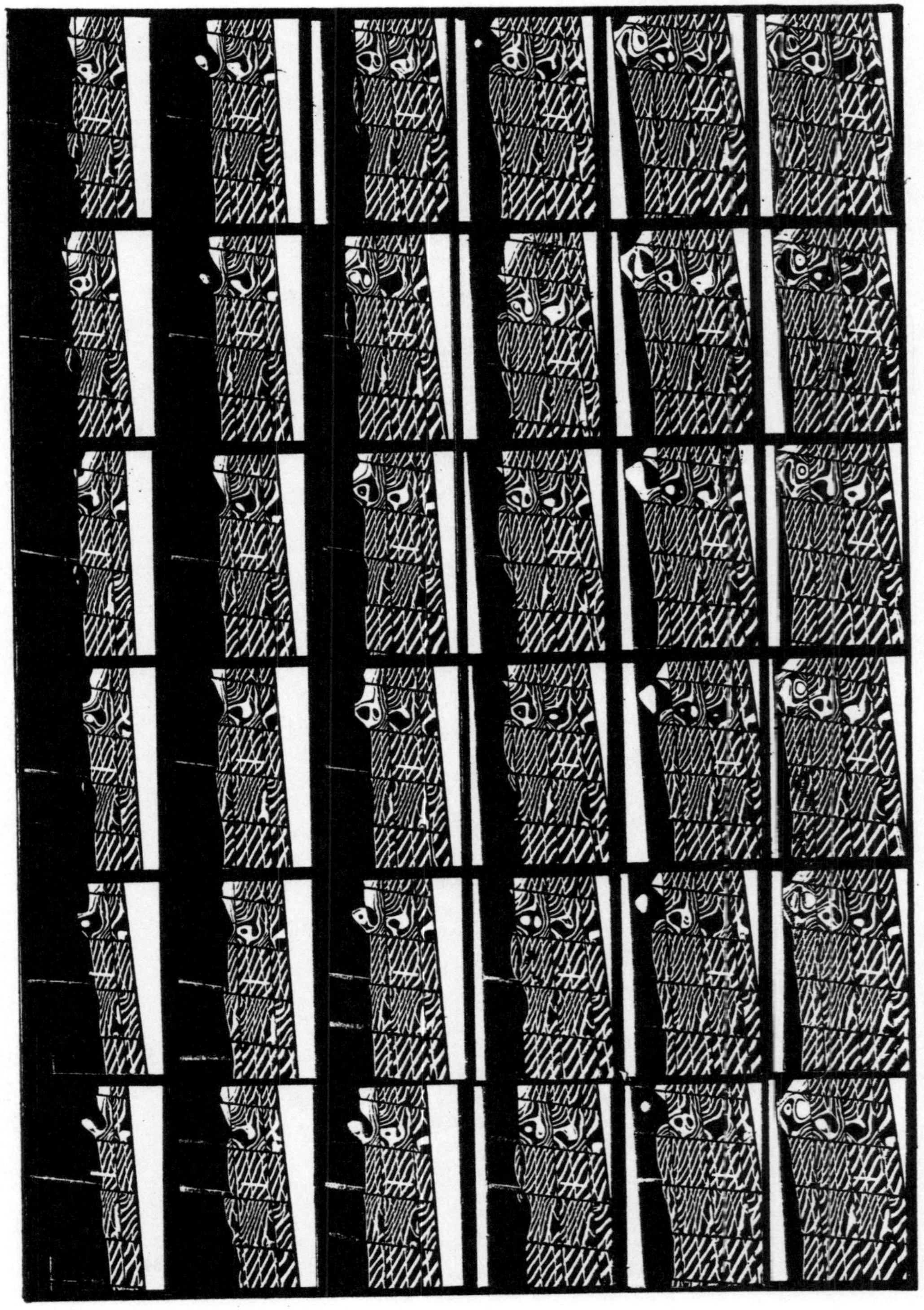

WITHOUT INTEGRITY
THERE IS NO CONSCIOUSNESS
WITHOUT CONSCIOUSNESS
THERE IS NO CONSCIENCE
WITHOUT CONSCIENCE
THERE IS NO REASON
WITHOUT REASON
THERE IS NO CLARITY
WITHOUT CLARITY
THERE IS NO VERITY
WITHOUT VERITY
THERE IS NO SIGNIFICANCE
WITHOUT SIGNIFICANCE
THERE IS NO INTUITION
WITHOUT INTUITION
THERE IS NO TRANSCENDENCE
WITHOUT TRANSCENDENCE
THERE IS NO EXPERIENCE
WITHOUT EXPERIENCE
THERE IS NO KNOWLEDGE
WITHOUT KNOWLEDGE
THERE IS NO DISTINCTION
WITHOUT DISTINCTION
THERE IS NO INSIGHT
WITHOUT INSIGHT
THERE IS NO SIGHT
WITHOUT SIGHT
THERE IS NO VISION
WITHOUT VISION
THERE IS NO NECESSITY
WITHOUT NECESSITY
THERE IS NO ENDEAVOR
WITHOUT ENDEAVOR
THERE IS NO CHANCE
WITHOUT CHANCE
THERE IS NO DISCOVERY
WITHOUT DISCOVERY
THERE IS NO ART.
WITHOUT ART
THERE IS NO DIMENSION
WITHOUT DIMENSION
THERE IS NO PERSPECTIVE
WITHOUT PERSPECTIVE
THERE IS NO ~~INTEGRITY~~ PERCEPTION
WITHOUT PERCEPTION
THERE IS NO PROPORTION
WITHOUT PROPORTION

WITHOUT ALL THIS : IT ISN'T ART

c BETHINA

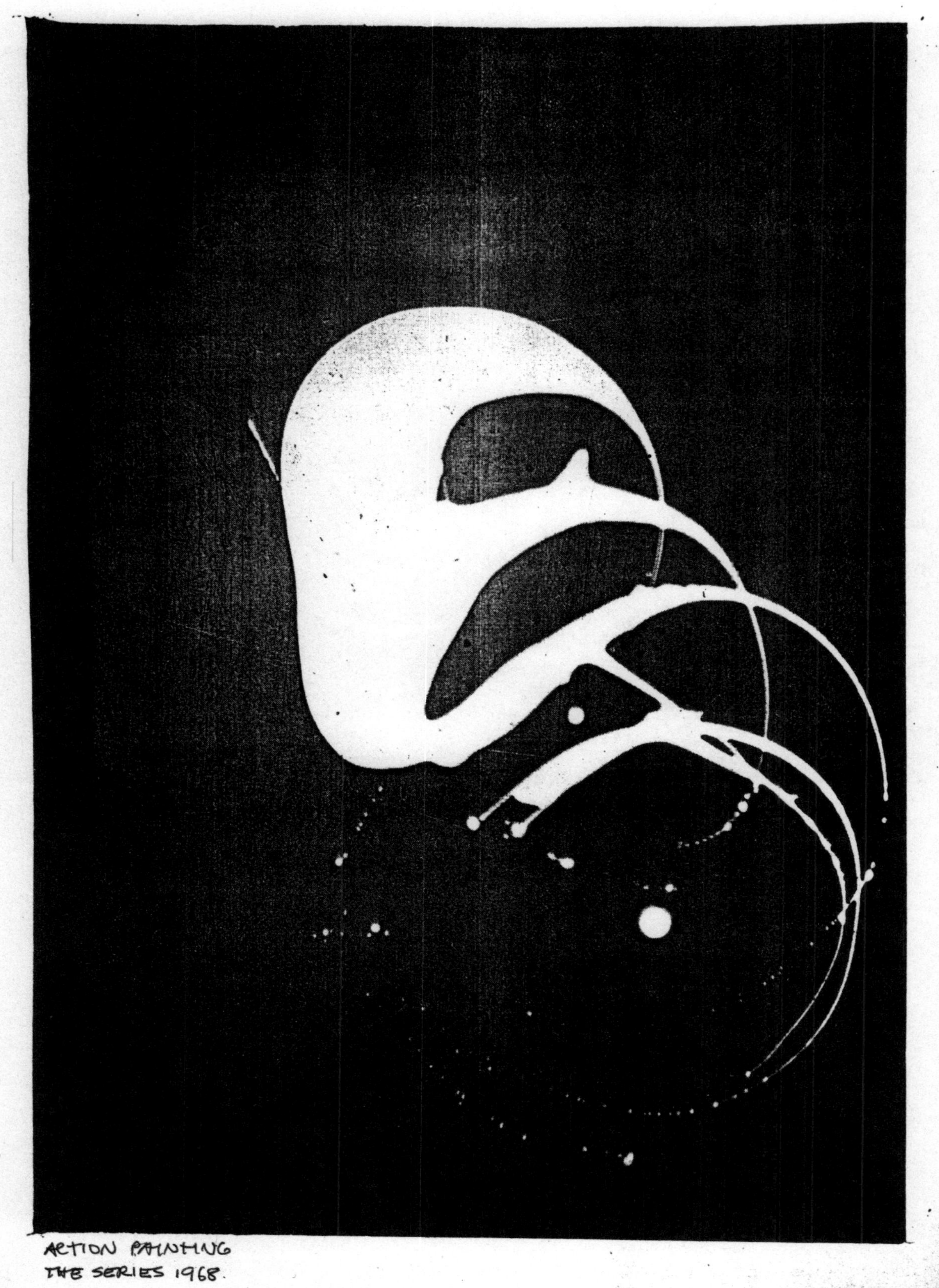

ACTION PAINTING
THE SERIES 1968.

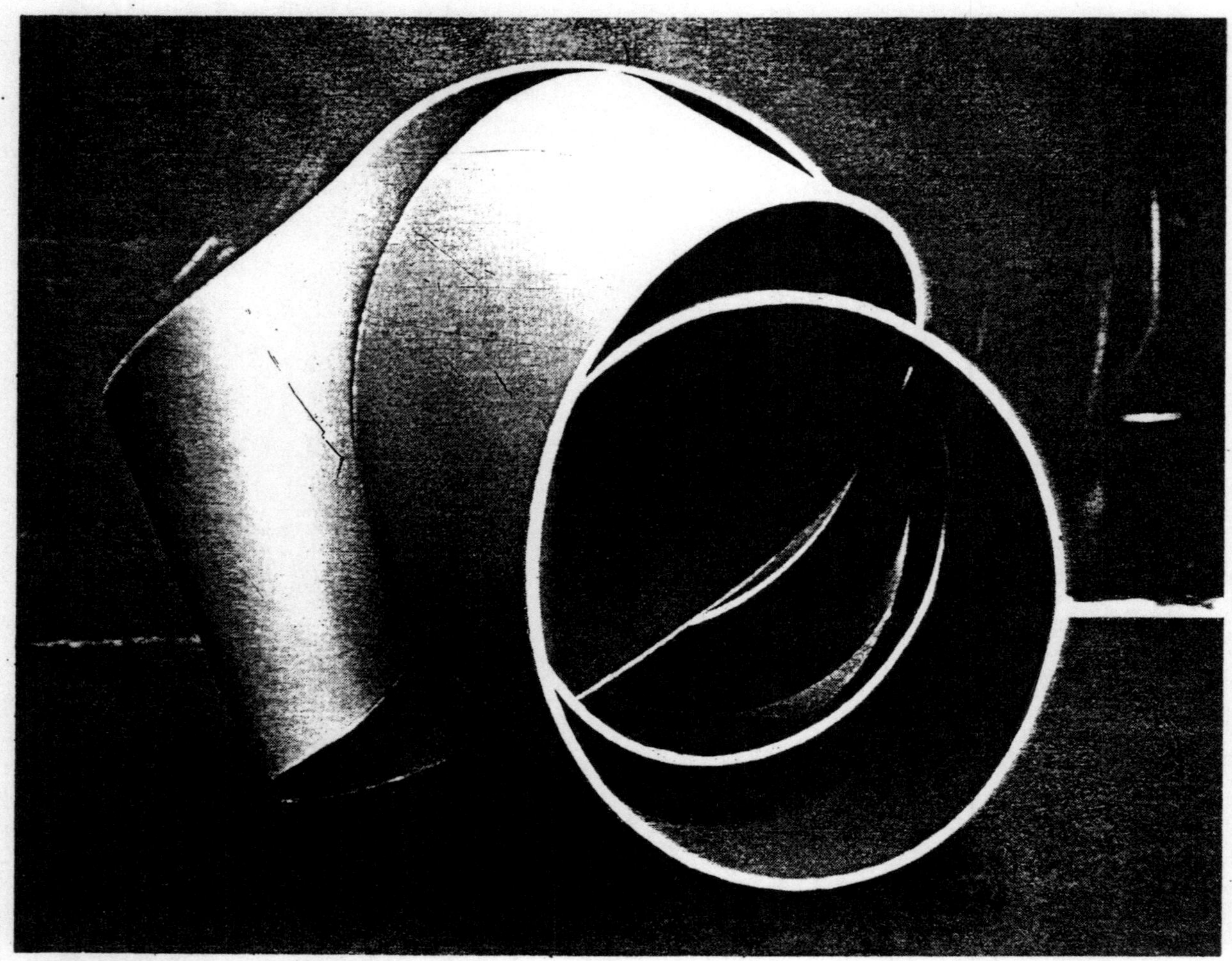

RETAKE/OUTTAKE the series

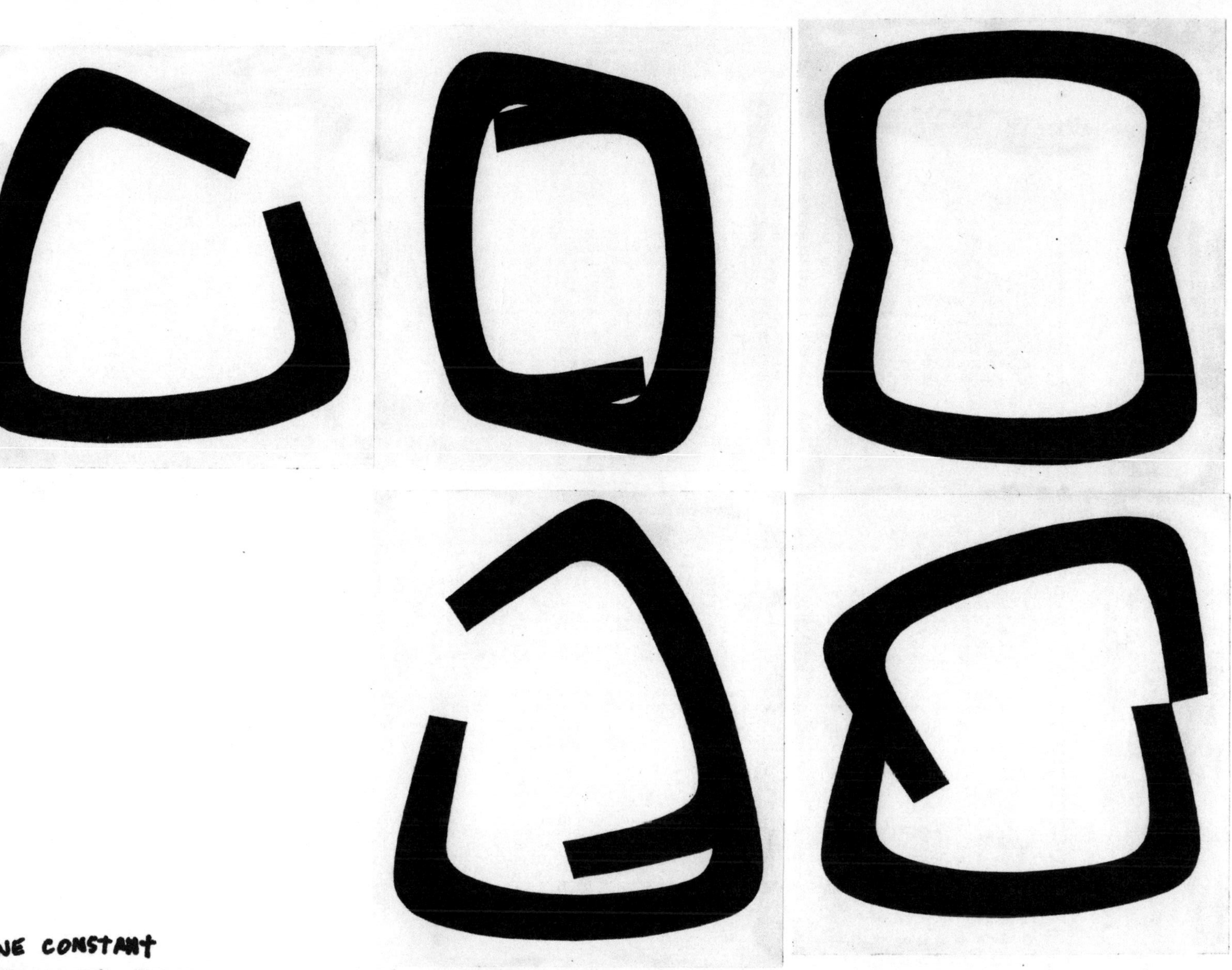

ONE CONSTANT

4-DIMENSIONAL STUDIES IN AUTO-REGENERATING ENERGIES

(I) 1 of 2 SETTING/HEADLINES/MISE EN SCENE

MISE EN SCENE / HEADLINE PROJECT / from THE FIFTH POINT OF THE COMPASS
1979–88 STUDIES IN RANDOM CONSTANT DEMOGRAPHICS ON 23 STREET

Headlines are collected all year for their critical comments and photographed once each year using the same model a ~~xxx~~ French scientist. ~~from the Institut Pasteur~~

●I- HELP
●II-I CAN'T HELP
●3 -THANKS
●4 -DEFIANT
●5 -GREED
●6 PEACE
●7 ALIVE
●8 FREE
●9 WANTED
I0 SHOOTOUT
II SNAG
●I2 SAVED
I3 WELCOME
I4 BOOM
●I5 WOW
I6 VANISHES
I7 FOOLISH
●I8 JINXED
I9 MARATHON
●20 (swastika)
2I SHOCKER
22 ROCKED
23 RAMMED
●24 SURVIVAL
25 OUTWITTED
26 SOLIDARITY
27 DEATH
28 PHEW
●29 FREED
●30 YES
●3I NO
●32 BUGGED
●33 SEIZED
34 COMEBACK
#% UNMASKED
●36 REBORN
●37 BELIEVE
38 CHAMPS
●39 WRONG
●40 NIGHTMARE

40 -COMING HOME
4I SUDDEN DEATH
42 WE'RE SAFE
●43 NEVER AGAIN
●44 PLAY BALL
45 DOWN SAFE
46 THEY'RE FREE
●47 HEAD-ON
●48 ITS-OVER
●49 NO-WAY
●50 AT LAST
5I MASS GRAVE
52 RANSOM CABS
53 THE KILLER
54 WHITE-OUT
●55 NOT YET
56 OUT WITTED
●57 D-E-E-P TROUBLE
58 NIAGARA FALLS
59 DEATH LEAP
60 SPAN-TASTIC
●6I STAND-OFF
62 HEART BREAK
●63 PRICES ZOOOM
●64 KEEP OUT
●65 IT'S WAR
66 WE'RE #I
●67 TOTALLY INVOLVED
I72 MAD OUT
I73

●68 - SAVED FROM DEATH
69 - MOMENT OF DEATH
70 - FIGHT FOR LIGHT
●7I - WHAT A NIGHT
●72 SLAIN BY MISTAKE
73 FOOD PRICES SOAR
74 WAR ZONE, USA
●75 THIS IS WAR
●76 NIGHT OF MADNESS
●77 THE IMPOSSIBLE DREAM
78 BEST OF ENEMIES
79 I MILLION CHEER
●80 EYEBALL TO EYEBALL
●8I TIME IS MONEY
●82 ROAD TO GLORY
83 ELEVEN INVISIBLE MEN
●84 LAW AND DISORDER
●85 LET'S GET TOUGH
●86 ITS TOO LATE
●87 WIN OR ELSE
●88 ITS A MESS
●89 WHAT A FARCE
90 WHAT A MESS
●9I MONSTER AT WORK
●92 I CAN'T HELP
●93 GASP FOR LIFE
●94 UNITED THEY STAND
95 HE WASN'T BLUFFING
●96 TRICK OR TERROR
●97 BACK FROM NIGHTMARE
98 OH, SO LOVERLY
99 GAME OF DEATH
I00 FLIGHT TO FREEDOM
I0I YONG YONG

●I02 TRIUMPH AND CRISIS
●I03 TRIUMPH.....AND TRAGEDY
I04 WORLD SERIES RAMPAGE
●I05 THANK YOU, AMERICA
I06 FEELS LIKE 0 BELOW
I07 DASH TO FREEDOM
I08 FURY OF ISLAM
I09 THE HOLY WAR
II0 THE COKE-BROKERS
III LOVE YA, METS
II2 THE SILENT FAREWELL
II3 CROSS MY HART
●II4 WE'RE NO. I

(II) 2 OF 2 BETTINA/HEADLINES/MISE EN SCENE

I15 — BACK FROM THE DEAD
I16 WE TOLD YOU SO
I17 RUN FOR YOUR LIFE
I18 IT WAS A PLOT
I19 HAVE PITY ON THEM
I20 PUT UP OR SHUT UP
I21 AM I GOING TO DIE, DADDY?
I22 WE DON'T NEED NEW YORK
I23 CHAOS AS $I FARE IS OK'D
I24 THE BEST OF ENEMIES
I25 ANOTHER DAY OLDER AND DEEPER IN DEBT
I26 LET THERE BE NO MORE WAR
I27 BACK FROM THE BRINK
~~I28xxxxxxxxxxxxxxxxxxxxxxxxxxx~~
I28 YOU DO DRUGS, YOU DO TIME
I29 WE WON'T TAKE IT
I30 REIGN OF TERROR LANDLORDS BUSTED
I31 FLOOD ZAPS EAST SIDE
I32 METRO-NORTH CRASH CHAOS
I33 TOXIC FUMES HIT GRAND CENTRAL
I34 A TRAIN FALLS APART ON TRACKS
I35 EARTHQUAKE RATTLES NEW YORK
I36 KILL AND BE KILLED
I38 THE CITY GOES 4th
I39 SEE YOU NEXT WEEK
I40 BACK FROM THE BRINK
I41 N.Y. (loves)CHRIS
I42 HOUSEXARREST PLAN FOR N.Y.
I43 LOTTO JACKPOT HITS 20 MILLION $
I44 PUT UP OR SHUT UP
I45 THE CHASE IS ON 24 HOURS A DAY
I46 THE BLAST THAT SHOOK NEW YORK
I47 WORK - OR BE FIRED
I48 COLDEST DAY OF CENTURY
I49 PUT UP OR SHUT UP
I50 HOLIDAY HELL IN PARADISE
I51 N.Y. POURS IT ON
I52 THE FURY OF MOTHER NATURE
I53 LAND OF THE FREEZE
I54 HEAT WAVE BAKES APPLE
I55 NO RELIEF 'TILL THURS.
I56 RAIN,RAIN AT LAST
I57 GET OUT OR ELSE
I58 HELL NO, I WON'T GO
I59 DAY OF THE JACKAL
I60 A STRIKE SO FOUL
I61 HELP ME, I'M BEING KILLED
I62 IT WAS ALL FOR NOTHING
I63 SHE SWIMS HER WAY TO GLORY
I64 HOMAGE TO A HERO
I65 WE WON'T TAKE IT
I66 GOD BLESS NEW YORK
I67 LADY SINGS THE BLUES
I68 BKLYN BRIDGE : A HAPPY I00th
I69 A BRIDGE TO OBLIVION
I70 THE GREAT N.Y. SPY GAME
I71 SAIL OF THE CENTURY
~~I72 THEXSILENTXFAREWELL~~

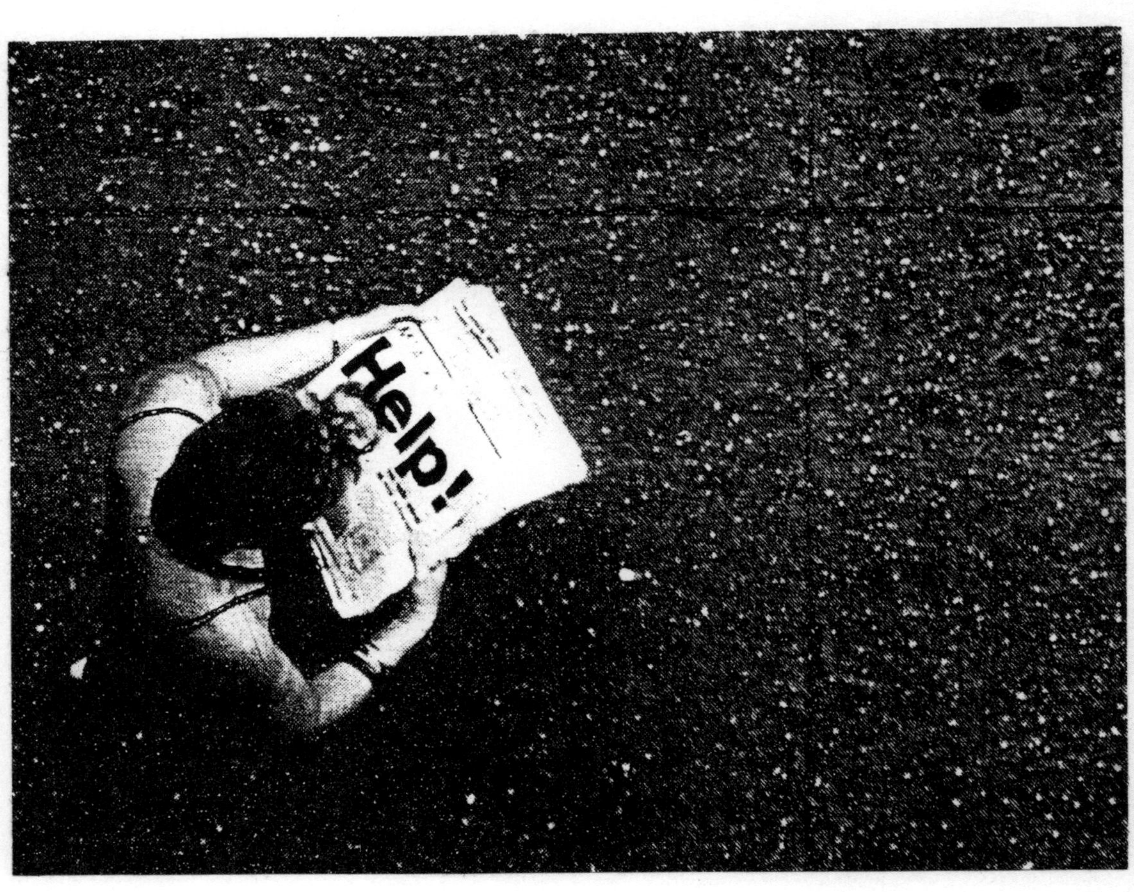
Help!

LAUNDRYMAN the series from THE FIFTH POINT OF THE COMPASS
studies in random constant
NEW YORK FROM A TO Z / DEMOGRAPHICS ON 23 ST.
1977- fixed focus/time lapse

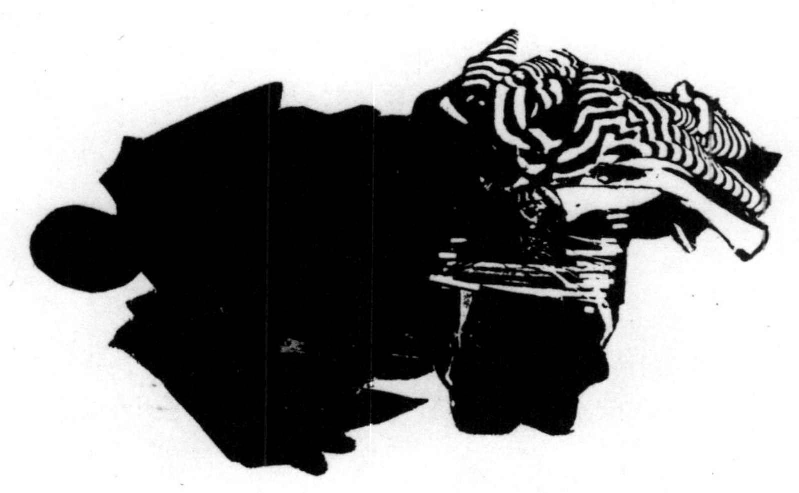

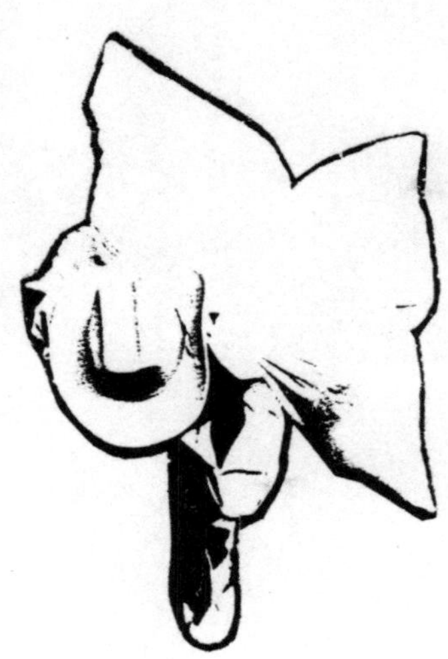

photography/wallforms

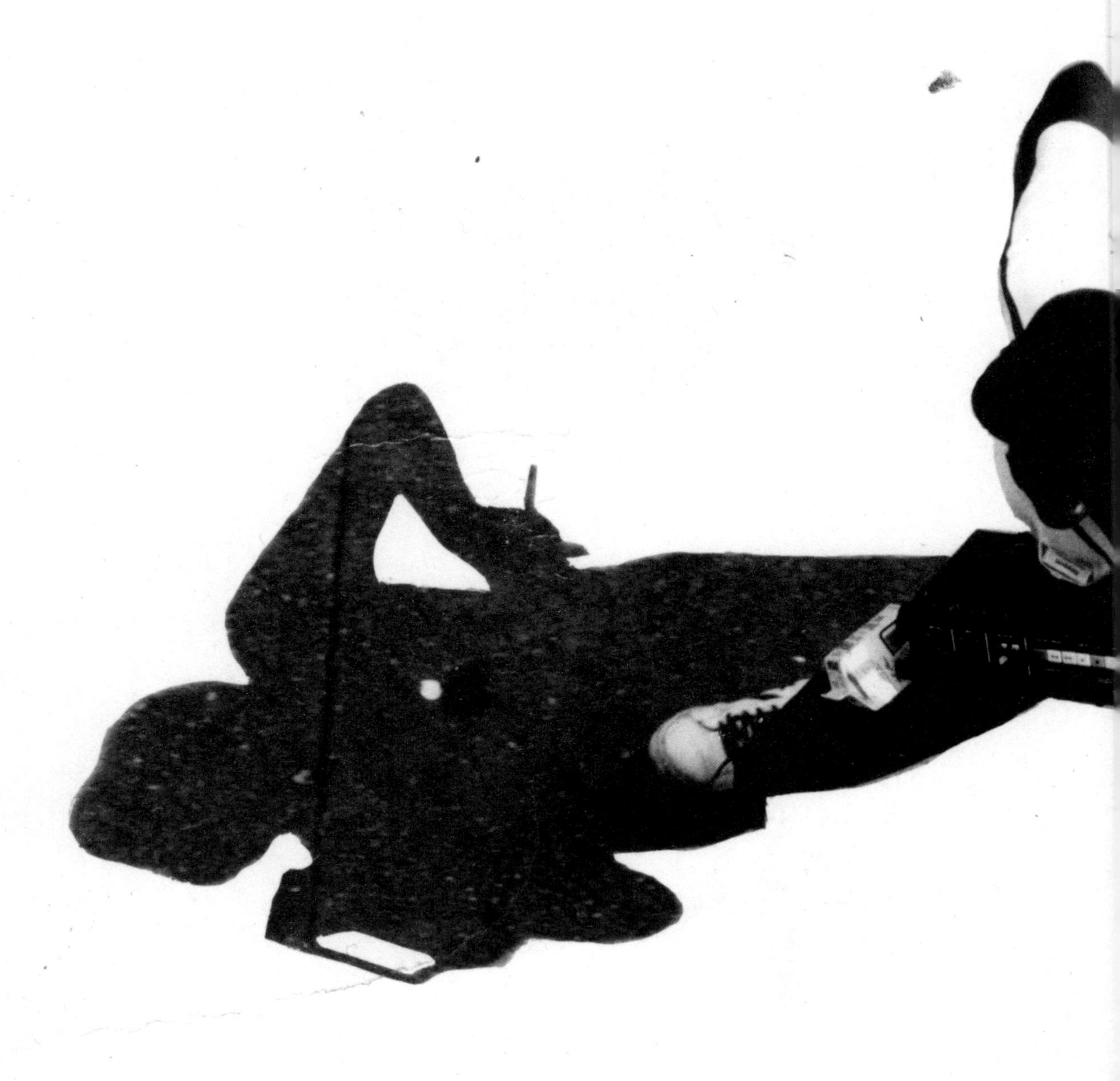

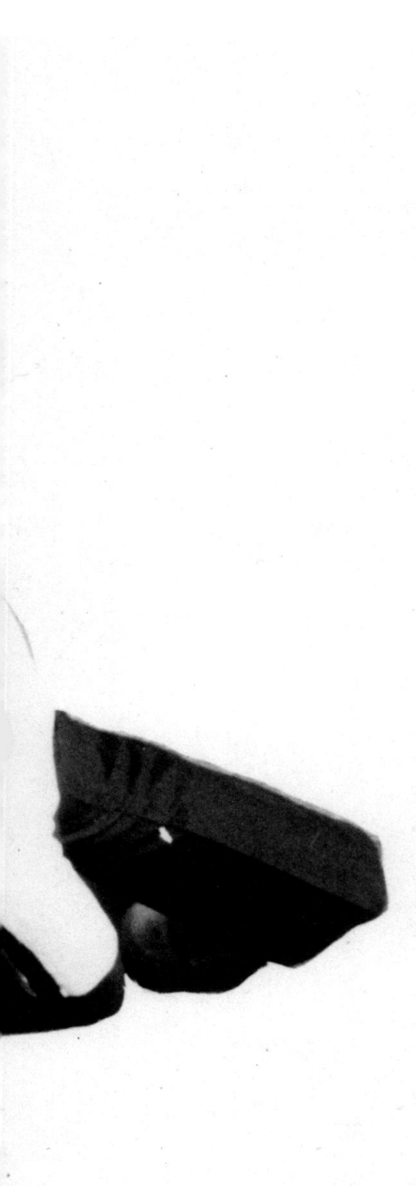

THE FIFTH POINT OF THE COMPASS / STUDIES IN RANDOM CONSTANT
NEW YORK FROM A TO Z / DEMOGRAPHICS ON TWENTY-THIRD STREET
FIXED FOCUS - TIME LAPSE / 1977- ongoing

R series exhibited O.K.HARRIS GALLERY 1980 / RAIN/RUNNER/READER/RADIO/RED (50 images each	published FOTO magazine SWEDEN three pages ----- April 1981

A-X

APPLE/AFRO/ADIDAS/ARTIST/ATTACHE
BOX/BAT/BALL/BALD/BOARD/
BUST/BOOKS/BOOTS/BOTTLE/BAUCH
BEER/BABY/BRAIDS/BETWEEN/BARELEGS
BAREFOOT/BARECHEST/BIG MAMA/BEADED
BLACK/BLONDE/BLOW/BALLOON/BICYCLE
BAREBACK/BACKPACK/BAG ON BACK/BABY ON BACK/SACK ON BACK
BAREBACK/BACKPACK/BAG ON BACK/BABY ON BACK/SACK ON BACK (sun/shadow)
CART/CAST/CANE/CASE/CRUTCH
CAP/CARTON/CAMERA/CIGARETTE/CHILD/CHAIR
COINS/COMB/COIF/COUPLE/COVER/COLOR CONTRAST
DOGS/DOLLARS/DELIVERY/(full/empty)DIALOGUE(serial)
DUFFEL/DRINK/EAT/EPAULETS/EMBROIDERY/EGGS/EYEGLASSES
FLAME/FLOWERS/FISHING/FRANKS/FASTFOOD
FAN/FOIL/FRISBEE/FILMCAN/FILING(cabinet)FRONTLOAD
GUM/GUITAR/GROCERIES/GREY/GARMENT(bag)/GARBAGE
HANDS: CLASPED/CROSSED/BEHIND BACK/IN BAG/ON HEAD/
HAT/ HAT IN HAND/HEAD/HAIR/HAIRCURLERS / HELMET /HAWAIIAN
HEART/HEADBAND/HARDHAT/HOSE/HIGHHEELS / HEADLINES(serial)
ICE CREAM/CONE/ICES/RED ICES/EAT ICE/ICE
JEANS/JACKET/JOCK/JUICE/JOINT/JUMPSUIT
110/22 KEYS/KHAKI/KNAPSACK/KNIT/KNEESOCKS/KISS

L-Z
LAUNDRYMAN(serial)
LAUNDRY/LUGGAGE/LOADED/LONG PKG/LEATHER/
LARGE/Man/woman) LIGHT/LABEL/LAVENDER/LADDER
MONEY/MANILA/METALLIC/MAIL/MILK
MUSIC/MASK/MATCH/MAILMAN/MILITARY/MOTHER & CHILD
NEWSPAPERS/NUMBERS/NAILS(toes/fingers)
OIL/ORANGE/OVER/OVERALLS/OFF-ON/ON HEAD/ OBJECT /OUTSTRETCHED
POINT/PAINT/PINK/PIZZA/PACKAGE
PLANT/PLAID/PRINT/PURPLE/PLASTIC Q-QUILT/QUENCH/QUARREL/
PAPERBAG/PATTERN/PUSHBABY/POCKETS(hands in)/PAIL/PART/PACK(six/eight)
Q— RAIN/RUNNER/READER/RADIO/RED/ROLLERSKATES/RIBBON
STRAW/STRING/STRAPLESS/STRIPE/STETSON
SACK/SATIN/SANDALS/SAILOR/SLICKER/SKATEBOARD
SNEAKERS/SUSPENDERS/SUIT/SHOES(in hand)SUNDAY TIMES
STRIDE/SHADE/SHAWL/SHIRT/SHOULDERSTRIPES/SHOULDERBAG
TANKTOP/T SHIRT/THONGS/TOILETTISSUE/TOENAILS /TOYS
TIME/TIED/TIDE/TATTOO/TWIST/
TENNIS/TRACKSHOES/TRACKSUIT/TOWEL/TV/TYPEWRITER /TRANSPORT
TATTOO CHARLIE (serial)
UMBRELLA/UNDERSHIRT/UNIFORM/
VACUUM/VISOR/VIRUS/VEST/VIOLET/VET
WOOD/WIND/WOMEN/WALLET/WHEELS
WINDOWWASHER/WHITE/WATERMELON/
WHISPER/WINGS/WHEELCHAIR/
X (marks the spot)
YO-YO/YAMALKA/YELLOW
26 ZEBRASTRIPE

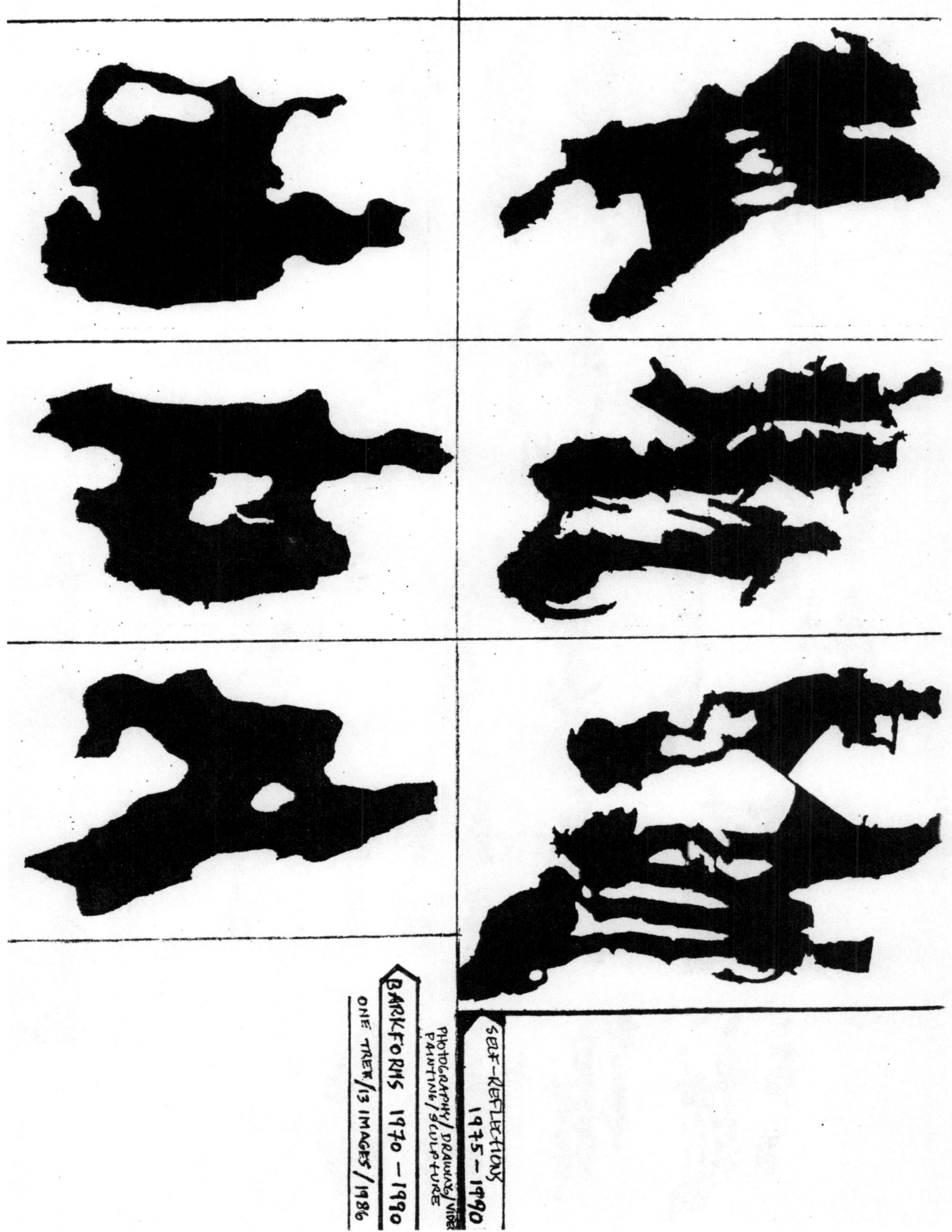
SELF-REFLECTIONS
1975 – 1990
PHOTOGRAPHY/DRAWING/VIDEO
PAINTING/SCULPTURE
BARKFORMS 1970 – 1990
ONE TREE/13 IMAGES/1986

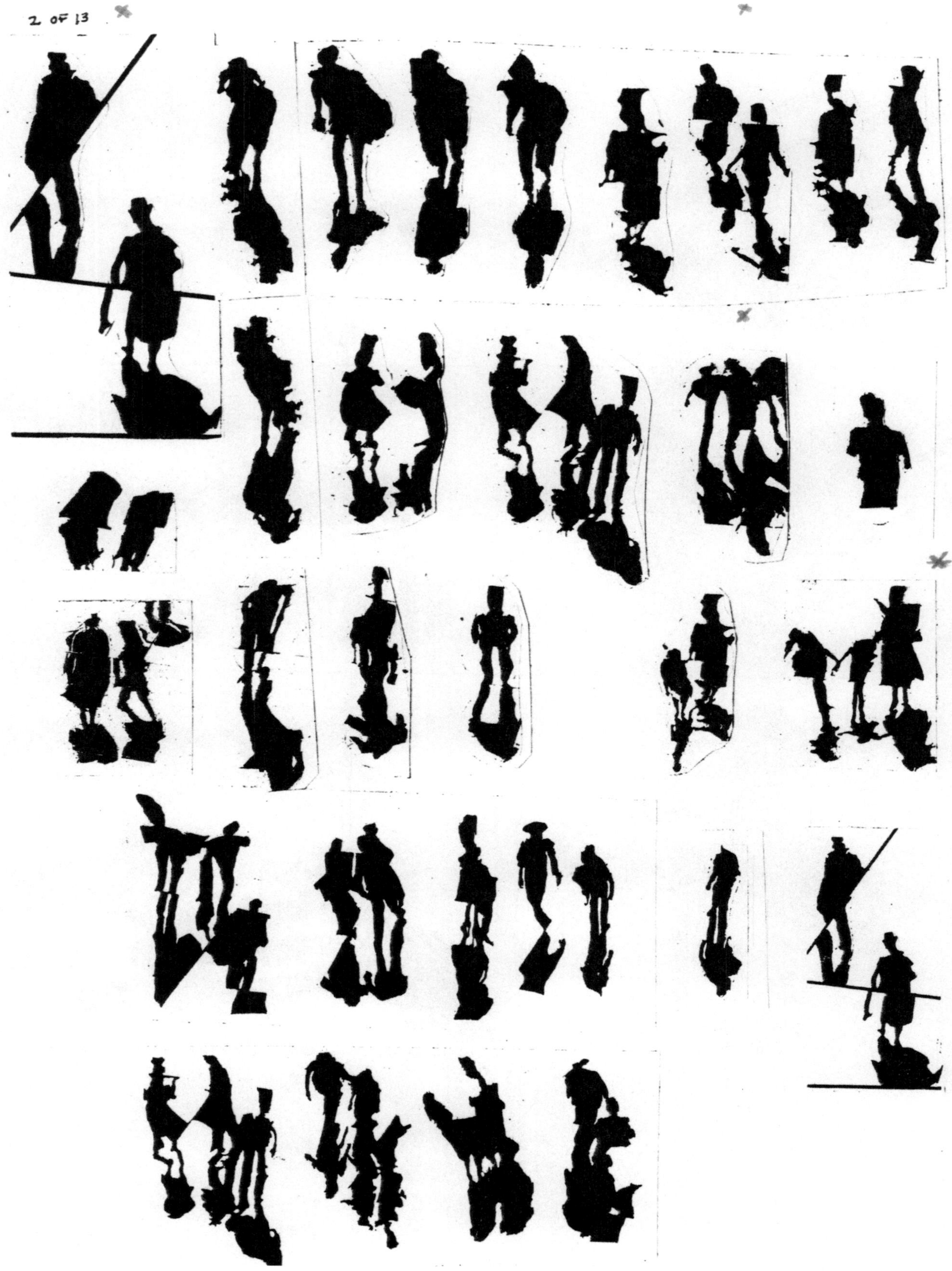
2 OF 13

MASTERWORKS OF THE LONDON PLANE / PARIS 1971

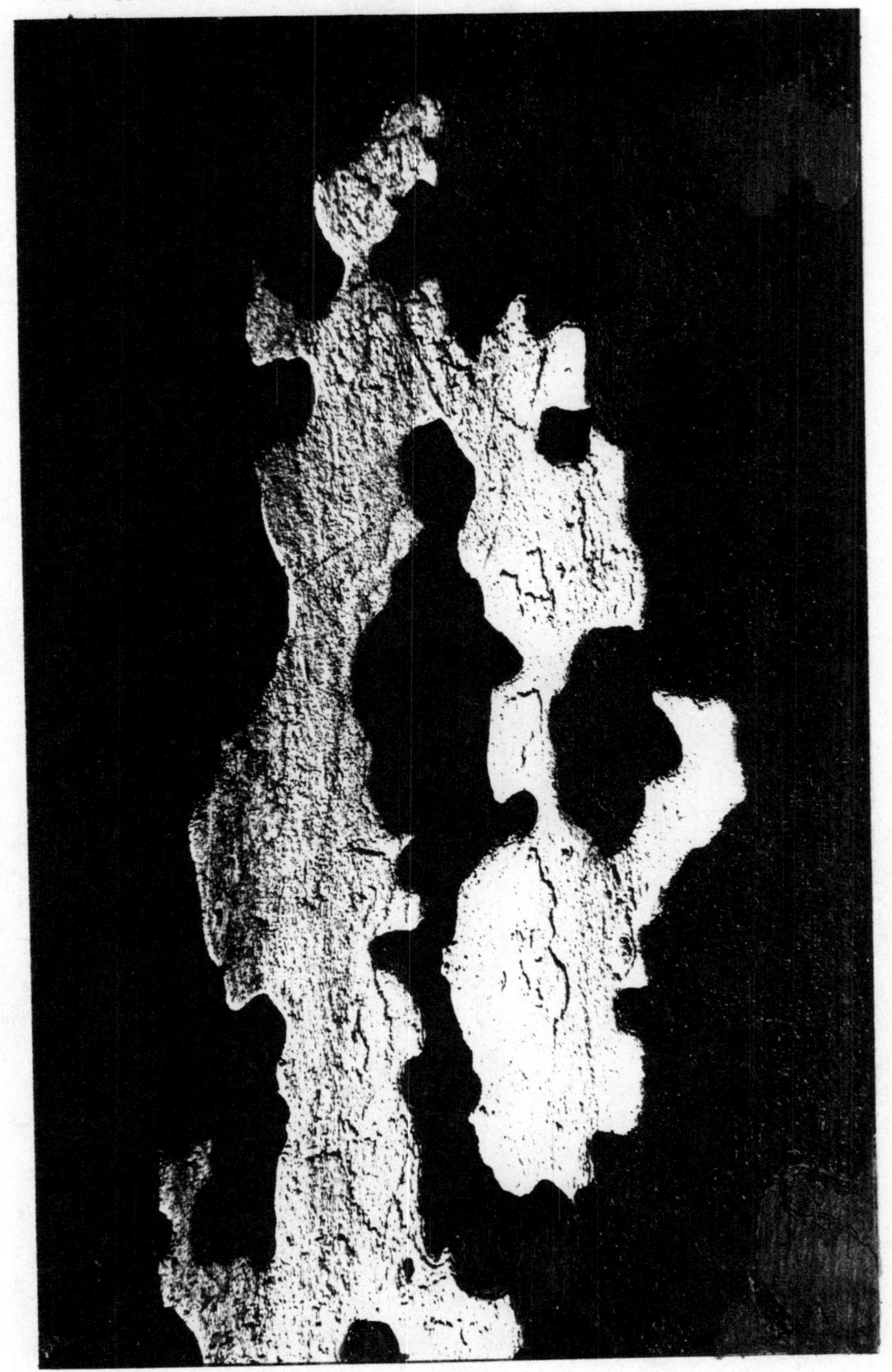

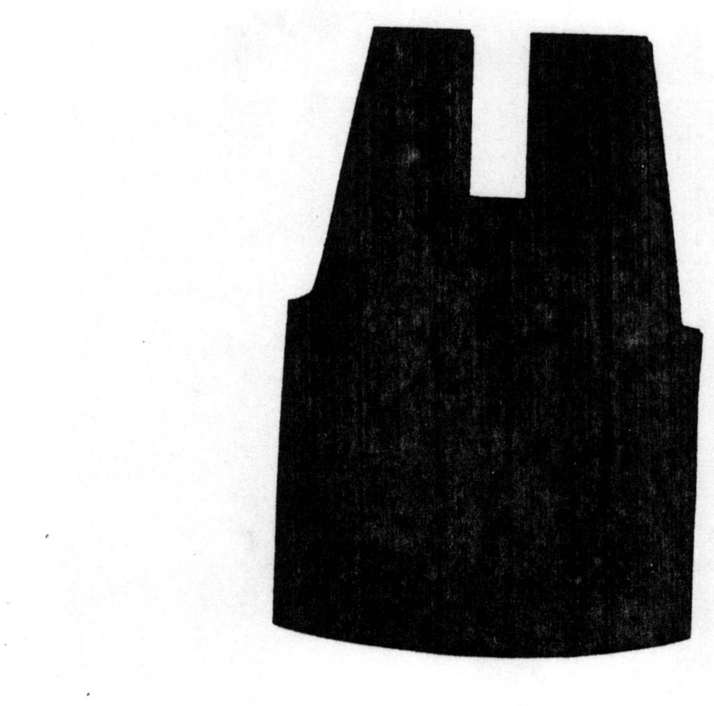

SHANGO / plane/curve/edge 1977-80
WEAPONS/THE CUTTING EDGE/STROKE/ NON-WAIVER
mirror-image KNOW THYSELF

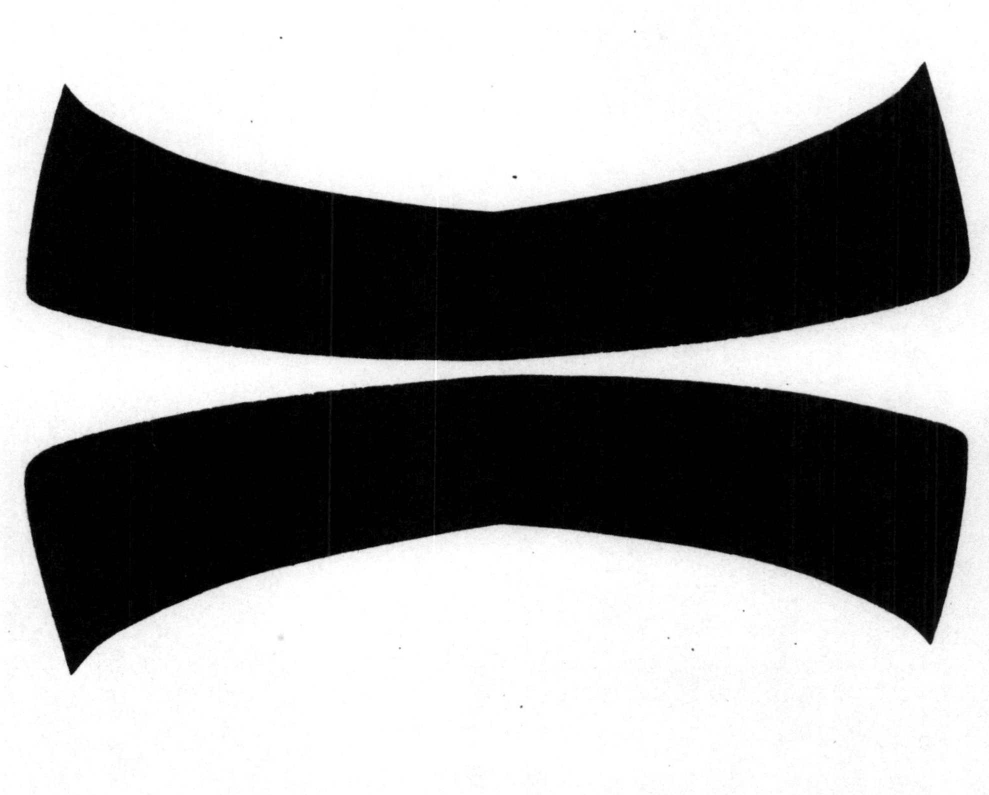

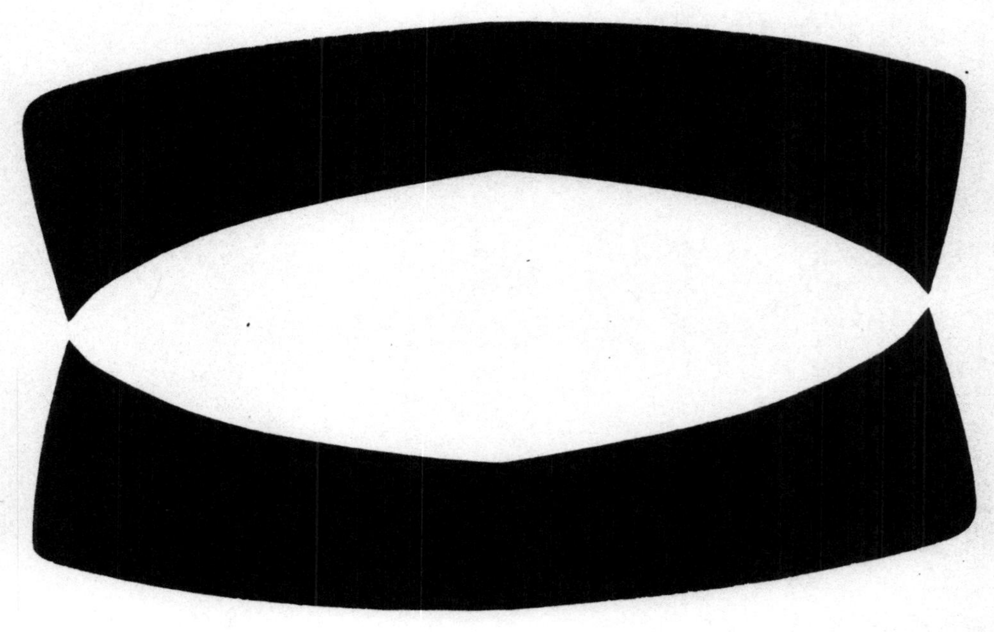

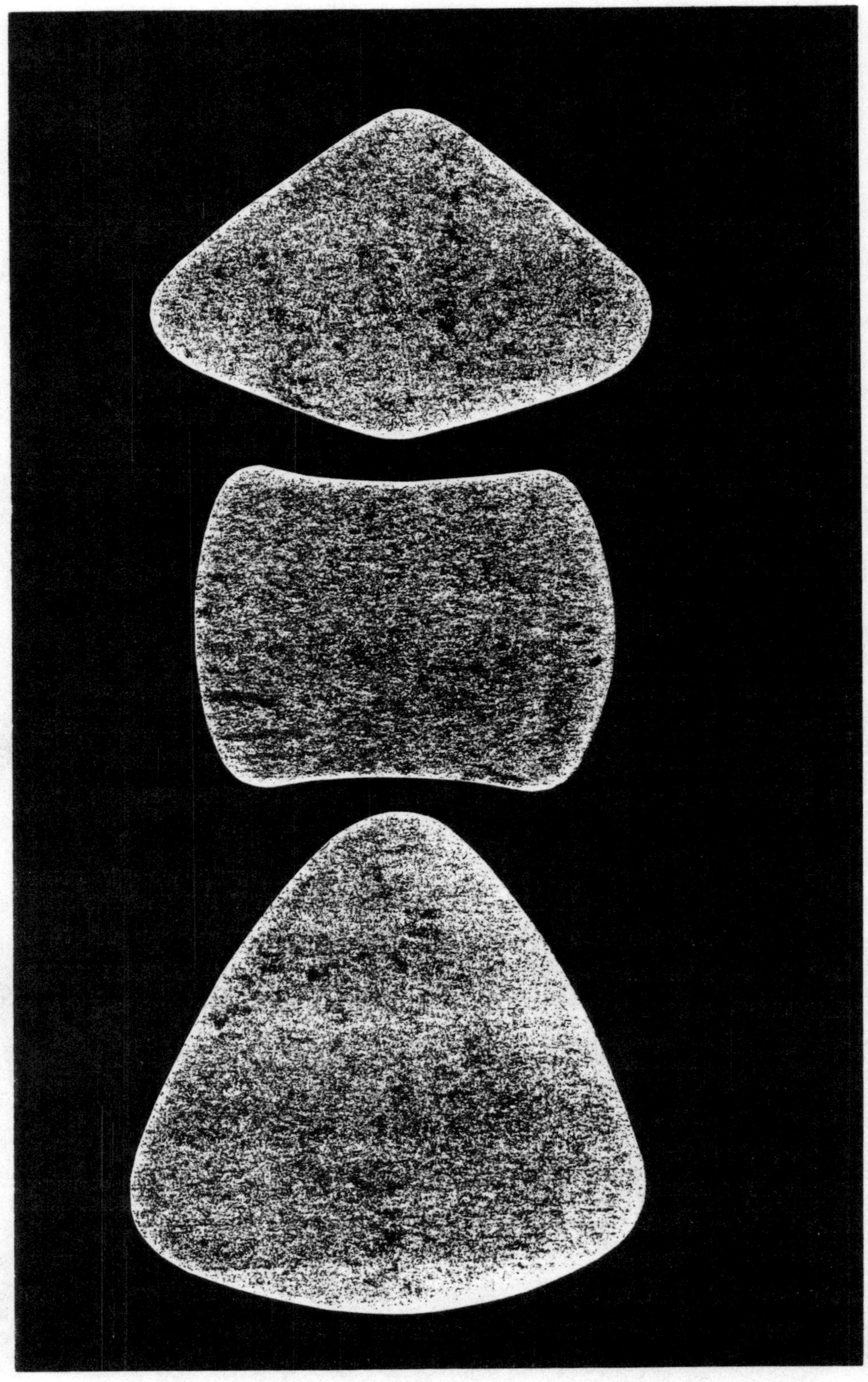

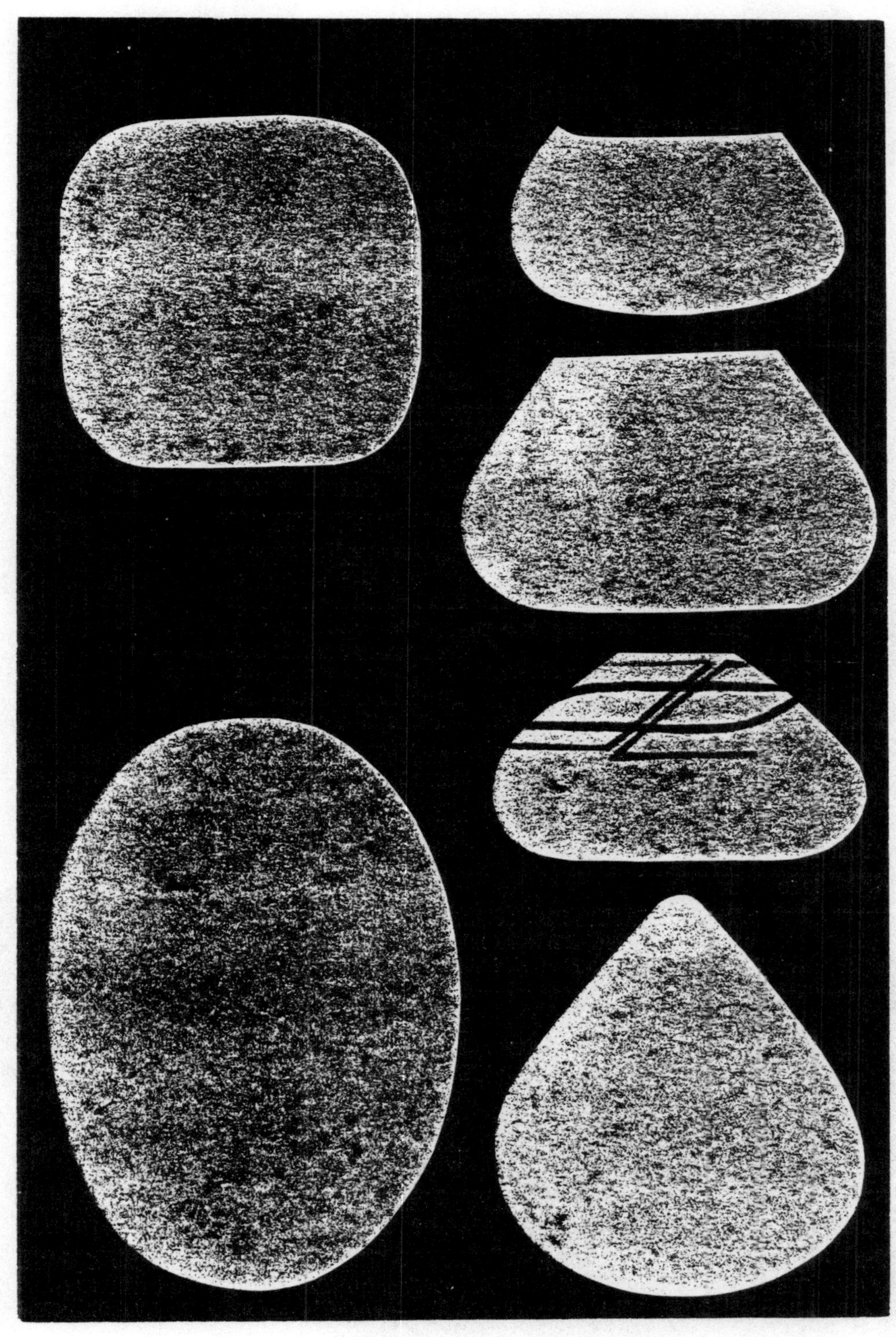

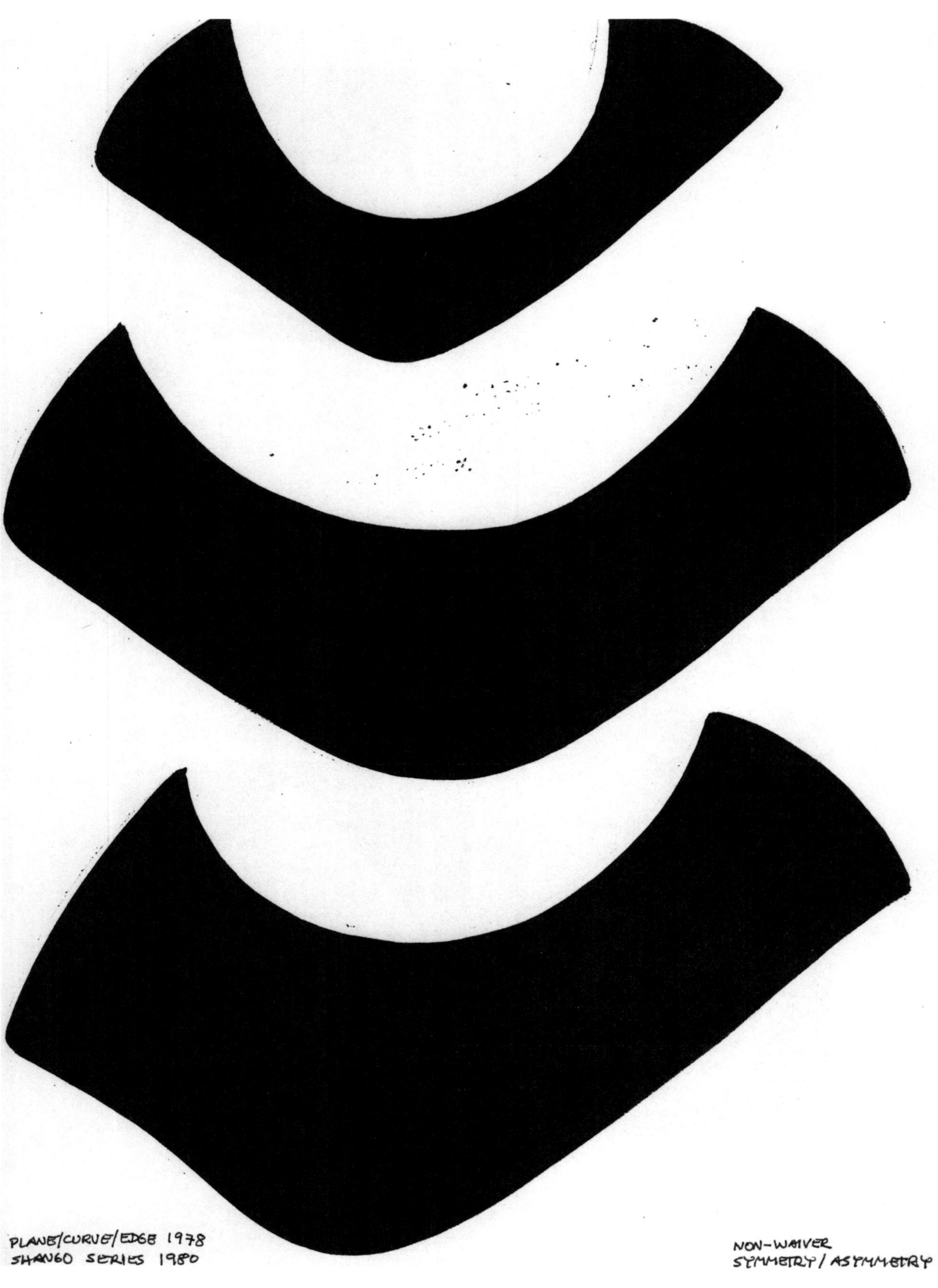
PLANE/CURVE/EDGE 1978
SHANGO SERIES 1980
NON-WAIVER
SYMMETRY/ASYMMETRY

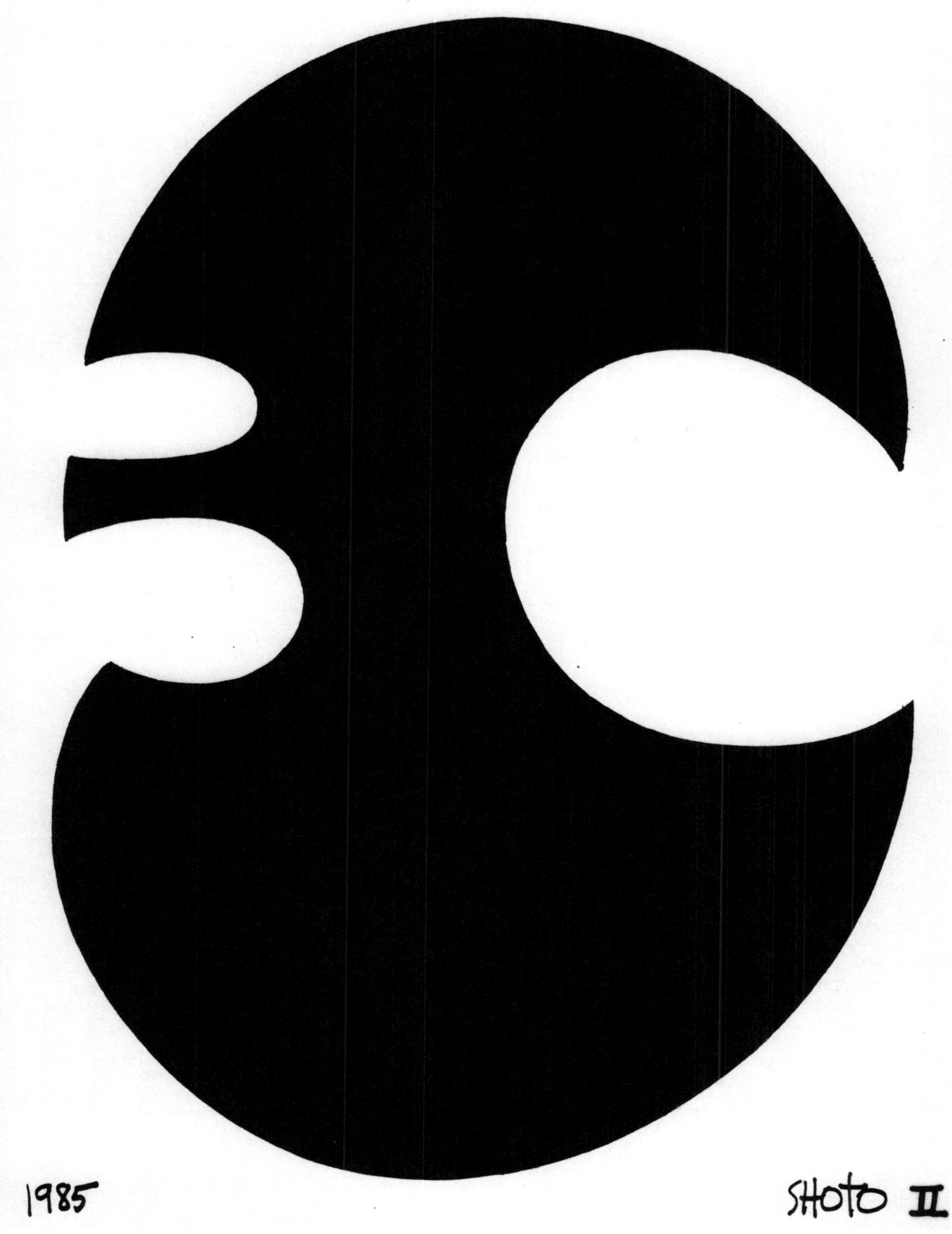
1985
SHOTO II

* THE FIFTH POINT OF THE COMPASS / studies in random constant
DEMOGRAPHICS ON 23rd STREET / NEW YORK from A to Z
fixed focus / time lapse fixed focus / serial image

RAIN / RUNNER / READER / RADIO / RED / ROLLERSKATES - - time lapse- 1977-1984
each title comprises fifty to one hundred images in color
RAIN is an installation piece of 500 images of mulptiple-patterned umbrellas
80 x 80 x 80 / 80 inches by 80 inches by 80 images / RED UMBRELLAS ONLY - 1977-1984

HEADLINES / READER - - - - STAGED PROJECT - -serial image1978-1984
headlines are collected all year for critical congruity and photographed once each year sequentially-using the same performer - installation piece of 300-500 images

WITHIN PREFIXED BOUNDARIES (the self-container) I AM DOCUMENTING DAILY URBAN ACTIVITIES IN FIXED FOCUS FROM THE FIFTH FLOOR. THE PAVEMENT GRID STRUCTURE BECOMES THE UNIVERSAL CONSTANT WITHIN WHICH INNER CITY ENERGIES ARE CONTAINED. IDENTIFYING FEATURES OF PASSING PEDESTRIANS ARE ISOLATED AT RANDOM AND ORGANIZED ALPHABETICALLY. SELECTIVE RETENTION.
THROUGH STRATEGIES OF REPETITIVE PROCESS,MULTIPLE IMAGES OF SIMILAR DISTINGUISHING CHARACTERISTICS ARE PRESENTED AS IKON. OBJECT. EVENT. SOCIO-HISTORY.
GESTURE AND INCIDENT, AT ONCE ORDINARY AND GLOBAL, ARE TRANSFORMED INTO PURE FORM AS THE HUMAN FORM BECOMES DEDIMENSIONALIZED. DEDIMENSION AS A STATE OF BEING.
REVEALED IS A MYSTIC COSMIC ENERGY.
THE STRANGE RECURRENCE BOTH WITHIN MY FIXED CONTAINER AND WITHIN MINUTES OF EACH OTHER - SPECIFIC CONSTANTS REPEATING THEMSELVES.
ie ; counting dollar bills as they pass directly below.
ONCE ELUSIVE TRANSITORY INAPPREHENSIBLE ENERGIES ARE HERE REPOSITED.
THIS PROJECT IS ABOUT EVERYMAN.
ONCE REMOVED FROM EXPECTED FRAMES OF REFERENCE - HE STANDS ISOLATED.
EVERYIMAGE. TO HELP US SEE OTHERS. TO SEE OURSELVES. TO SEE AT ALL.

RESTRAINING STRUCTURES

* FINITE STRUCTURES / ONE OUT OF A POSSIBLE 1,048,576 1968-1984
random penetration of four equal constants by eight elements of progressive displacement

architecture/wallforms/volumes/graphics/book/film/sculpture/painting/drawings/etcetera

UNDERLYING THE EVER-CHANGING FORMS GENERATED WITHIN THIS PROJECT IS THE SAME GRID STRUCTURE AS EMPLOYED ABOVE. THIS PREVAILING CONSTANT ENABLES ME TO EXPLORE FOUR-DIMENSIONAL STRATEGIES WITH MAXIMUM ARTICULATION DESPITE THE LIMITATIONS OF RIGID DISCIPLINE. IMPOSED CONSTRAINTS ARE SYNONYMOUS WITH EXPERIENTIAL PROCESS.
CONSTANTLY CHANGING WITH DEGREES OF RECEPTIVITY ARE THE POSSIBILITIES OF ENDLESS SELF-EXTENSION. THE WAYS IN WHICH WE ARE SUBJECTED TO AND ACHIEVE DIMENSION THROUGH CHALLENGE. ABSOLUTES ARE CHALLENGED WITH MULTI-DIMENSIONAL CONSTANTS.
YOUR LIMITATIONS ARE DETERMINED BY THE REALITIES OF YOUR CHOICES.
FINITE SOLUTIONS ARE BUT TENTATIVE ACKNOWLEDGEMENT OF INFINITE ALTERNATIVES.
HUMAN POTENTIAL IS EXPLORED. NOT AS PROPORTIONATE TO HUMAN CONDITION, BUT AS PROPORTIONATE TO HUMAN SCALE.

SINGLE-LINE DRAWINGS / ONE HAIR

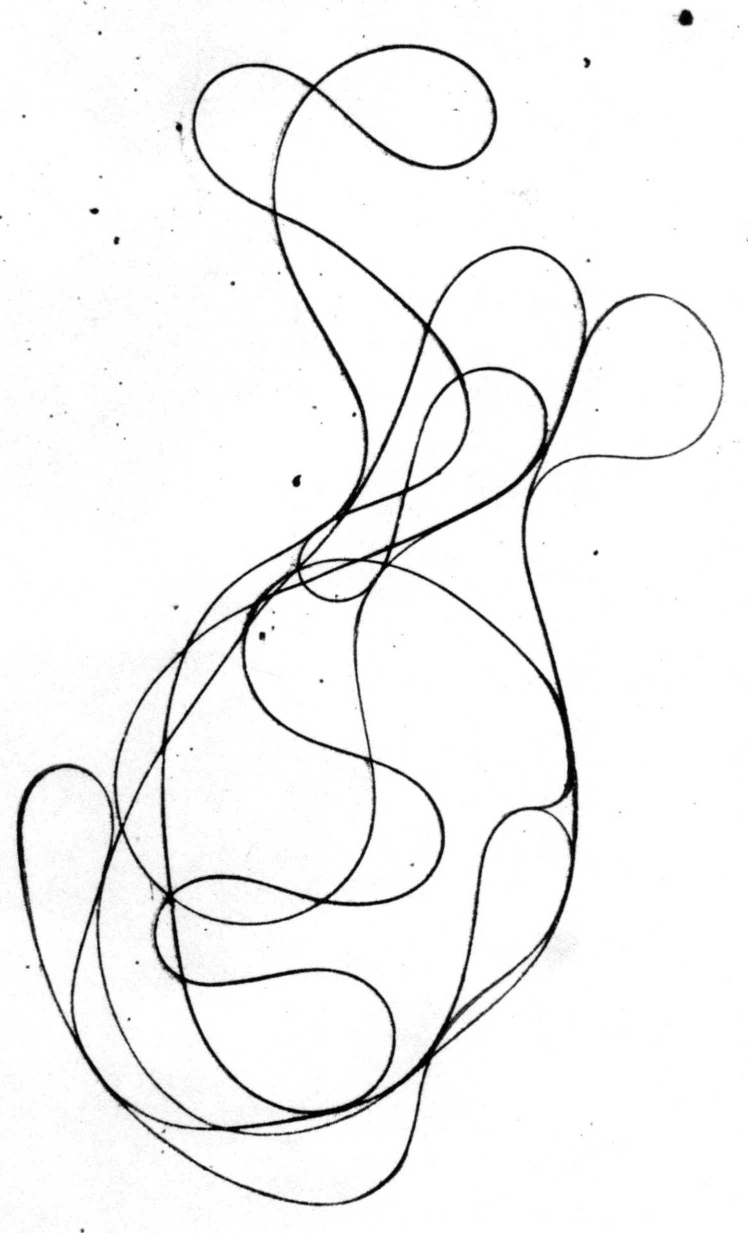

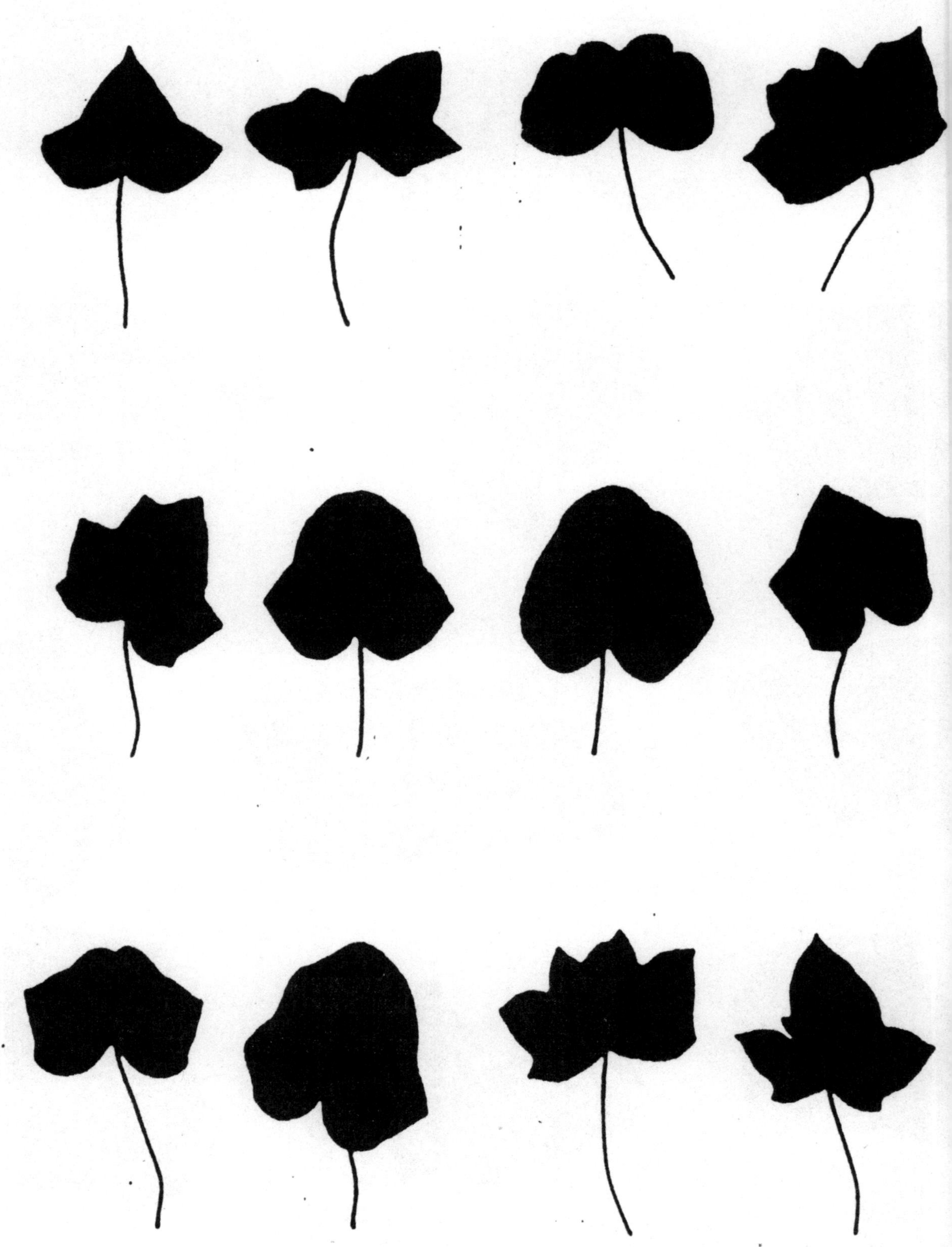

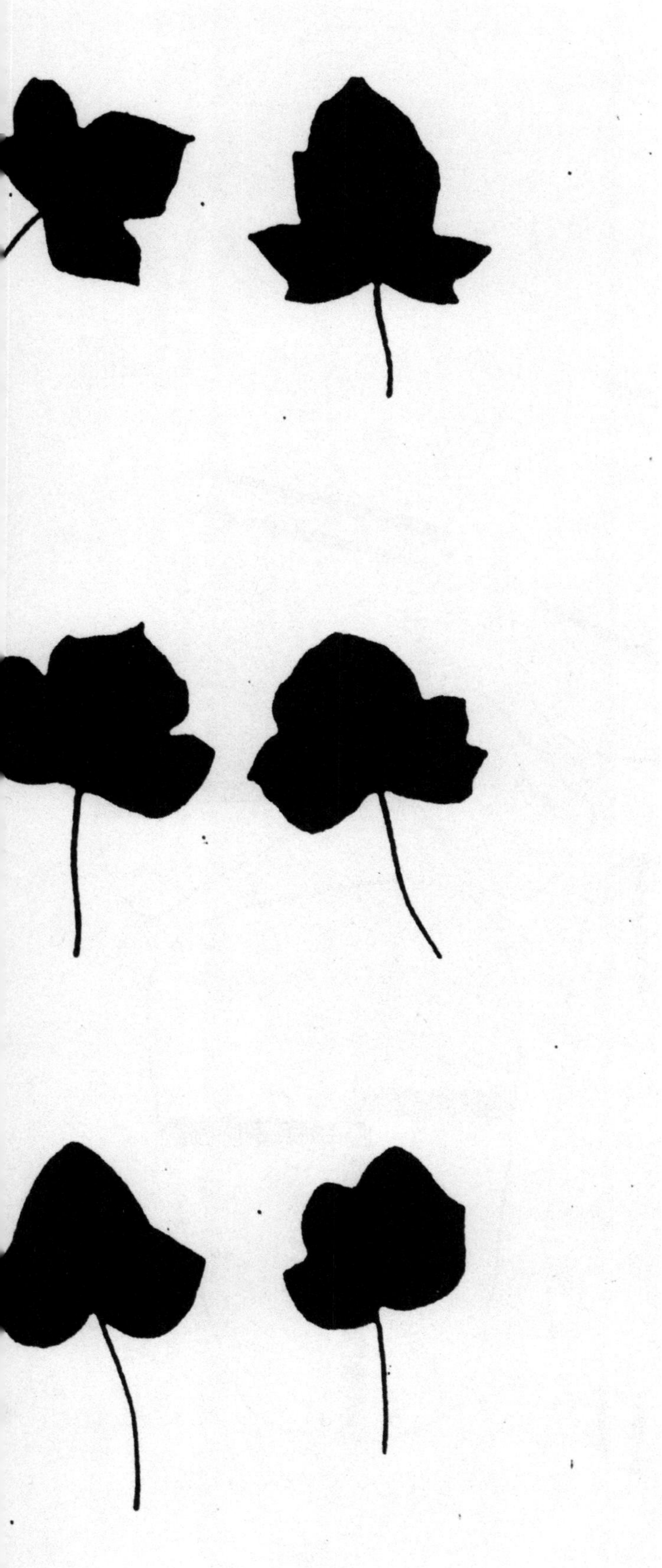

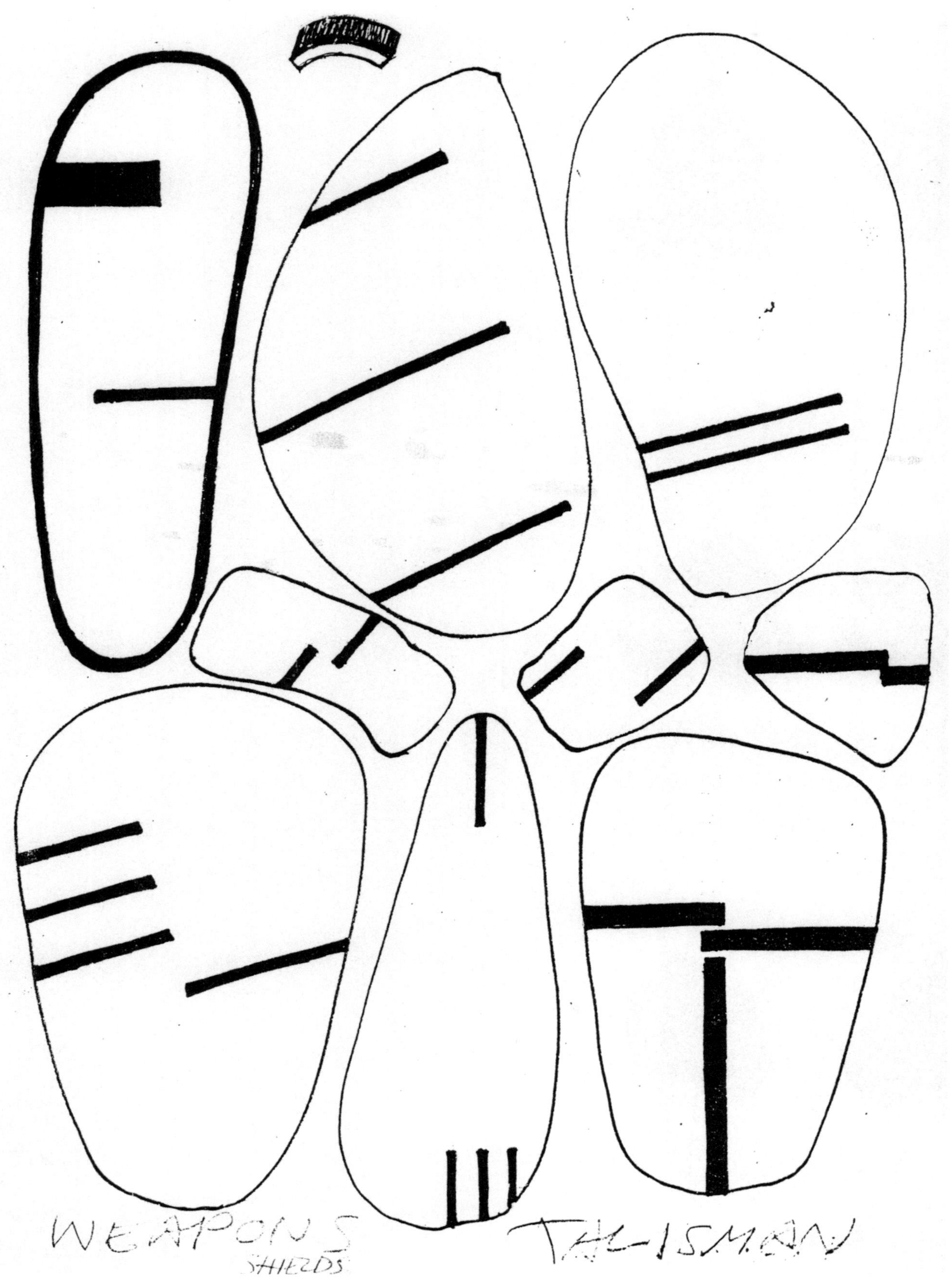
WEAPONS
SHIELDS
TALISMAN

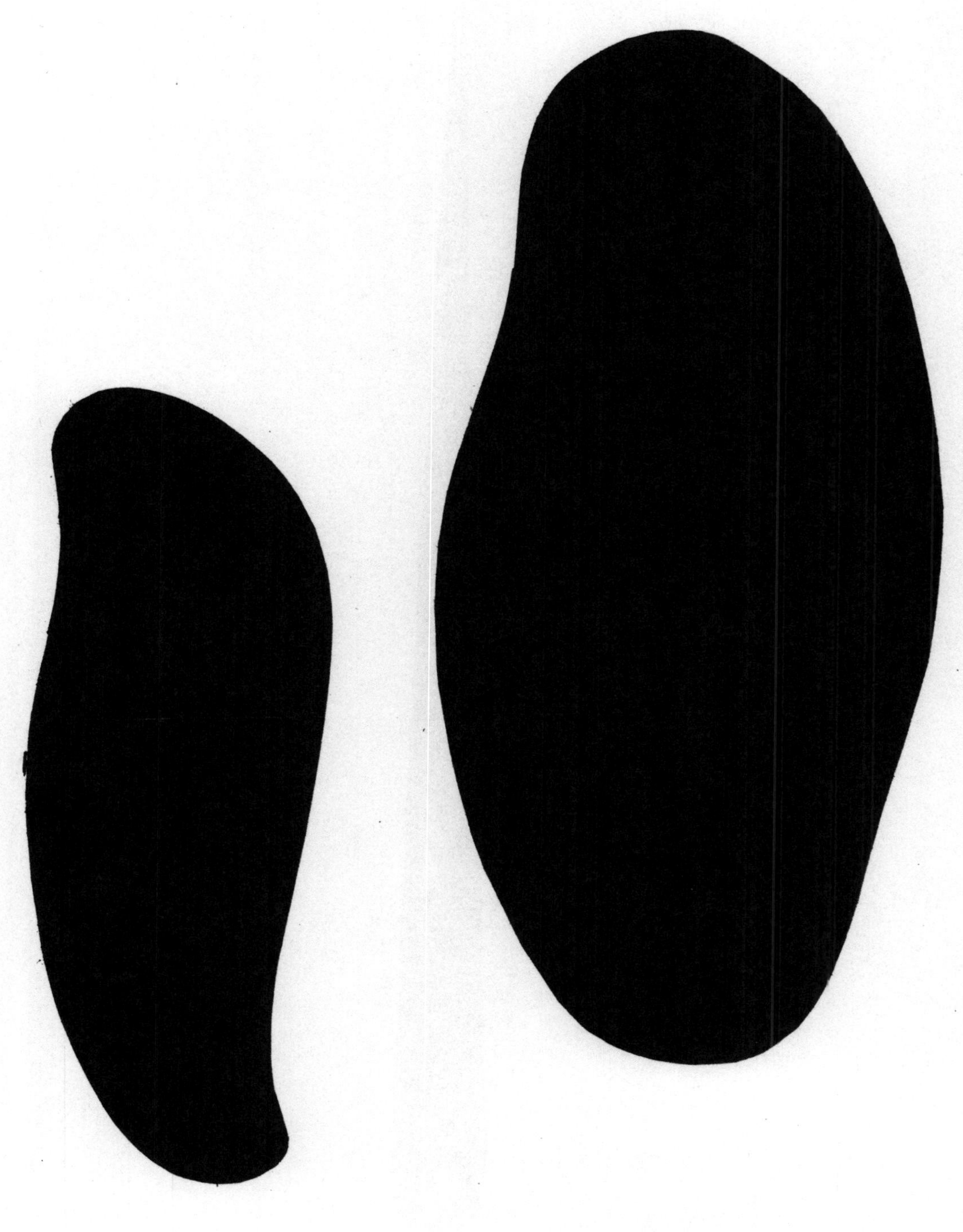
PIT
MANGO

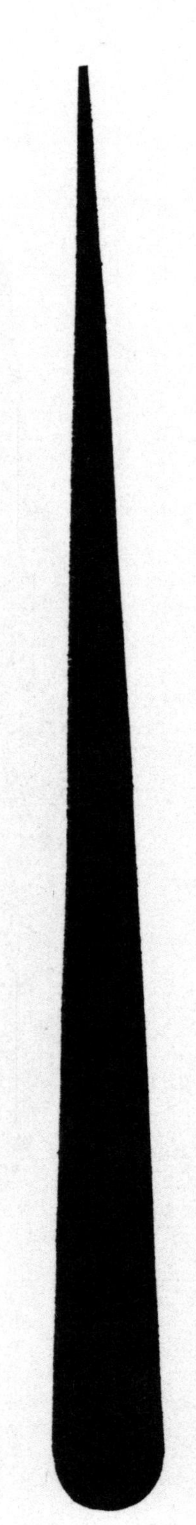

FLEAU

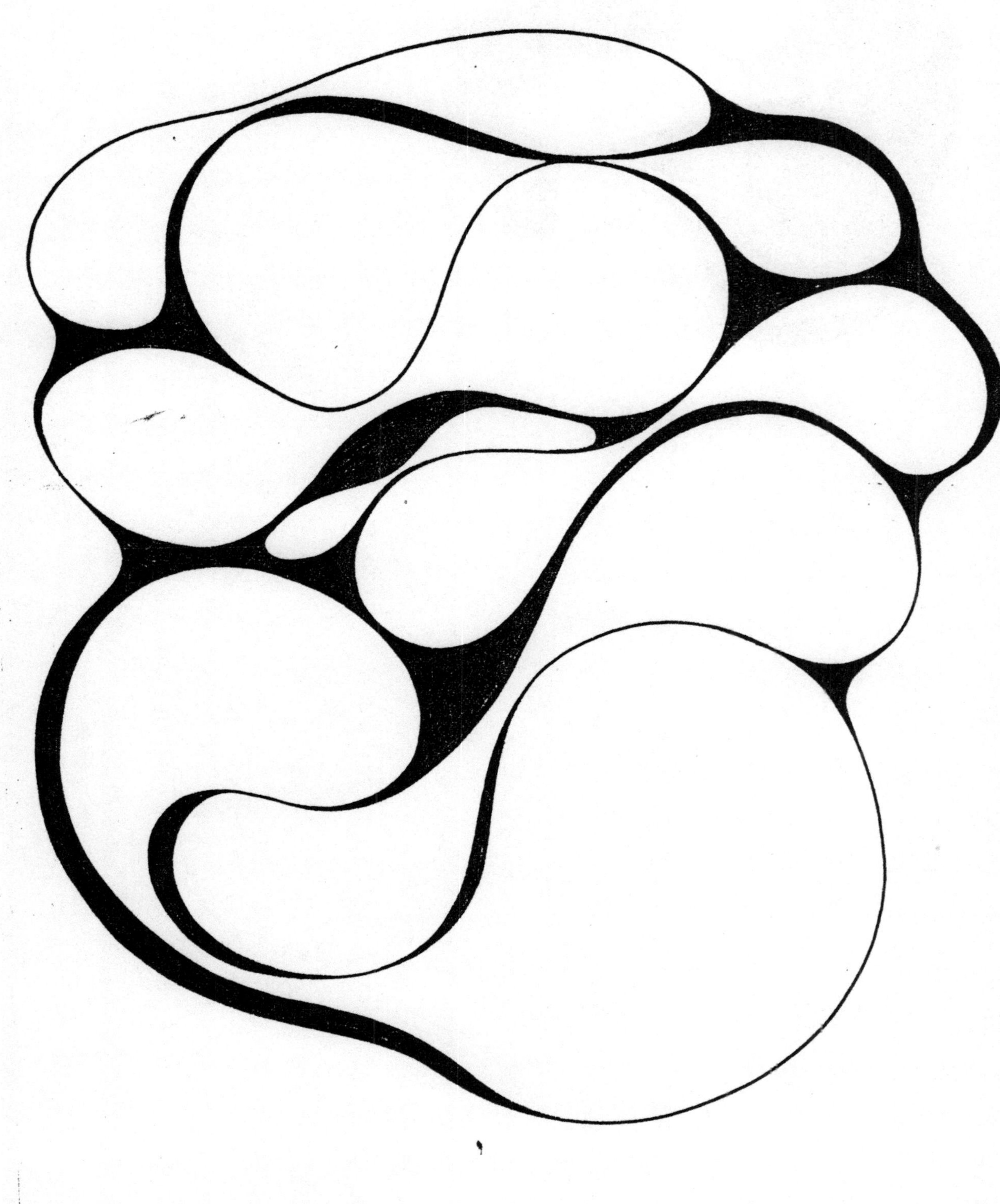

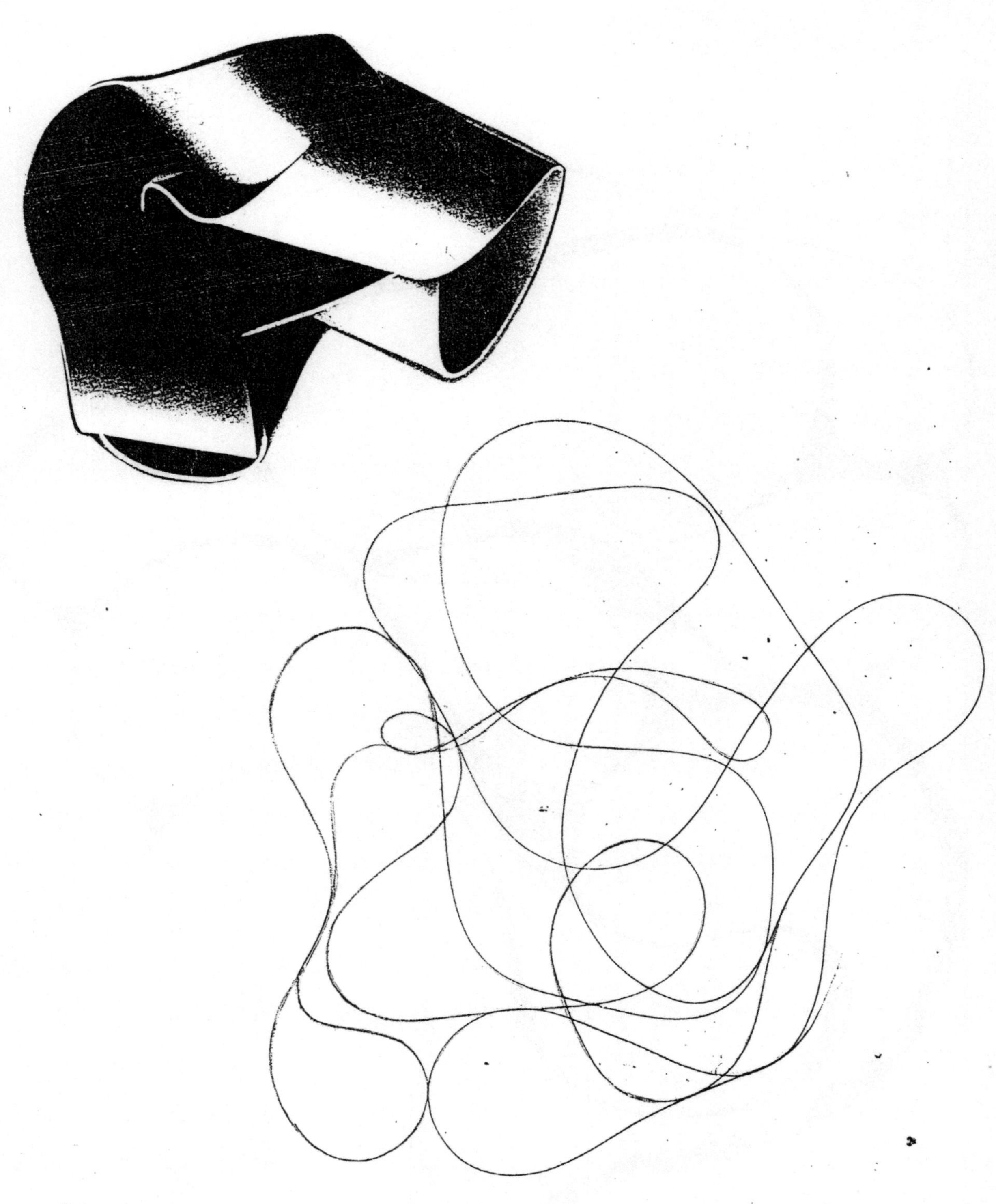

SCULPTURE

LIST OF SLIDES

BETTINA/BASHYI
222 west 23 St.
NEW YORK,N.Y.IOOII

I - 5 restructure/seastructure 1973 from euclidean to non-euclidean curve with developable absolute

ONE CONSTANT

four-dimensional studies in auto-regenerating energies

These are IO" models for monumental sculpture
both walk-under and architectural spaces
They were executed while ill in bed during one year 1973.
They are composed of eighty-six equal parts glued together one at a time.
Each is an indentical circular form.

---

6 SHANGO series of shrine objects * NON-WAIVER 1980/8I

ONE CONSTANT/ balance points KNIFE EDGE PLANE/CURVE/EDGE

These are 3' - 6' models in wood to be cast and fabricated in other materials. Because my woodworking shop was forced to close after a sizable rent increase , I was forced to execute these models while on a liquid diet (not having eaten solid food for one full month).

---

7 RETAKE/OUTTAKE series of filmtwists 1983/4

ONE CONSTANT (Io-I4" models)

This project derives from my experience with the medium of film.
The material is railroad-board models to be realized in steel and stone and monumental sculpture. Originally planned for the CITY OF LA.

---

8 CONTINUUM / ONE CONSTANT (20" models) 1968-85

wood models

These are planned for monumental sculpture in stone, etc.
Other models are gates and drive-under sculpture / always site specific

---

9 FINITE STRUCTURES/ ORTHOGON series 1969-

LINE/MASS/VOLUME studies for architecture

solid state and skeletal structures/volumetric spaces
mass/paintings

RANDOM PENETRATION OF FOUR EQUAL CONSTANTS BY EIGHT ELEMENTS OF PROGRESSIVE DISPLACEMENT

23 out of a possible I,048,576

Marble award ITALY I970 to execute this project in part/BLACK AND WHITE MARBLE which evolved from CONTINUUM.
Presented at INTERNATIONAL PHYSICS SUMMER SCHOOL,Varenna,Italy
SIX TO THE EIGHTH POWER

IO FRENCH KEYS PARIS I970 became KEYS & KEYHOLES series KNOW THYSELF series

Figurative series began at this time on paper tablecloths of Paris.
Each figure (99 in KEY series) can be any site specific size.
These are drawings(created to be cut as keys when I was denied the possibility of purchasing actual keys for purposes of exhibition in France).Actual key series numbered 99 but the drawing was not predetermined, but strictly random. These exist in models/wood.

USURP

CLONE

SEIZE

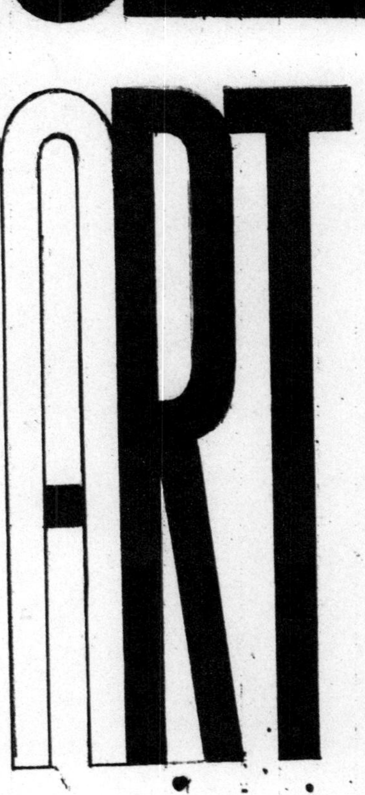

BENEVOLENT PREDATOR ACUITY

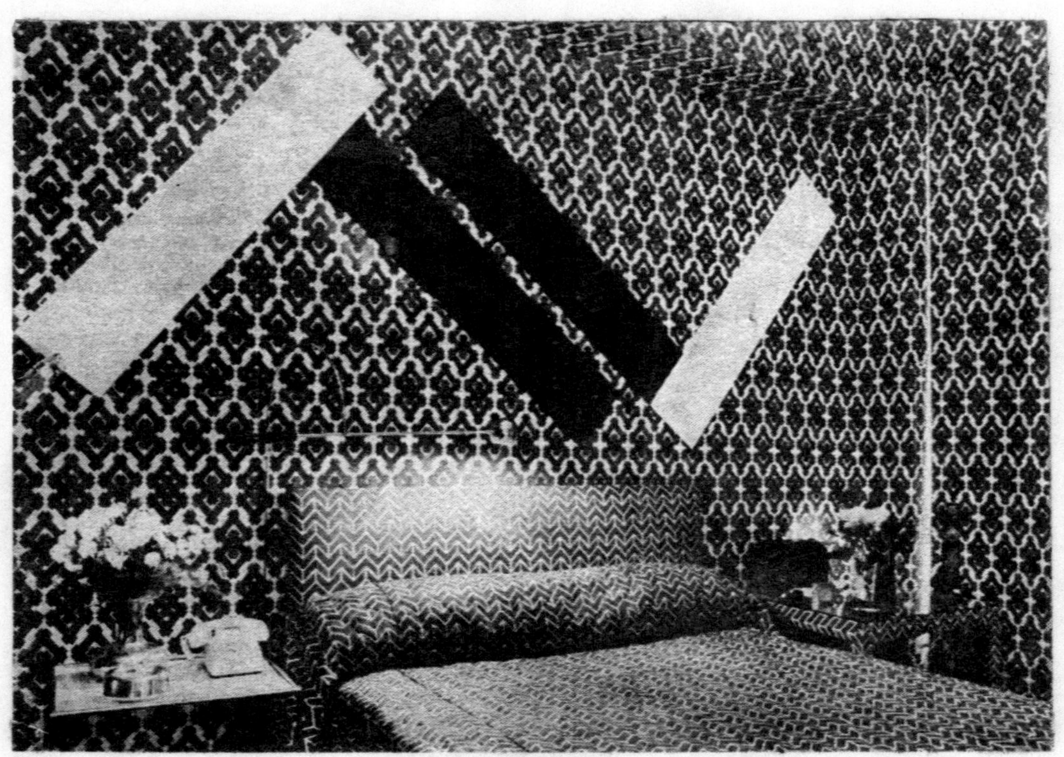

BITTER BROWN & WHITE
FOUR ELEMENTS 1:5

1969

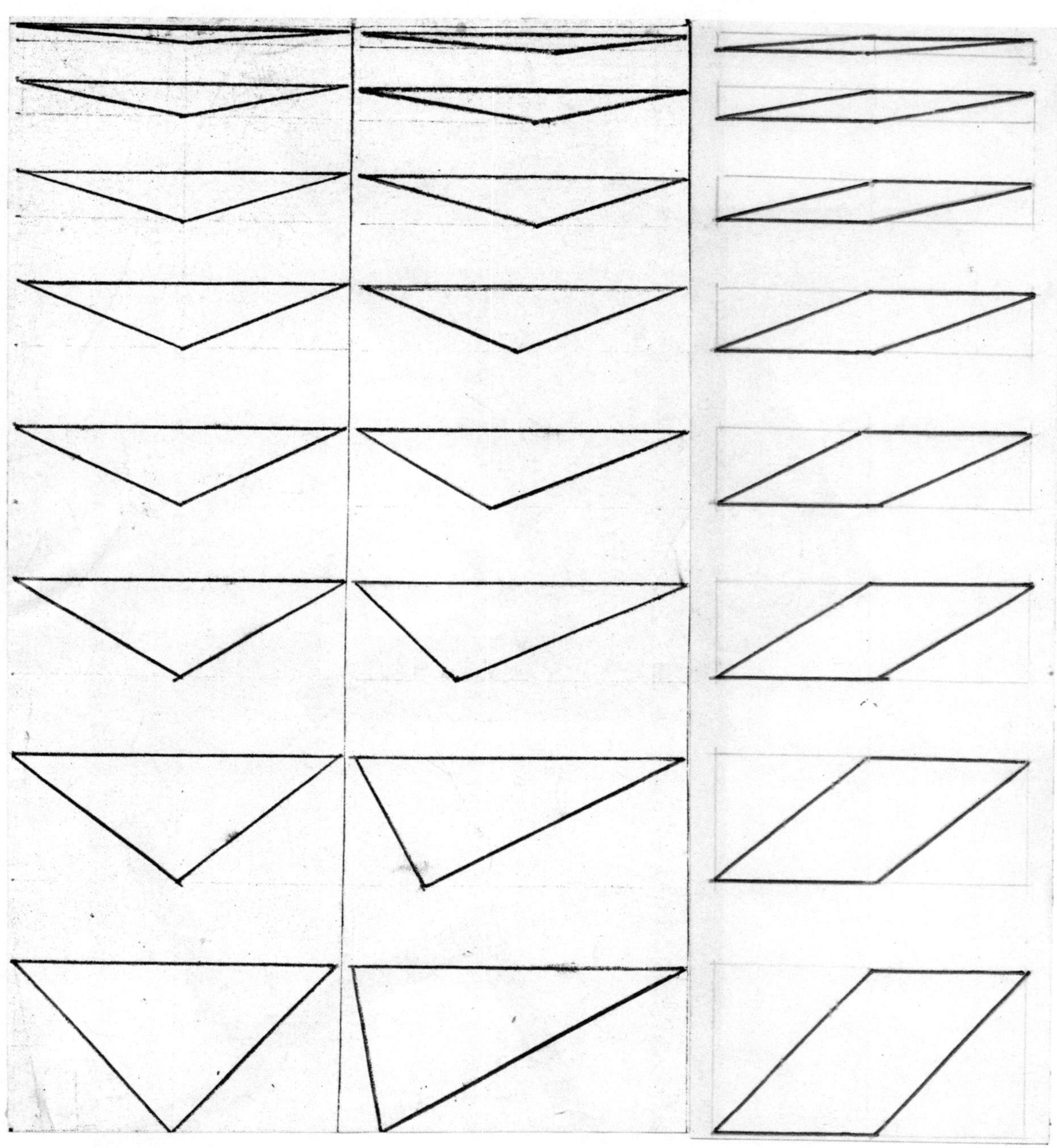

DEDIMENSION
of a three-dimensional orthogon

FINITE STRUCTURES 1969-

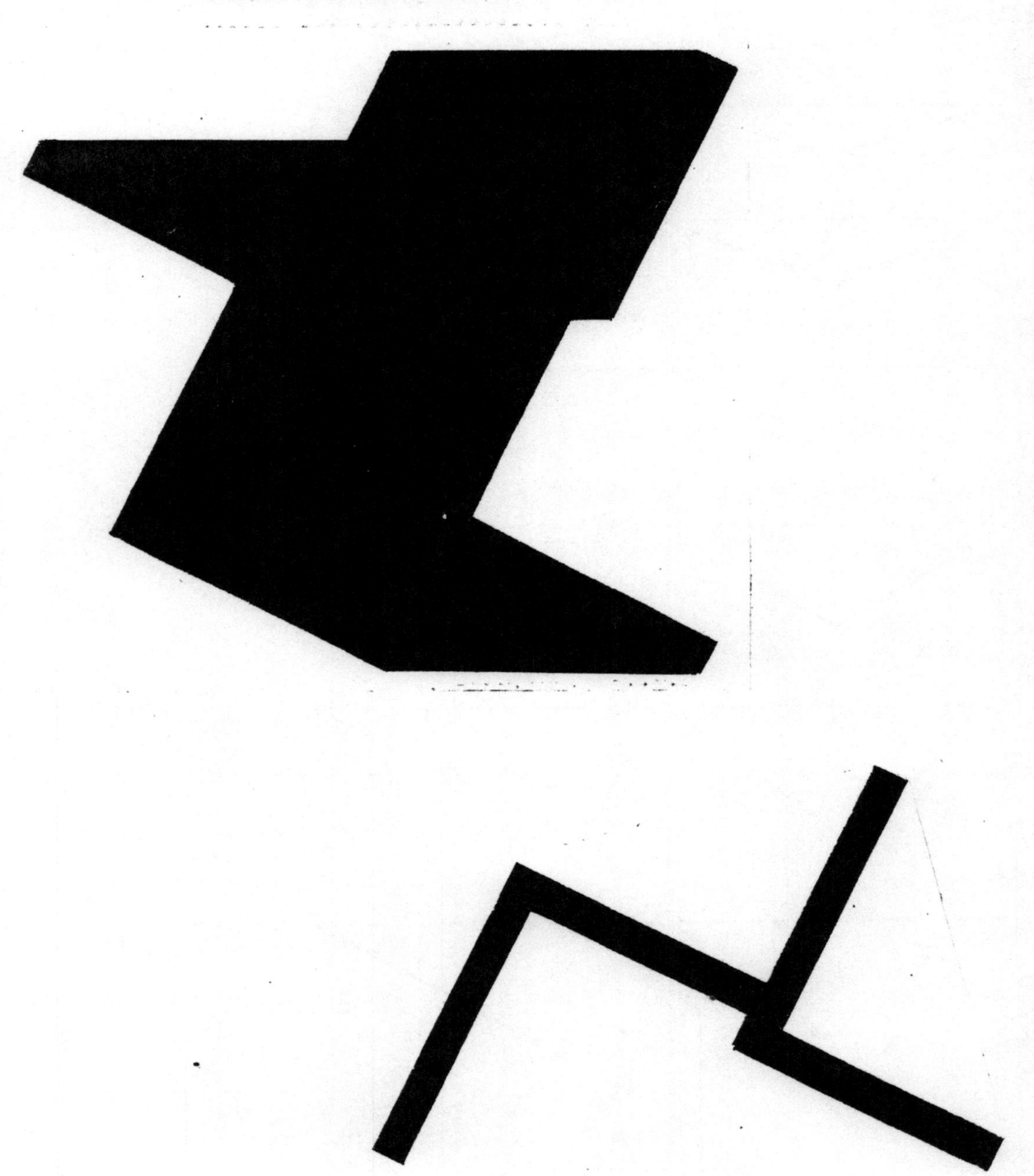

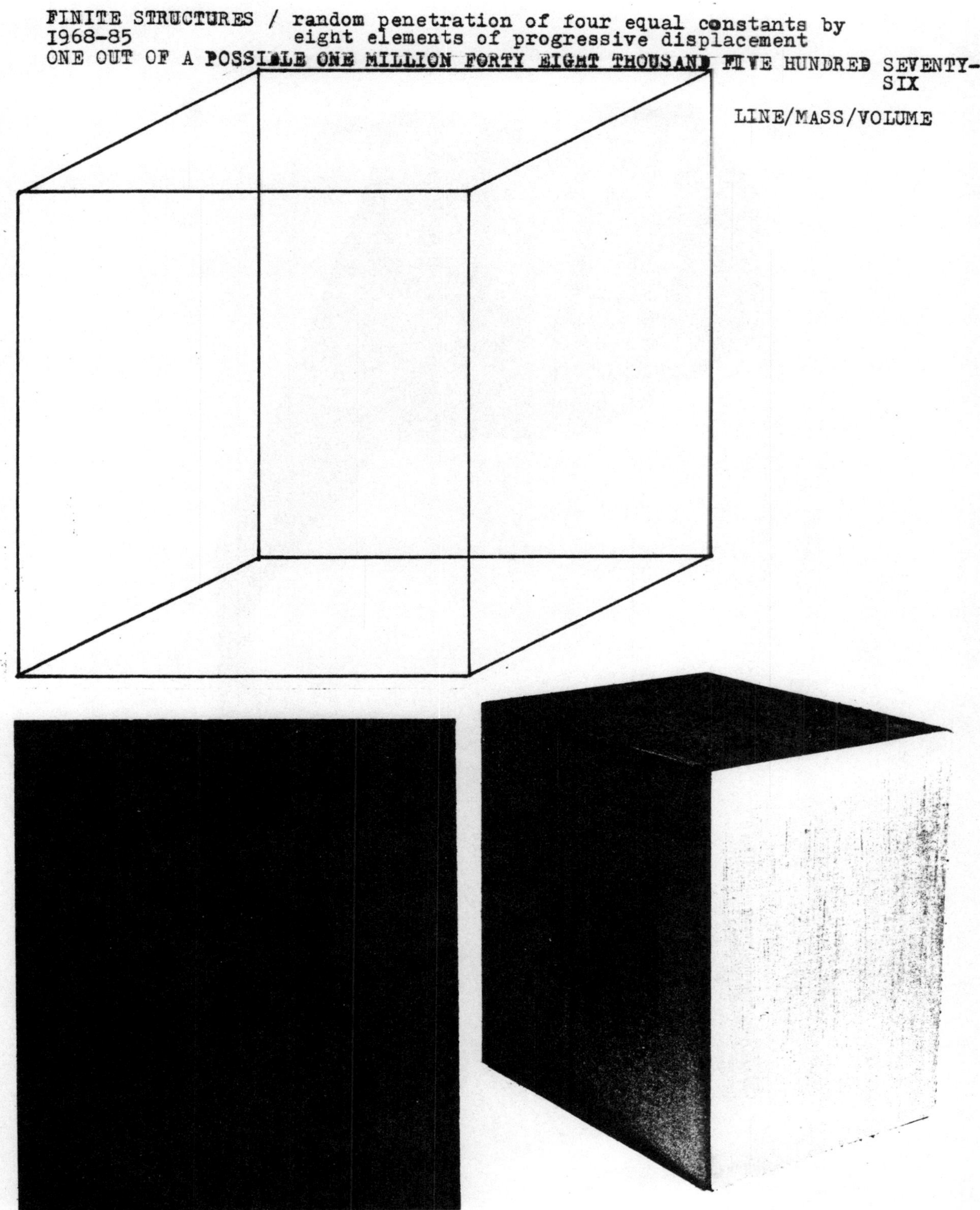
FINITE STRUCTURES / random penetration of four equal constants by
1968-85 eight elements of progressive displacement
ONE OUT OF A POSSIBLE ONE MILLION FORTY EIGHT THOUSAND FIVE HUNDRED SEVENTY-SIX
LINE/MASS/VOLUME

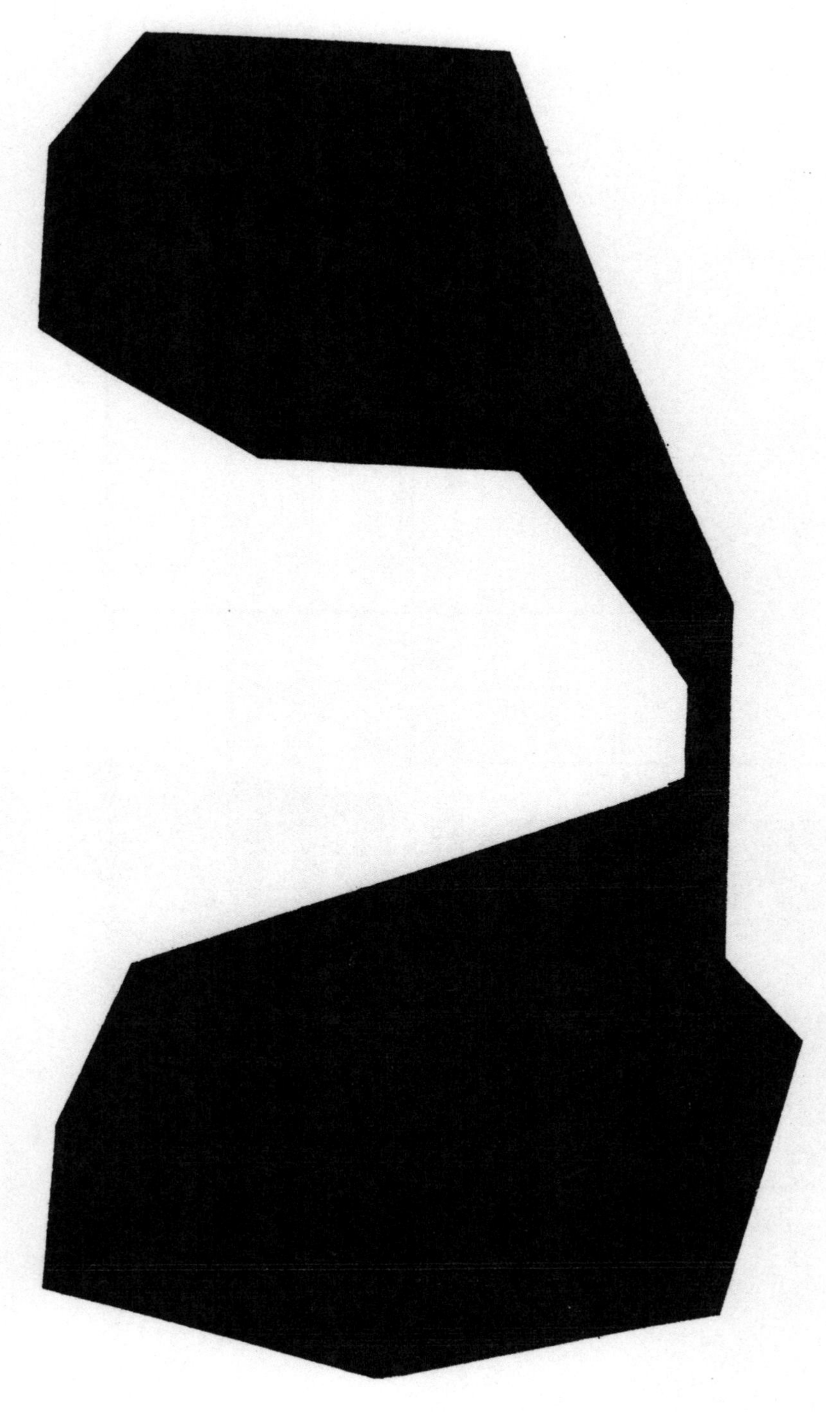

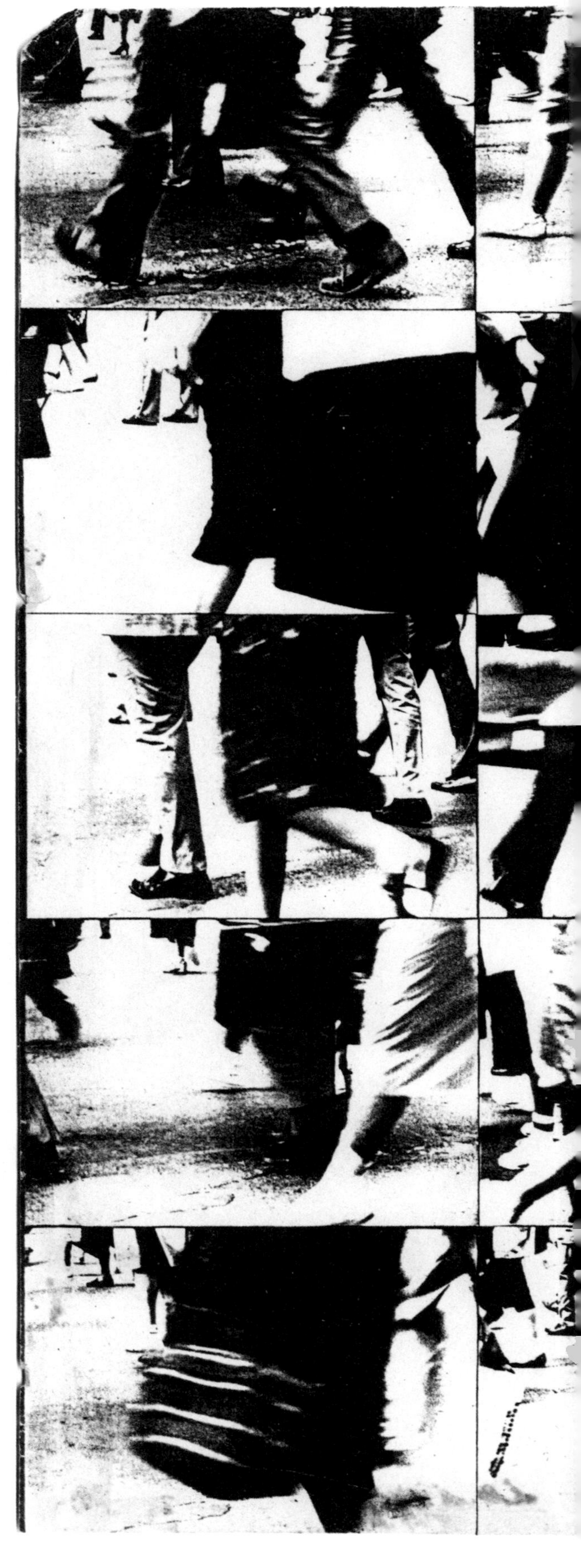

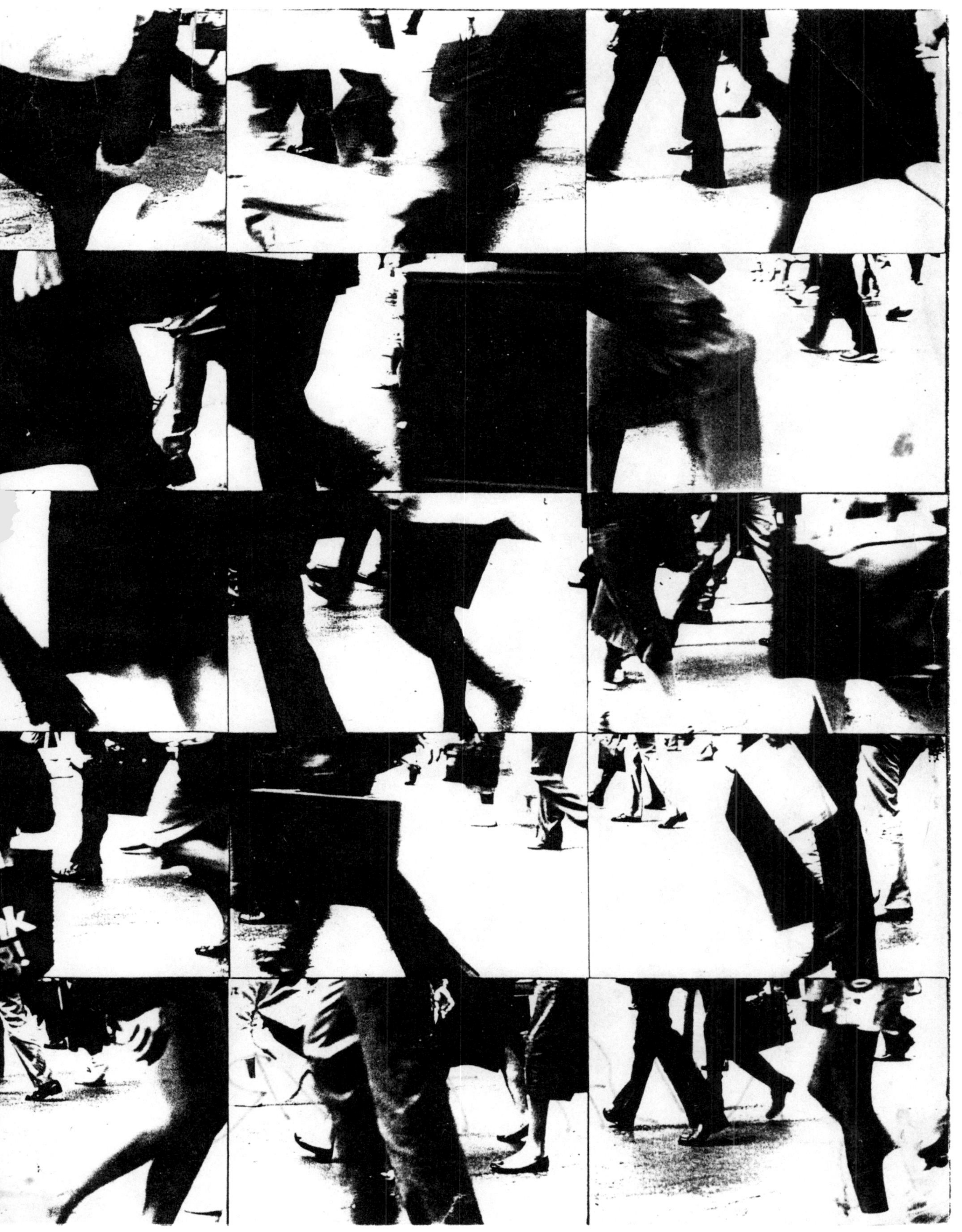

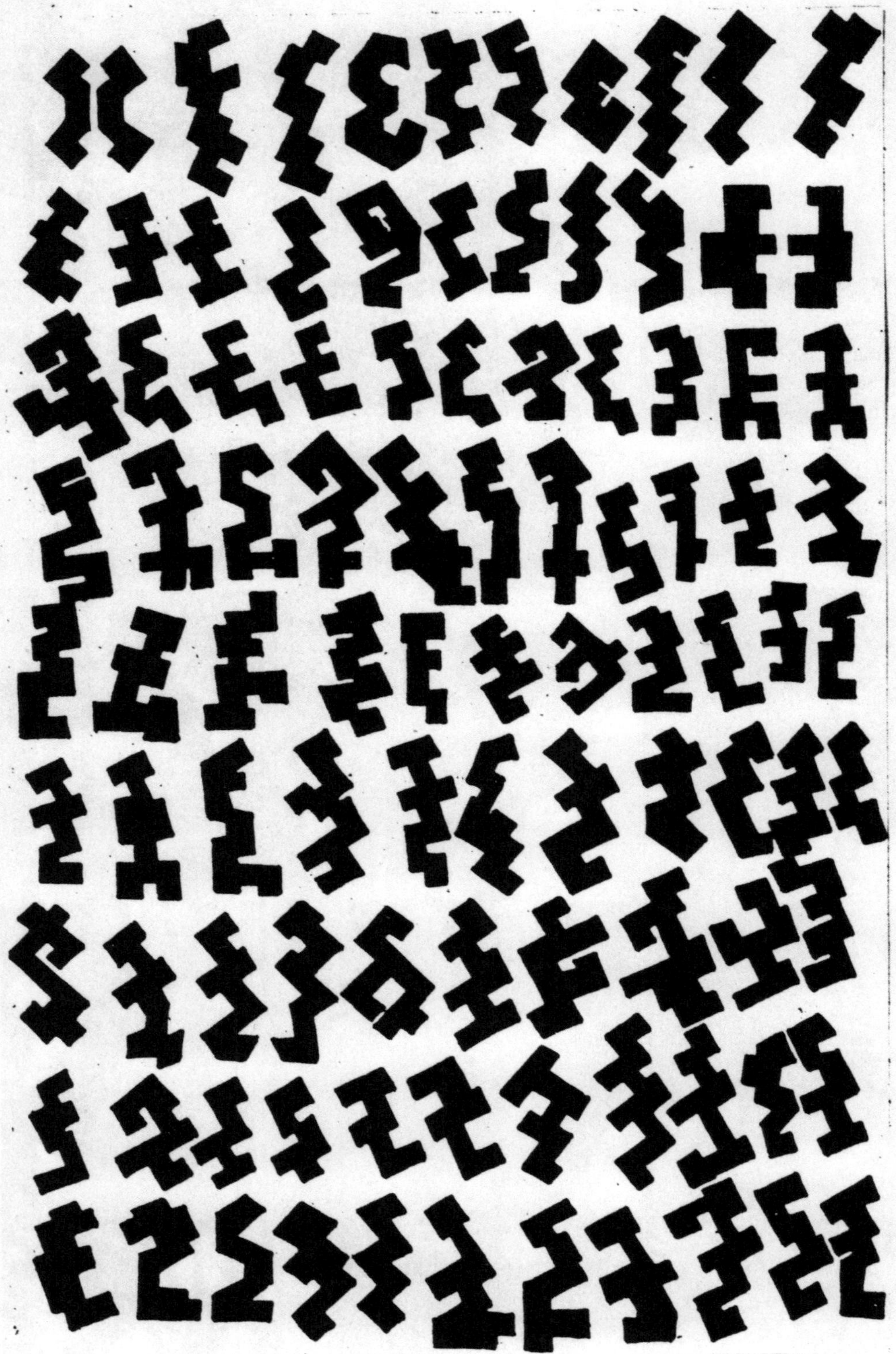
KETS / PARIS 1970
DRAWING/SCULPTURE

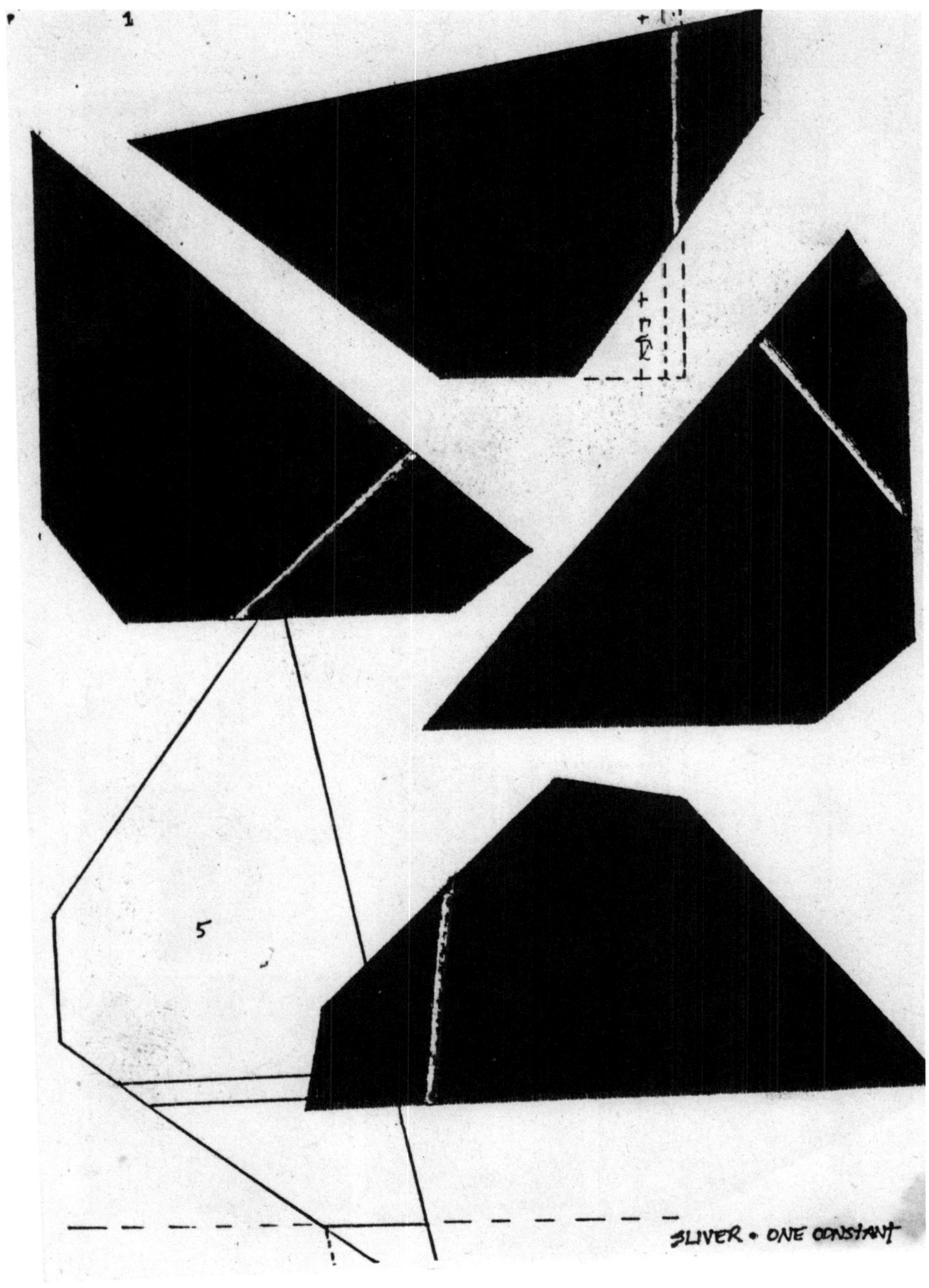
1
5
SLIVER • ONE CONSTANT

FINITE STRUCTURES 1969 - random penetration of four equal constants by eight elements of progressive displacement.

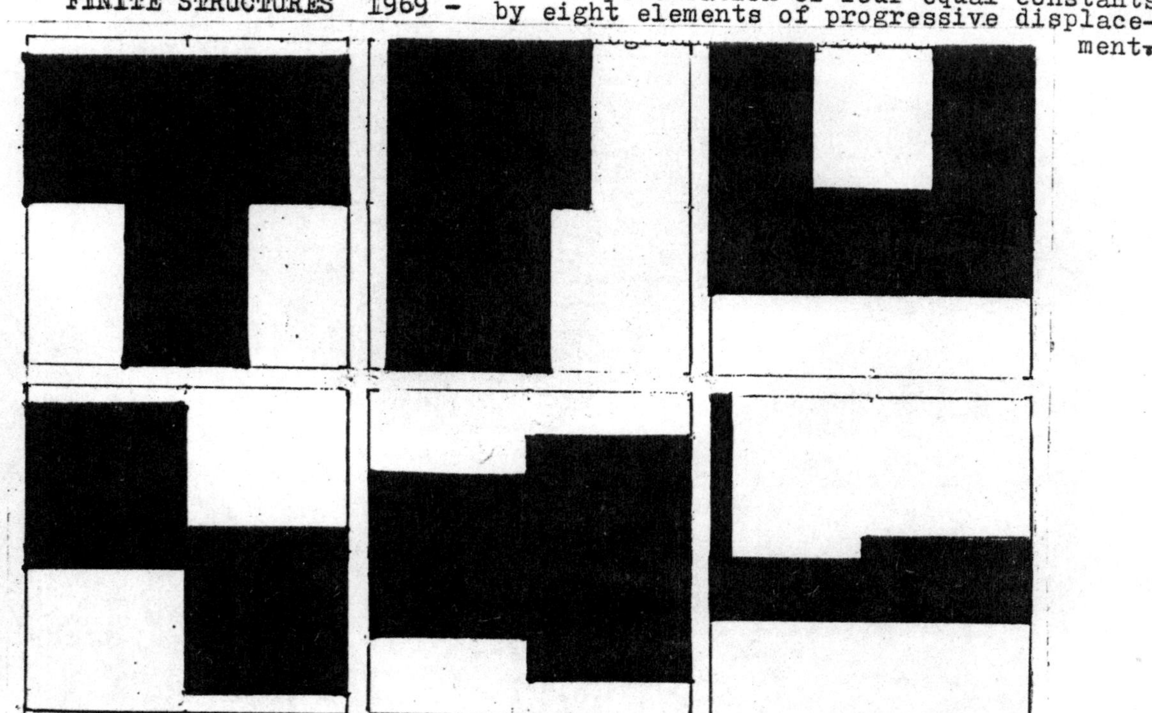

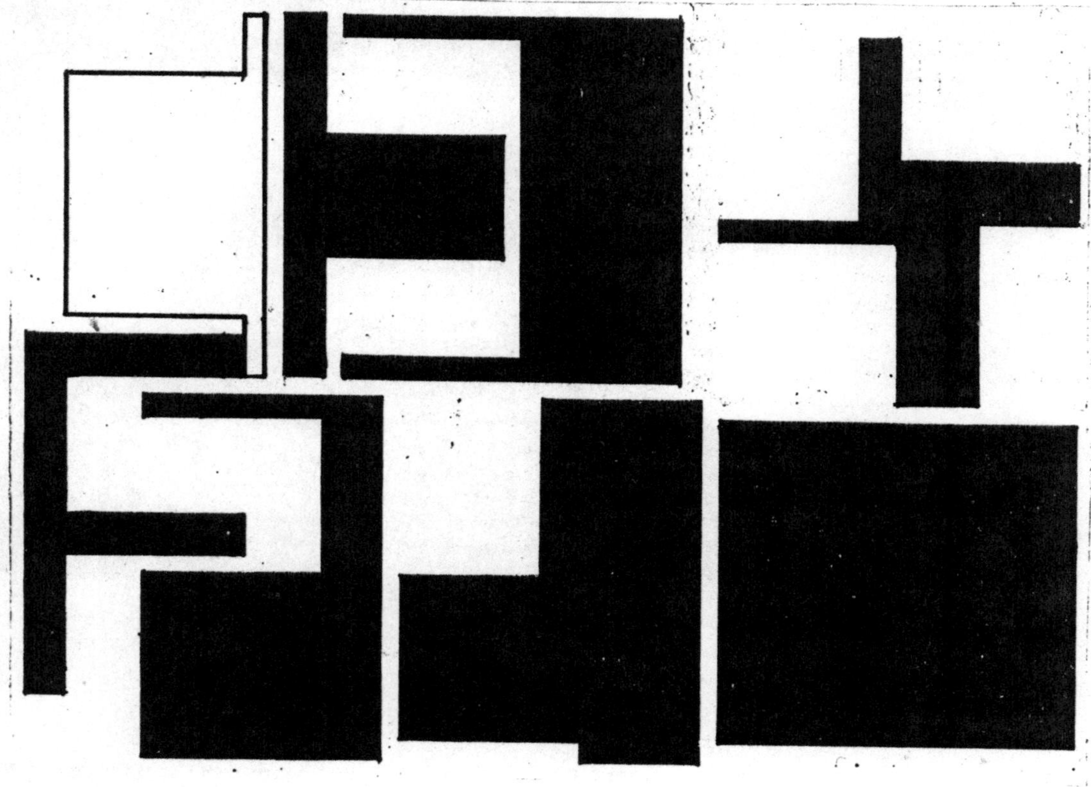

TITLES :

STUDIES IN RANDOM CONSTANT

THE FIFTH POINT OF THE COMPASS/DEMOGRAPHICS ON 23 ST.
RED AND GREEN
TAXI
CANAL/LAGOON
VENETIAN WINDOWS
VENETIAN TRANSPORT
ITALIAN STONE HEADS
TURKISH TRANSPORT
TURKISH TILES
BOSPHORUS BOATS
ON THE BOSPHORUS

NEW YORK FROM A TO Z
BOAT DETAILS
FISHING BASKETS
MARATHON
HALLOWEEN
EASTER
PARADE OF SAIL 1976
1986
BOTANICAL GARDENS
HEADLINES

ISTANBUL/VENICE/BYZANTIUM
ACUTE/OBTUSE/RIGHT : THE ANGLE IN PARIS
CONSTRUCT/DESTRUCT : THE PARISIAN EXPERIENCE
CRYSTAL/EIFFEL/PALM/LEAF/TREE/ PATTERNS OF GROWTH
ESCALIER
THE FIFTH POINT OF THE COMPASS/STUDIES IN RANDOM COSTANT
NEW YORK FROM A TO Z / DEMOGRAPHICS ON TWENTY-THIRD STREET
PHENOMENOLOGICAL NEW YORK/ URBAN ENERGY STRATEGIES
TRAFFIC PATTERNS / INTERNATIONAL
ASPHALT ART
STREET ART
INSIDE THE STRUCTURE / PARIS/NEW YORK
BERLIN ARCHITECTS
PORTRAITS
AUTO-RITRATTO
BRITISH MAN-HOLE COVERS
BARKFORMS PARIS/NEW YORK ONE TREE/13FORMS
BYZANTINE MOSAICS
PATTERNS OF GROWTH : STRUCTURAL STUDIES IN LINEAR TRANSPC
PARKING LOT / HAIR /MASTS/THE ITALIAN LINE
AN EYE FOR AN EYE / OFF THE FRAME
PARIS KEYS
DIALOGUES / LINE/MASS/VOLUME
ESCALIER
ABSOLUTE FORM
DISPLACED ABSOLUTE
RESTRUCTURE/SEASTRUCTURE/CRUSTACEAN
UNTITLED / SPLASH/DRIP
RETAKE/OUTTAKE
SHANGO / DOUBLE-AXE SHRINE OBJECT
NON-WAIVER
PLANE/CURVE/EDGE
CONTINUUM / ONE CONSTANT
FINITE STRUCTURES / LINE/MASS/VOLUME/ISOMETRY
WORDWORKS I/II/III/IV/V
CONSTRUCT/DESTRUCT
PENETRATION/DISLOCATION/RELOCATION
PENETRATION/ELEVATION
PENETRATION/DISLOCATION/RELOCATION/INTEGRATION
THE ANGLE /
TWNTY-FOUR INCONSTANTS FROM ONE CONSTANT
ONE DOZEN EGGS / EVOLUTIONARY SYSTEMS/ B/W
HALF A DOZEN EGGS / TWO-LINE LIMITATION
TWO-LINE LIMITATION / SHEN SERIES / WELDED STEEL
SHEN SERIES / DIVISIBLE TOTALITIES
PROGRESSIVE DISPLACEMENT
FIELD THEORY / ONE CONSTANT
IN MEMORIAM : OPTIONS FOR AN ABSOLUTE / CRUCIFORM
DOUBLE-CROSS
TWO EQUAL ELEMENTS SEEN FROM THIRT-SIX POINTS OF VIEW
THE OPEN CUBE

FACTS ....AND THE SPACE BETWEEN

(a whole'nother story)

FINITE STRUCTURES /THEORY:1969

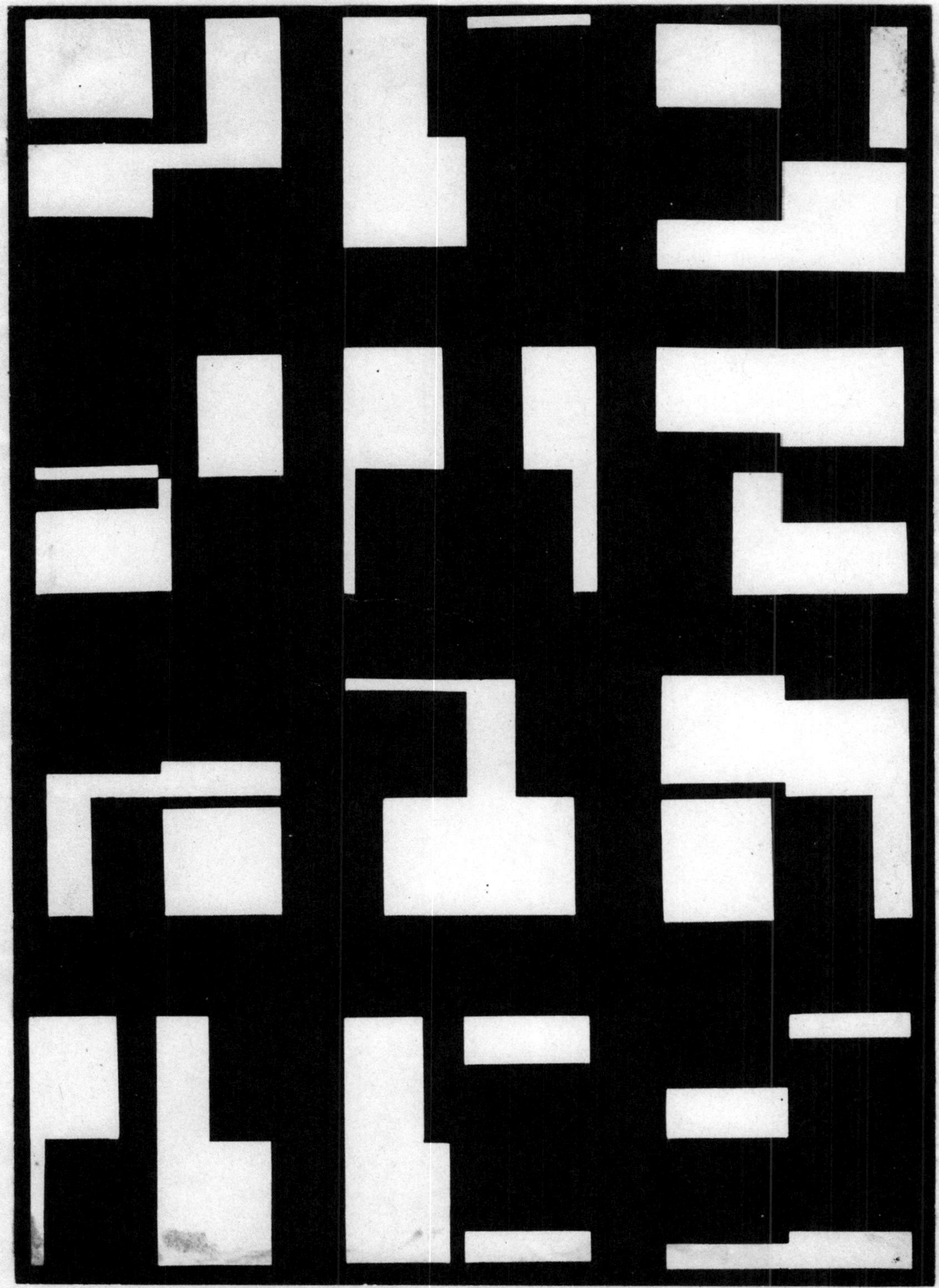

12 studies for painting/sculpture/mural THEORY:1969

FINITE STRUCTURES / PLAN XVIII (18) 1969 —

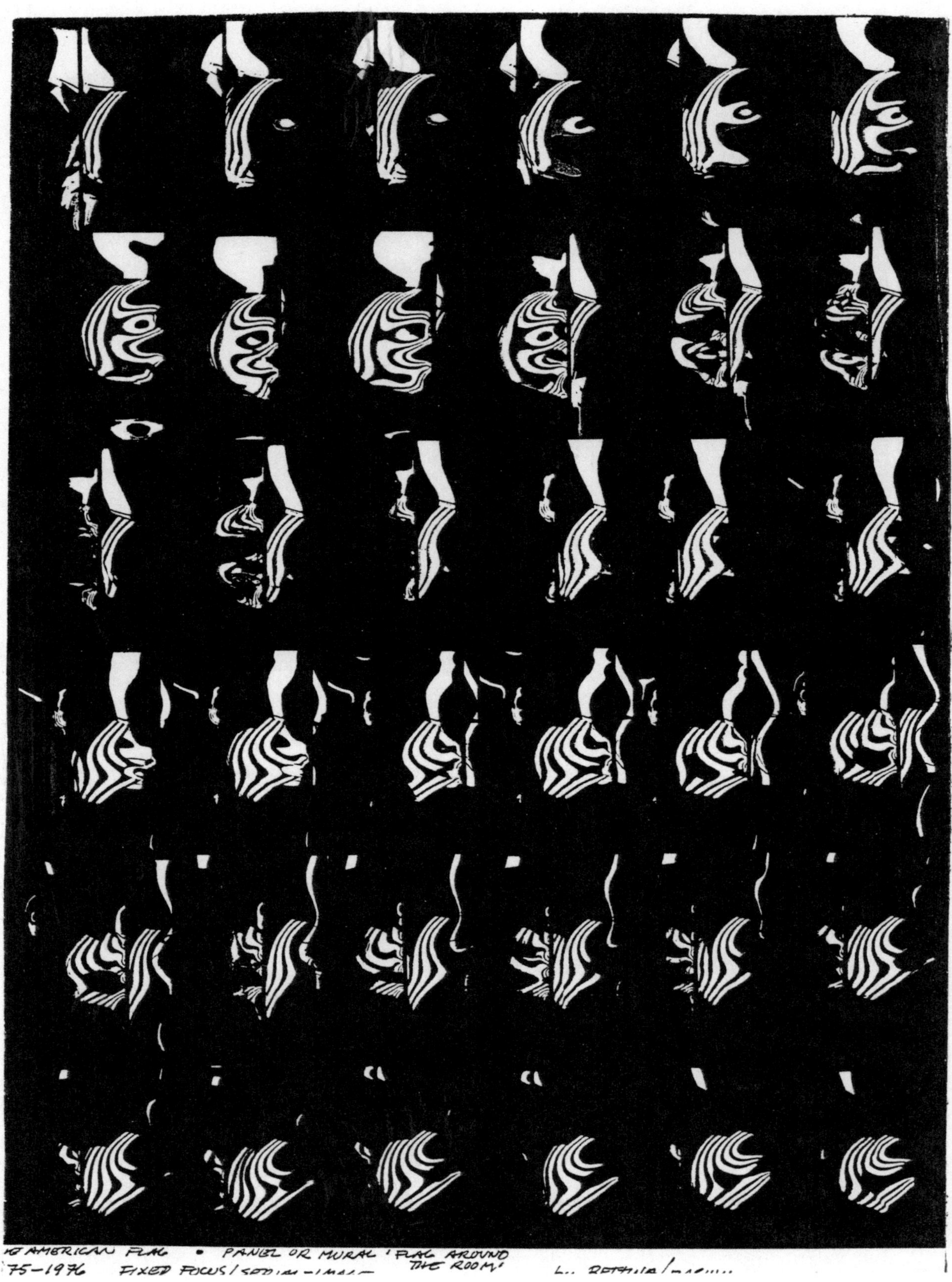
AMERICAN FLAG • PANEL OR MURAL 'FLAG AROUND THE ROOM'
75–1976 FIXED FOCUS/

Photography

"I was on the balcony, thinking about jumping, because everything seemed to be going missing I couldn't find this and that. Then I looked over the balcony, and I saw these people walking below me. Men carrying packages on their backs, shadows in front. And I thought ... I'd like to capture that. You find mystical coincidences when you concentrate on something hard enough. Something else comes into being, reinforcing what preceded it."

THE FIFTH POINT OF THE COMPASS / NEW YORK FROM A TO Z /
studies in random constant / fixed focus- time lapse 1977-85
O.K.HARRIS GALLERY - NEW YORK 1980 * RAIN/RUNNER/READER/RADIO/RED/ROLLER

NEW YORK FROM ABOVE / NEW YORK FROM BELOW / GRID CONSTRAINT
MAN WITH BOXES/MAN WITH BRIEFCASE/RUNNING MAN

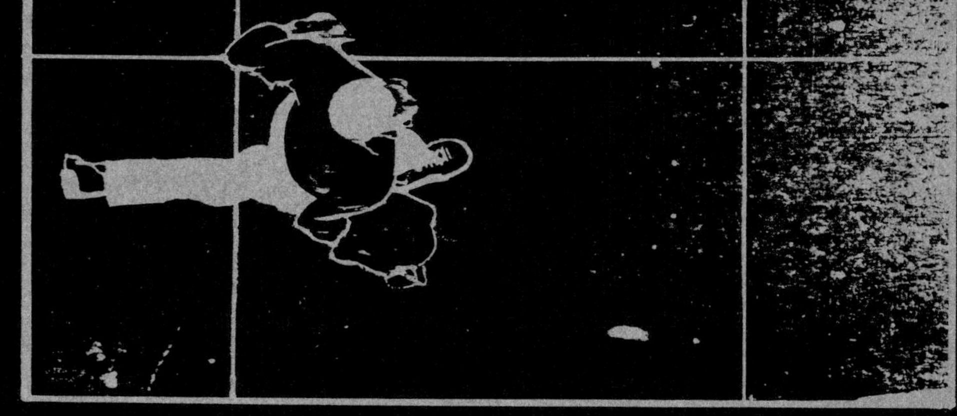

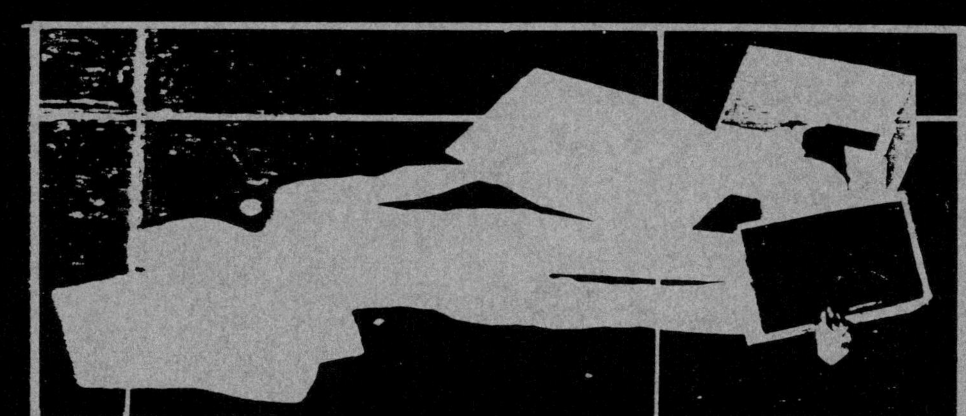

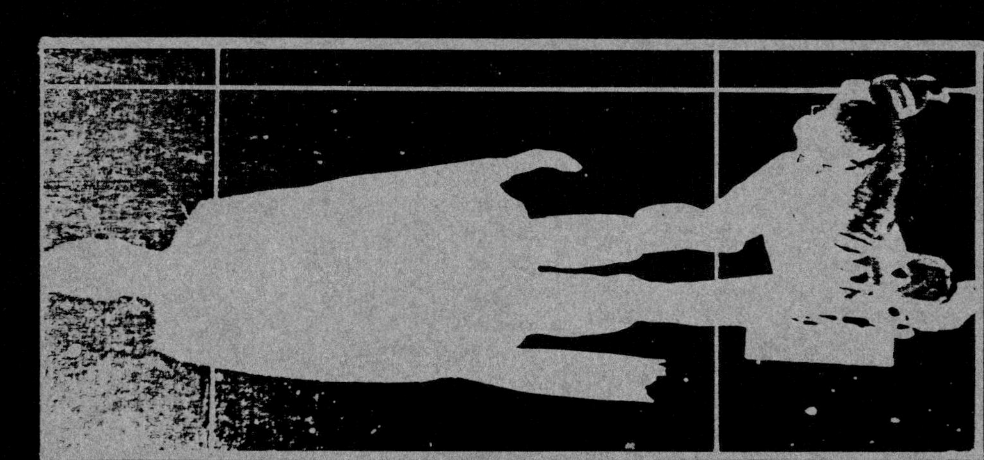

THE FIFTH POINT OF THE COMPASS
studies in random constant

FIXED FOCUS

29 BOXES
I6 IMAGES
I5 MINUTES
2 MEN
I HANDTRUCK

Pages 70–73: From the series *The Fifth Point of the Compass / New York From A to Z, Studies in Random Constant, Fixed Focus–Time Lapse*, 1977-85

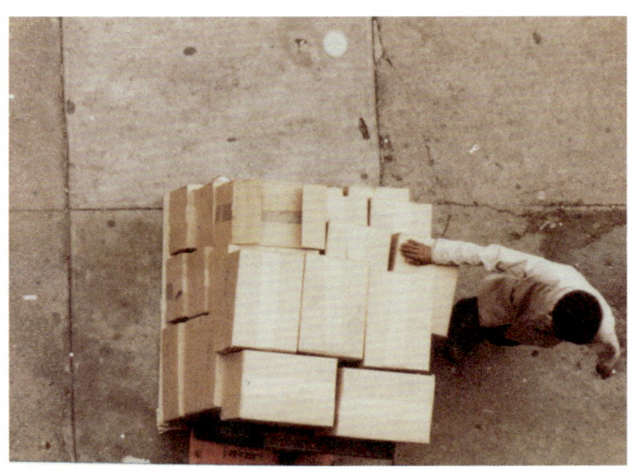

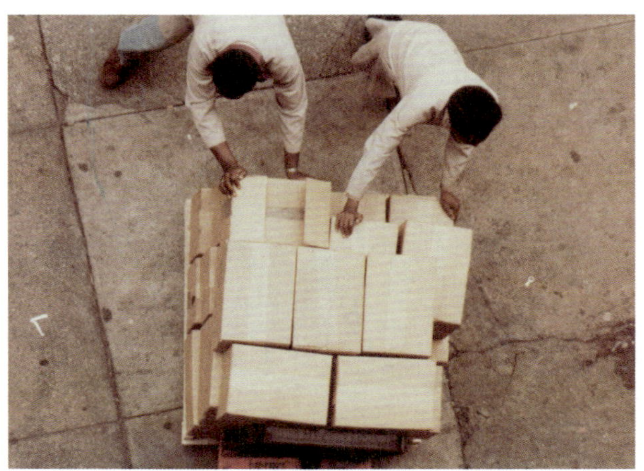

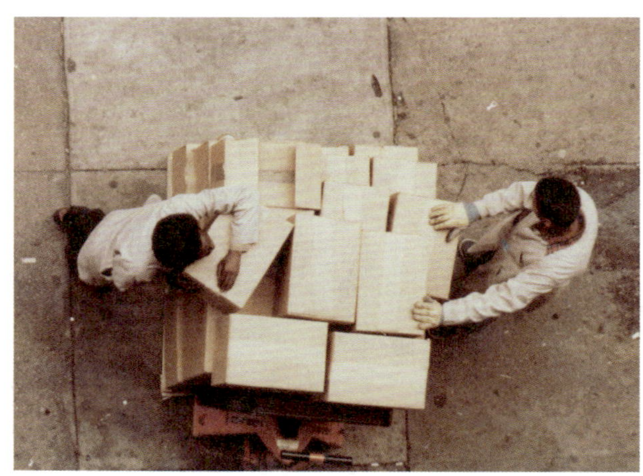

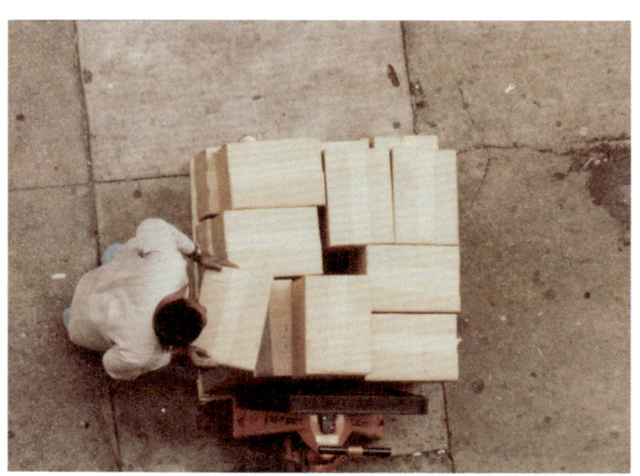

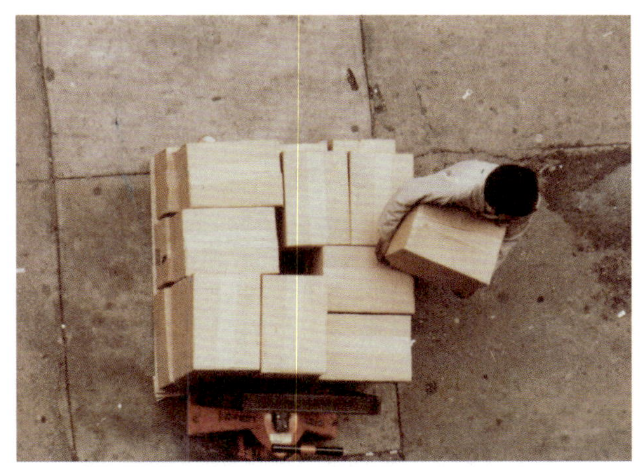

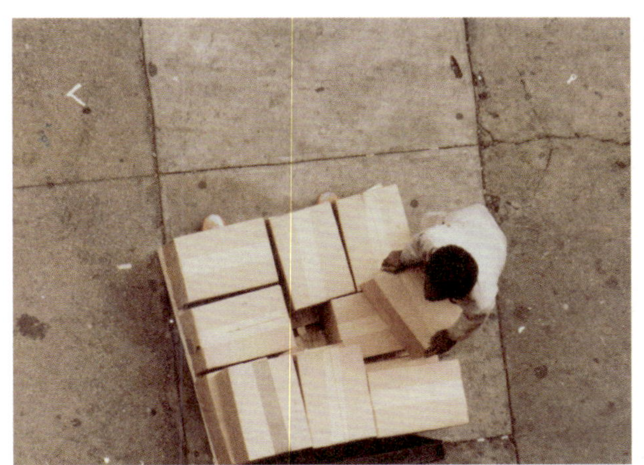

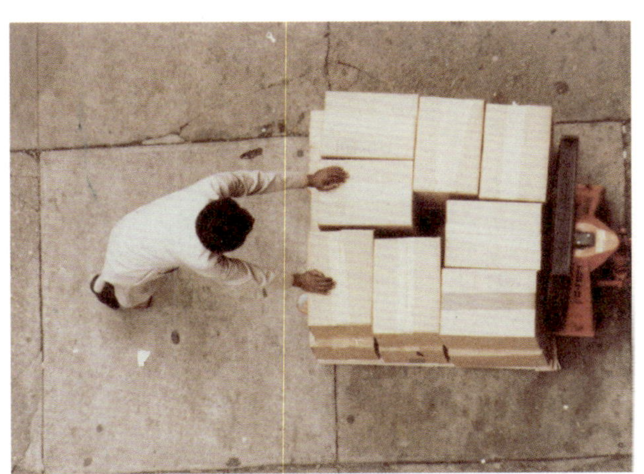

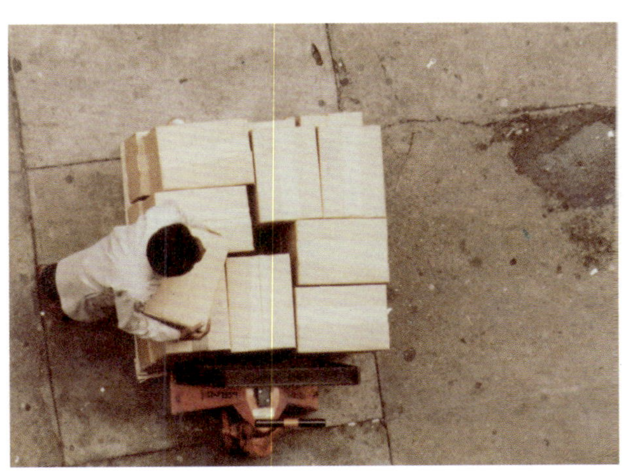

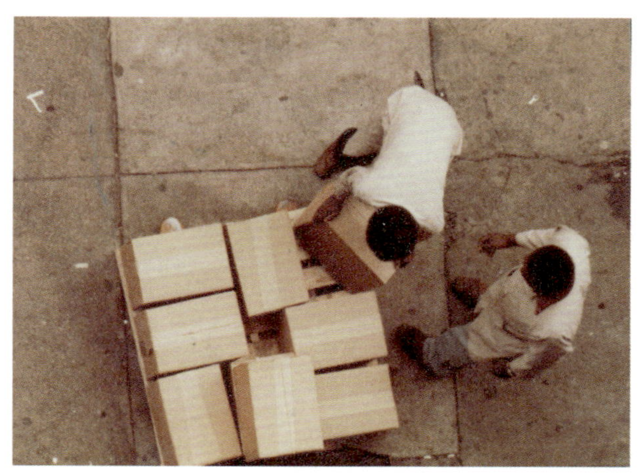

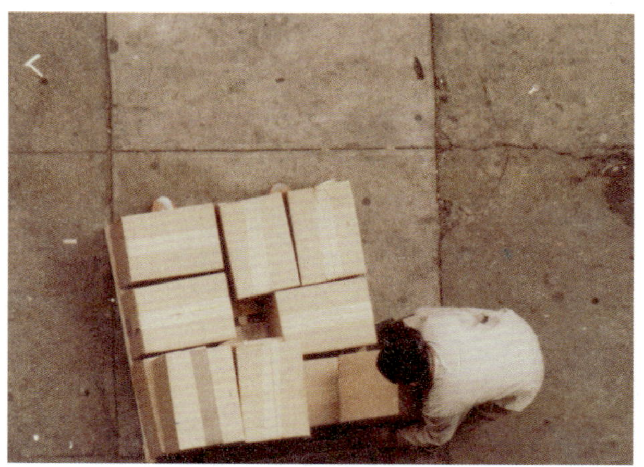

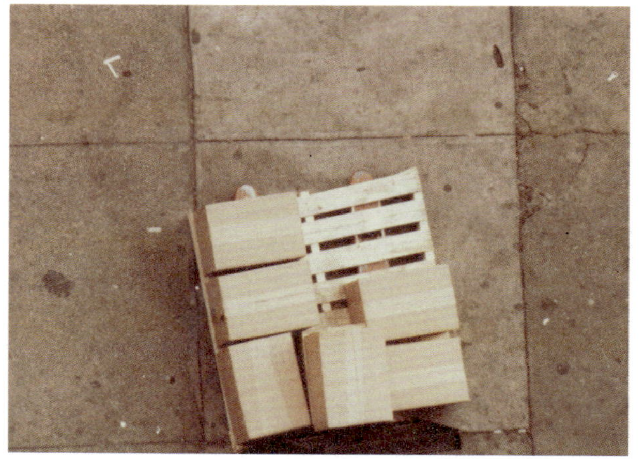

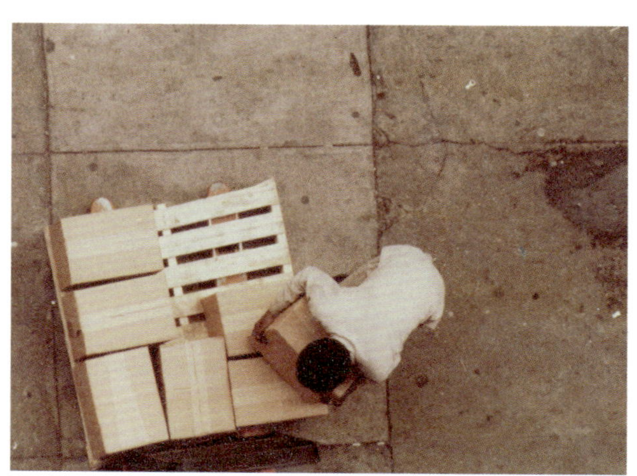

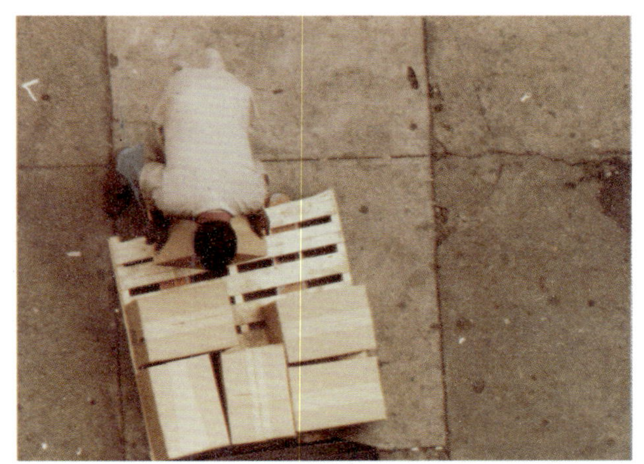
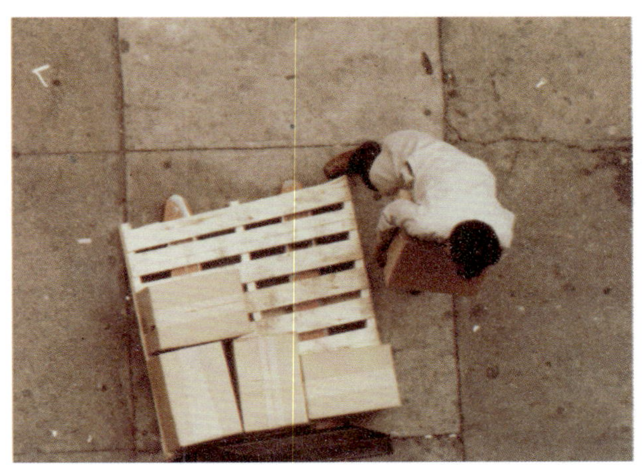
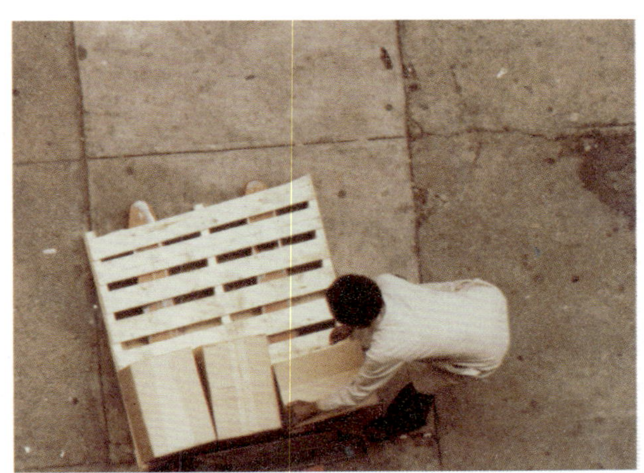
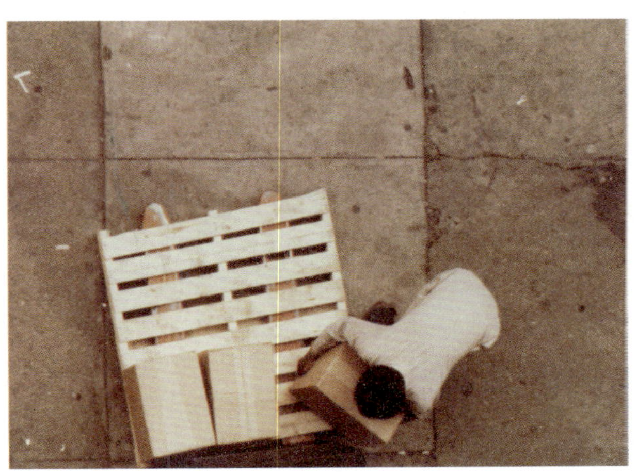

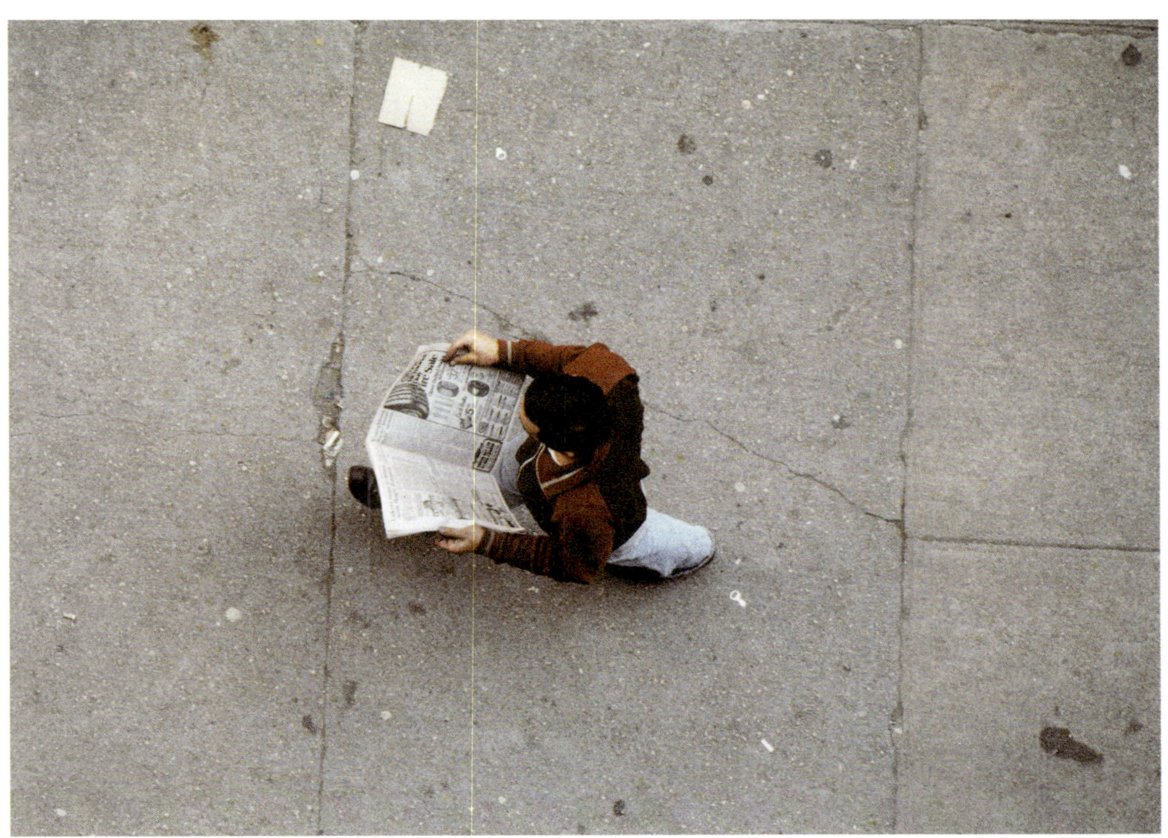

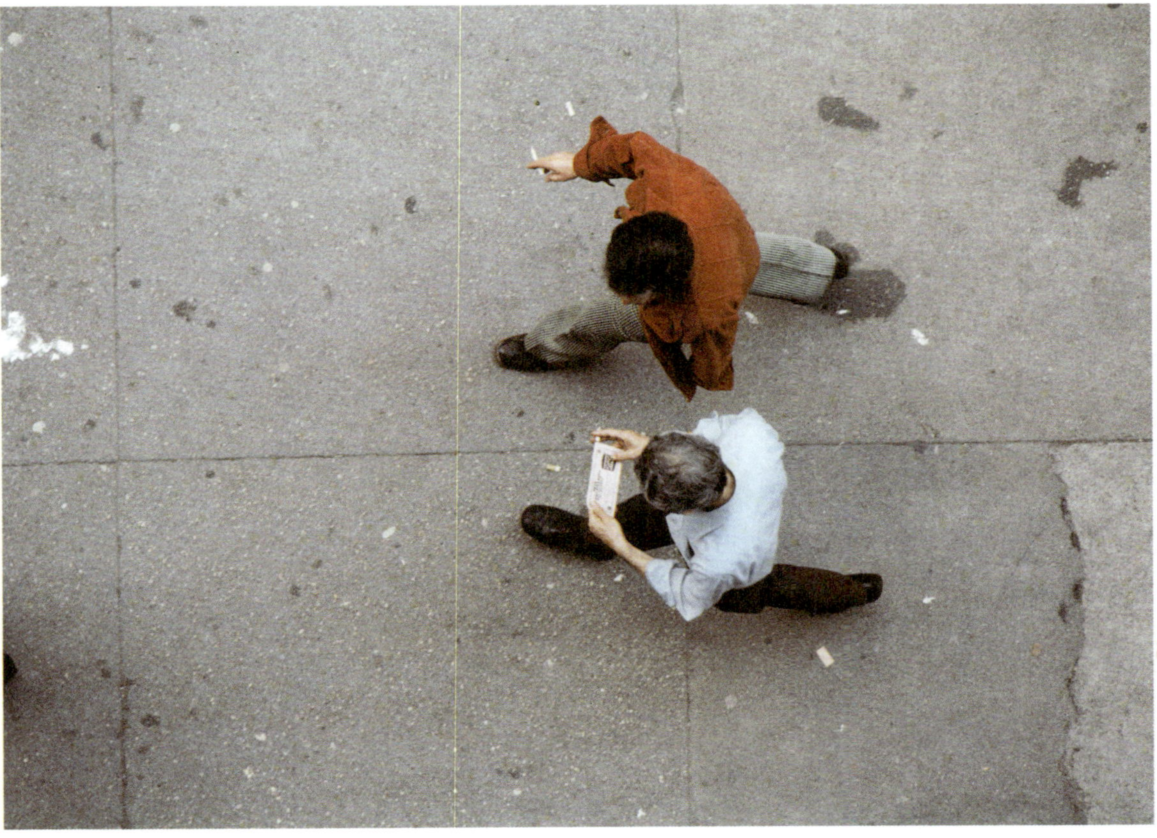

Pages 75–87: From the series *The Fifth Point of the Compass / New York From A to Z, Studies in Random Constant, Fixed Focus-Time Lapse*, RAIN, RUNNER, READER, RADIO, RED, ROLLER, 1977–85

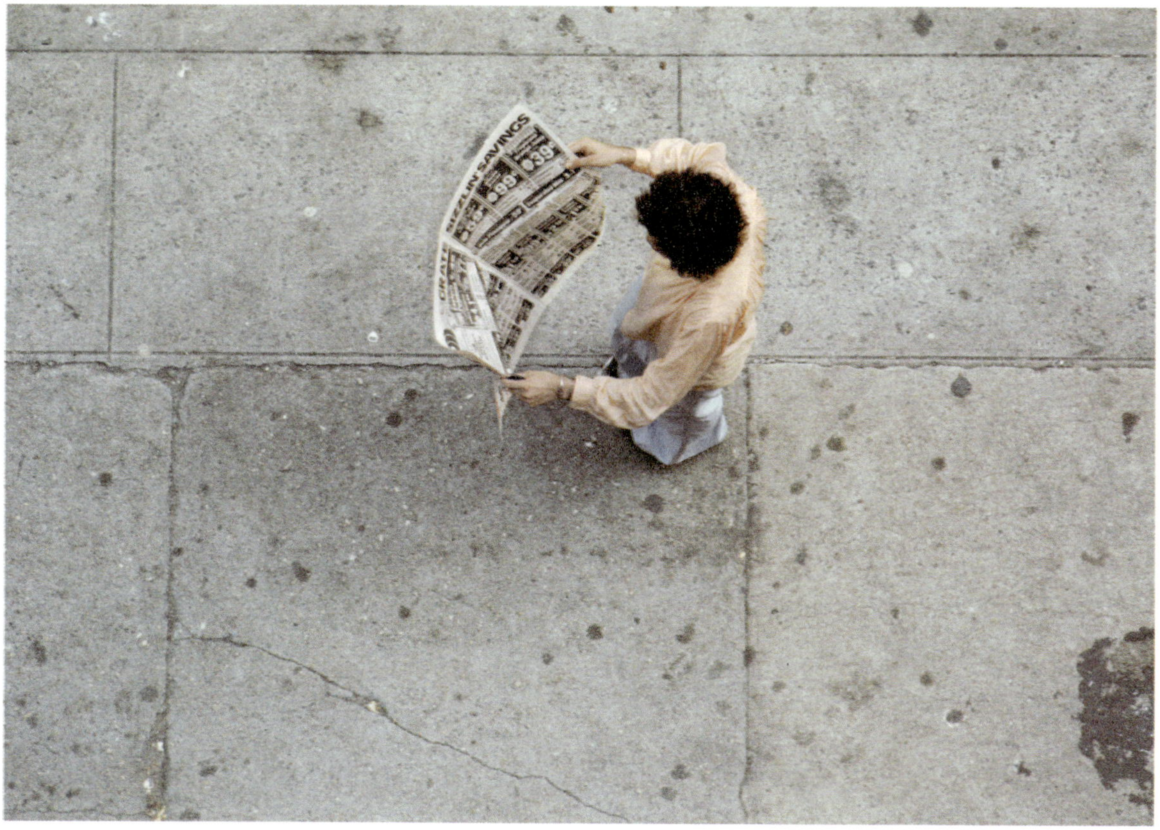

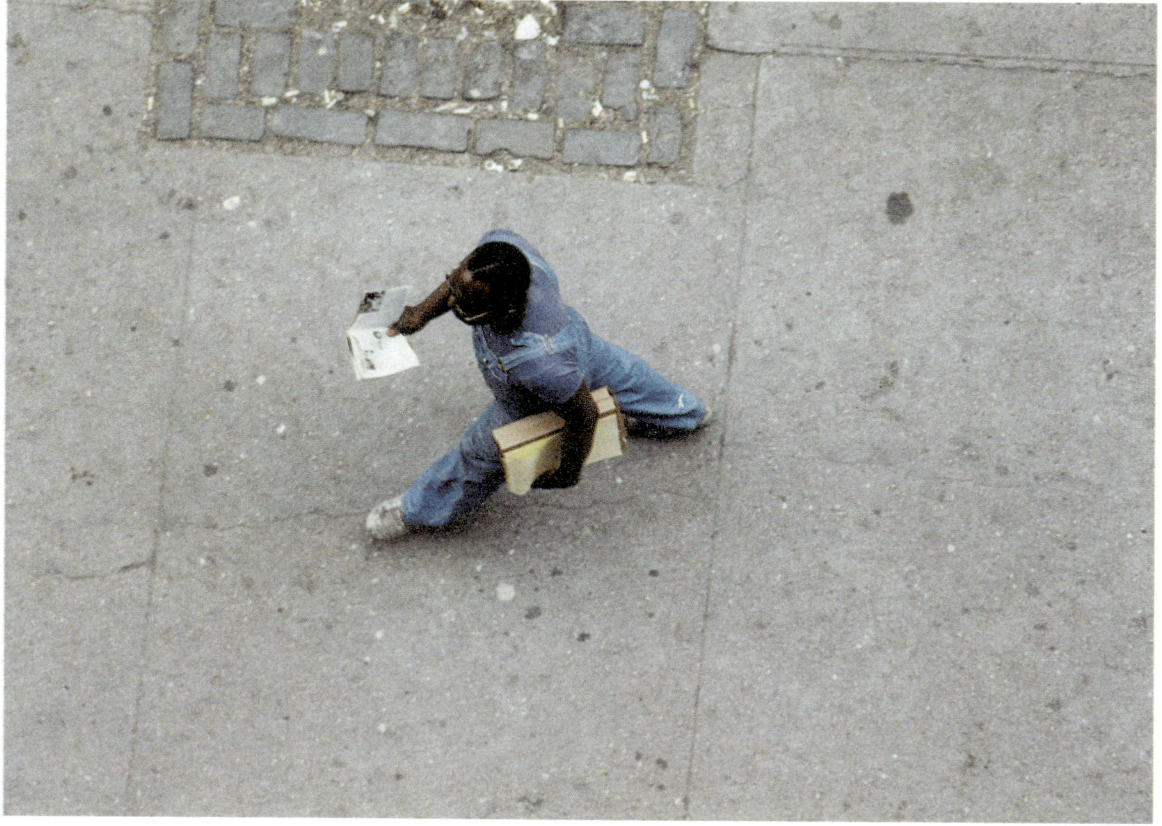

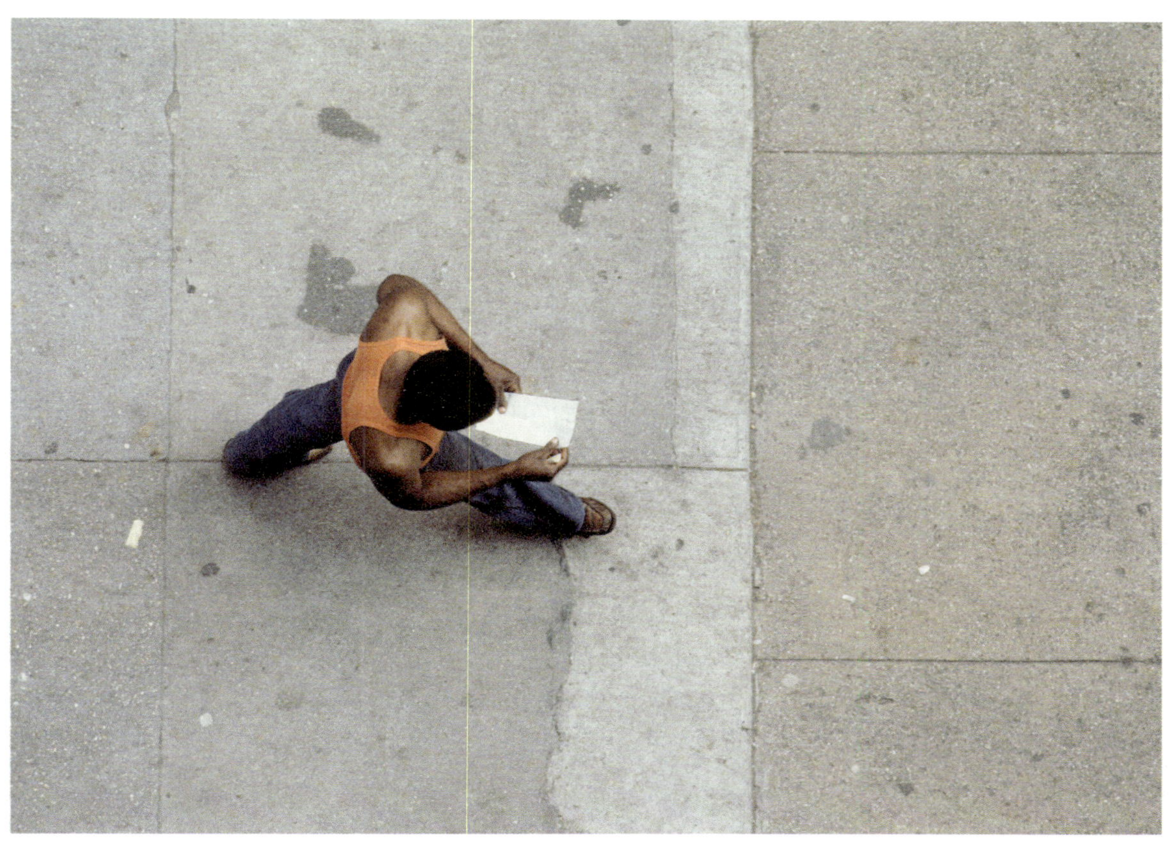

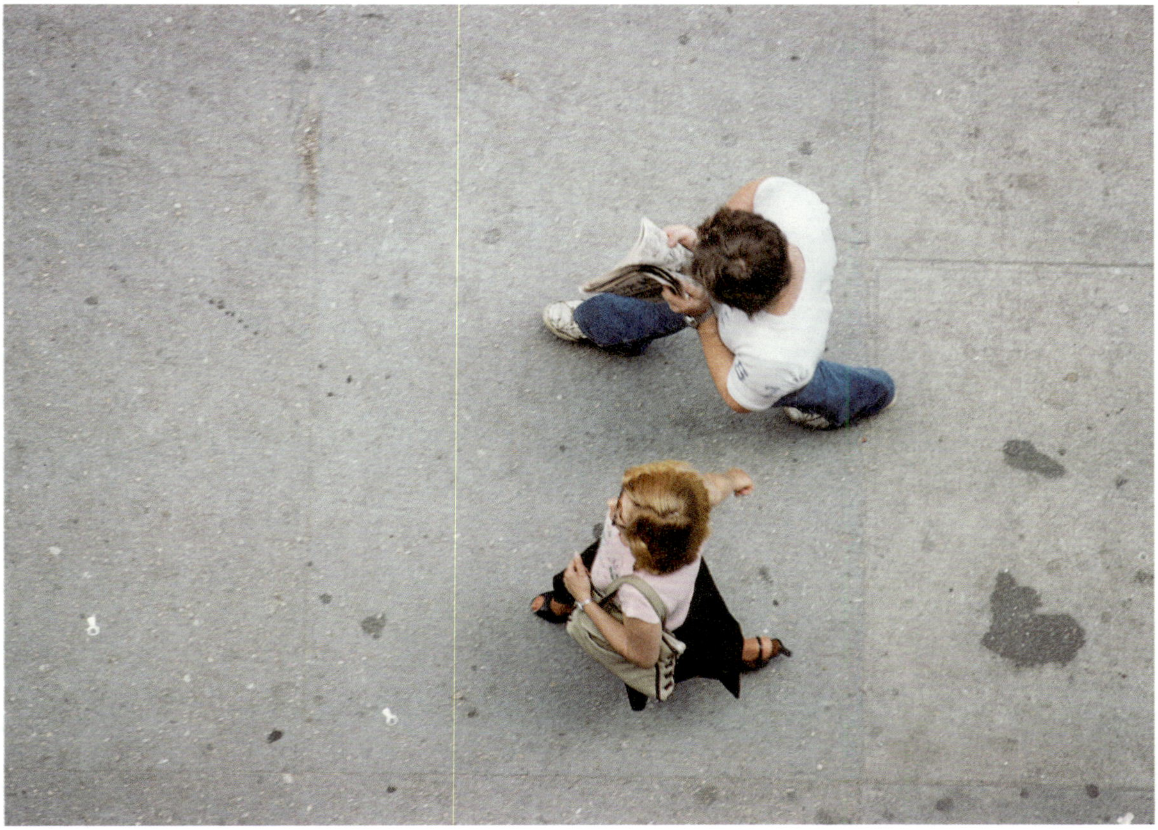

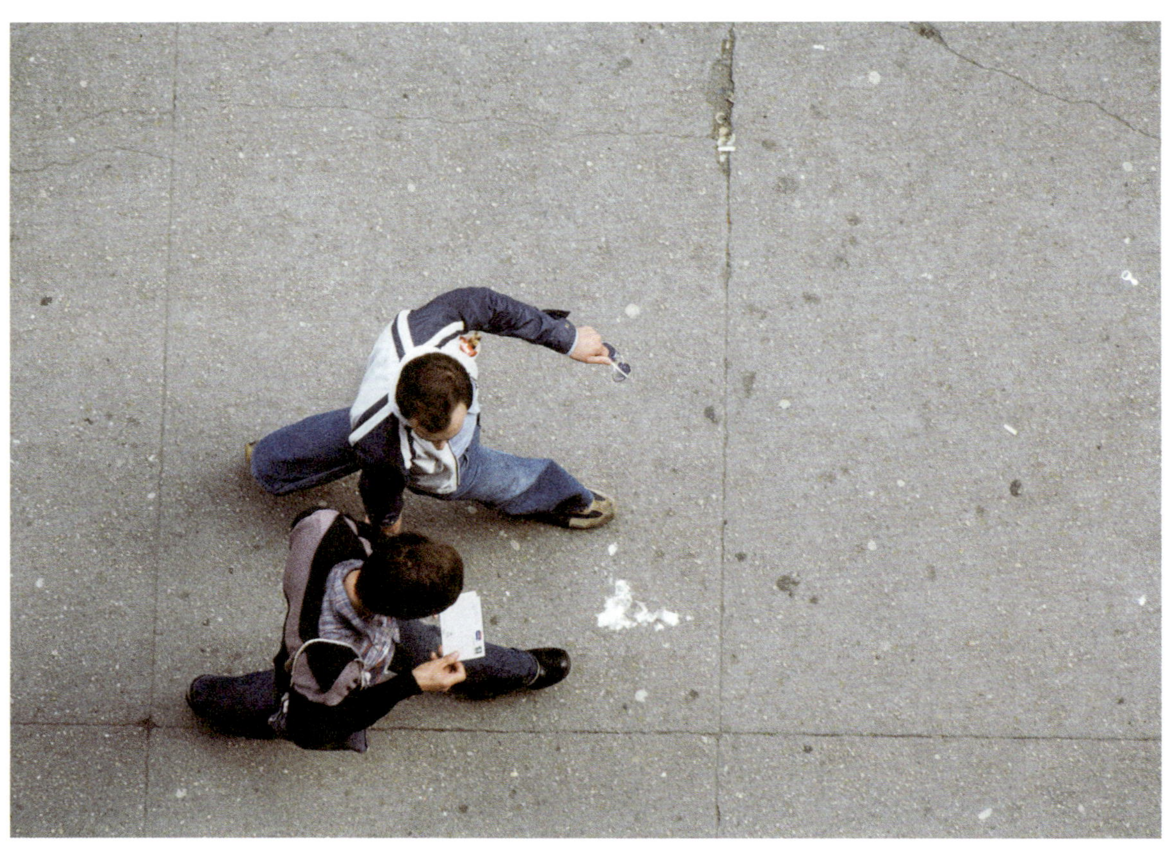

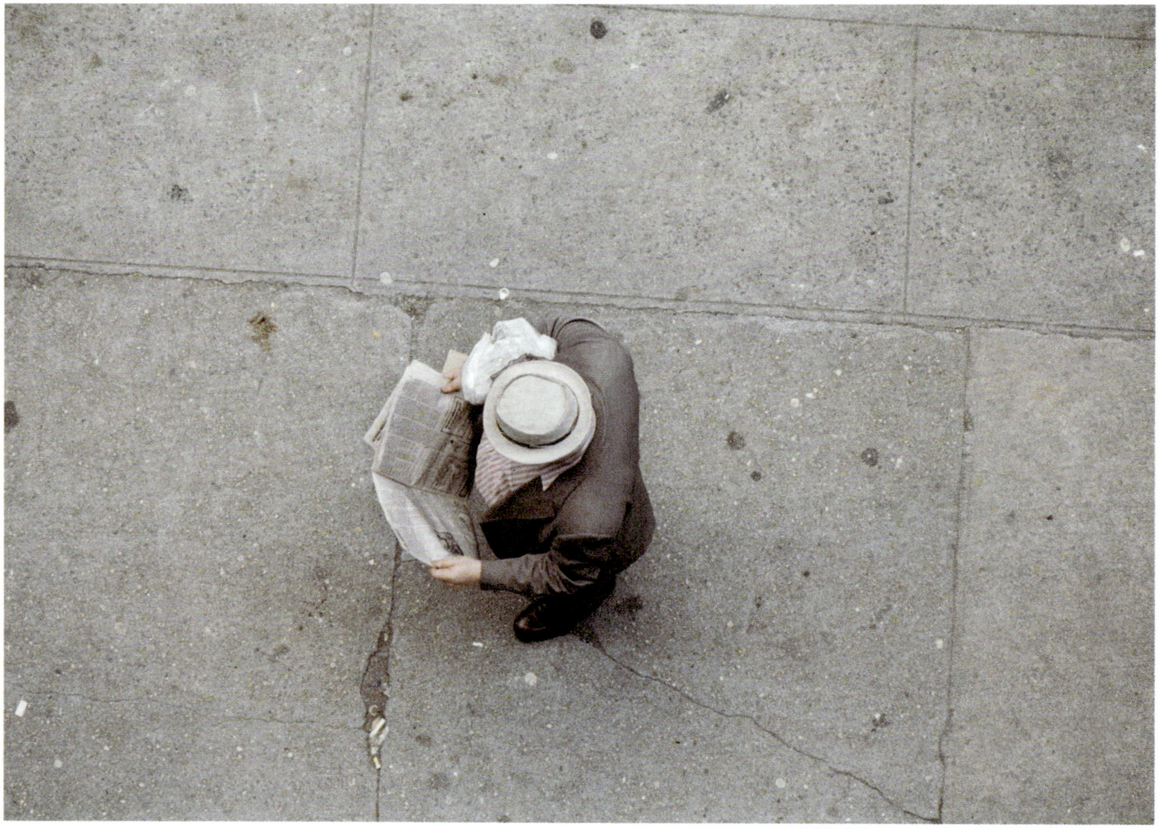

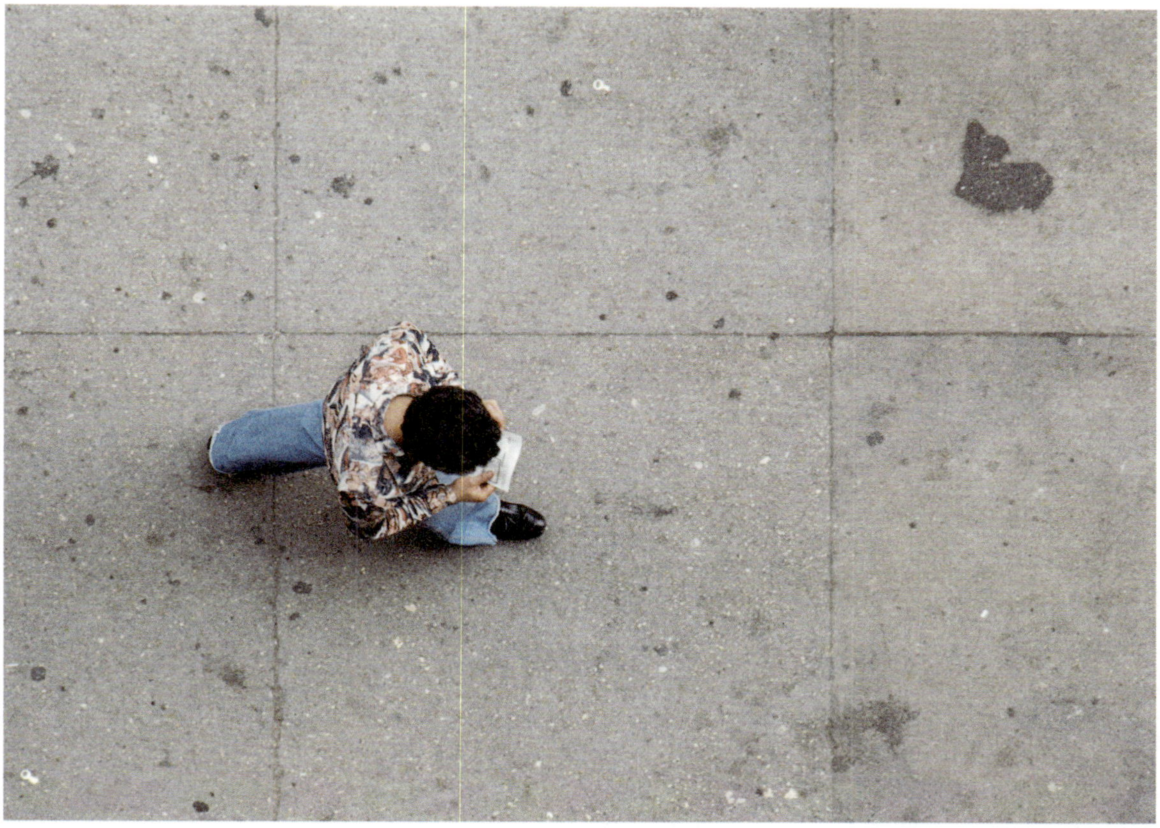

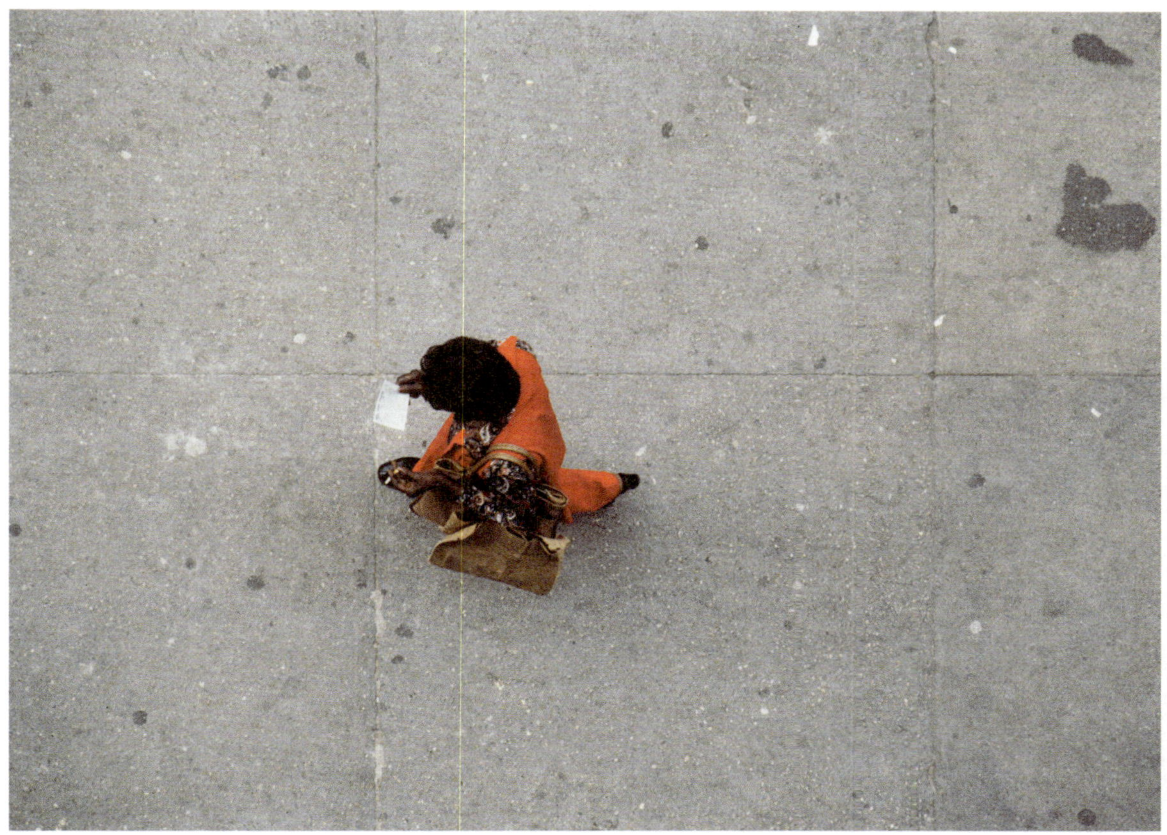

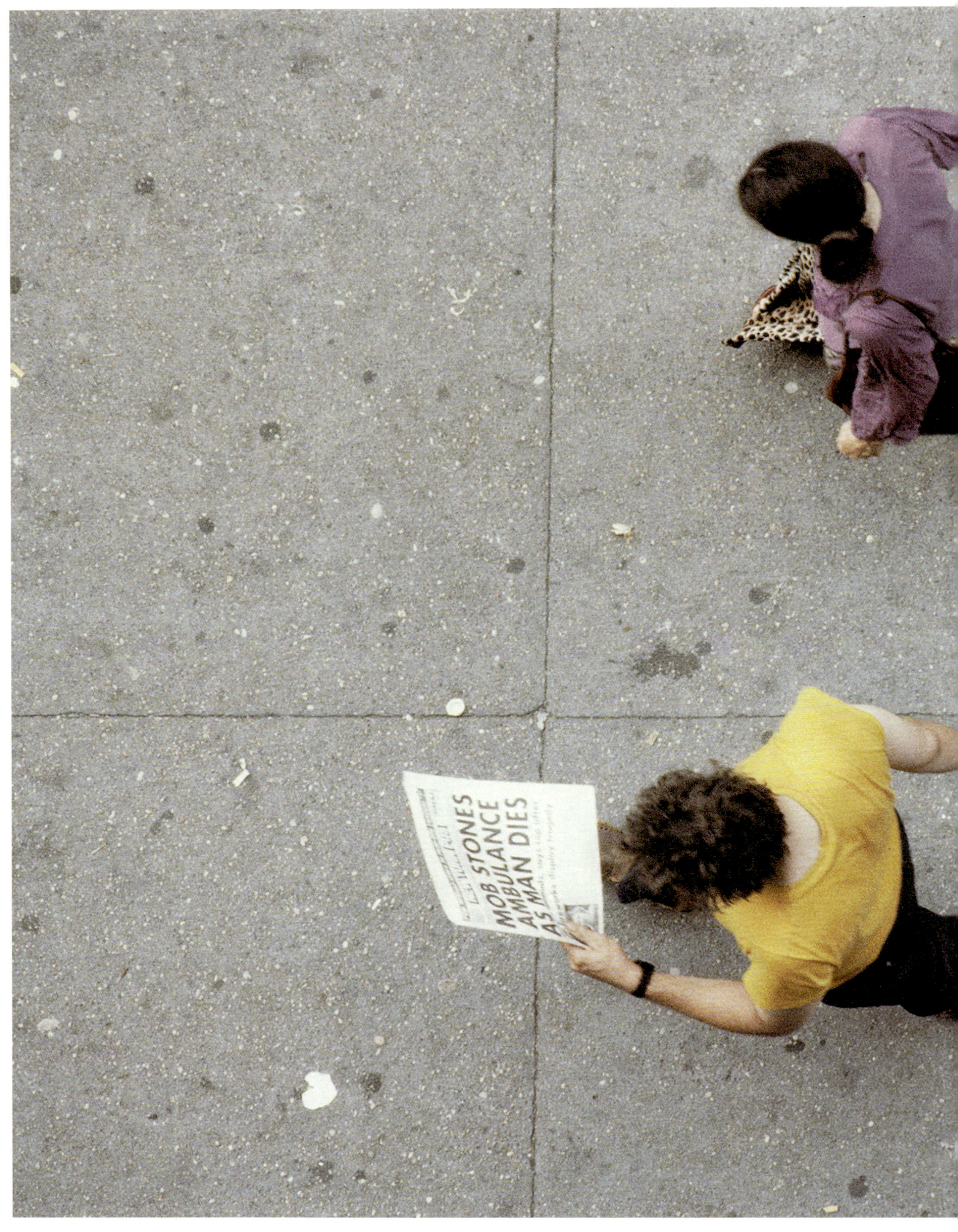
MOB STONES
AMBULANCE
AS MAN DIES

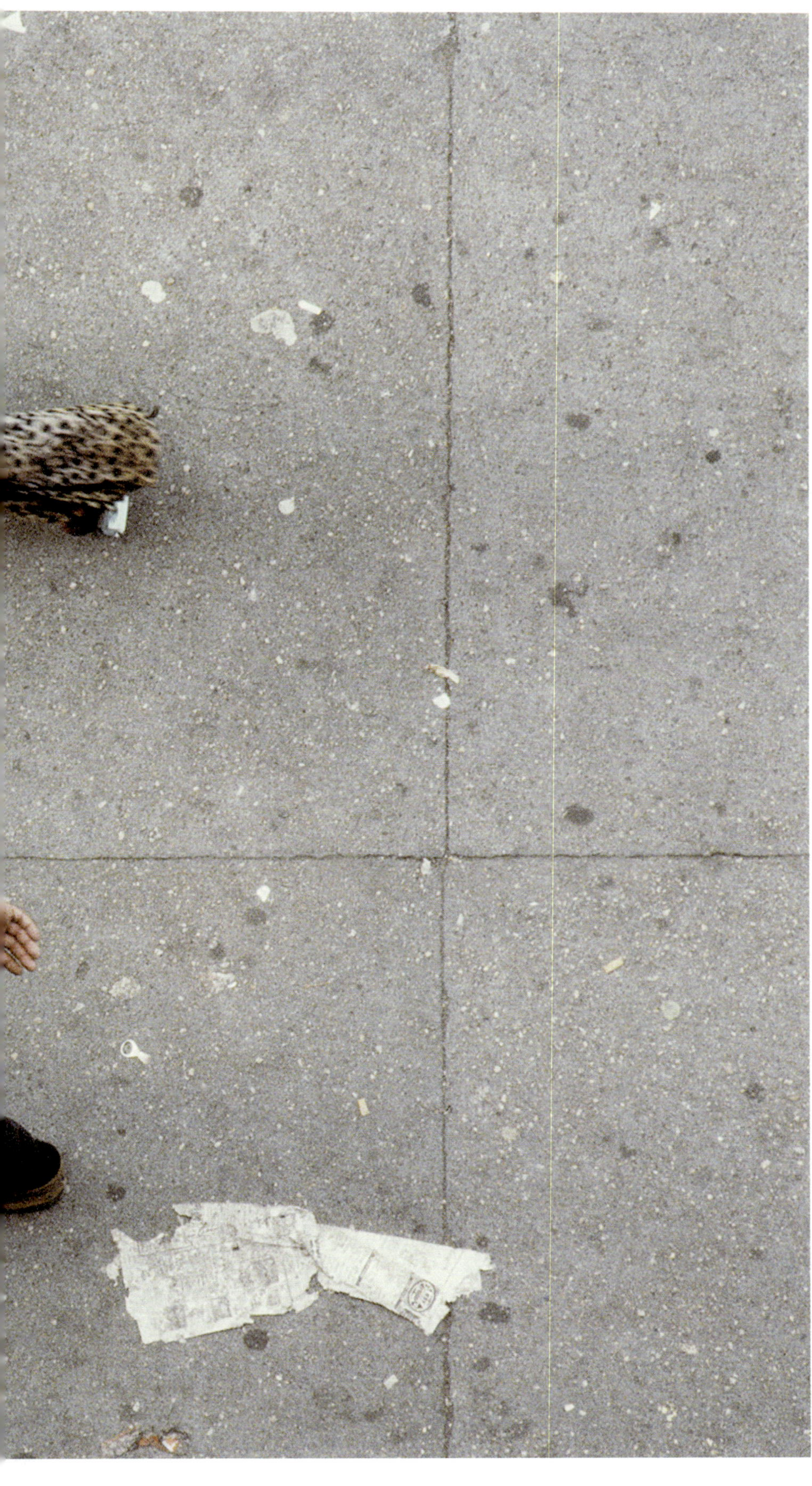

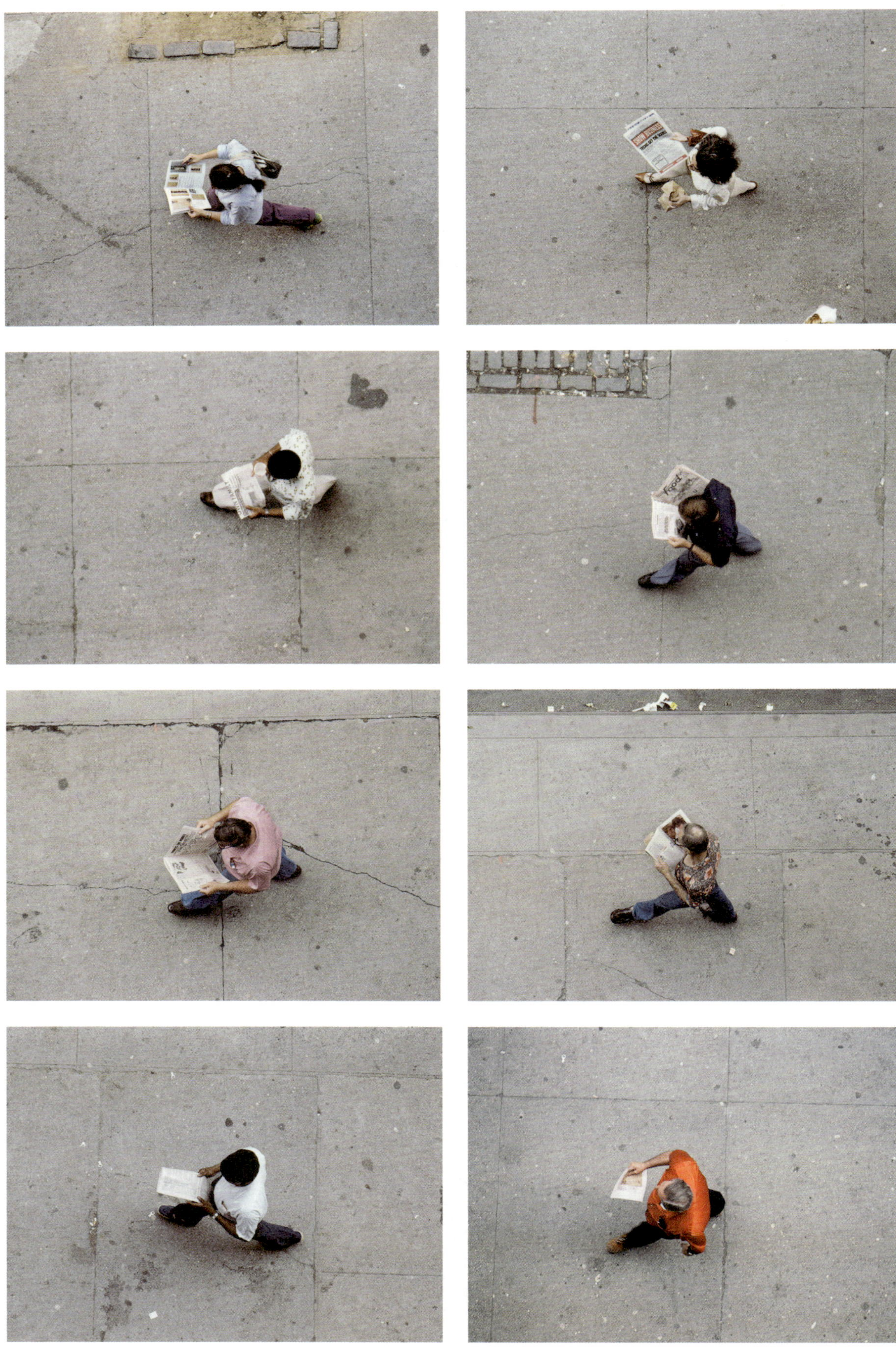

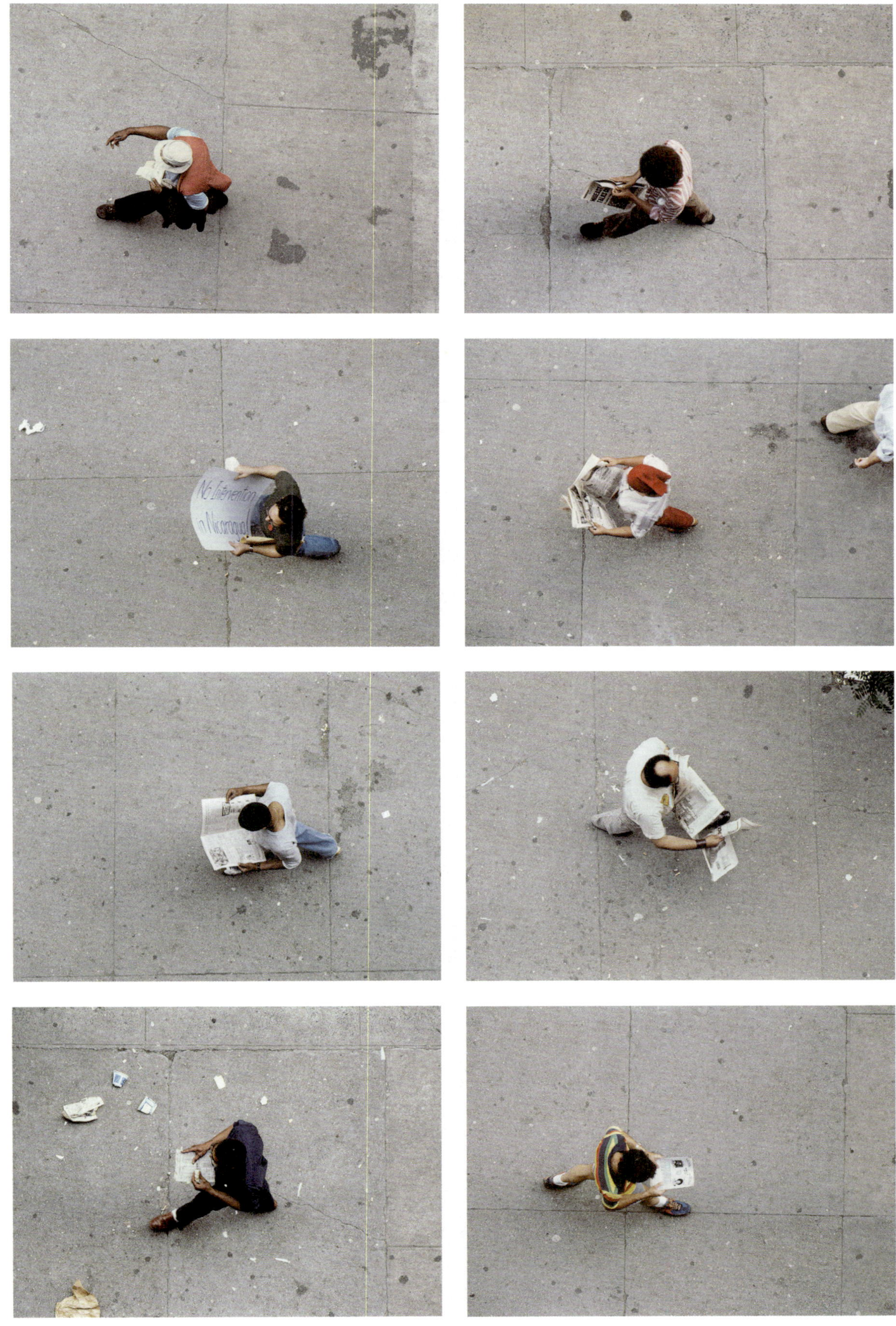
No Intervention
in Nicaragua!

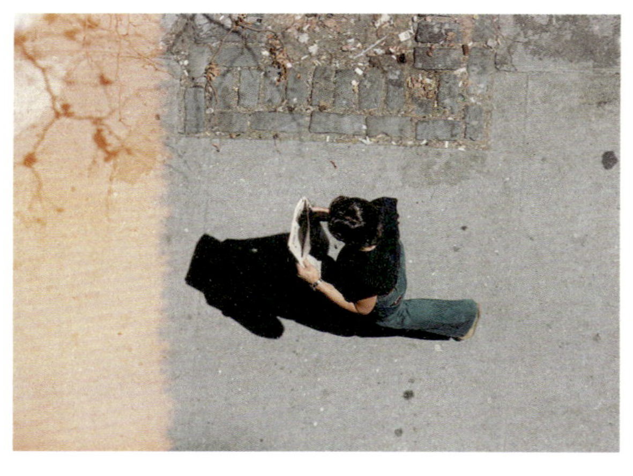
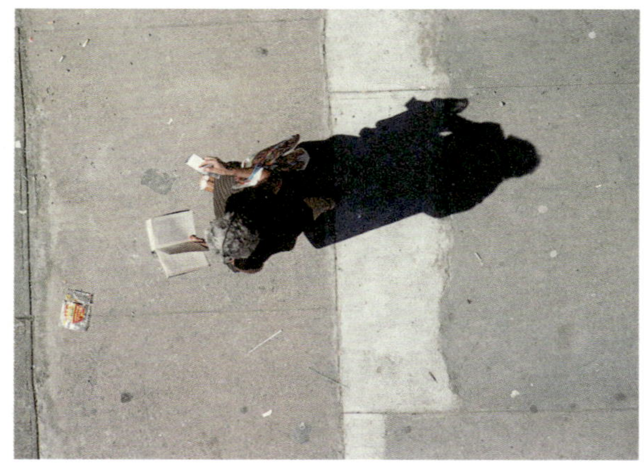
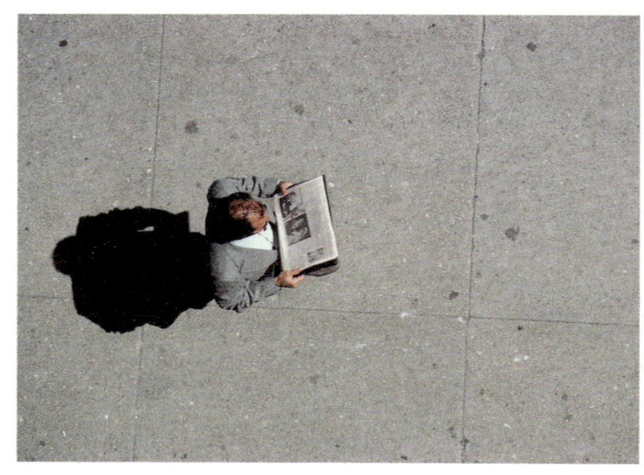
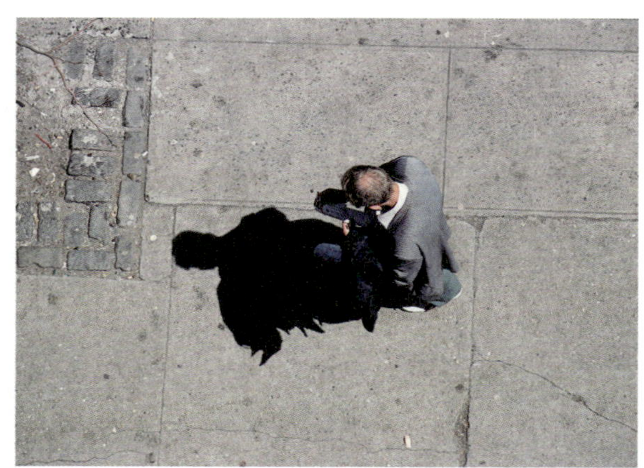
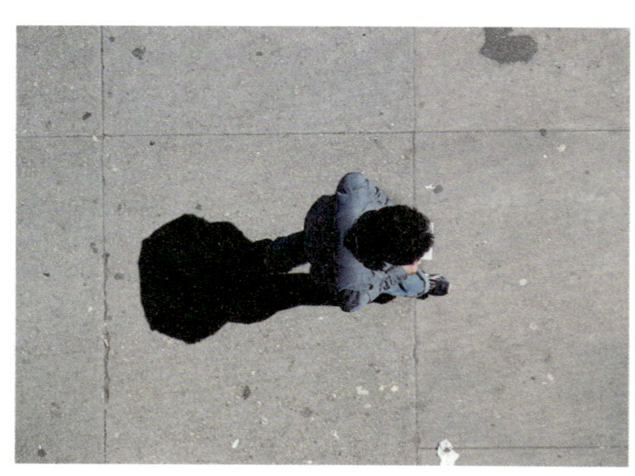
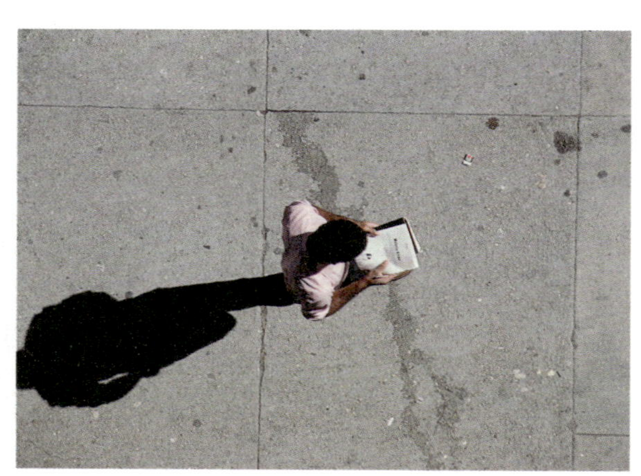
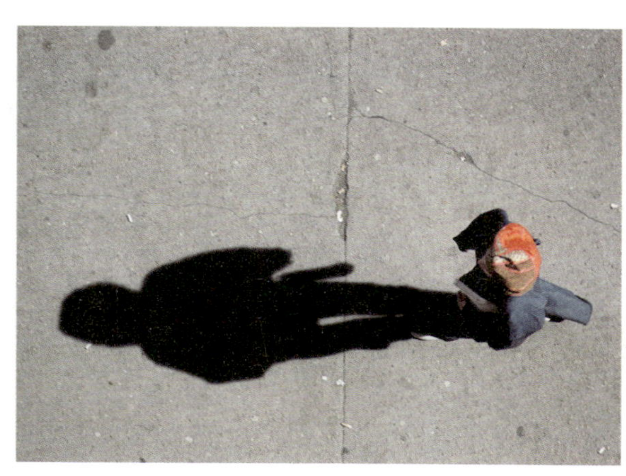
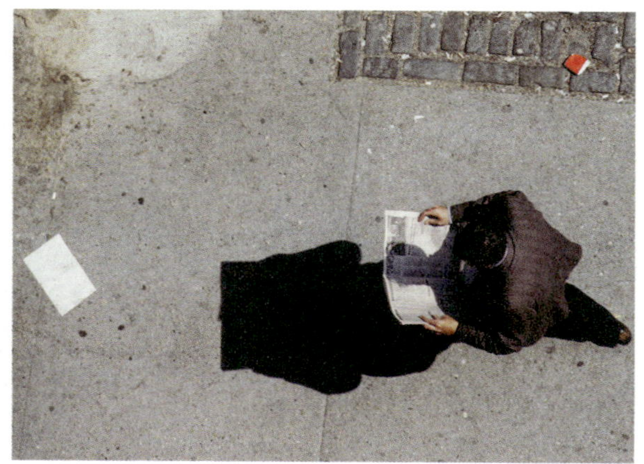

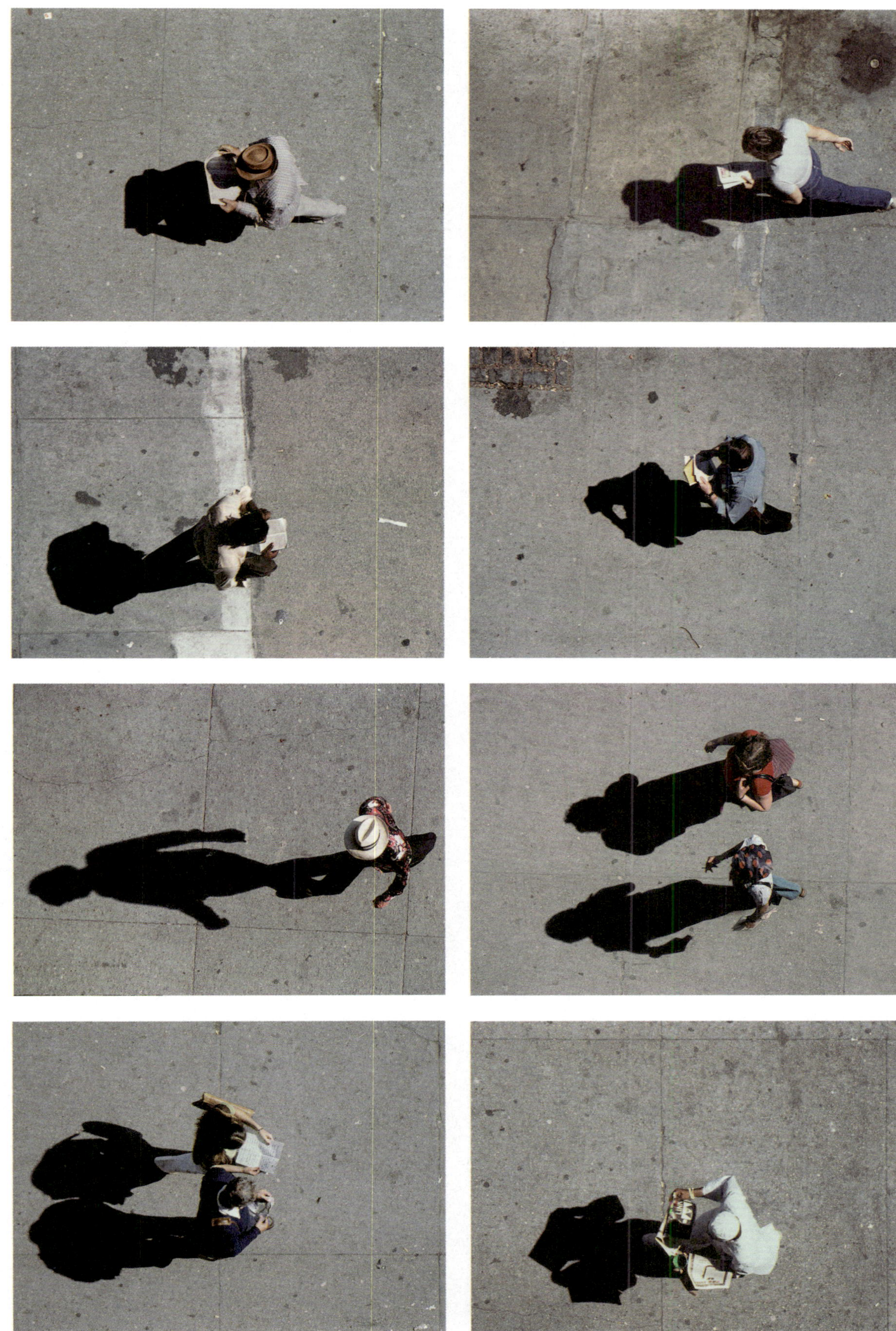

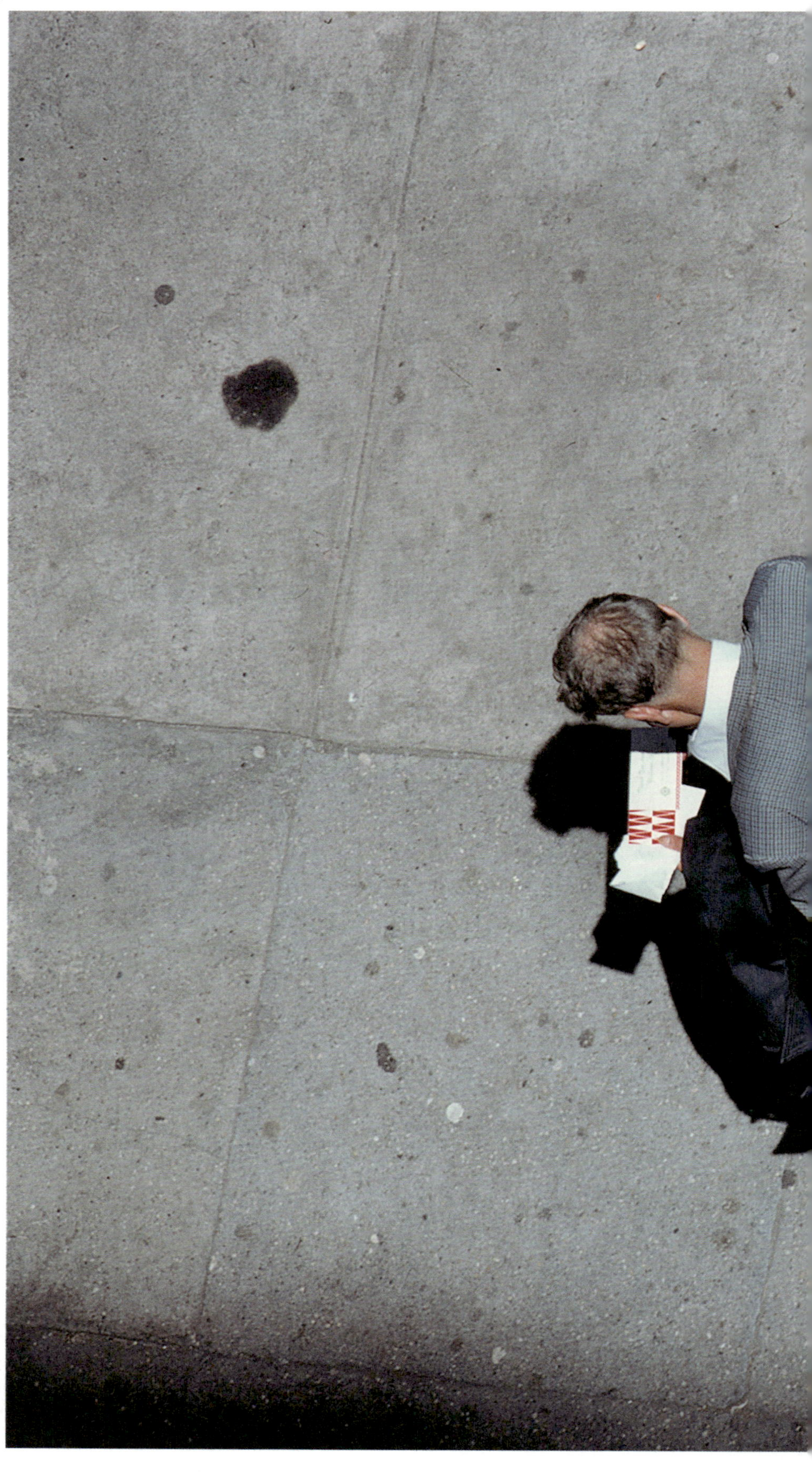

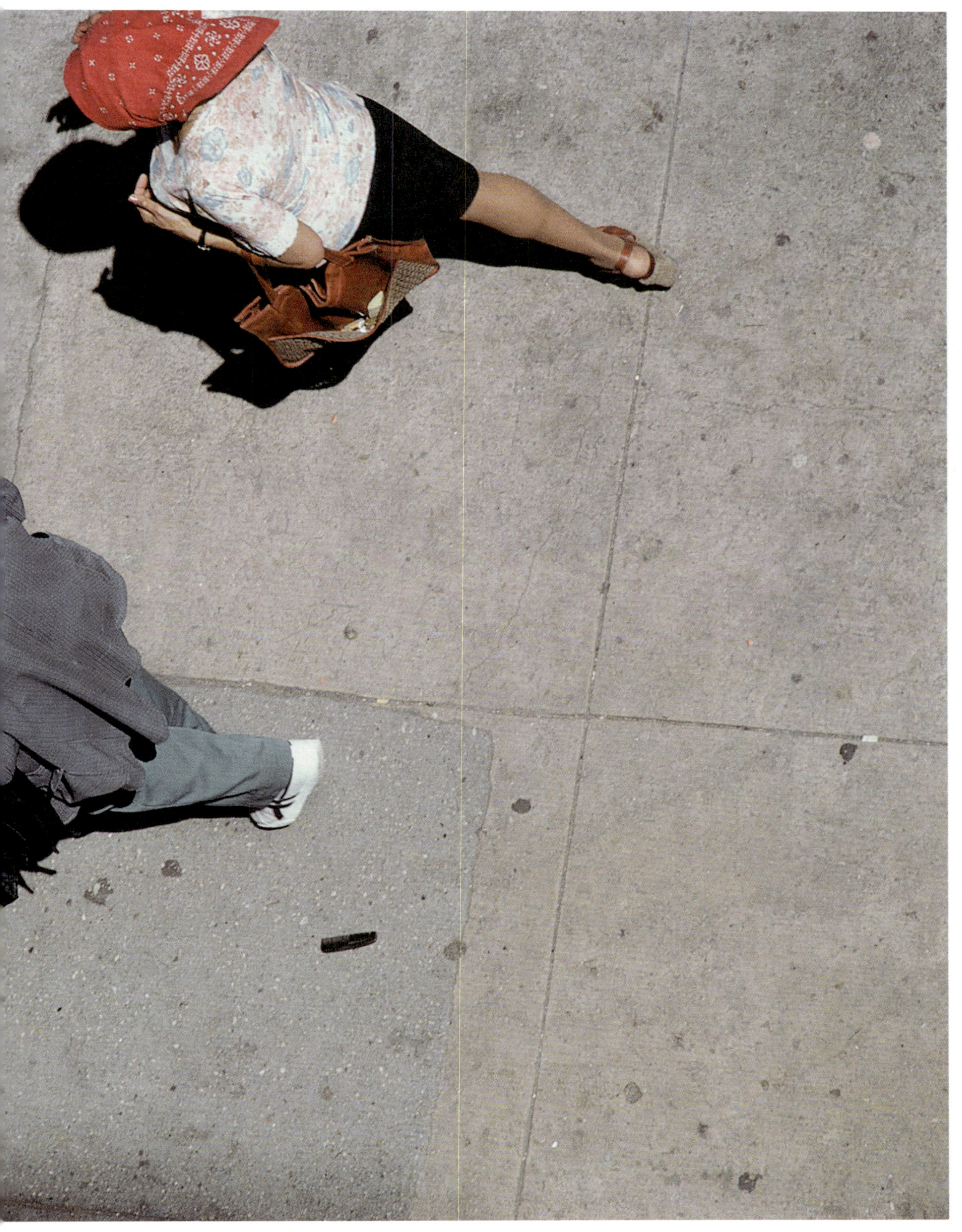

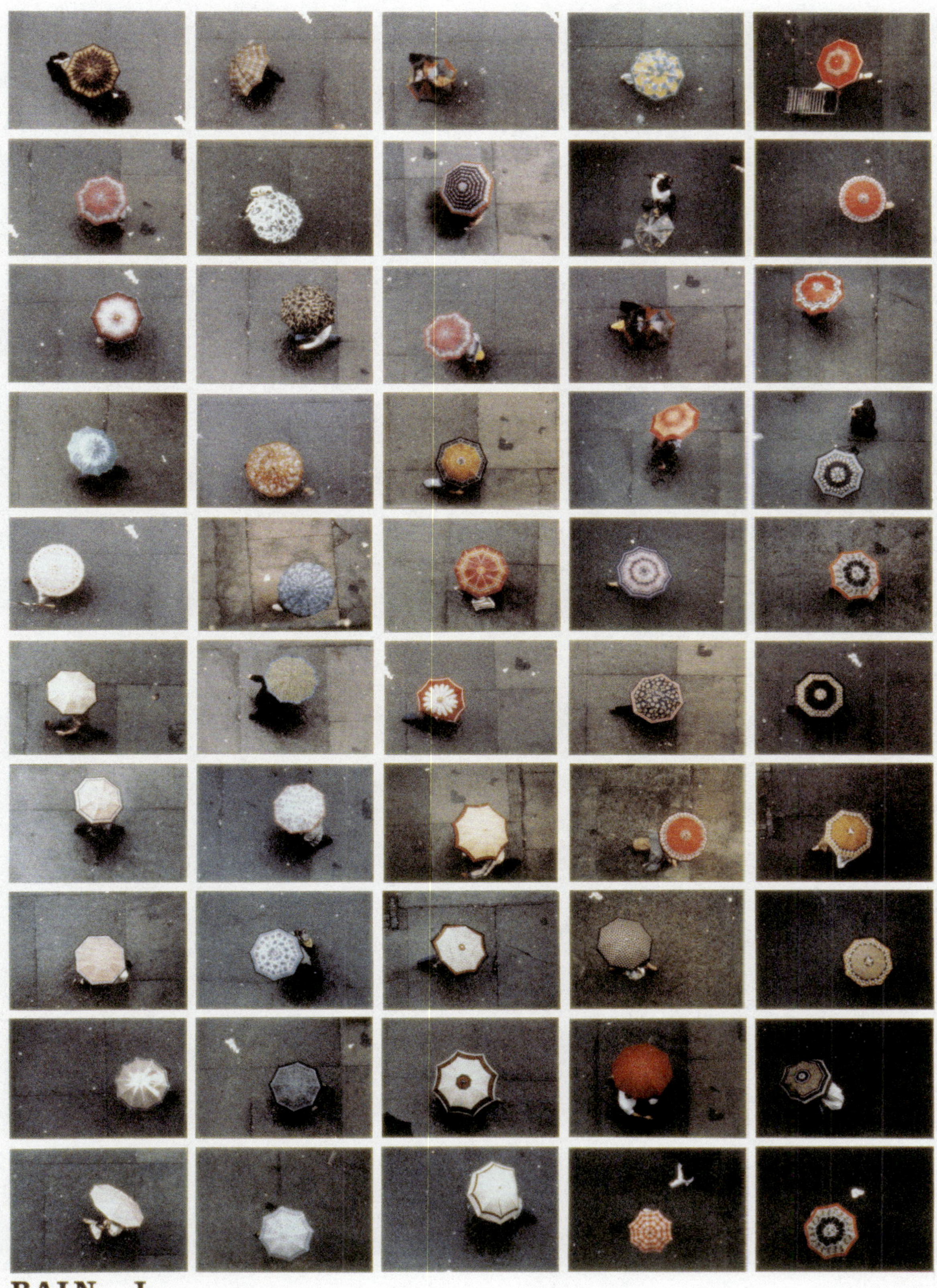

Pages 89–90: Testsheets, *The Fifth Point of the Compass / New York From A to Z, Studies in Random Constant, Fixed Focus–Time Lapse*, RAIN, RUNNER, READER, RADIO, RED, ROLLER, 1977–85

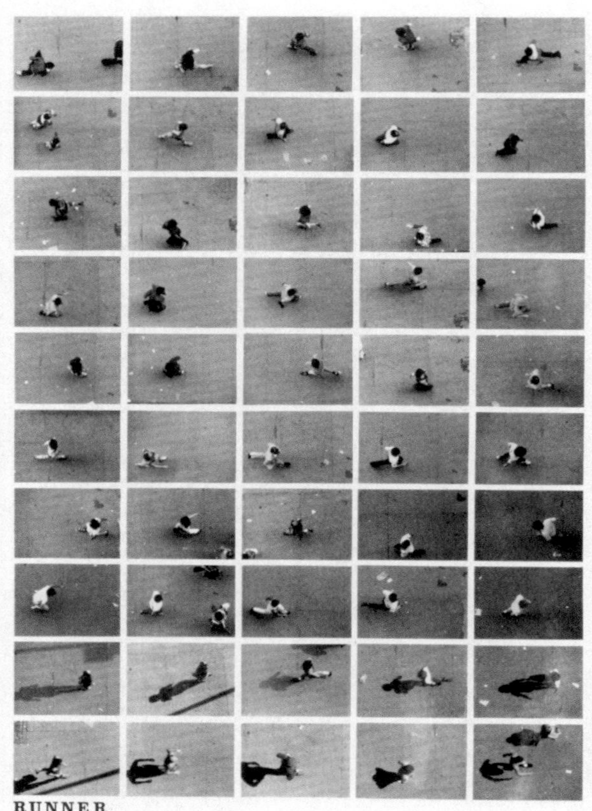
RUNNER

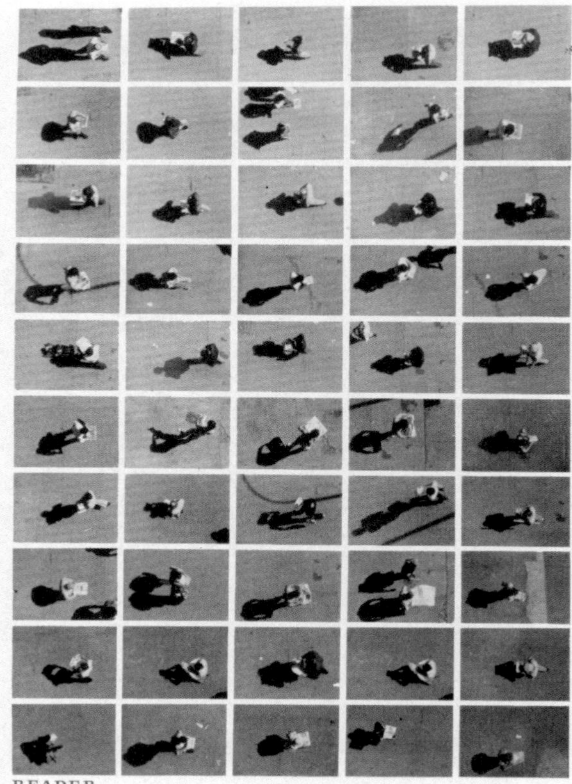
READER

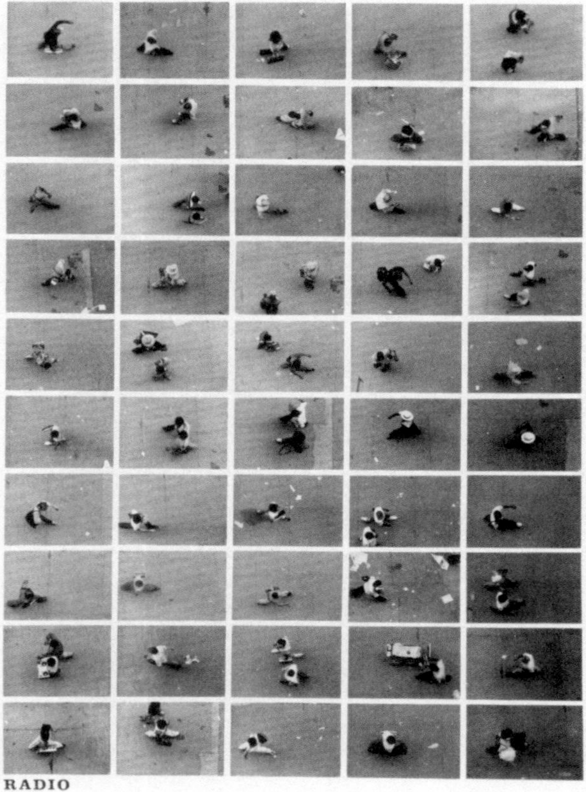
RADIO

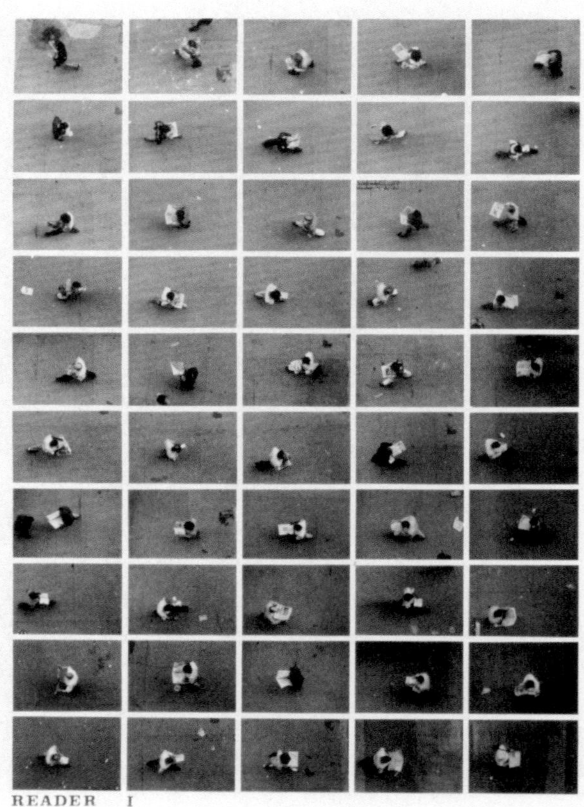
READER I

III-
FORM ///
HATS ///////
JKT IN HAND /
JKT ON SHLDR//
JKT ON ARM III
CROSSED ARMS I
HANDS ON WAIST I
HANDS/HANDS BEHIND BACK /
HANDS IN PKTS //
hand in bag /
hand to face/
hand to head /
headband / (outstretched/point)

IV-
BABY IN ARMS ///
BABY ON BACK /
MOTHER & CHILD ///
FATHER & CHILD /
CHILD ////////
PUSHBABY ///////
COUPLE /////////
ARM IN ARM ///////
HAND IN HAND //

V
OBJECTS ///////
STREETSWEEPER //
WINDOWWASHER /
DELIVERY //// empty/full
BOARDS /
LONG TUBES //
BOX /////
SACK ON BACK ///
CART ///
* chairs/ladder

VI-
BETWEEN /
BICYCLE /////
BOTTLE //
BAREBACK /////
BACKPACK ///
BAG ON BACK ///
SHLDRBAG //
camera //
cap /
contrast colors /
BAGS BOTH ARMS /
PLASTIC BAG IN HAND//
PAPERBAG / 3
FRONTLOAD //
GARMENTBAG /
cane /
coins /
dollars /// (bills)

VII-
AFRO /
fishing //
plant /
glasses in hand / on head /
helmet-/-------hardhat /
jeans /
mail -/--------manila /
overalls /
point /
plaid //
skateboard /
stride /
string /
scarf /
thongs /
visor /
yellow / - anklesocks /
kneesocks /
ADIDAS /
flowers ///
luggage /
over //
twist //
pink /
stetson /
stripe /
strapless /
sunday times /
tennis /
vacuum /

VIII-
BUST //
LONG SKIRT /
CANE /
PRINT /
printblouse shirt //
printscarf ///
plaid /////
violet/lavender /
orange / yellow / turqgreen /
WOMEN ///////
HAIR ///
FEMME ////
HIGHHEELS /
PATTERN /////
SHAWL / SATIN /

IX-
RED ////////////////////// I9
READER //////////////////////////////// 28

X- RUNNER /////////// II
RADIO XX //////////// I2
ROLLER // 2

XI-
ISTANBUL 23 XI
VENICE 20 XII
VENETIAN WINDOWS XIII

RAIN 40
parasol /
clear /
black //
blue /
green /
white //
beige ///
assorted //
red /////
yellow /
yellow/red/green/blue /
multi red white blue black red/yellow/green
printallover
printborder border

SEQUENTIAL 27 94 situations
//////////////////////////
//////////////////////////
//////////////////////////
//////////////////// 94

STRUCTURE -
BRANCHES / EIFFEL / METRO / SCRAP

Index of slide categories, *The Fifth Point of the Compass / New York From A to Z, Studies in Random Constant, Fixed Focus-Time Lapse*, RAIN, RUNNER, READER, RADIO, RED, ROLLER, 1977-85

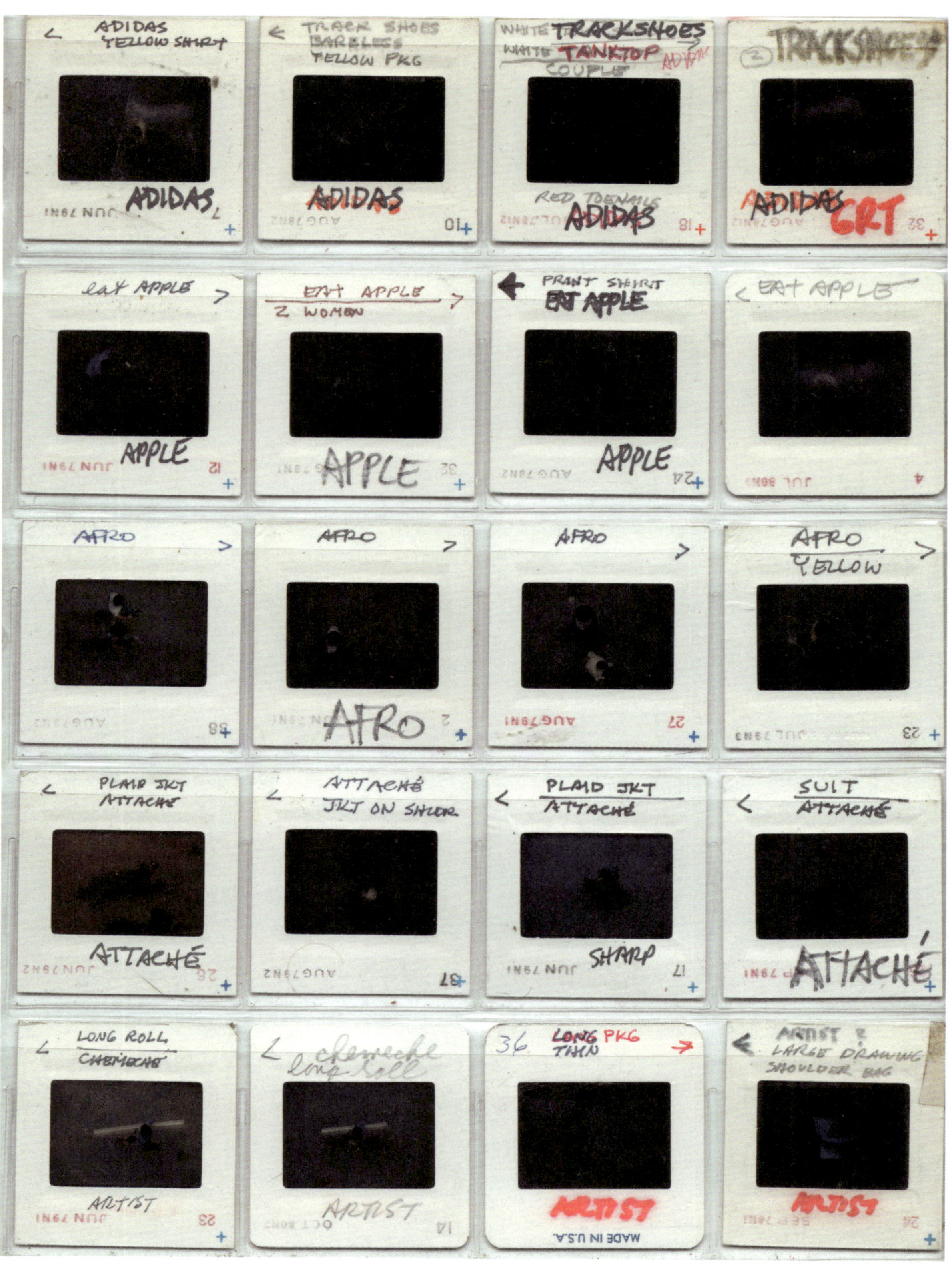

Slides from ***The Fifth Point of the Compass / New York A to Z, Studies in Random Constant, Fixed Focus–Time Lapse***, RAIN, RUNNER, READER, RADIO, RED, ROLLER, 1977–85

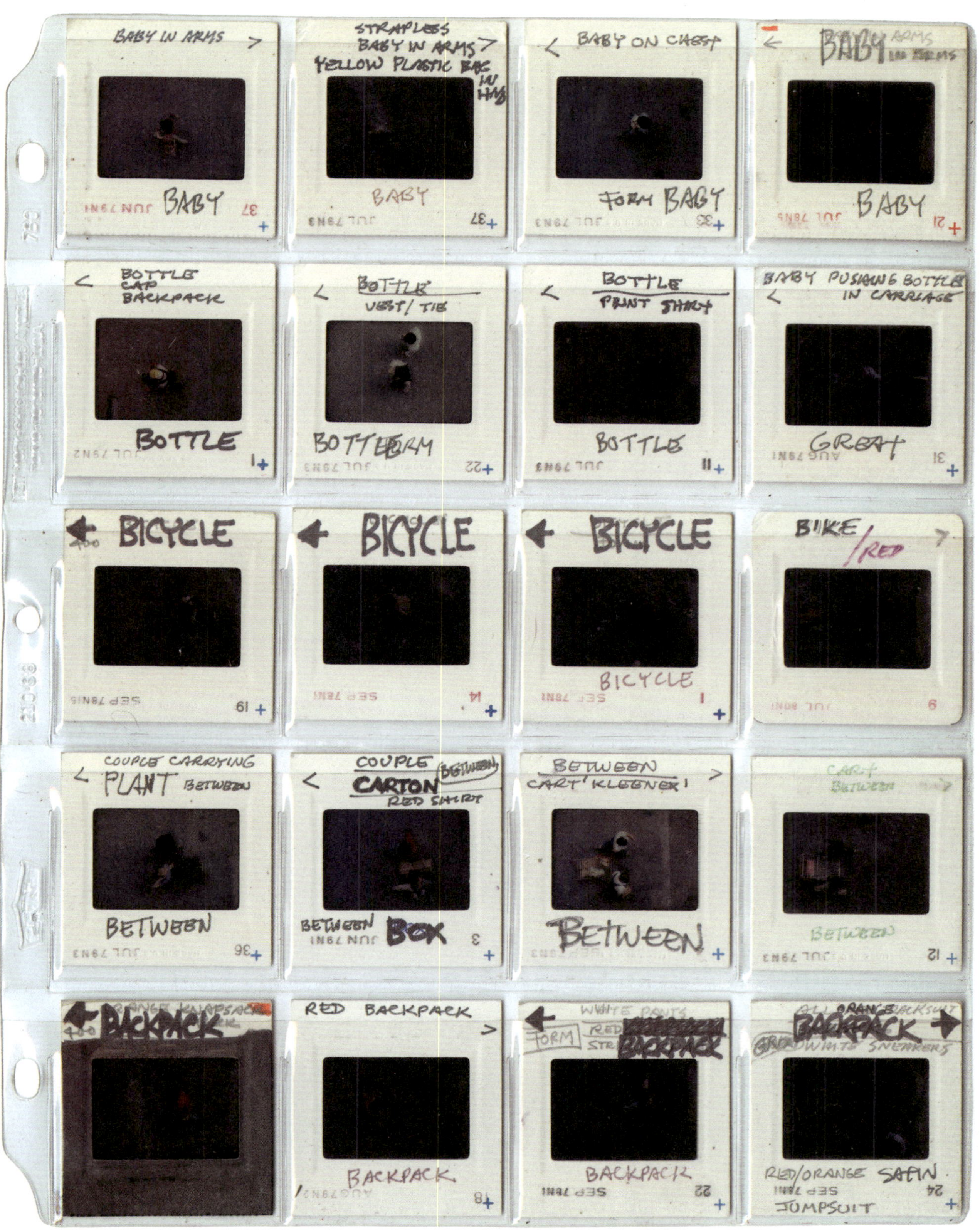

BABY IN ARMS
BABY
STRAPLESS BABY IN ARMS
YELLOW PLASTIC BAG
BABY
BABY ON CHEST
FORM BABY
BABY
BABY
BOTTLE CAP BACKPACK
BOTTLE
BOTTLE VEST/TIE
BOTTLE PRINT SHIRT
BOTTLE
BABY PUSHING BOTTLE IN CARRIAGE
GREAT
BICYCLE
BICYCLE
BICYCLE
BICYCLE
BIKE /RED
COUPLE CARRYING PLANT BETWEEN
BETWEEN
COUPLE CARTON BETWEEN RED SHIRT
BETWEEN BOX
BETWEEN CART KLEENEX
BETWEEN
CART BETWEEN
BETWEEN
BACKPACK
RED BACKPACK
BACKPACK
FORM BACKPACK
BACKPACK
BACKPACK
WHITE SNEAKERS
RED/ORANGE SATIN JUMPSUIT

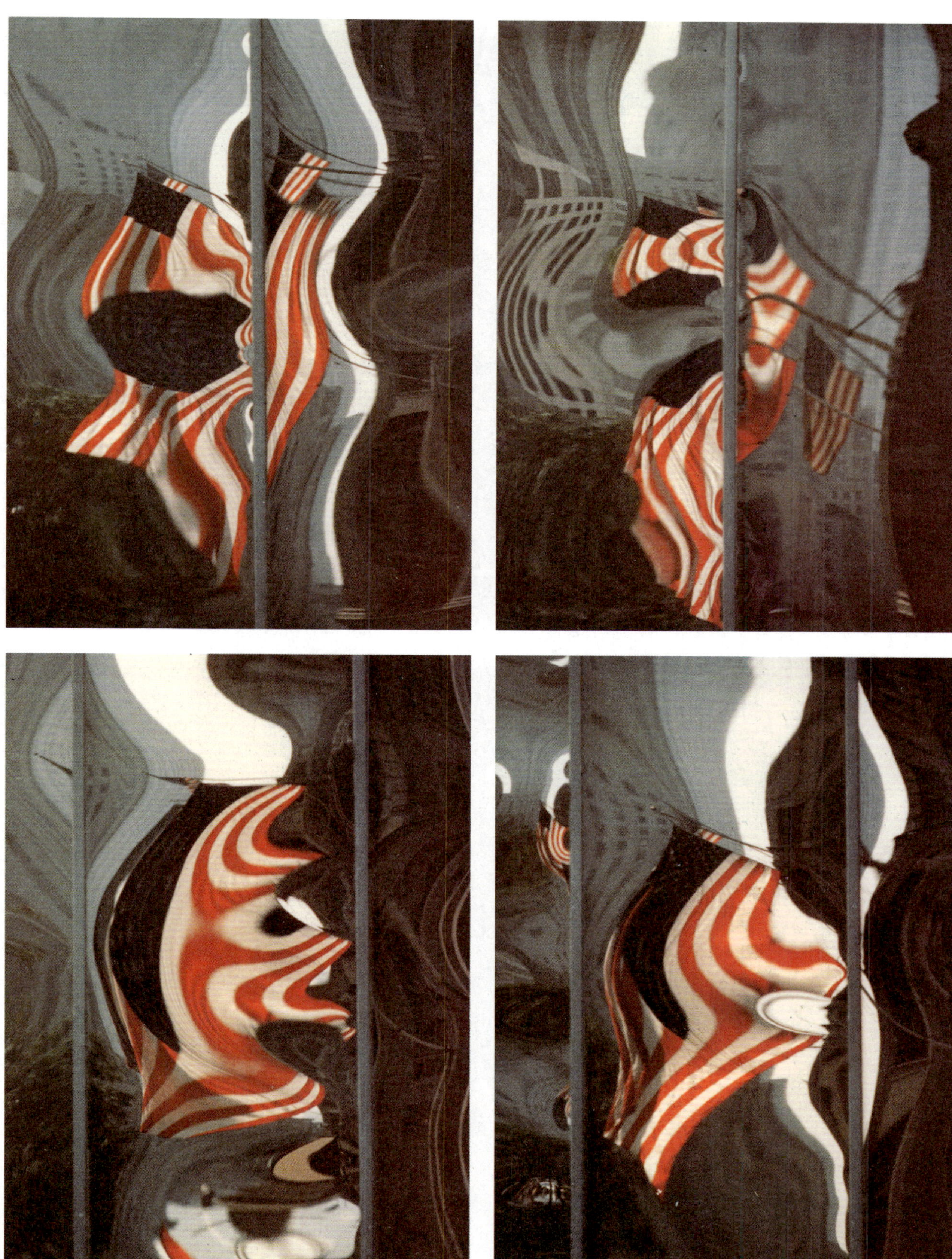

The Flag from the series *Four-Dimensional Studies in Auto-Regenerating Constants*, thirty-six-image sequence, 1975

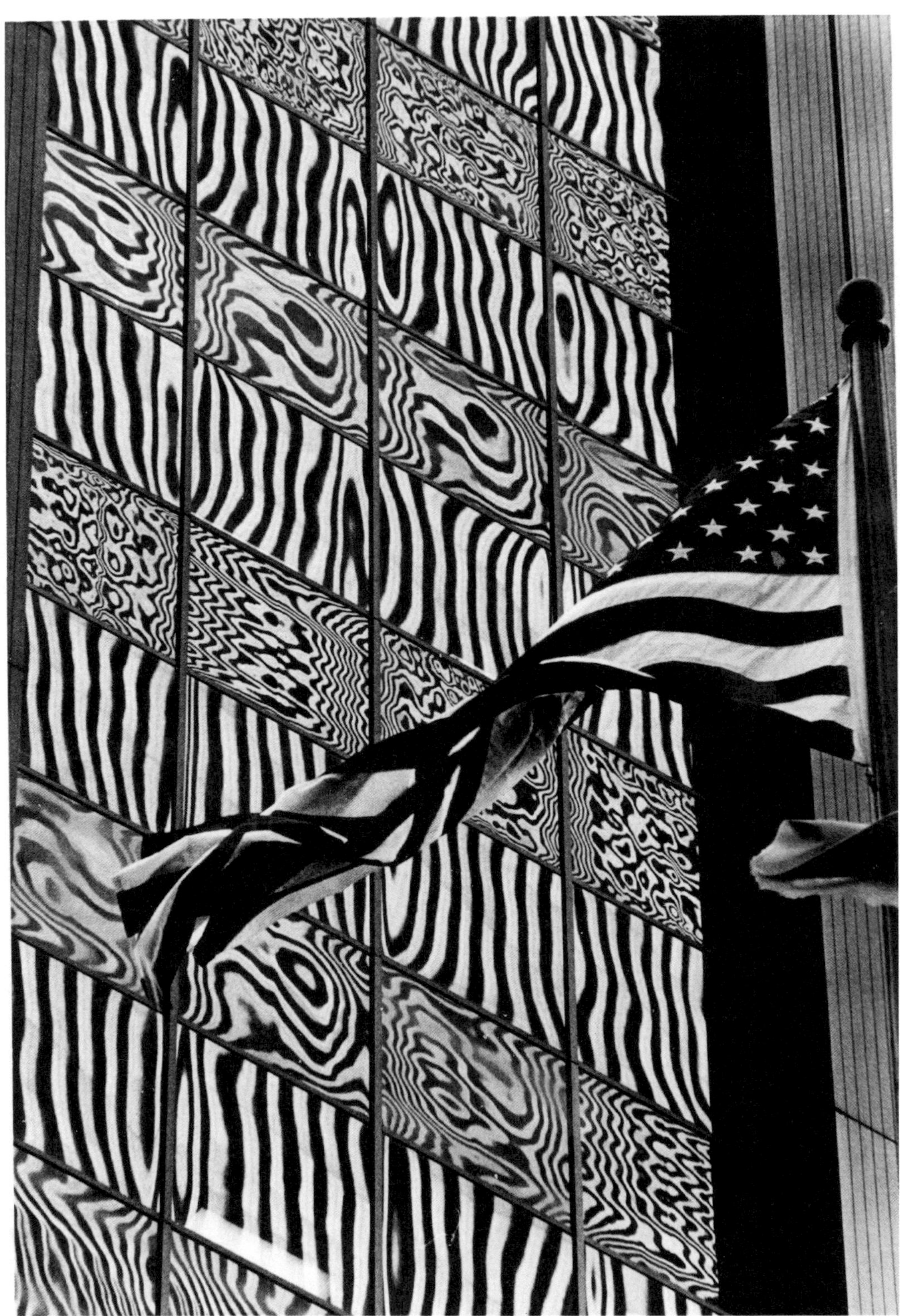

 Corporate Wave-Maker, from the series *Phenomenological New York*, New York, 1972–86

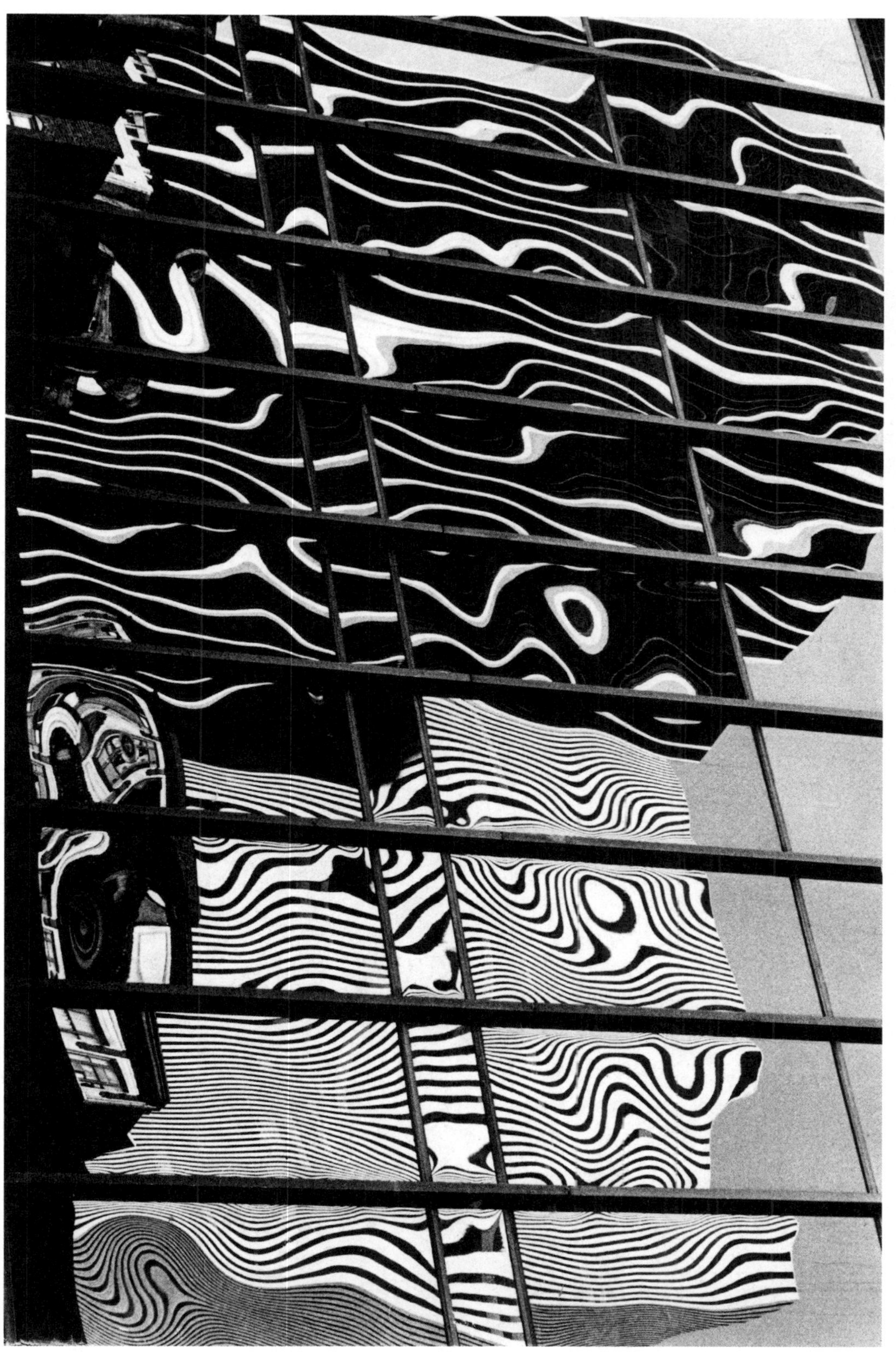

Traffic Patterns, from the series *Phenomenological New York*, New York, 1972–86

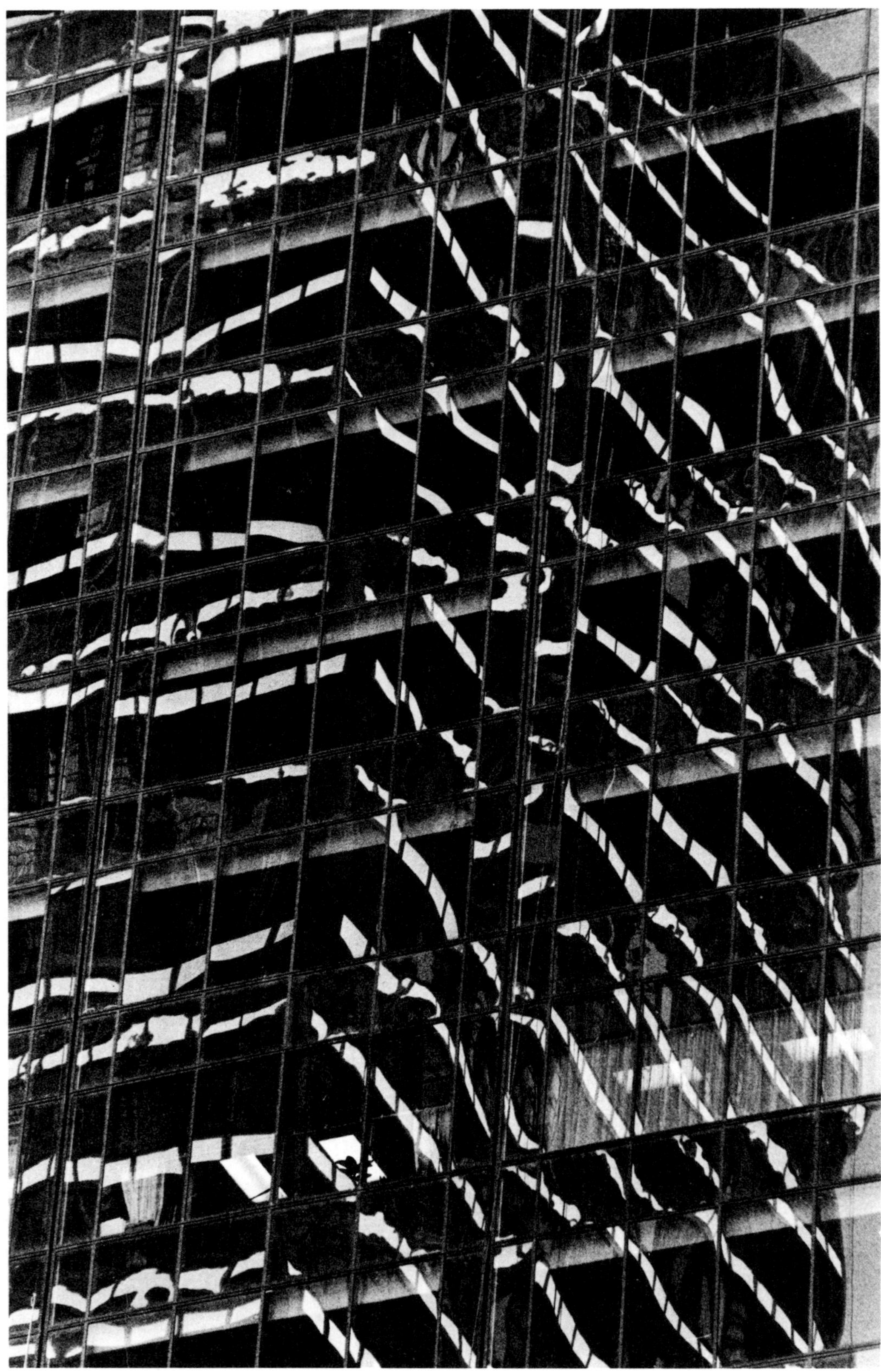

 Pages 98–99: From the series *Phenomenological New York*, New York, 1972–86

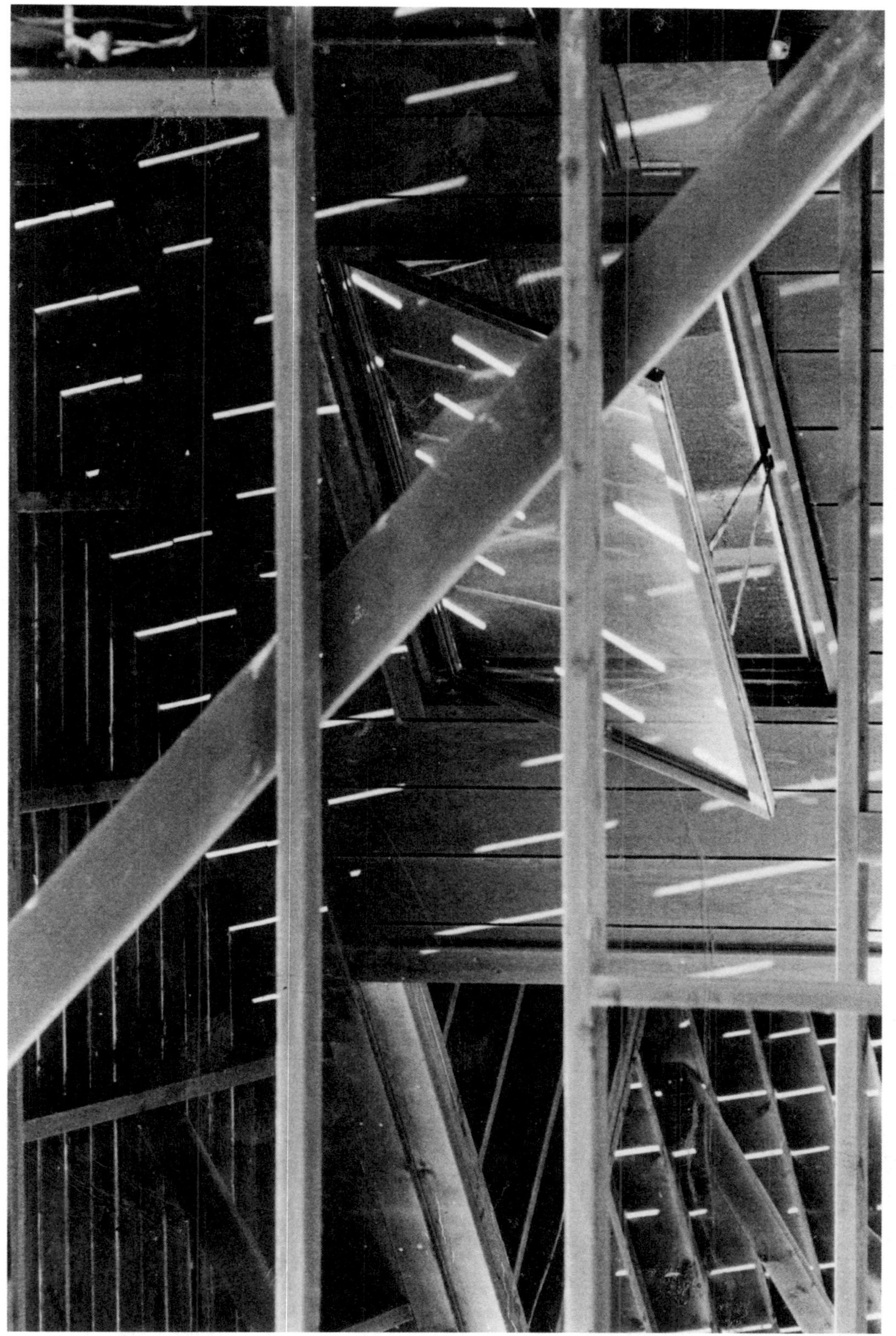

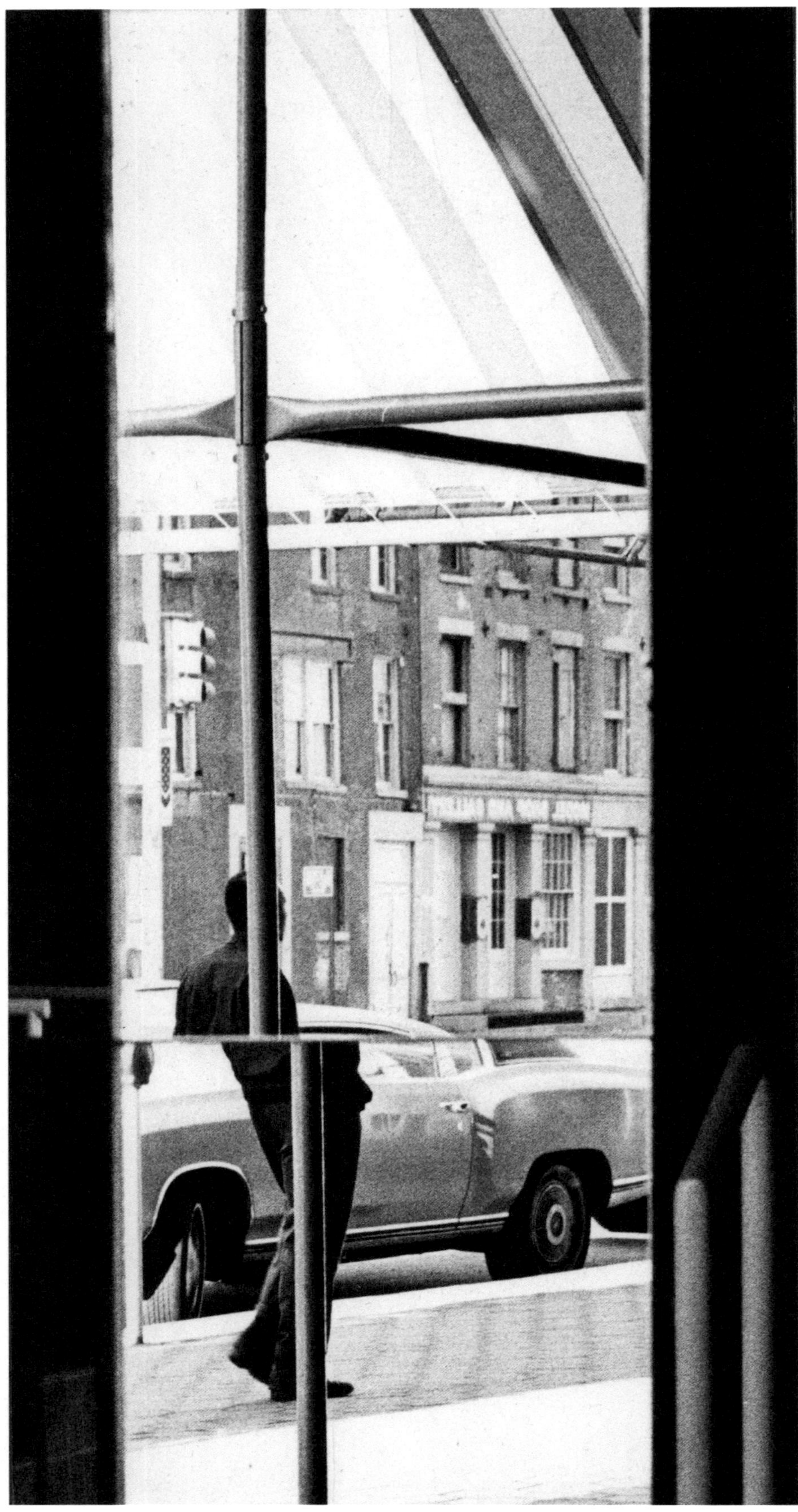

Relocation from the series *Self-Regenerating Energy Strategies Documented*, 1972–76

Film

"I started photographing distortions in the architecture. Not reflections. If you go to certain buildings at certain hours when the light is just right, you'll find fantastic surrealism."

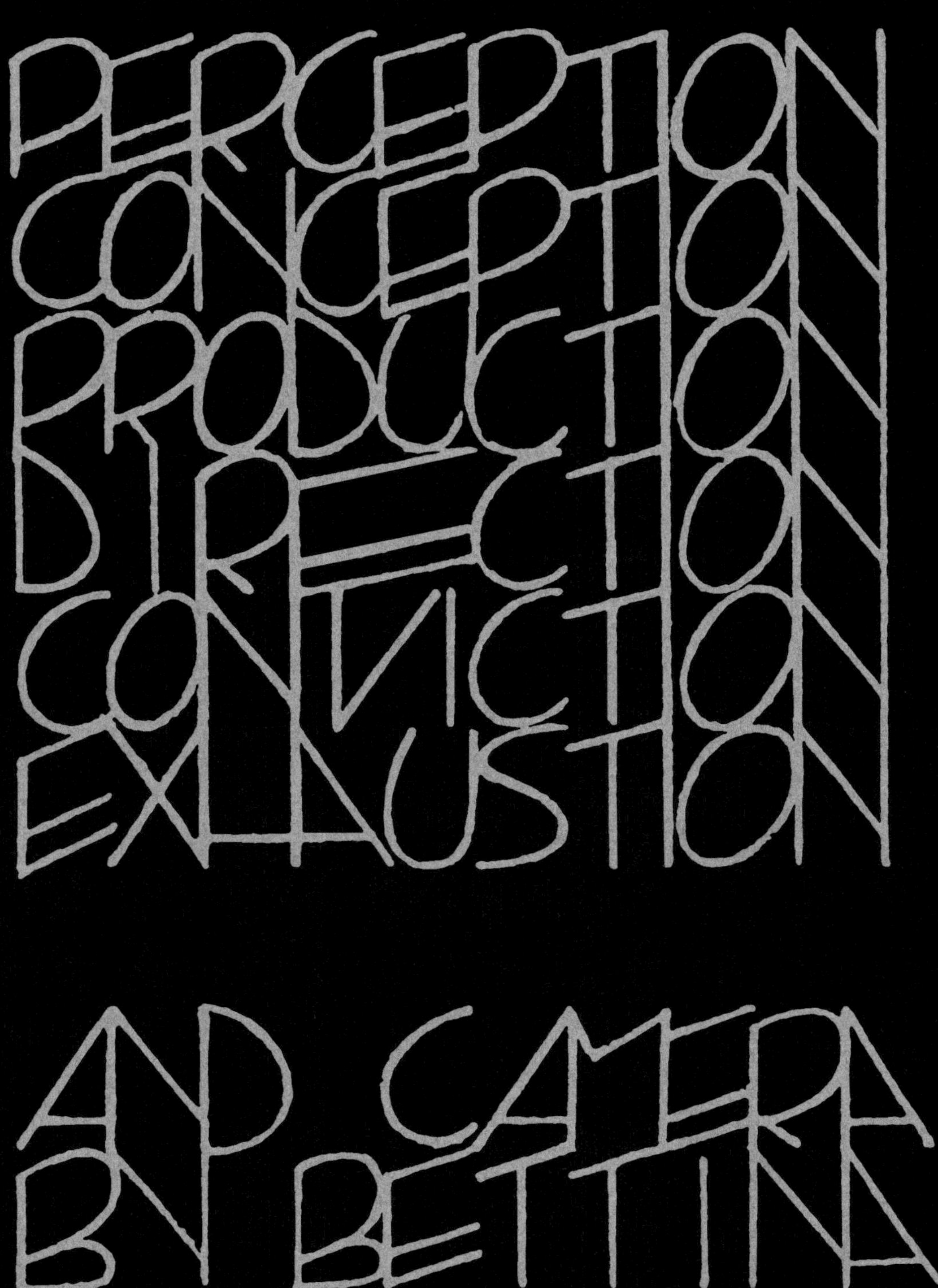

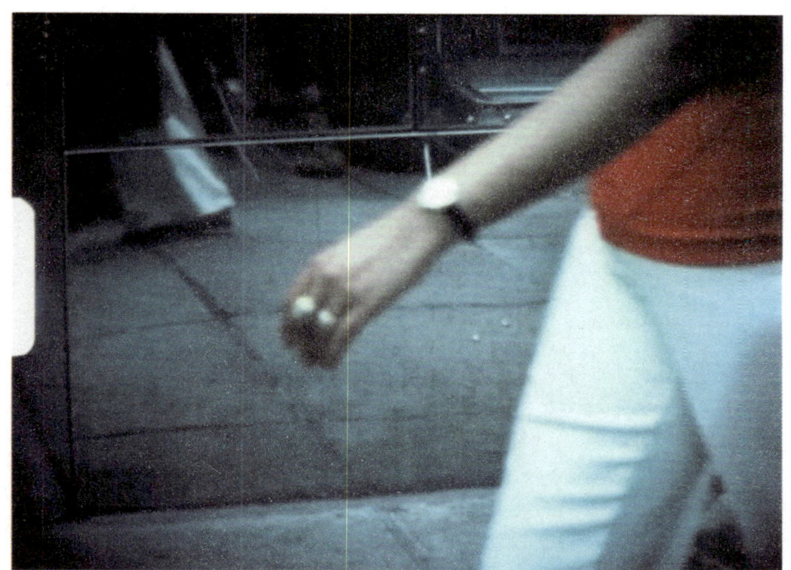

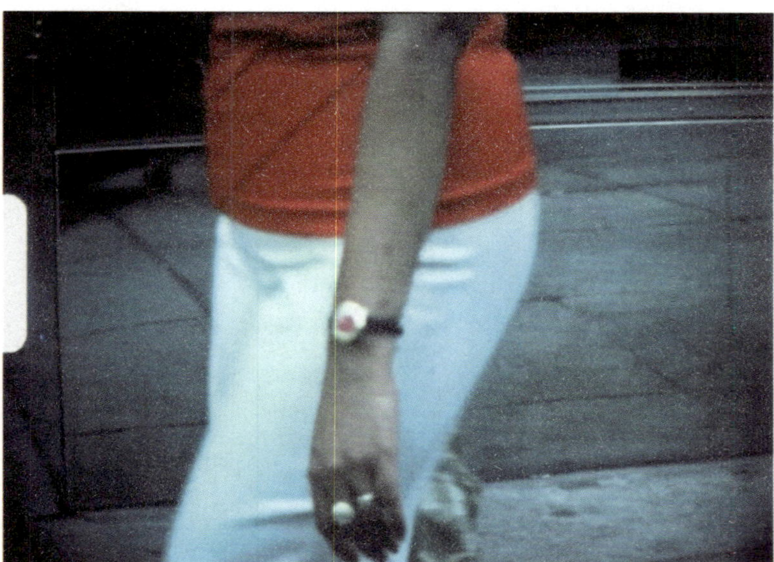

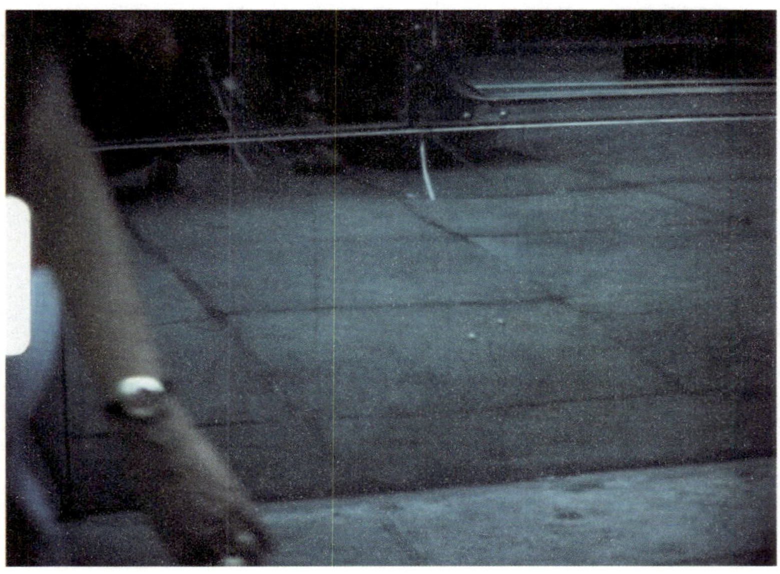

Pages 103–17: Stills from *The New York Phenomenology, Urban Energy Strategies*, 8mm film and unedited footage, 1976-77

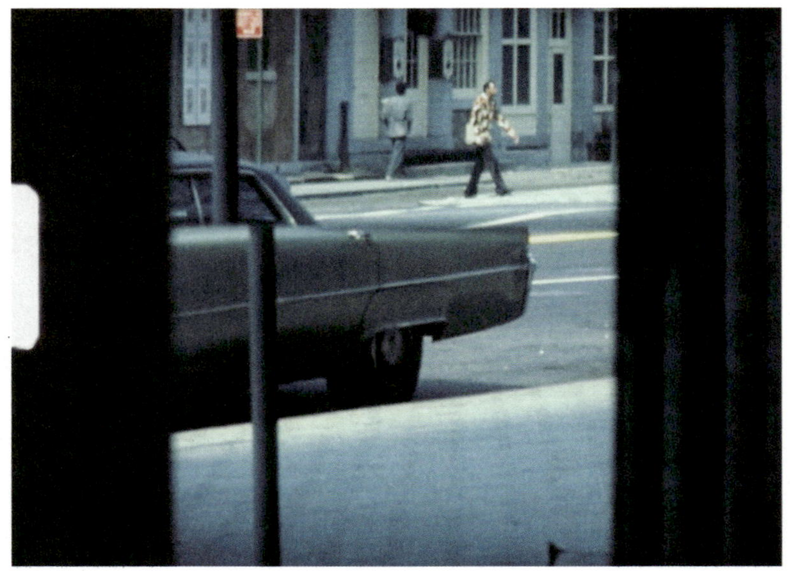

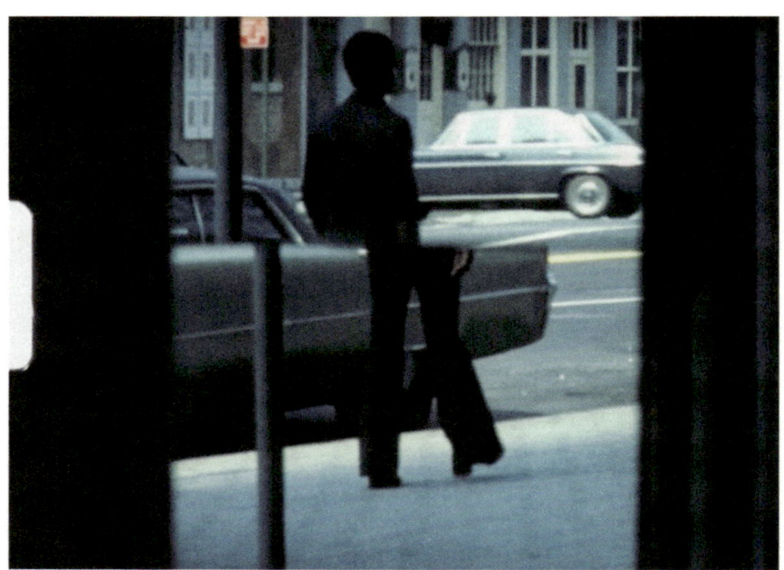

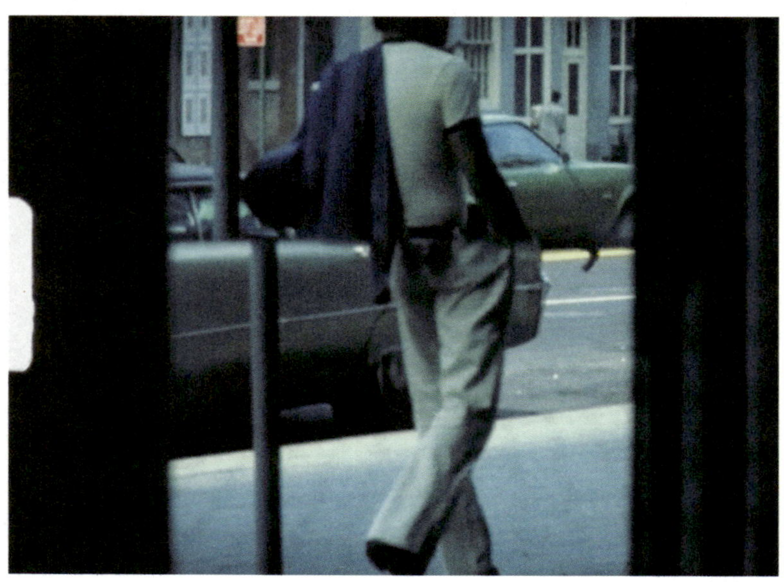

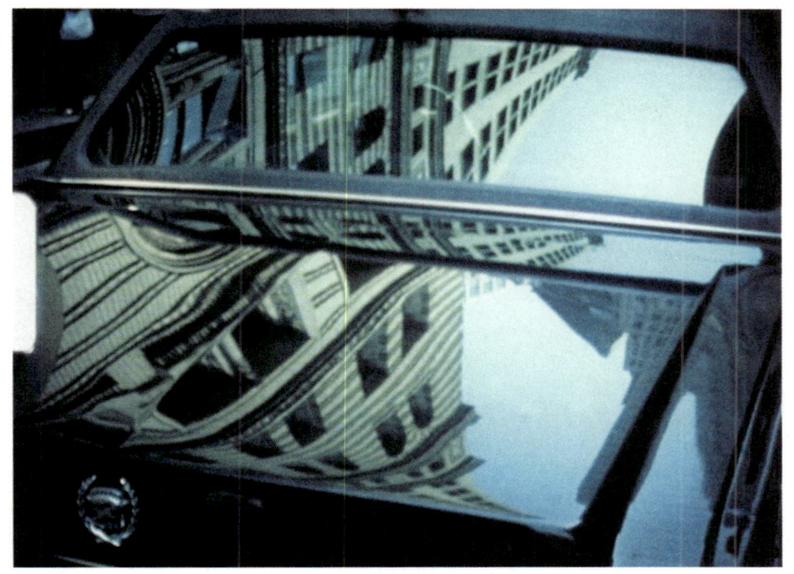

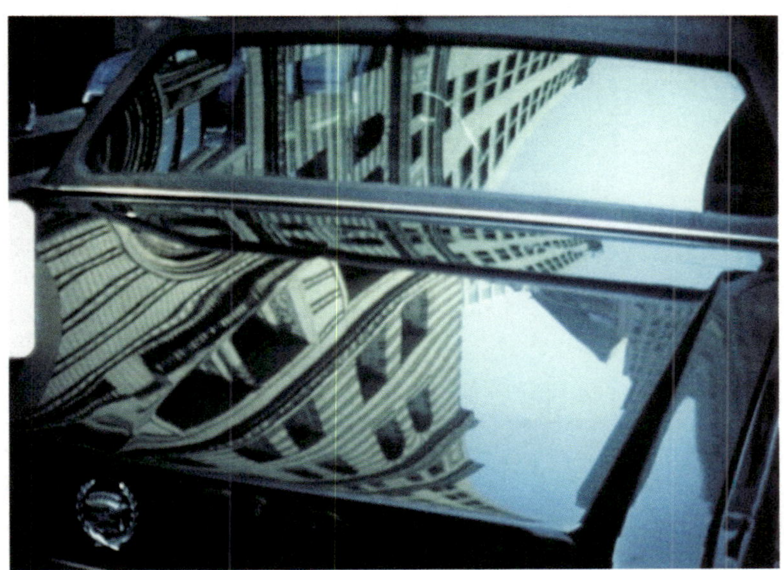

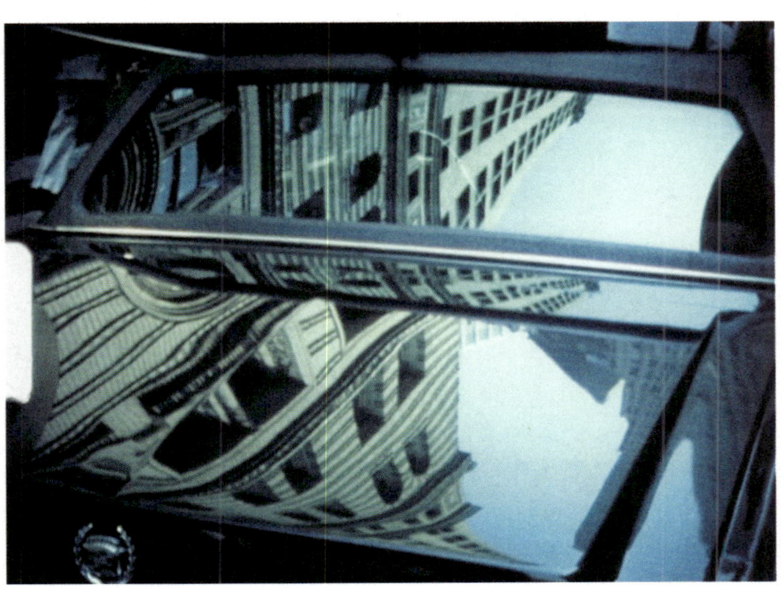

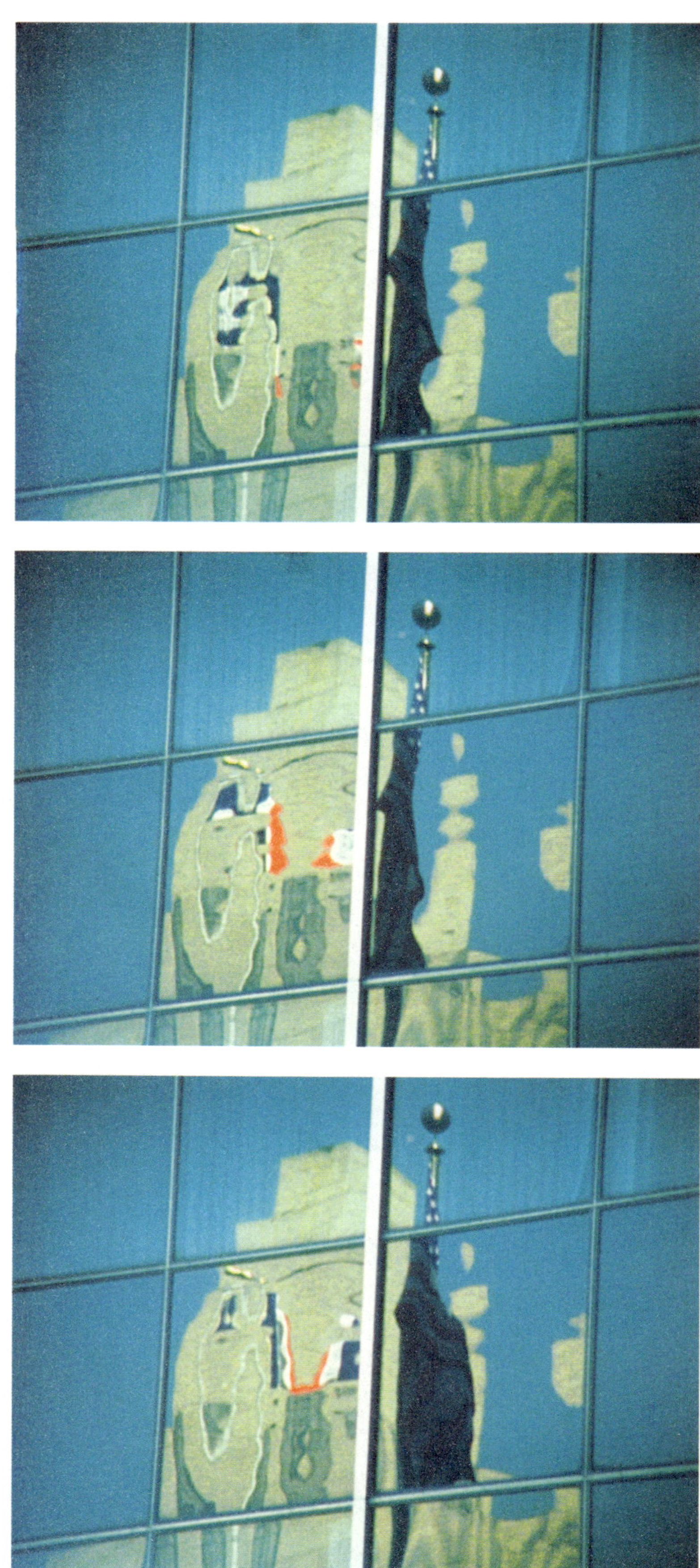

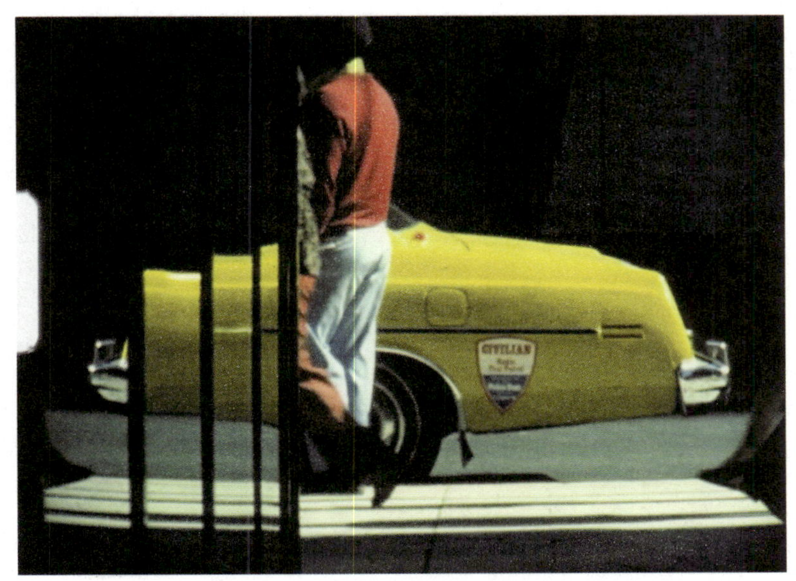
CIVILIAN

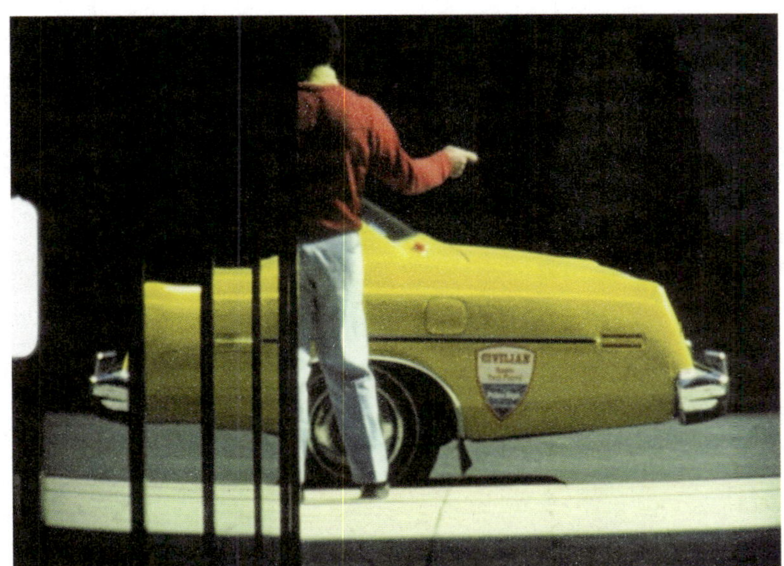
CIVILIAN

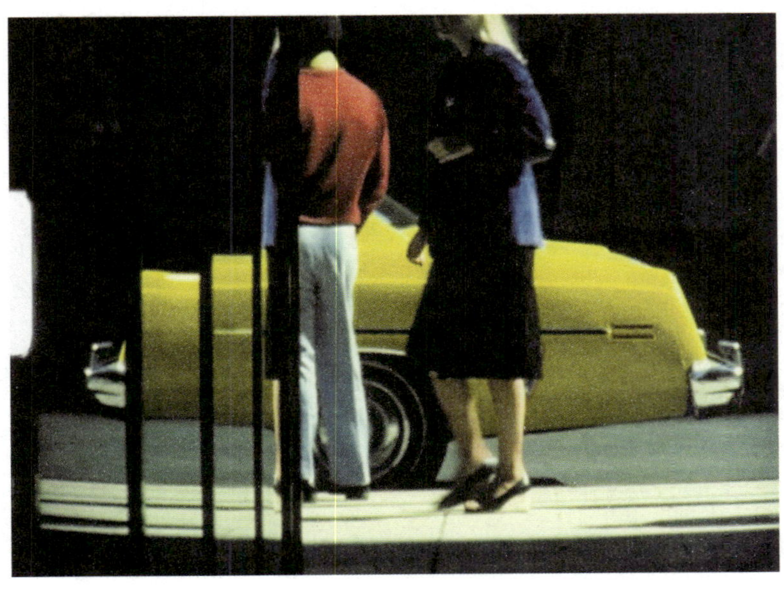

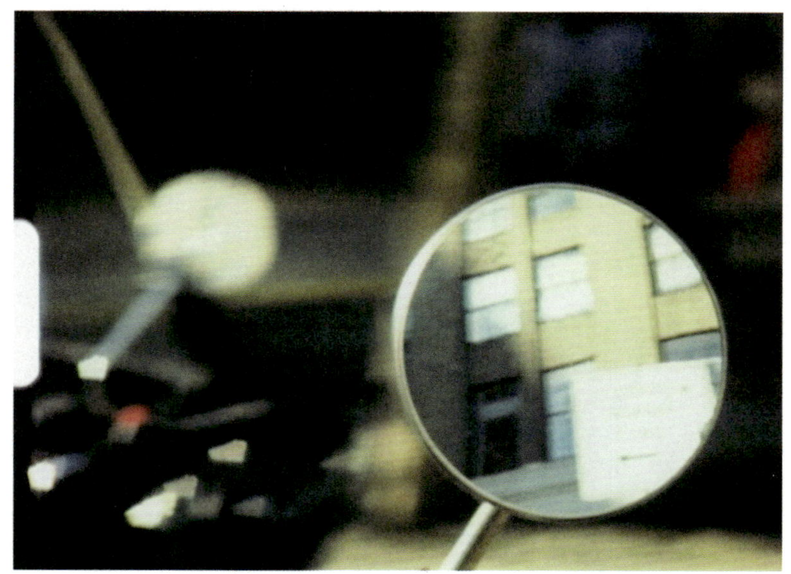
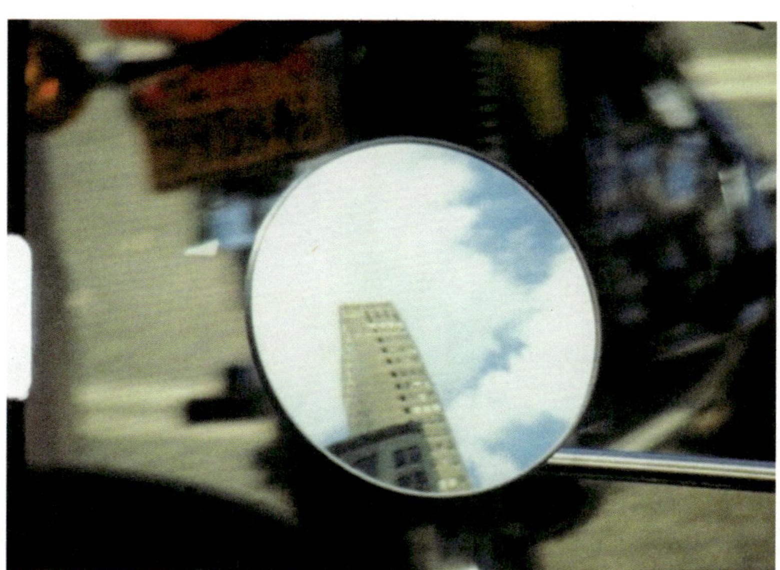
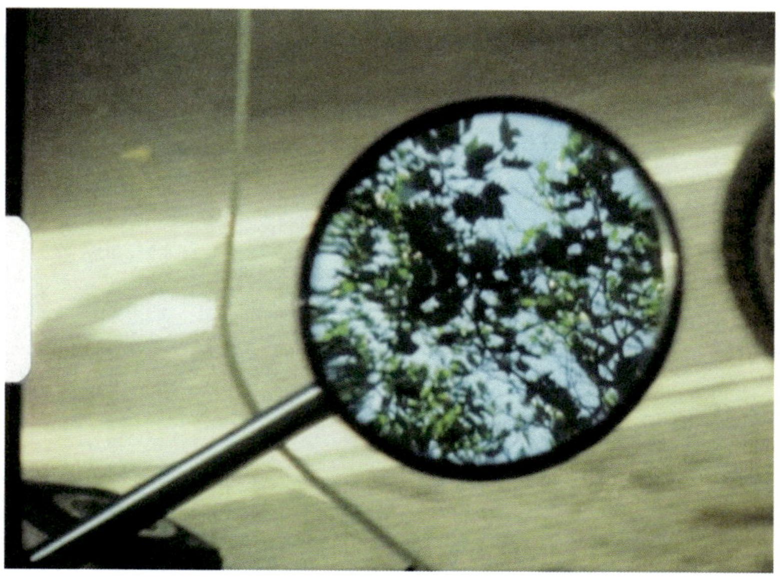

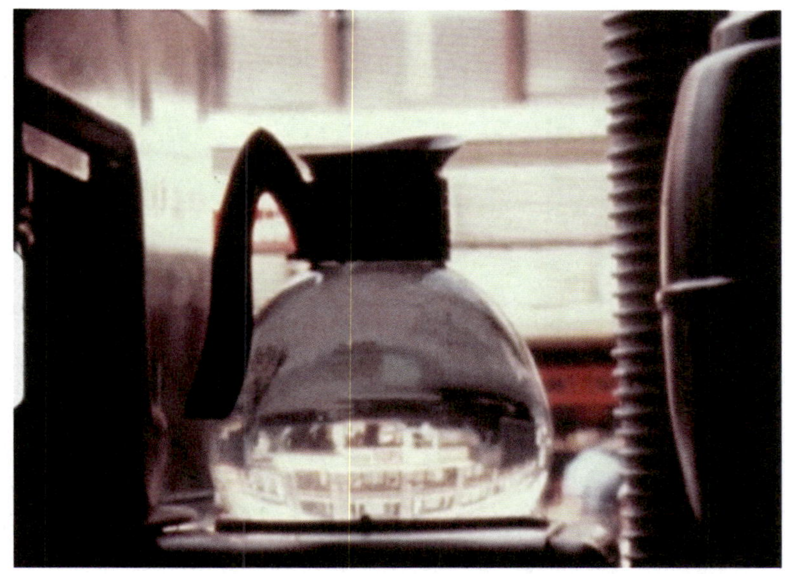

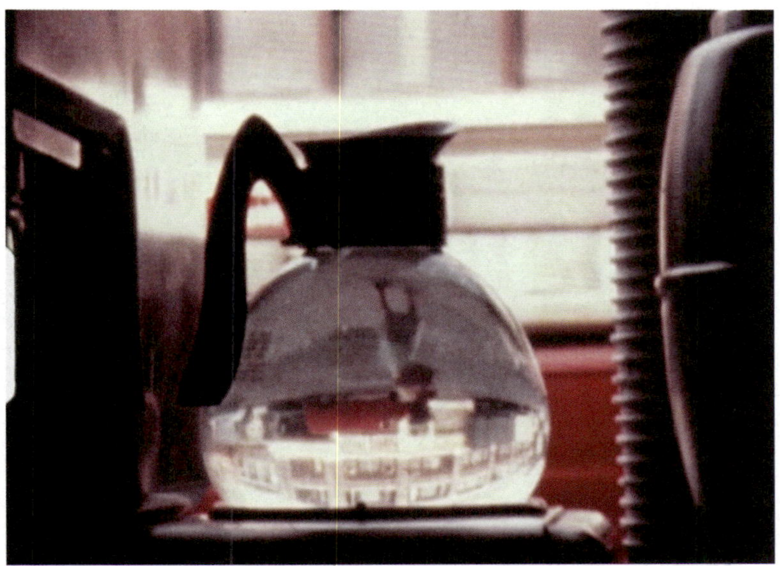

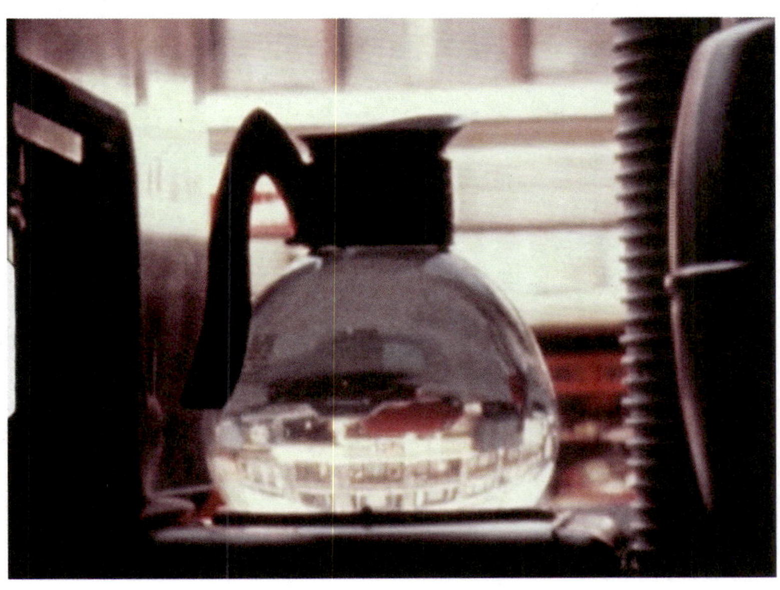

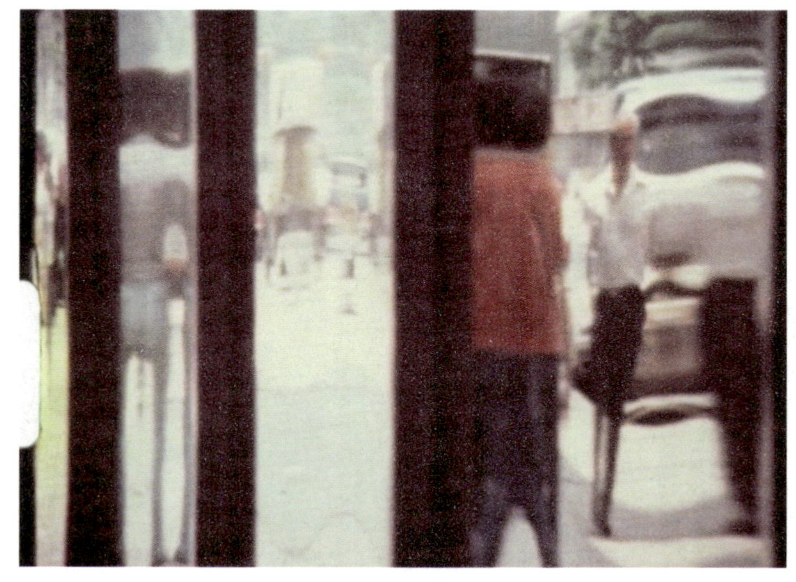

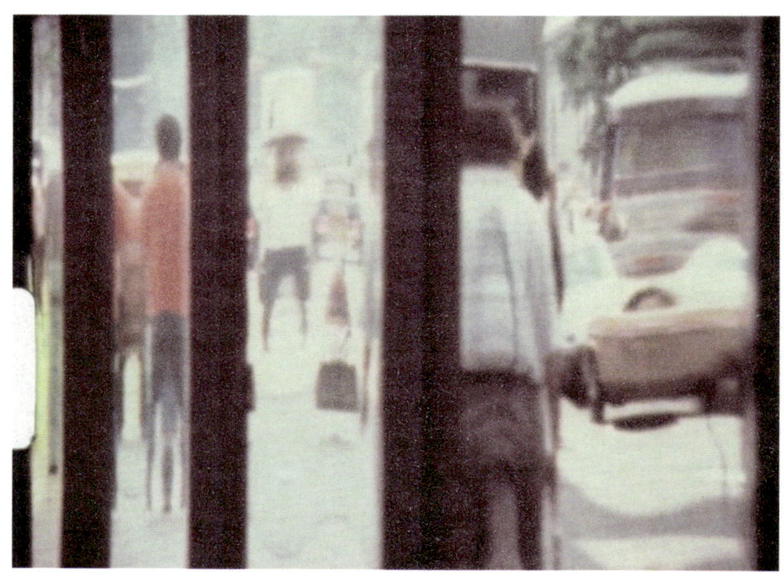

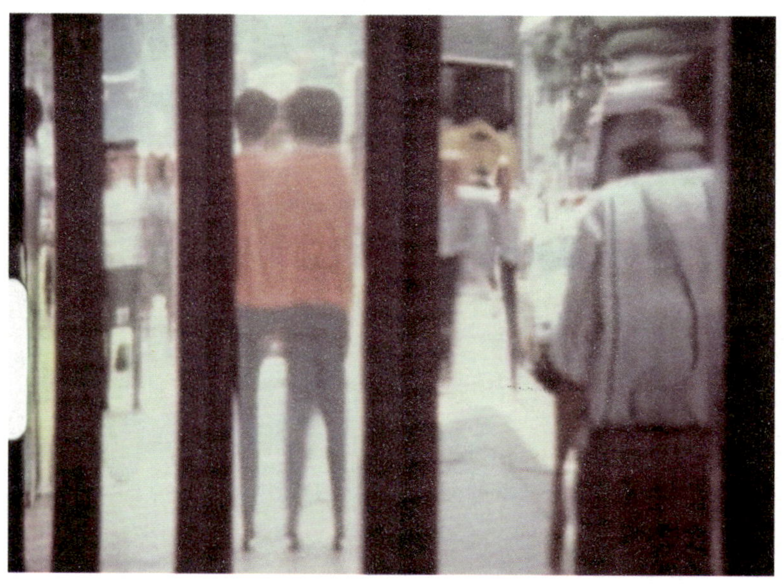

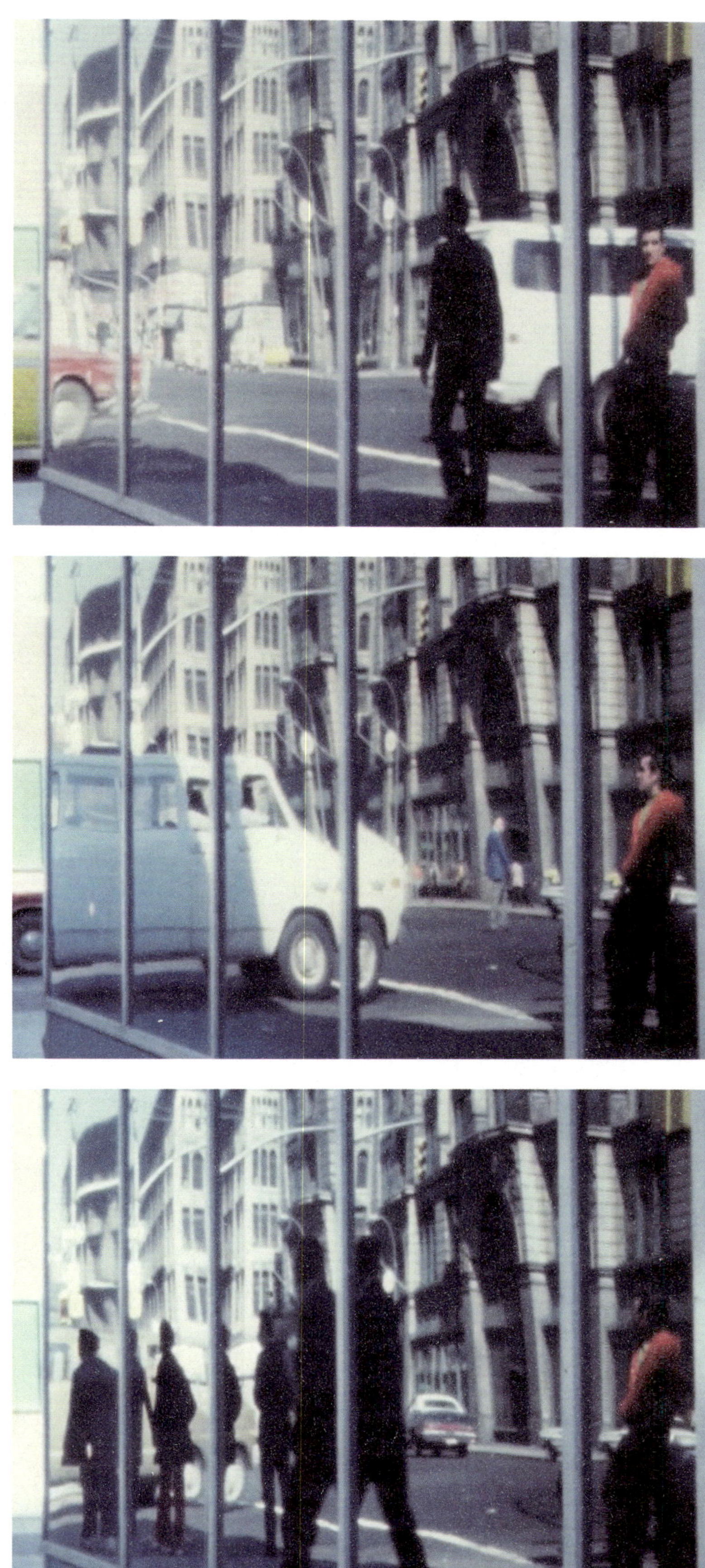

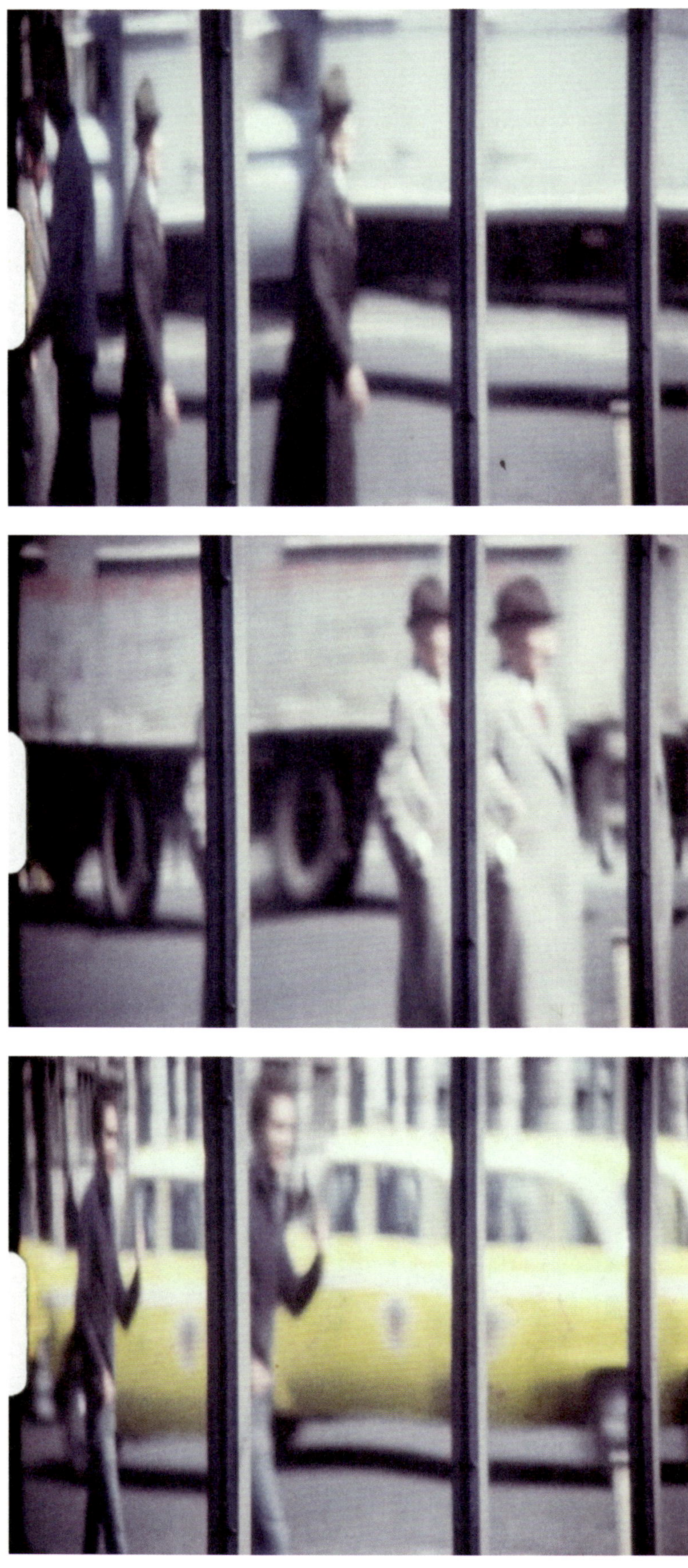

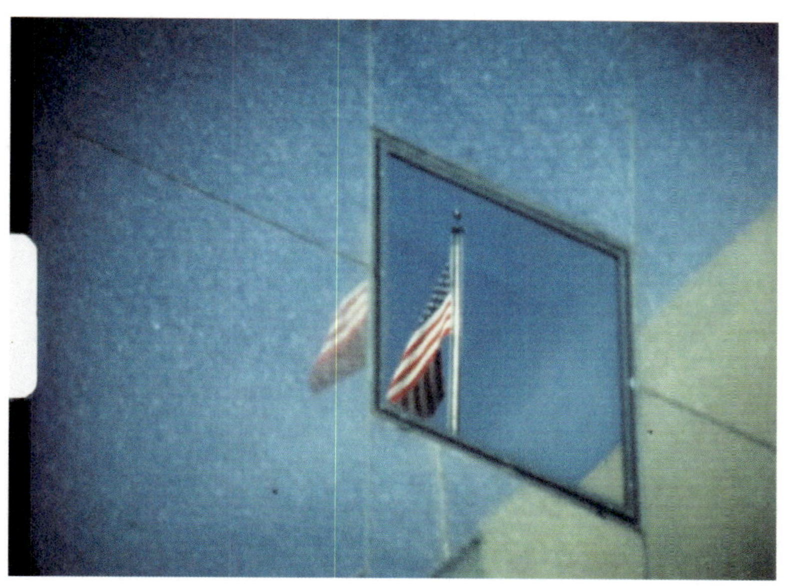

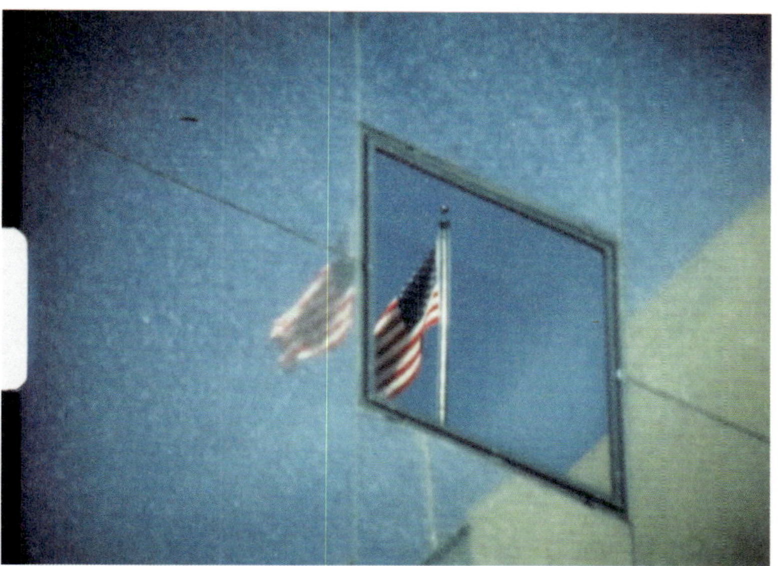

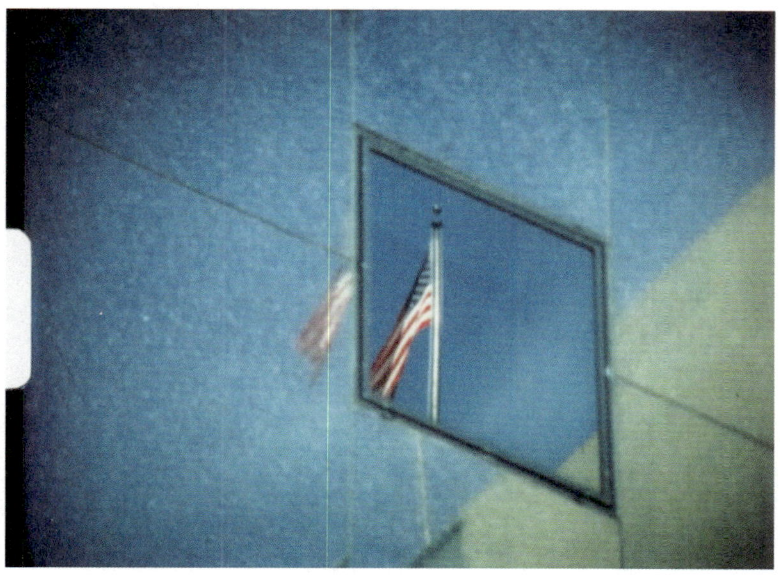

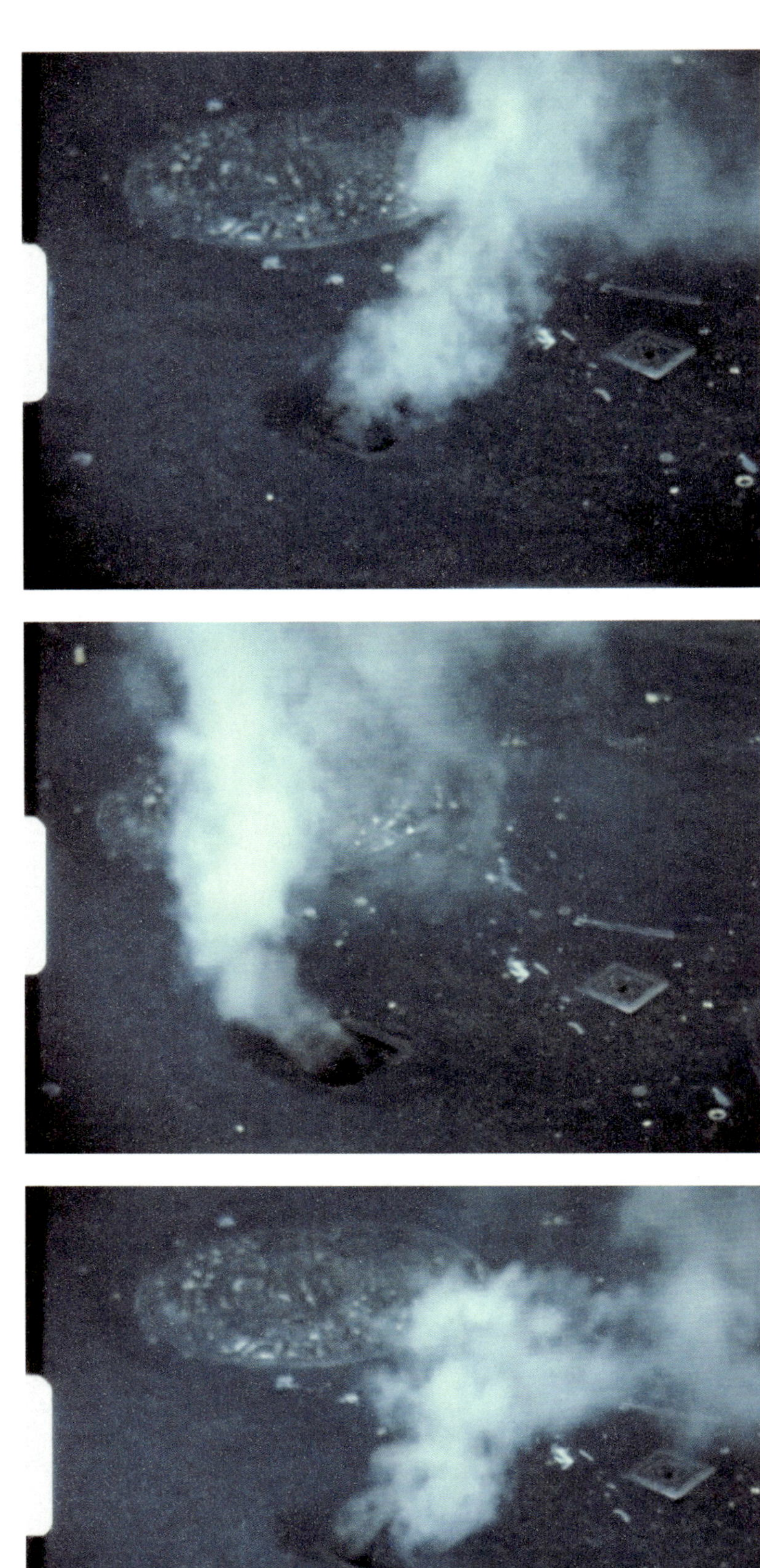

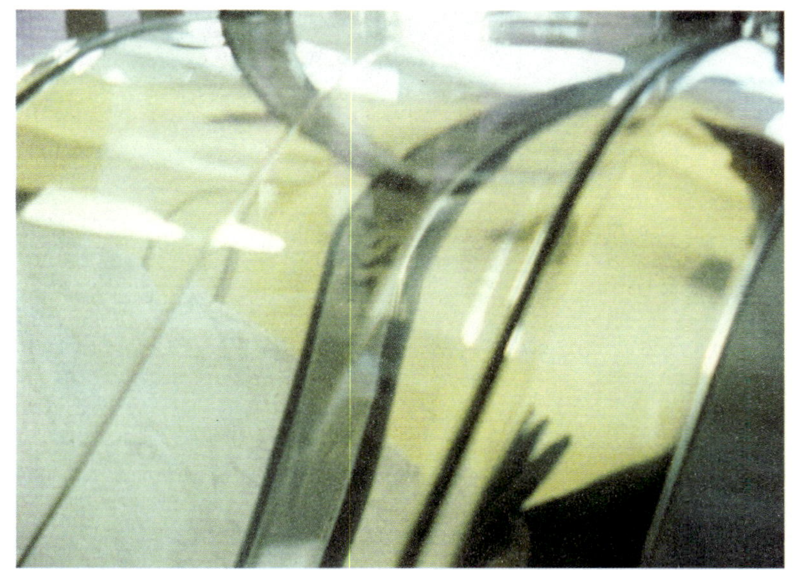

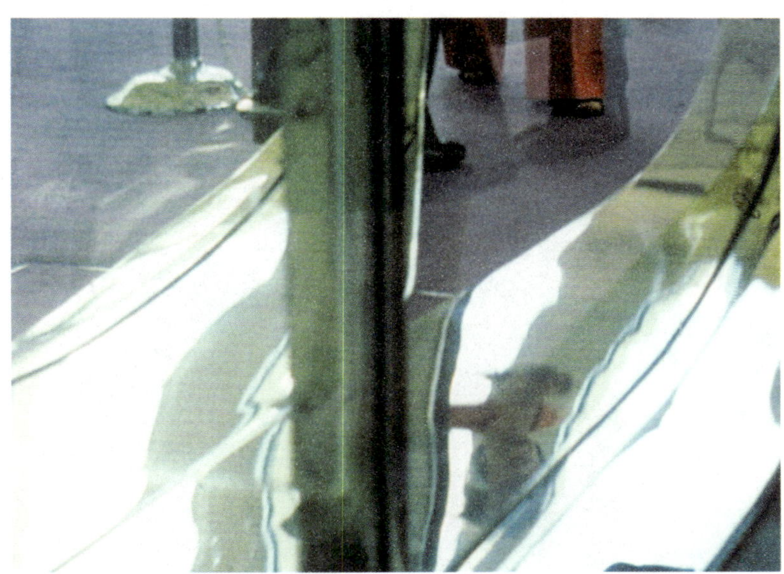

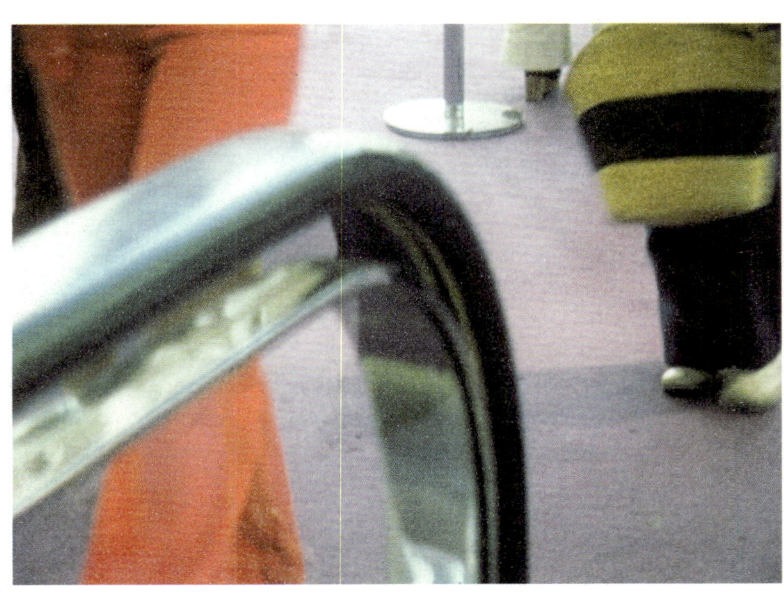

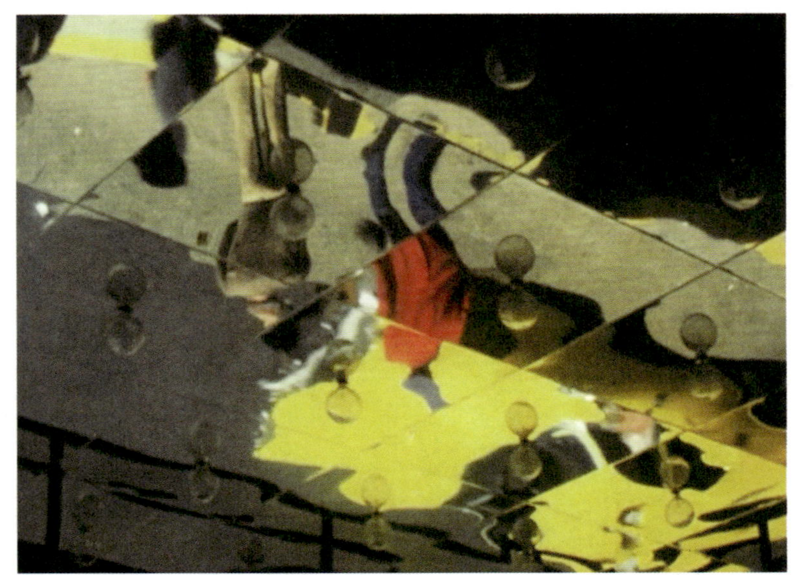

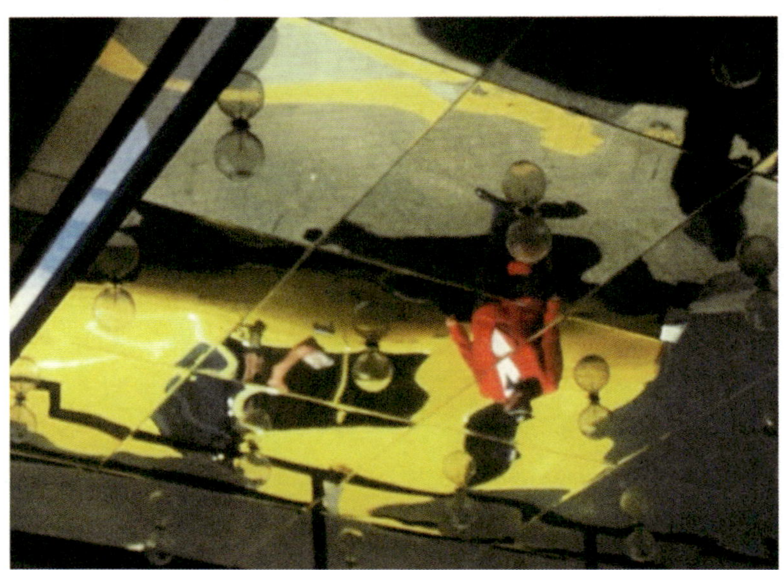

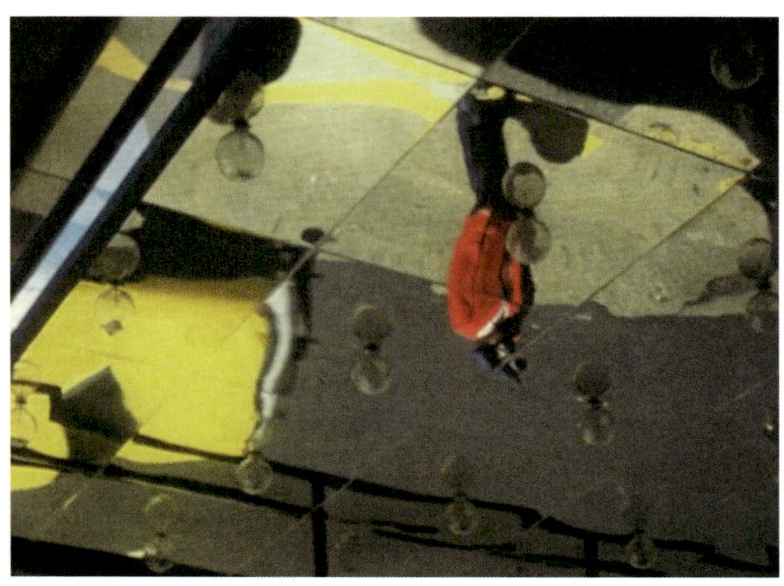

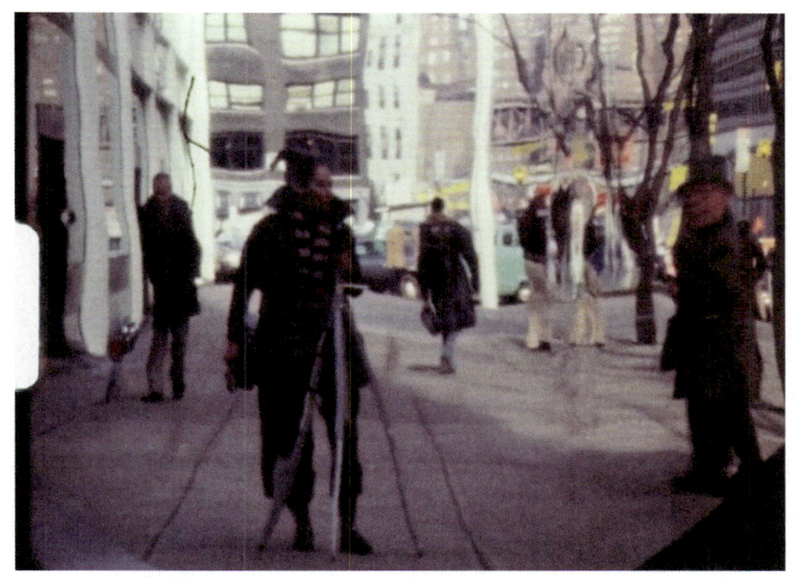

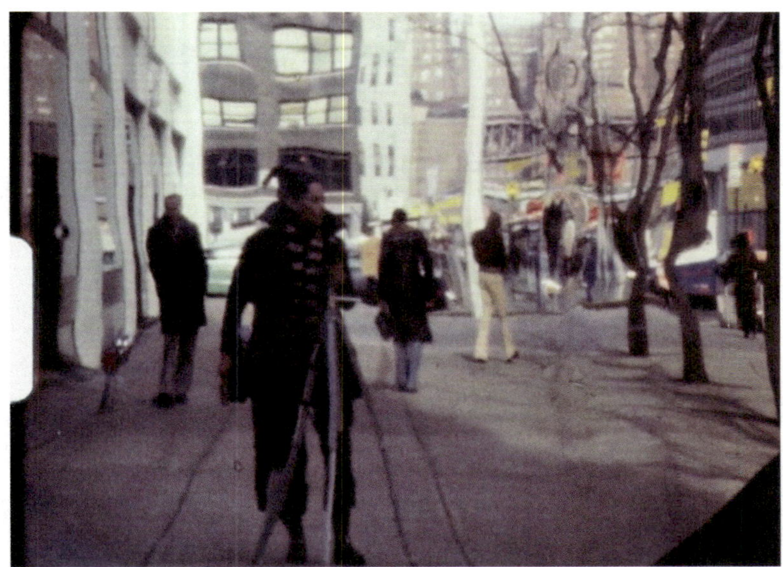

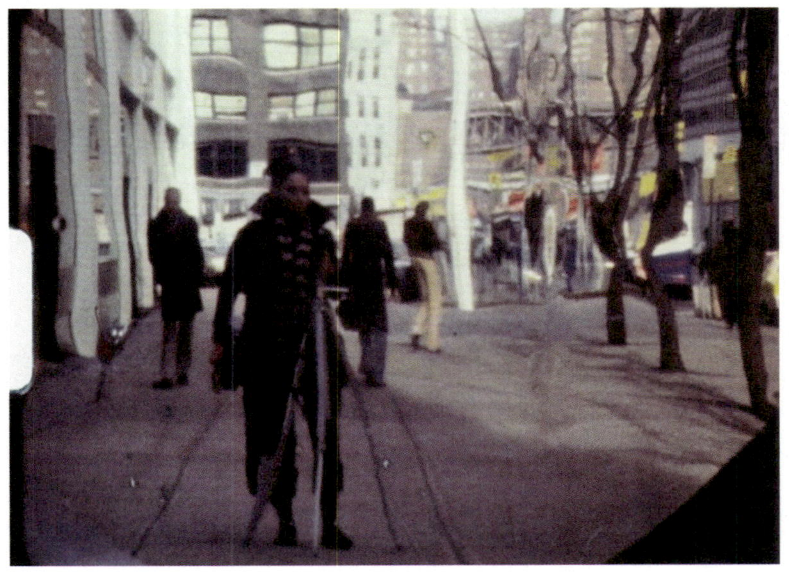

Identifying numbers for BETTINA's film on distortions in N.Y. in super 8 / video-transfers.

SUYAMA COLOR LAB INC 55 west 42 street 869.3355 #1-8

#I (stripesover) 7 /22 bill of lading ready 7/23
2 IO 87 suy33 4388 G855 585IL 7/24 jul 24
I59emF20H6 585IL OI-468-00-8

#2 (stripesover) I58emF20H6
2 I0 87 suy 33 7/22 4500 G 855 jul 22
585IL OI-468-00-8

#5 (halfshadowover G2I IO
2 I0 87 suy 33 jul23 4502 G 855 G2I I0
585IL OI-468-00-8

#3 stripesover G22B8
2 IO 87 suy33 jul24 4384 G 855 585IL OI-468-00-8

#4 stripesover G22B8
2 IO 87 suy33 jul24 450I G855 585IL OI-468-00-8

#6 PLAZA G22H4
2 I0 87 suy33 jul24 4507 G 855 585IL OI-468-00-8

#7 FT G22H4 torn leader
2 I0 87 suy 33 jul24 4506 G855 585IL OI-468-00-8

#8 (FT) G22H4
2 IO 87 suy33 jul24 4508 G855 585IL OI-468-00-8

#9 HALFOVER S4 120 S4120 158emF29H6
env X237 314 6I 8/I/86 PA 7/25 237289

#IOHALFOVER S4 I06 158em F29H6
env x237289 6I 8/I/86 PA 7/25 237346

#II TAXIOVER S4I09 158emF29H6
env x237346 6I 8/I/86 PA 7/25 237291

#I2 (GEO) S4 I08 158emF29H6
env x254303 6I 8/I/86 PA NY JAF INC 7/25 237314

#I3 (GEO) 158emF29H6
8/I/86 PA 7/25 254303

MAILED AND PROCESSED IN CALIFORN KODAK PALO ALTO

PROFOTO

#I4 (highway) envelope 2 II 29 / 7I88-G837 / OCT 27 /
585IL / OI-468-00-8 /
inside box K24H5 / outside envelope ∆ D-865

#I5 (chockfull) env. 2 II 29 / 7I88-G837 / OCT 27 ?
585IL / OI-468-00-8
inside box K24H5 / outside ∆ H-7I8

#I6 (chockfull) env. 2 II 29 / 7I89-G837 / OCT 27
585 IL / OI-468-00-8
inside box K24H5 / outside ∆ D-865

Identifying numbers for Bettina's film on distortions in New York, in Super 8, video transfers

Drawing & Painting

"My work was originally two-dimensional. But after the fire—when I had to start all over again—I found, psychologically, that two dimensions weren't sufficient. I began working with solid material ..."

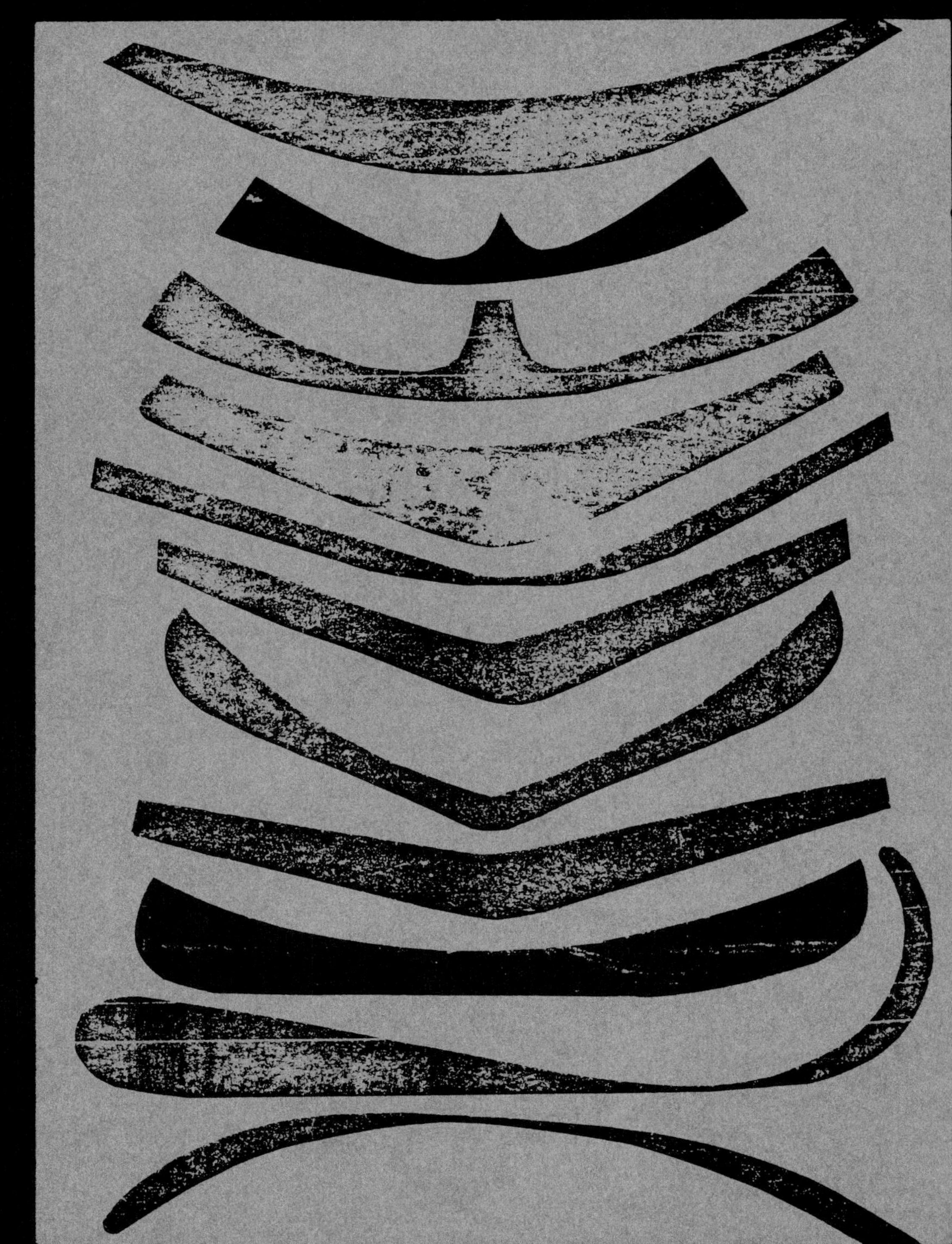

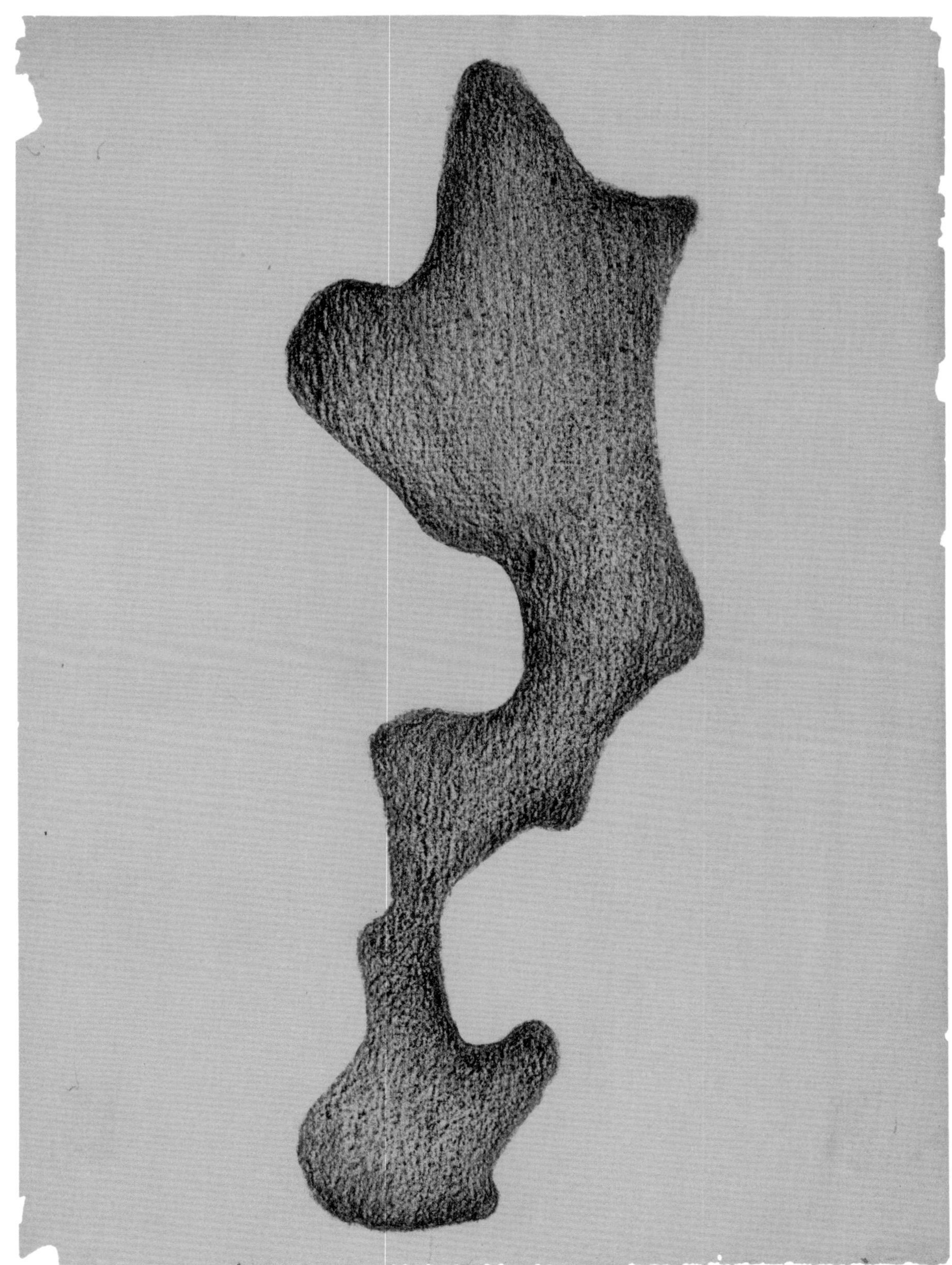

Pages 121–27: From the series *Barkforms*, charcoal on paper, 1970–90

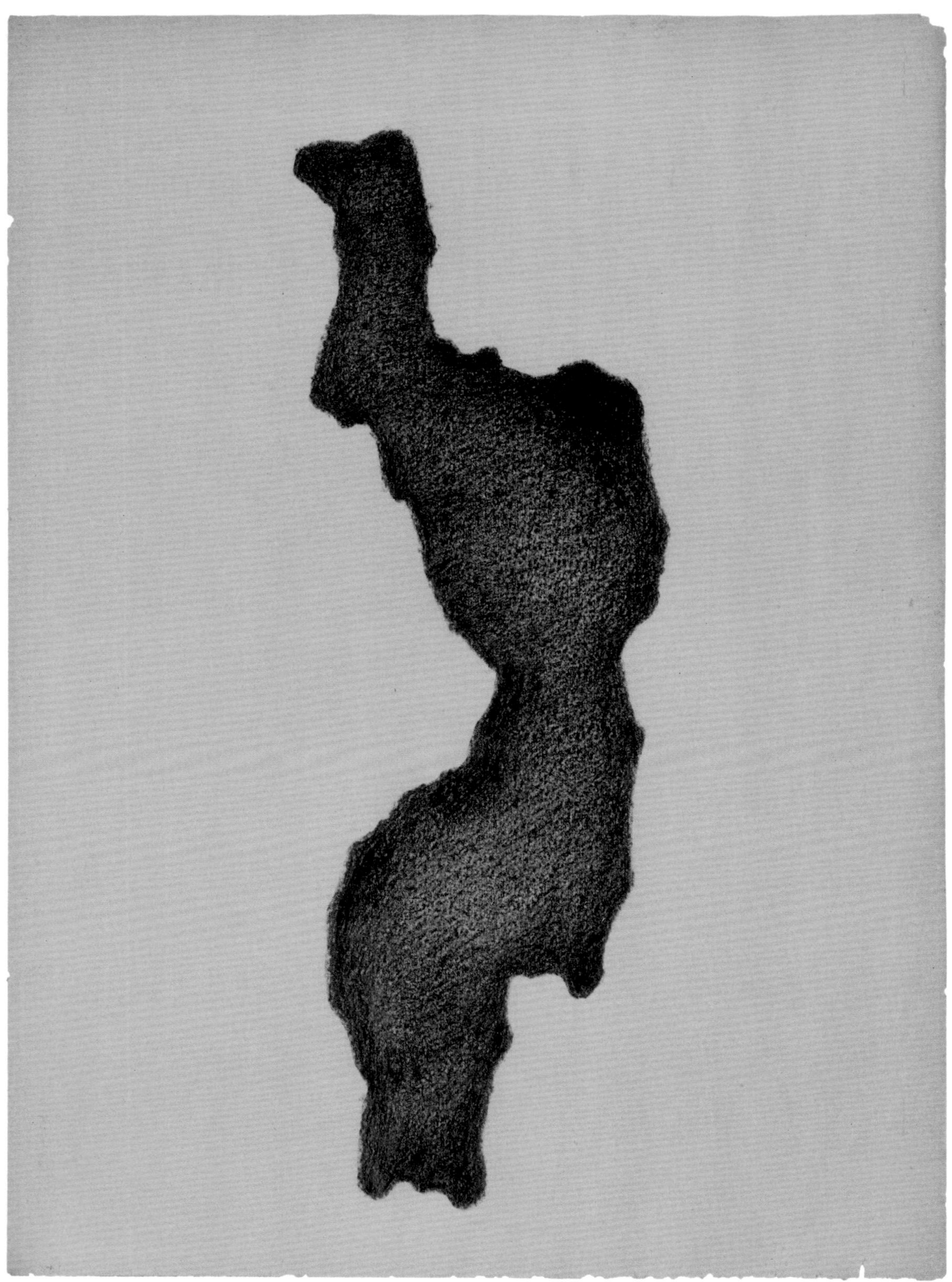

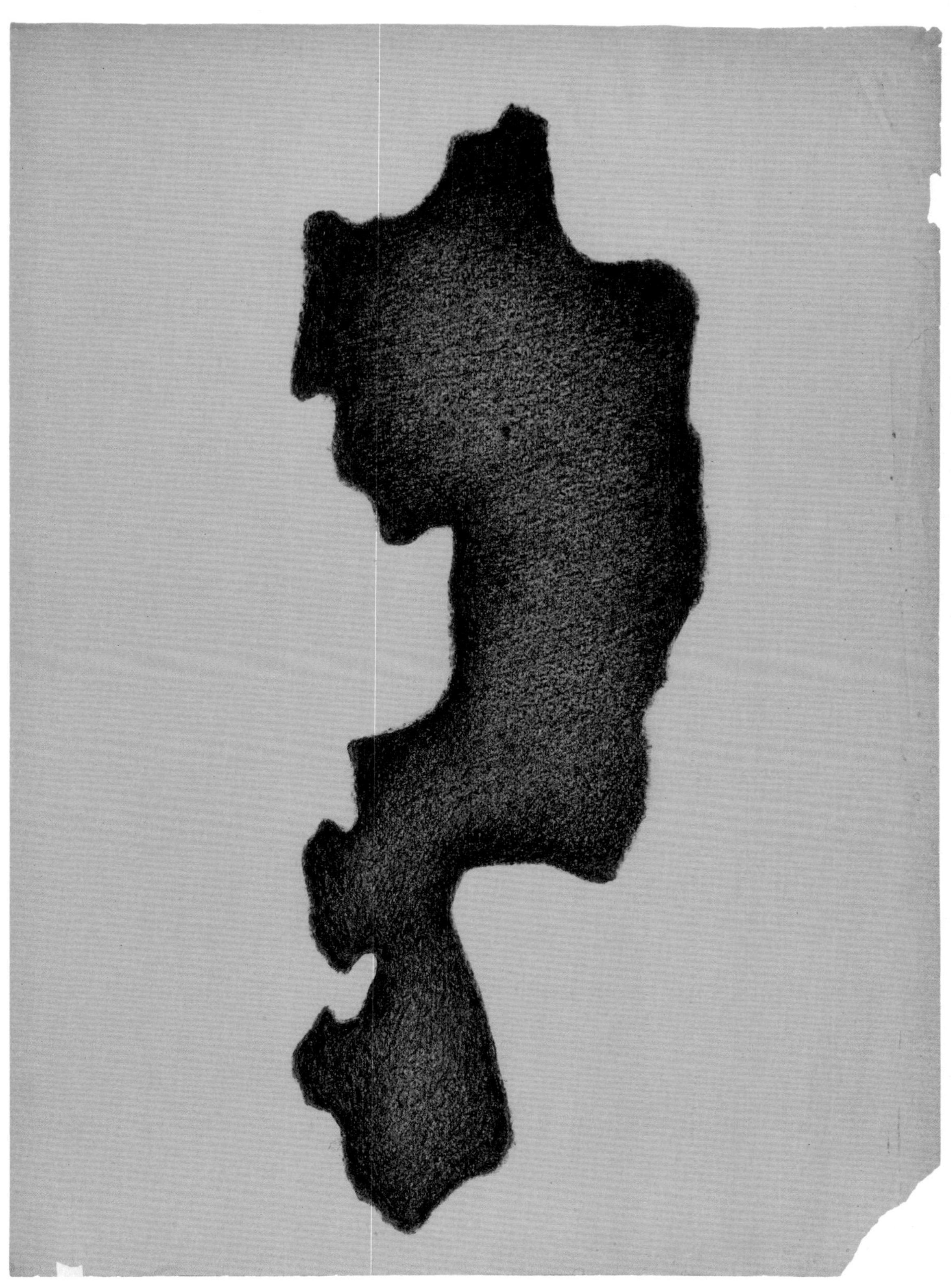

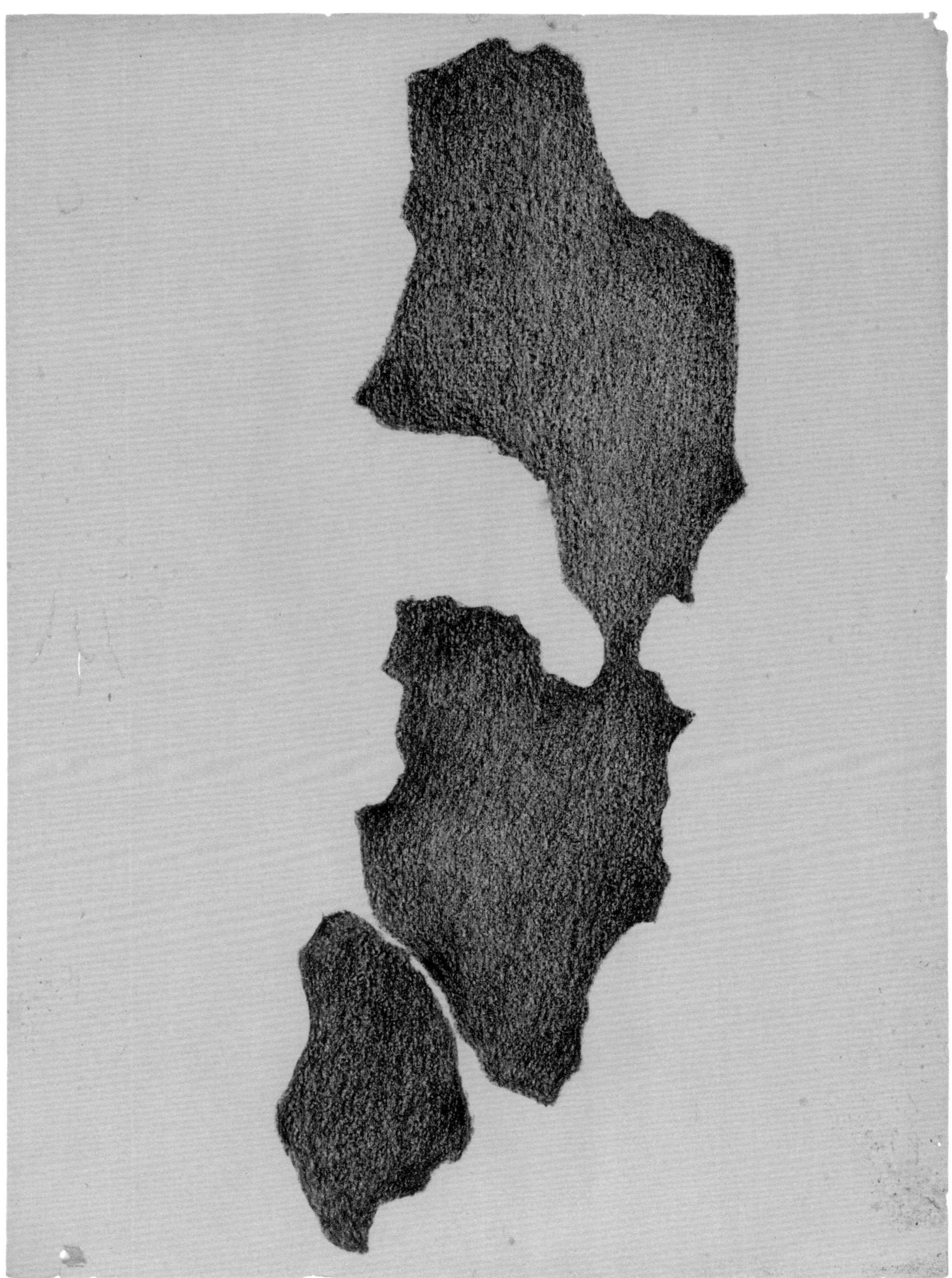

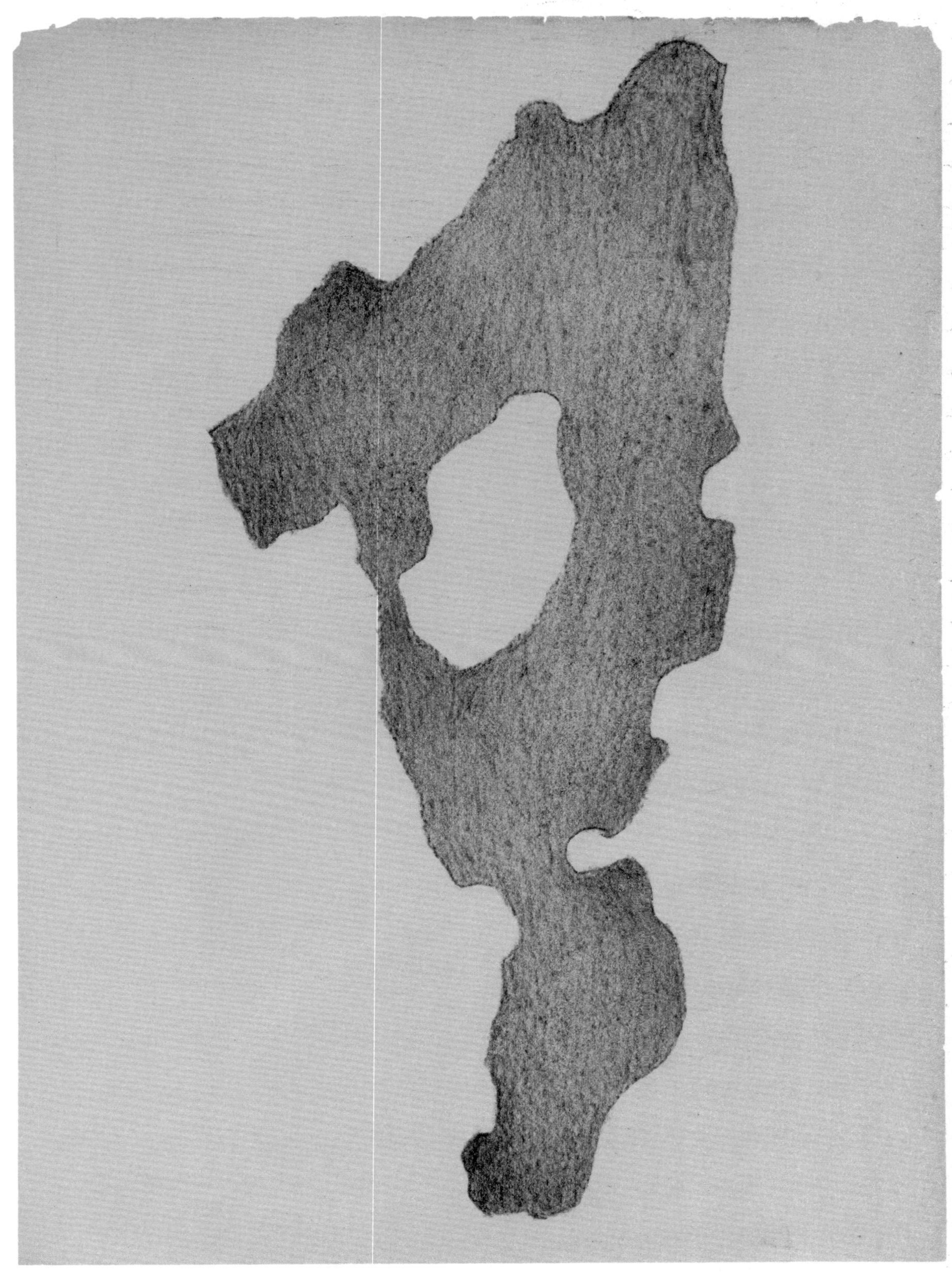

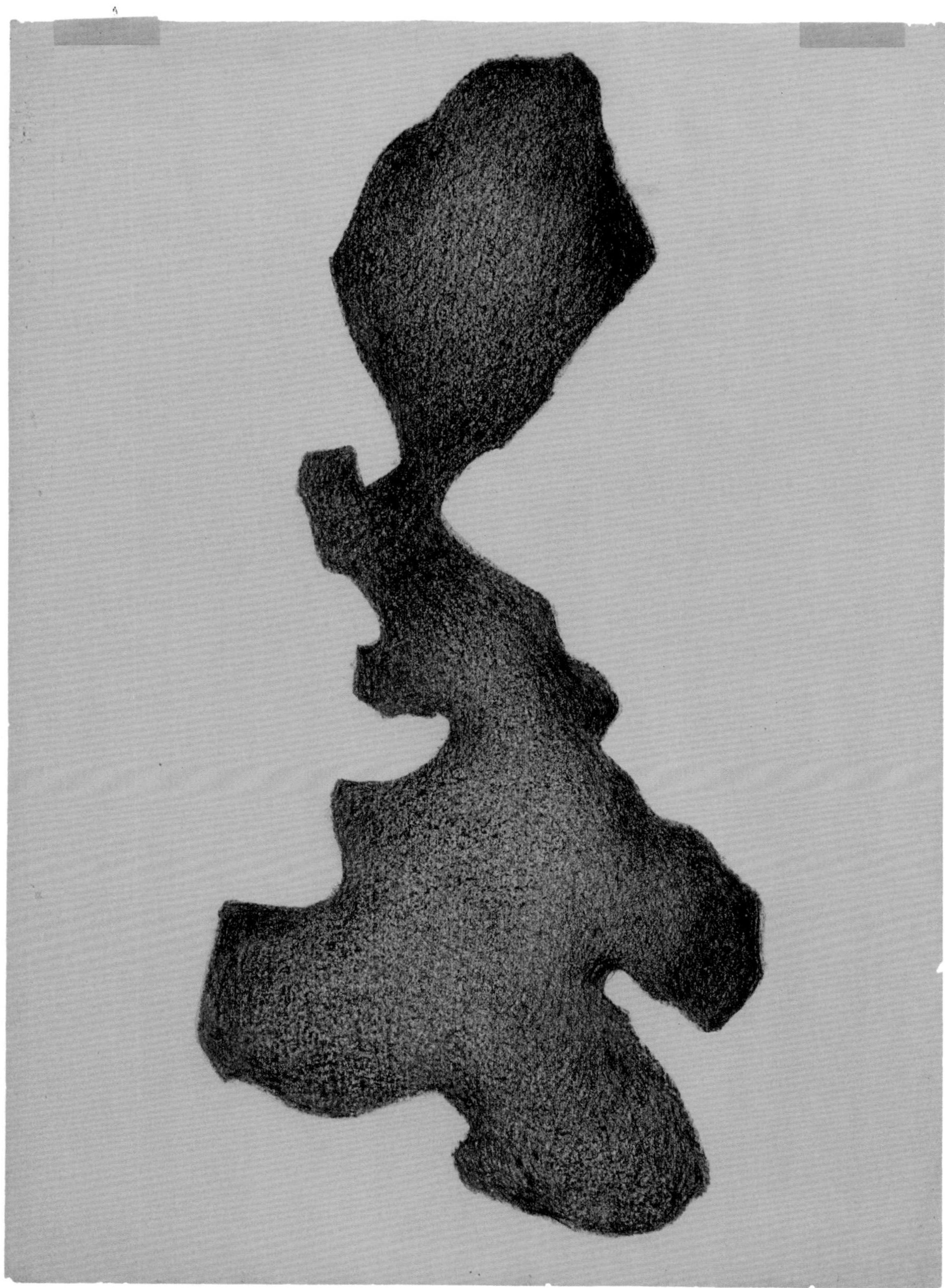

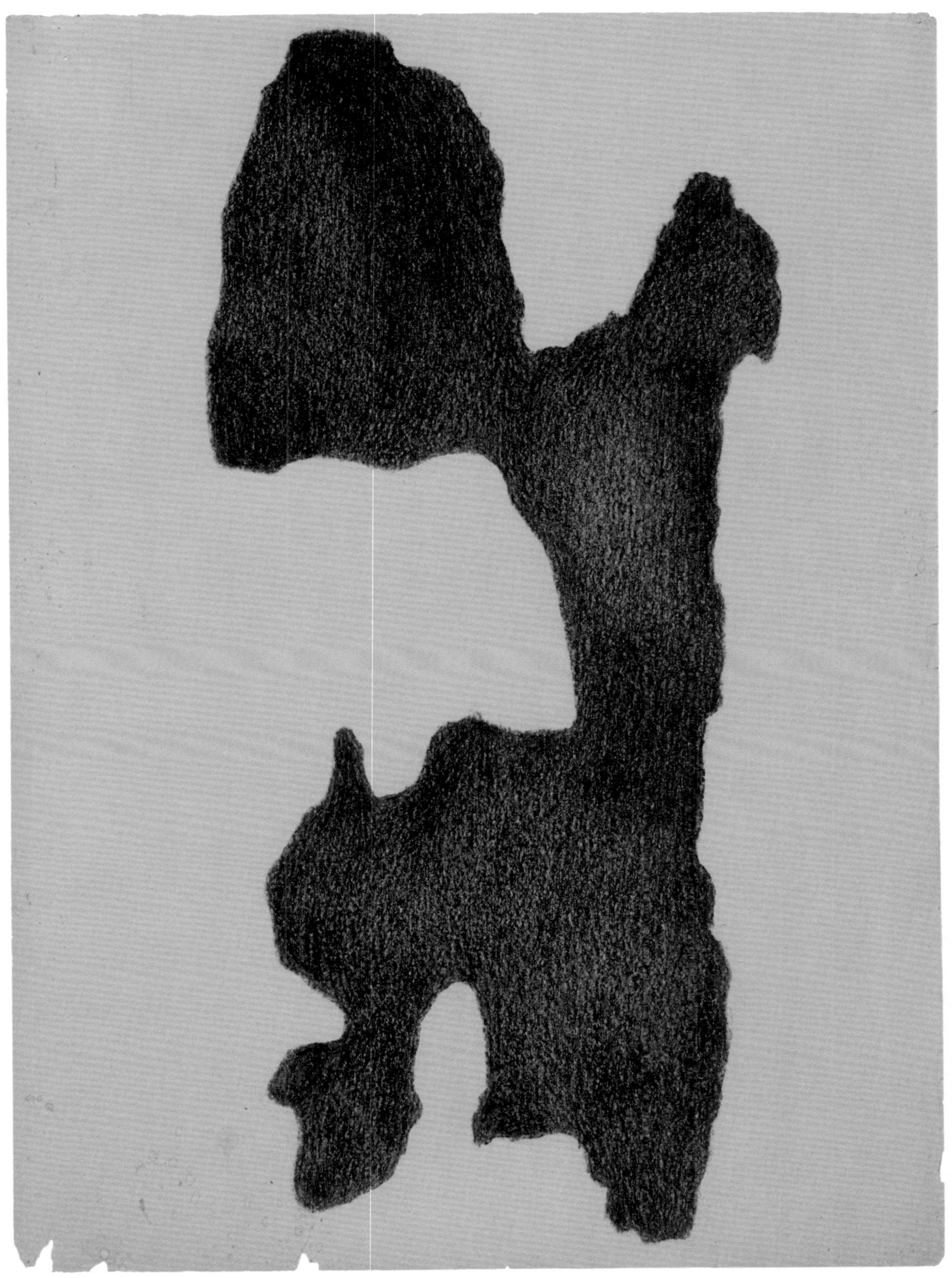

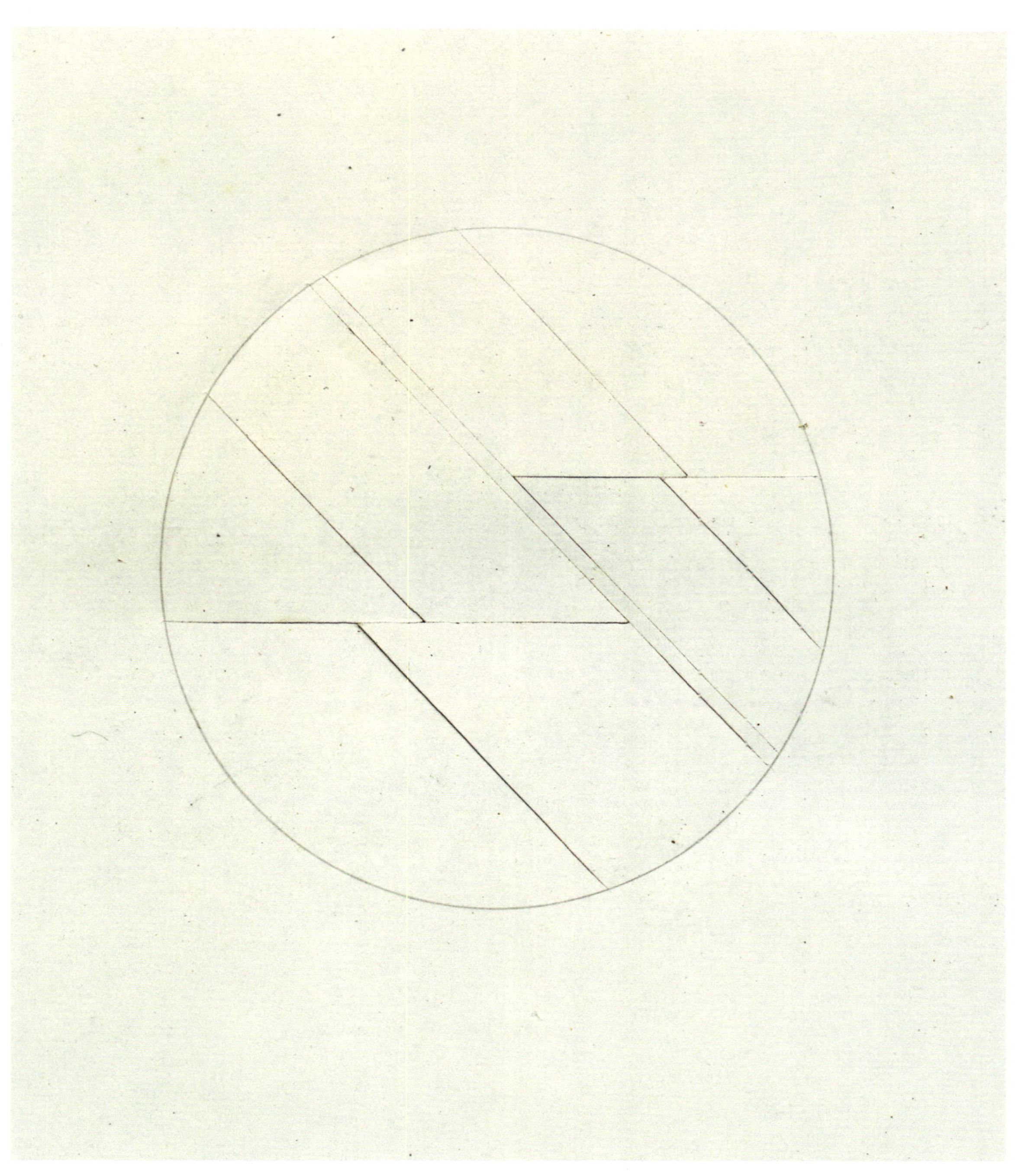

Pages 129–31: From the series *GroundBreakers*, cut paper, 1967–84

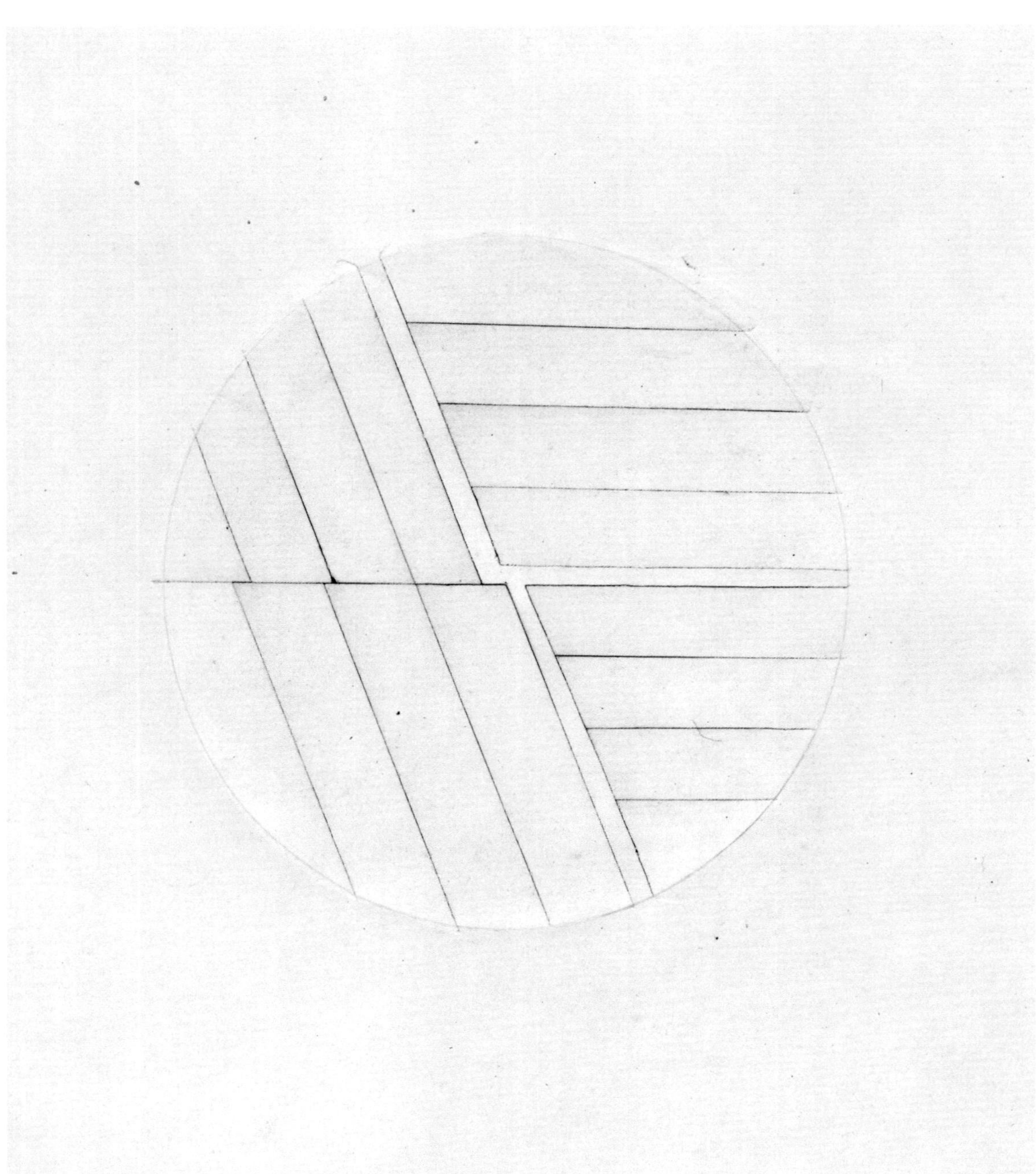

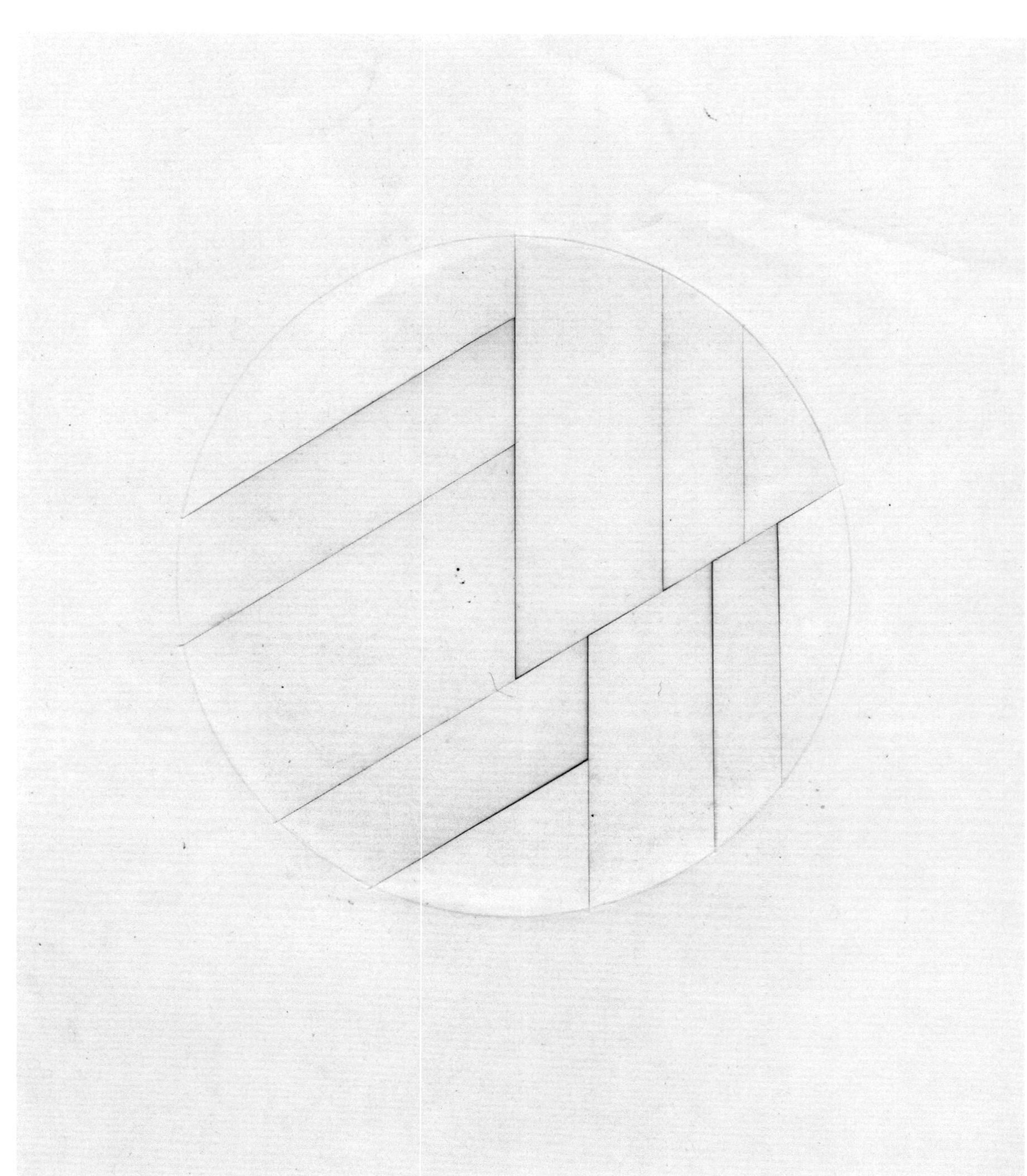

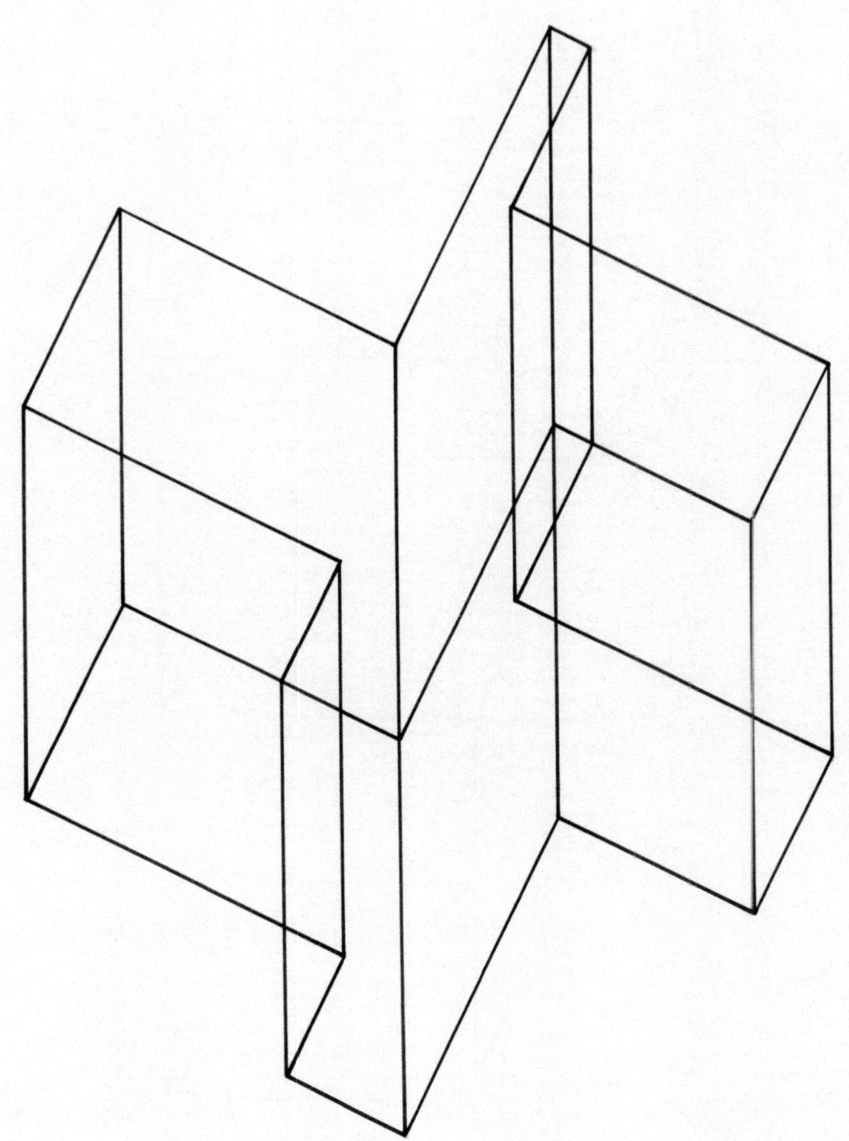

Pages 133–42: *Finite Structures*, ink on paper, 1968–83

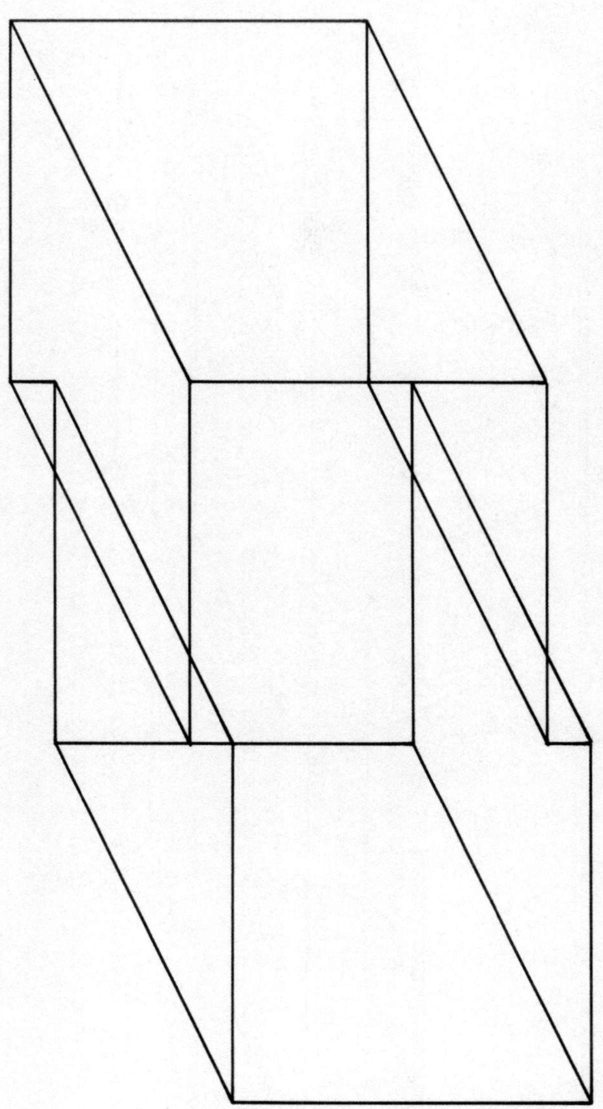

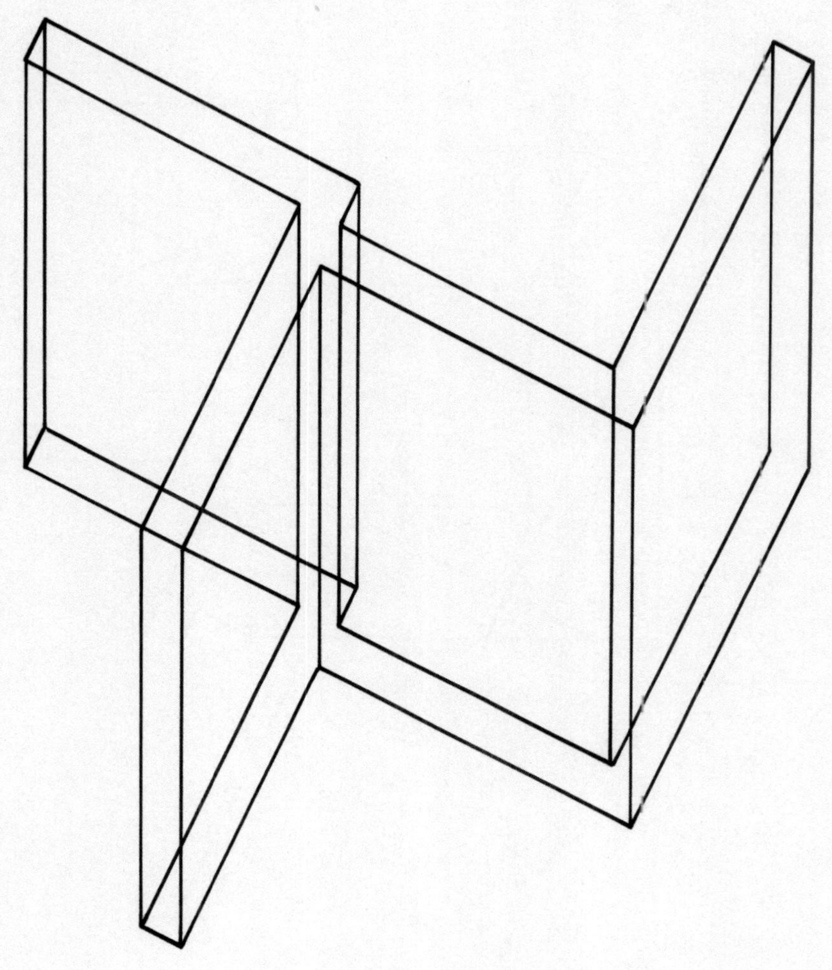

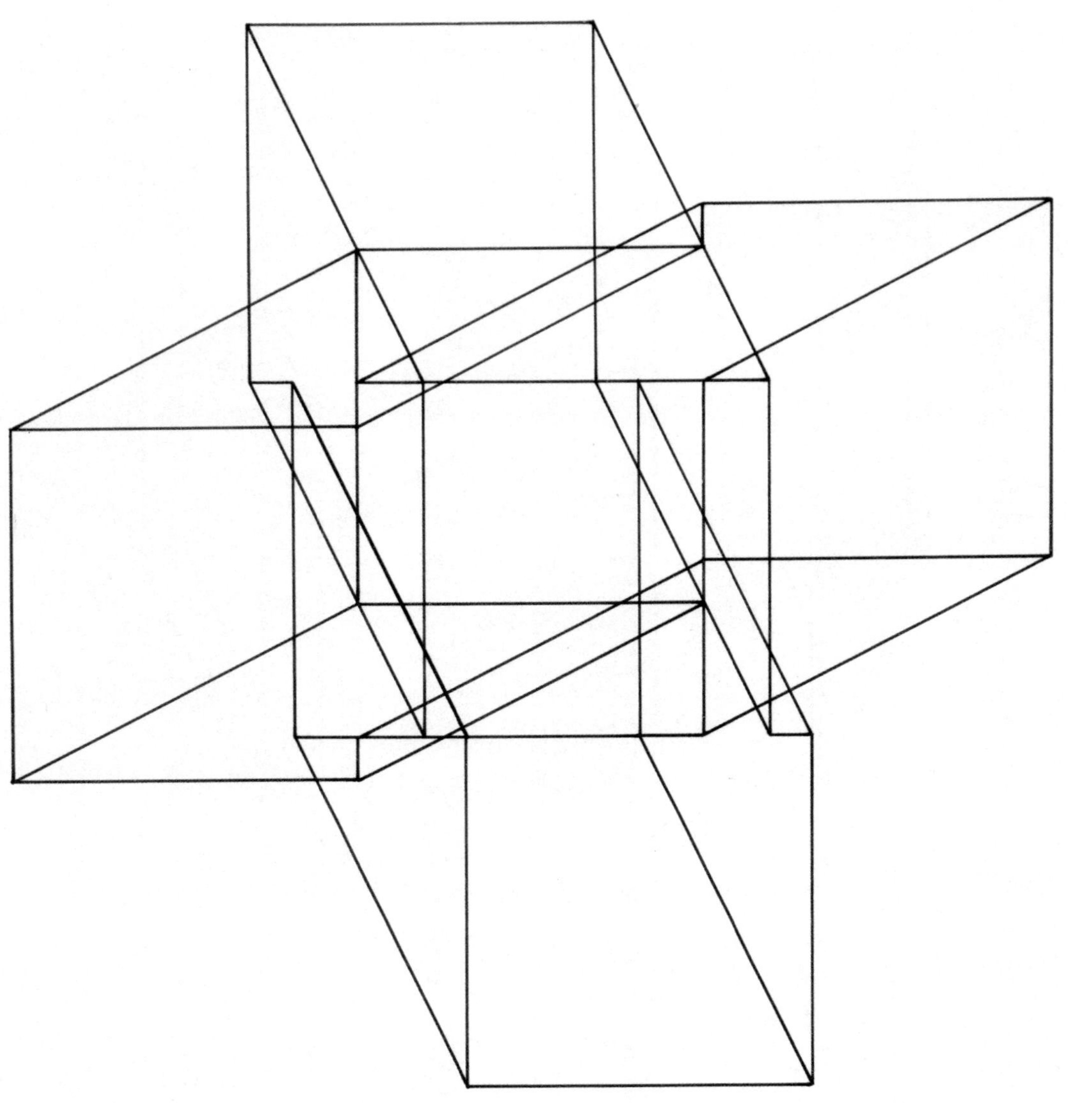

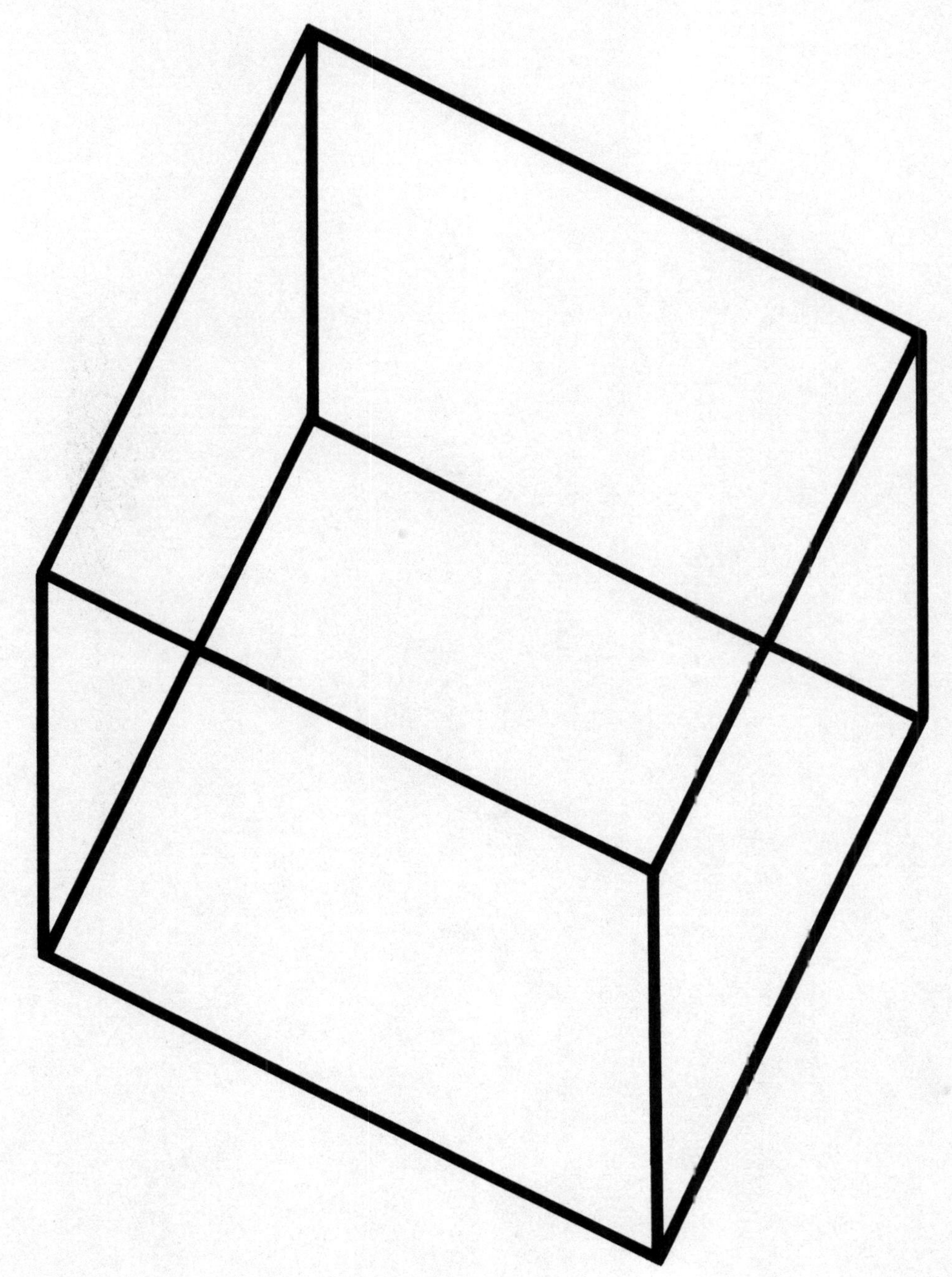

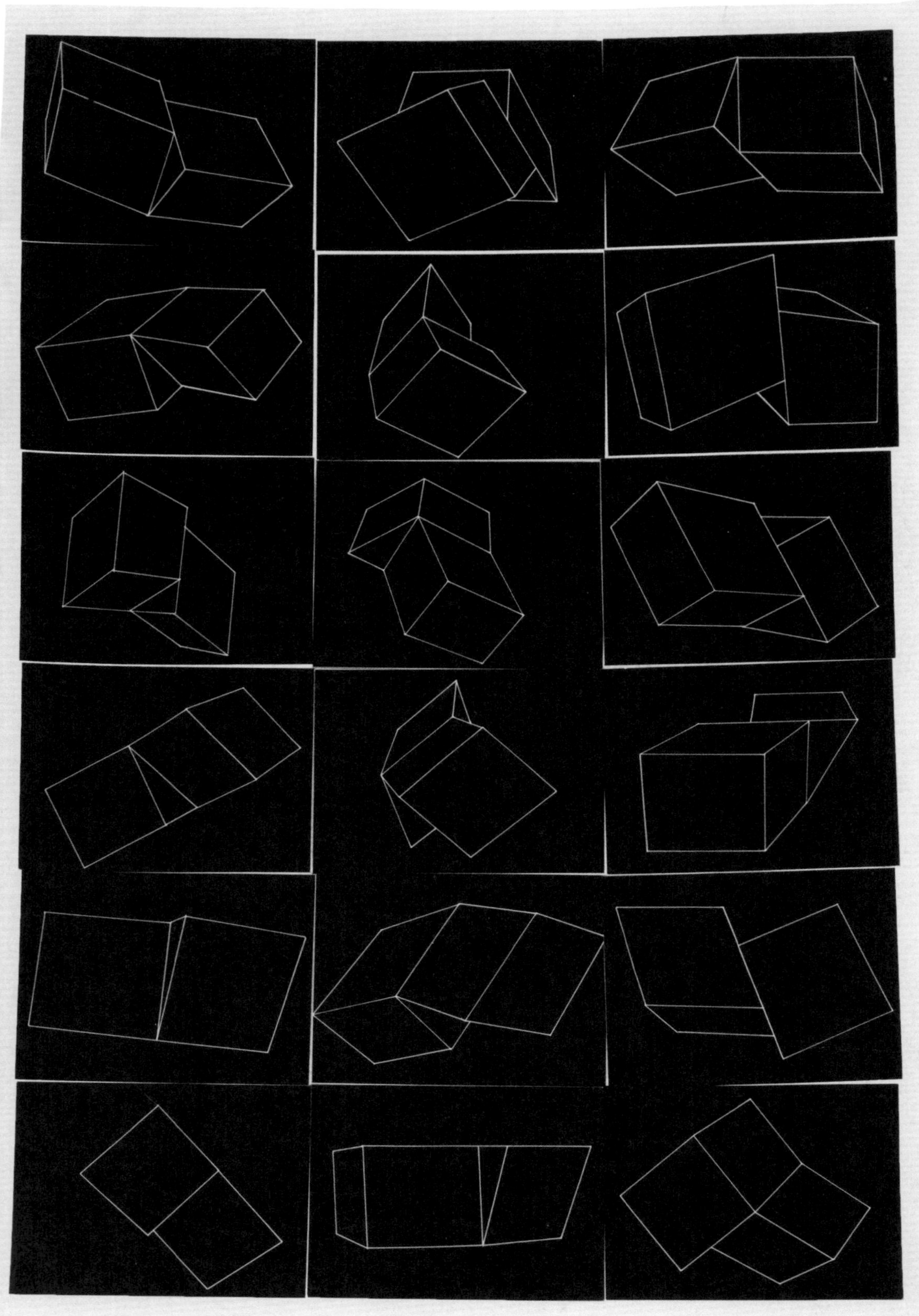

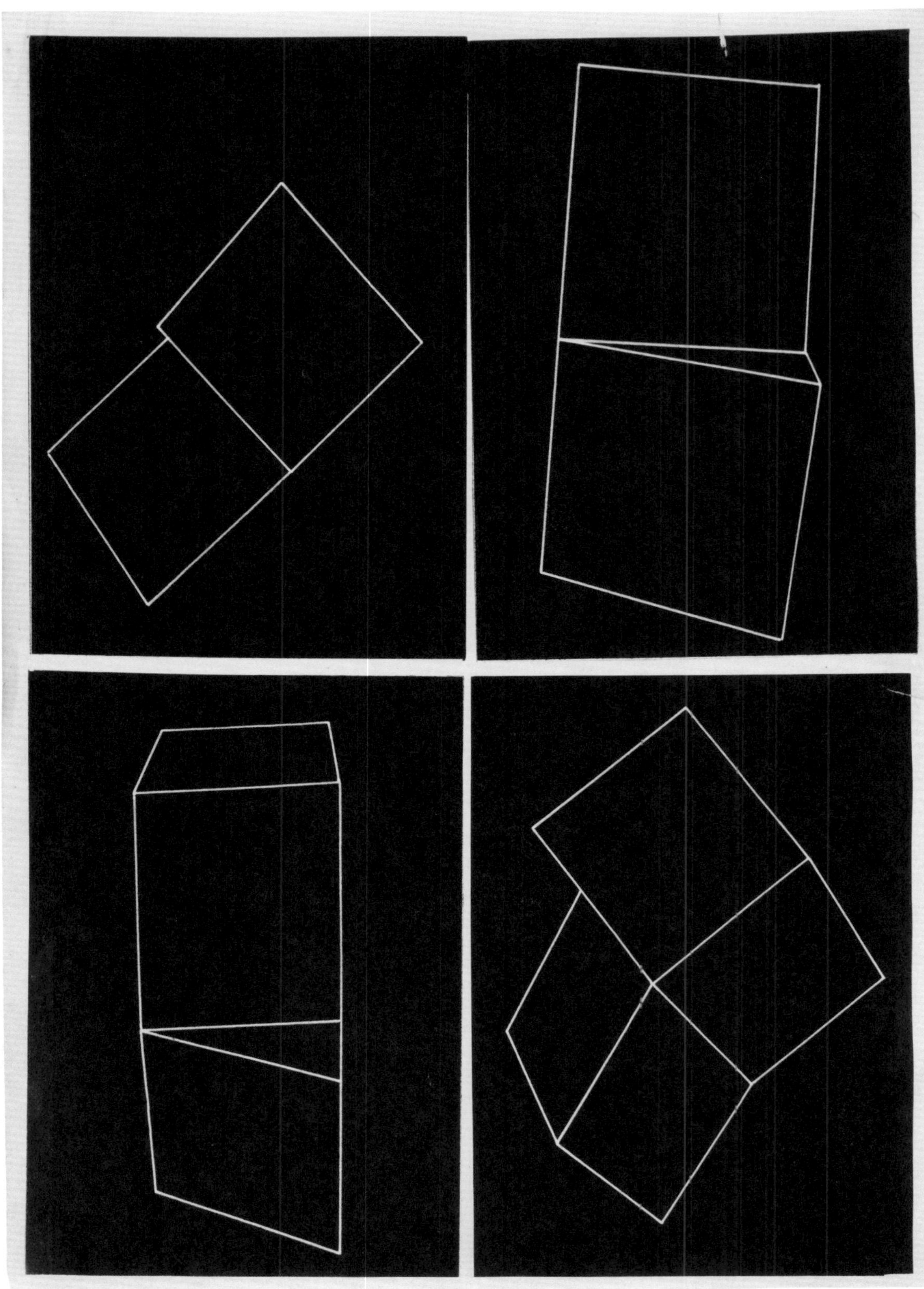

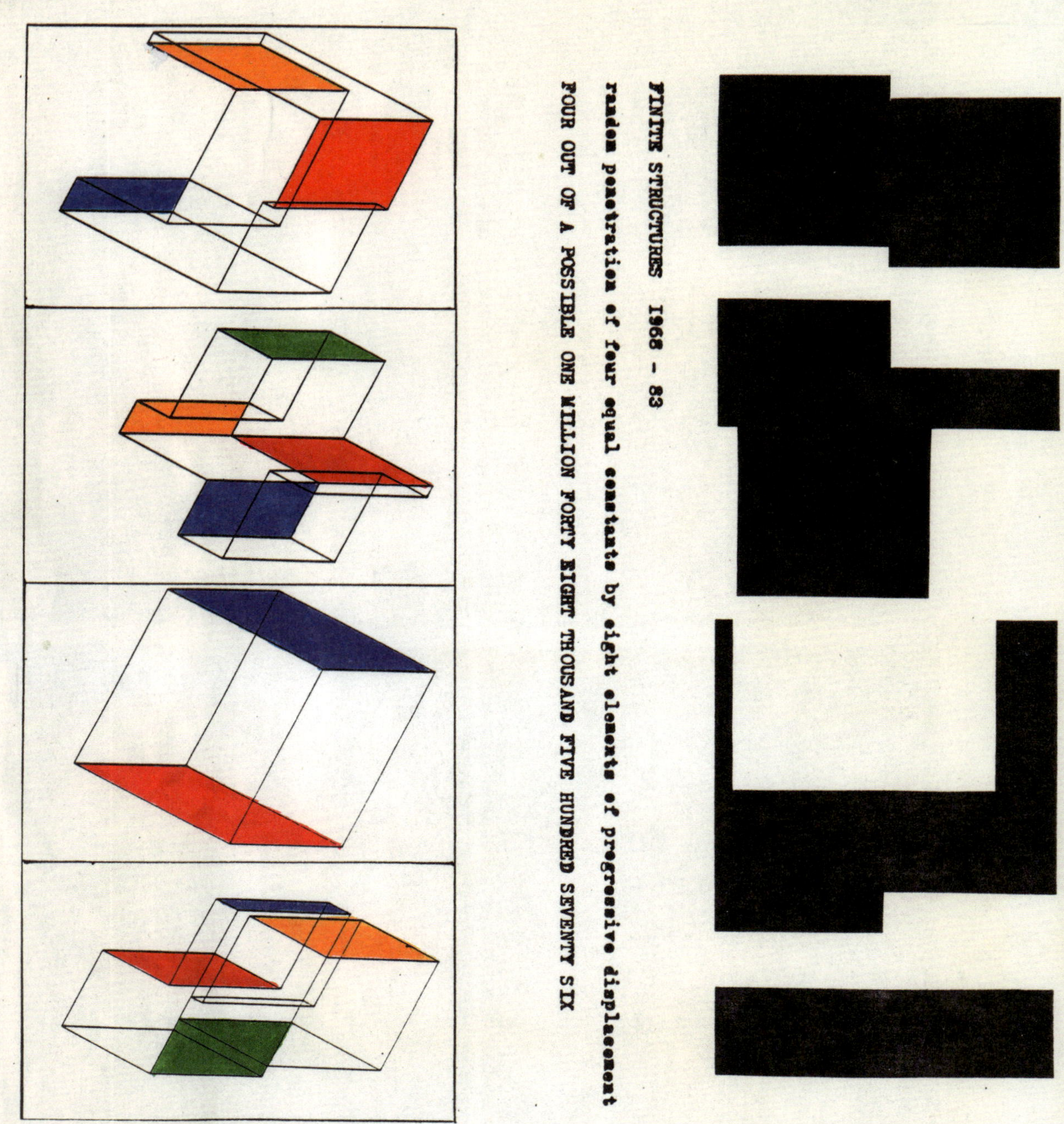

drawing/painting/sculpture/film/graphics/architecture/etc

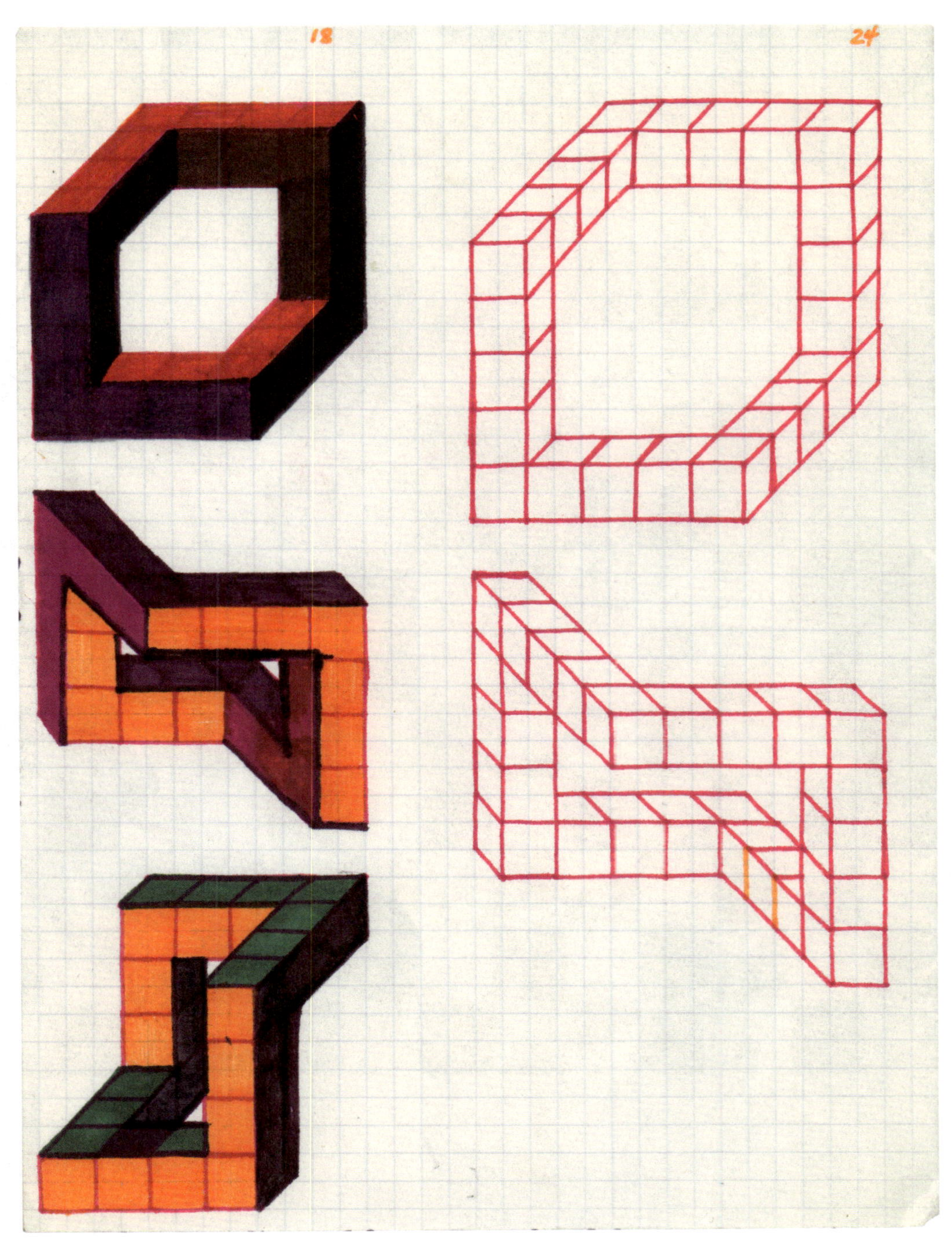
18
24

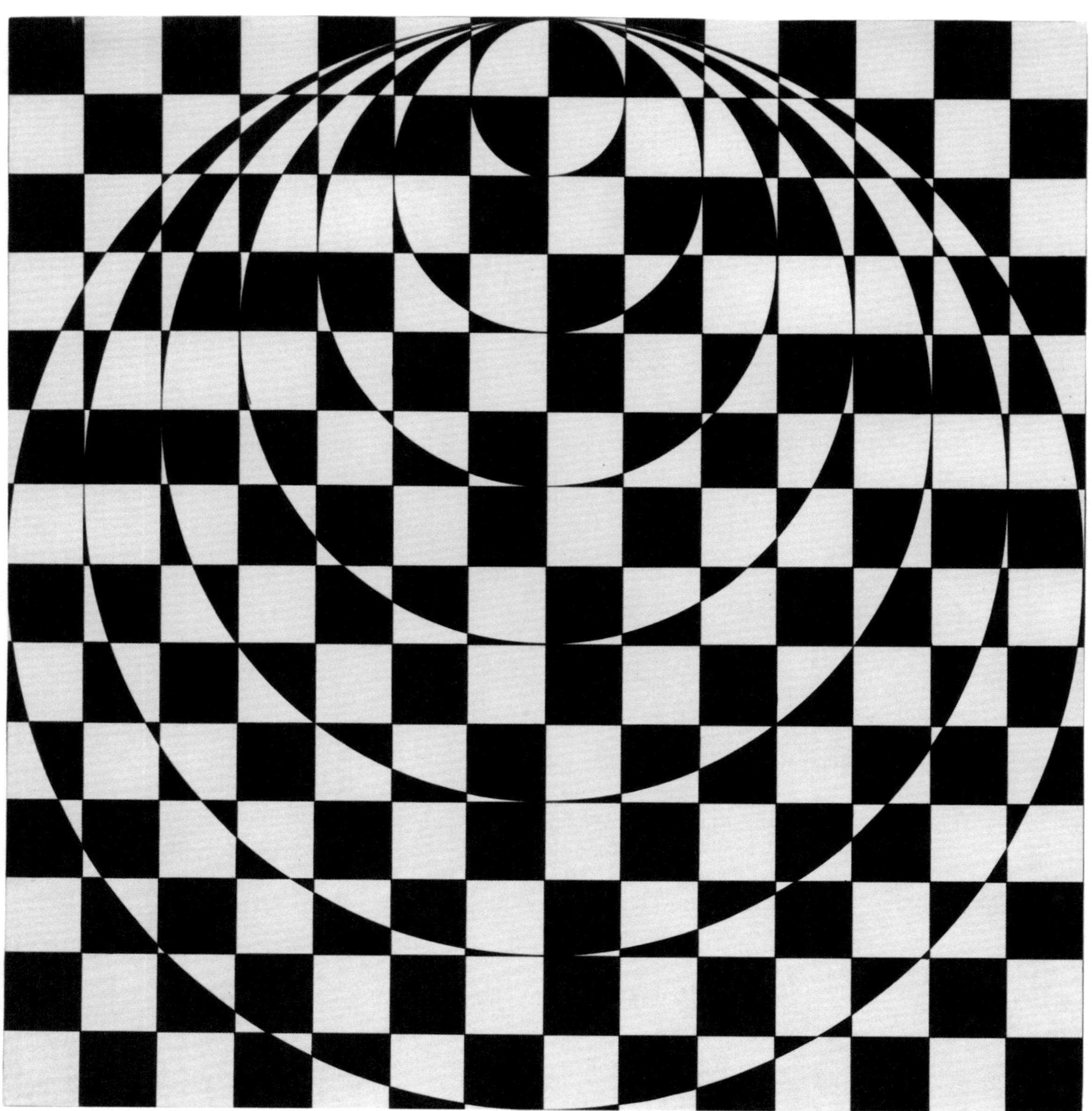

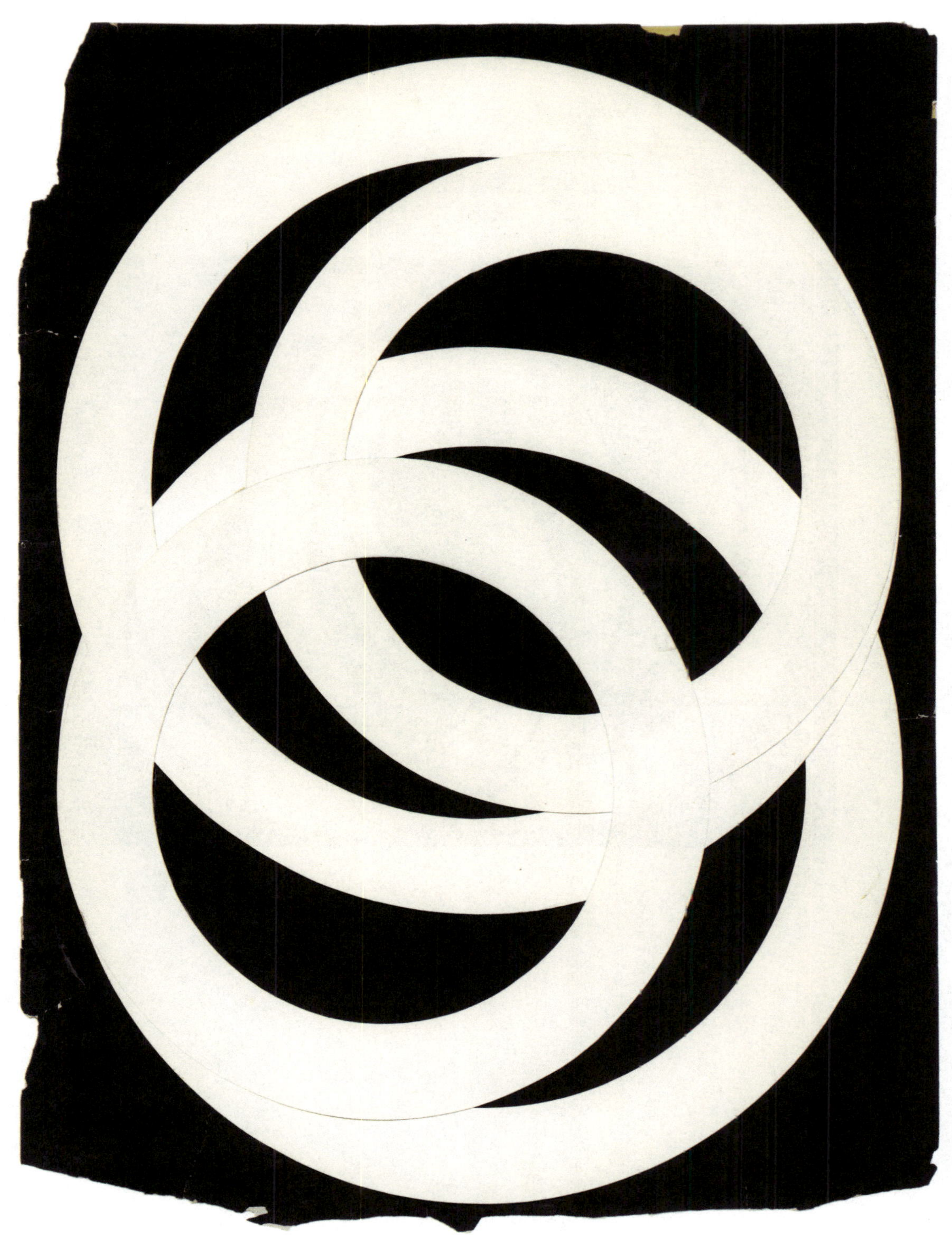

Pages 143–45: Sketches for *Projective Generation*, 1971

PROJECTIVE GENERATION
VITRAUX PARIS 1971

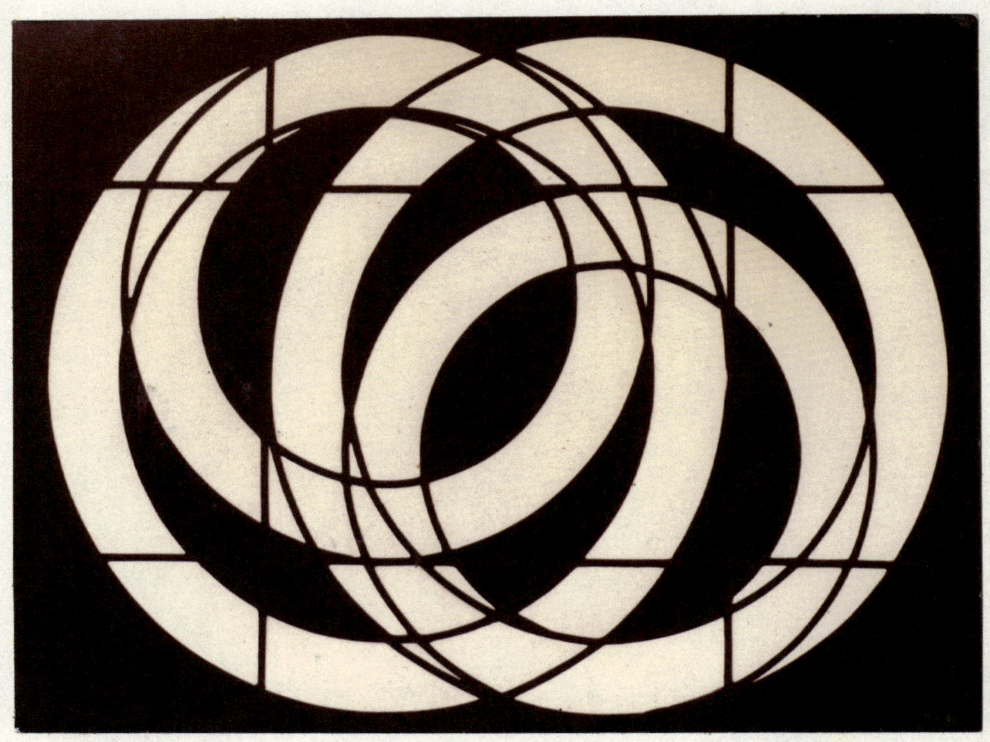

VITRAUX PARIS 1971

noir/blanc opaque/translucent lead/glass 50/50

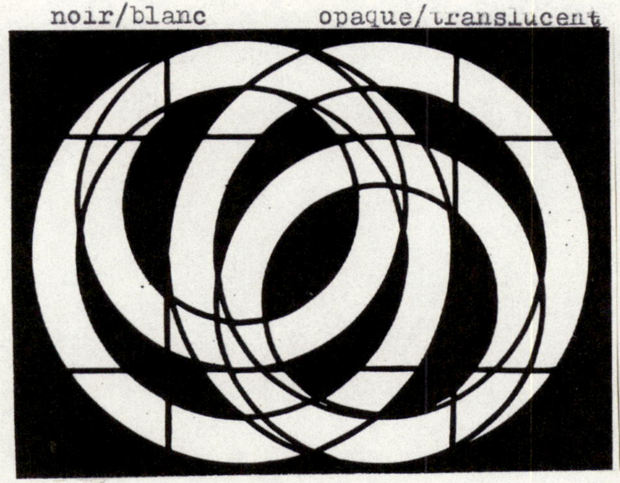

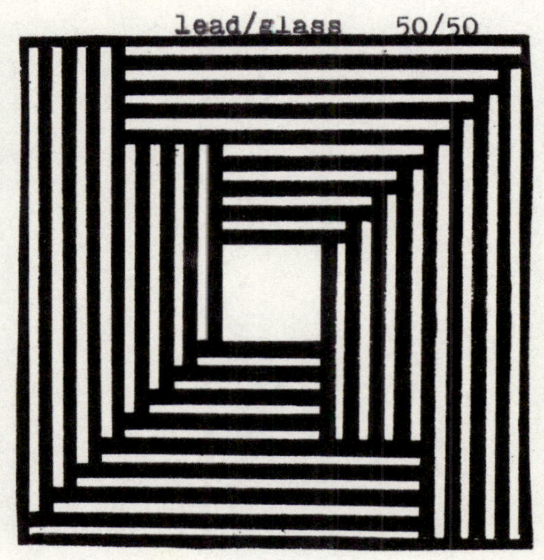

33 colors / verre ancienne / faux camaïeux

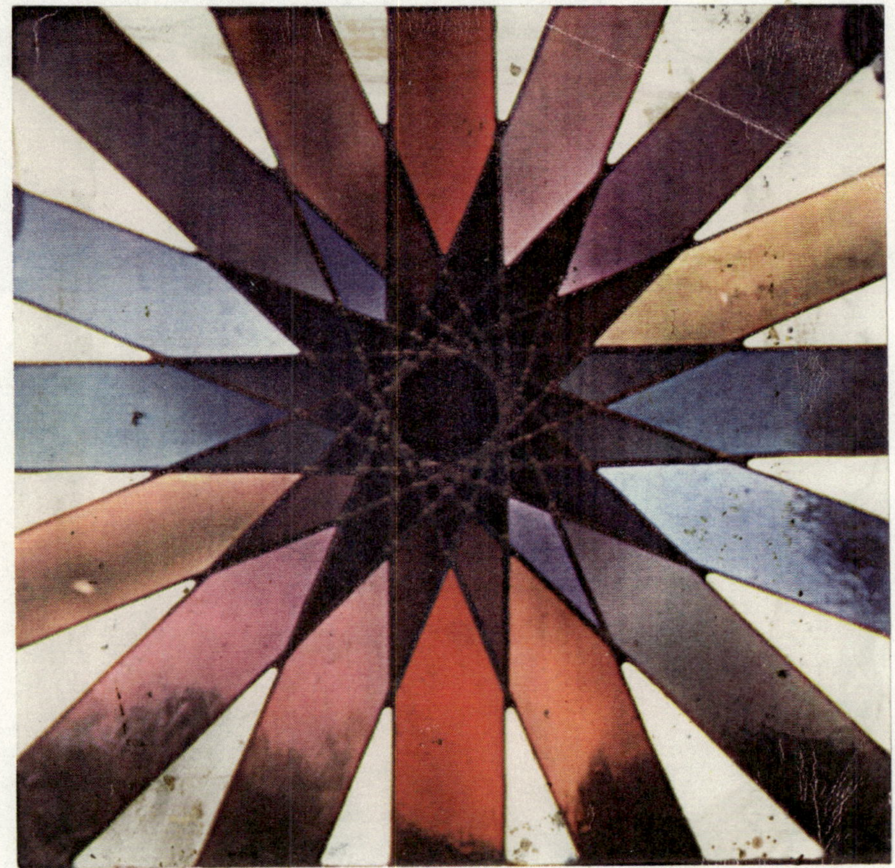

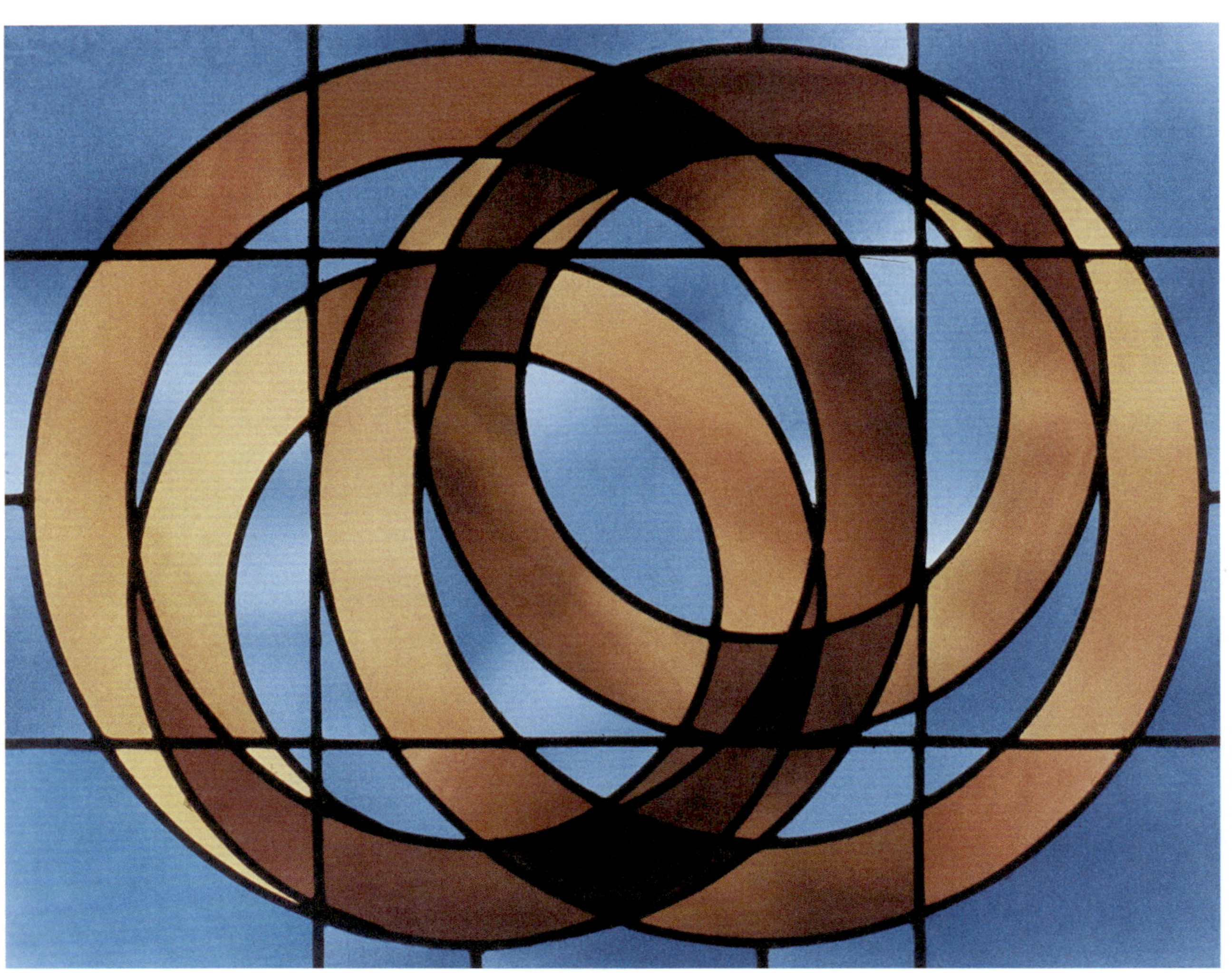

 Pages 146–53: From the series *Projective Generation*, stained glass panel, Ateliers Loire, Chartres, 1971

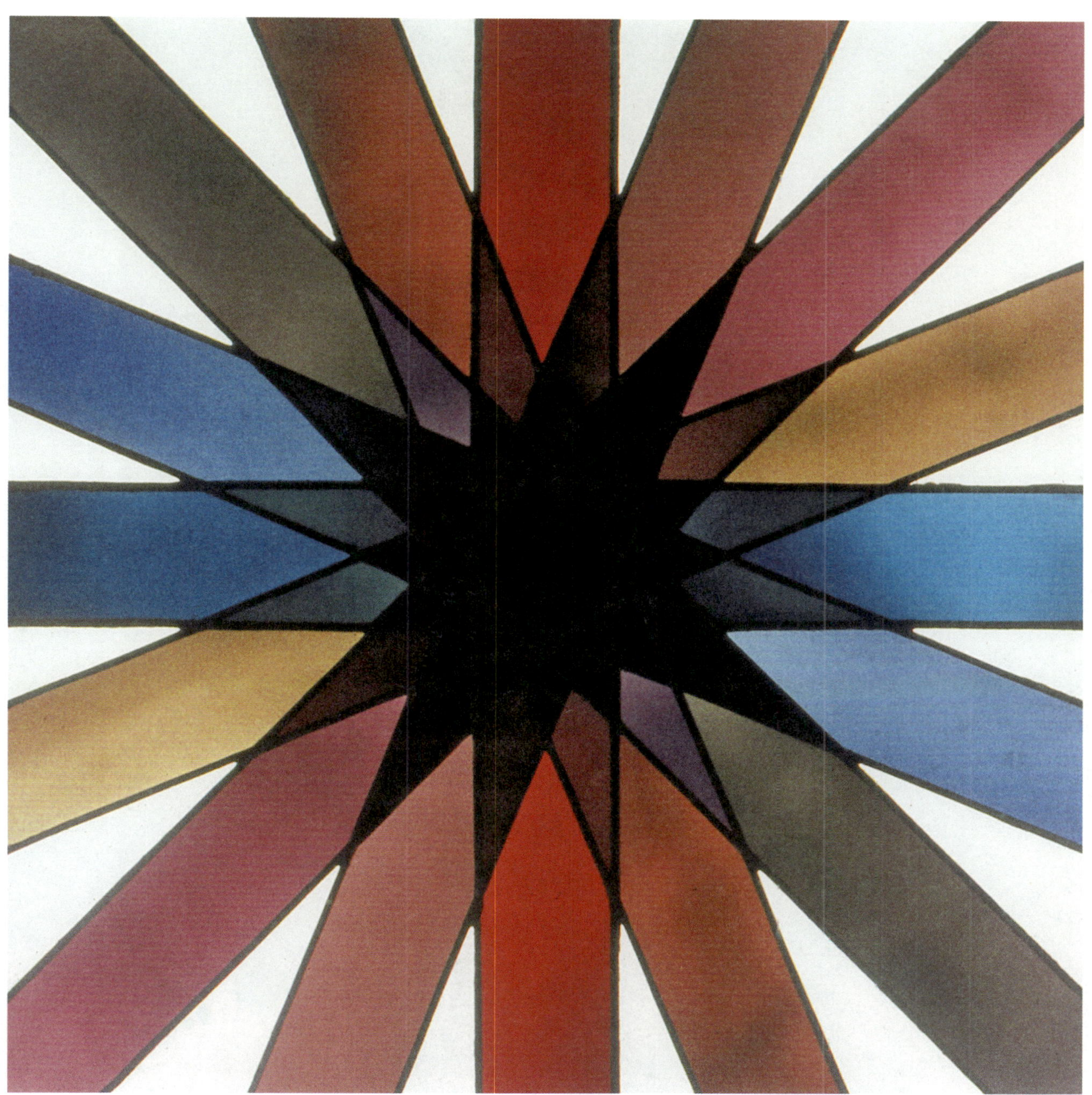

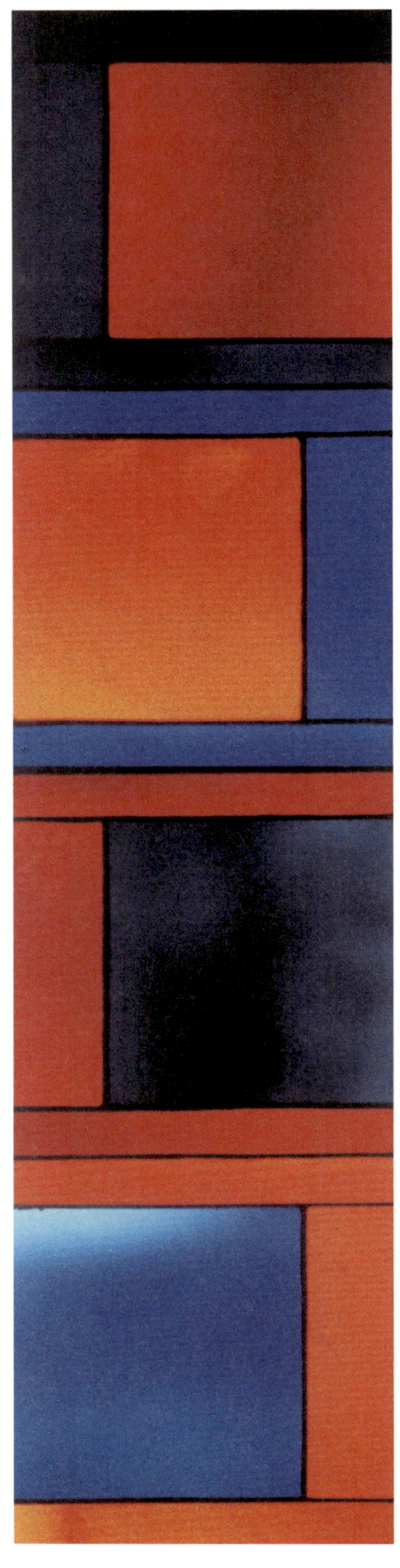

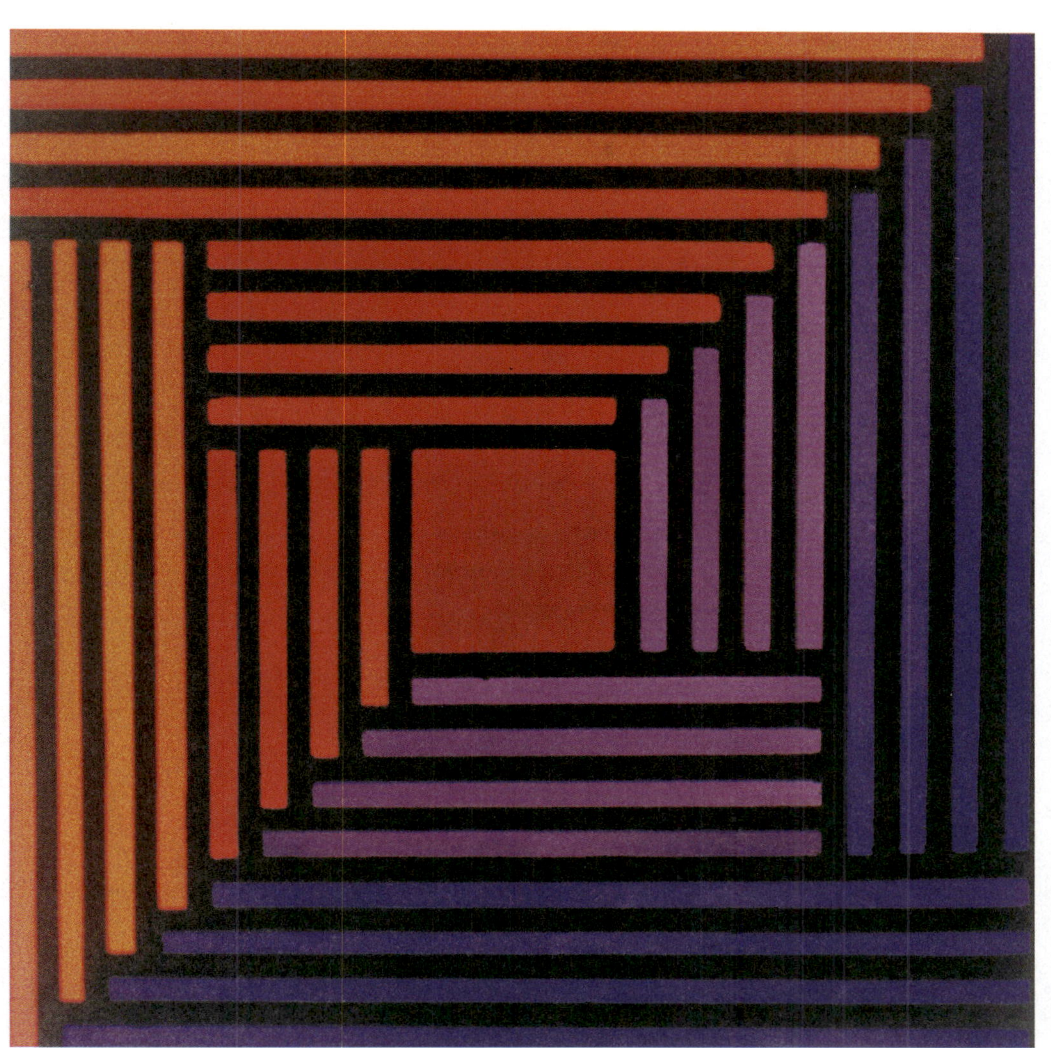

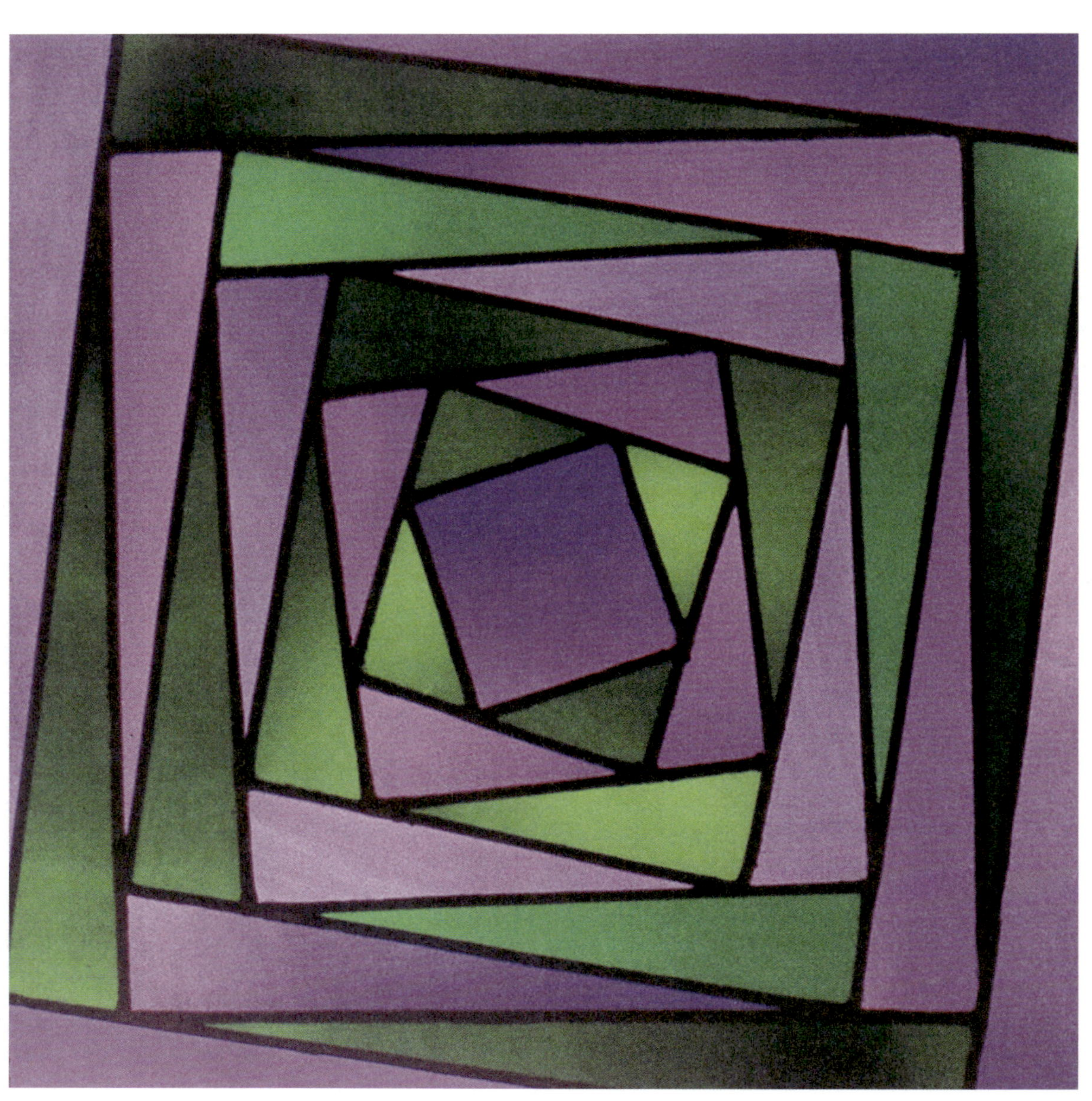

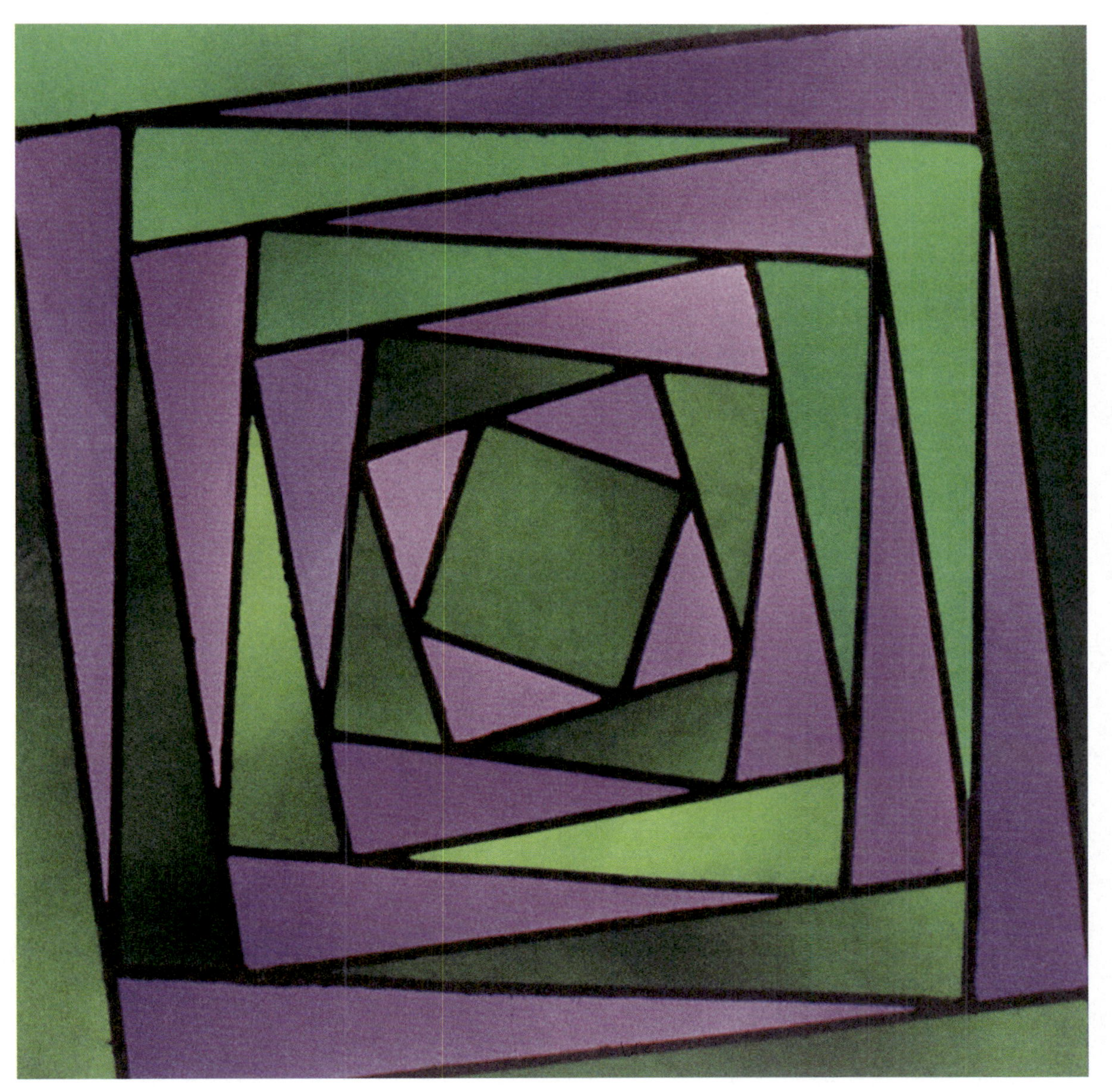

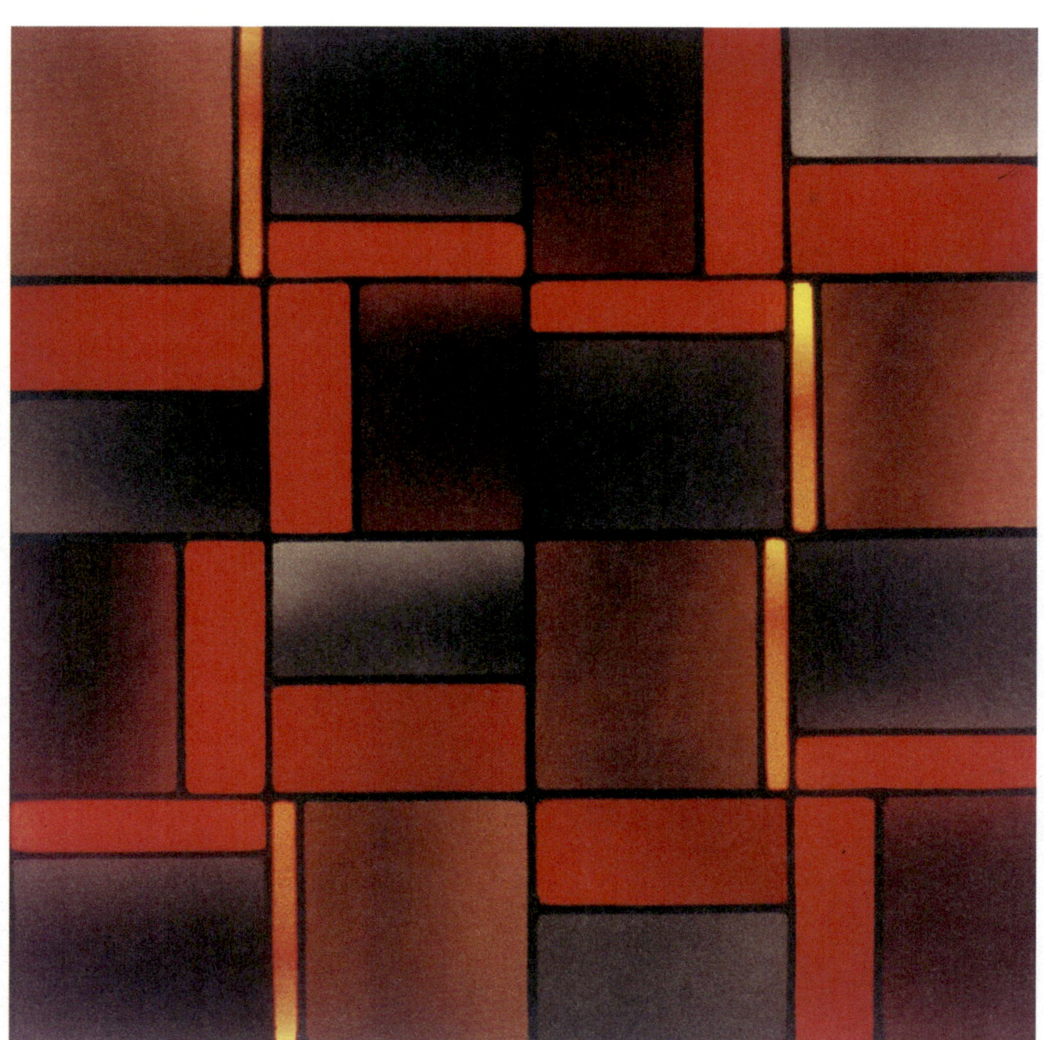

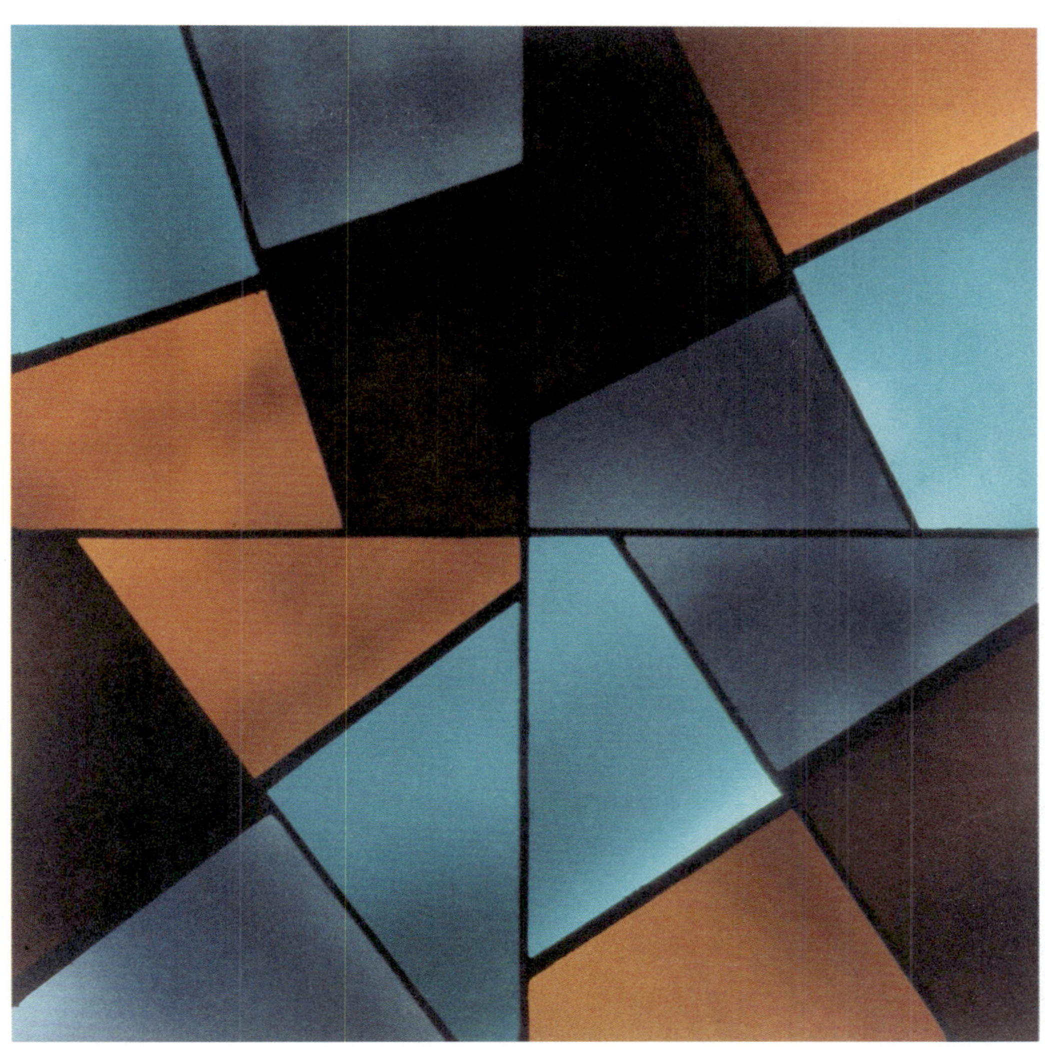

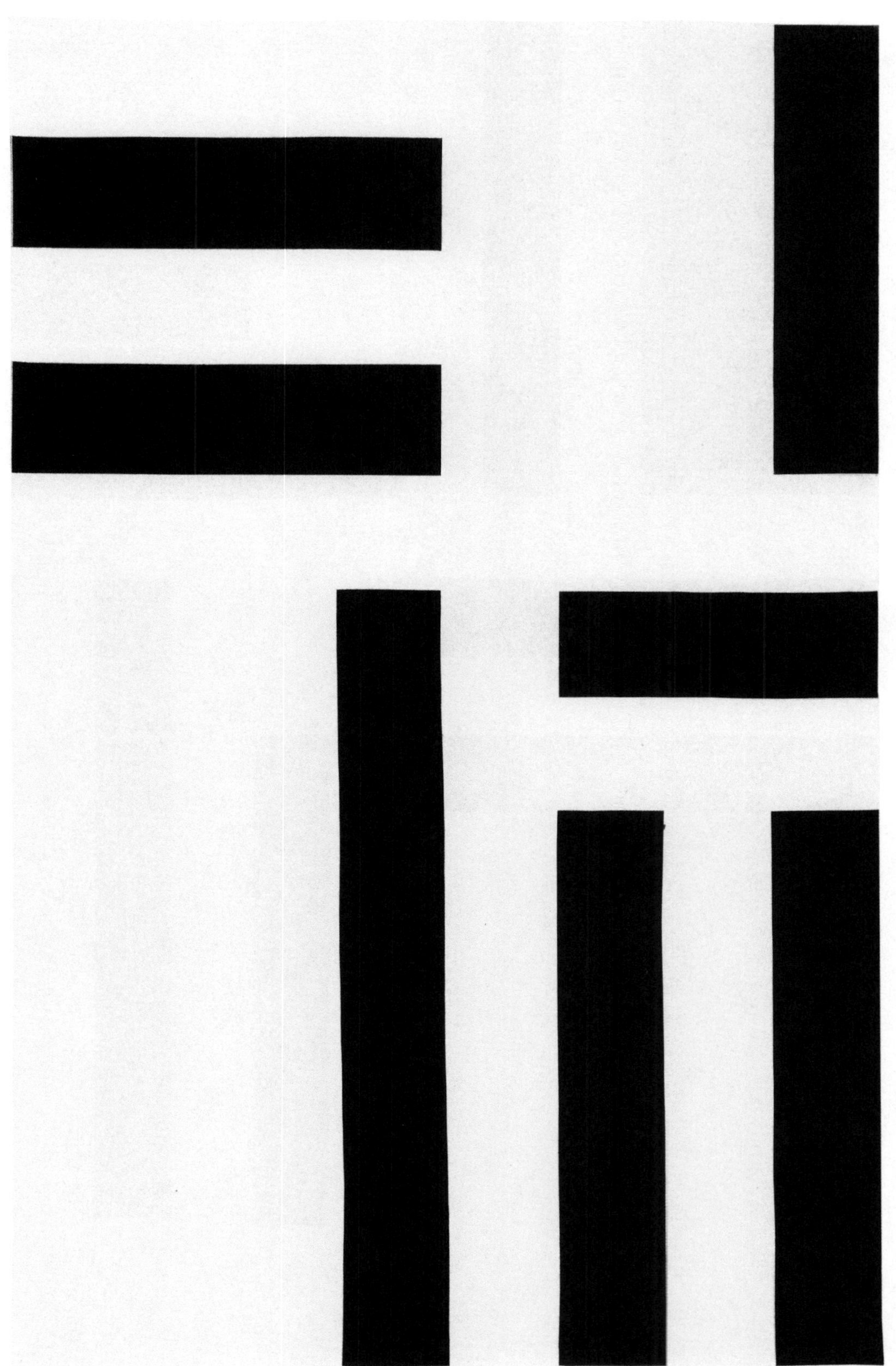

Pages 155–64: From the series *Paintings with Tape*, date unknown

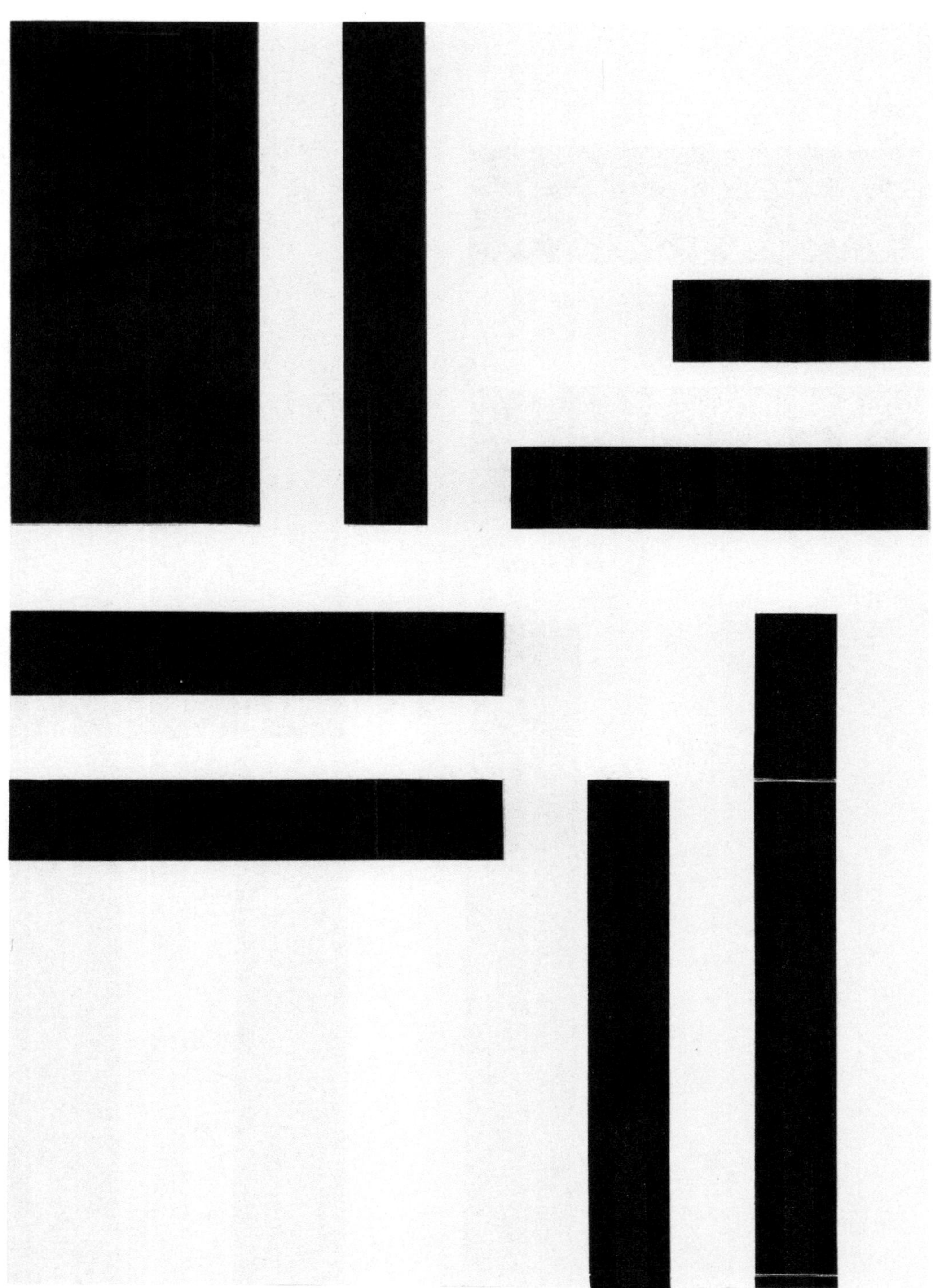

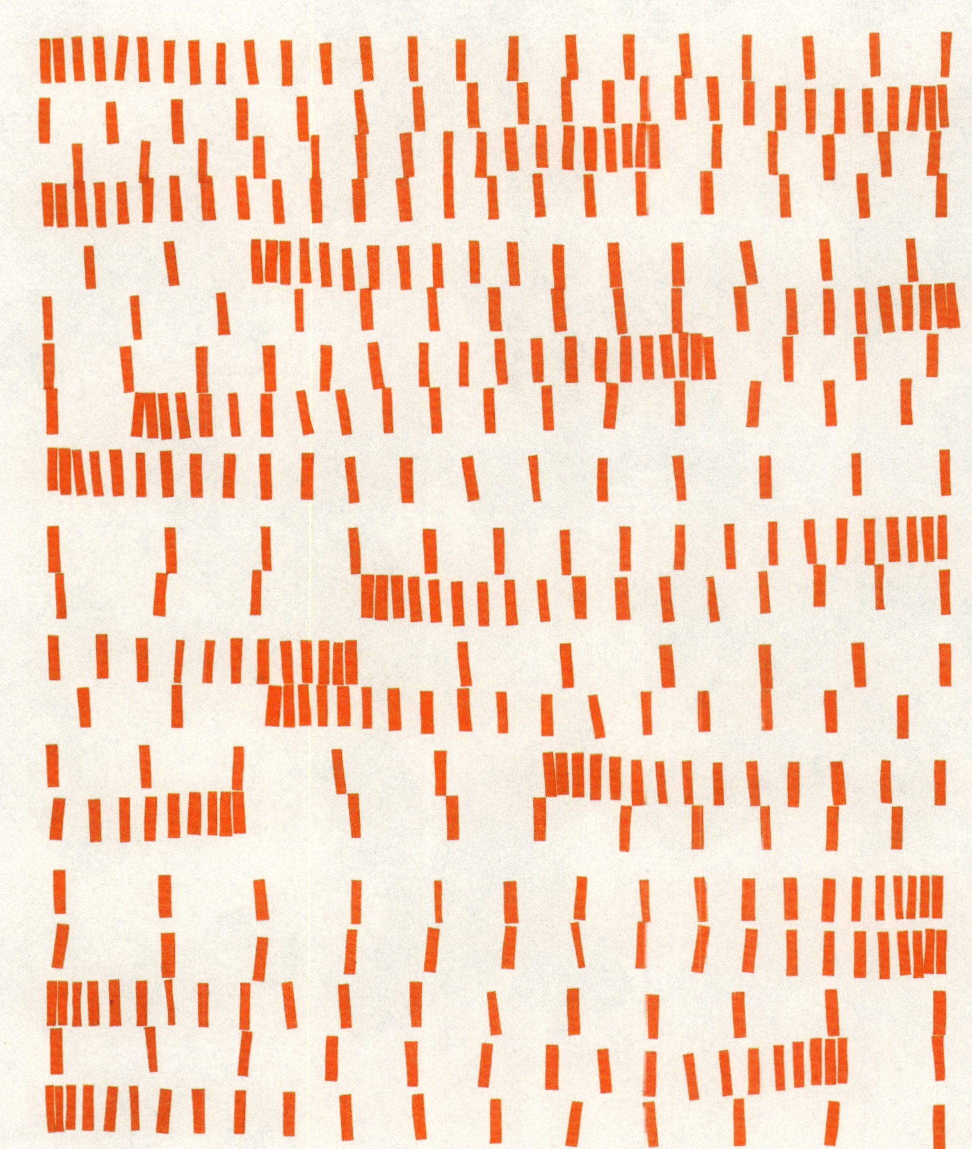

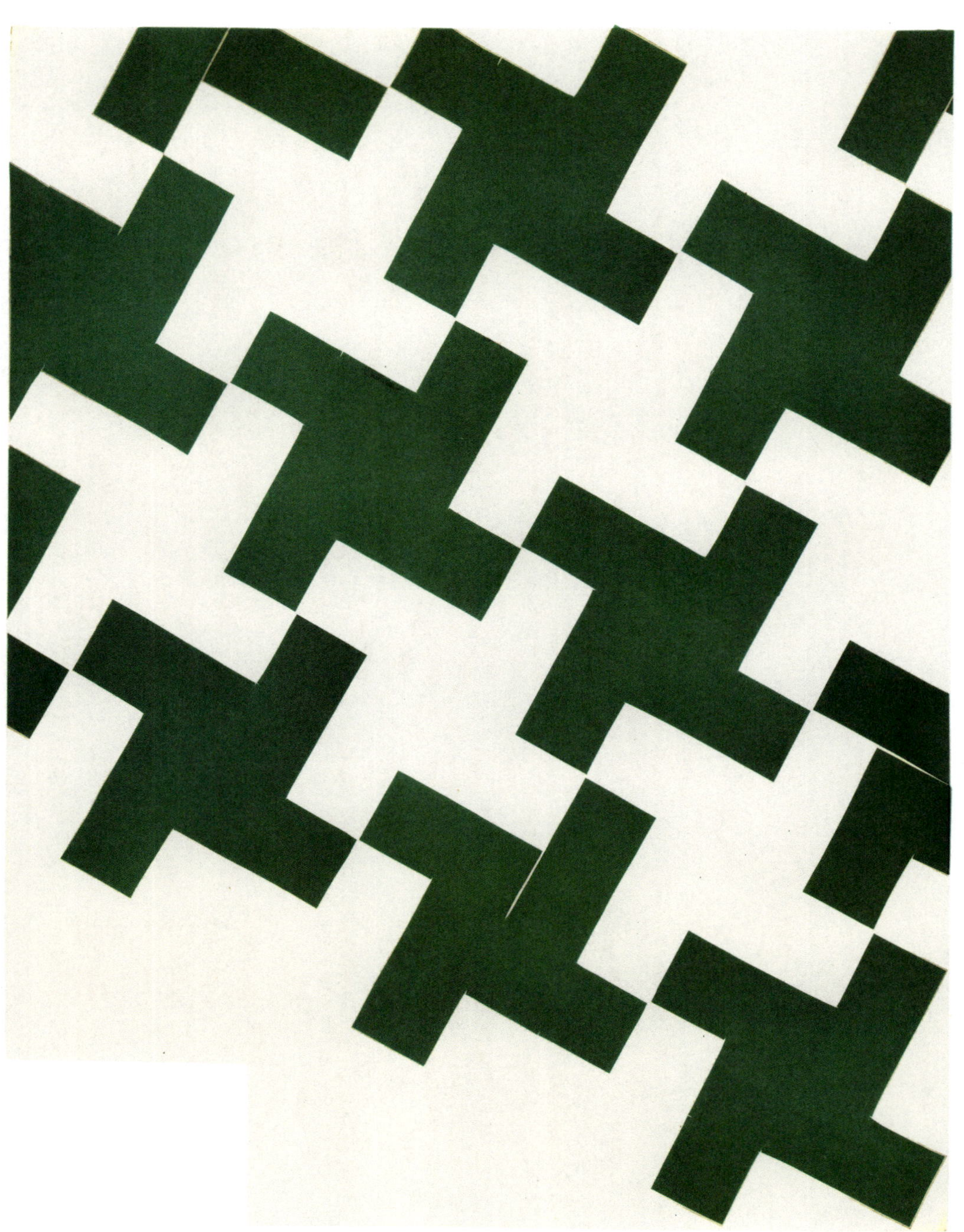

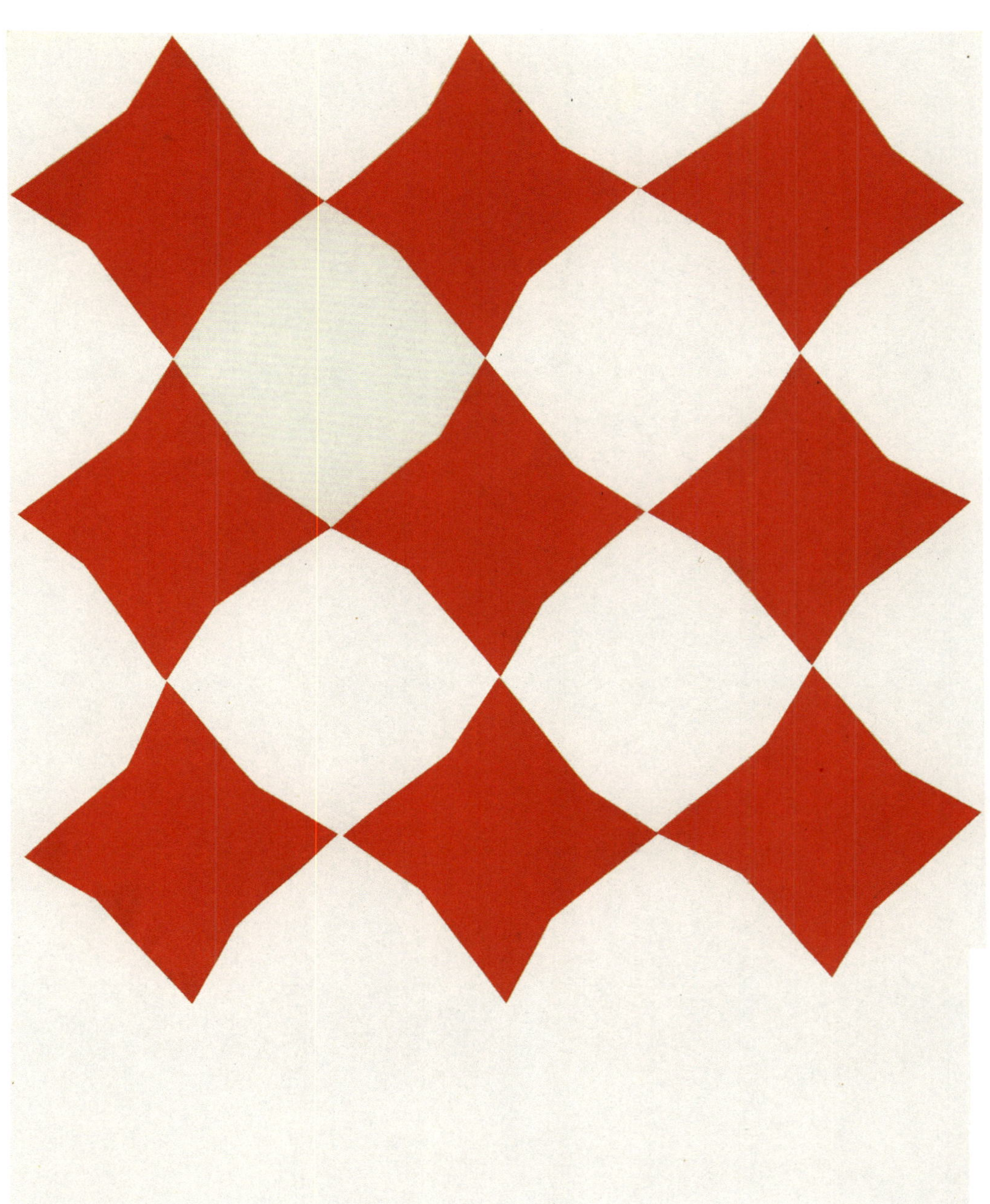

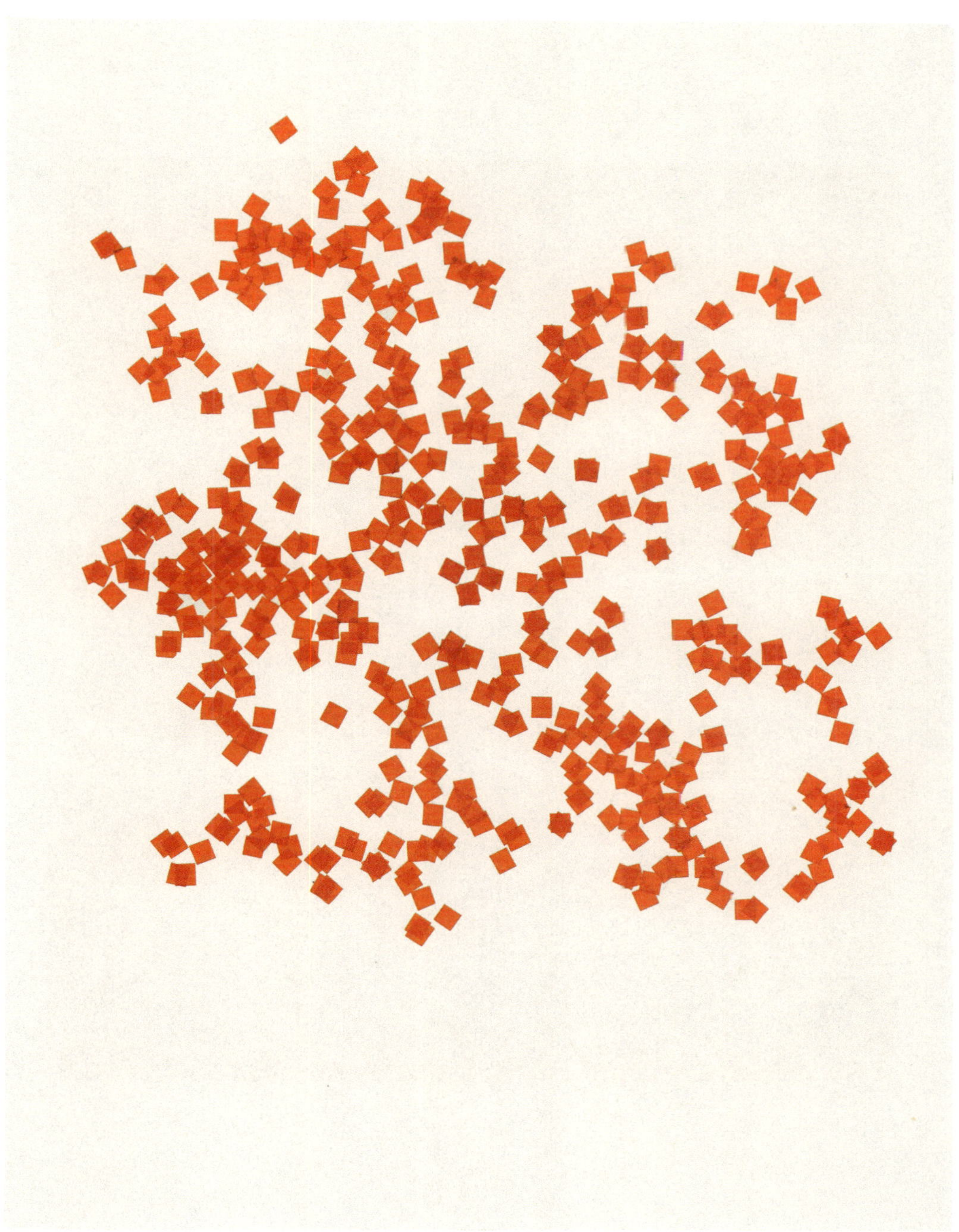

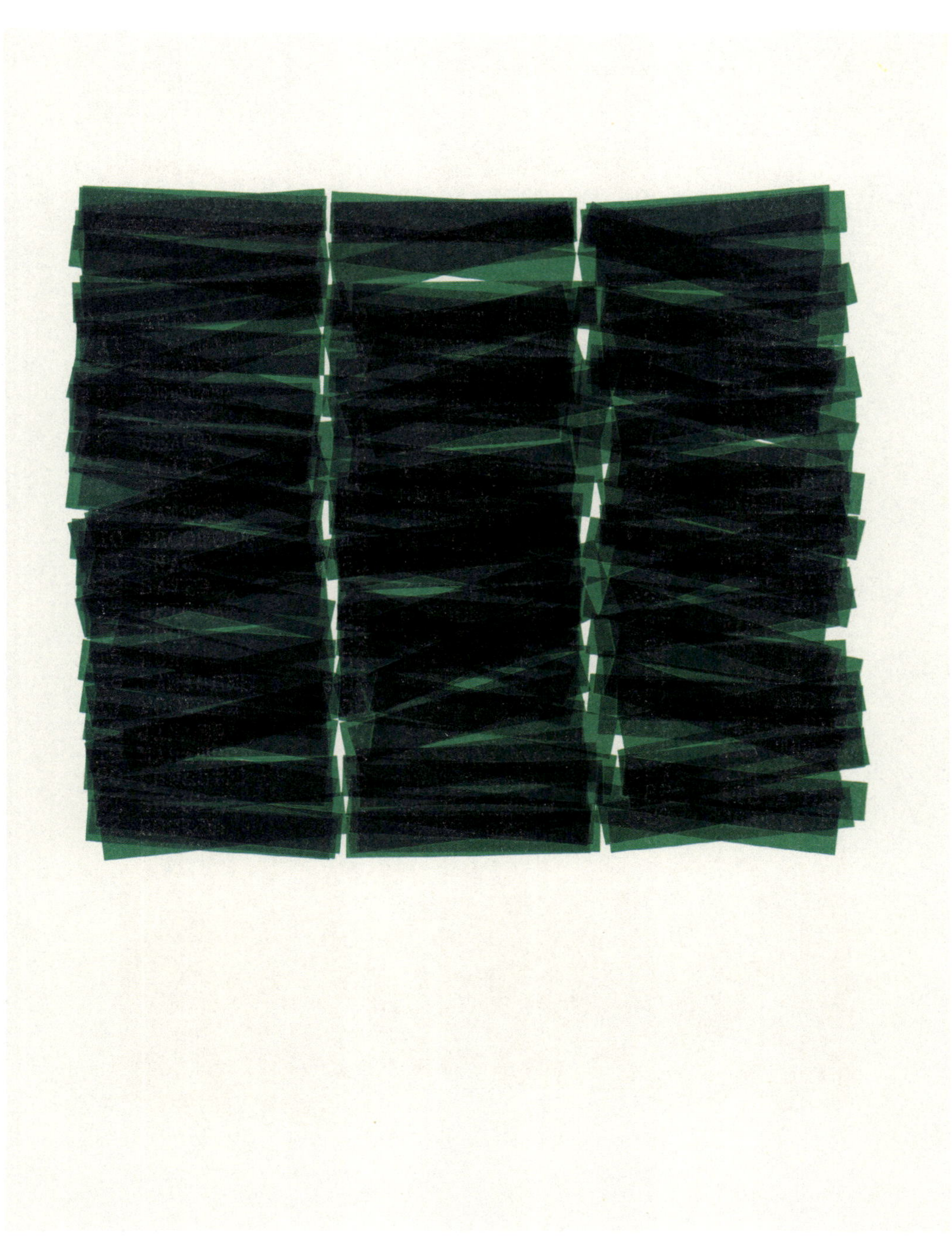

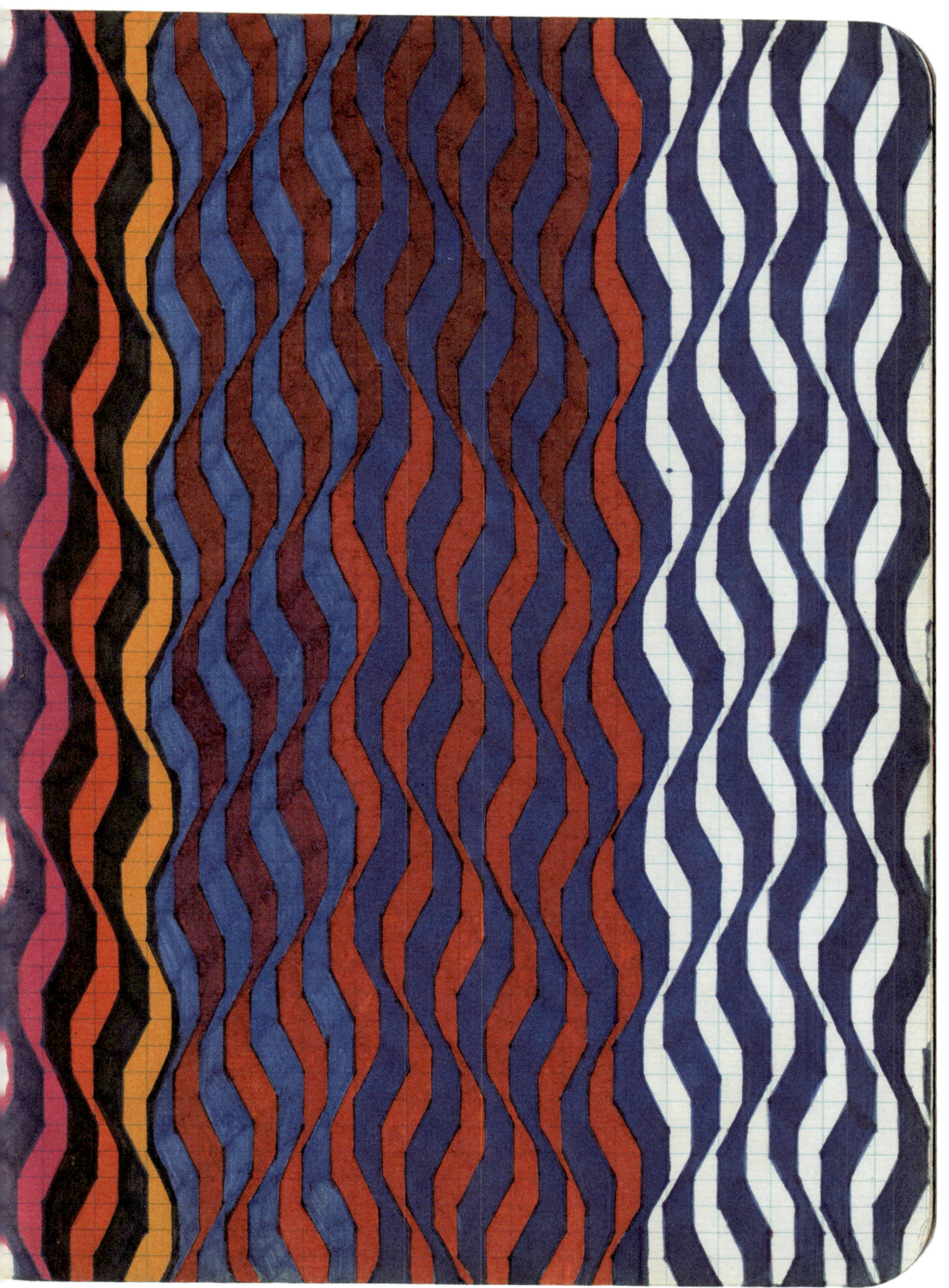

Pages 167-84: Drawing notebooks, 1970s

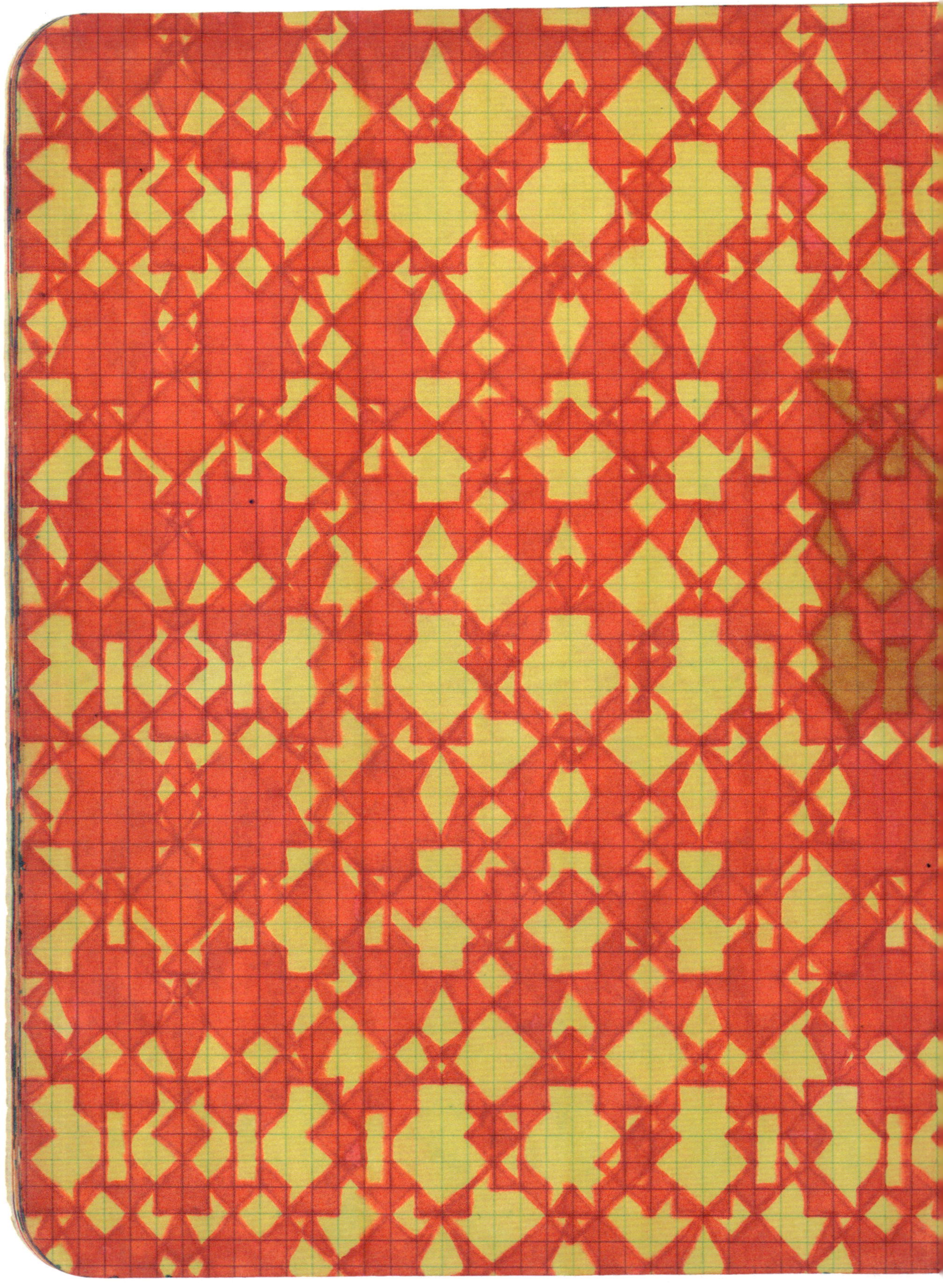

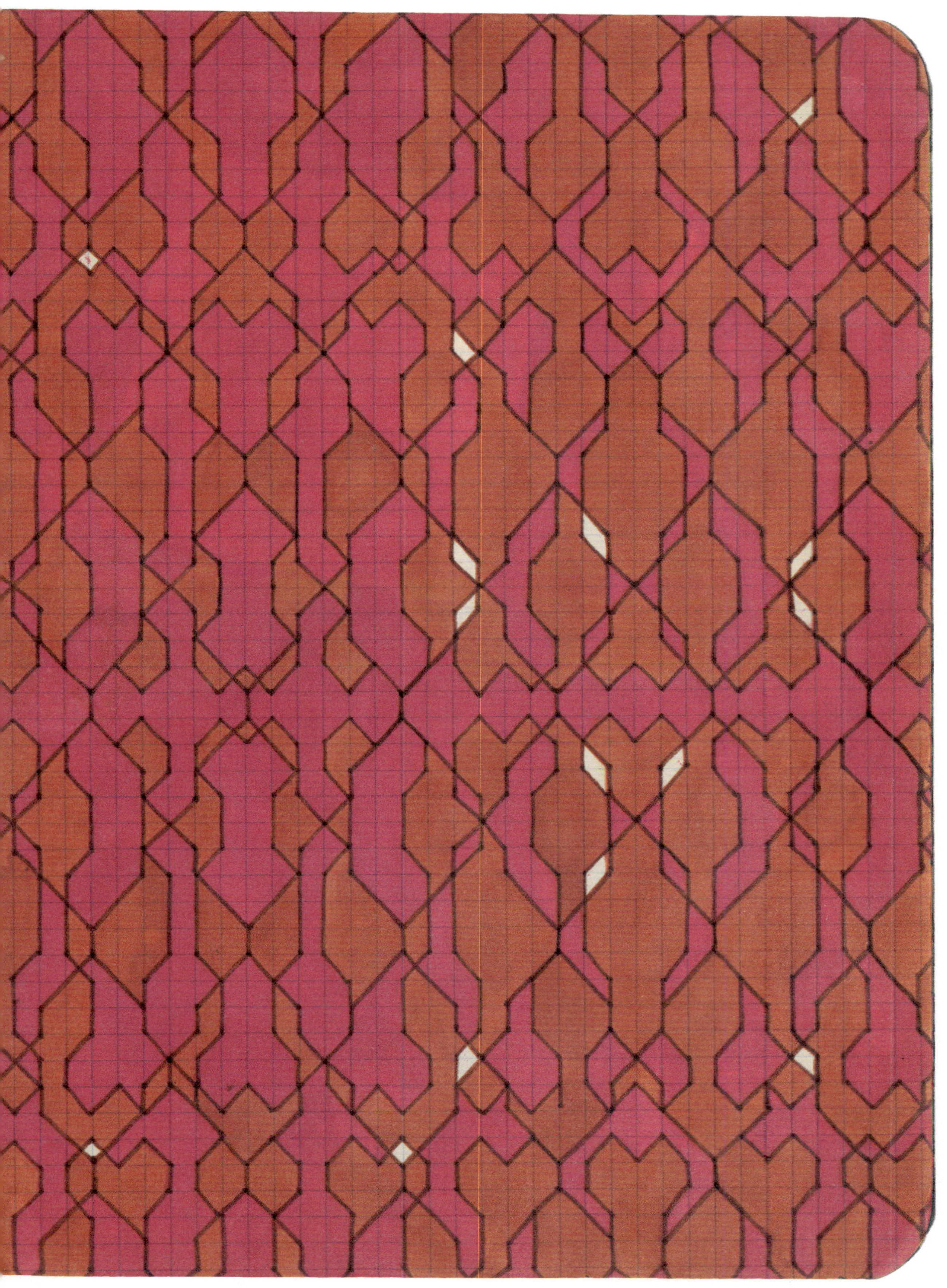

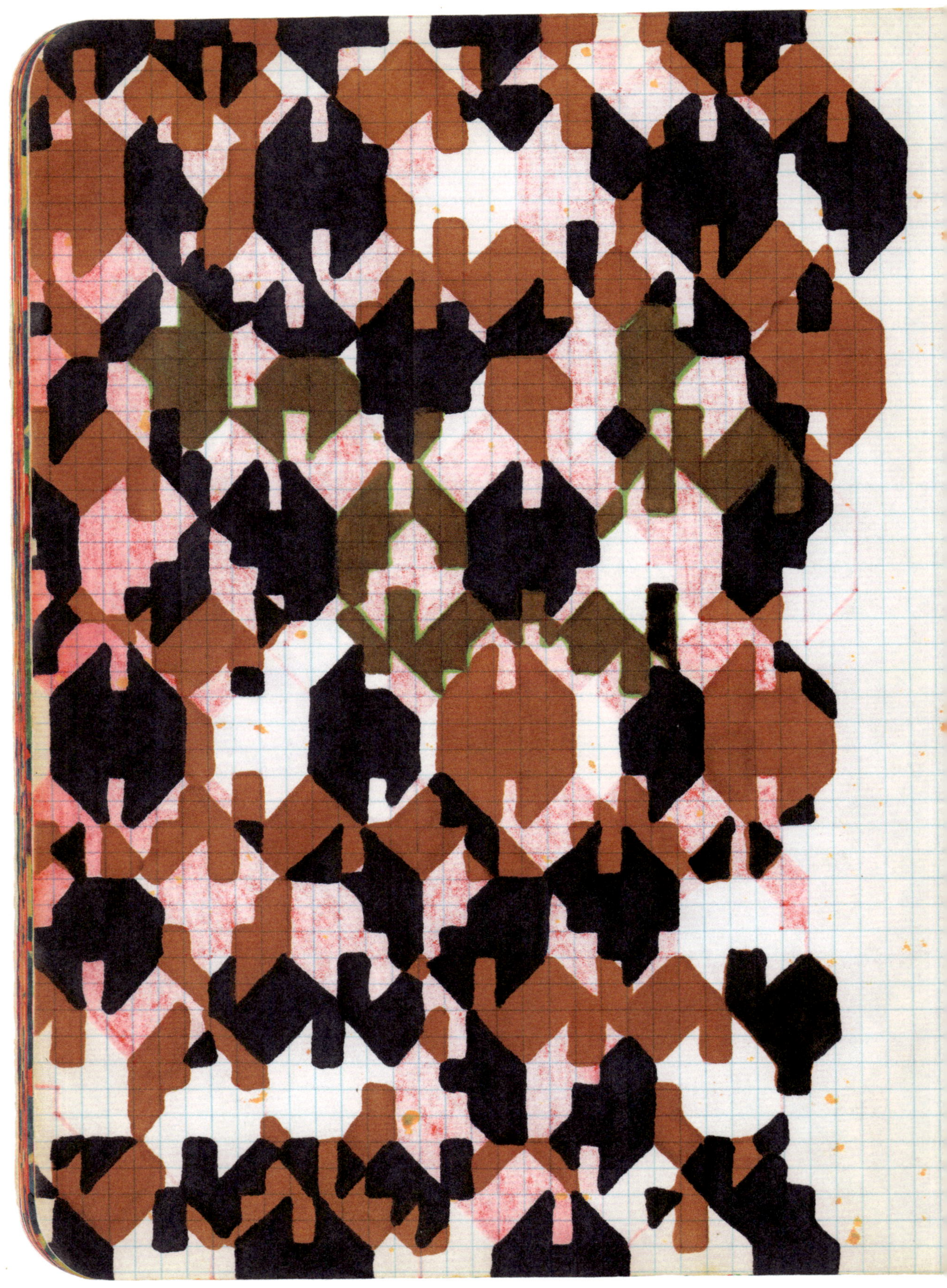

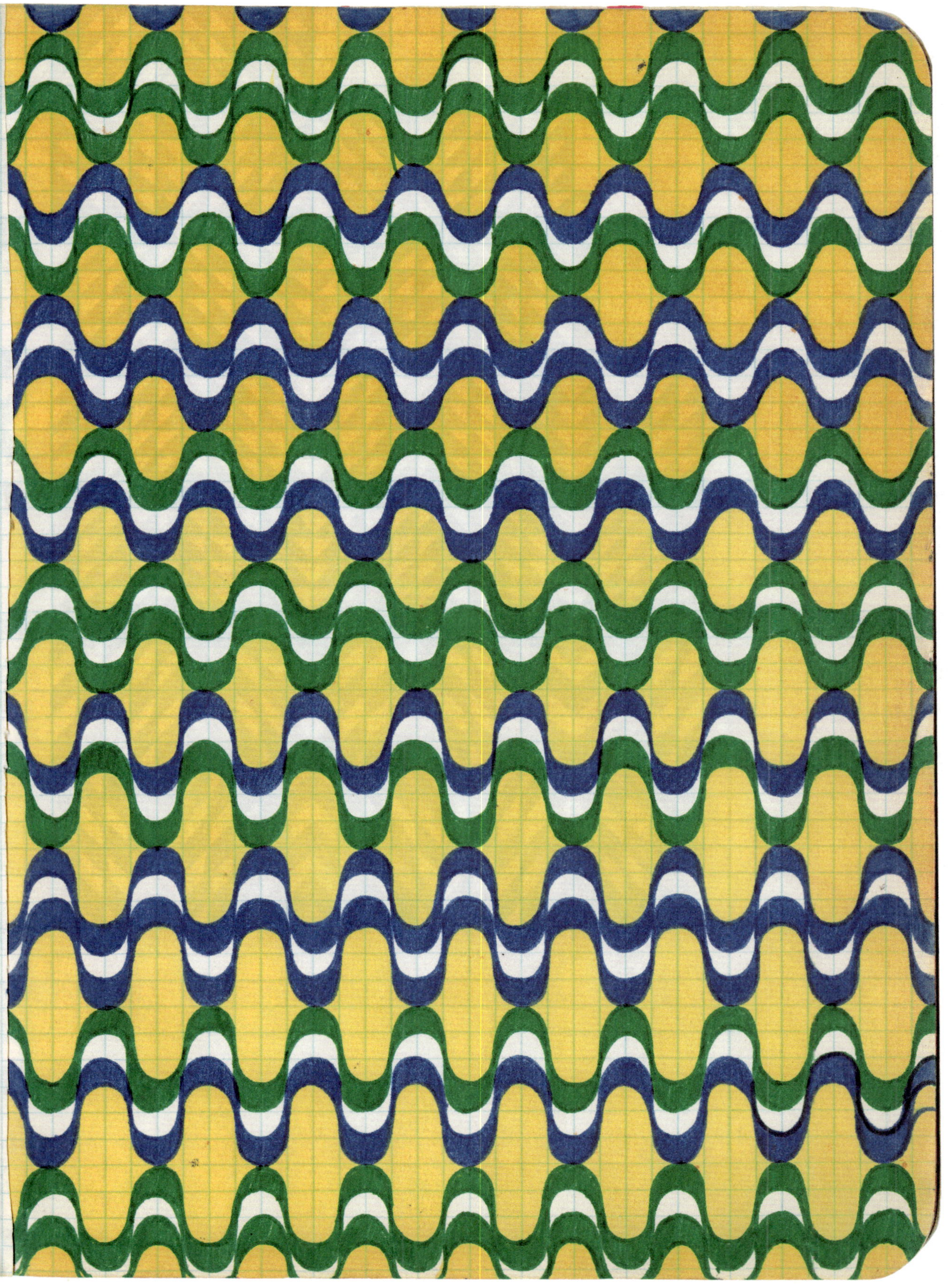

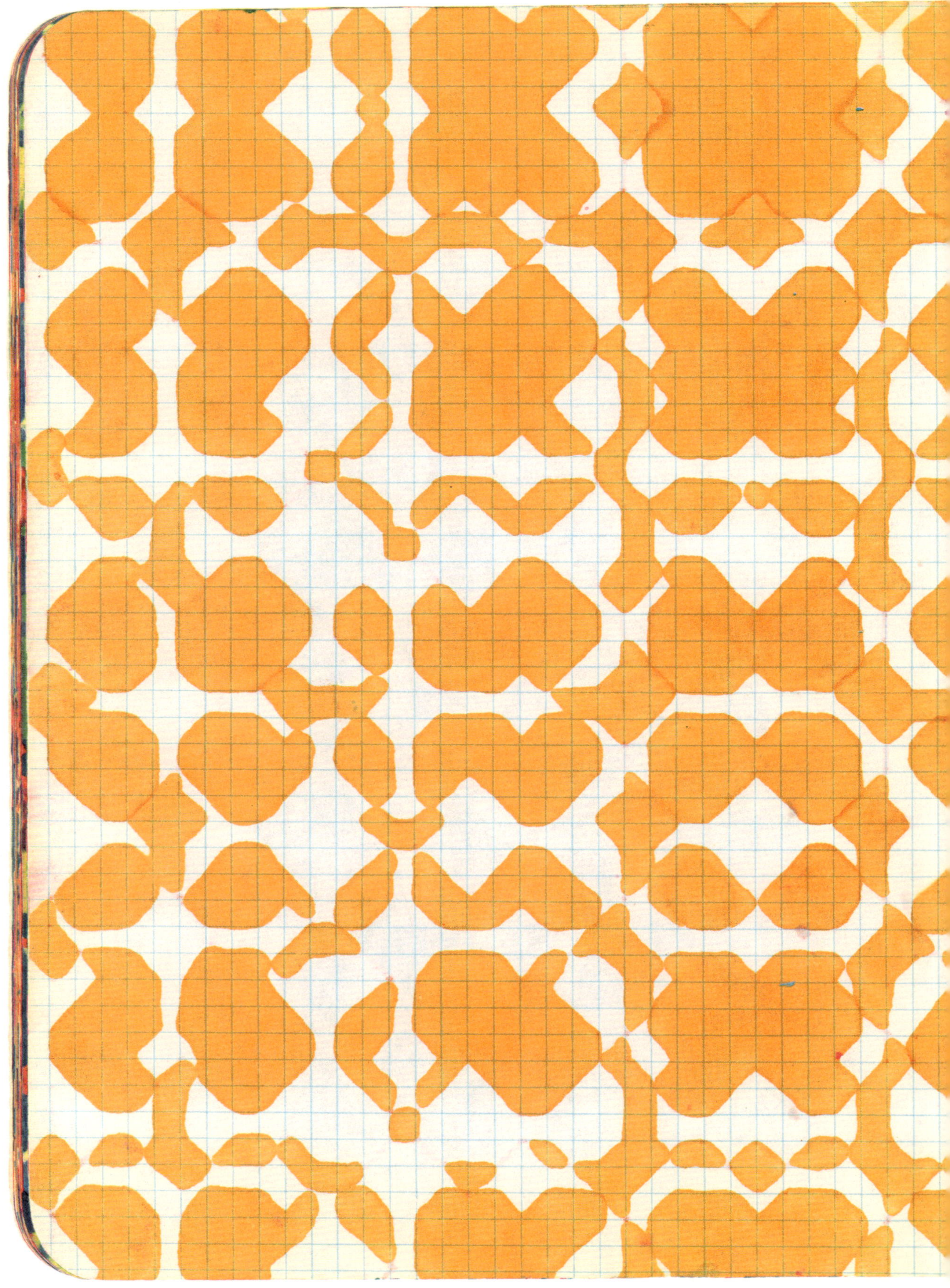

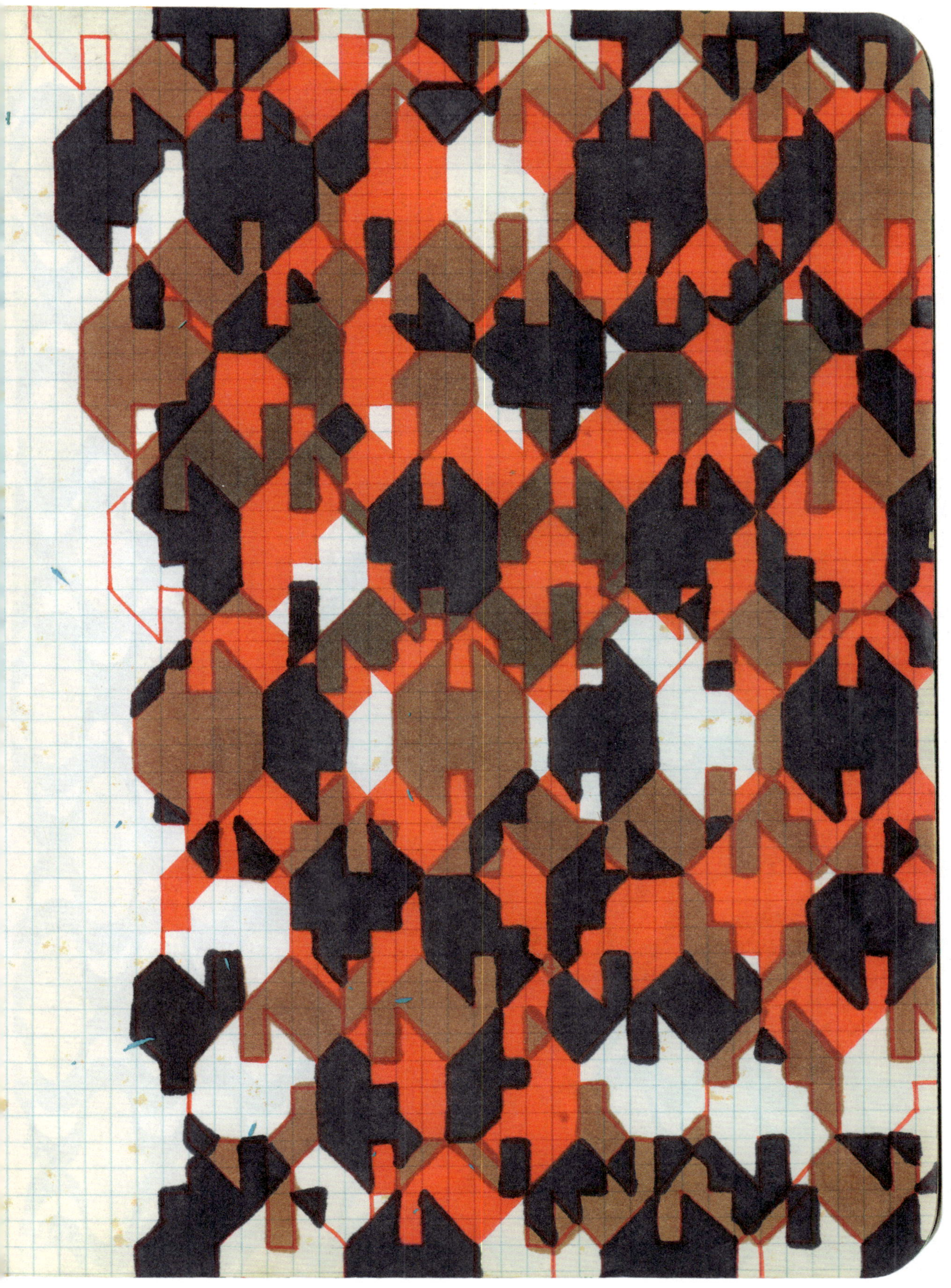

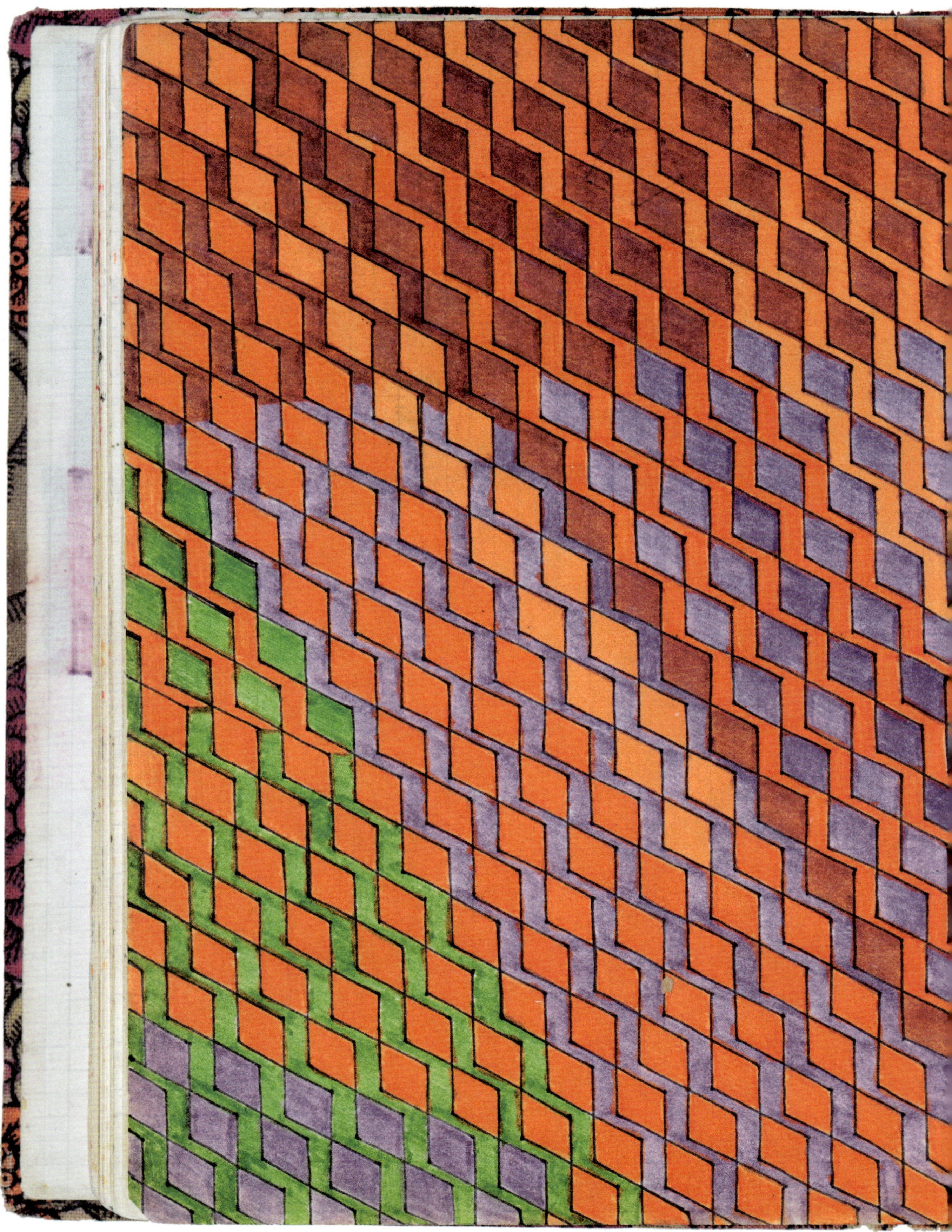

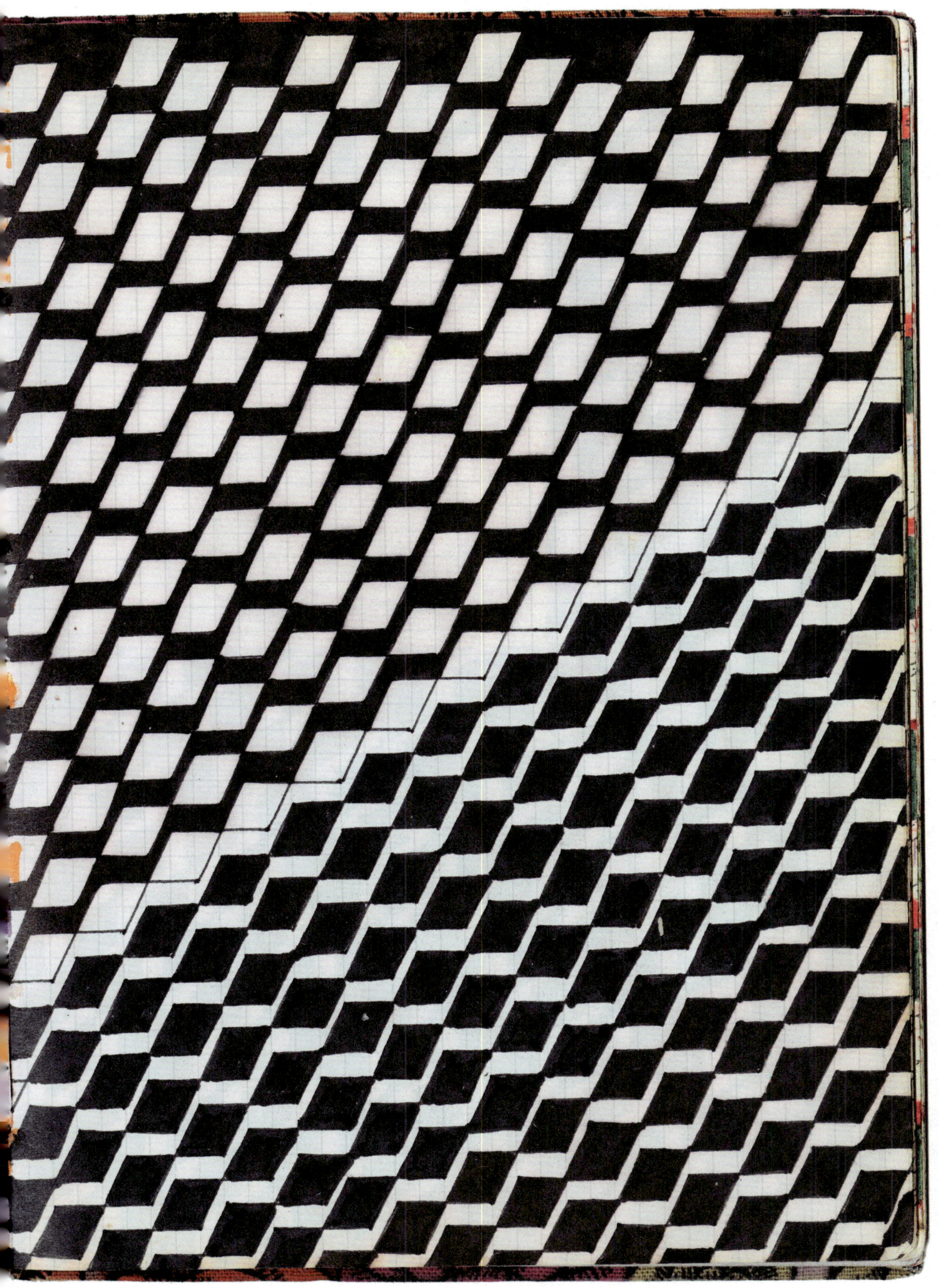

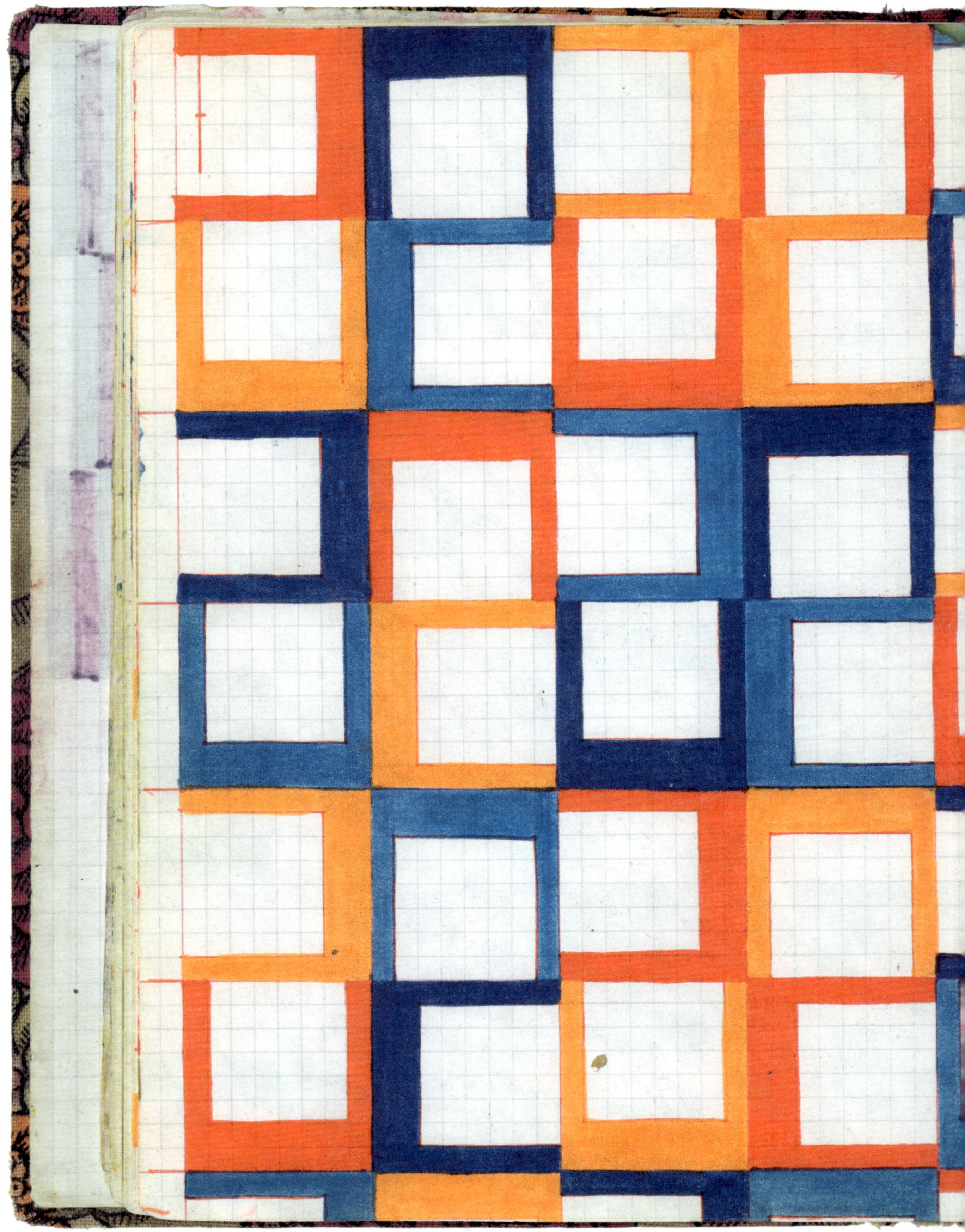

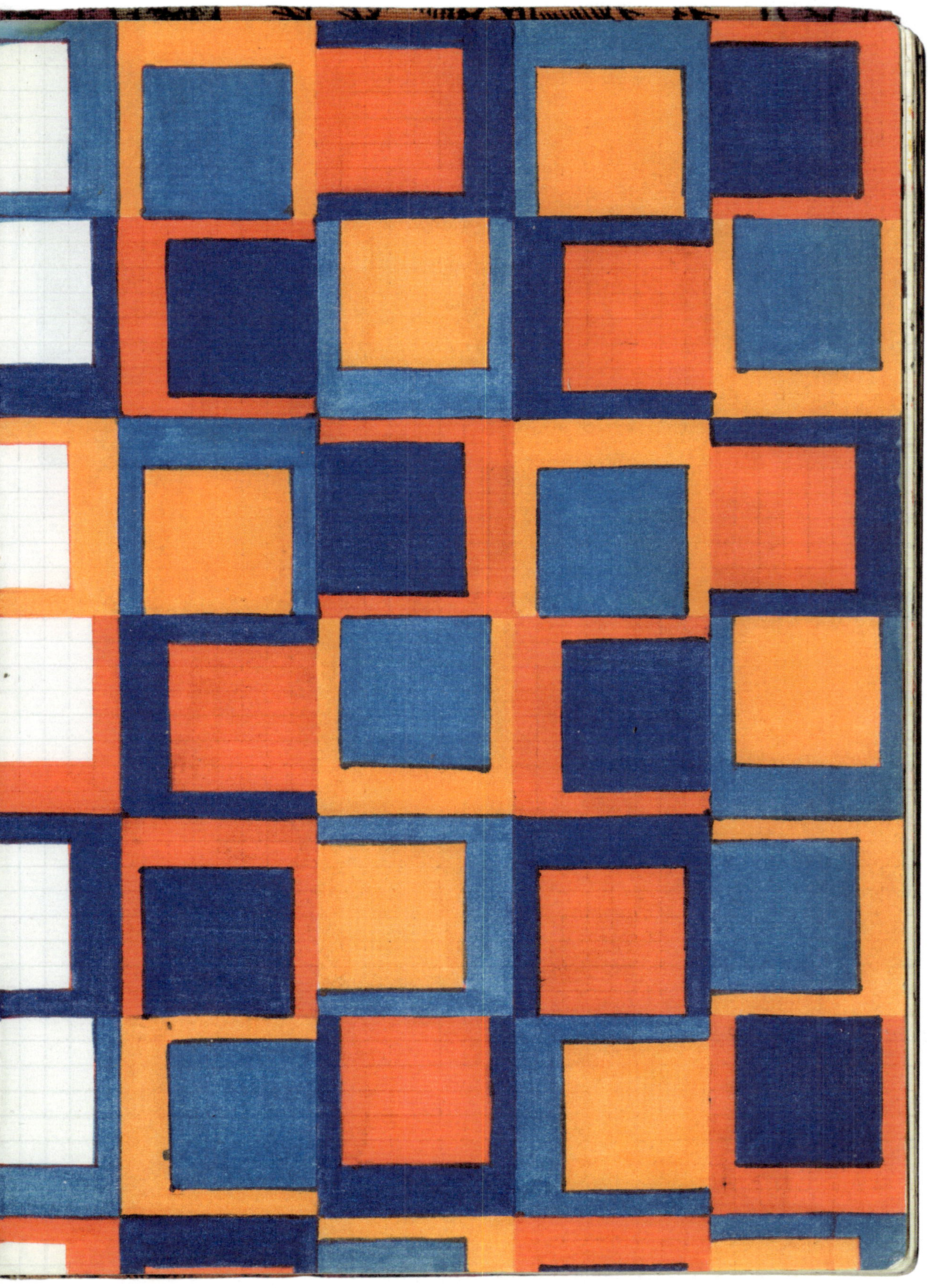

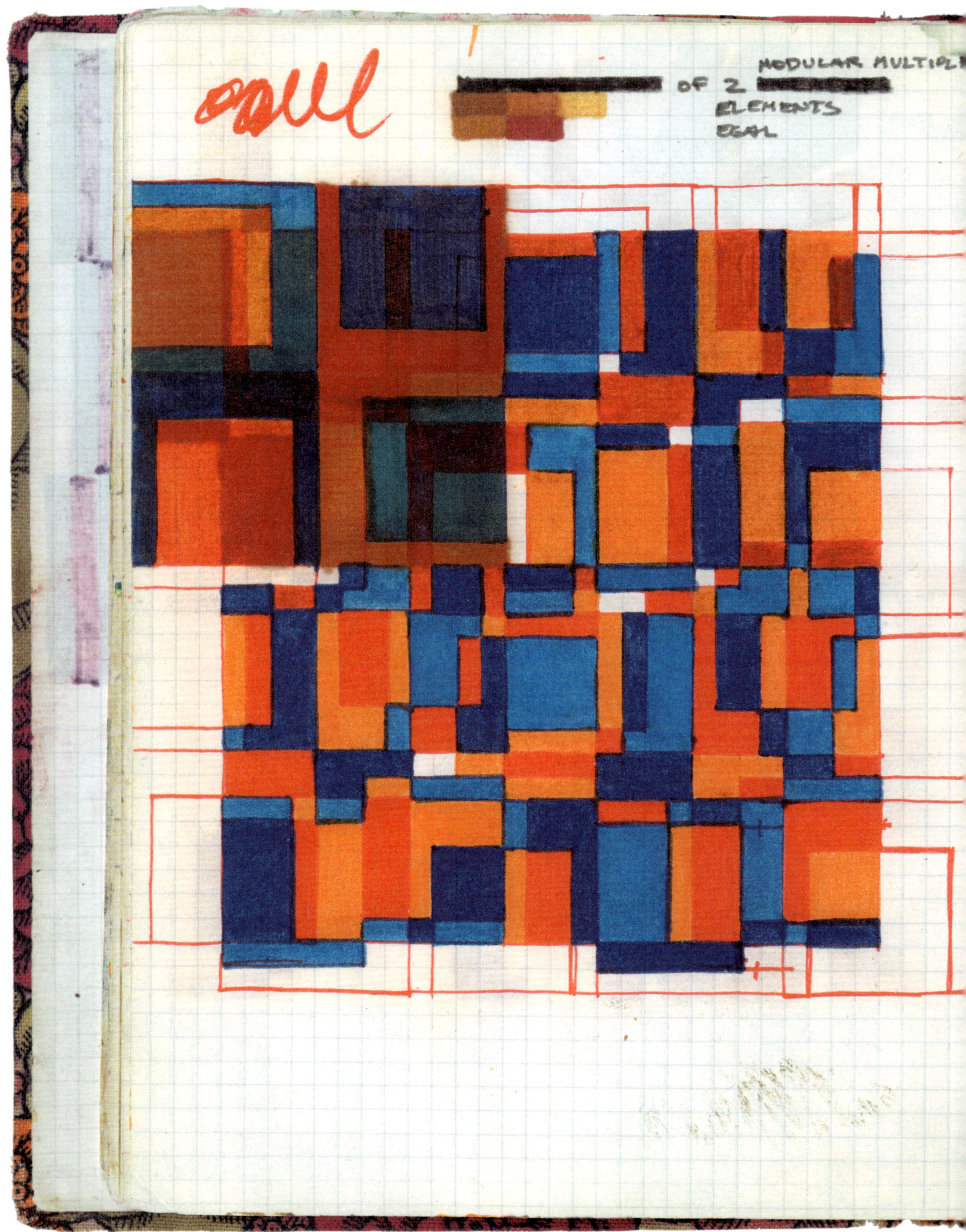
MODULAR MULTIPLE
OF 2
ELEMENTS
EGAL

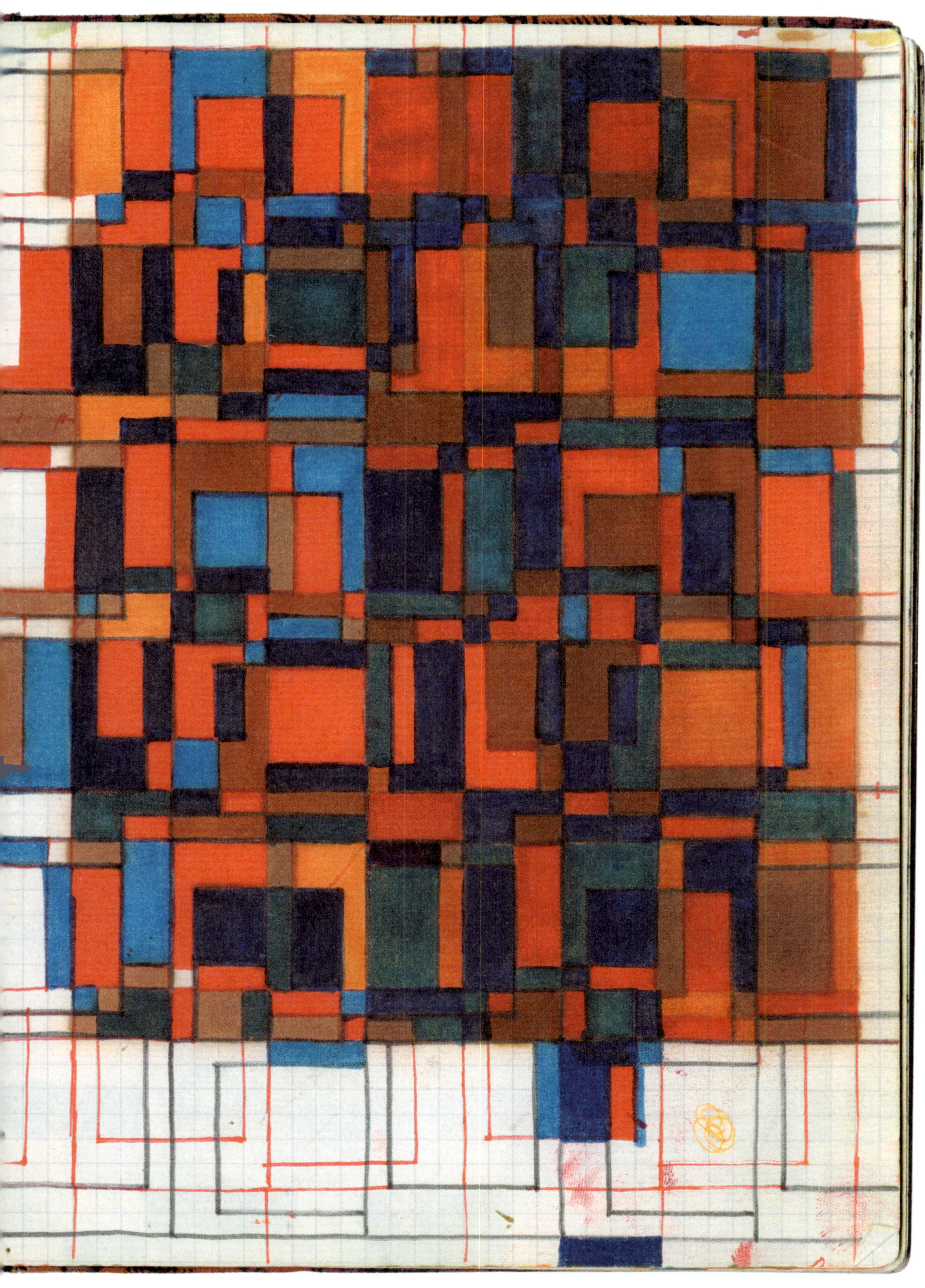

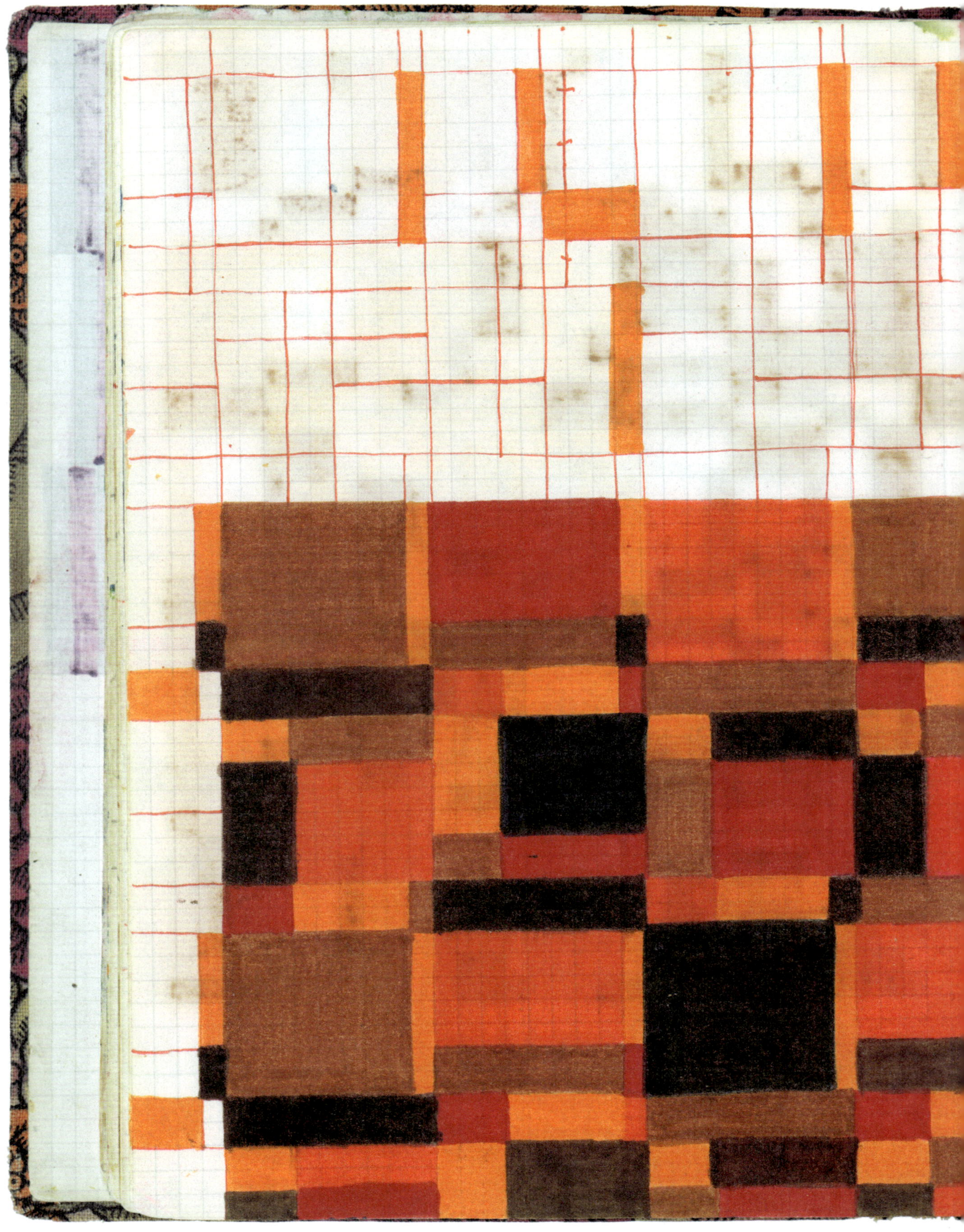

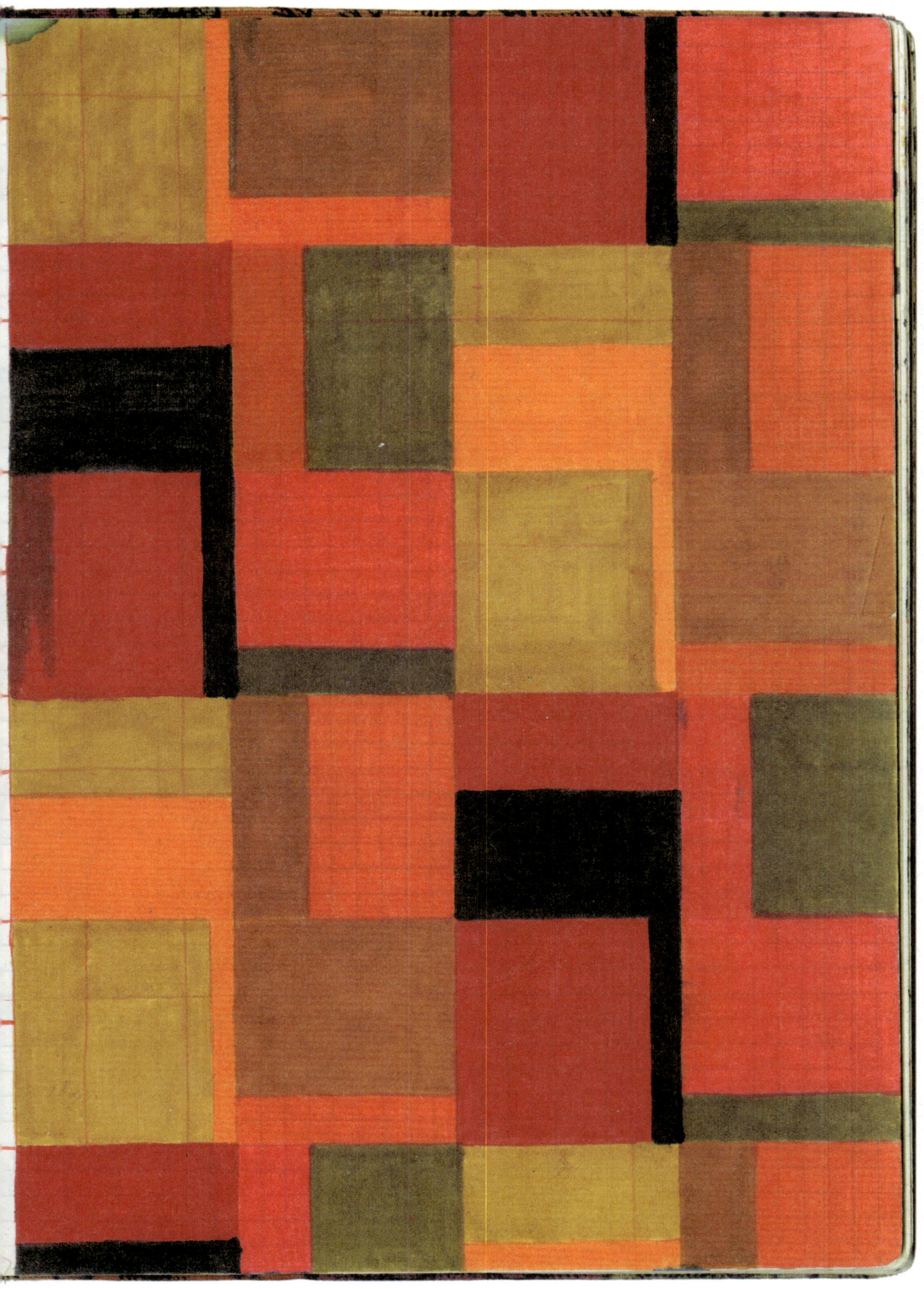

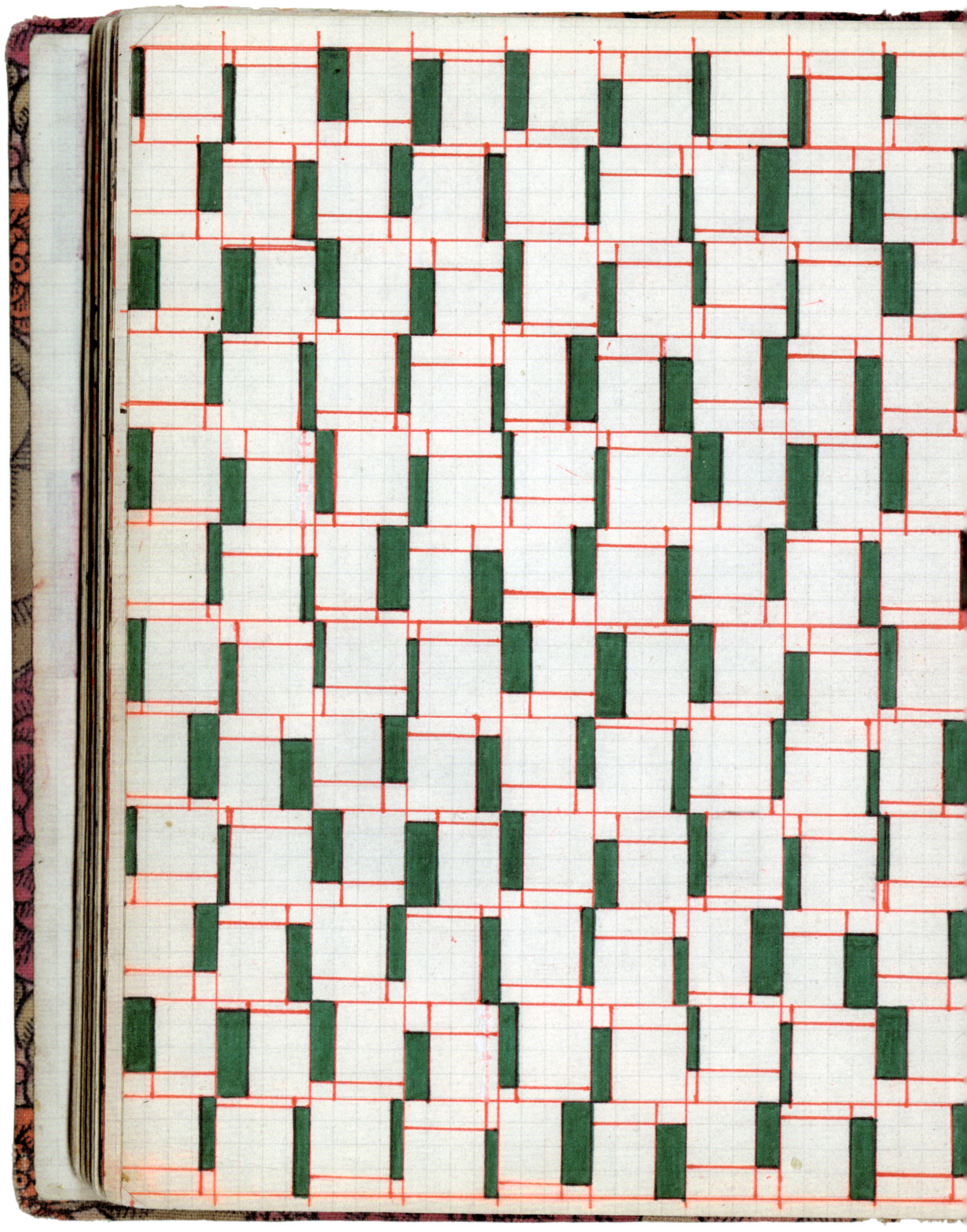

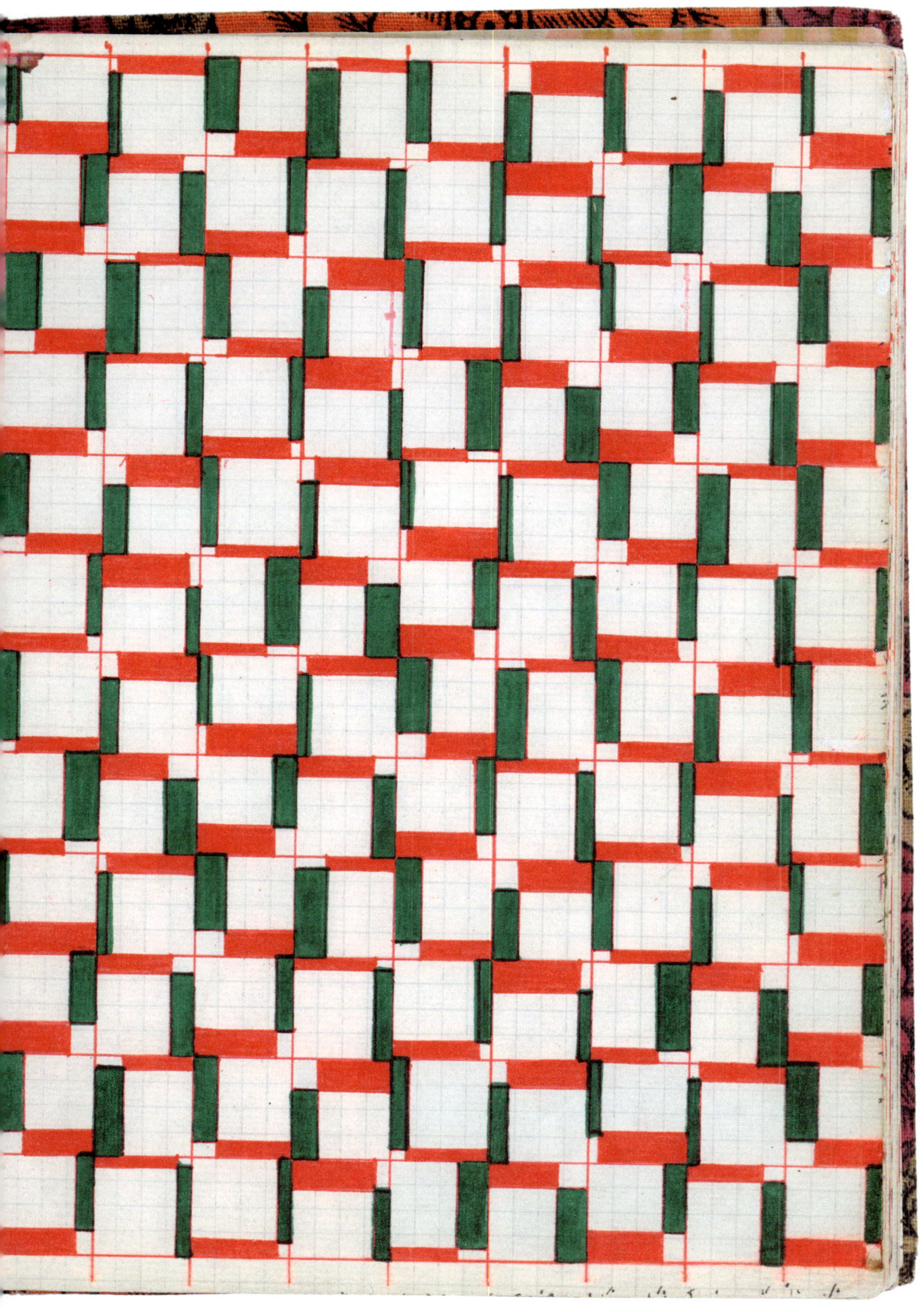

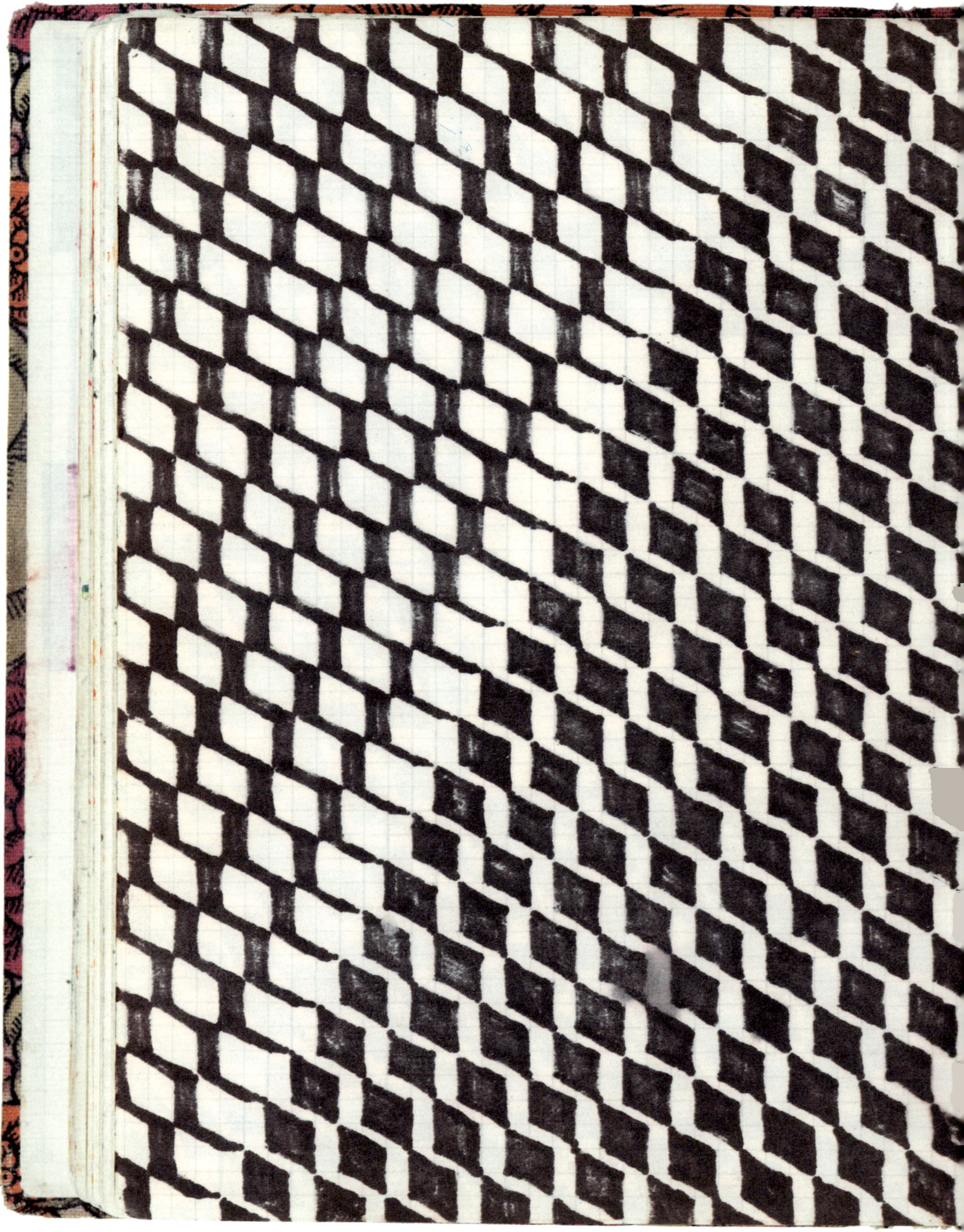

Albums

"I couldn't stop. It just kept coming, kept flowing through me. The only way you could do beautiful things like that is by isolating yourself from reality, from friends, from the messy situation out there. And when you isolate, you allow divine energy to flow. And once you find that you're not going to allow anyone into your studio to interfere with it."

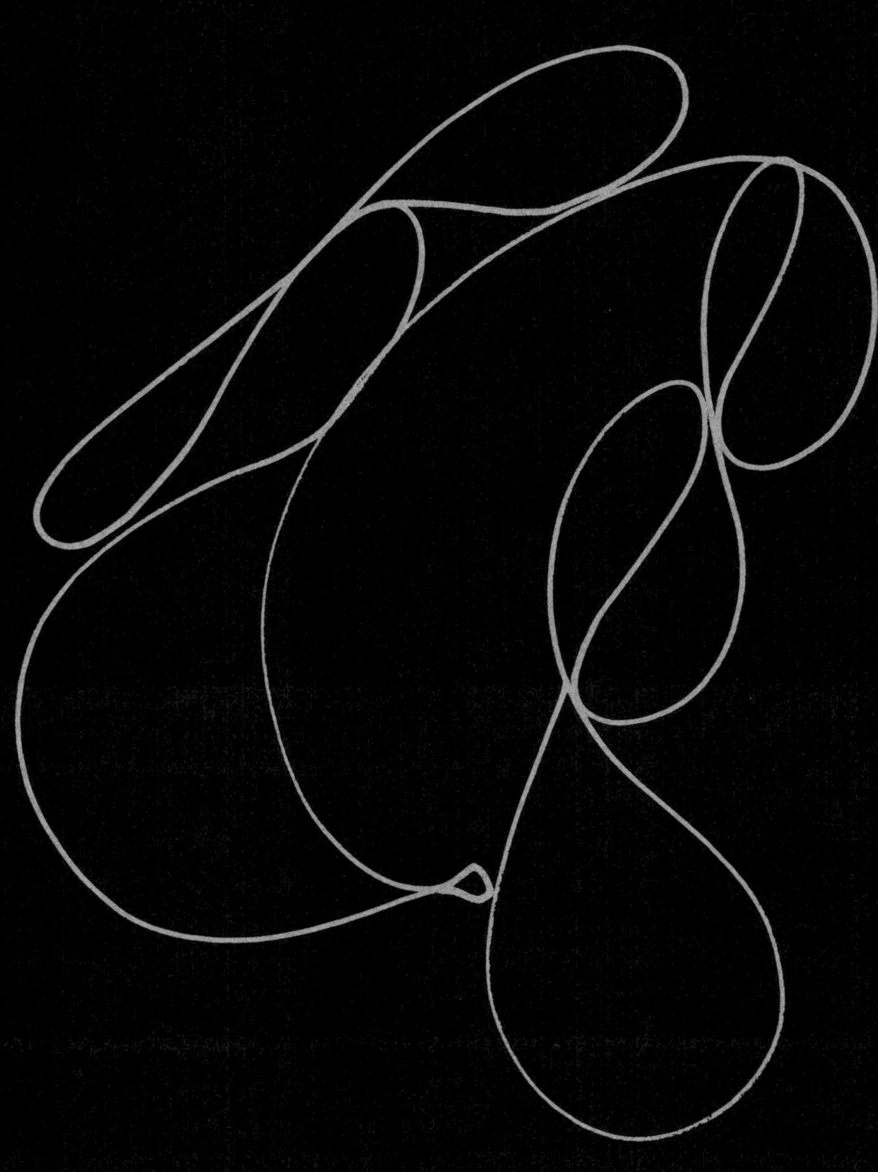

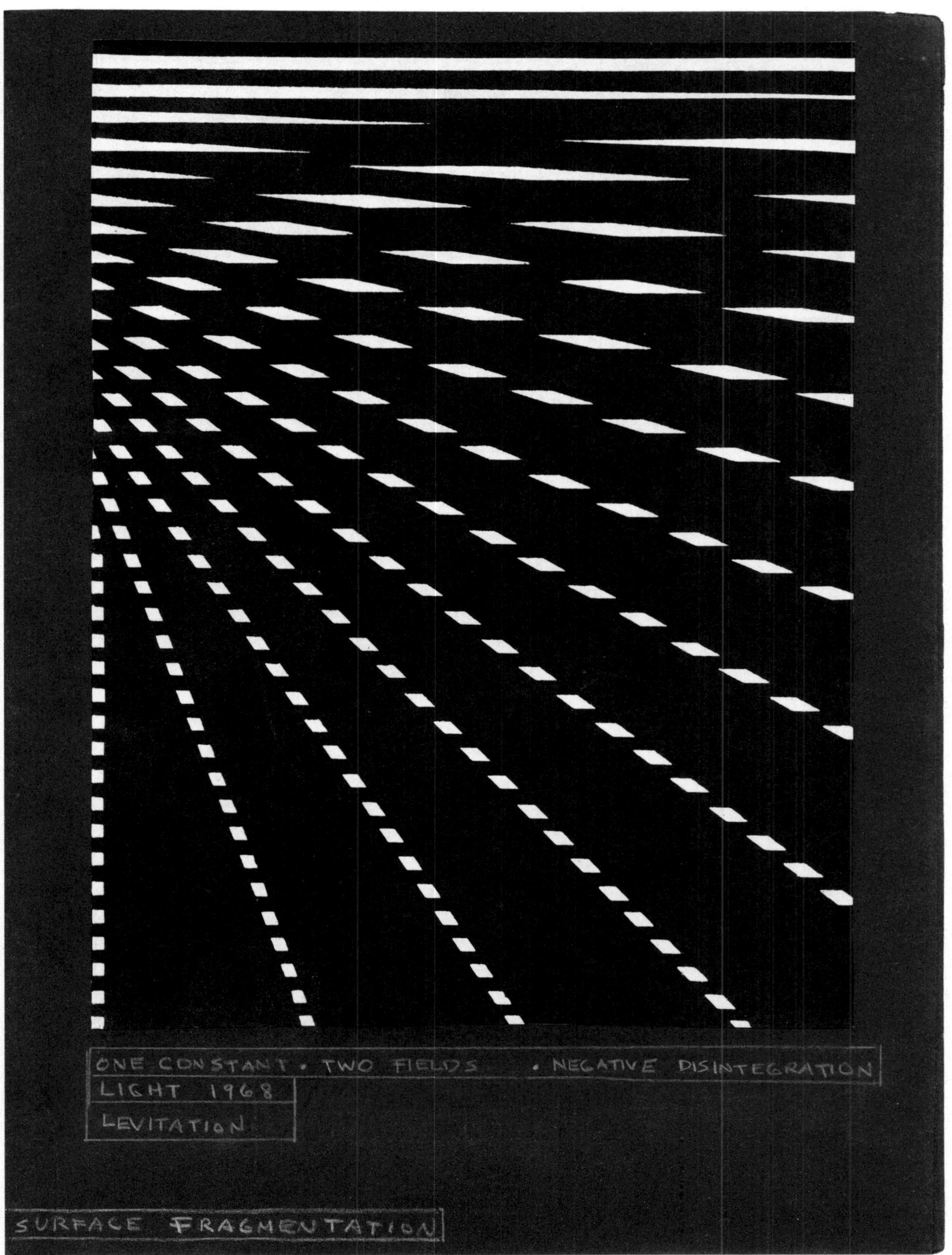

Pages 187–226: Photoalbum portfolios, 1965–75

PUBLIC STAIRWAY · PHOTO PARIS 1970
INFINITY FIELD

PUBLIC STAIRWAY. PHOTO PARIS 1970

LEVITATION

AN INFINITY CORRIDOR

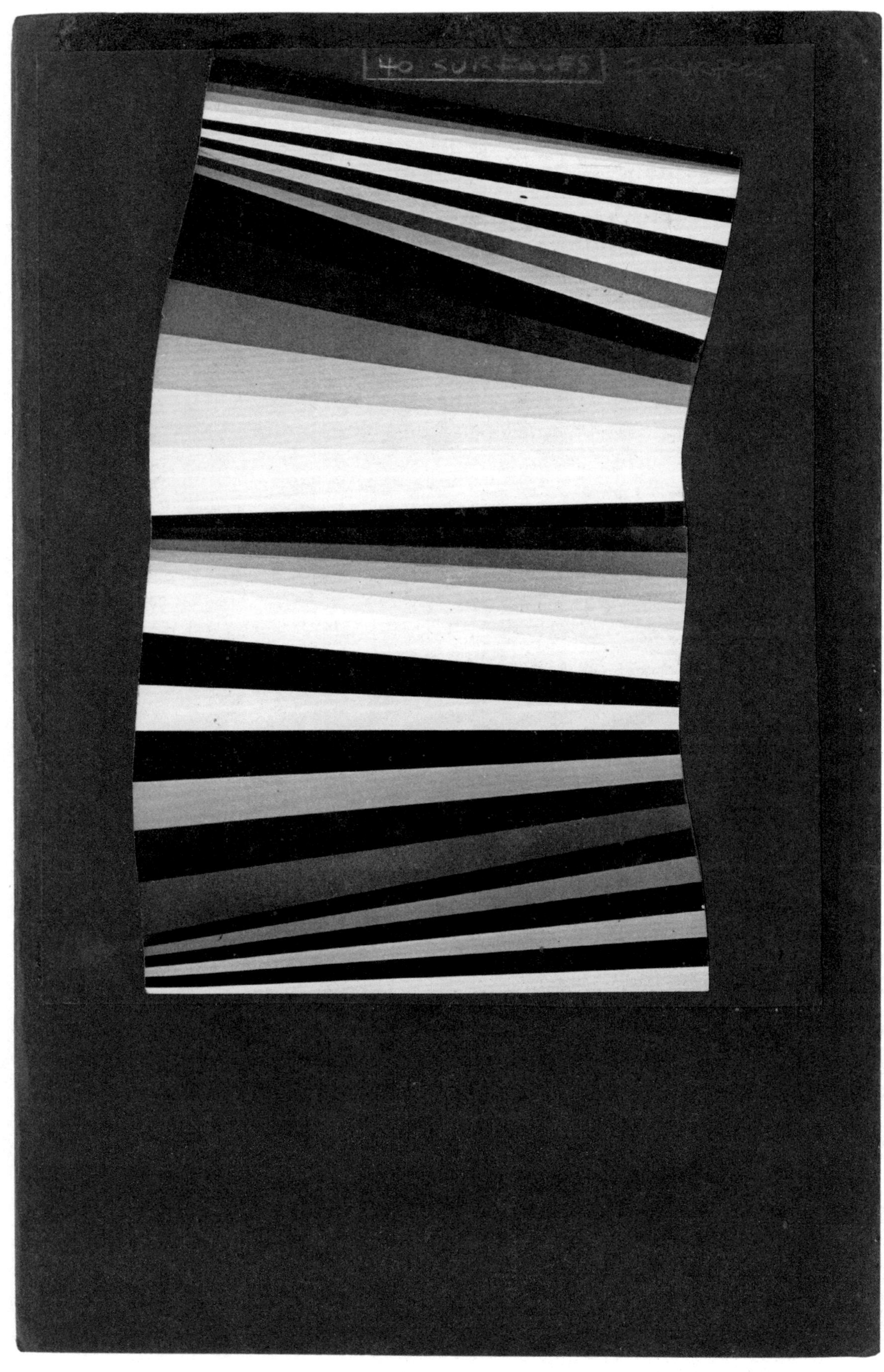

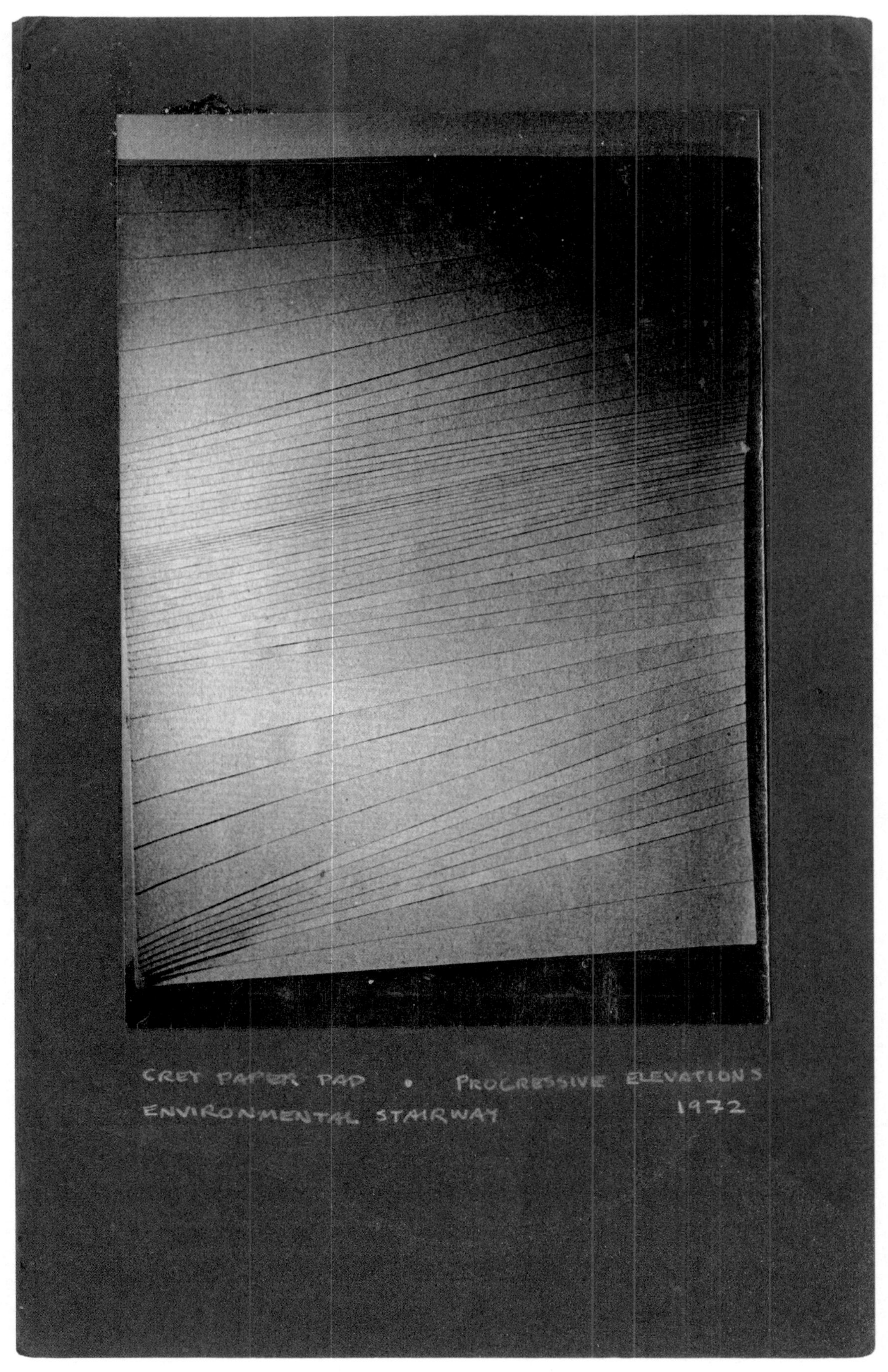
GREY PAPER PAD • PROGRESSIVE ELEVATIONS
ENVIRONMENTAL STAIRWAY 1972

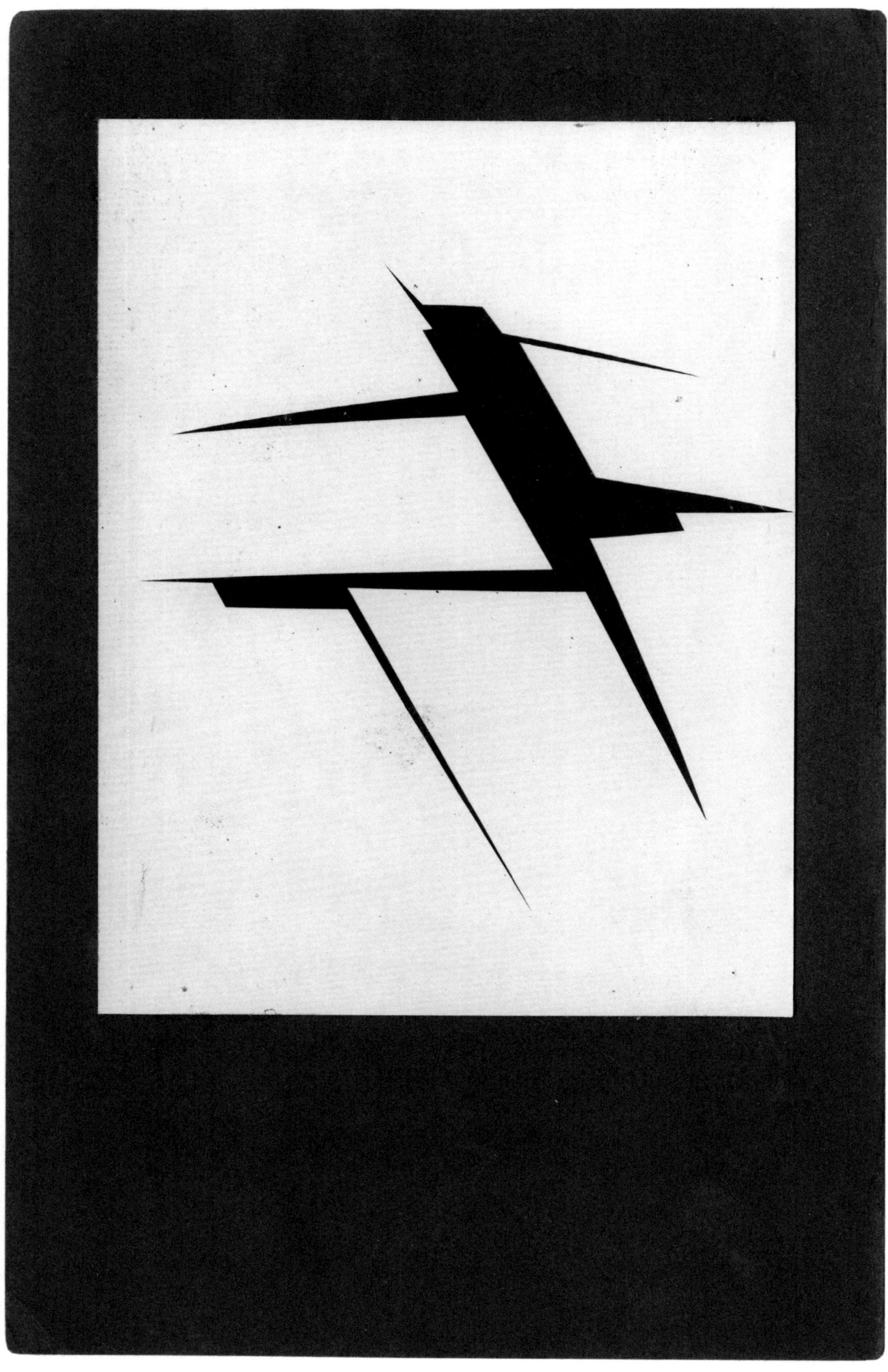

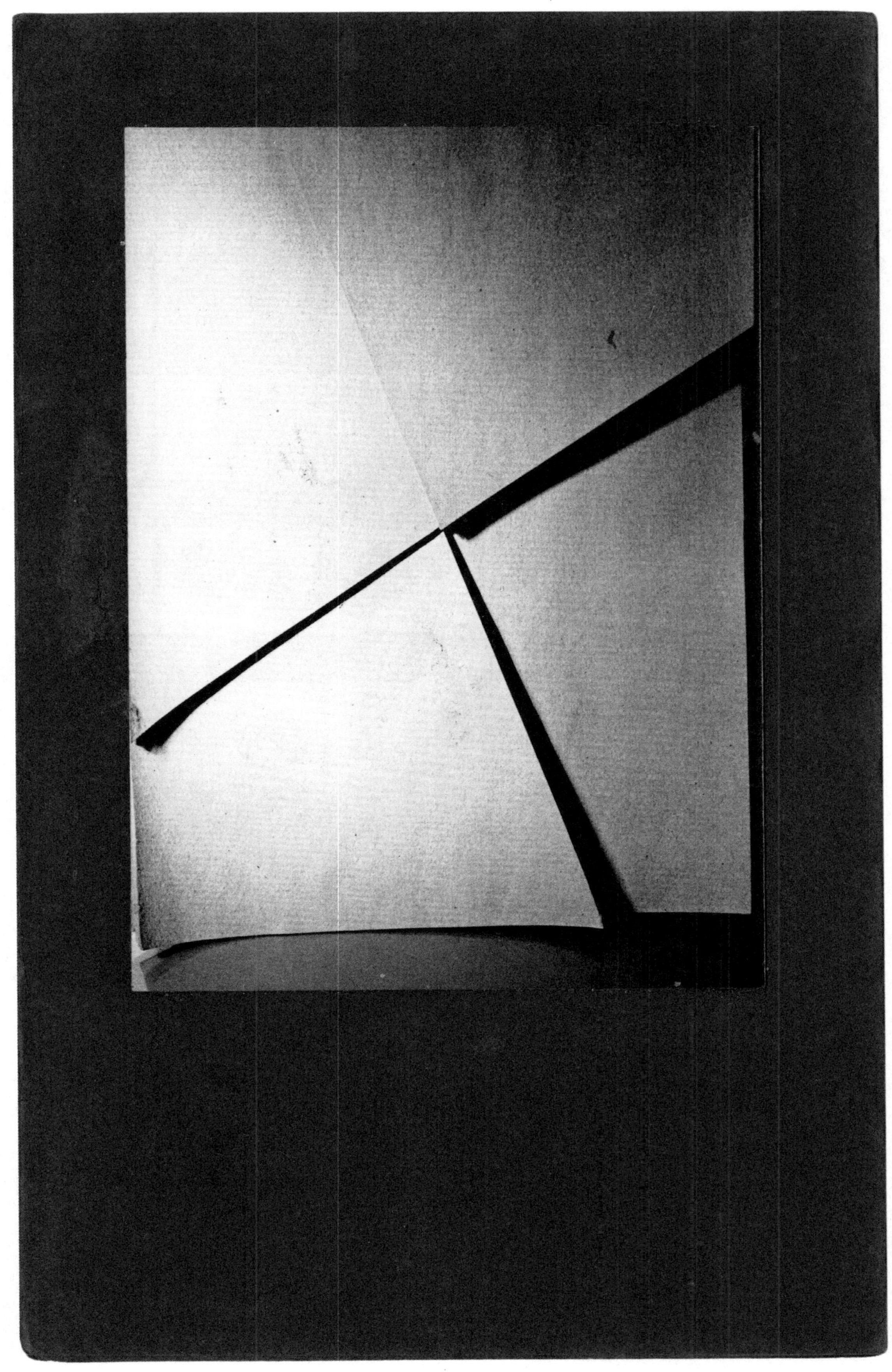

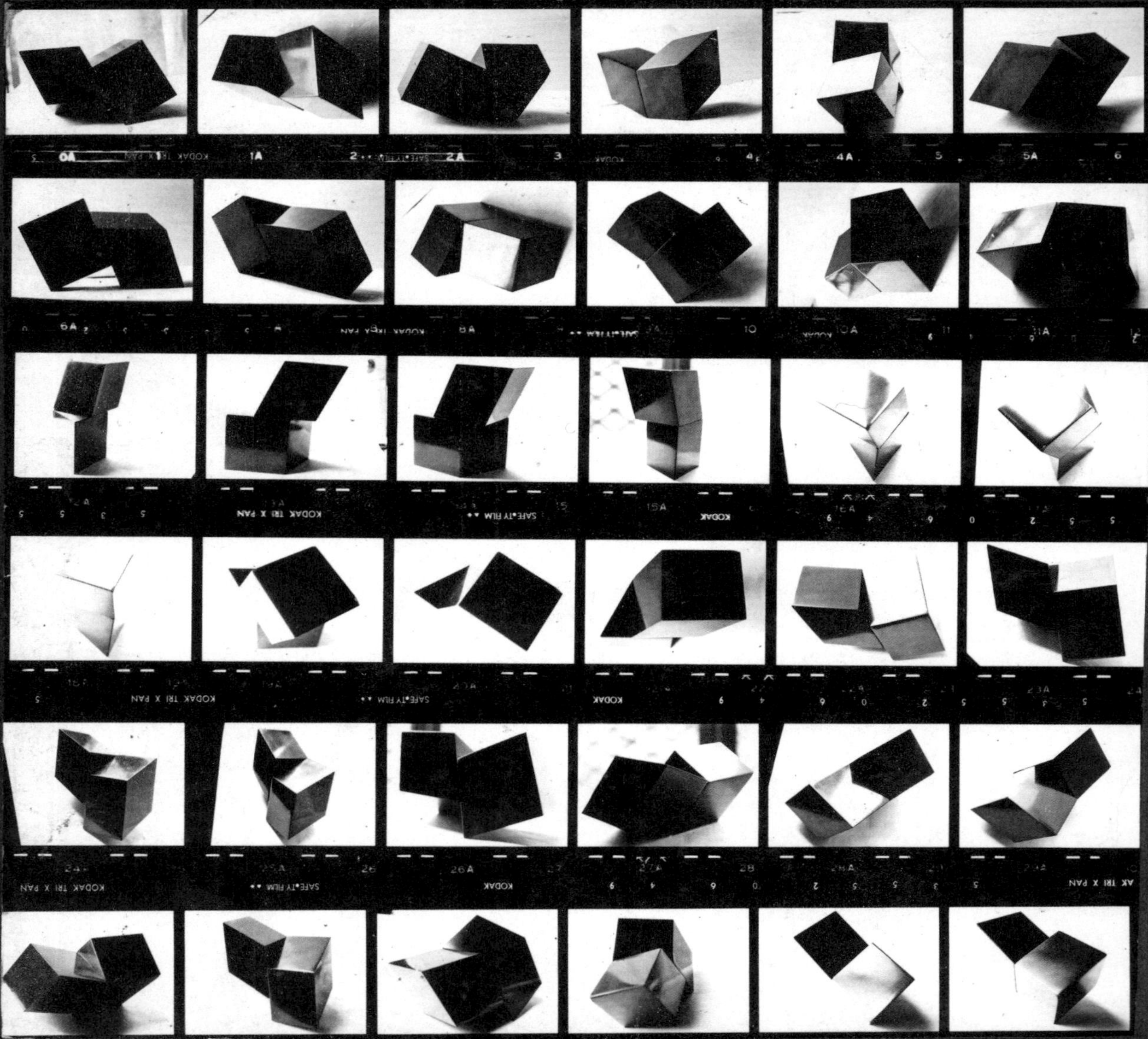

MARBLE ITALY 1970

2 EQUAL ELEMENTS
36 POINTS OF VIEW

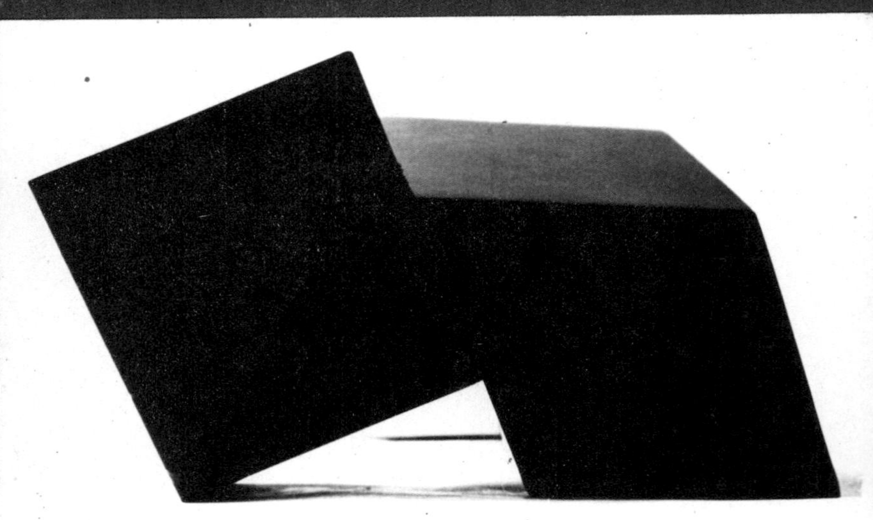

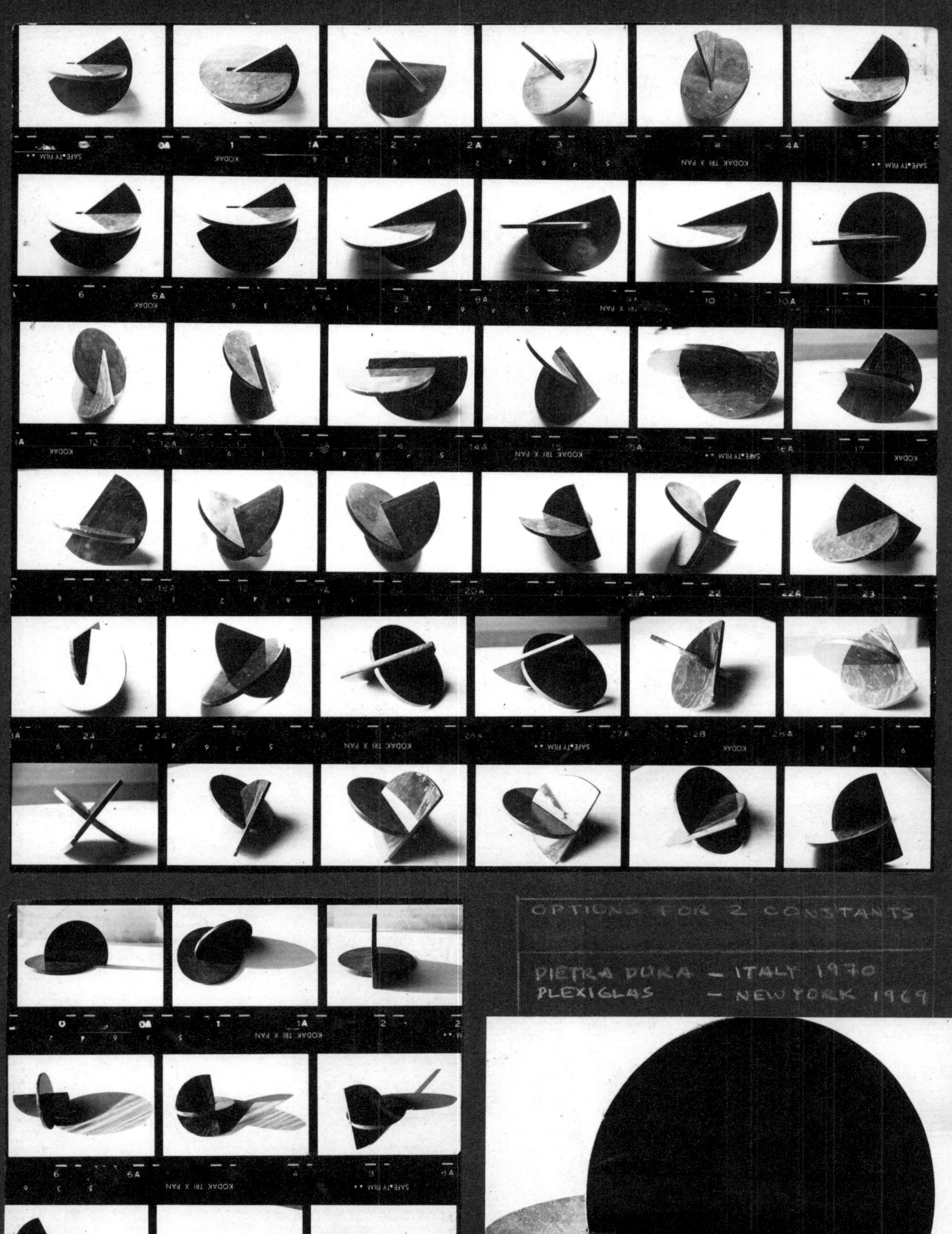
OPTIONS FOR 2 CONSTANTS
PIETRA DURA - ITALY 1970
PLEXIGLAS - NEW YORK 1969

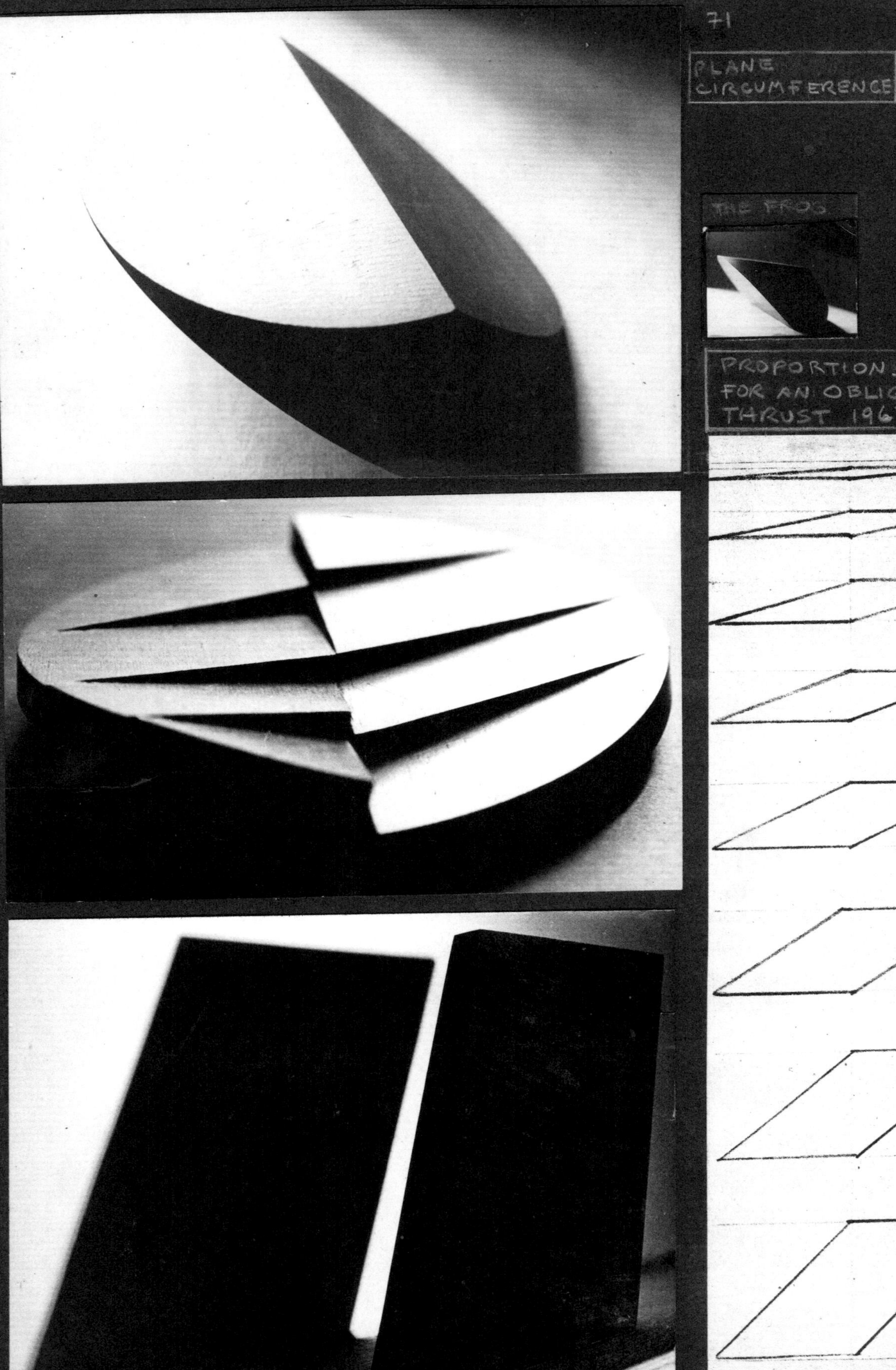
71
PLANE
CIRCUMFERENCE
THE FROG
FOUR CON
PROPORTIONS
FOR AN OBLIQUE
THRUST 1963-73

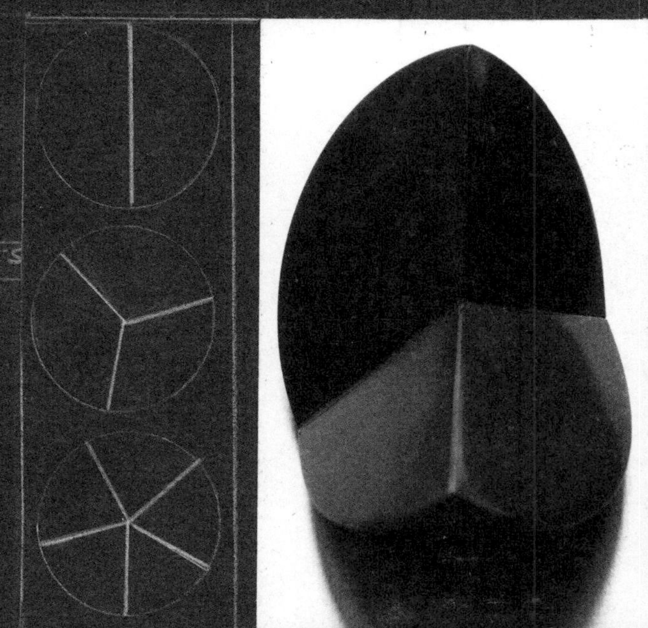

SYSTEM FOR PENETRATION OF A SPHERE · RELOCATION · 1970
MARBLE, ITALY

TEN SURFACES –
EIGHT BALANCE POINTS
SIX POUNDS OF BRASS WOOD 1968
TWO EQUAL ELEMENTS – MARBLE 1970
COPPER, BRASS, ALUMINUM 1971
FROM 'DISPLACED ABSOLUTE' SERIES
MUSEUM OF MODERN ART 1971

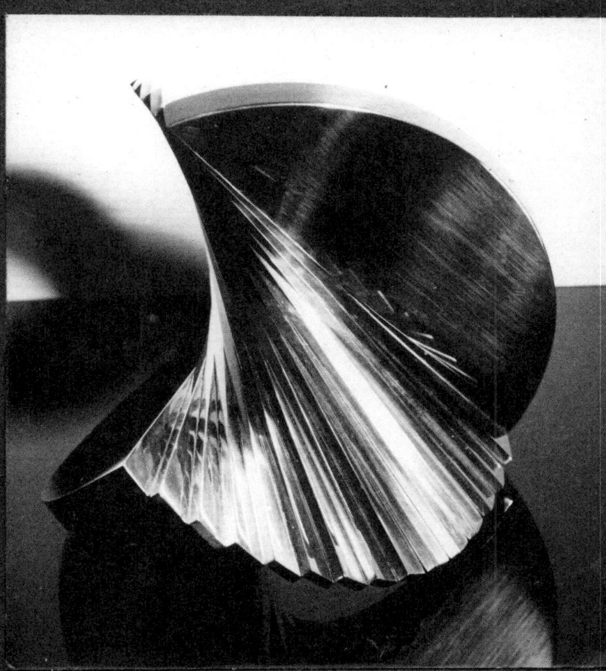

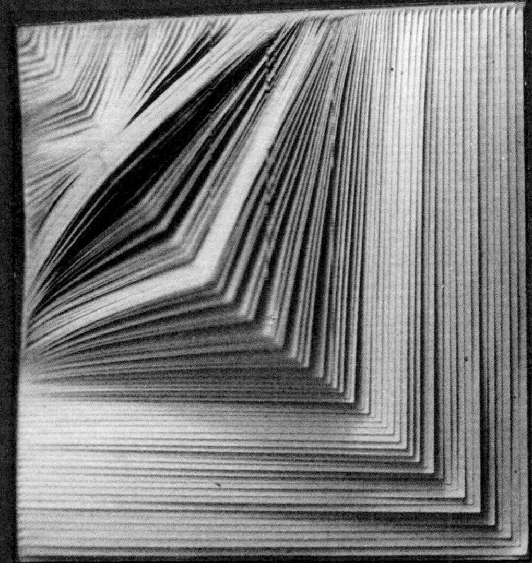

PAPER PAD, 1973
100 SURFACES $1.35

PARTIALLY DEVELOPED ABSOLUTE · 1971 · MOMA

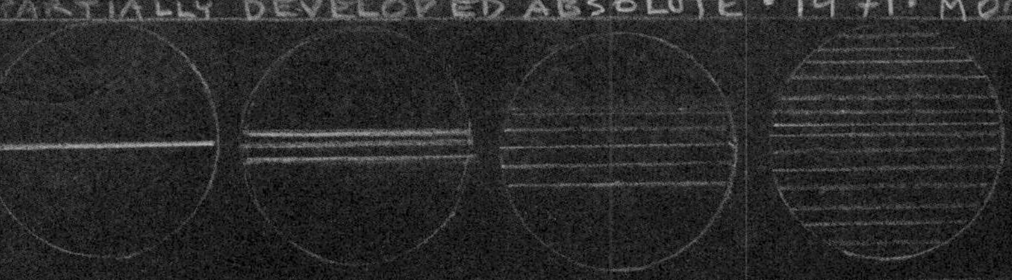

II

II

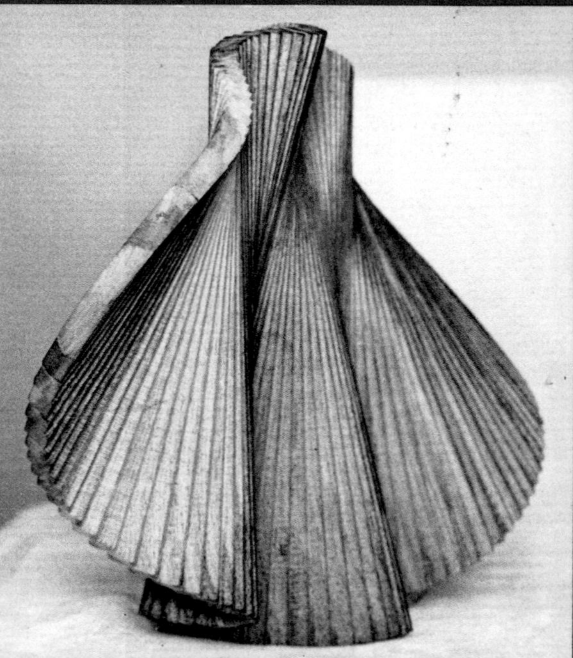

RESTRUCTURES

OPTIONS FOR A DEVELOPABLE ABSOLUTE

1972 - 73

-ONE CONSTANT-

BEACH STRUCTURES

FROM EUCLIDEAN TO NON-EUCLIDEAN CURVE

SUITE OF 13

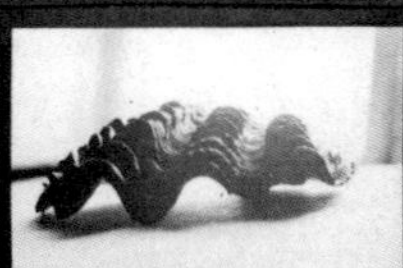

ORGANIC 1974

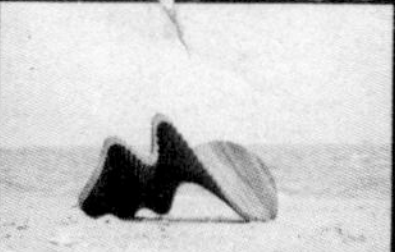

#4 1972

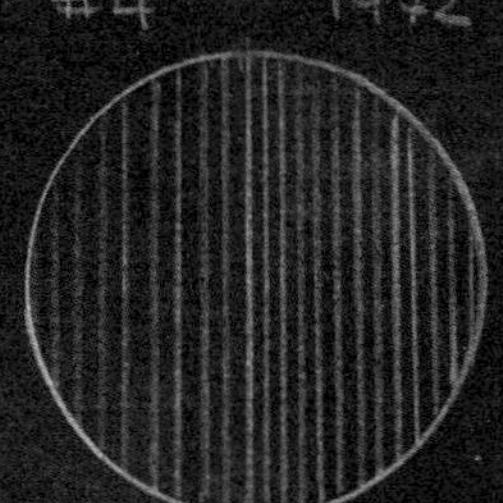

I

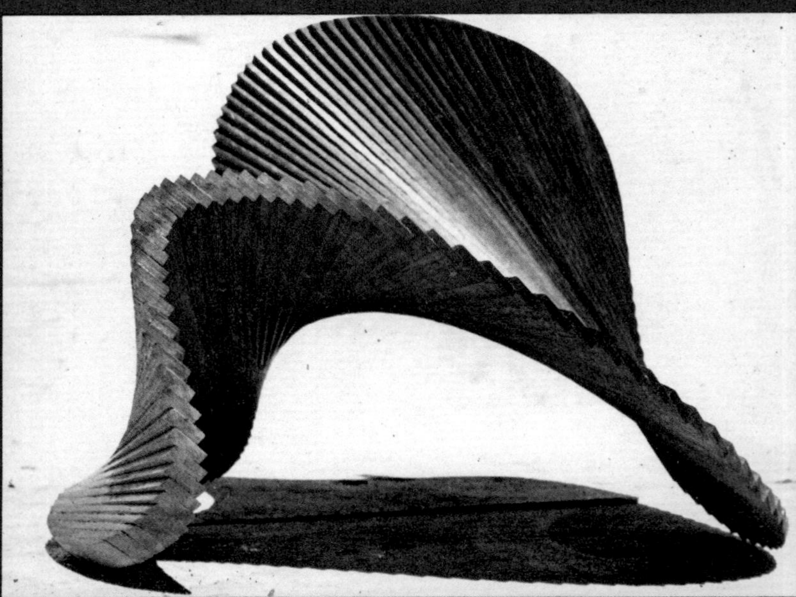

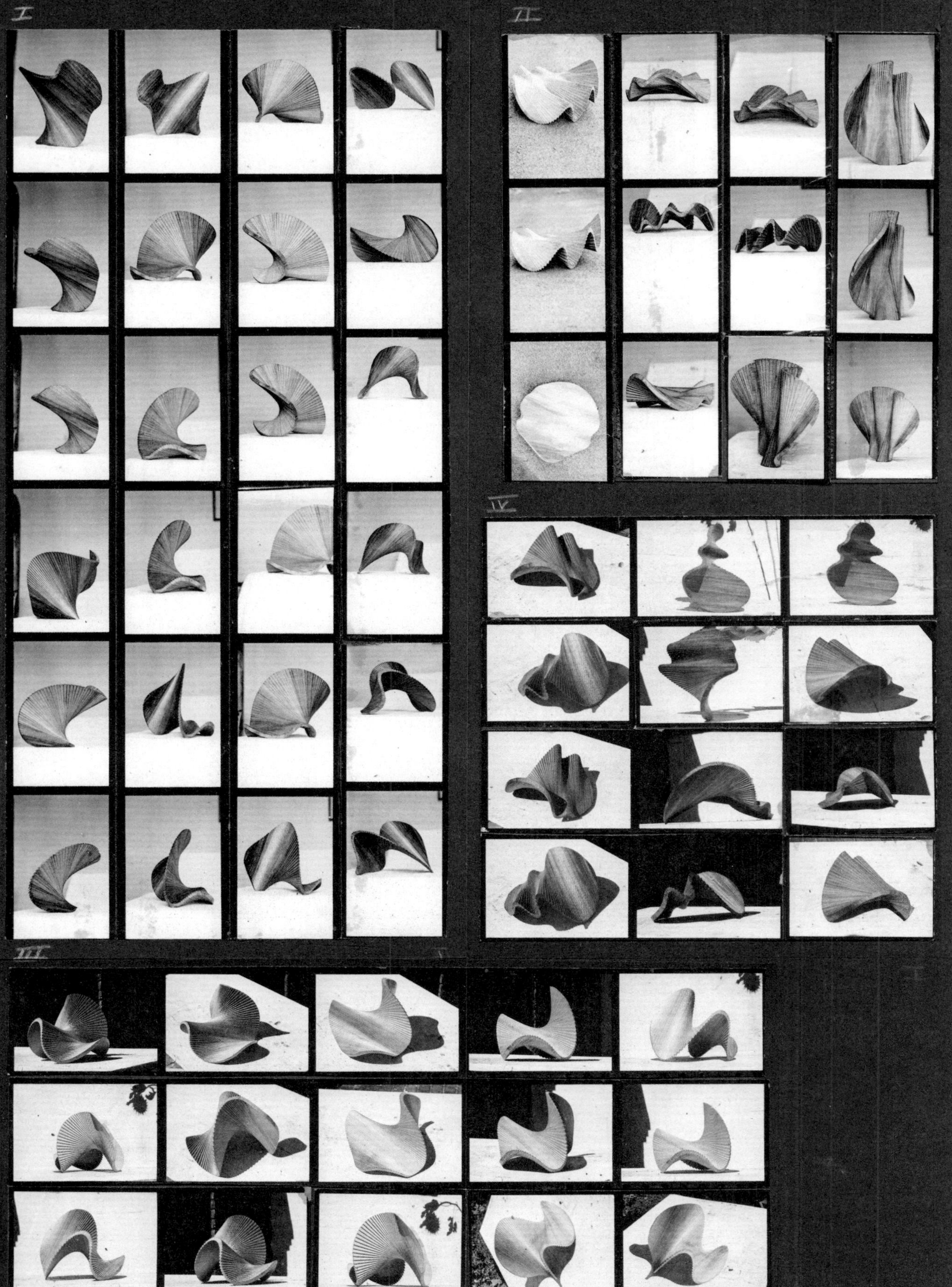
I
II
IV
III

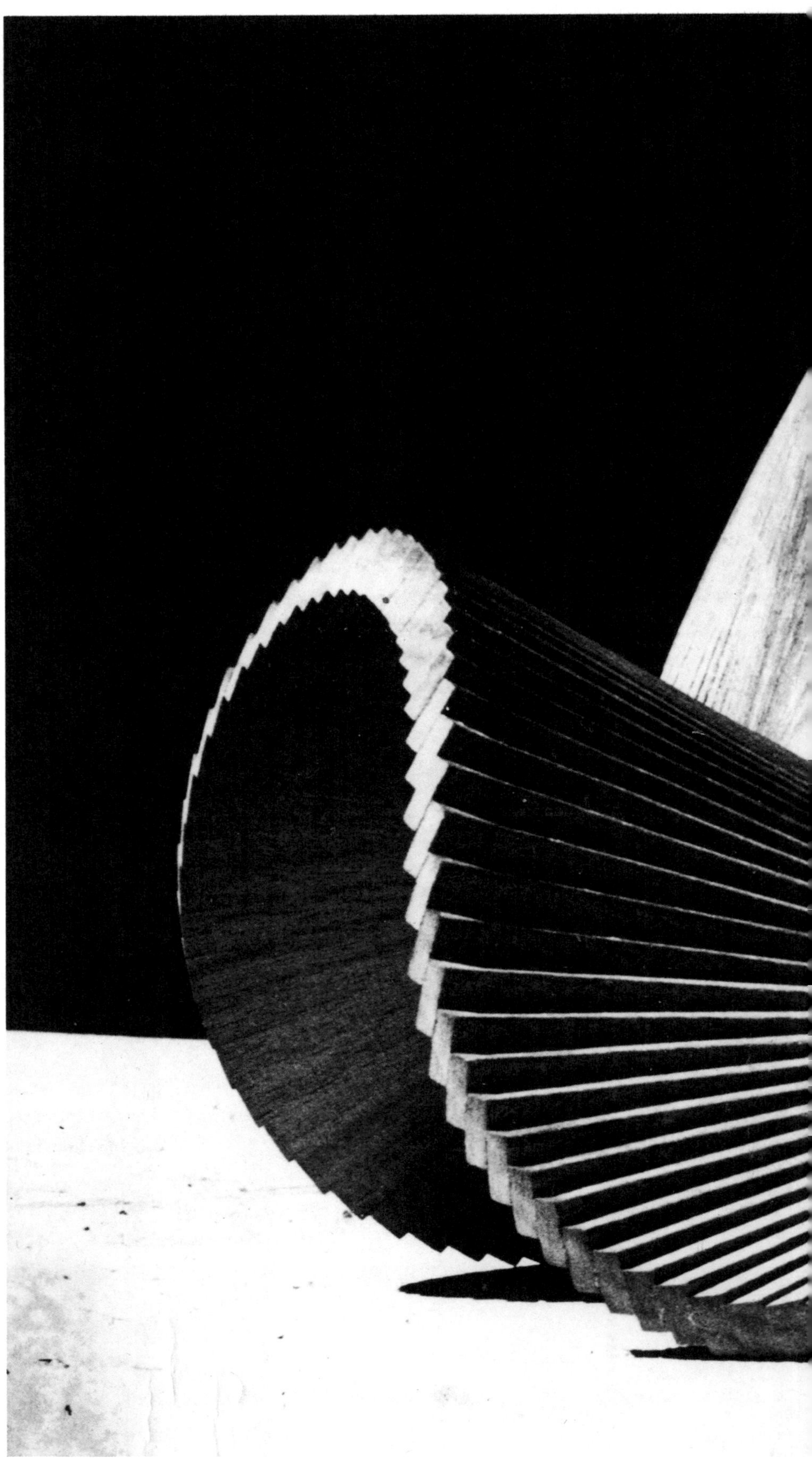

Detail of the album ***RESTRUCTURE / SEASTRUCTURE***, 1972–73

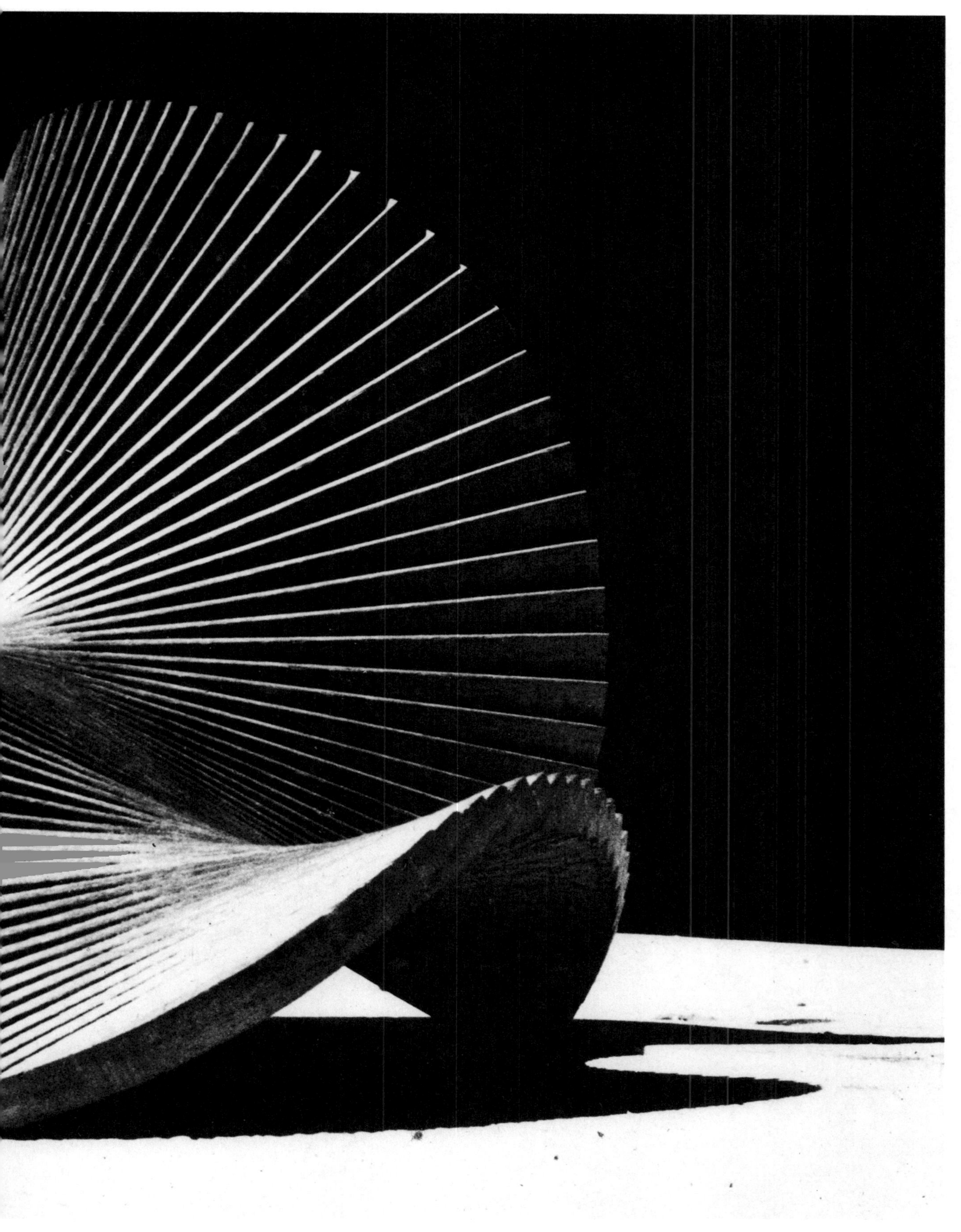

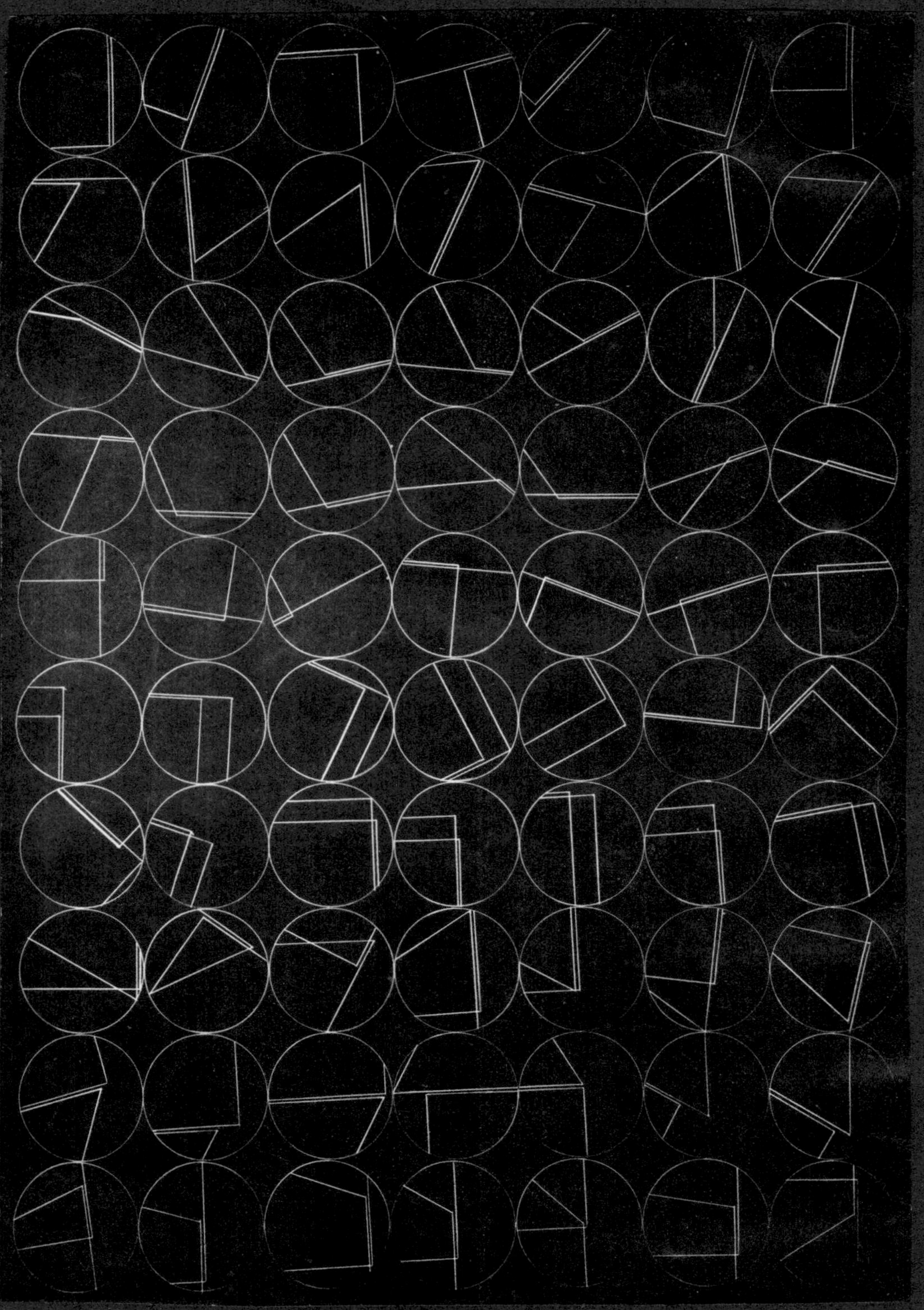

DRAWING 1968
ENGRAVING 1967

TWO-LINE LIMITATIONS
PARALLEL OPTIONS

ONE FIELD
CONTAINED WALL DRAWING

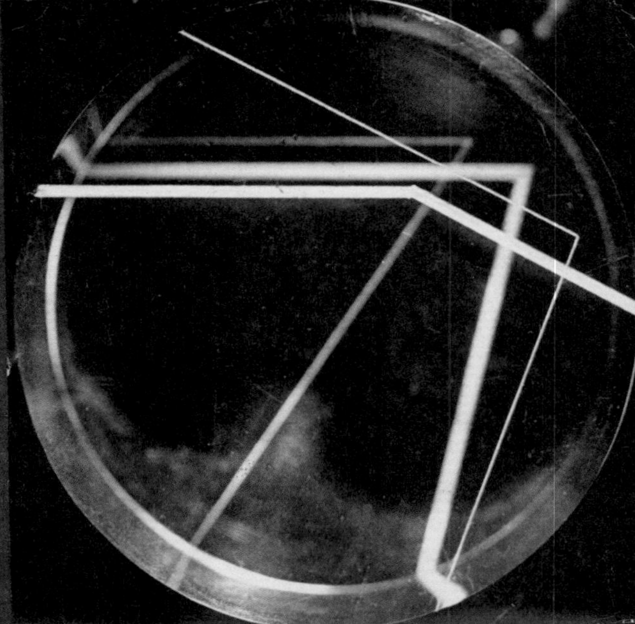

LEVITATION • 1968 • INCISED

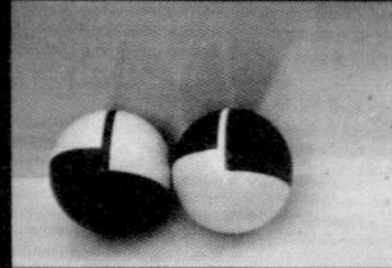

MARBLE ITALY
1970

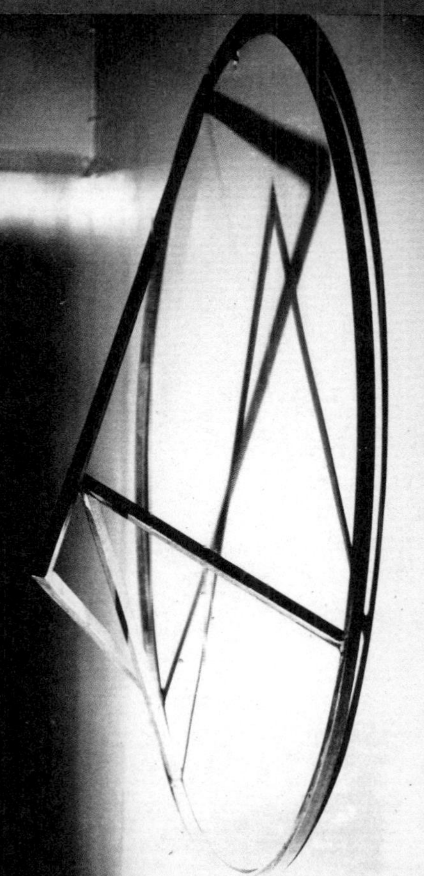

WELDED STEEL • 1973-4

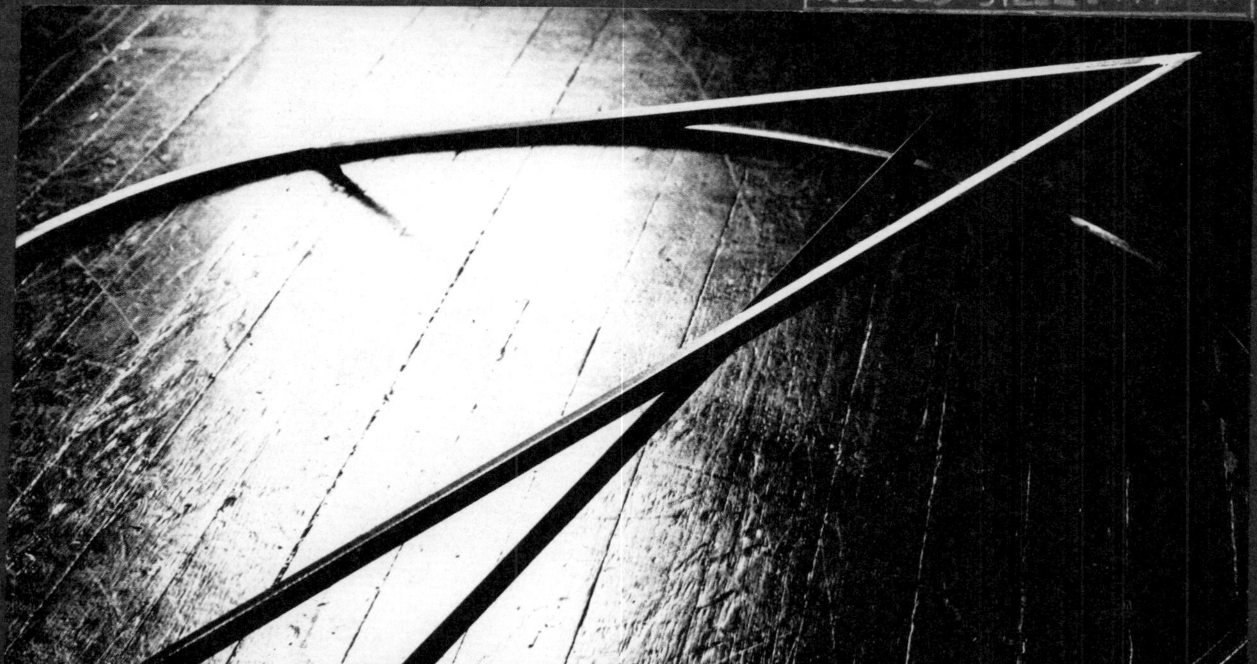

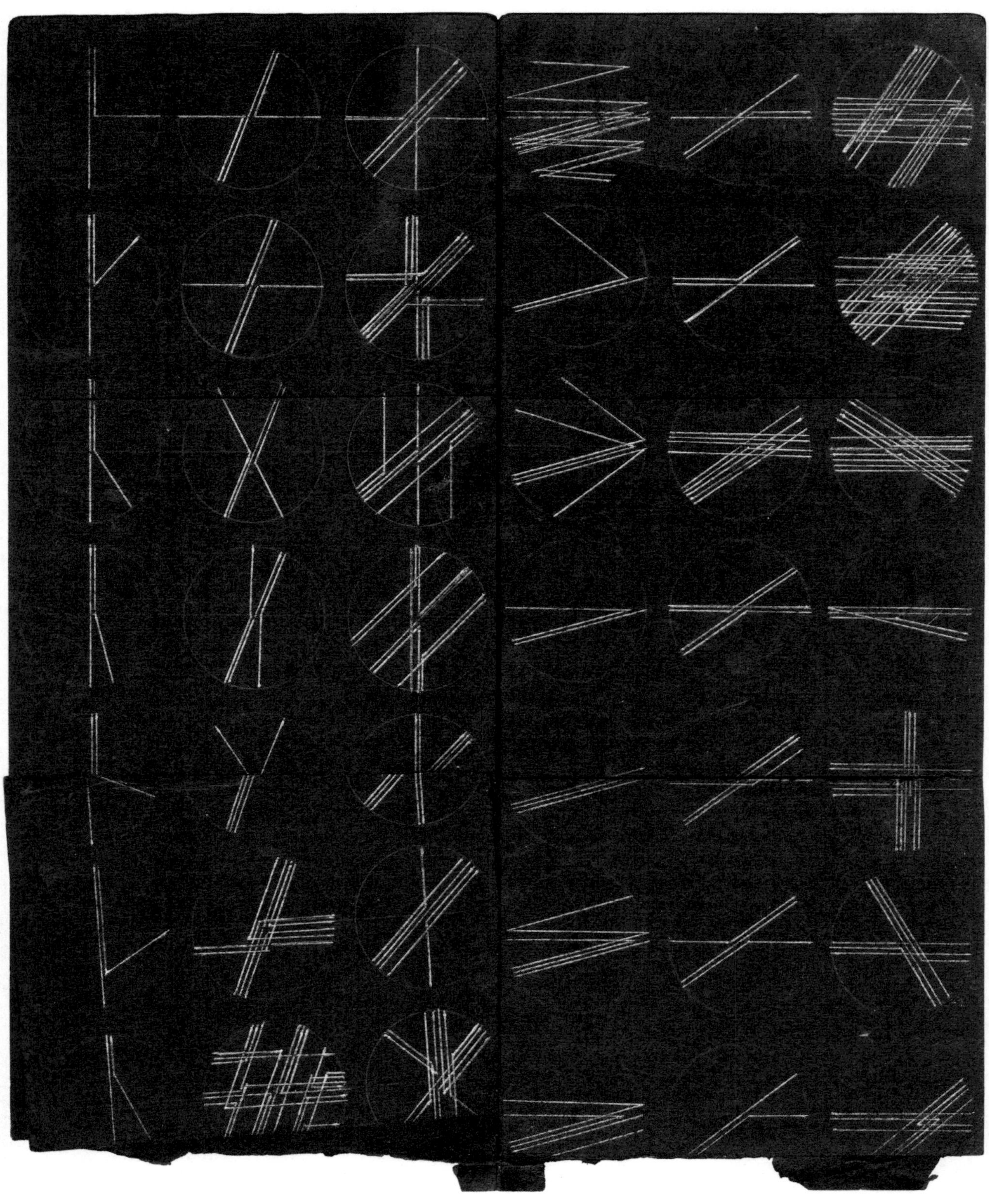

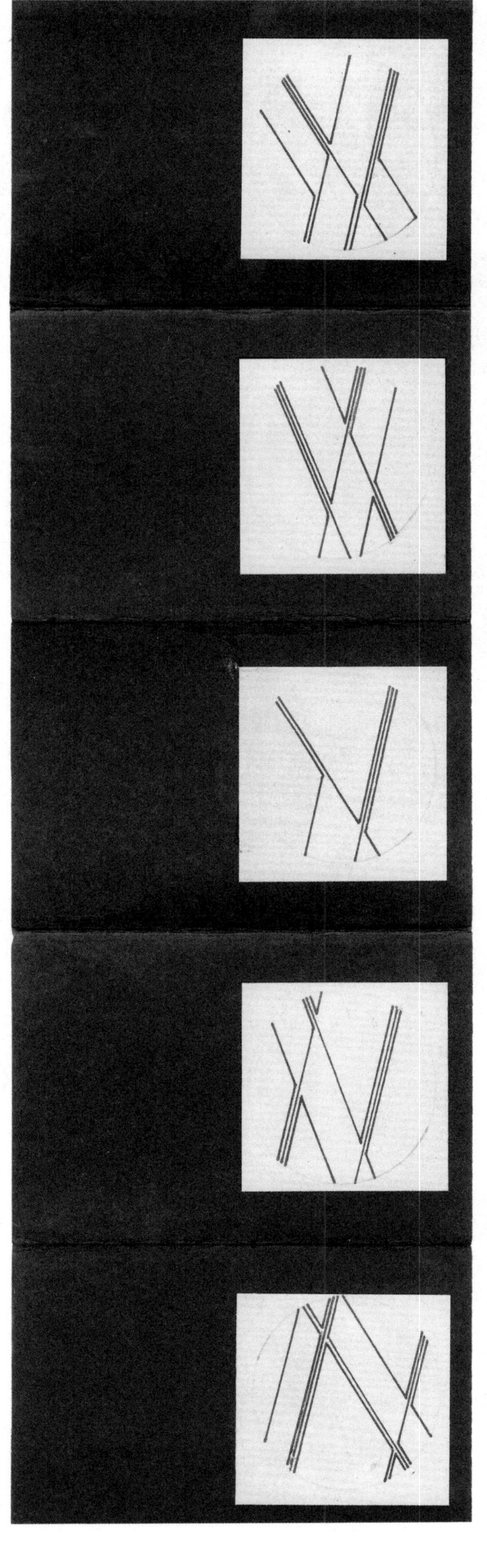

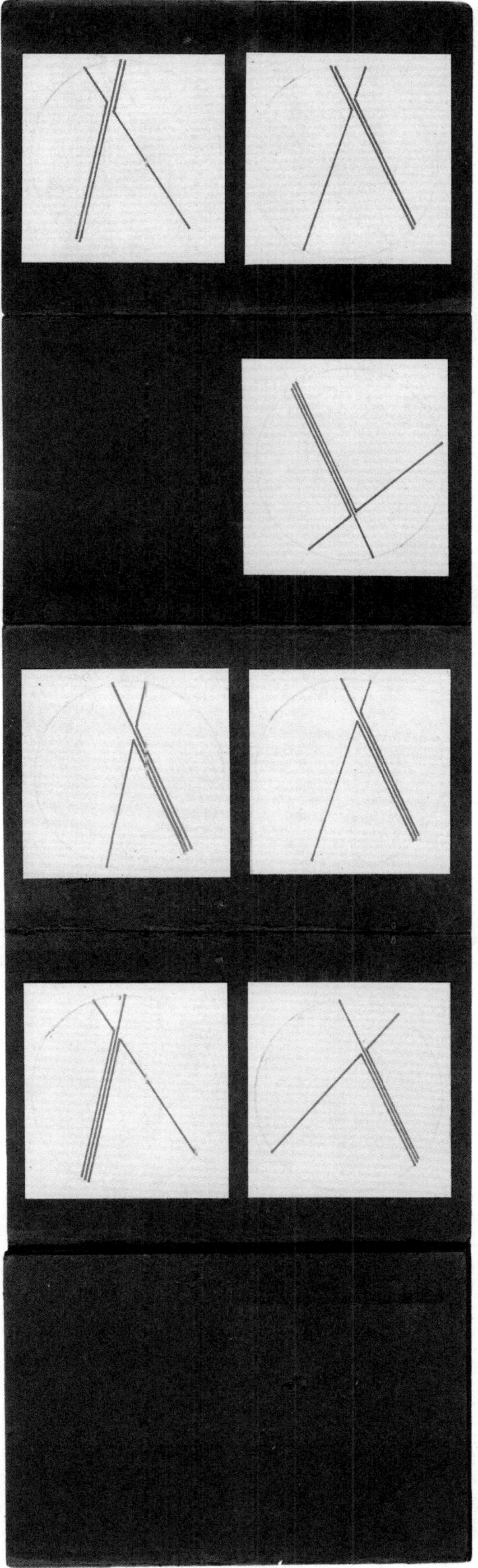

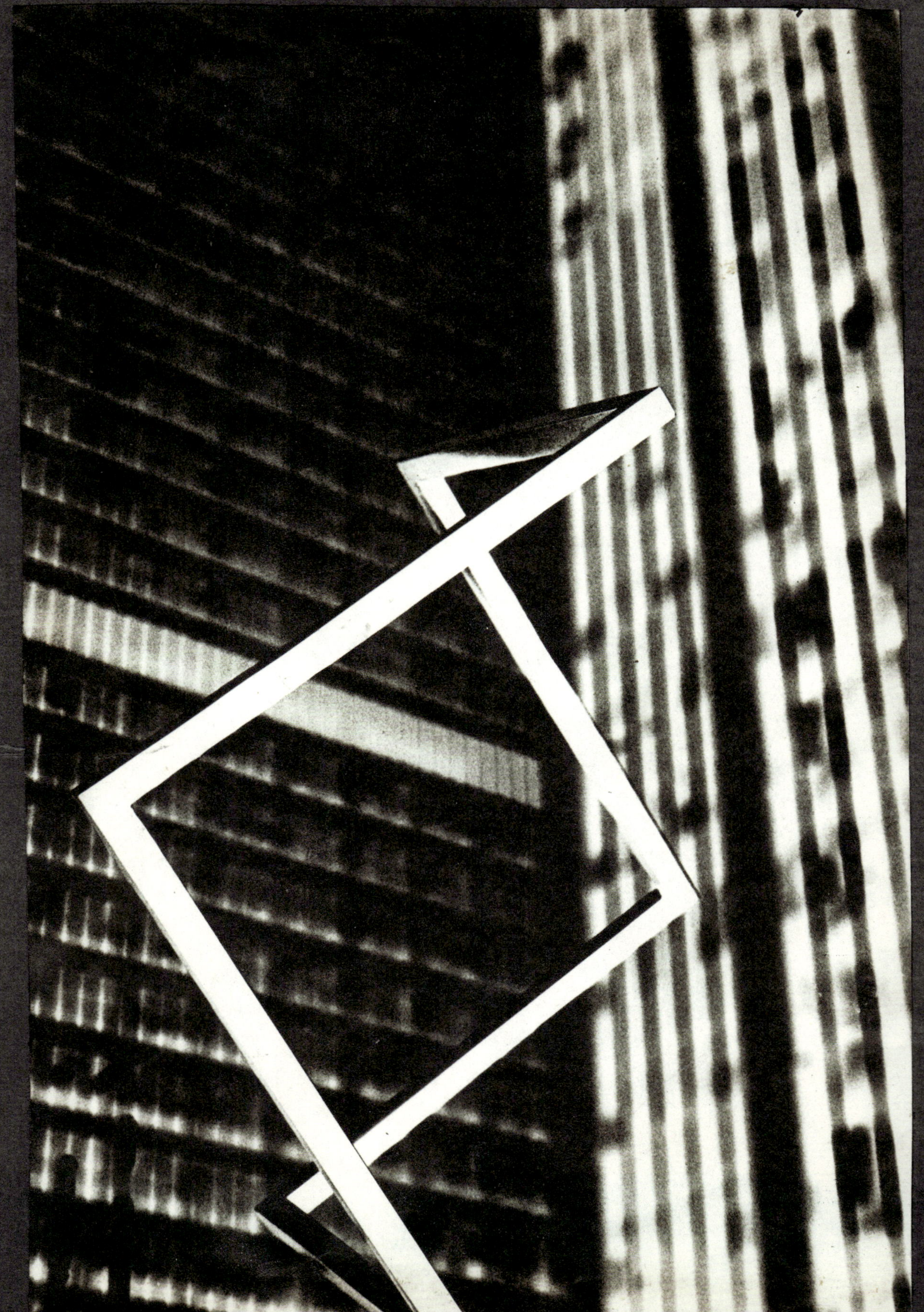

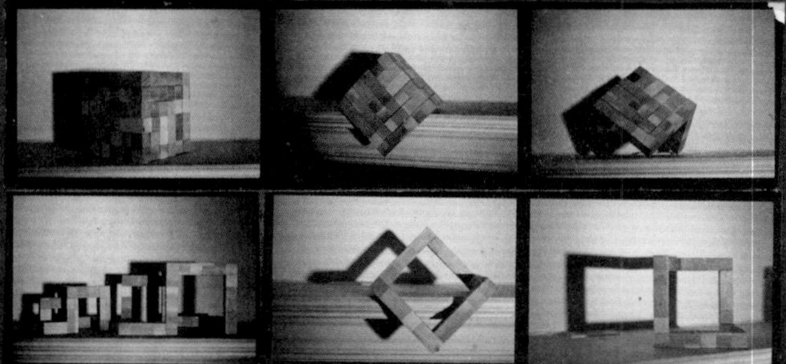

ONE CUBE BUILT UP WITH 11 OPEN CUBES OF PROGRESSIVELY CHANGING PROPORTIONS OF SPACE AND MATTER BUILT UP WITH 152 EQUAL ELEMENTS

WOOD MODELS 1971
ALUMINUM MODEL 1971

ONE CONSTANT SEEN FROM 36 POINTS OF VIEW • 1972 STEEL PAINTED RED

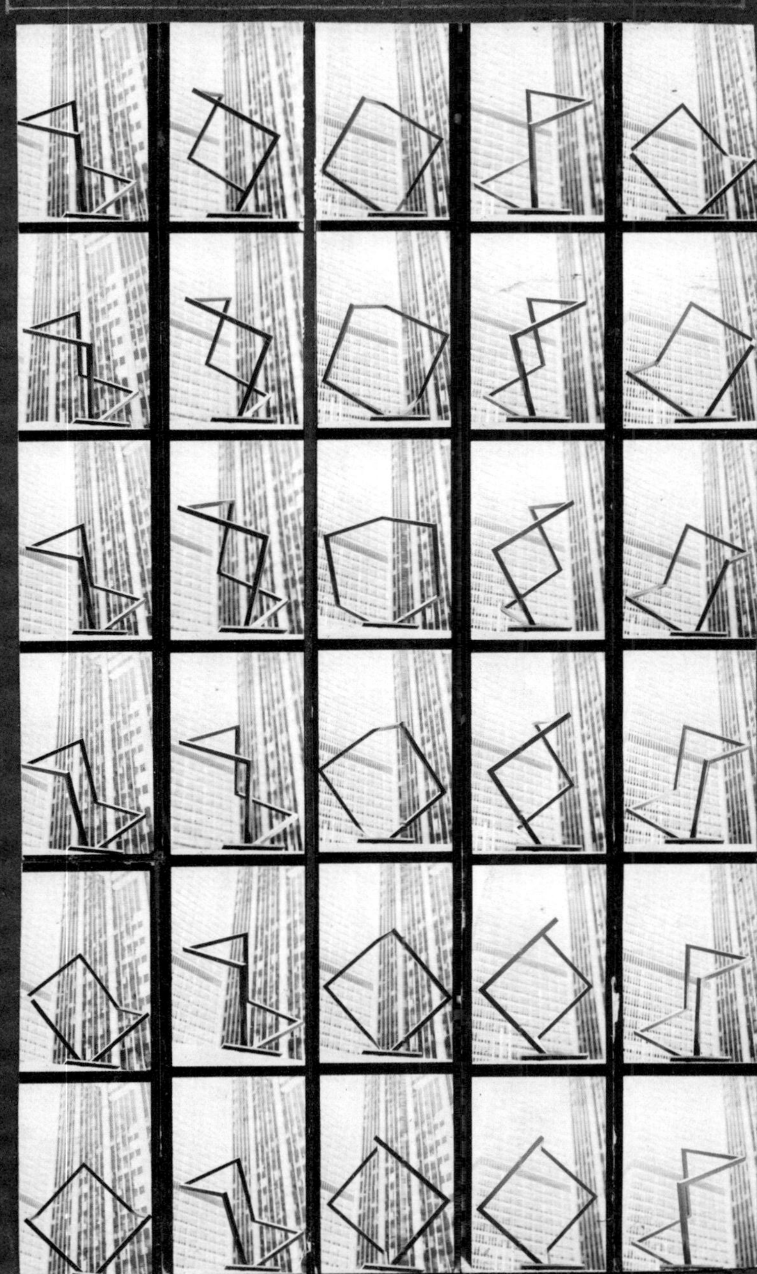

CONCRETIZING THE SPATIAL REDEFINITION OF ONE CUBE SEEN FROM 36 POINTS OF VIEW 1972

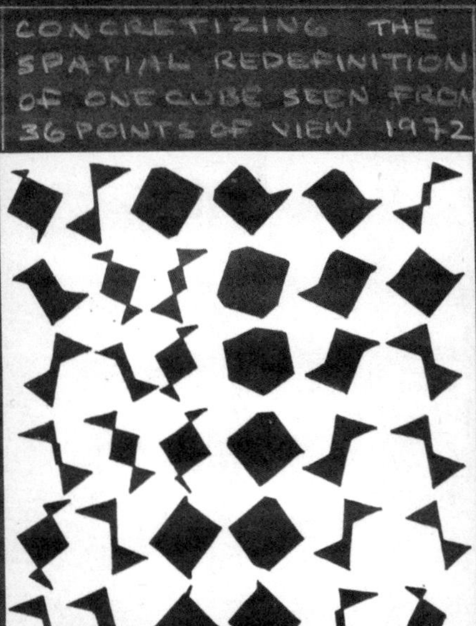

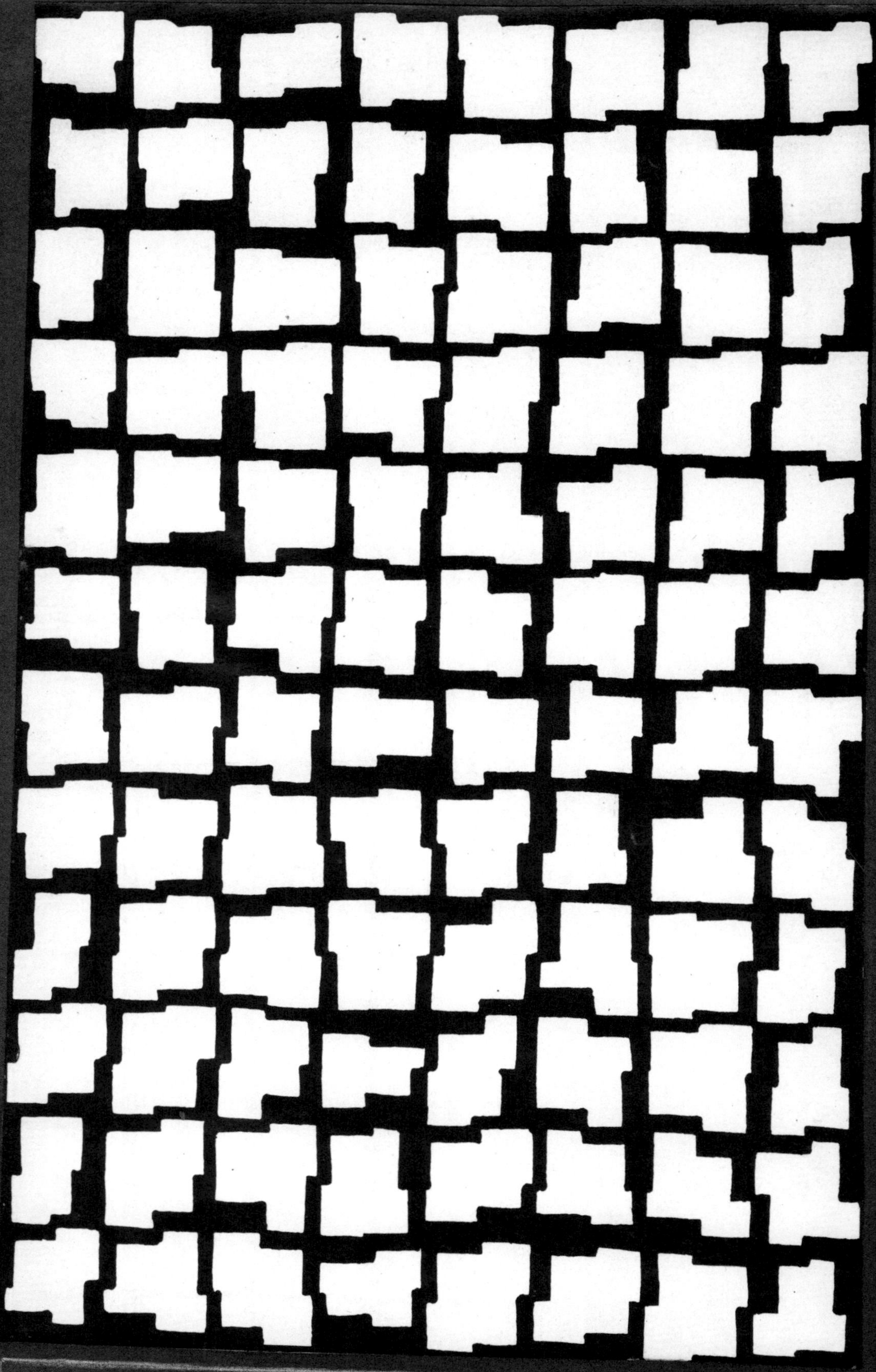

RANDOM PENETRATION BY FOUR
CONSTANTS OF PROGRESSIVE DISPLACEMENT
OF A FIELD OF 96 EQUAL ELEMENTS 1965

WHERE SPACE
BECOMES MASS
BECOMES MATTER

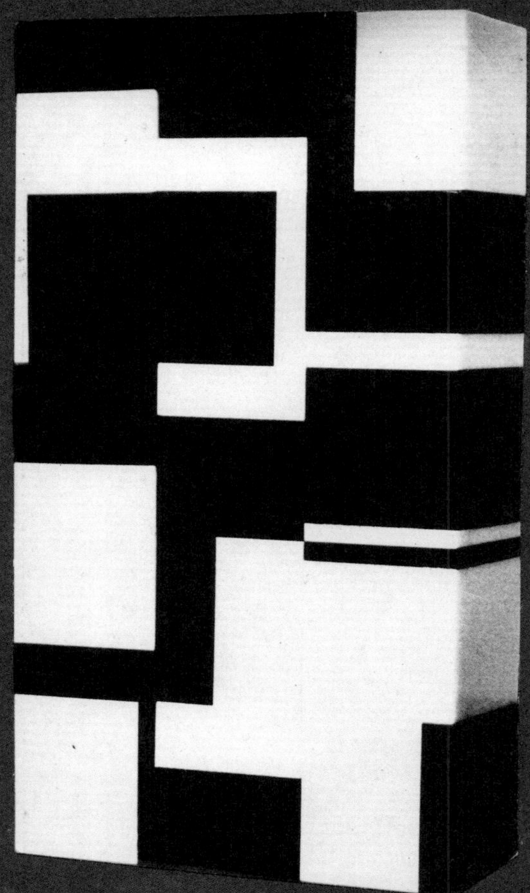

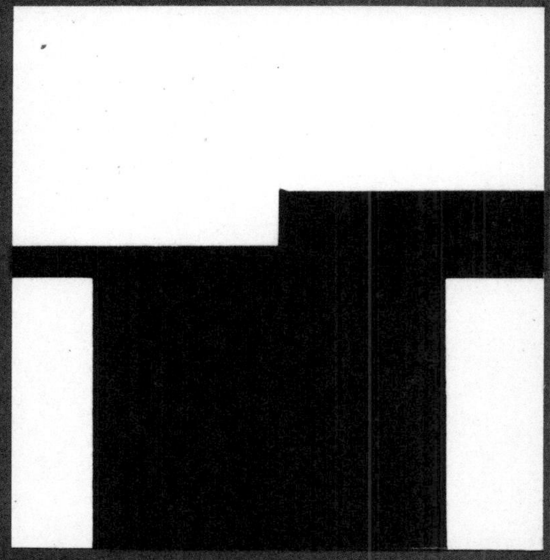

1 OUT OF A POSSIBLE 1,048,576
WHERE SPACE BECOMES MATTER
BECOMES VOLUME • 1965–1975
INTERIOR EXTERIOR SPACE
THE INSIDE–OUTSIDE HOUSE 1970

CONTAINED POSSIBILITY
STRUCTURE
LIMITATION: 281,792,804,290
MARBLE CONSTANTS • 1970
= VOLUME RELOCATION • ITALY
COMPUTER PROGRAMMED • 1974
16 MM FILM 1975–6
= INTERCHANGEABLE FOCUS
MASS LEVITATION
CONCRETE SPACE

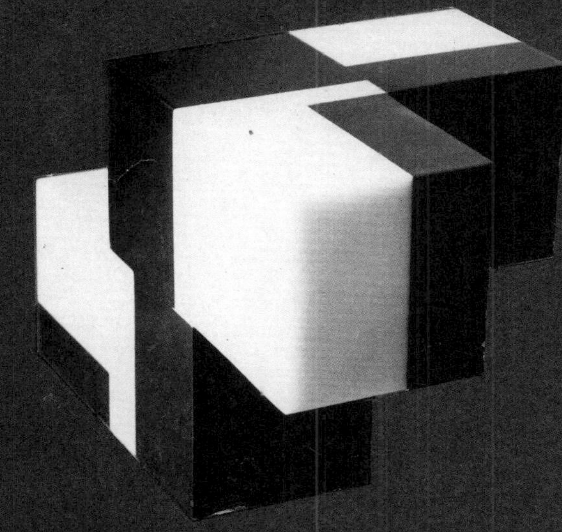

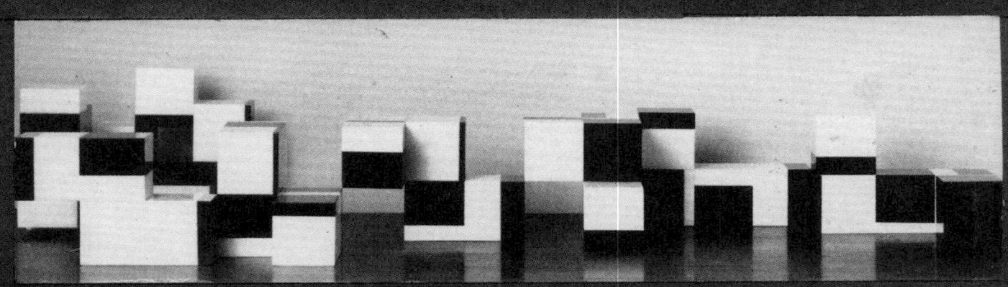

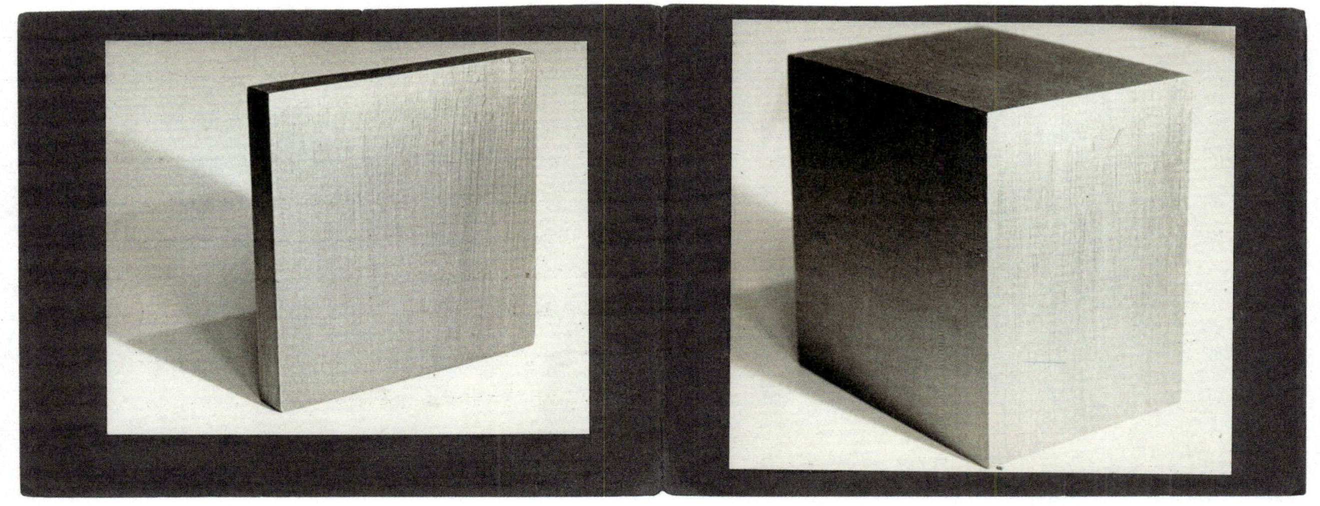

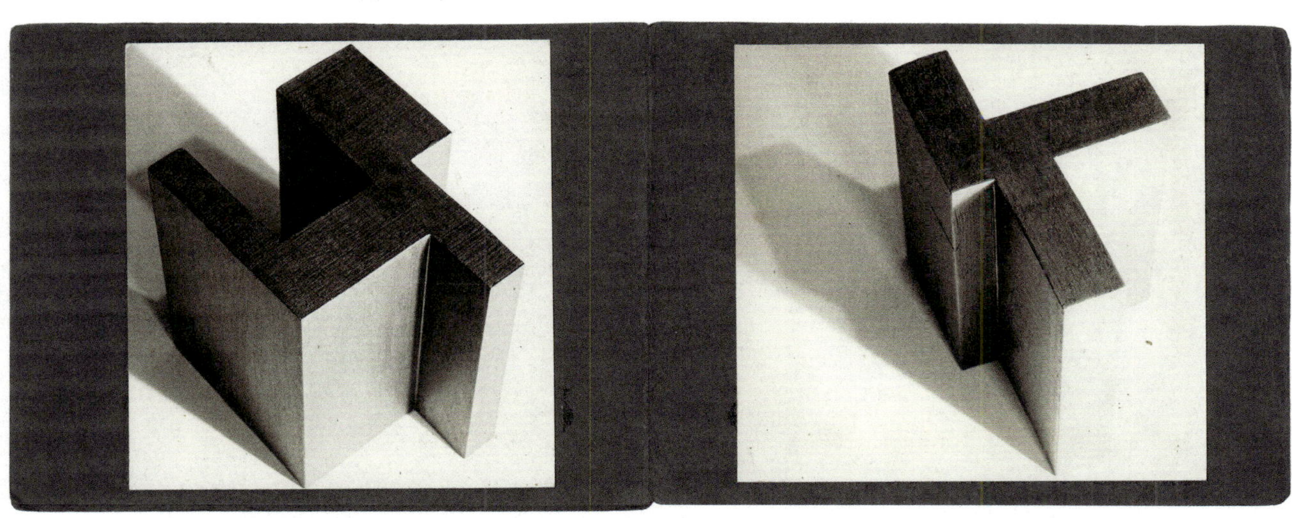

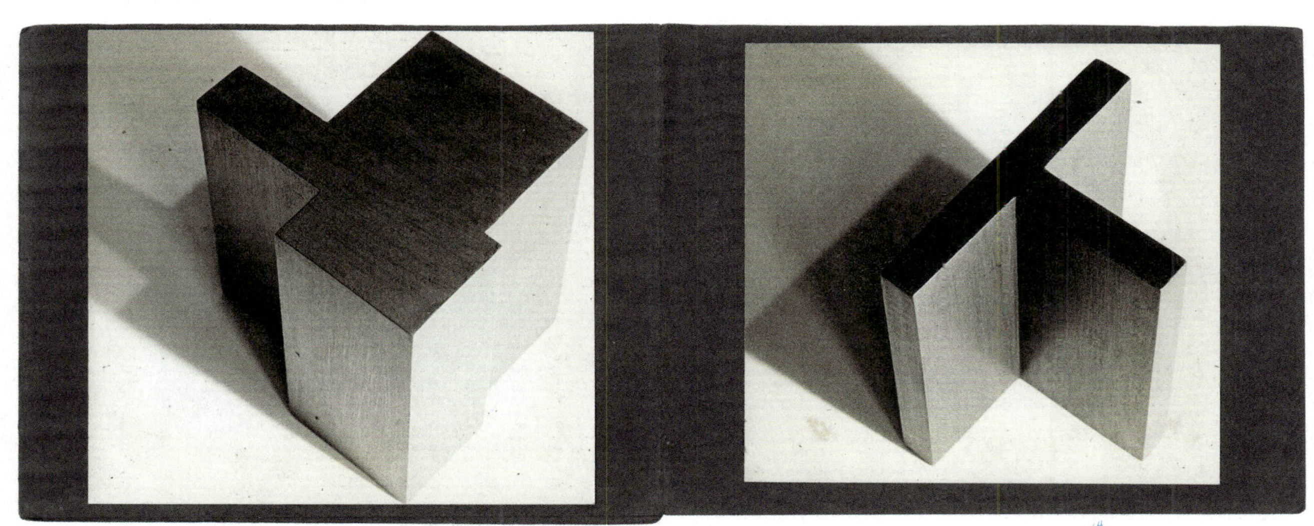

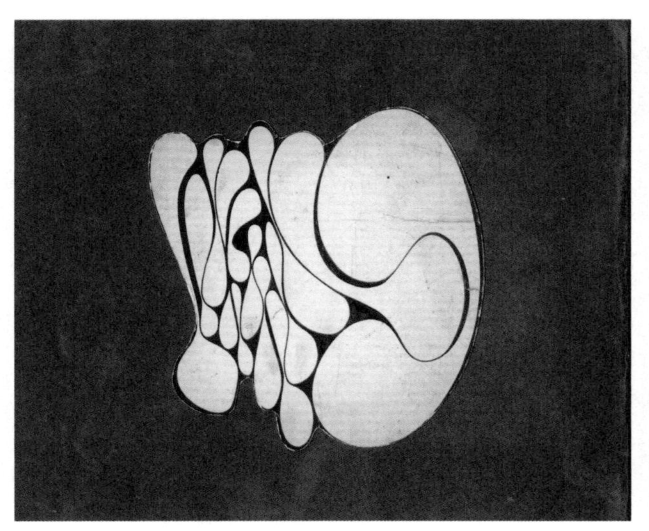

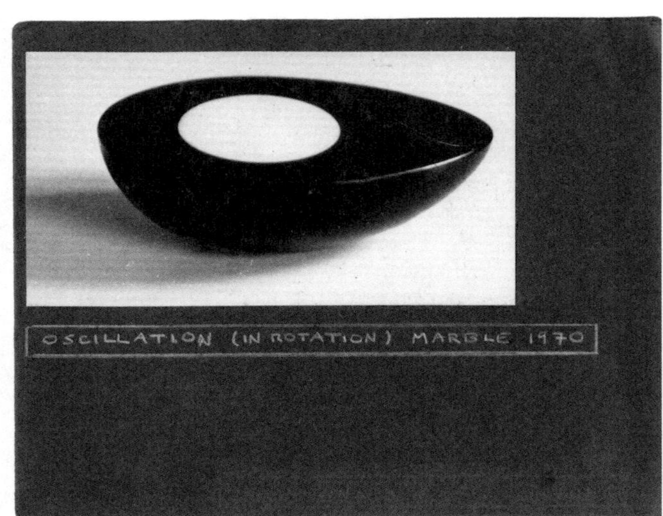
OSCILLATION (IN ROTATION) MARBLE 1970

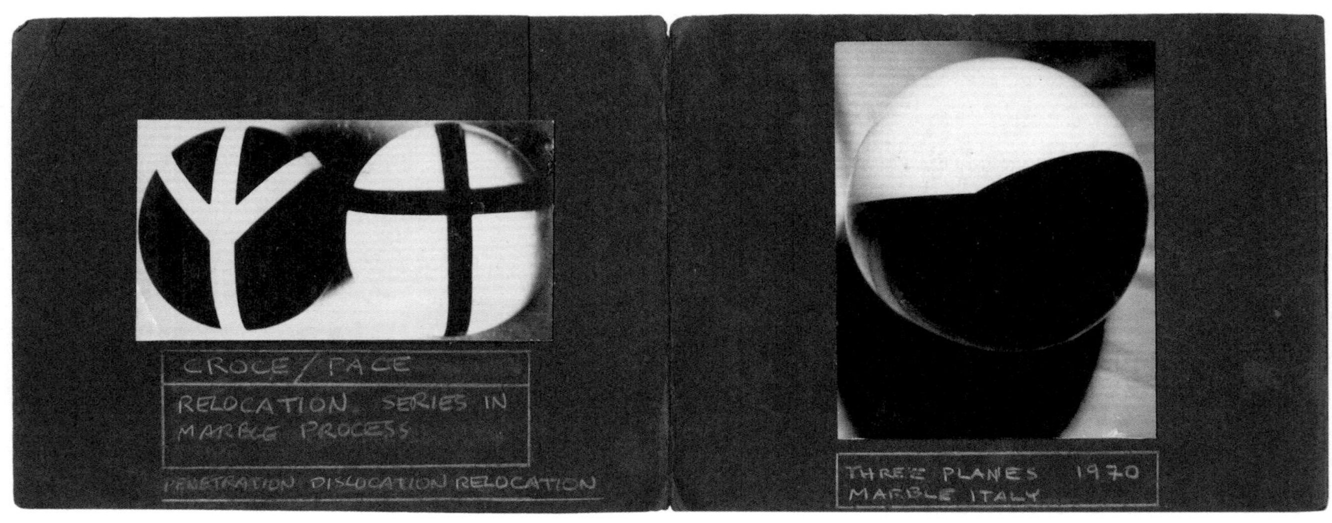
CROCE / PACE
RELOCATION SERIES IN
MARBLE PROCESS
PENETRATION DISLOCATION RELOCATION
THREE PLANES 1970
MARBLE ITALY

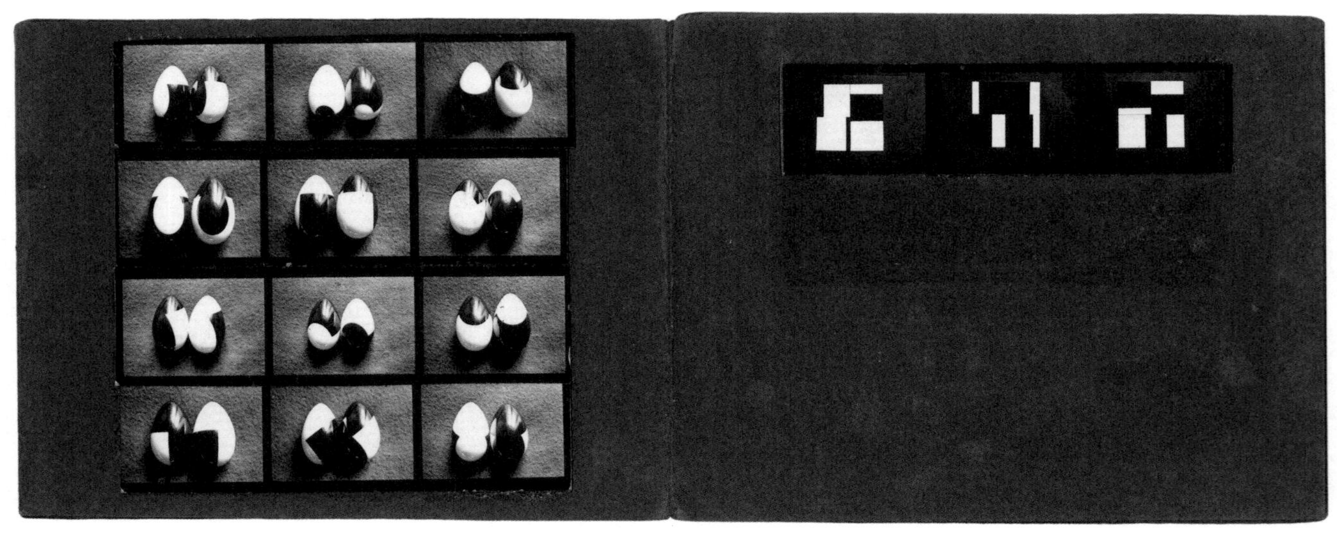

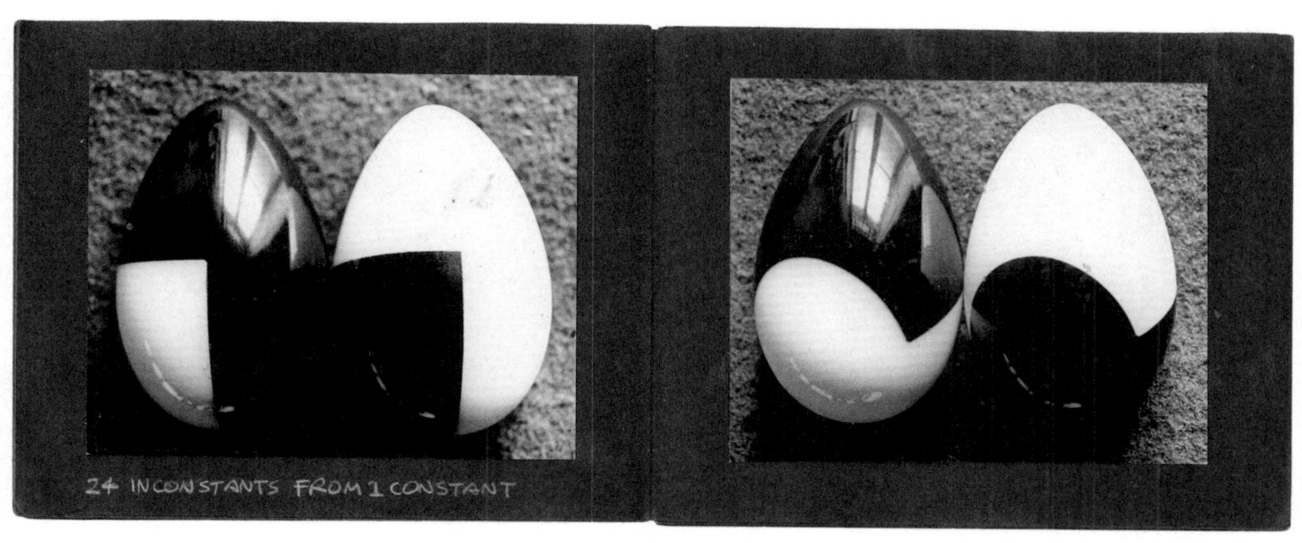
24 INCONSTANTS FROM 1 CONSTANT

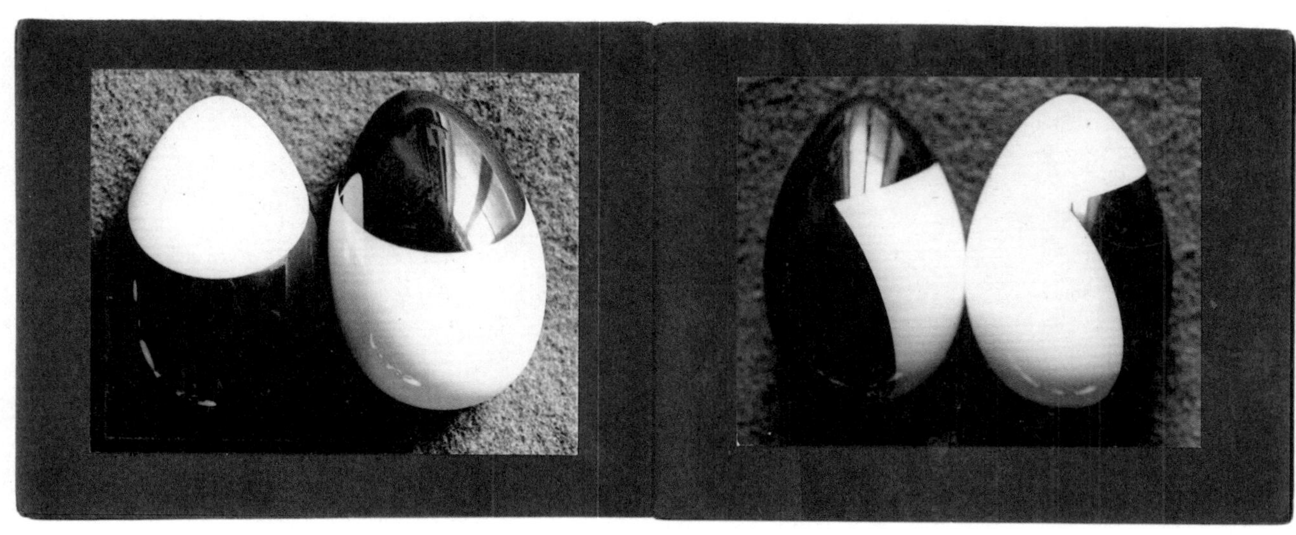

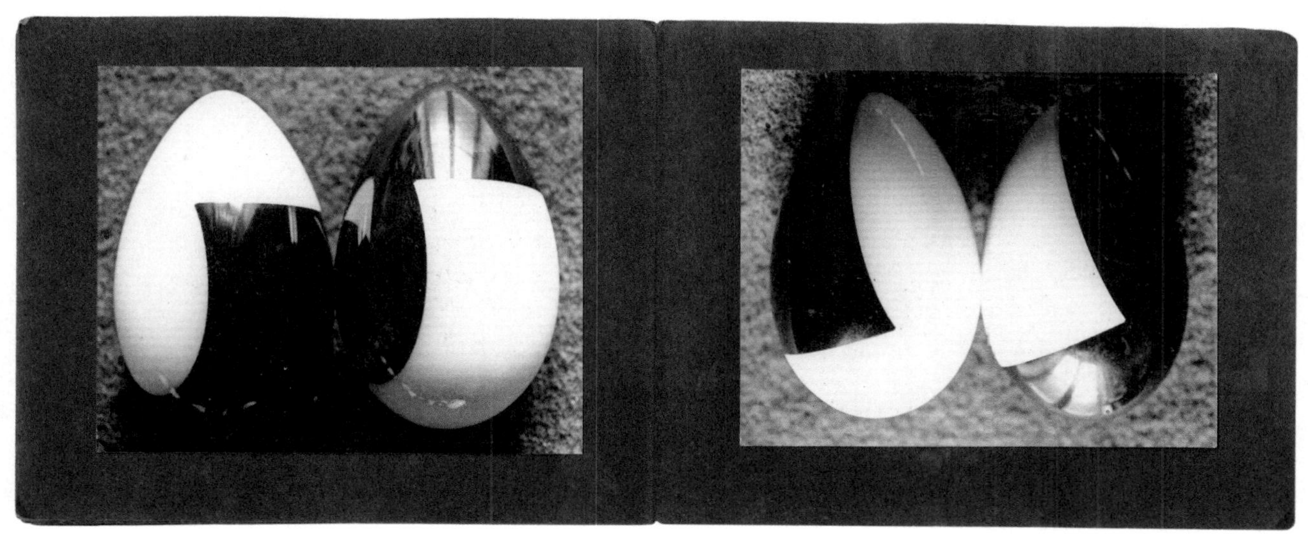

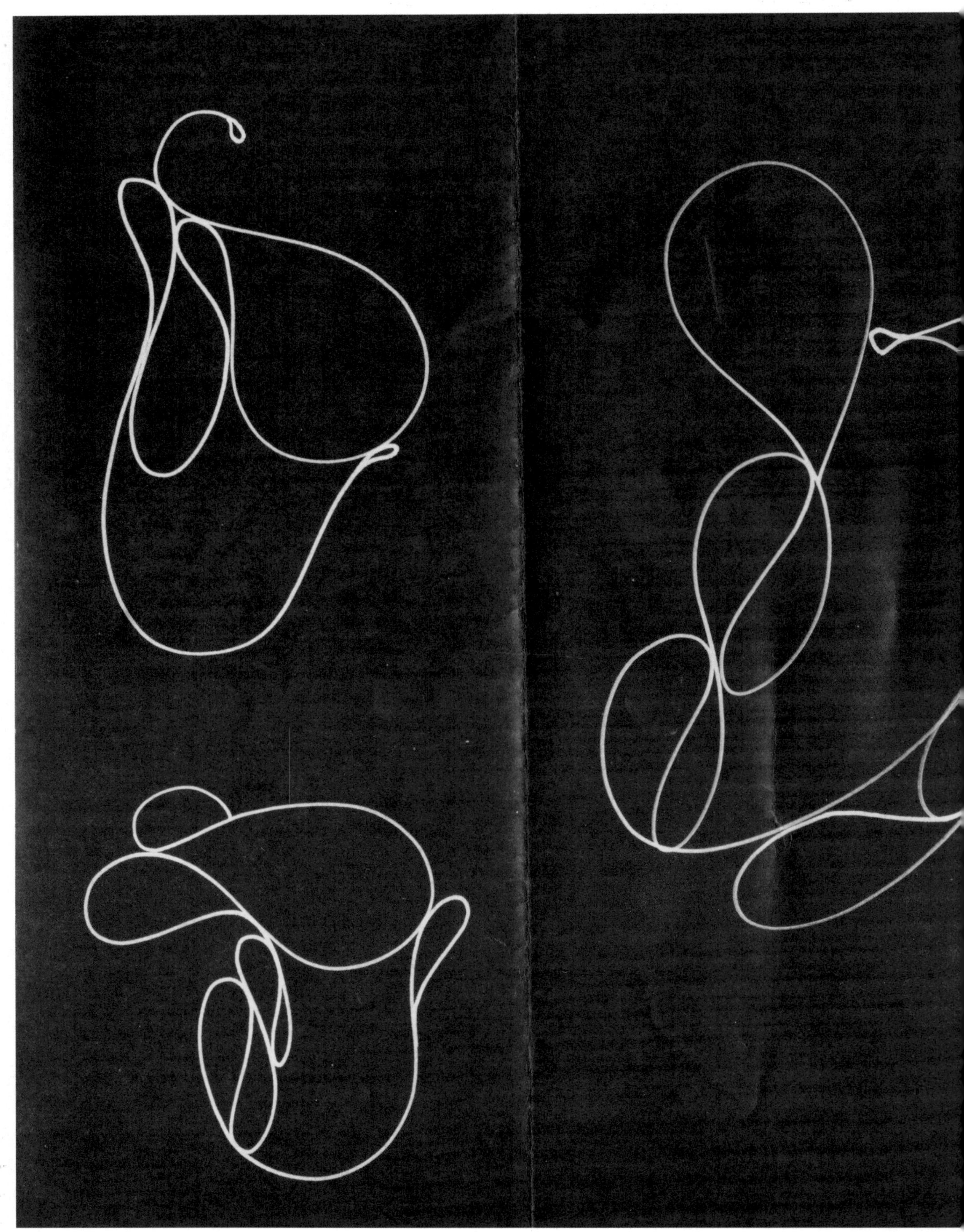

Two hours in the life of one hair photographed in the sink at one-minute intervals while agitated by running water—extending the experience with line drawing, 1974

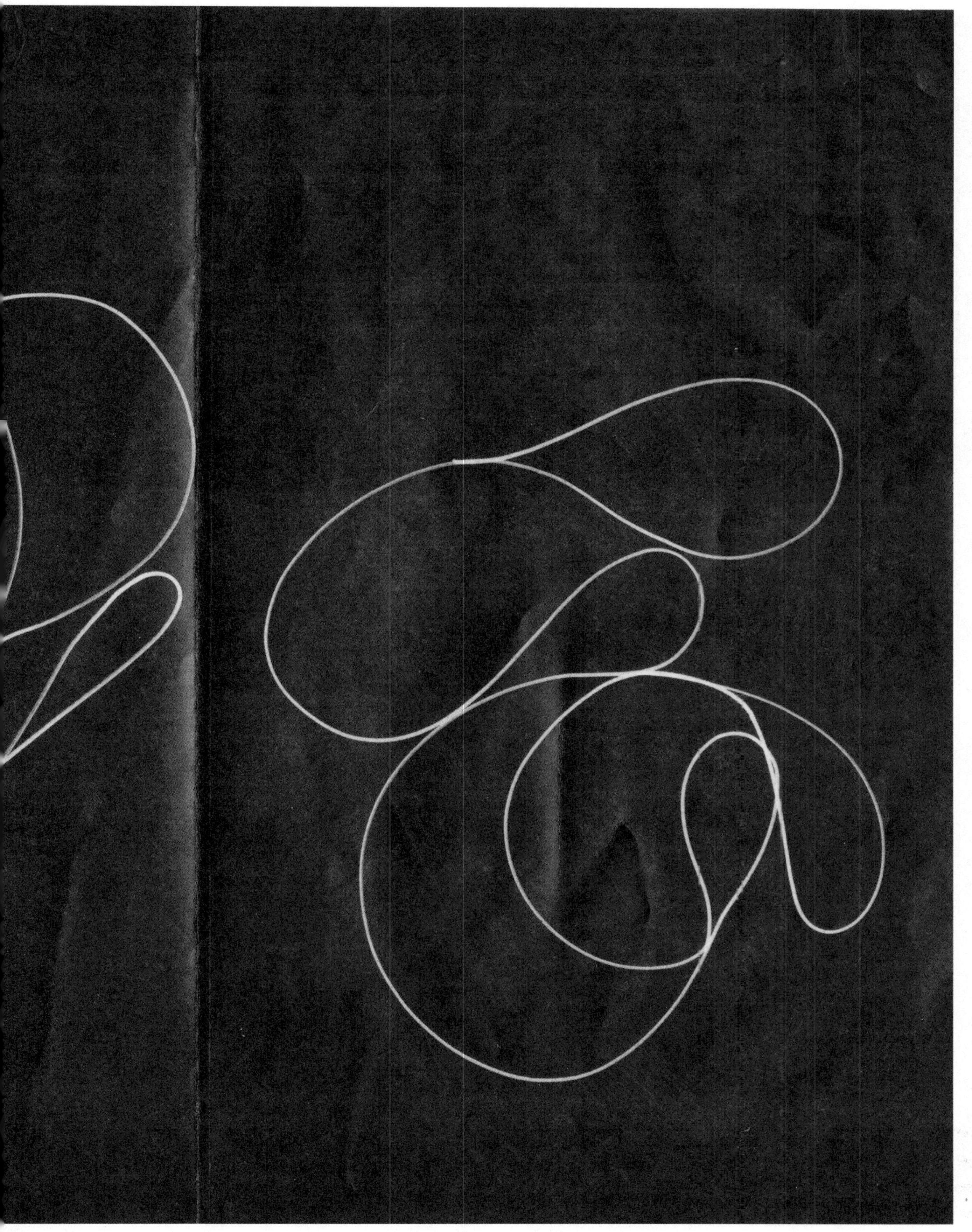

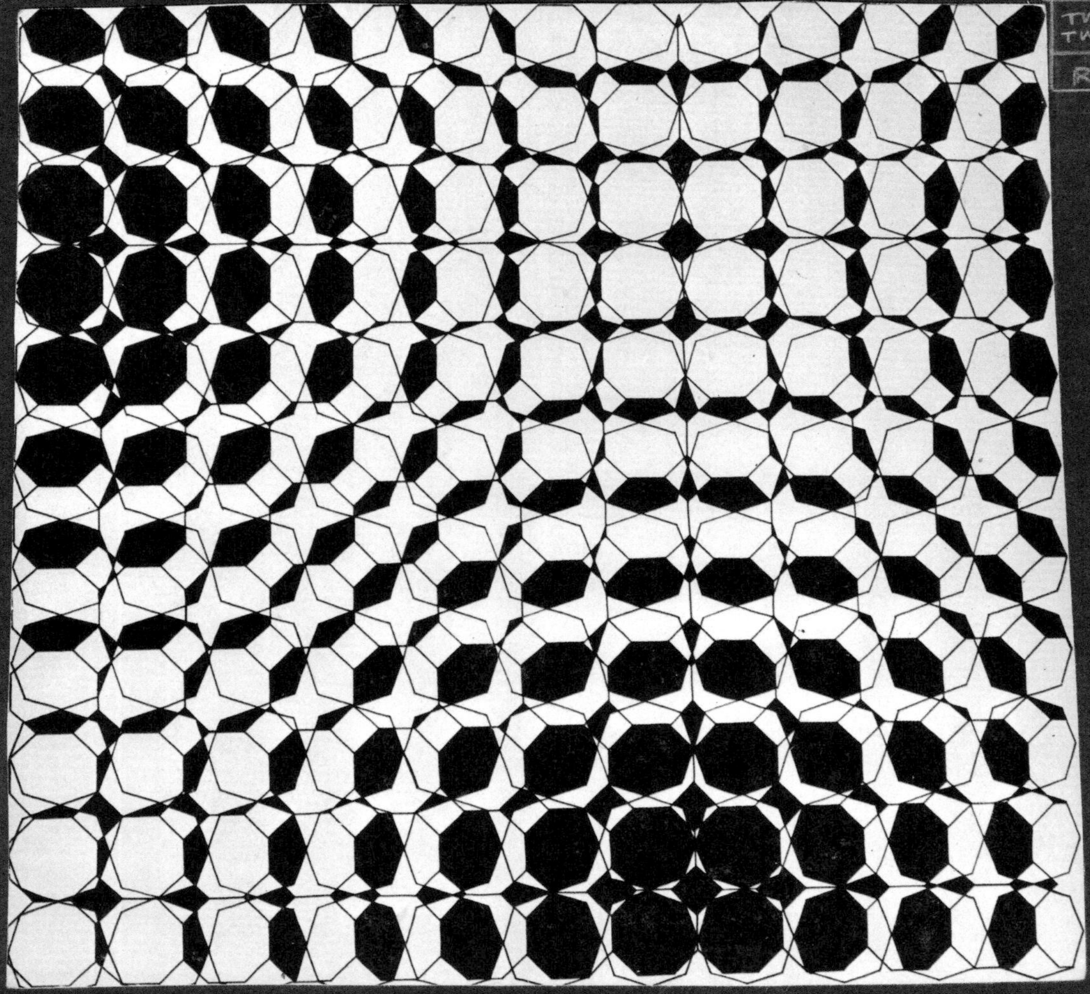

TWO CONSTANTS
TWO SURFACES

REPLICATION

ONE CONSTANT
THREE SURFACES

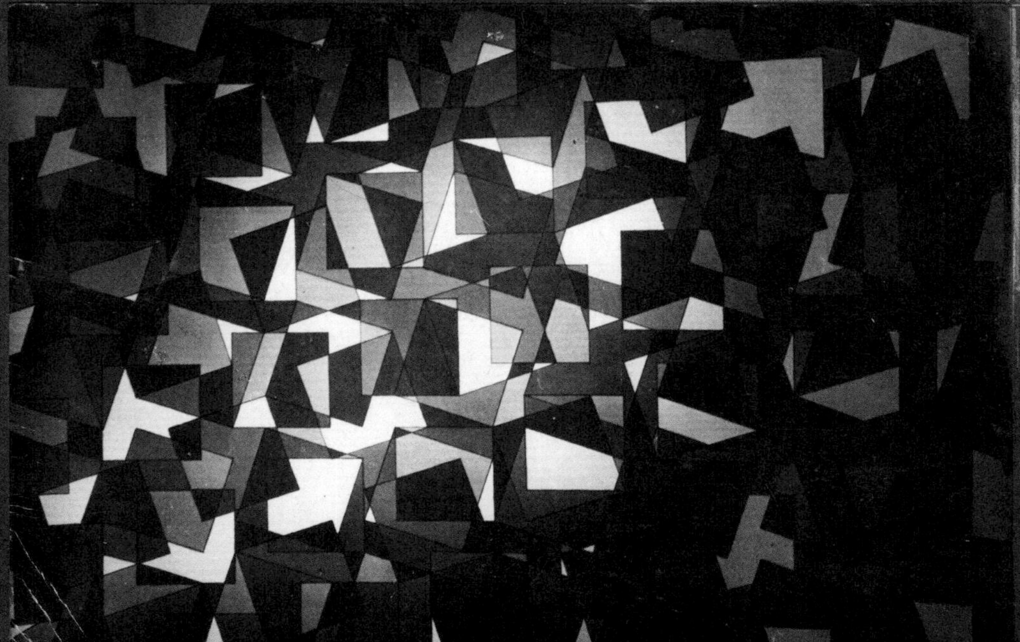

EVOLUTION THRO
CONTINUITY

LINEAR TRANSPOR
HUMAN RELATION

MULIPLE FIELD

THEORY LONDON 1

RECONSTRUCTE
1967, 1968 AF
DESTROYED BY F

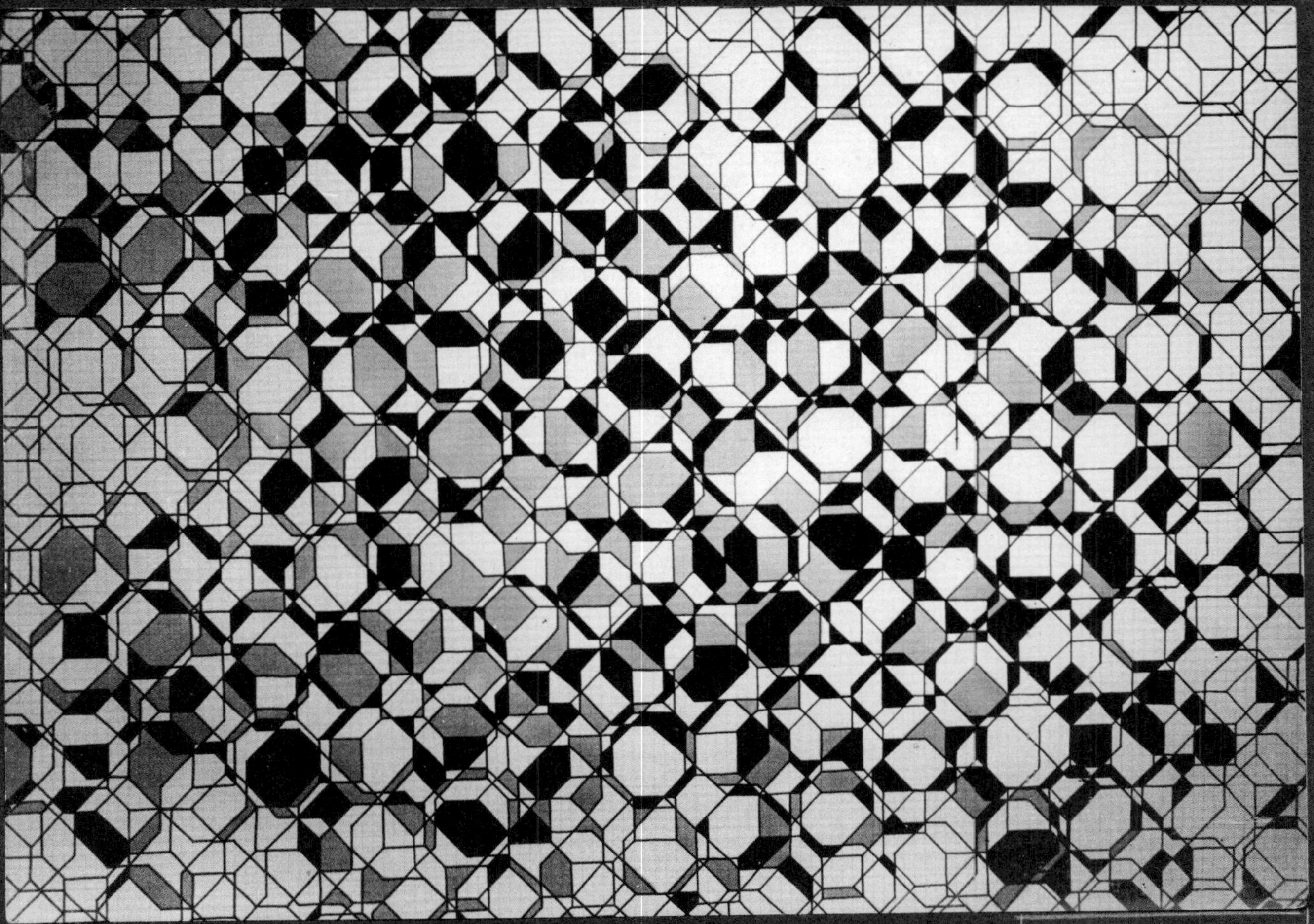

THREE CONSTANTS
THREE SURFACES

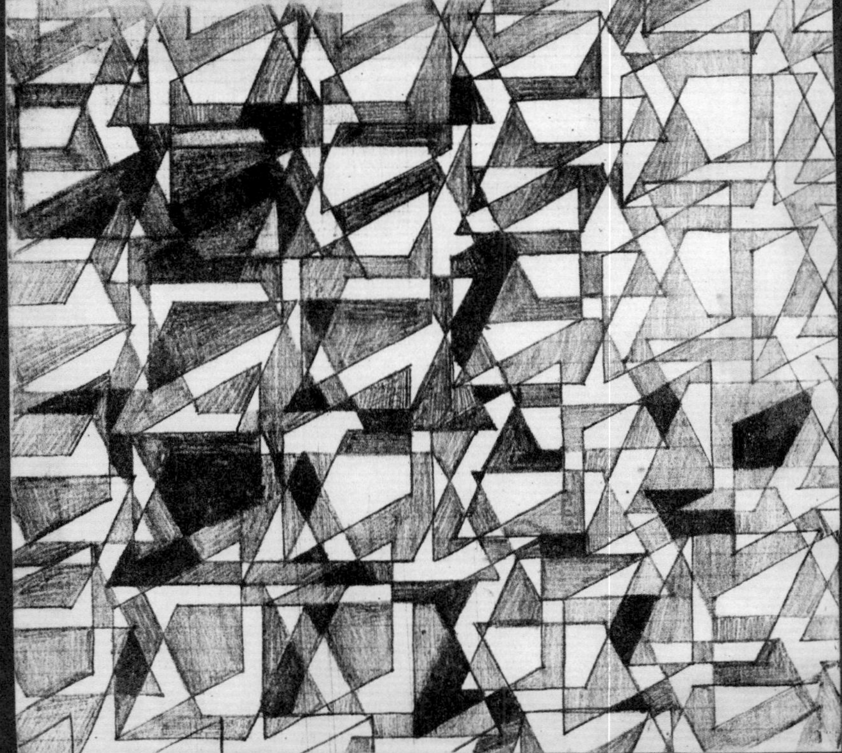

ONE CONSTANT

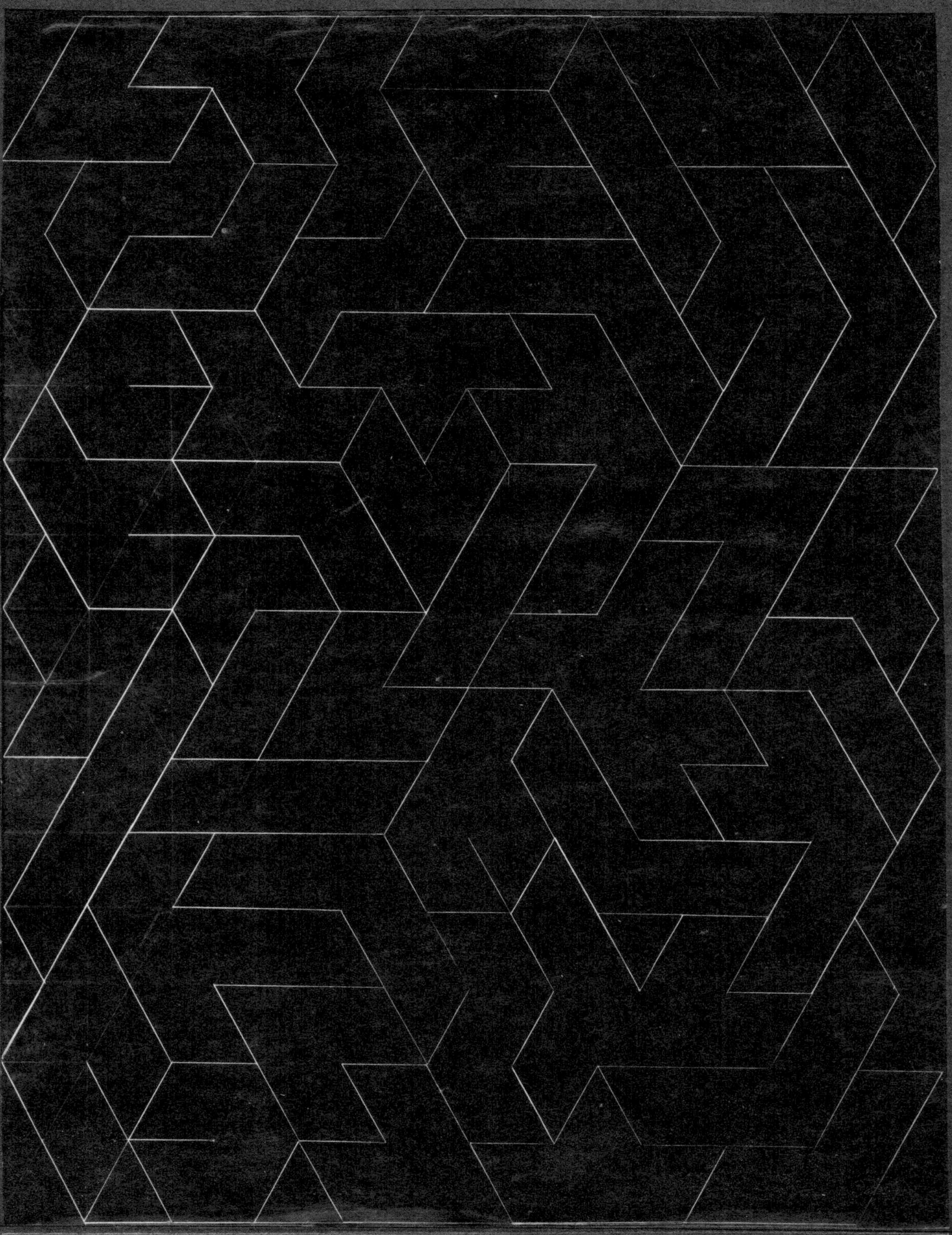

FIELD THEORY · 1962 LONDON

ONE CONSTANT
INFINITY FIELD 1974

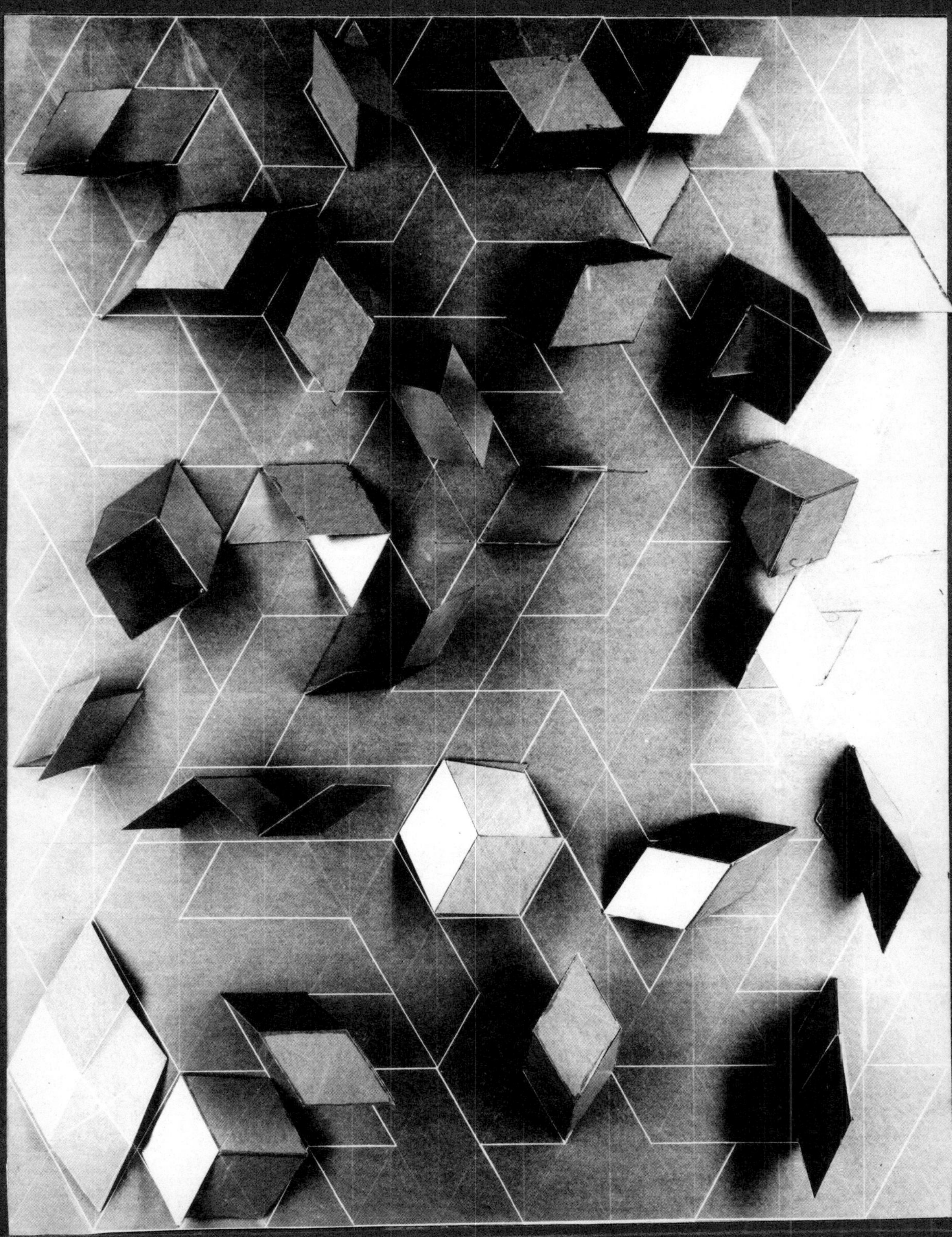

ONE CONSTANT 1969 —
EXTRACTIONS/ELEVATIONS FROM CONTINUITY FIELD

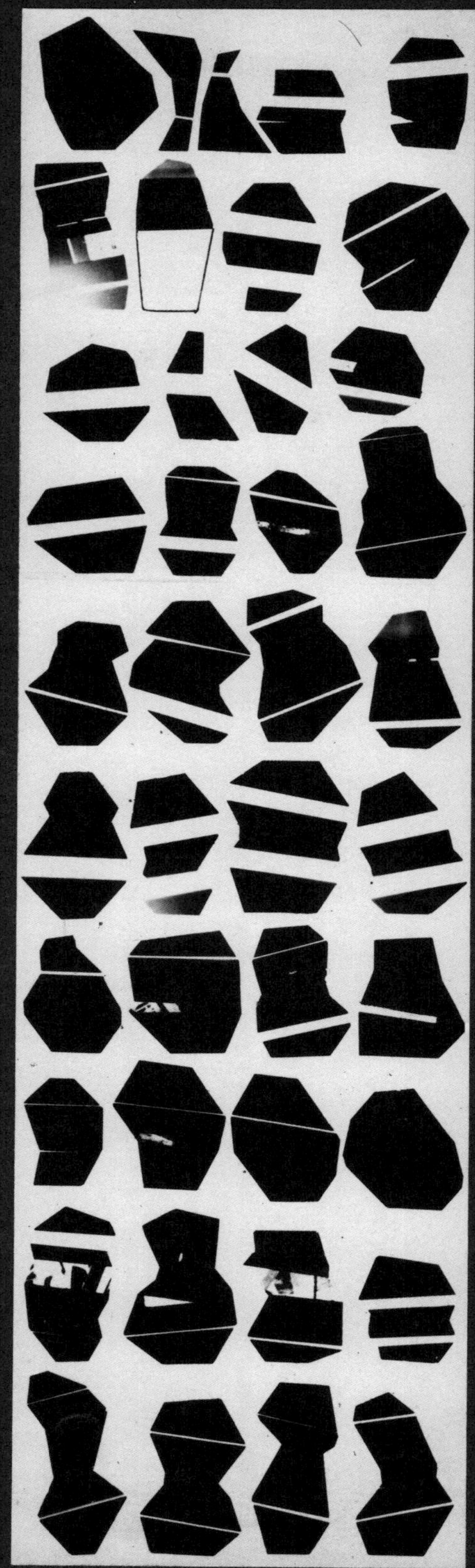
NUGGETS 1970 PARIS

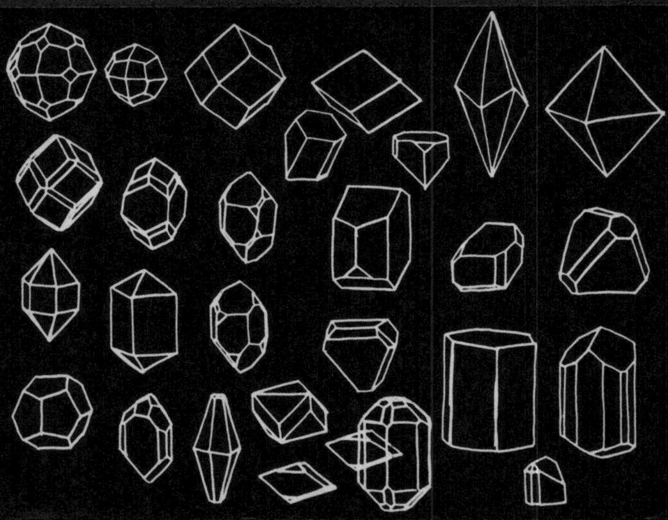

STUDIES IN CRYSTAL MORPHOLOGY -1972-

PLANE SYMMETRY AND ASSYMETRY IN ORGANIC AND NON-ORGANIC STRUCTURE

ORGANIC CONFIRMATION

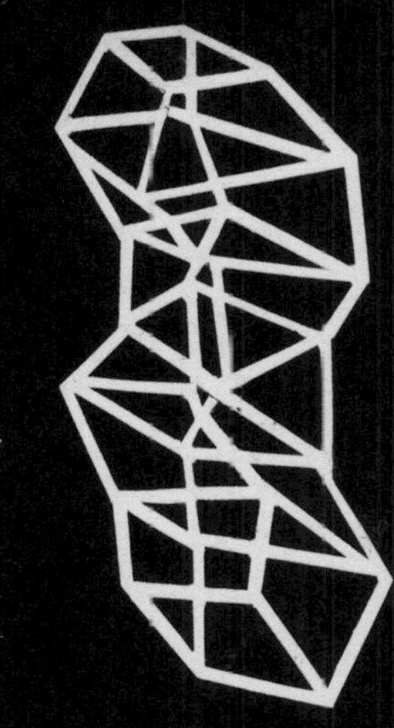

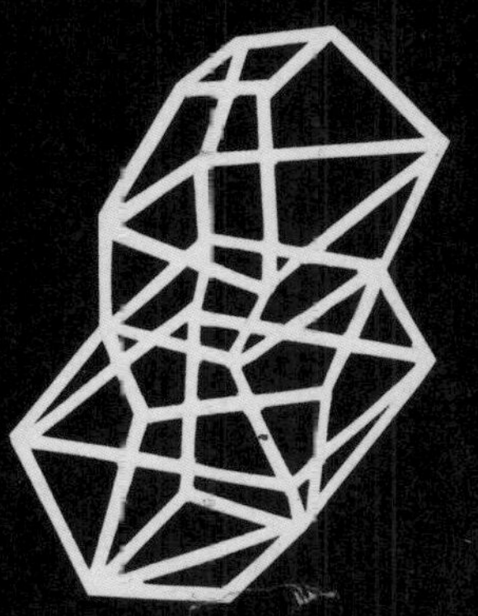

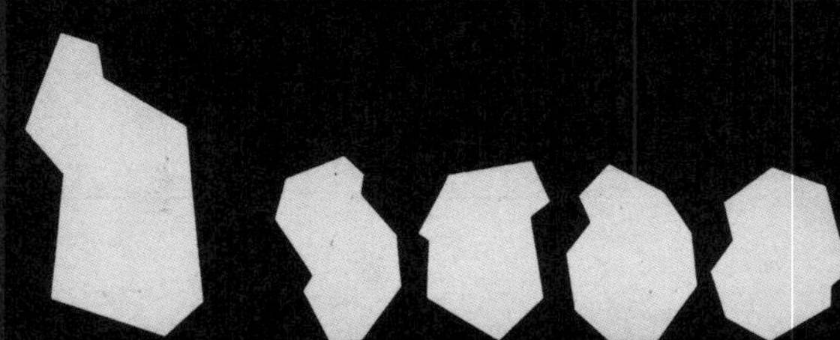

WHERE SCALE DETERMINES ATTITUDE 1970

OPTIONS FOR OPEN STRUCTURE WITH NO TWO PARALLELS 1971

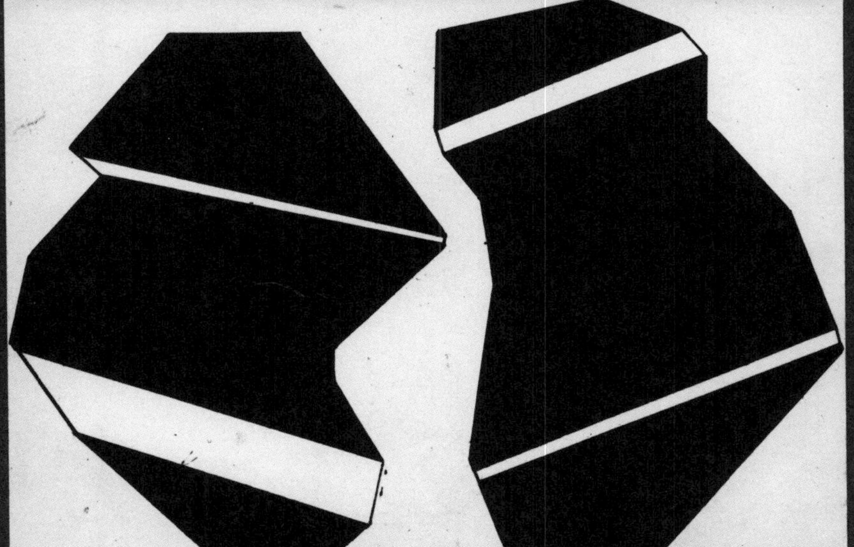

30 + 30 SURFACES 1970

14 PLANES OF BALANCE-1971- NOT PHOTOGRAPHED

DETAIL FROM STUDY AT LEFT - 30 + 30 SURFACES

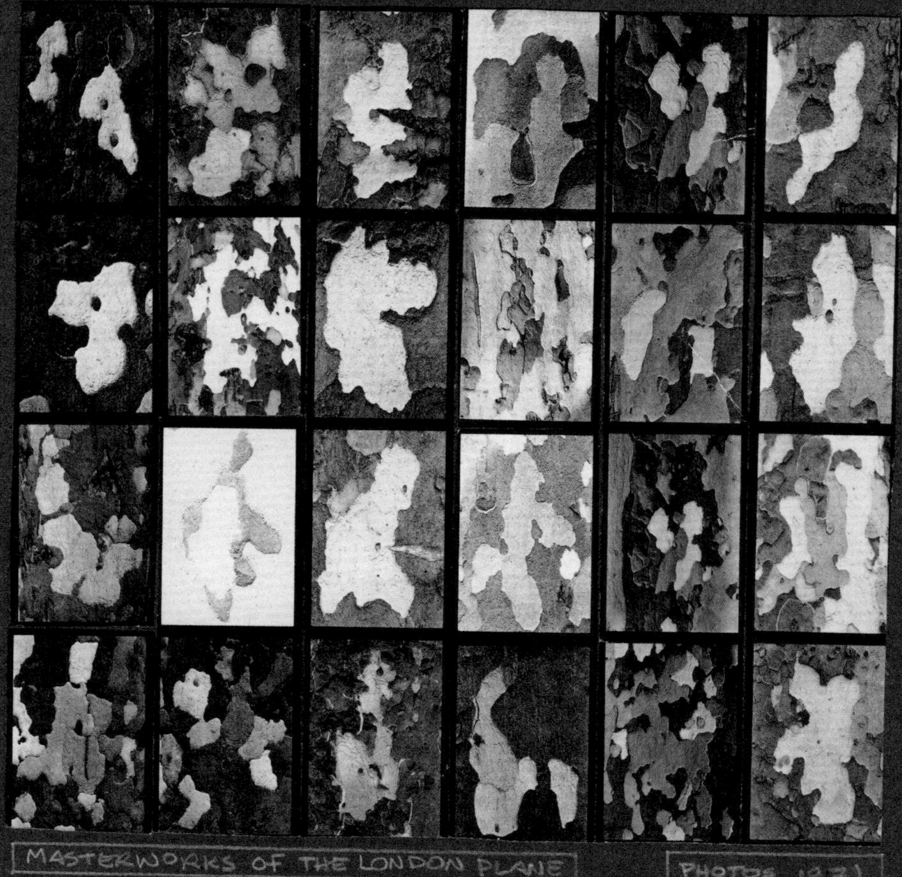

MASTERWORKS OF THE LONDON PLANE

PHOTOS 1971

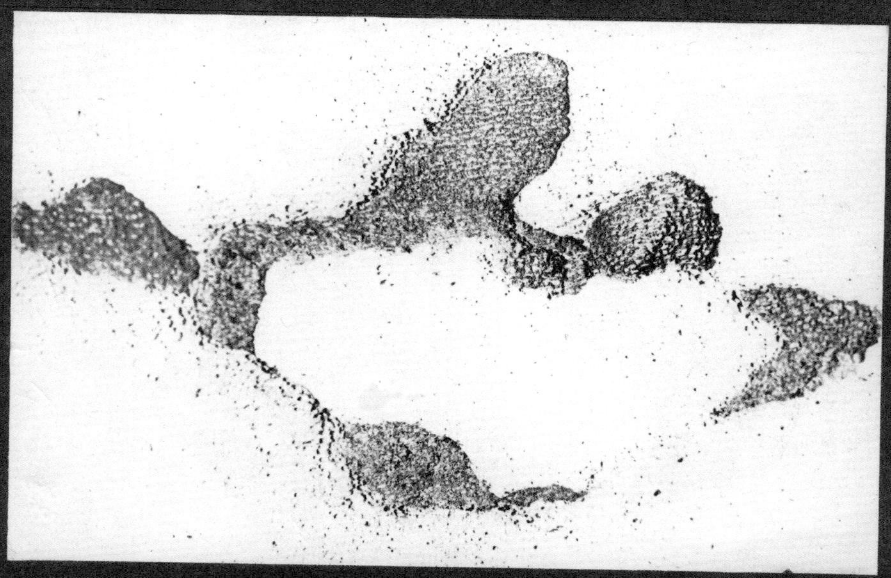

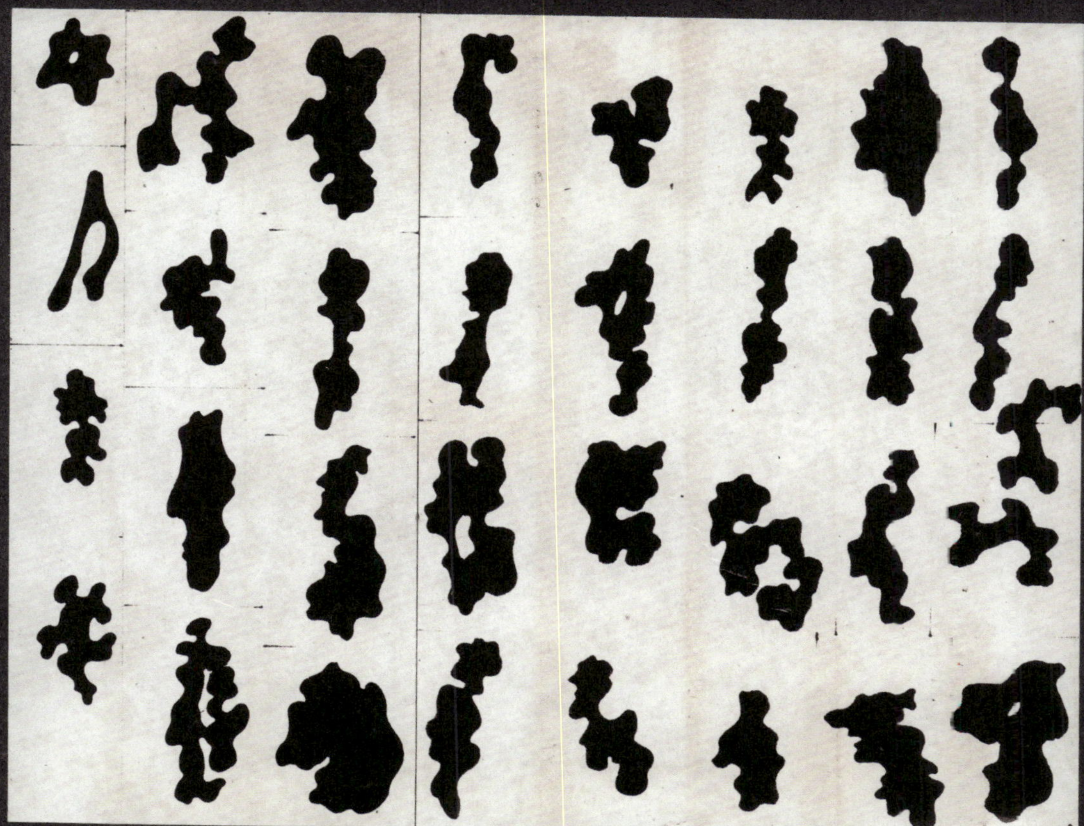

EXCERPT FROM PHOTOS

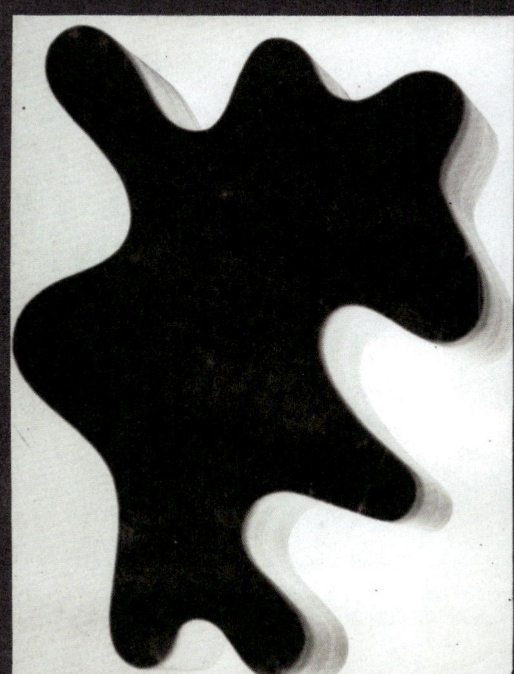

1,000 PHOTOS OF FACE AND FIGURE — ORGANIC + ISOLATED ELEMENTS FOR REDEVELOPMENT

PARIS 1970-71

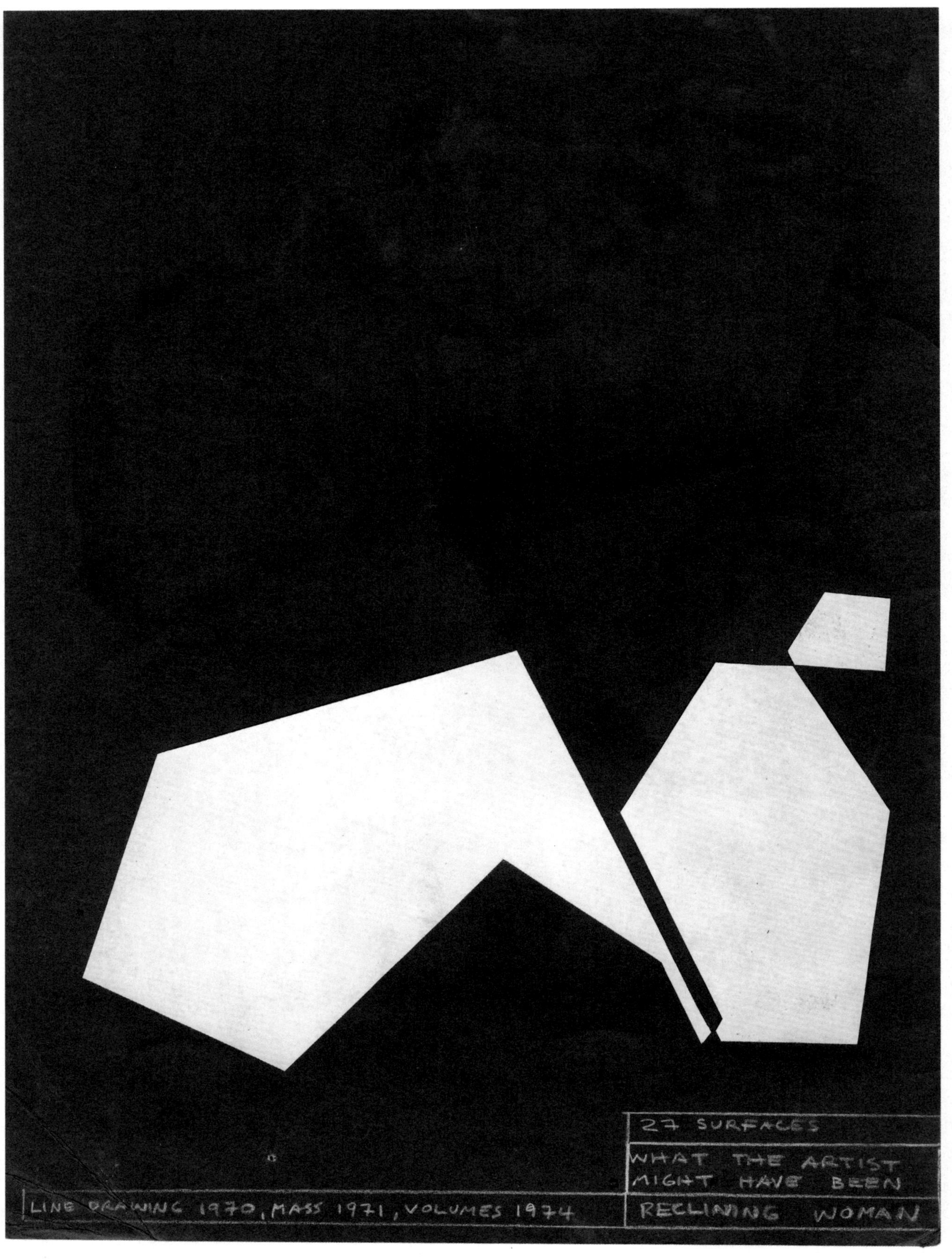

Reclining Woman, from the series *27 Surfaces, What the Artist Might Have Been*, 1970

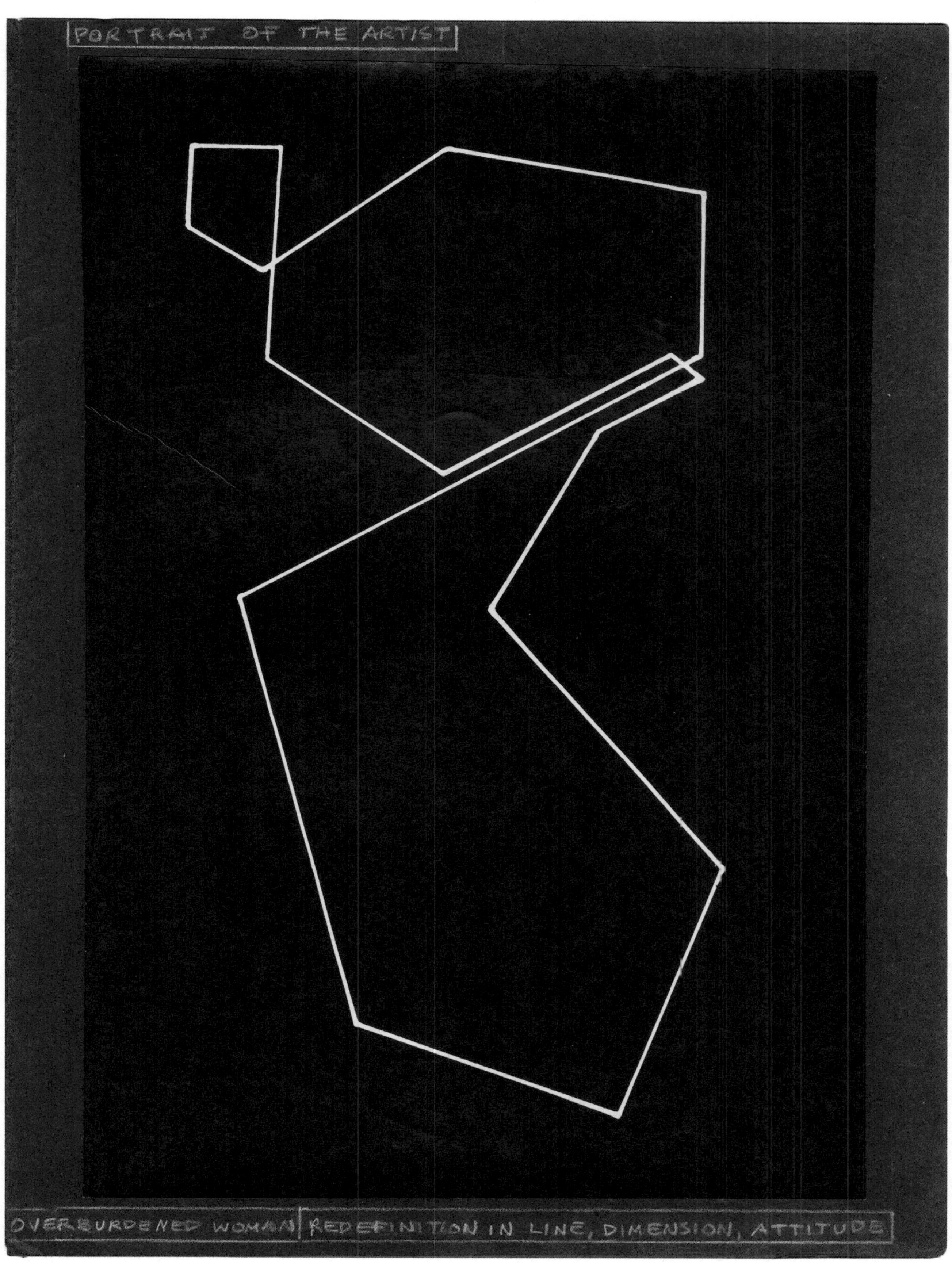

Overburdened Woman, from the series *27 Surfaces, What the Artist Might Have Been*, 1970

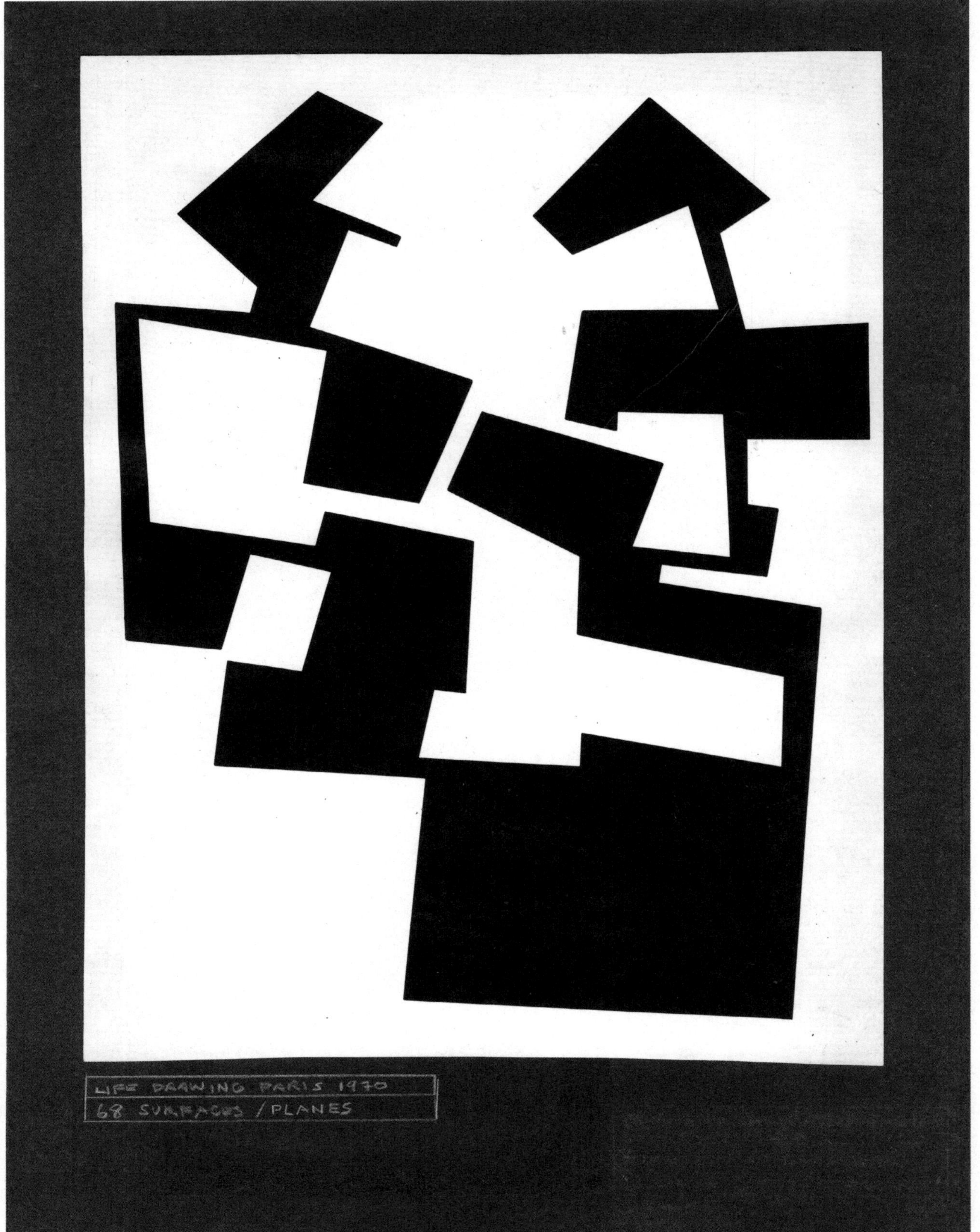

 68 Surfaces / Planes, Paris, 1970

Sculpture

“I made a dozen eggs using one angle. I used black and white stone. I cut through both stones at the same time using a jig, and then I replaced the white bits with black and vice versa with glue, then turned it on a lathe ... I didn’t know what was going to develop. I just felt that this was what I had to do ... And then I discovered that by using my intuition, whatever forces encouraged me to do that, I developed more intuition. My intuition seems to come from some outside energy, cosmological, if you will. It told me to do this.”

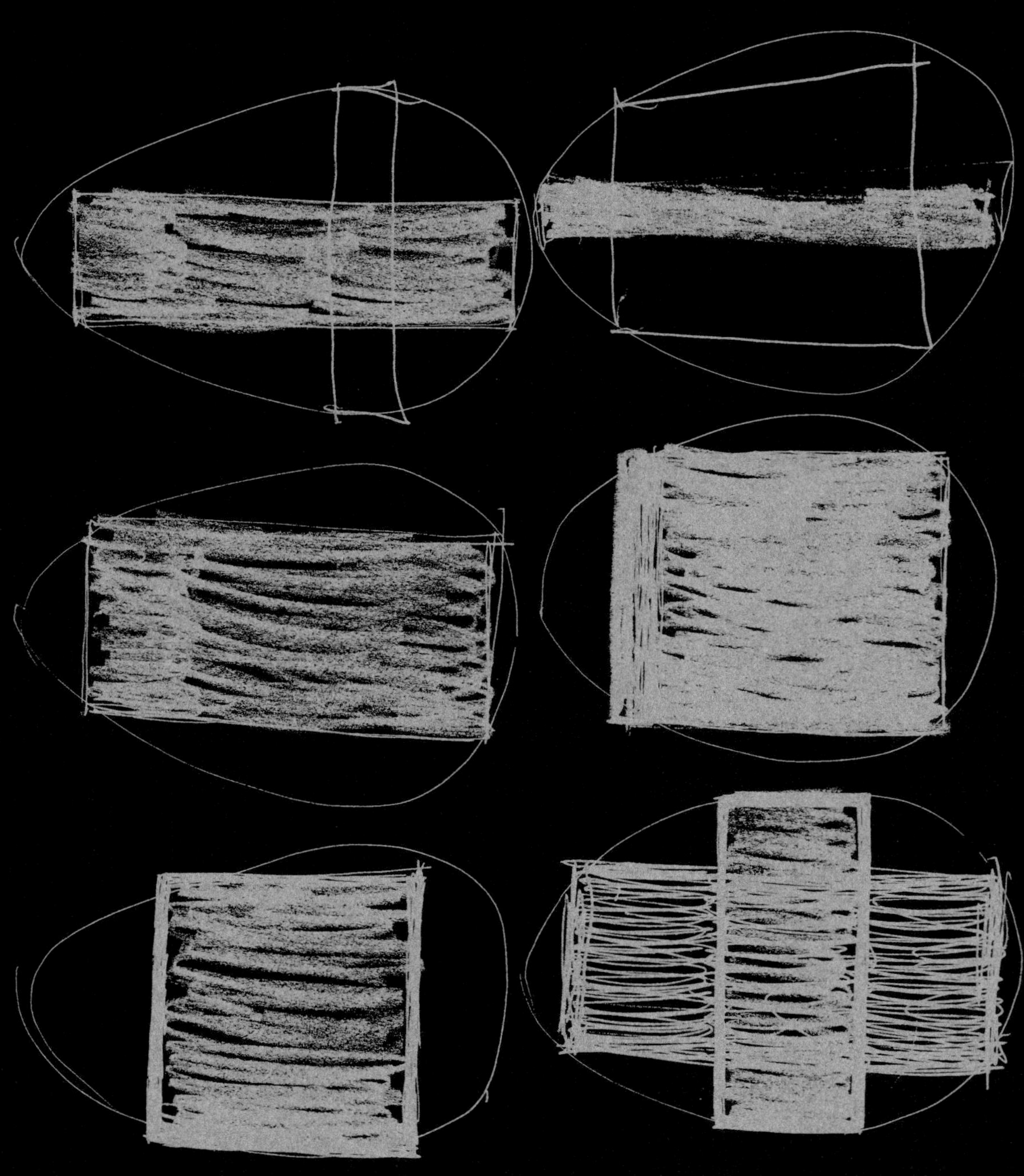

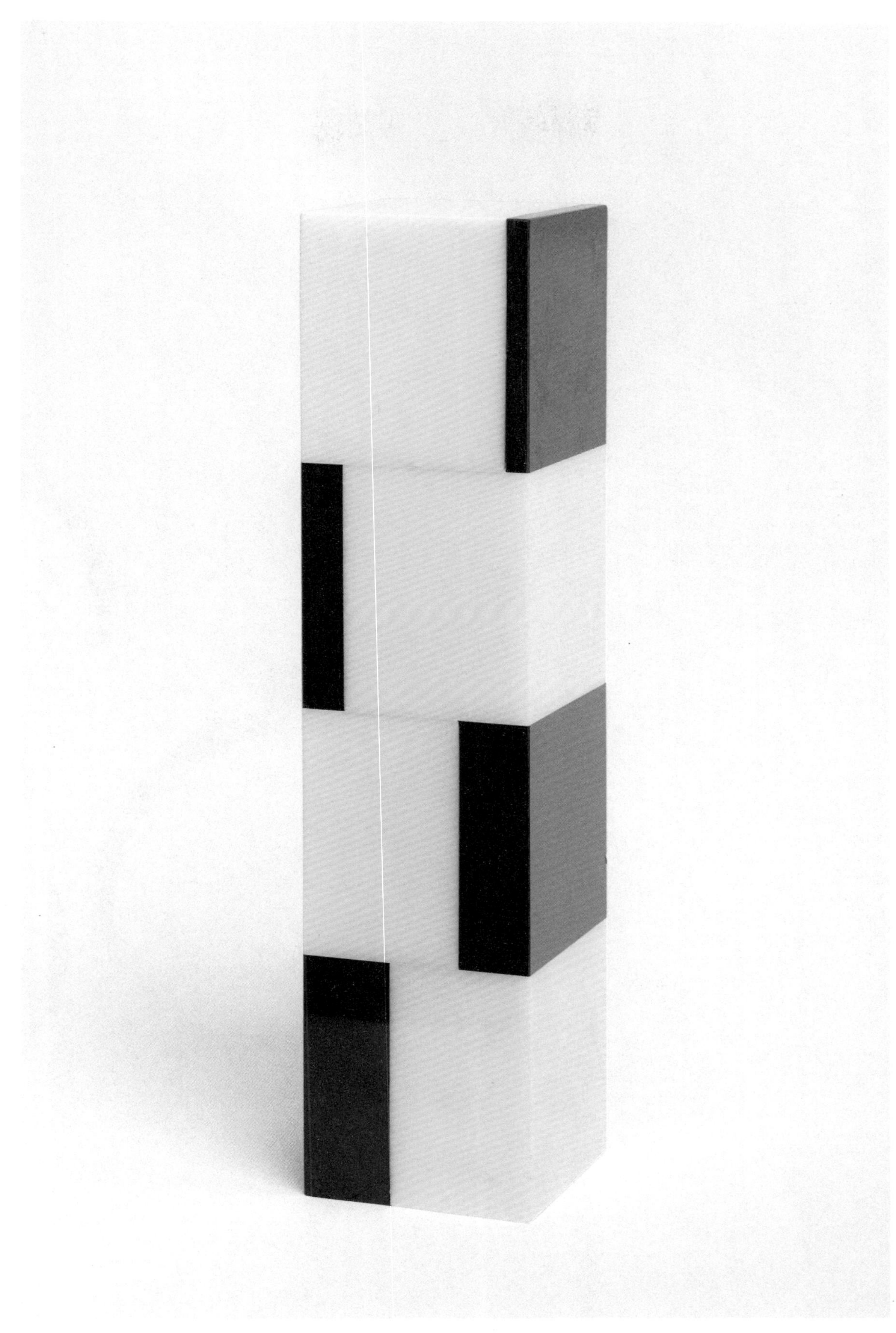

Mass Levitation. Concrete Space. Where Space Becomes Matter, Matter Becomes Volume**,**
from the series *The Inside-Outside House*, marble, 1965–75

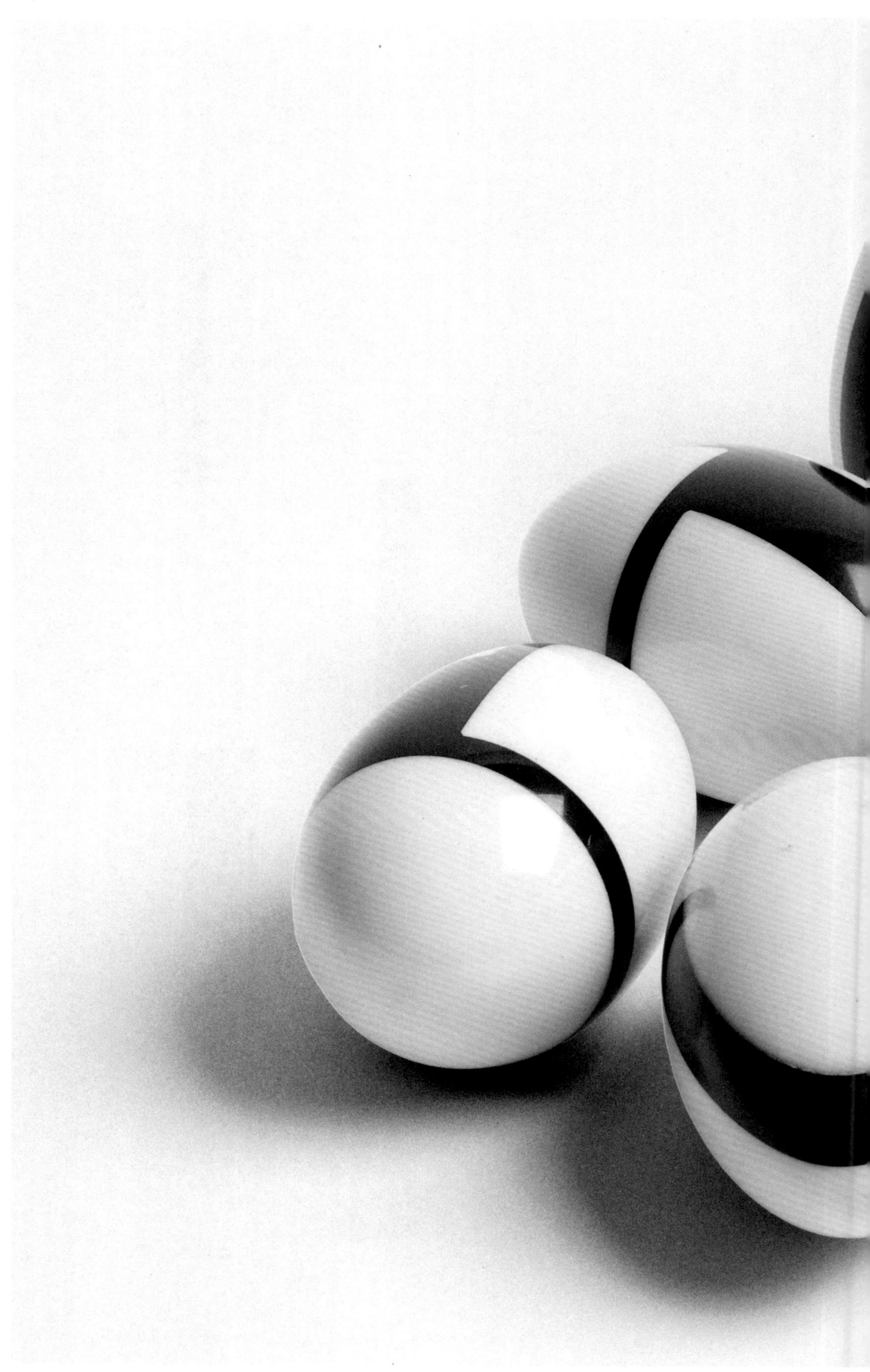

From the series *Options for an Angle: 24 Inconstants from One Constant*, marble, 1970

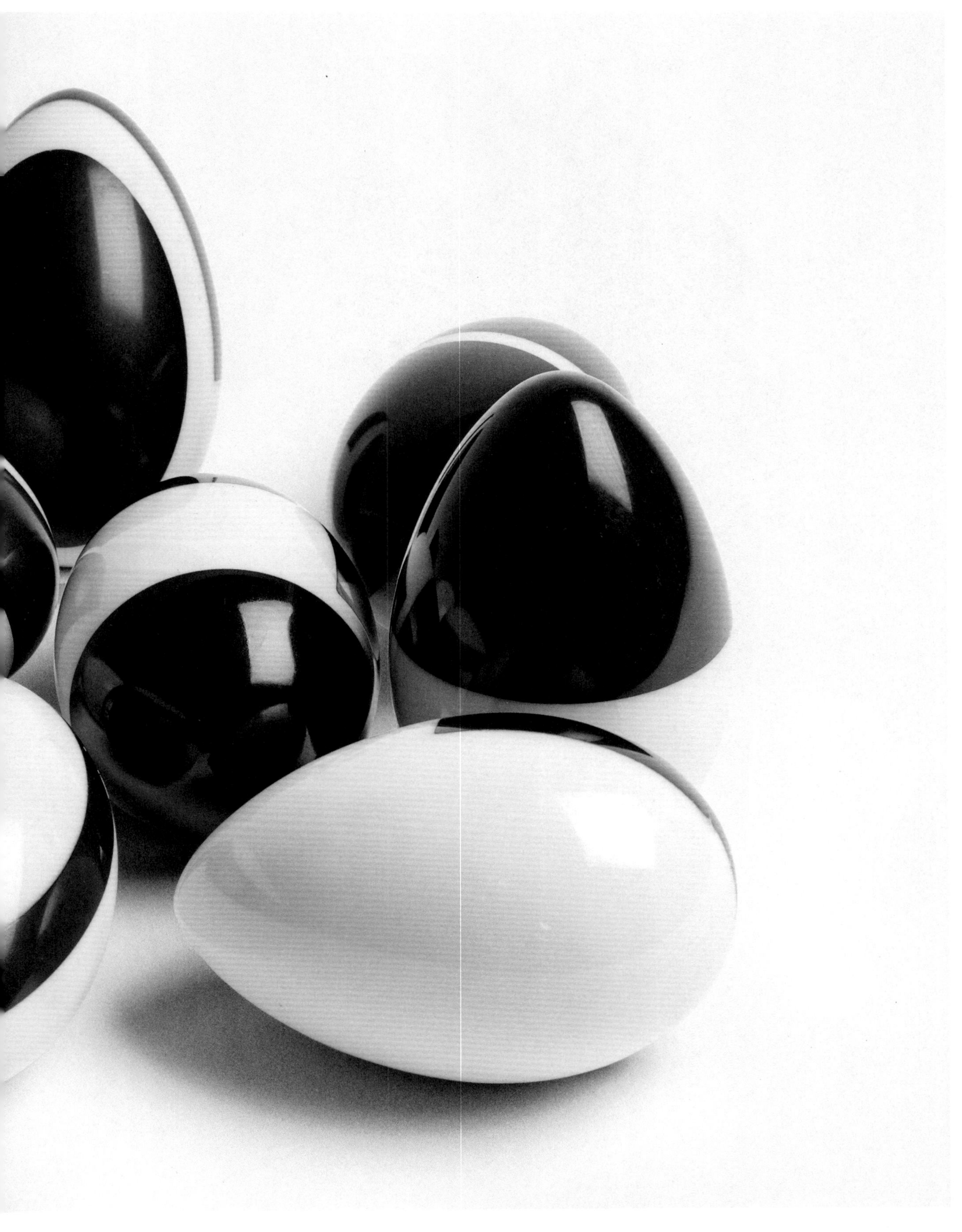

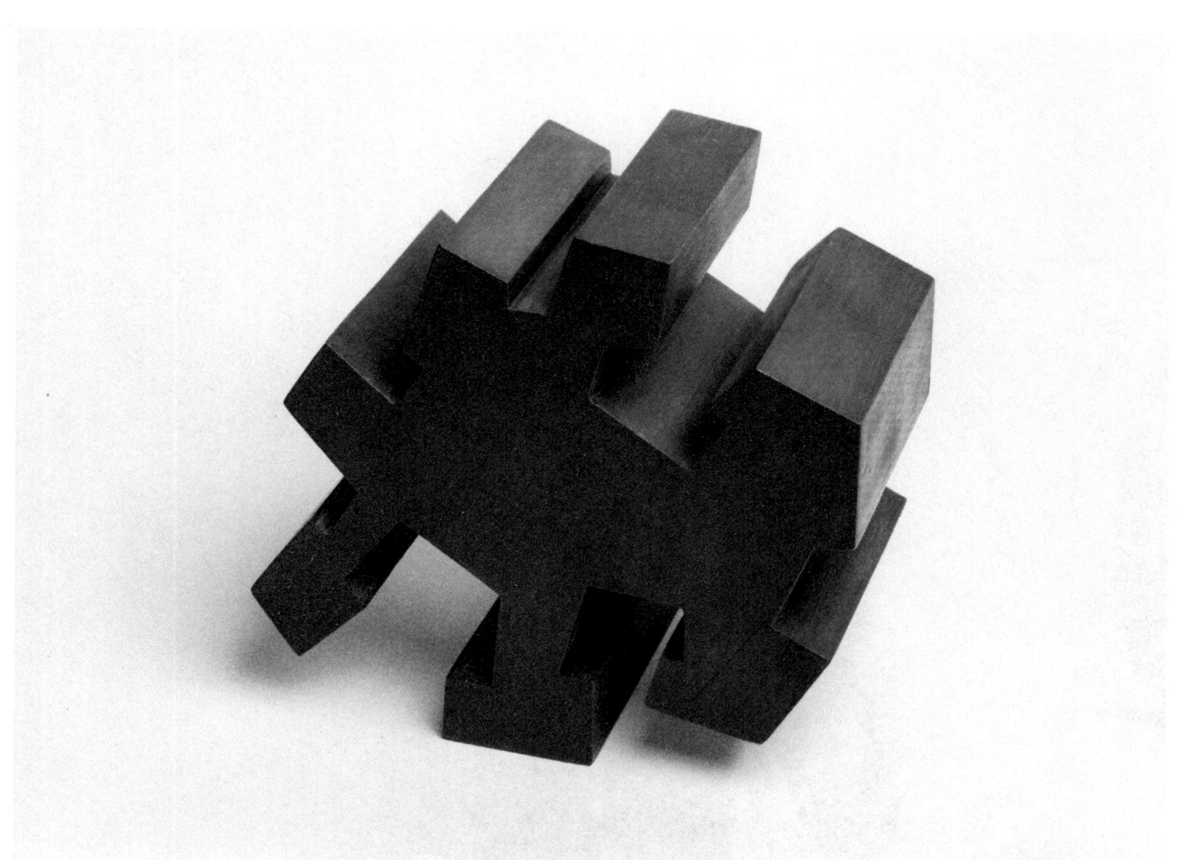

 From the series *French Keys*, wood model, 1970s

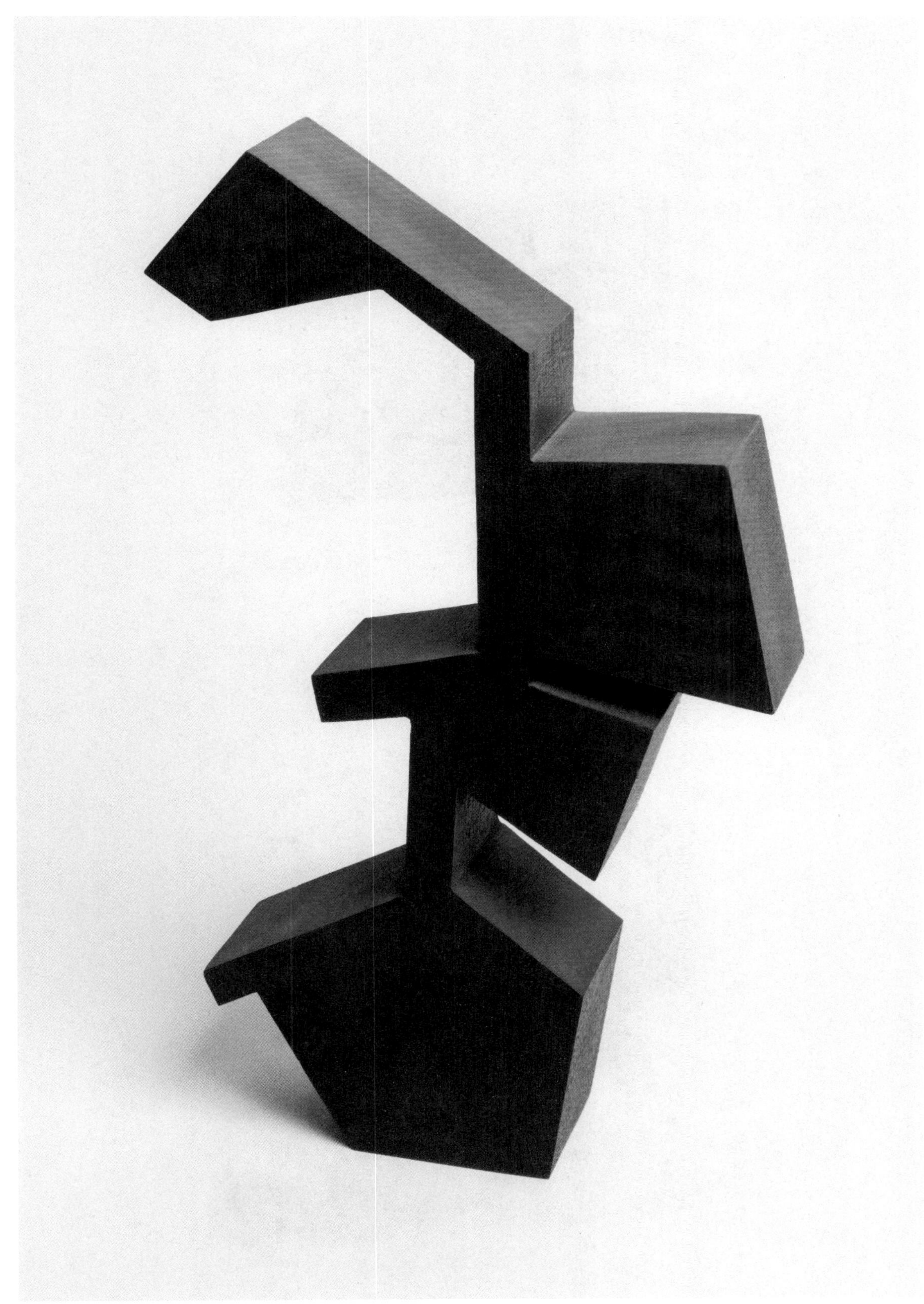

From the series *French Keys*, wood model, 1970s

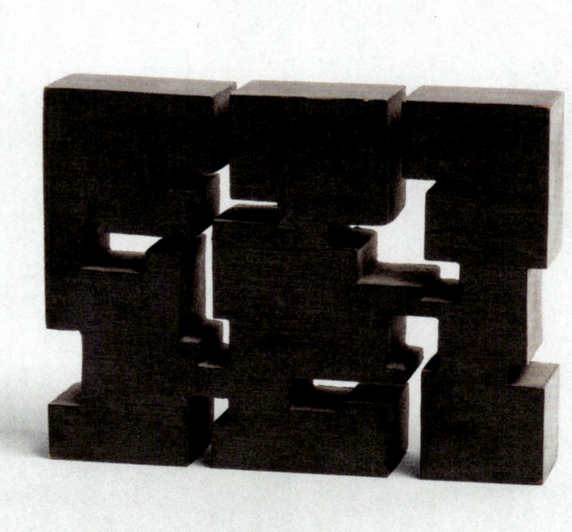

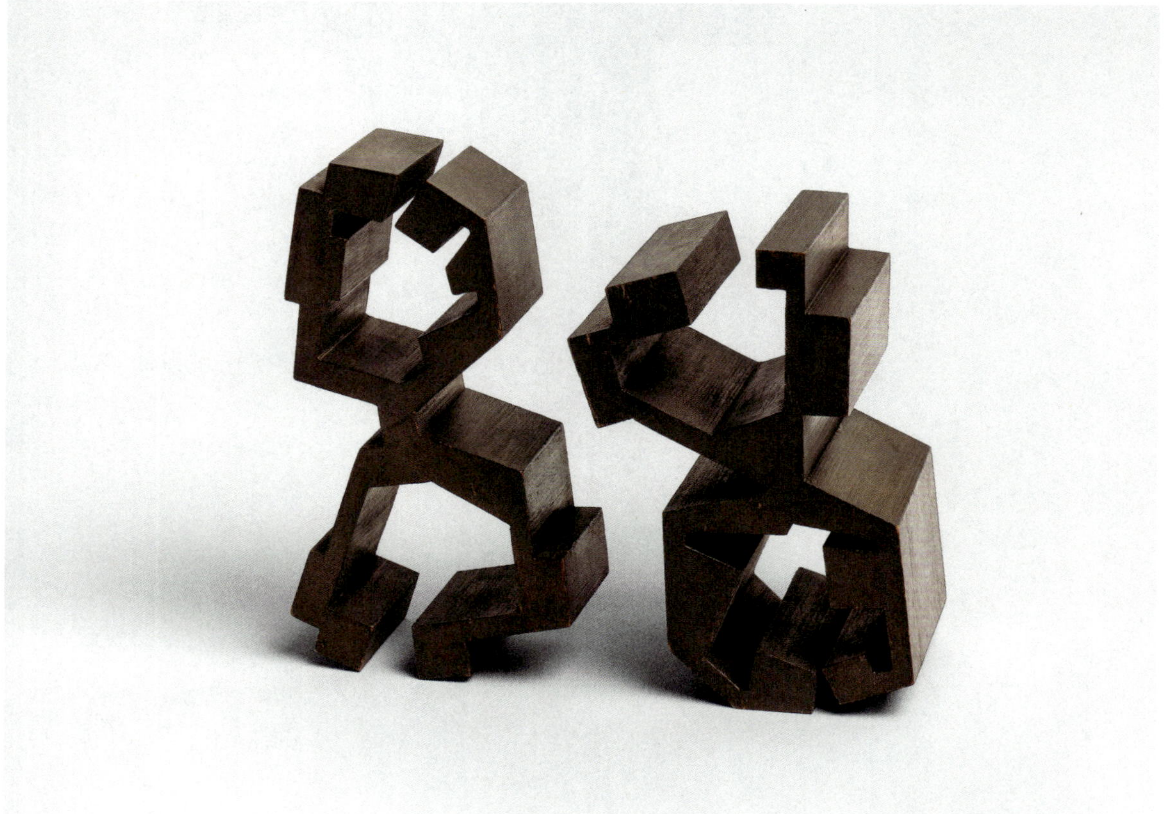

Top: *Dialogue in Line, Mass, Cubic Volumes, Remplir l'espace*, 1972
Bottom: *Five Points of Equal Balance*, from the series *French Keys*, 1971

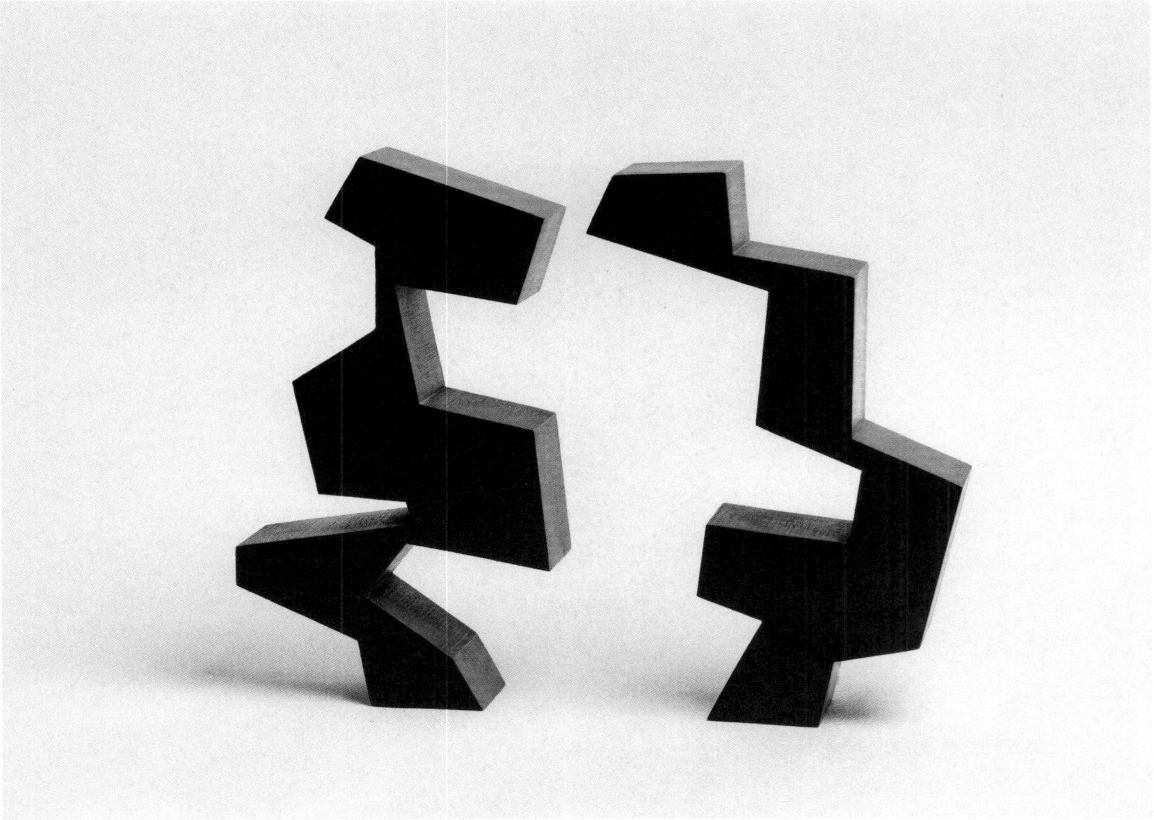

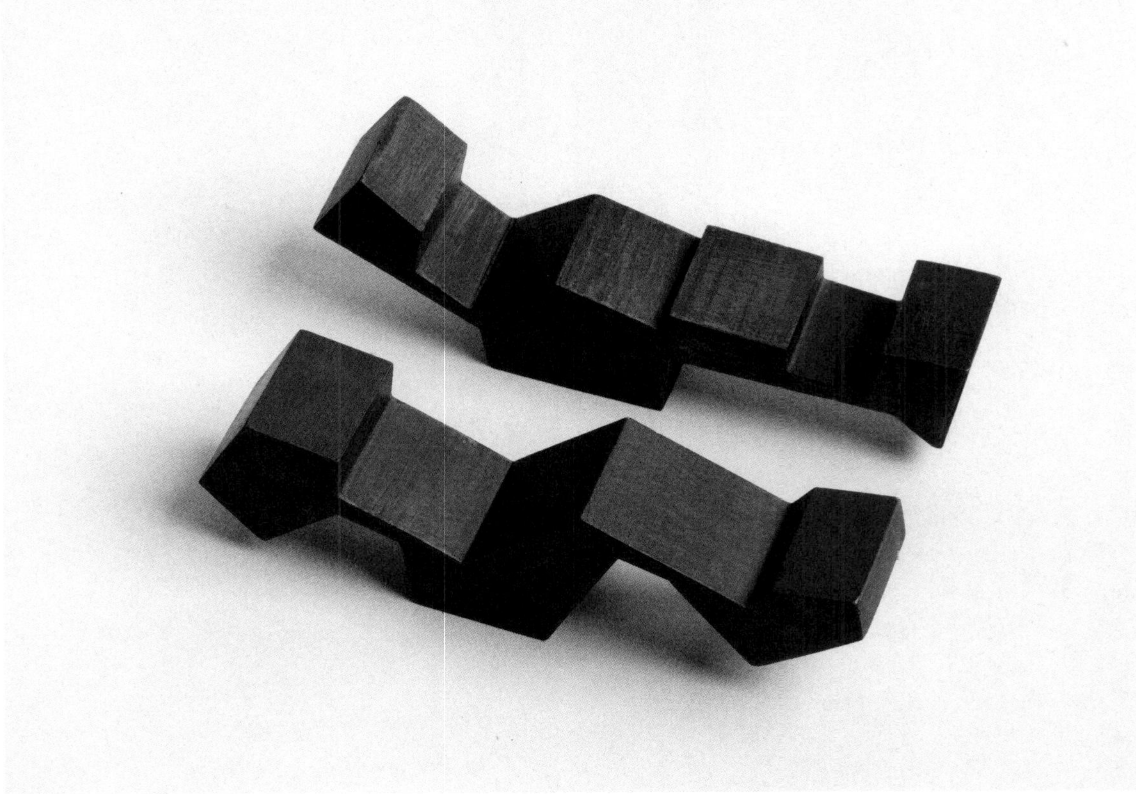

Top and bottom: ***Five Points of Equal Balance***, from the series ***French Keys***, 1971

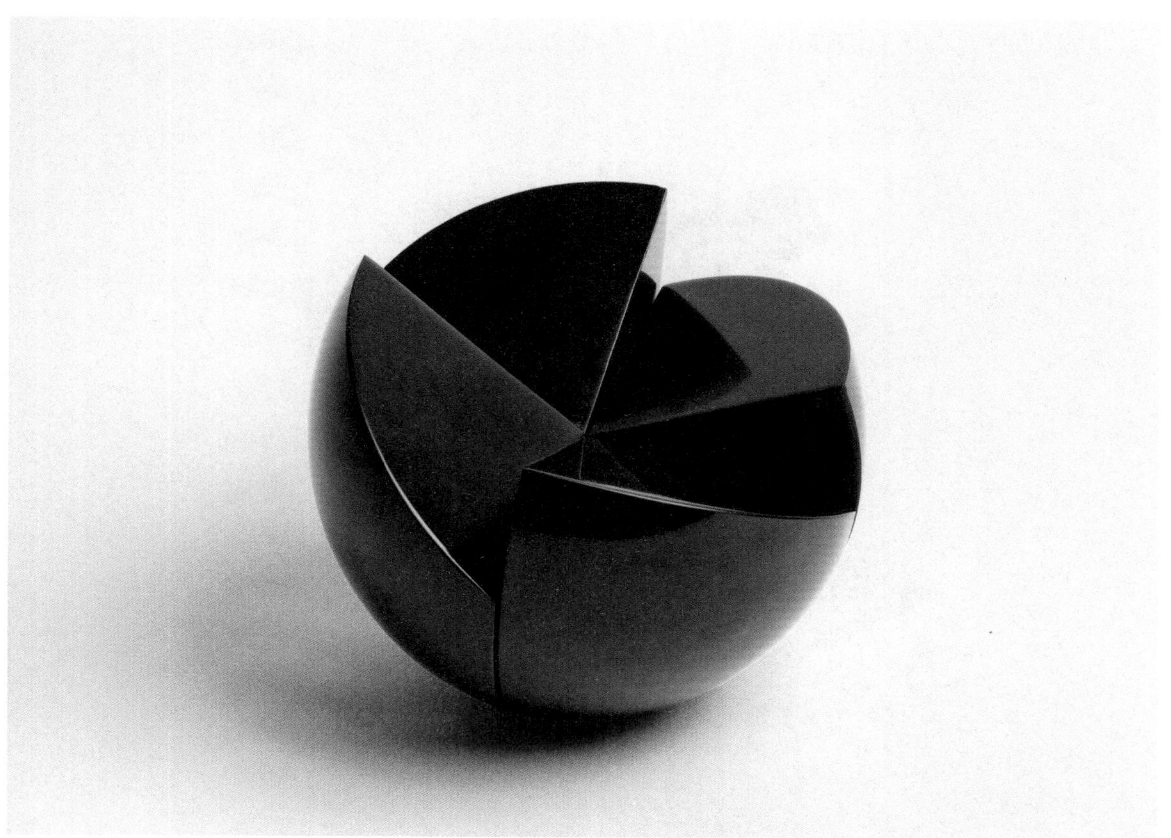

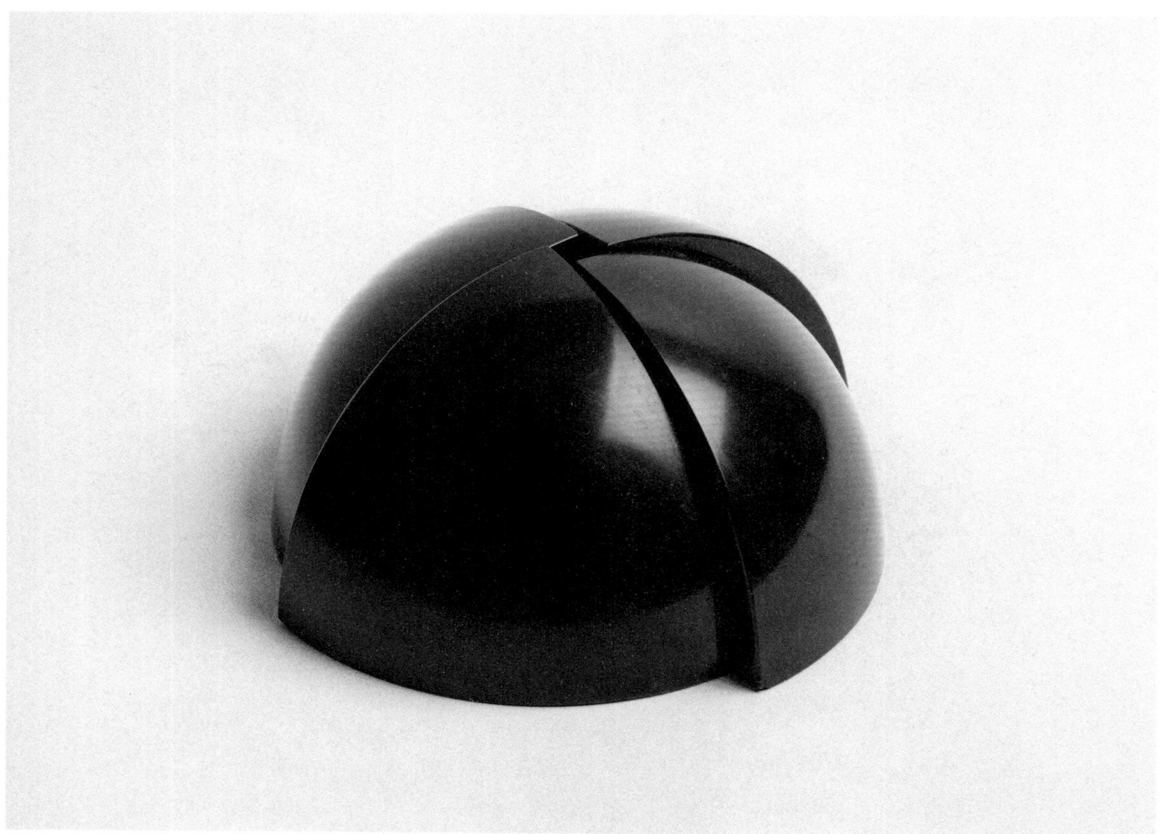

 Top and bottom: Untitled, marble, 1970s

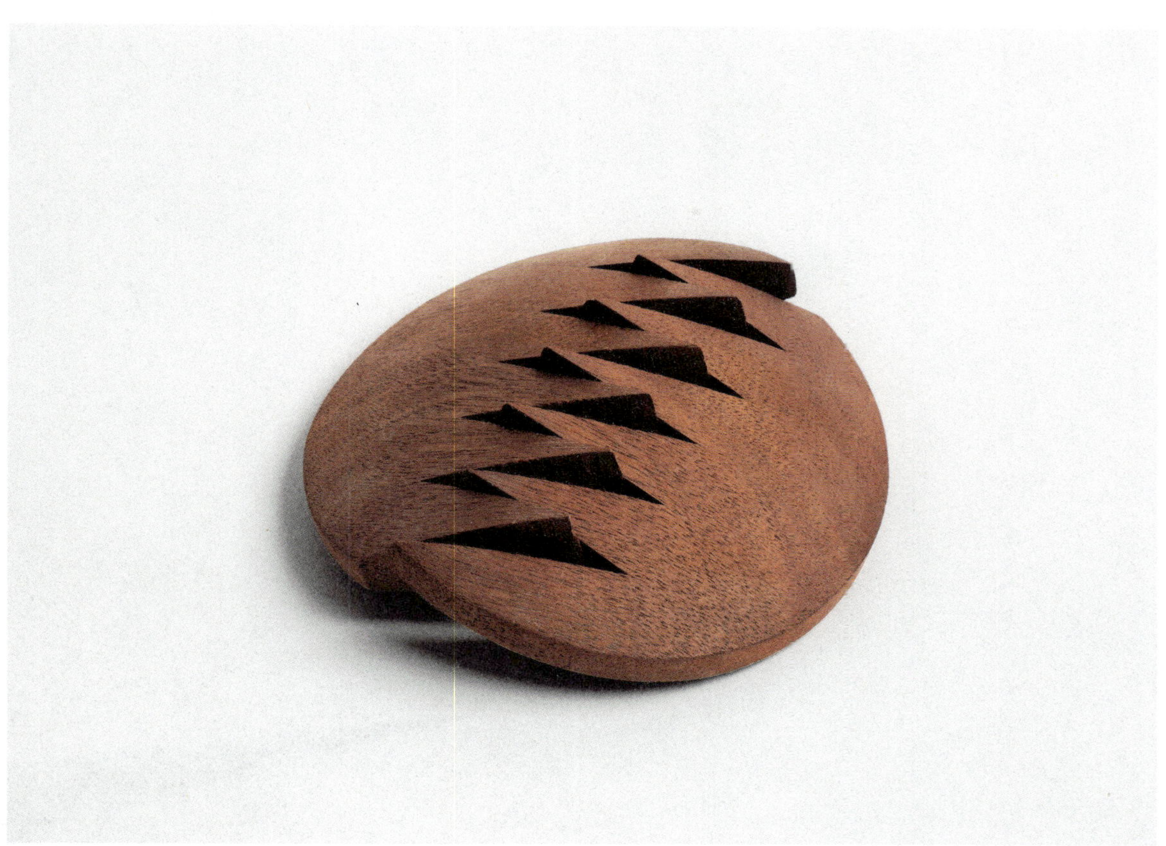

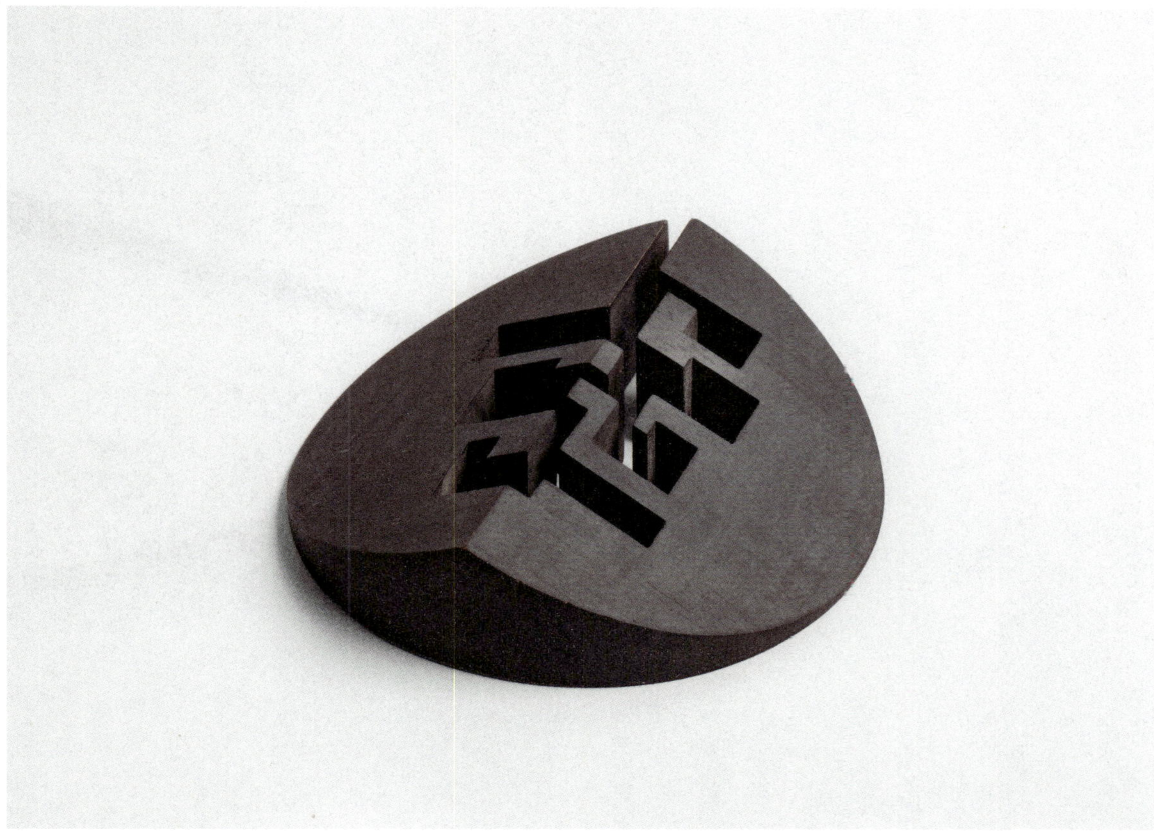

Top: *Clasped Hands*, wood model, 1972
Bottom: Untitled, wood model, 1970s

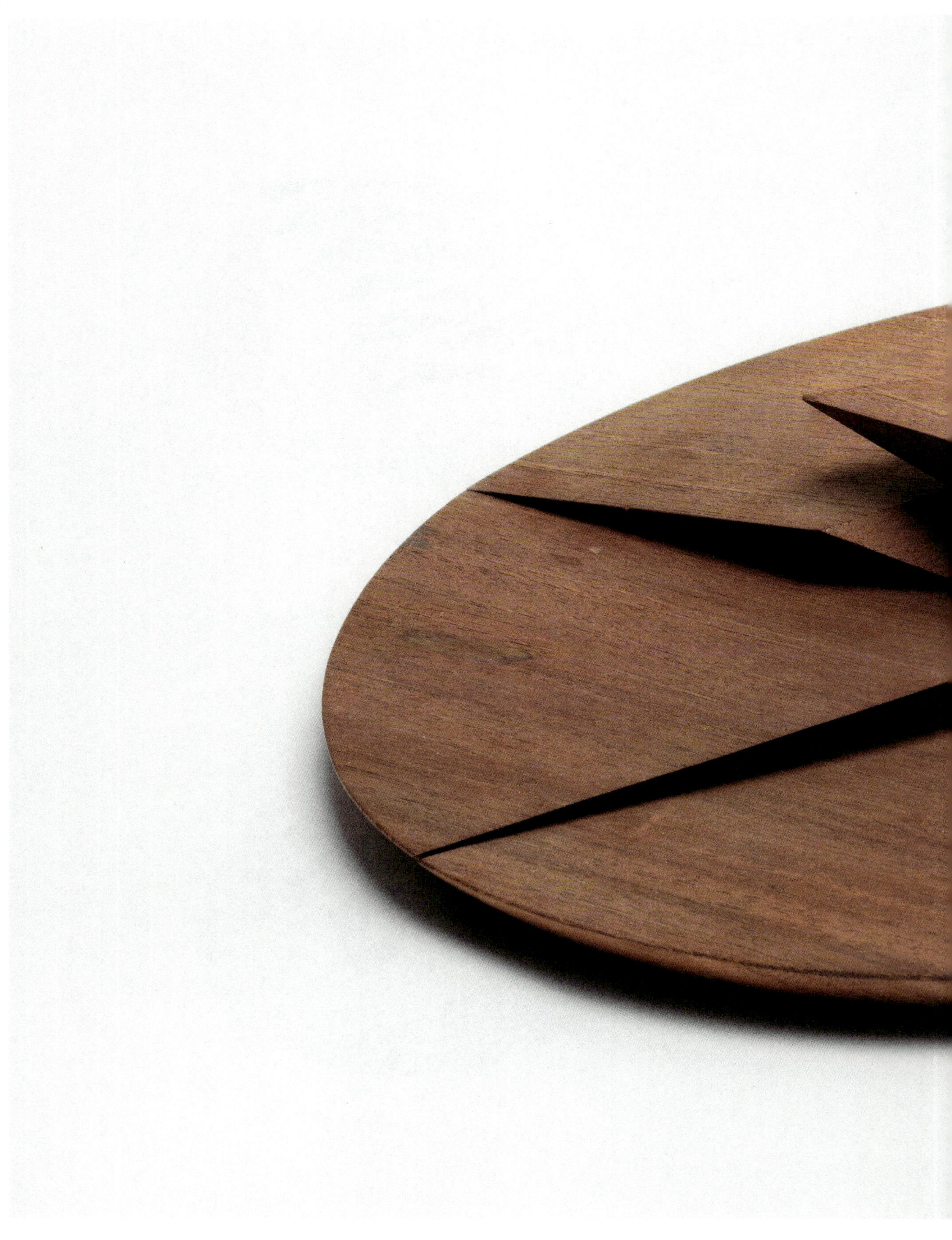

 Untitled, wood model, 1970s

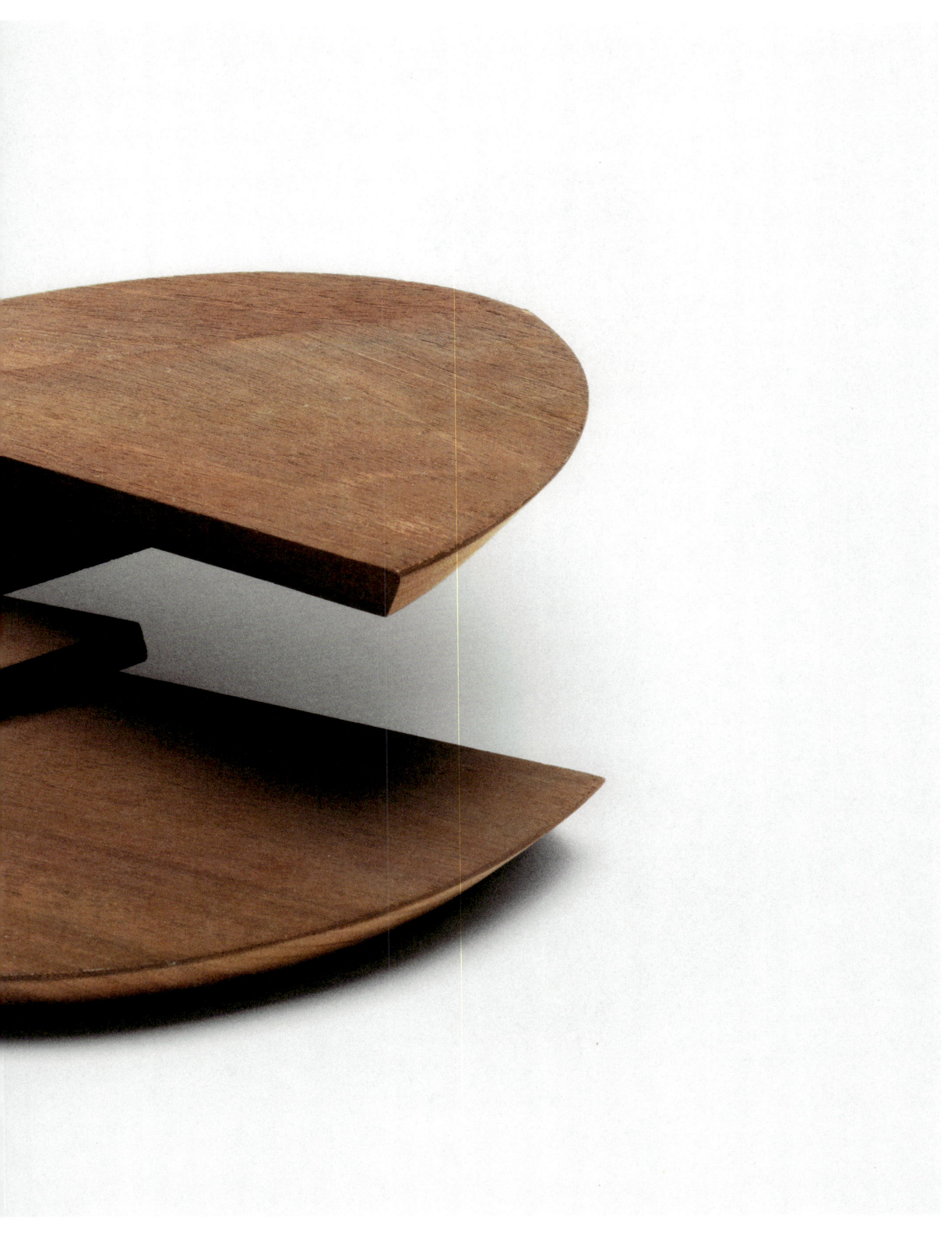

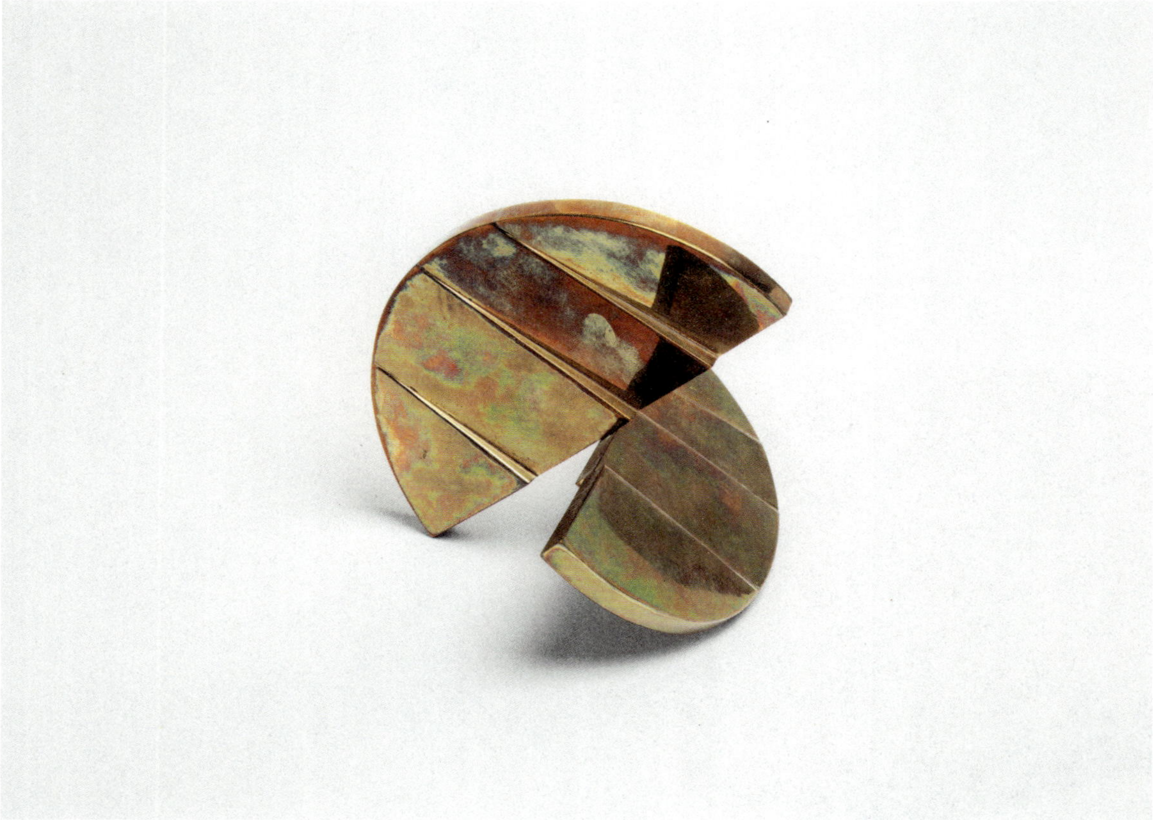

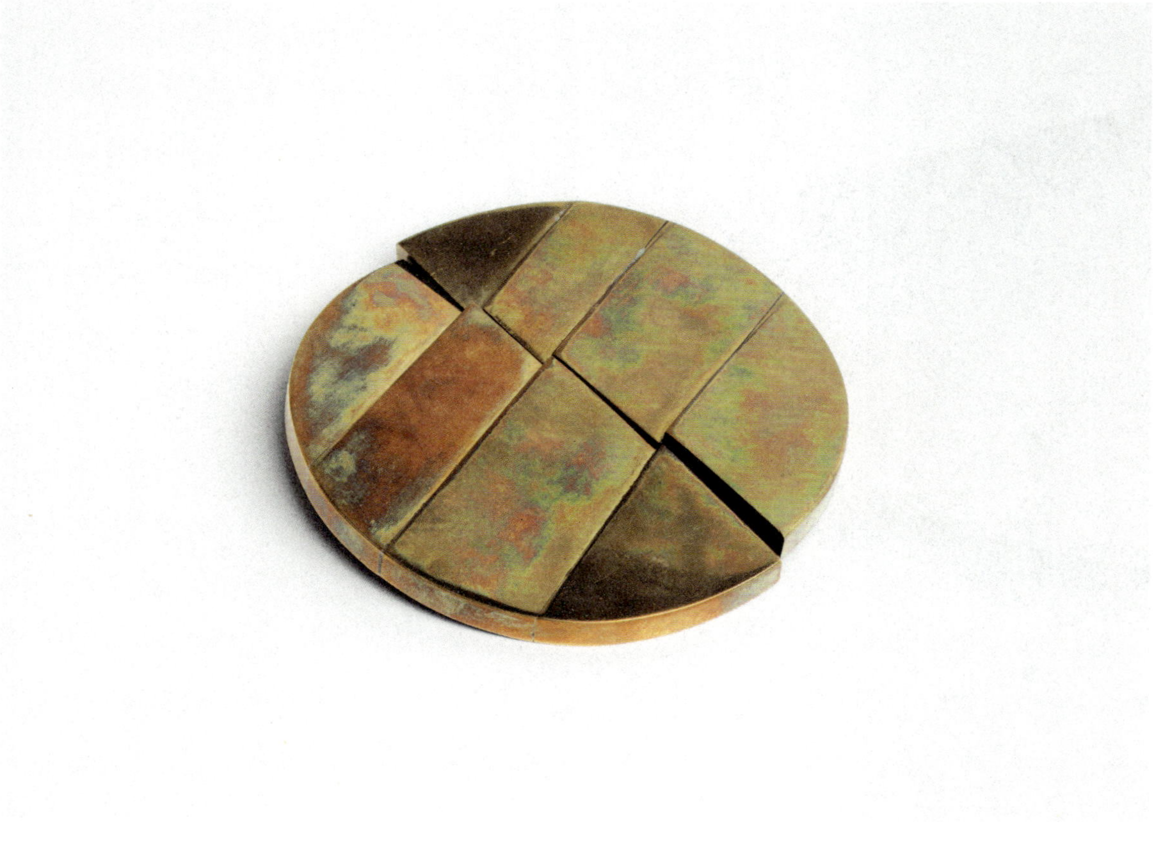

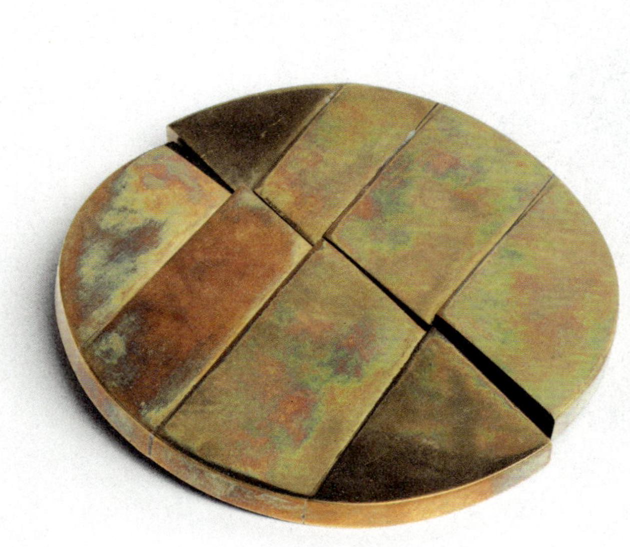

 Top and bottom: Untitled, brass model, 1970s

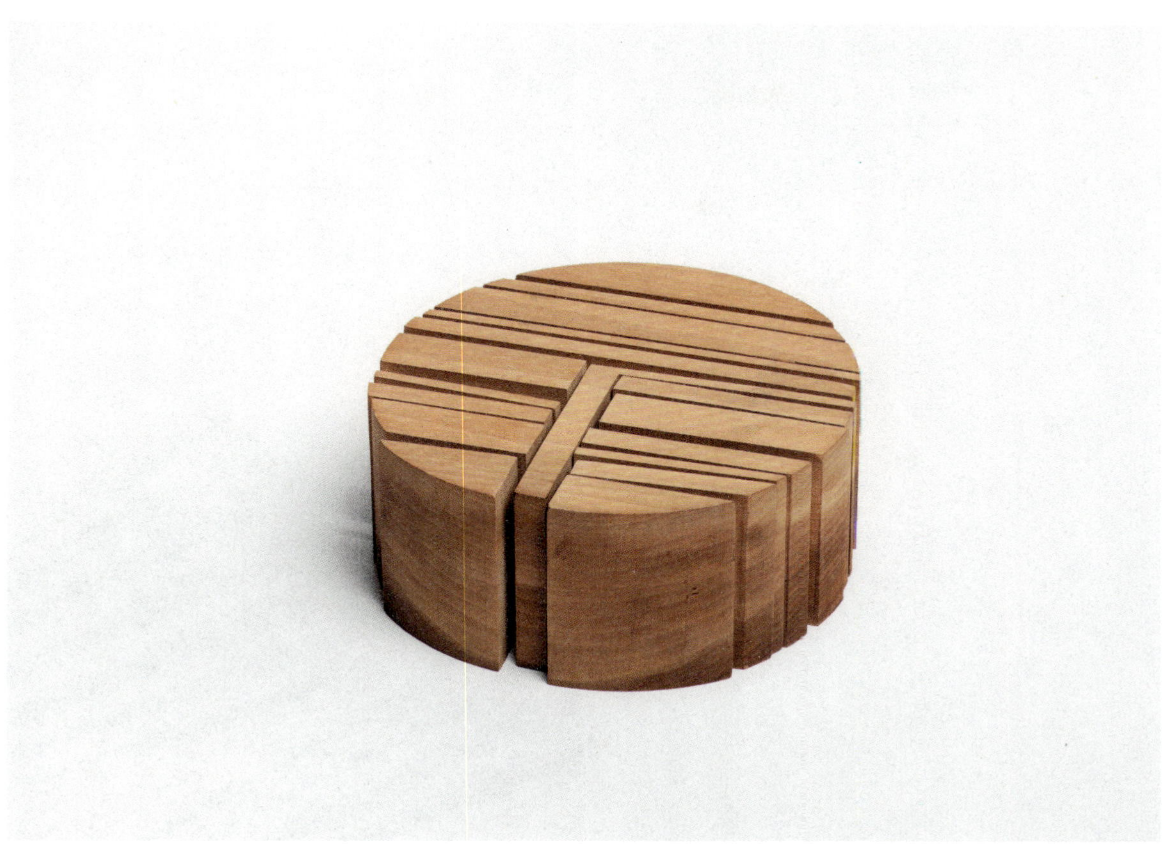

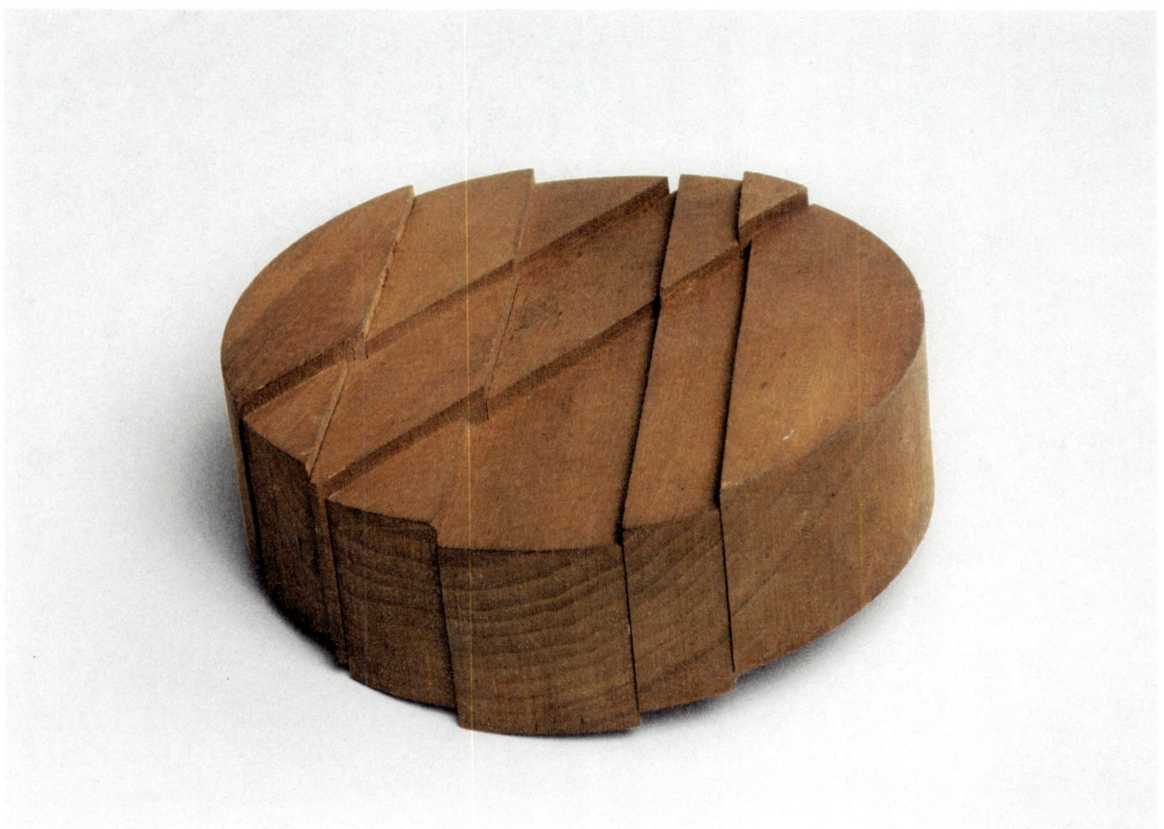

Top: Untitled, wood model, 1970s
Bottom: Untitled, wood model, 1967–73

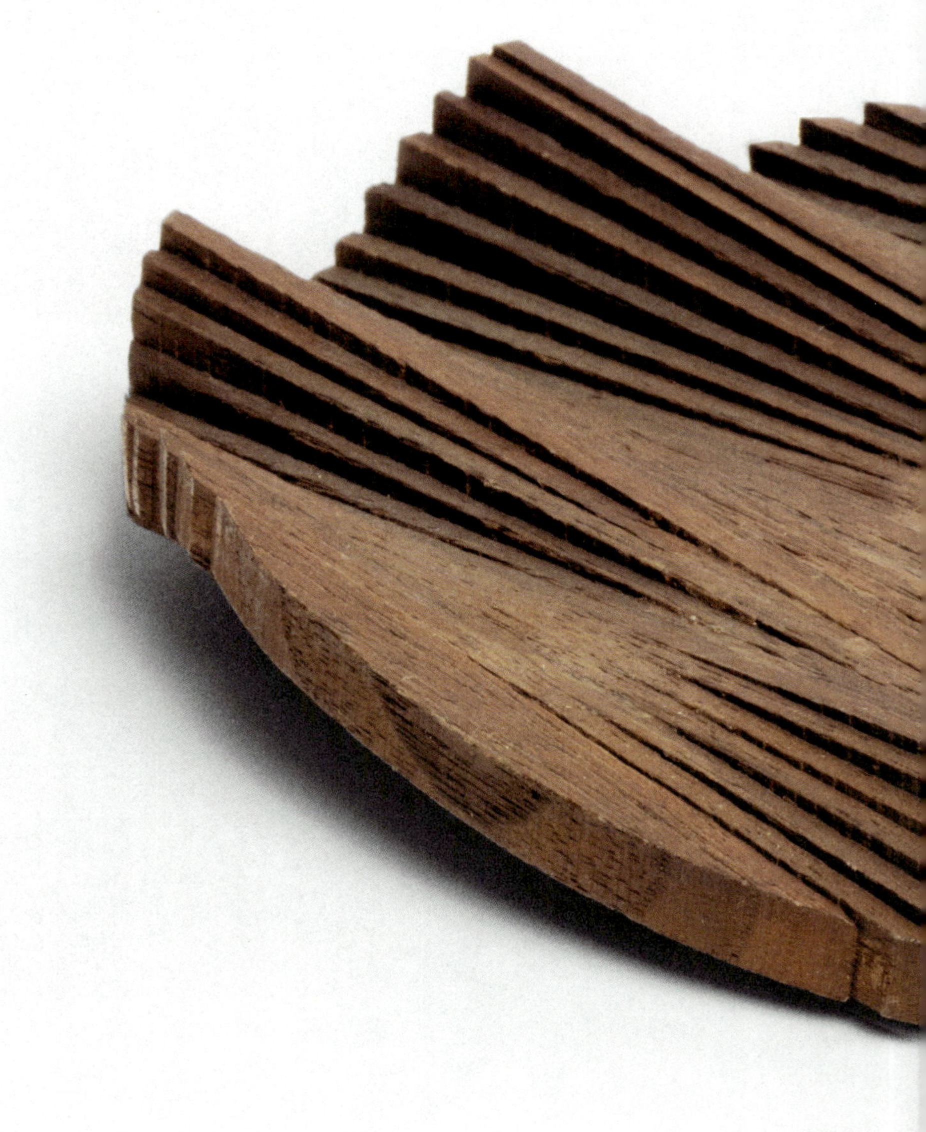

Euclidean to Non-Euclidean Restructures. Options for a Developable Absolute. 1972–73
From the series *One Constant. Euclidean to Non-Euclidean Curve.* Suite of thirteen

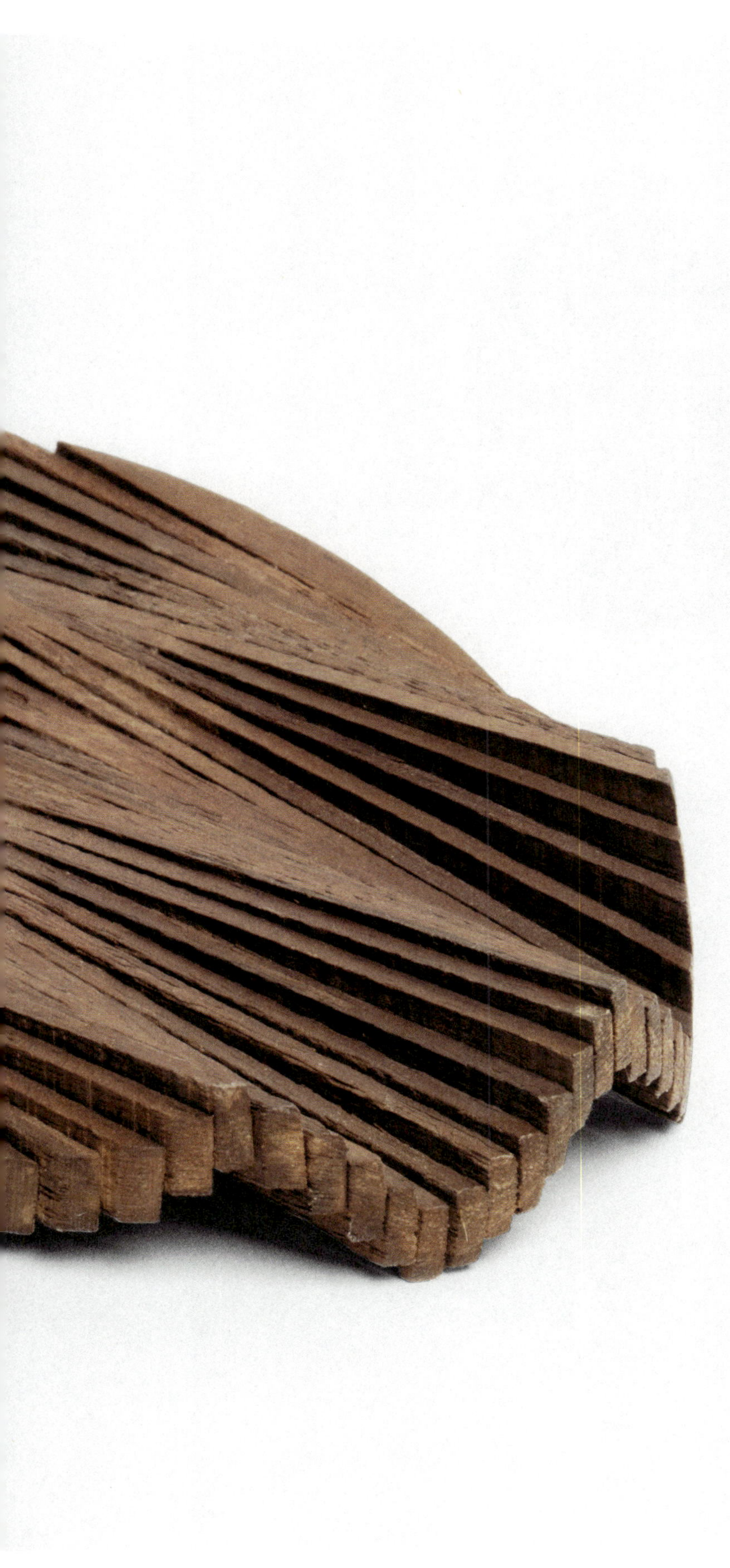

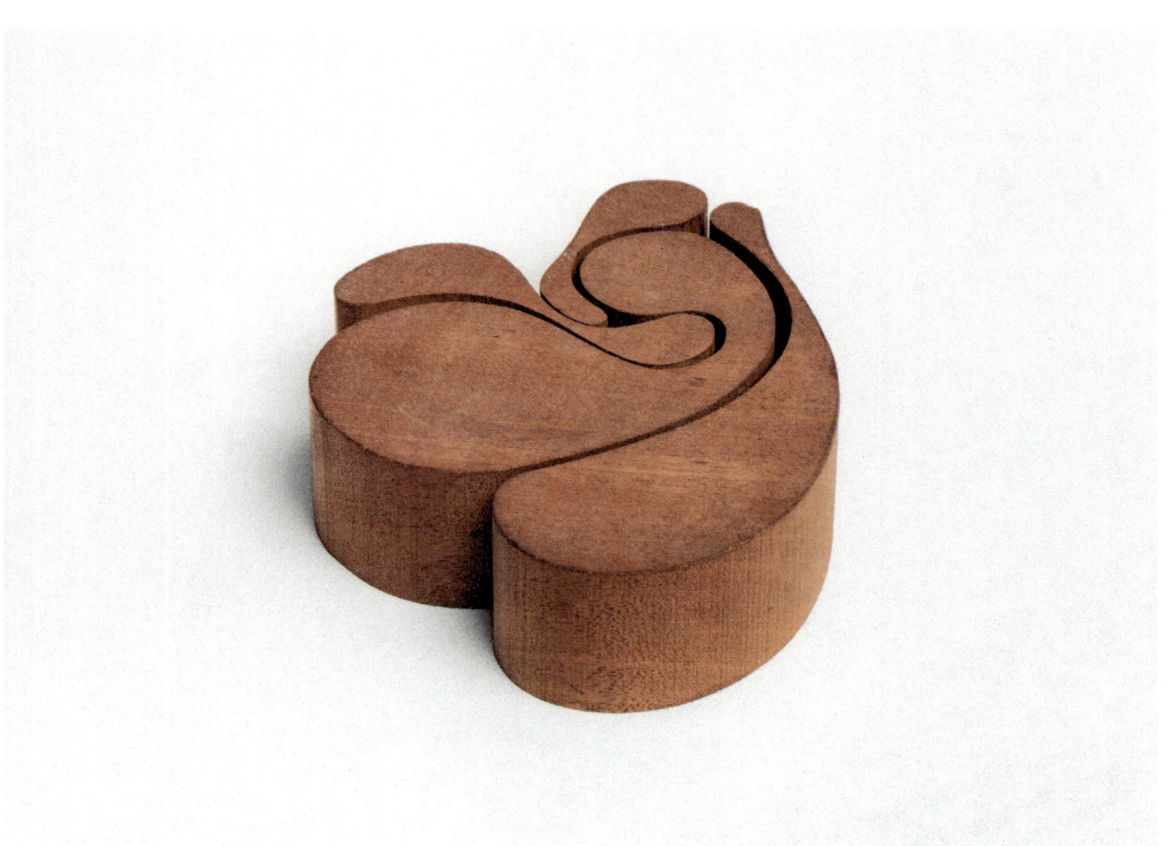

 Untitled, wood model, 1970s

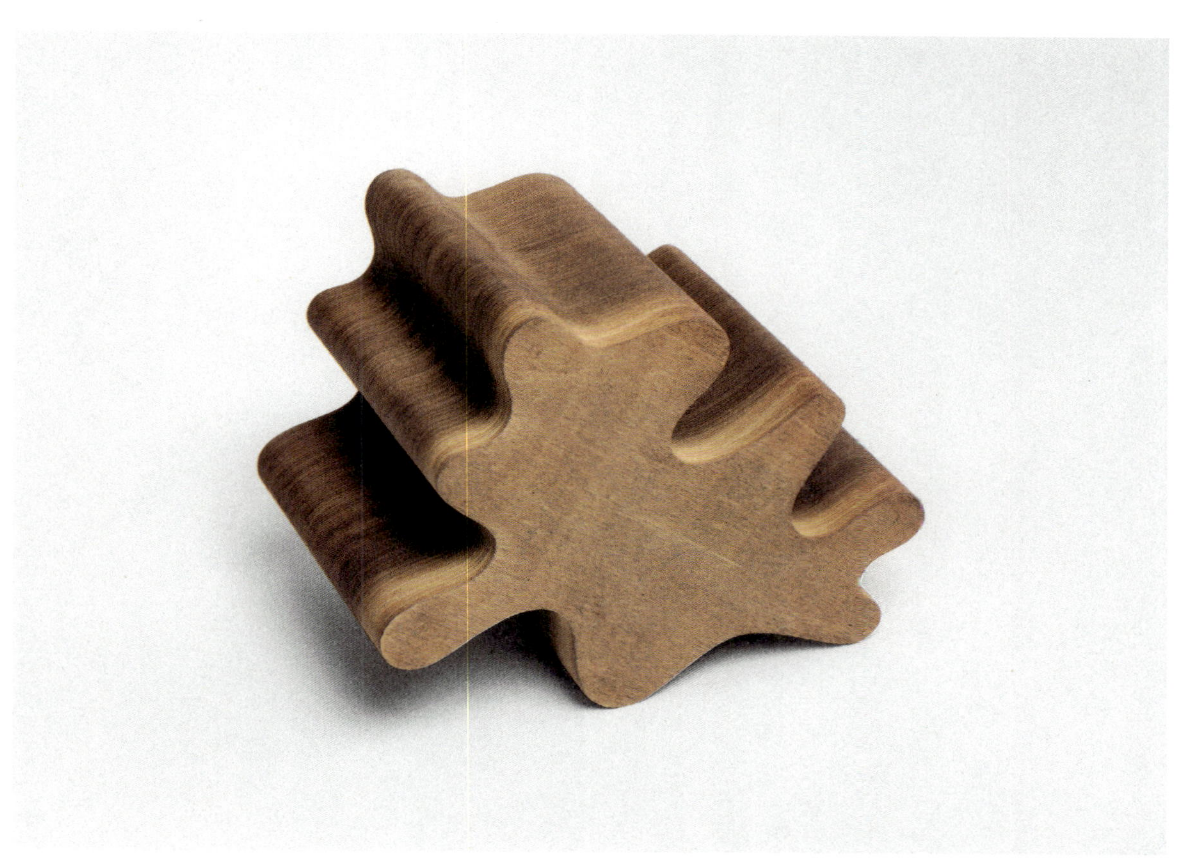

Untitled, wood model, 1970s

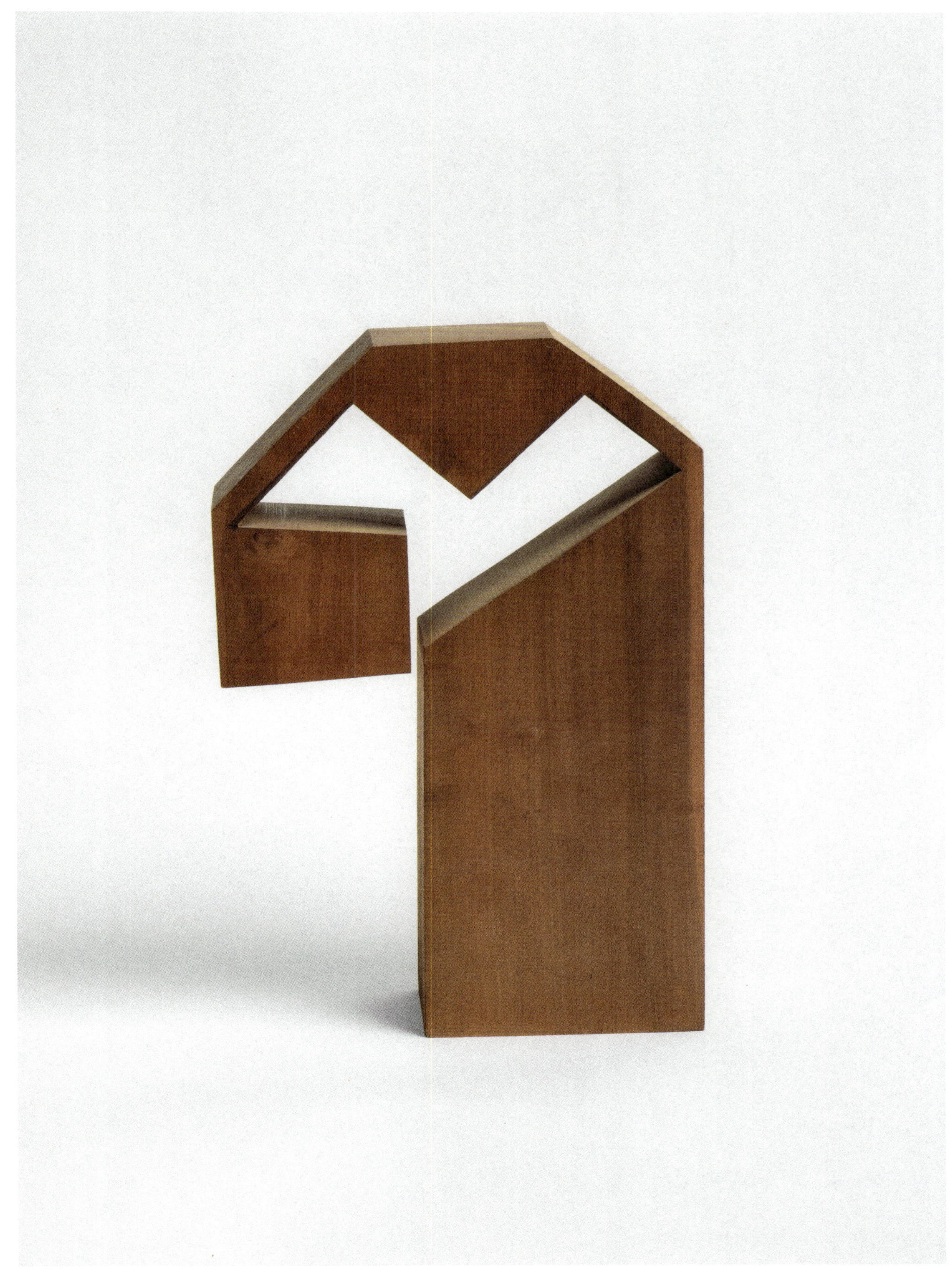

From the series *French Keys, Finite Structures*, 1970

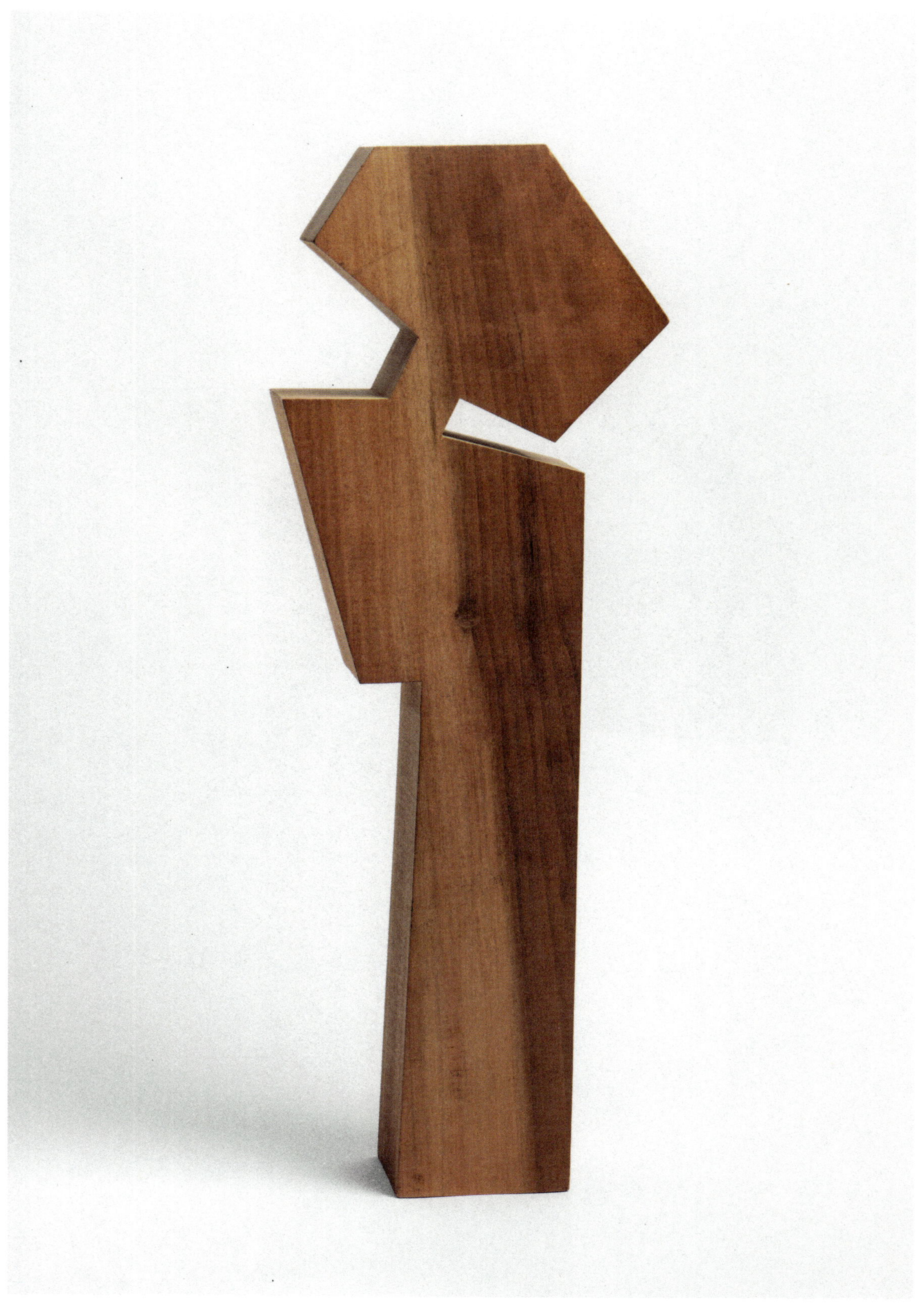

 From the series *French Keys, Finite Structures*, 1970

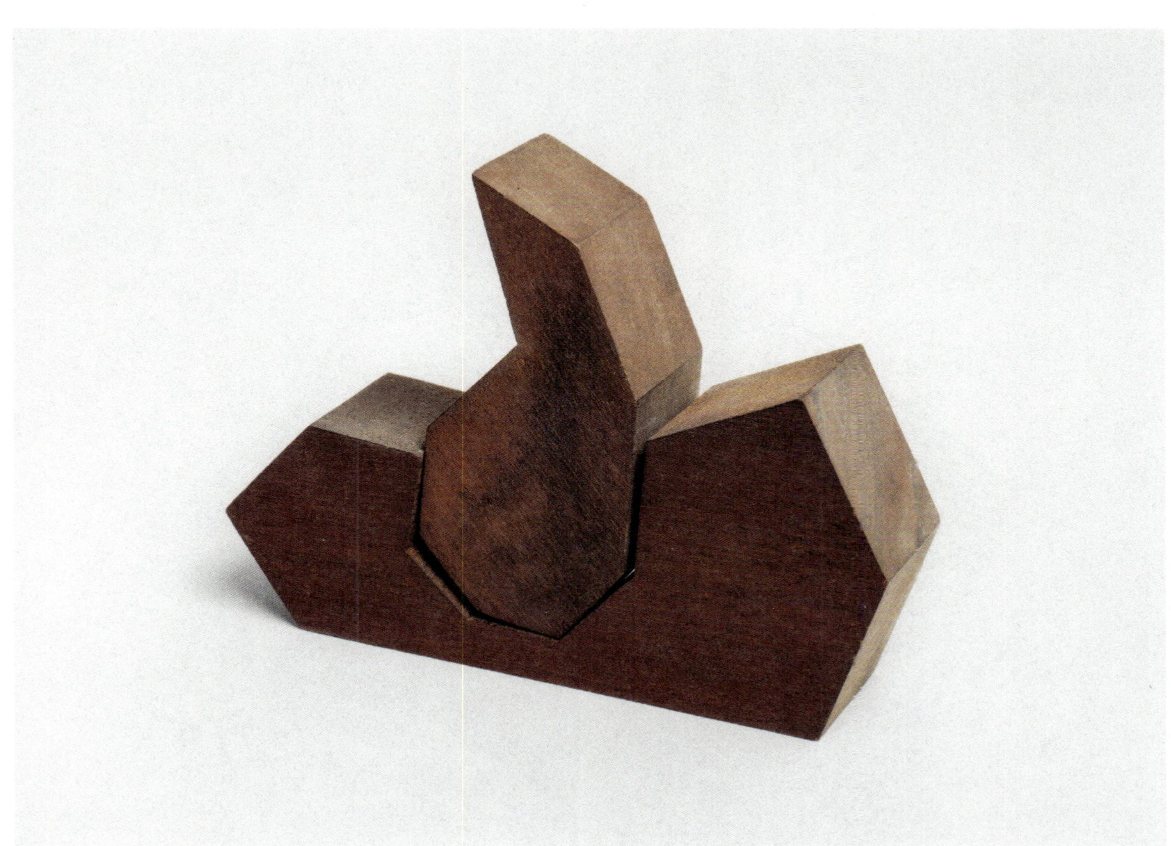

Untitled, wood model, 1970s

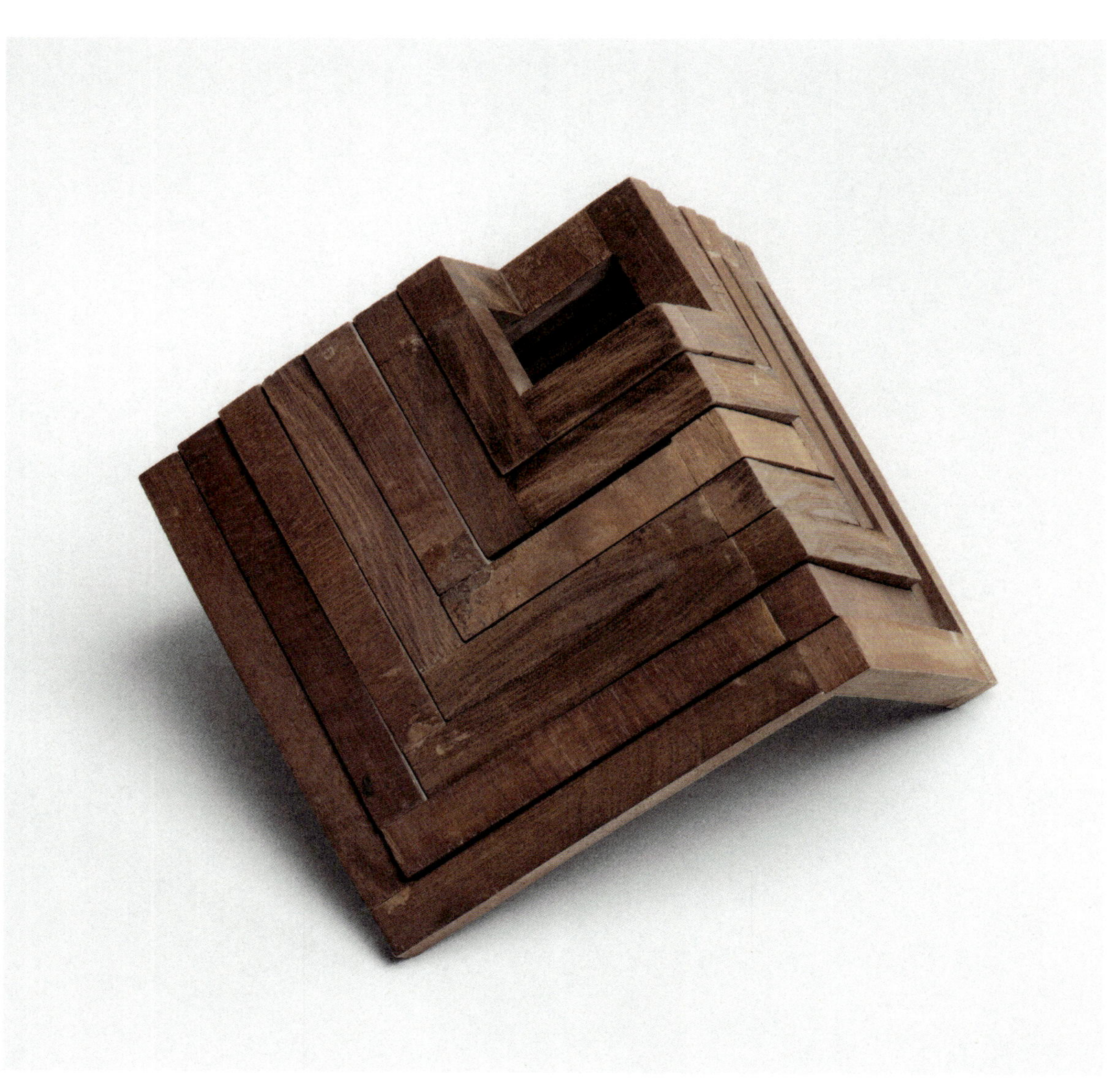

One Cube Built with Open Cubes of Progressively Changing Proportions of Space and Matter, Built-up with 152 Equal Elements, wood model, 1971

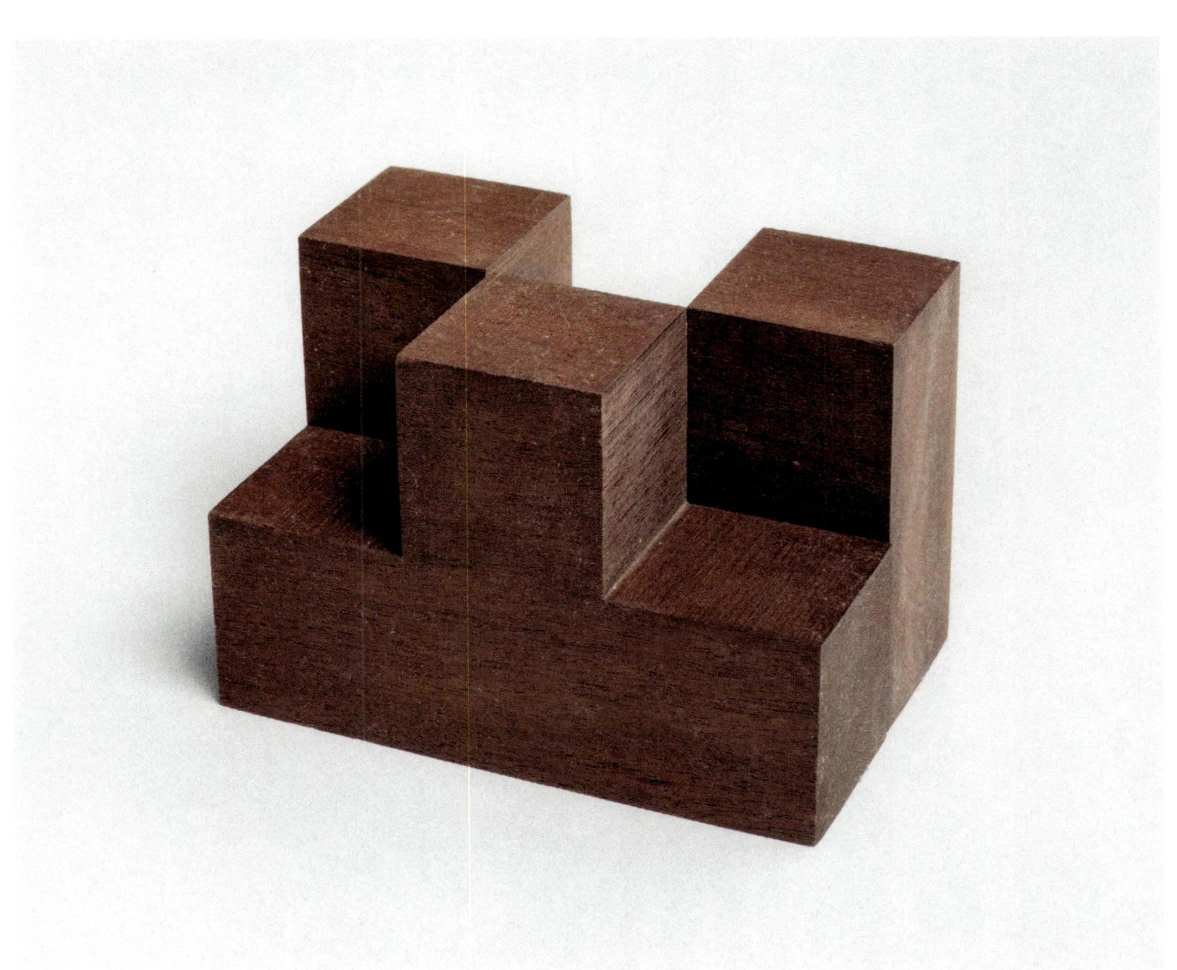

Untitled, wood model, 1970s

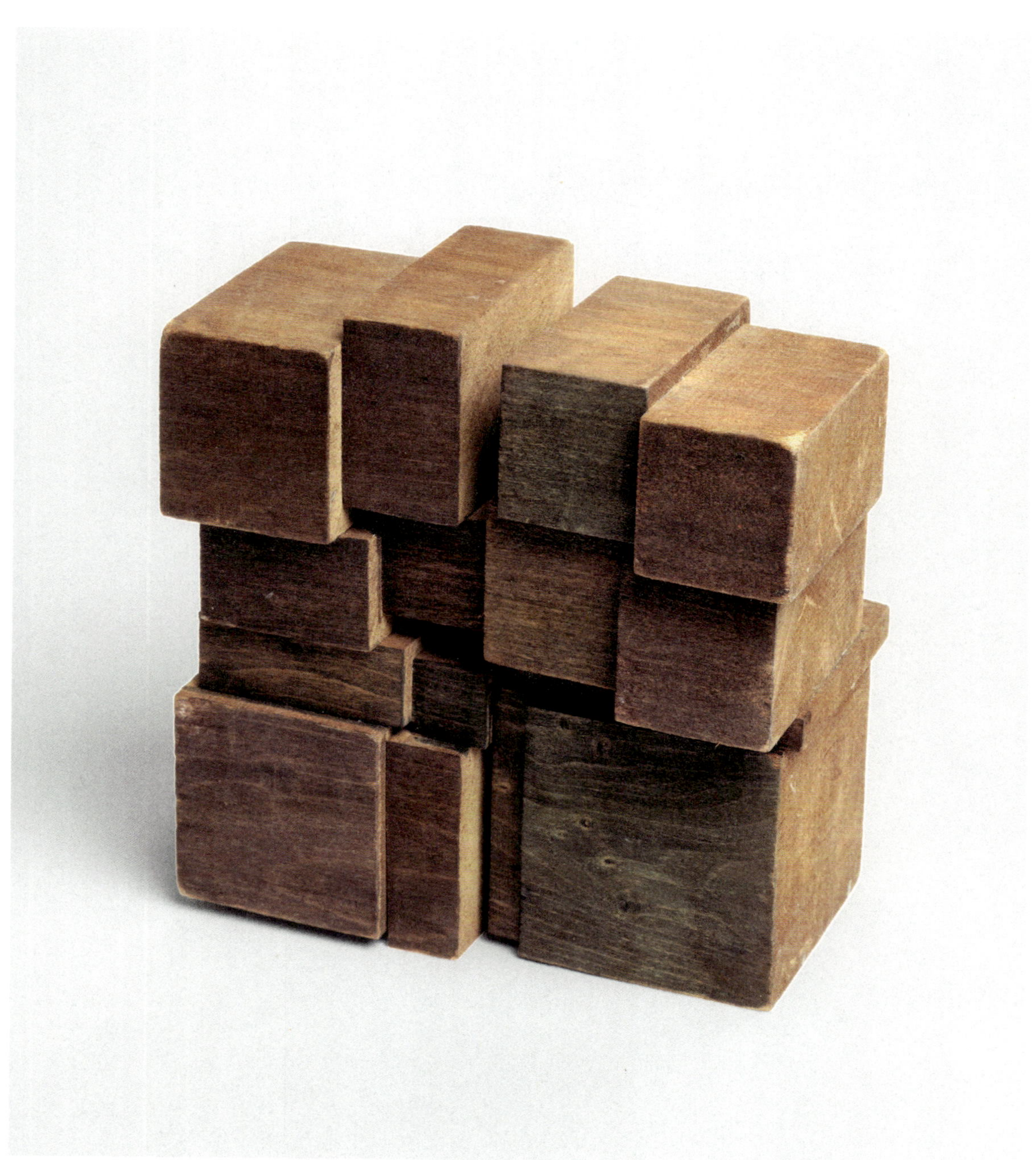

Untitled, wood model, 1970s

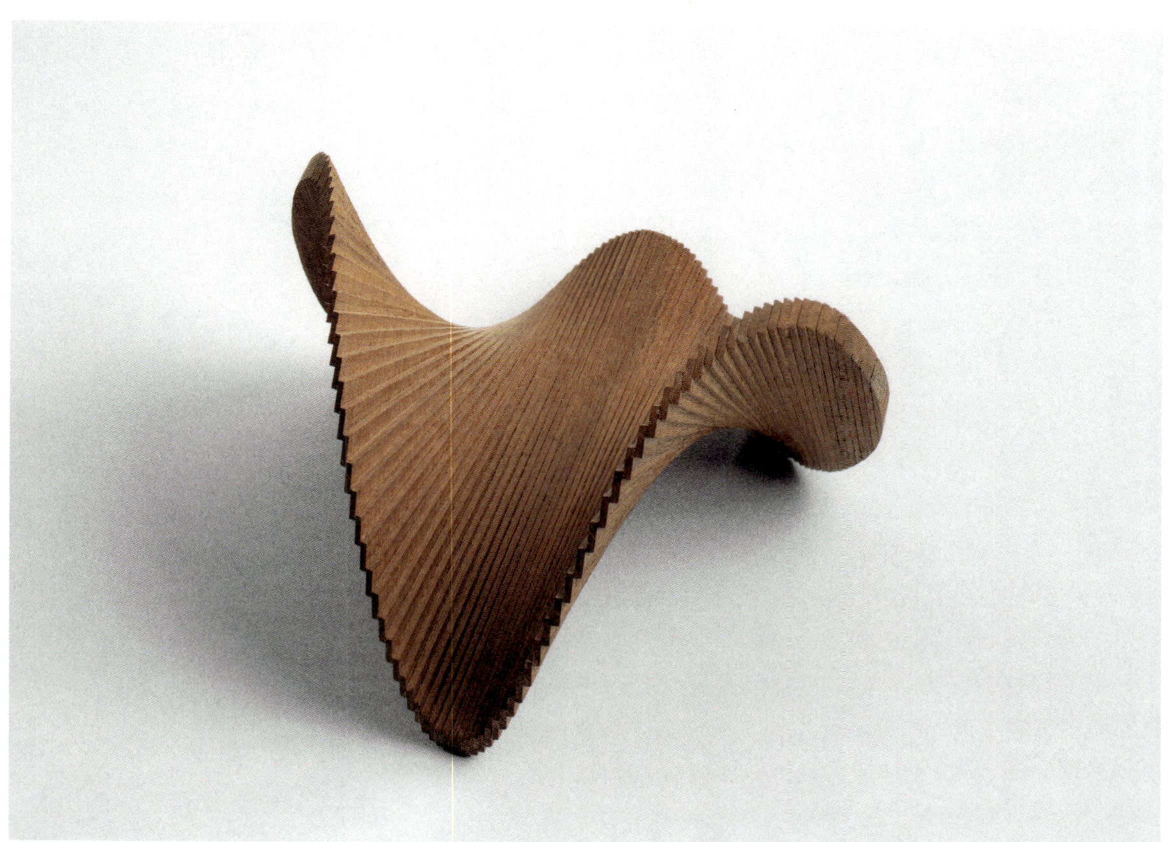

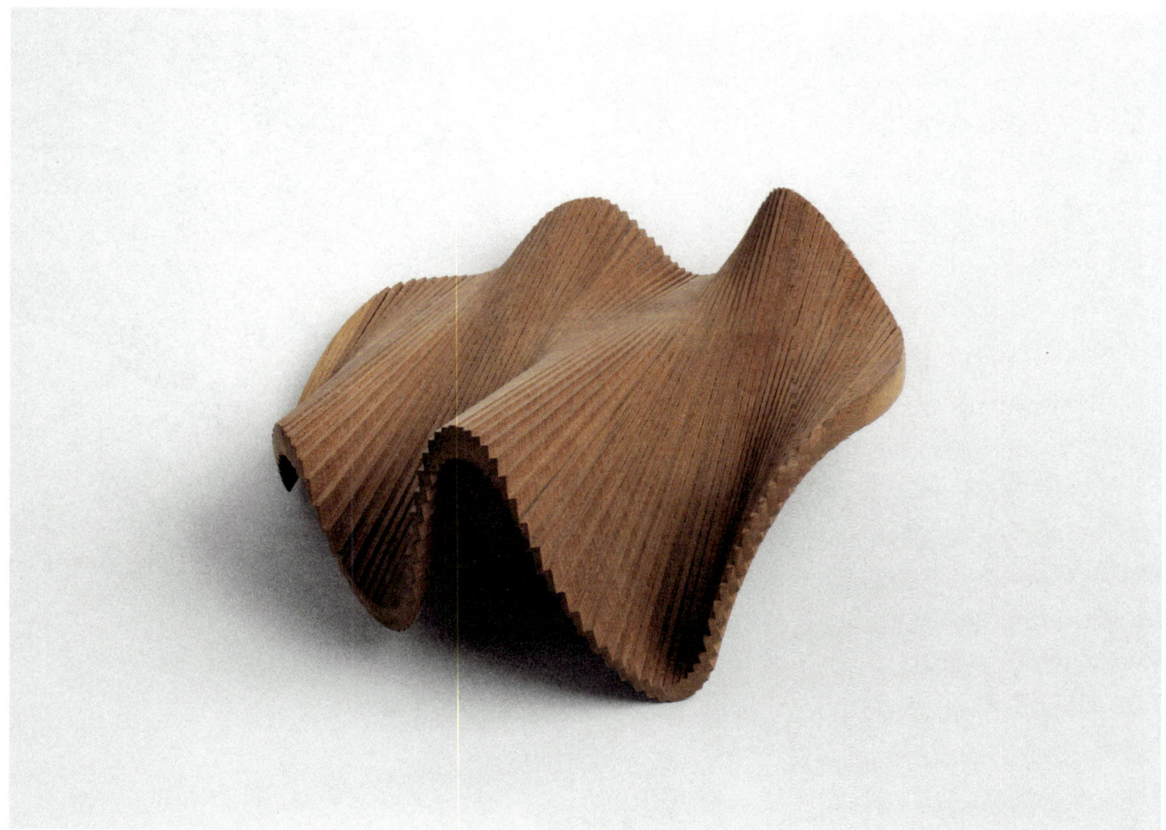

Pages 255-58: ***Euclidean to Non-Euclidean Restructures. Options for a Developable Absolute,*** **1972-73**
From the series ***One Constant. Euclidean to Non-Euclidean Curve.*** **Suite of thirteen**

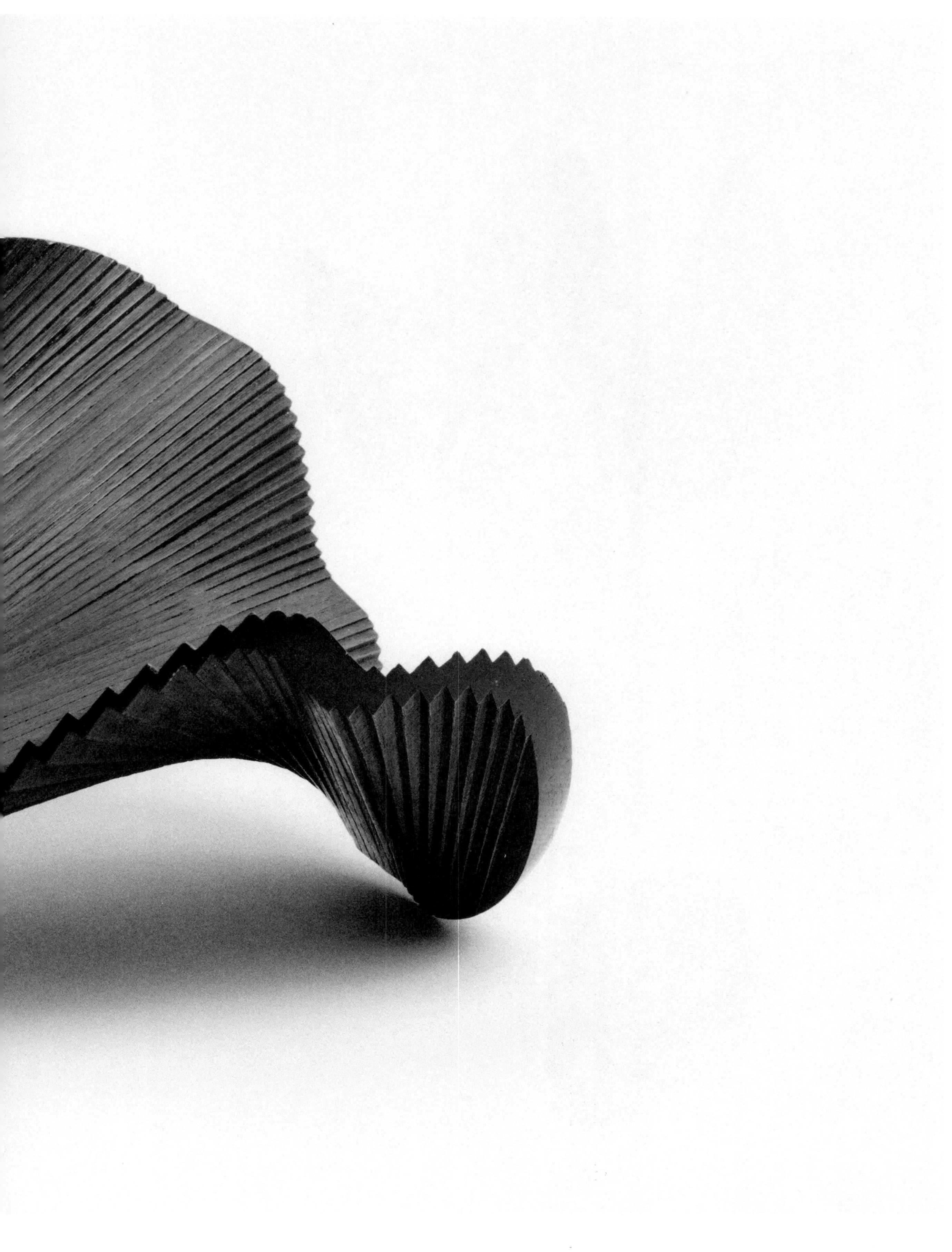

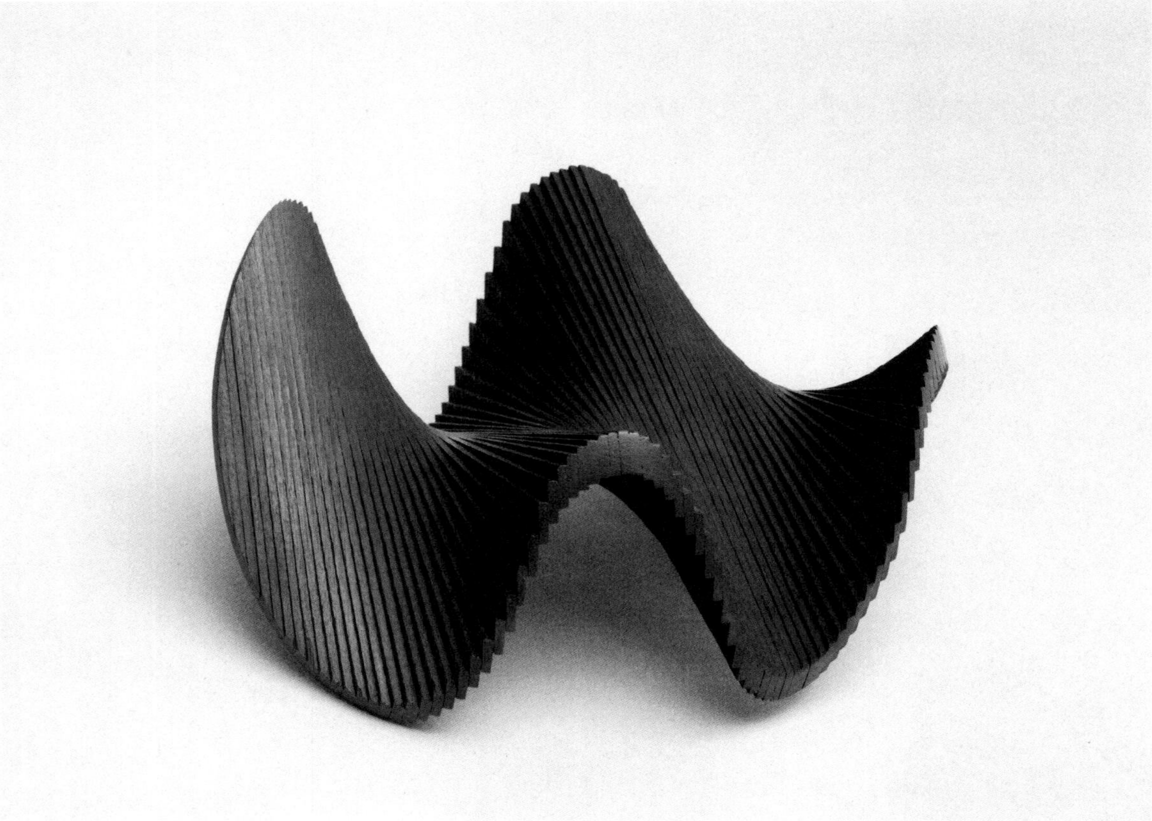

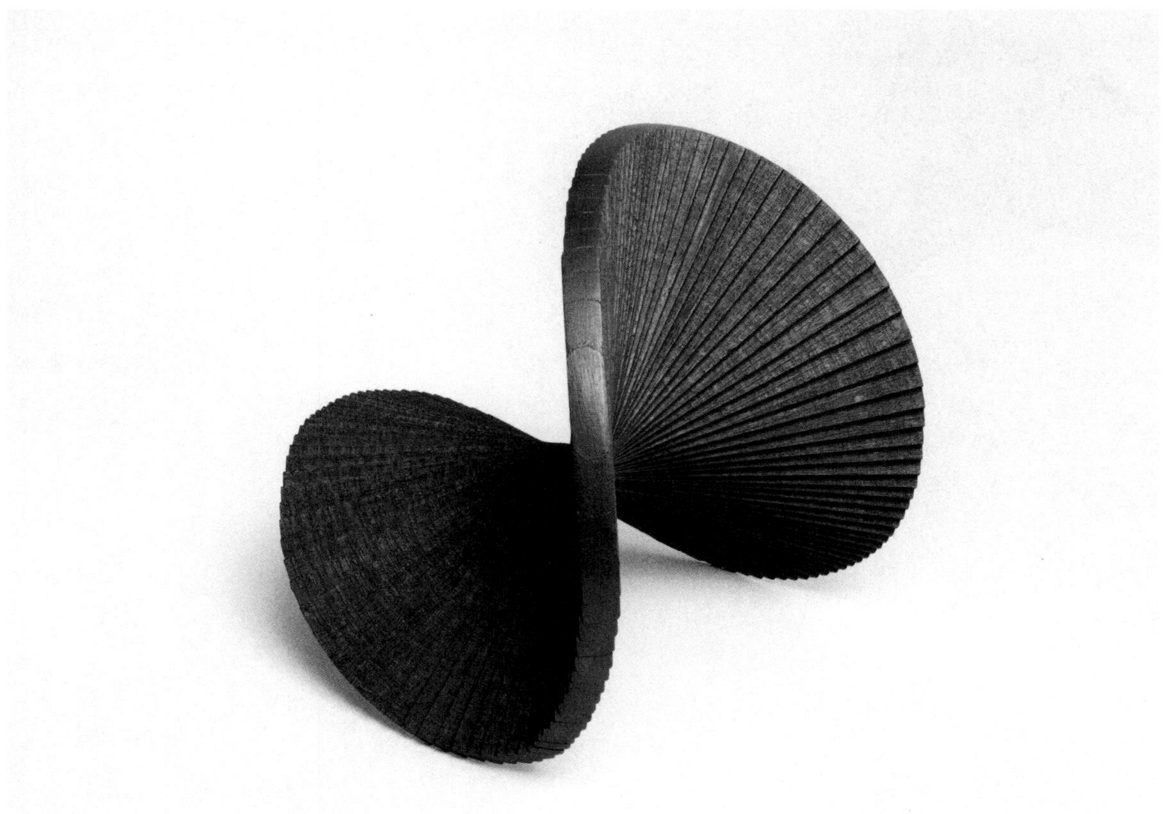

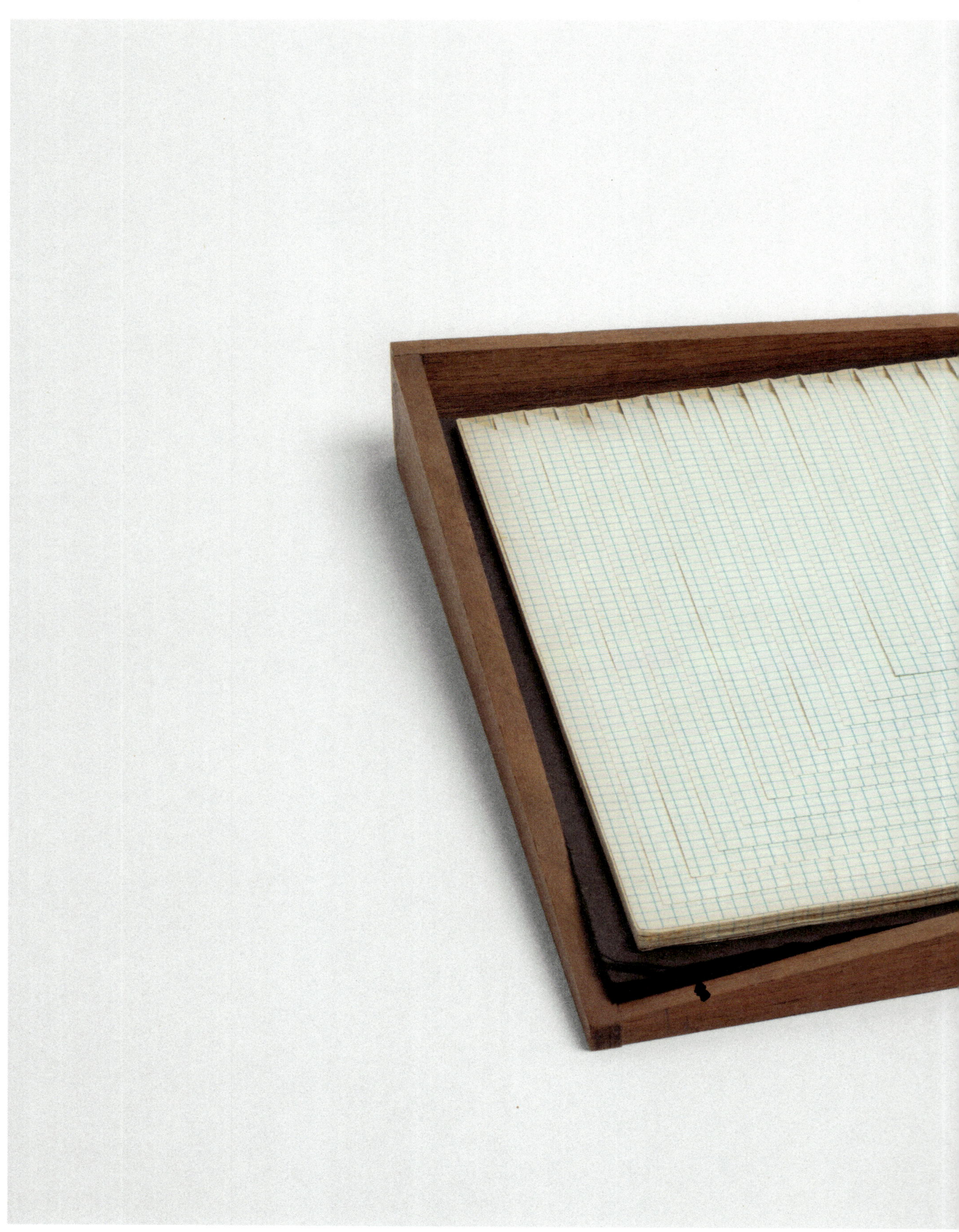

 From the series *Paper Pad. 1000 Surfaces*, 1970s

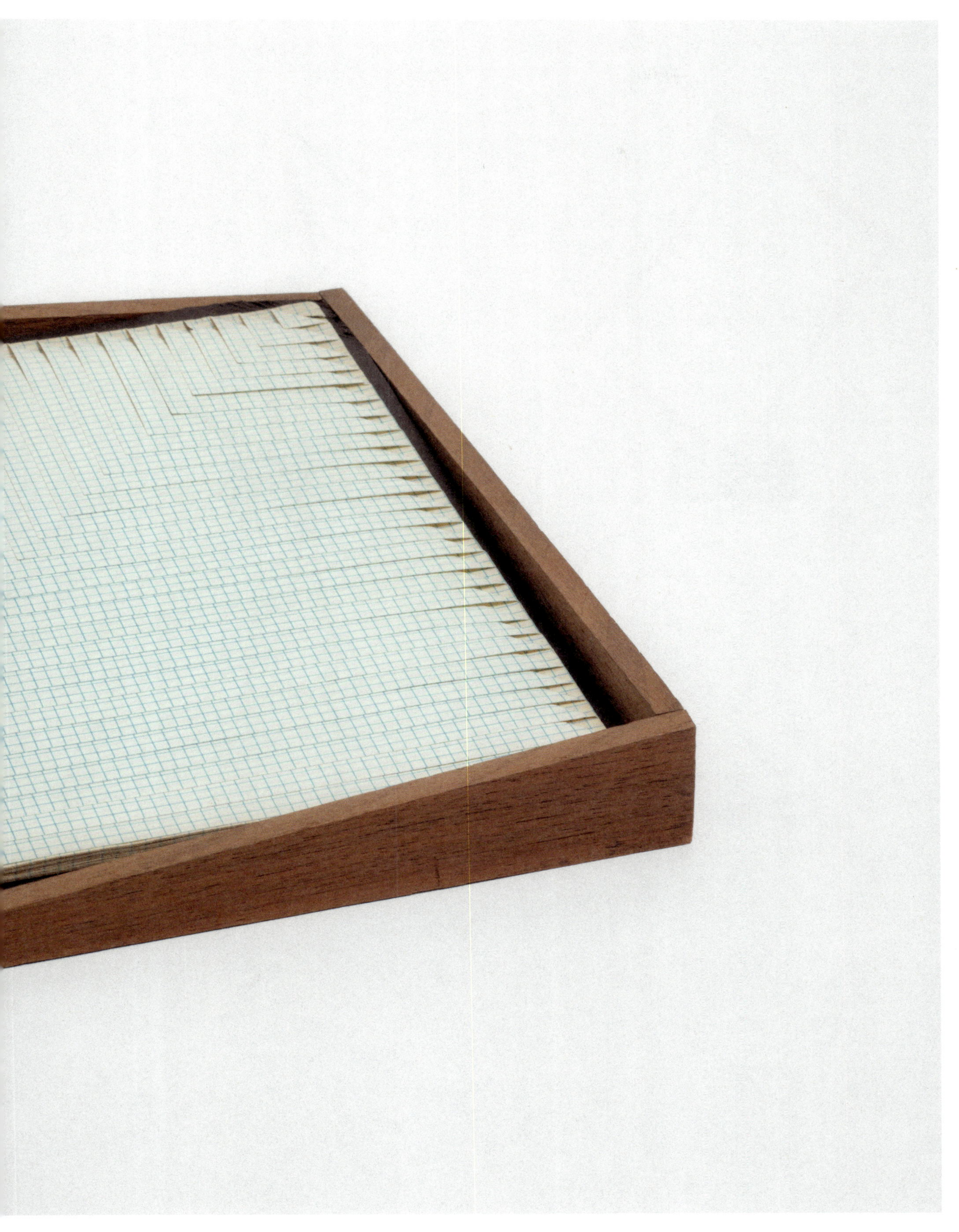

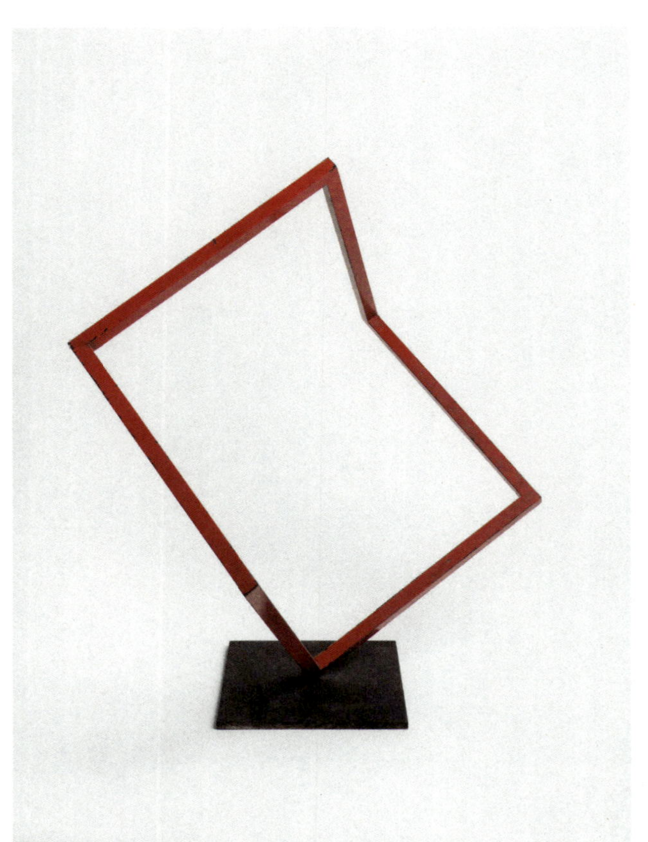

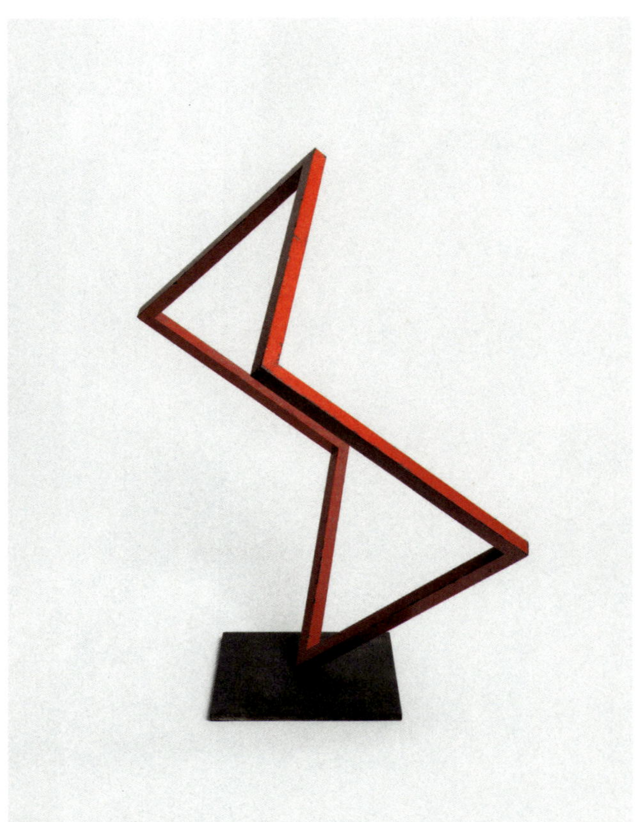

 One Constant Seen from 36 Points of View, steel painted red, 1976

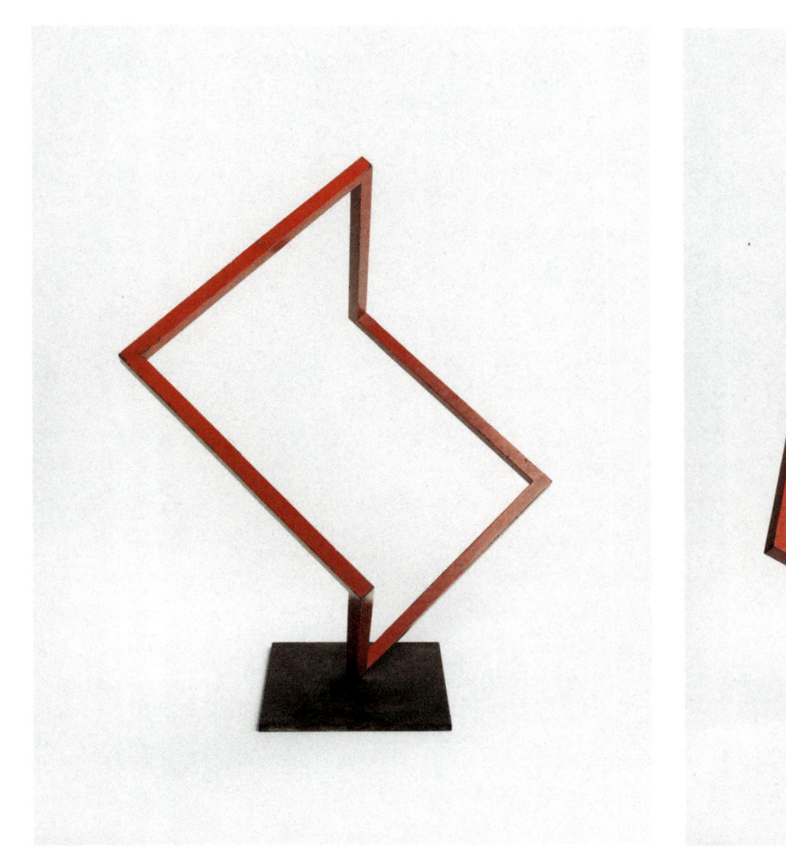

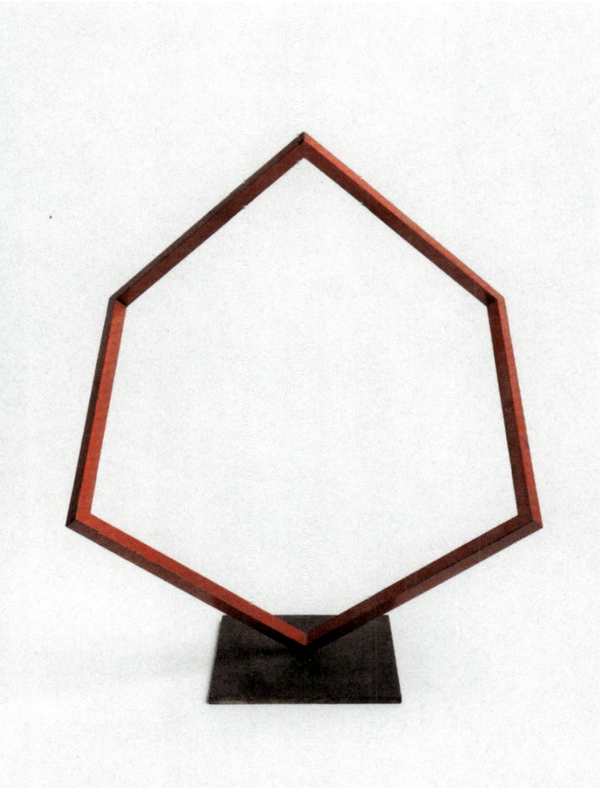

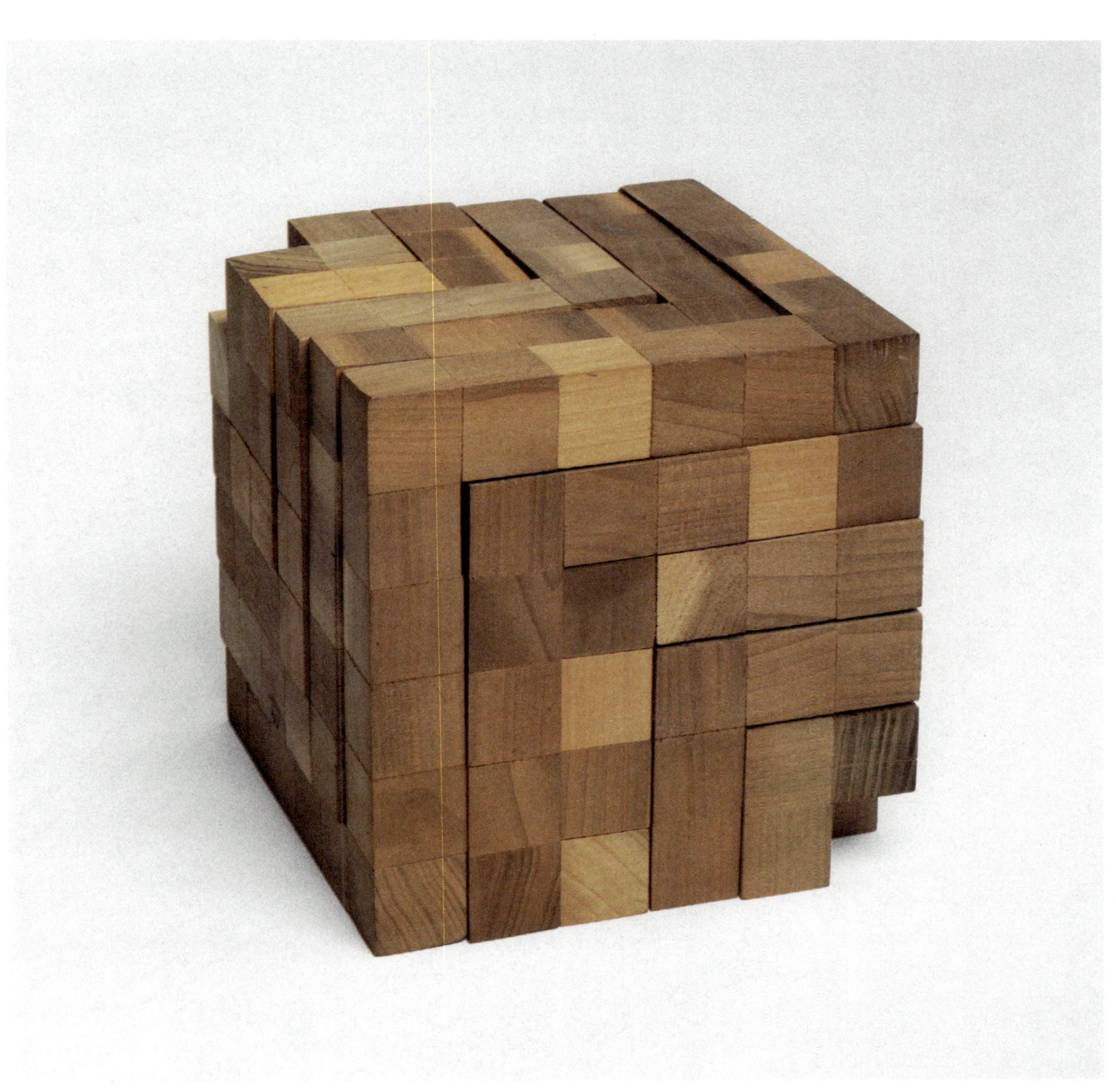

One Cube Built with Open Cubes of Progressively Changing Proportions of Space and Matter, Built-up with 152 Equal Elements, wood models, 1971

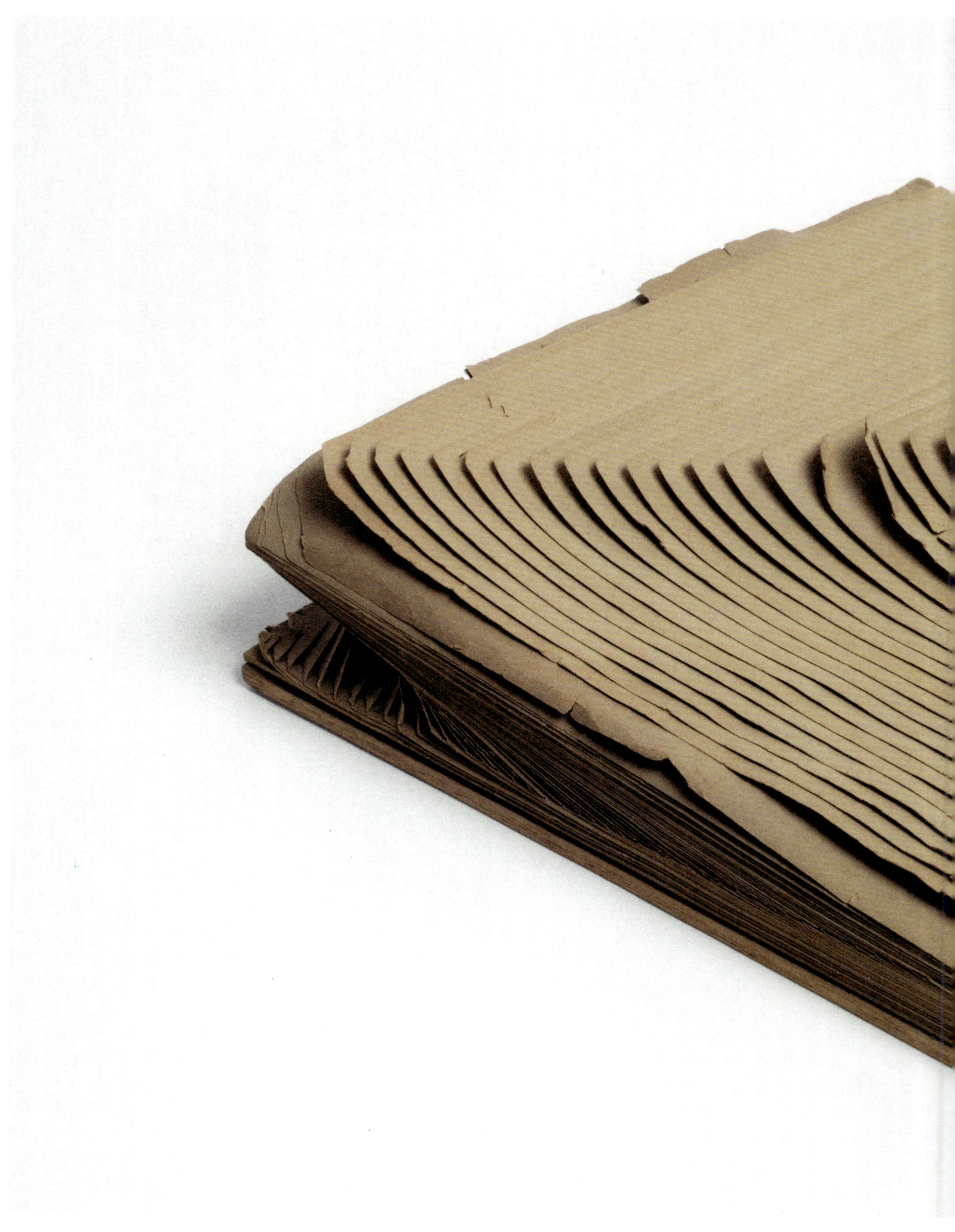

 From the series *Paper Pad. 1000 Surfaces*, 1970s

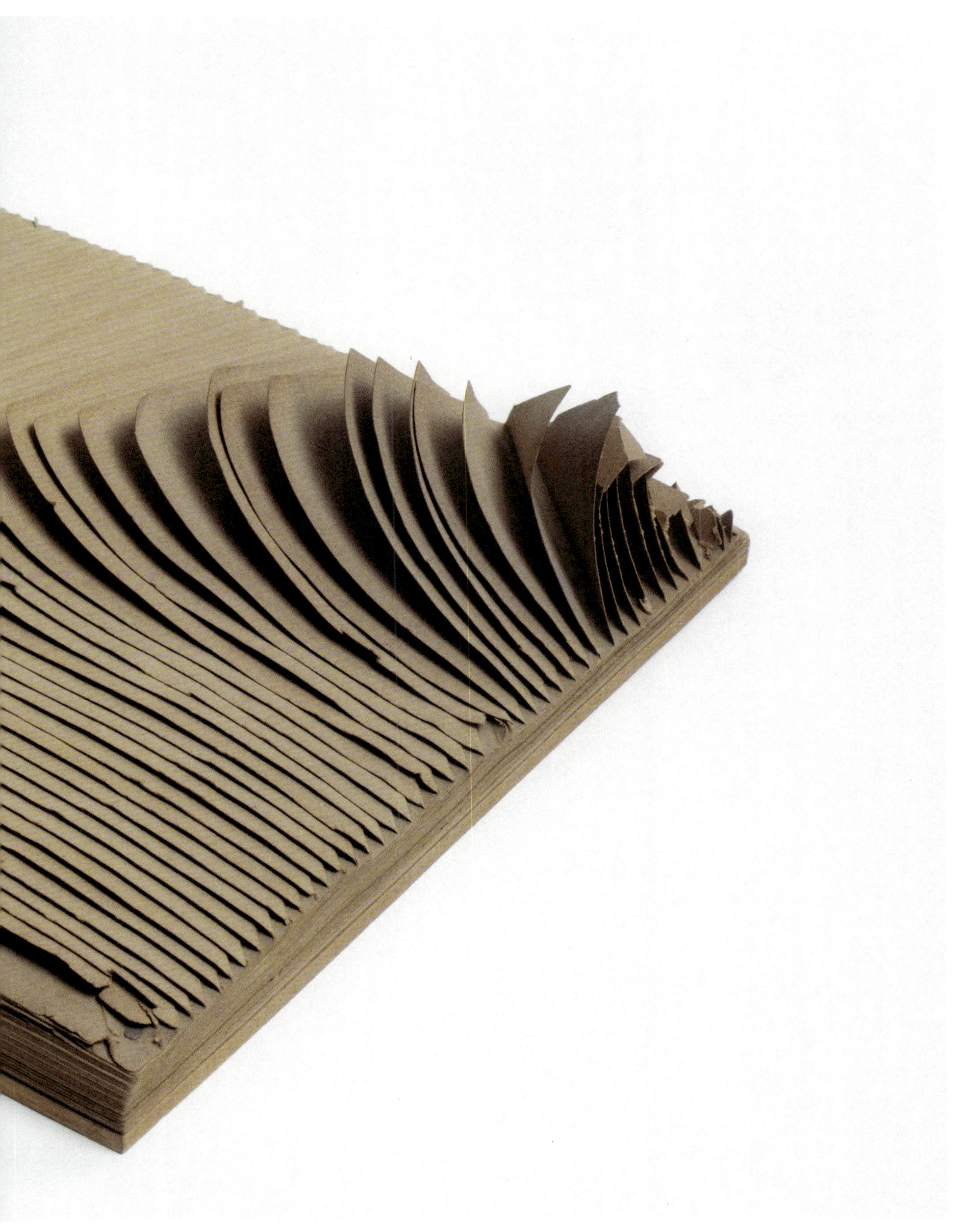

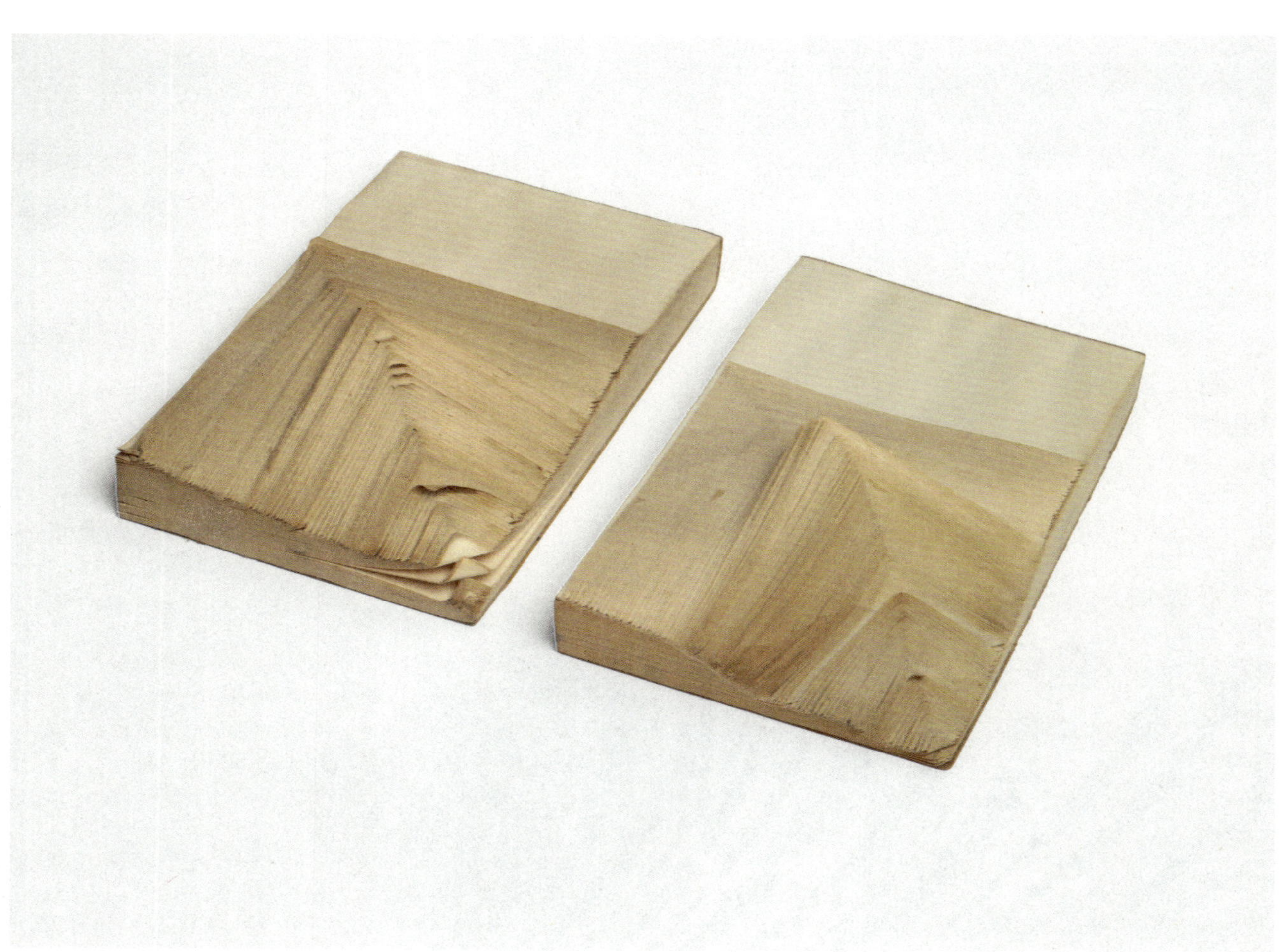

 From the series *Paper Pad. 1000 Surfaces*, 1970s

Texts

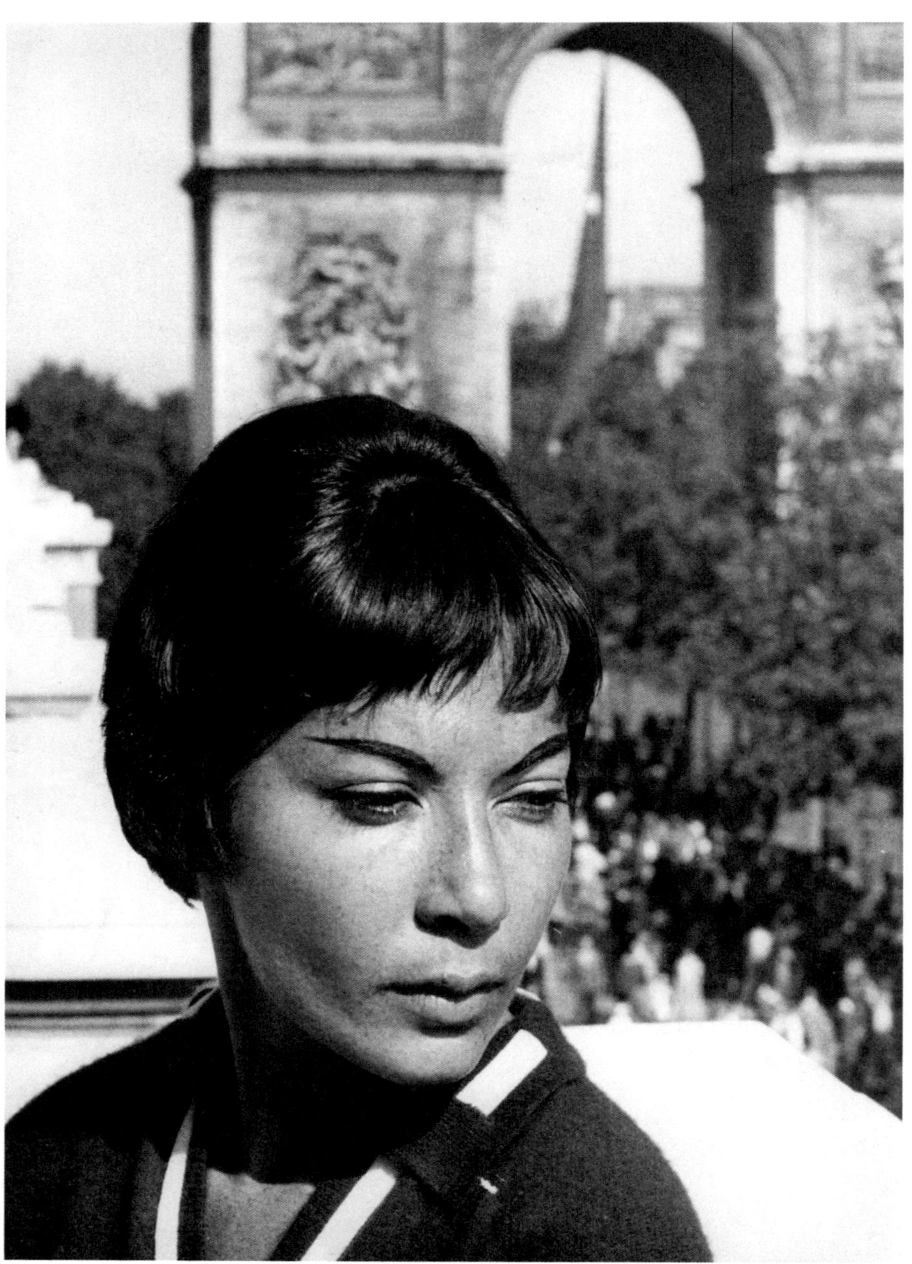

 Bettina, Paris, ca. 1957

Bettina, Volume One

Yto Barrada

It has been seven years since I met Bettina. She became an admired friend, and even now, there's just so much I don't know about her.

It all began on an evening in 2015, when my neighbor in Brooklyn, the Dutch filmmaker Corinne van der Borch, was showing some of her films in her workspace. She screened *Girl with Black Balloons*, her 2010 film about an artist named Bettina—namely, the artwork she had lost in a fire and her life in the Chelsea Hotel. Bettina is a striking character, and I couldn't stop thinking about her artwork, of which you caught only glimpses scattered throughout the film. I wanted to know more. I found some *New York Times* articles about Bettina and other hotel residents who were struggling to stay in their homes after the hotel had been sold and was being renovated, and I heard about another film, *Bettina* (2008), by Sam Bassett, but I couldn't track him down (I later found out he was a neighbor). I managed to see Bettina's Super 8 film *Phenomenological New York* (1976–86) and its images of people walking in the streets and going to work, reflected on urban surfaces. It was amazing. I very much wanted to meet this artist.

I first met Bettina at a Coney Island hospital, where she was being treated for dehydration. We sat in the hospital dining room. It's impossible to miss Bettina's total sovereignty or her sense of humor. She was very New York: she would snap at you with a smile, play with language. Soon after, I visited her at the Chelsea Hotel. The building was a construction site, with plastic barriers, dust, and noise. Bettina's front door was plastered with xeroxes of word art made on a typewriter. As instructed, I opened the door to her apartment without knocking, and then announced myself in the small corridor filled with an assemblage of miniature xeroxed versions of her favorite artworks—at the threshold of her visual grammar. There were miniatures of the photos she shot from her balcony of the recurring actions of street-level passersby; abstract cutout shapes in black and white; xeroxed word works potently stacked atop one another; leaves of New York City trees laid out in grids; and much, much more ...

Inside, Bettina sat on a twin bed, surrounded on three sides by industrial metal shelves. One sees Bettina and understands that some disaster has taken place, long ago. Nobody begins with this kind of withdrawal. The shelves were piled with art supplies, materials, boxes of artwork, giant wooden shapes, her books and magazines, and photo boxes. Her bedroom opened onto a second room, whose door was open to a balcony overlooking Twenty-Third Street. There, stained glass windows overlooked the street, and the sun shone through onto tables covered with wooden, brass, and marble sculptures made by Bettina. The heater was on full blast. The radio was tuned to NPR. I had to move slowly, turning sideways to navigate through the obstacle course of boxes and piles of papers, to reach the one available red stool in front of her daybed. As I asked about her work, another obstacle appeared: Bettina insisted that all her work had been lost in a fire. In 1966, she said, her studio in Brooklyn burned down, her cat died, and she lost decades of work. She moved to the Chelsea Hotel and started from scratch, remaking everything. Now, she said, she won't show anybody her work—it's all gone. But looking around, I could make out the outlines of a prolific body of work, covered with dust.

I began to visit her regularly, just to talk, and did not see much more of her work in those boxes.

I was not the first to encounter this conundrum. In getting to know Bettina, one sees her talent all around and hears countless wonderful stories of her artwork and the life she led in dedication to it, while sitting with her total reticence to share the work or even acknowledge that it still exists. The hotel room sits in a kind of suspended animation, held in an obscure, melancholic dimension outside of space and time.

Two years after my initial visit, Bettina's brother Morty called Corinne. He was moving to Israel and had some artworks of Bettina's in his basement. I joined Corinne to visit Morty in the Rockaways and inspect Bettina's works. There were sculptures, many in marble, from the 1950s, '60s, and '70s, along with boxes of films, papers, photographs, and beautiful portraits of Bettina in her thirties. Every box I opened confirmed what we all suspected: Firstly, that this artist had created an incredible body of work that somehow very few people had seen; and secondly, that many pieces were damaged. We called Bettina from Morty's kitchen and planned to bring everything to my studio to take inventory of this archive. As Corinne and I packed Bettina's fragile works for their move to Brooklyn, it was clear that something was beginning.

Back at my studio, I started looking carefully through the work, trying to piece together Bettina's story, which felt like the nocturne of a modern soul. The Xerox portfolio, the black-and-white sculptures ... She grew up in a New York family originally from Austria, and she attended the Girls' Commercial High School in Prospect Heights, Brooklyn. Her dad had a music store in the East Village. In her twenties she declined a scholarship to Parsons and lived in Europe, where she designed textiles, made art, and developed a rigorous and demanding approach to her work. Then there was the fire in her live-work space overlooking the Brooklyn-Queens embankment that took all her artworks and her cat. There were the Chelsea years, the rebuilding of works in stone and other fireproof materials ... her legendary renown as the *most beautiful woman at the Chelsea Hotel*, at a time when every artist and musician passed through a room there. But what about showing her work? There was a show with Ivan Karp at the OK Harris gallery in SoHo, in 1980, and then a gap of forty years. Somehow, through all this, Bettina had persisted in leading a life entirely dedicated to her art.

By this point, I was obsessed with seeing the unseen in Bettina's apartment: what was inside those boxes. But she was totally uninterested in doing all that unpacking and showing of work. Her answer was not even a question: "Why." Beyond my own eye wanting more, I didn't have an answer. Only then did I start thinking about a show, which my team began imagining by sending a small selection of images to people in the arts: curators, gallerists, and friends. "Please look at this," we said. "I think it's amazing. How and where can we show her work?" We got very few responses, most of them questions: Was there any documentation of the works that were destroyed via photos or exhibitions that she did? Was the recreation of her destroyed works all done from memory? The fire had destroyed all of her work and was a traumatic experience for her. For me the idea that an artist is recreating her own work due to the fact that all of it was destroyed is fascinating.

Our colleagues needed clarity about Bettina and her work, chronology, and story. By then, I understood that clarity wasn't so easy. The partial answers didn't trigger what we needed: a place to show Bettina's work. And only once we had that could I open those damn boxes, start research and documentation, and put the puzzle together. It was a catch-22.

A new friend of Bettina's, Varun Khanna, had met her outside the hotel and been struck by the phenomena that was Bettina. He sent me images of some black portfolios Bettina had shown him—indexes containing references to many series of her artworks. But her apartment at the Chelsea was so densely packed with her art that I didn't know where to start. Though it had clearly been organized at some time, the system was nonlinear and opaque. Bettina's neighbor, Sam, who had made the 2008 film about her, worked with her on a big cleanup in 2006, but entropy had since reclaimed the space. I managed to scan some of her drawings and collages, but without a show, she wouldn't give me permission to open the boxes, so I still had no real access to her work.

A pillar during Bettina's life was Rachel Cohen-Lunning, a friend who still lives at the hotel—a talented jewelry and eyeglasses artist. Rachel visited Bettina daily for many years to help her with the mechanics of living. She is a rock, deeply trusted by Bettina and demanding when it came to her well-being. But in 2008, the new owners of the hotel, eager to rid themselves of this last generation of long-term residents, arranged for health authorities to visit the apartment, which they had deliberately long stopped maintaining. Based on the conditions of her apartment collection, the authorities decided that Bettina could not care for herself and appointed her brother Morty as her official guardian.

So Morty, Rachel, Corinne, Varun, and I had all been caught in Bettina's suspended animation, the parallel world that she had created. Even as life took us in different directions—Corinne moving across Brooklyn, Varun moving back to Oslo—we were all troubled by a shared sense of urgency that Bettina's work must be shown, and soon. Despite months of brainstorming how we could exhibit her work, we couldn't come up with anything that had the grandeur of Bettina's oeuvre or of the artist herself.

Then an opportunity arrived. In 2018, I had been invited to make new work for the inaugural exhibition at the Lower Manhattan Cultural Council's (LMCC) new space on Governors Island in New York Harbor.

I made a small project, but the show wasn't coming together properly. The curator and writer for the show, Omar Berrada, is a good friend of mine, and I had spoken to him about Bettina and my doubts about the exhibition I had planned. Then I had a lightbulb moment: maybe Bettina could save me. I called Omar and asked, "What if we made it a two-woman show?" Just raising the possibility of a real show could provide the excuse we needed to finally go through her work and make selections—to escape the catch-22. Omar met Bettina, and they connected right away.

A four-handed show? Bettina, looking at her work and mine side by side, said no and yes and no and then: yes. Now there was tremendous time pressure to conduct some kind of inventory so we could choose the right works. Finally, though gradually, Bettina allowed us into the archive in her apartment so we could begin the selection process. With this new access, I shared the task of making a more comprehensive inventory with my studio manager Marina Caron—who was first vetted by Bettina, of course.

Sorting through the works felt like walking into the final shot of *Citizen Kane*, with the crates piled beyond the edge of the frame ("What have you been doing all this time?" "Playing with a jigsaw puzzle."). We worked in Bettina's apartment at the Chelsea Hotel over that summer, compiling a document that detailed hundreds of artworks, with many more yet to be inventoried. As Bettina gave us access to her archive, she opened up, just a bit, about her life, sharing stories of her work with marble artisans in Italy; the carpenter near the Chelsea with whom she made her wooden sculptural series; designing textiles in London and Paris; drawing and photographing in Istanbul; the beautiful car she drove around Europe. In all her stories one thing was clear: art and life were one. As we took frantic notes, Bettina continued to work in parallel, going through her old work and producing new work for the exhibition. We selected around eighty works for the show, and she reluctantly permitted us to take the pieces to Governors Island for cleaning, preparation, and exhibition.

Rachel was essential in the success of our visits, helping us with scheduling and communication. An artist herself, she acted as a staunch advocate for Bettina's creative will throughout the curatorial process, standing firm on concerns Bettina expressed, following up on proper care of the works, and contributing suggestions and encouragement. Omar helped me explain our plan to Bettina: that this exhibition would introduce the city and the world to her work, and that we hoped much more would follow. The title of the exhibition, *The Power of Two Suns*, came from a film I made and included in the show, about weathering machines used to simulate the impact of the sun, wind, water, and salt on textiles over time. Now that Bettina was on board, we were able to play a kind of chess game, bringing forward pieces of hers in response to mine, and finding works that shared a direct connection and relevance to our overlapping artistic concerns. As she made her moves, I could see her ruminating on materials and things, giving form to her choices without ever trying to reorder the chaos of the world she had lived in.

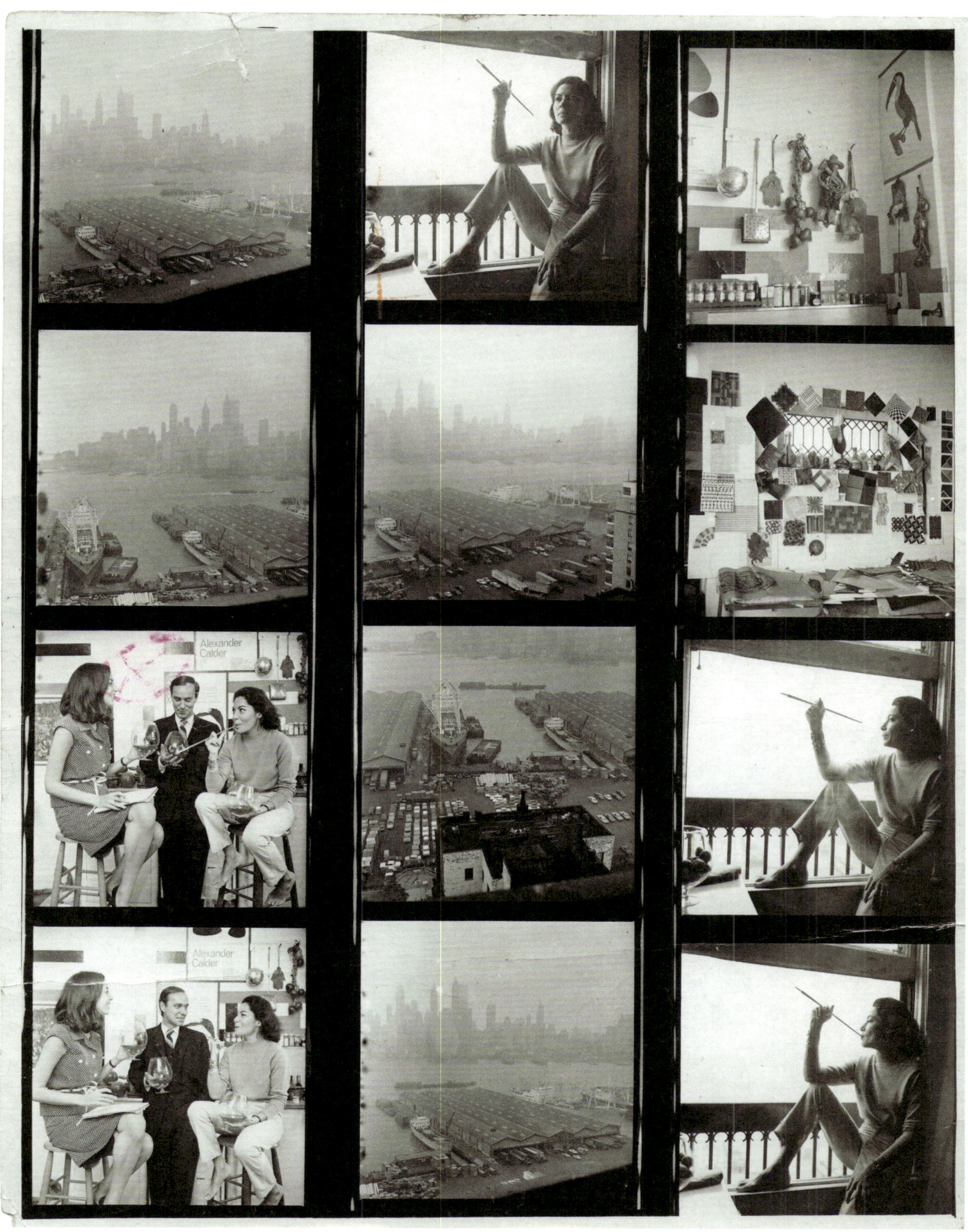

Pages 275–77: Bettina's studio in Brooklyn Heights before the fire
Contact sheet, from *Home Furnishings Daily*, 1966

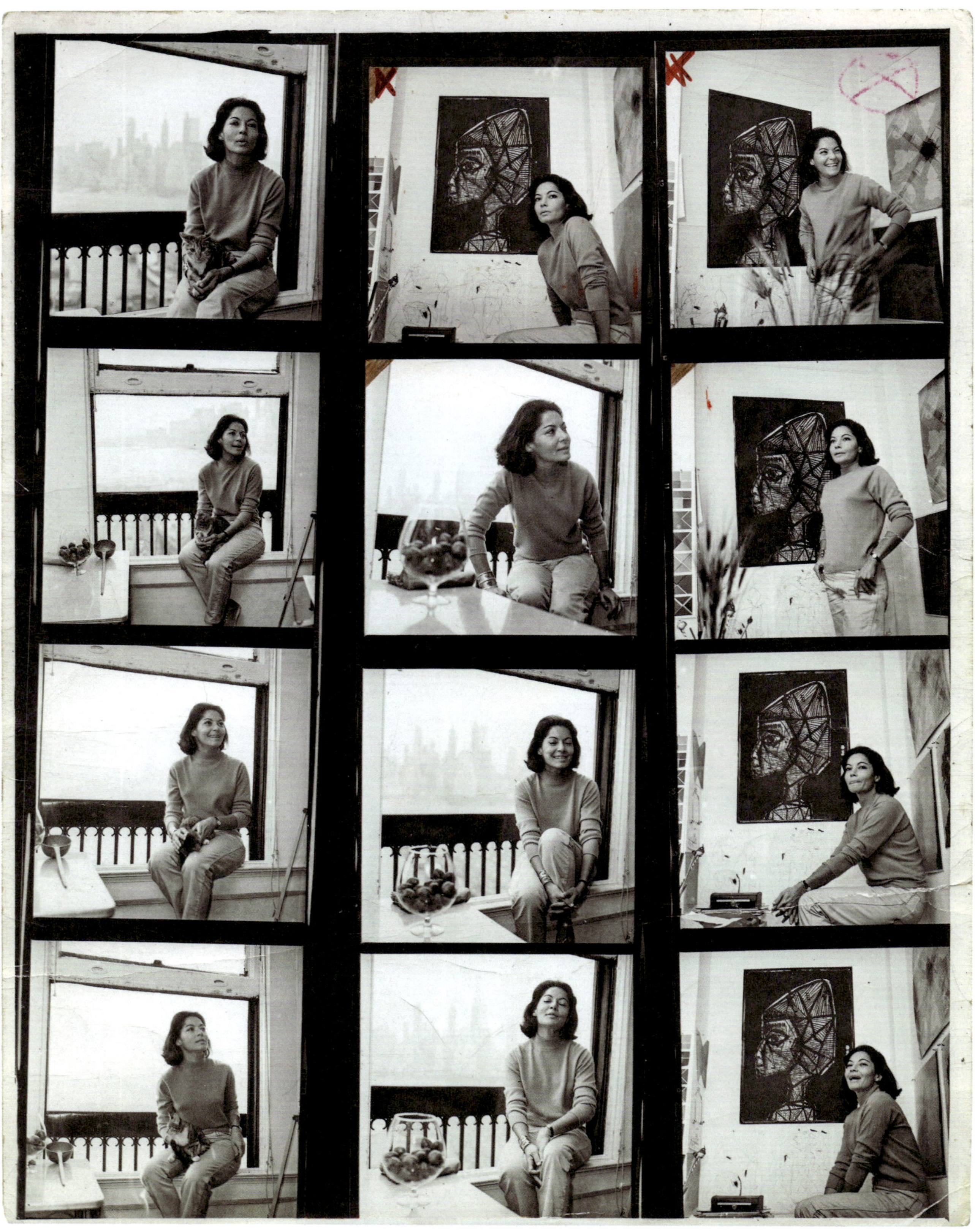

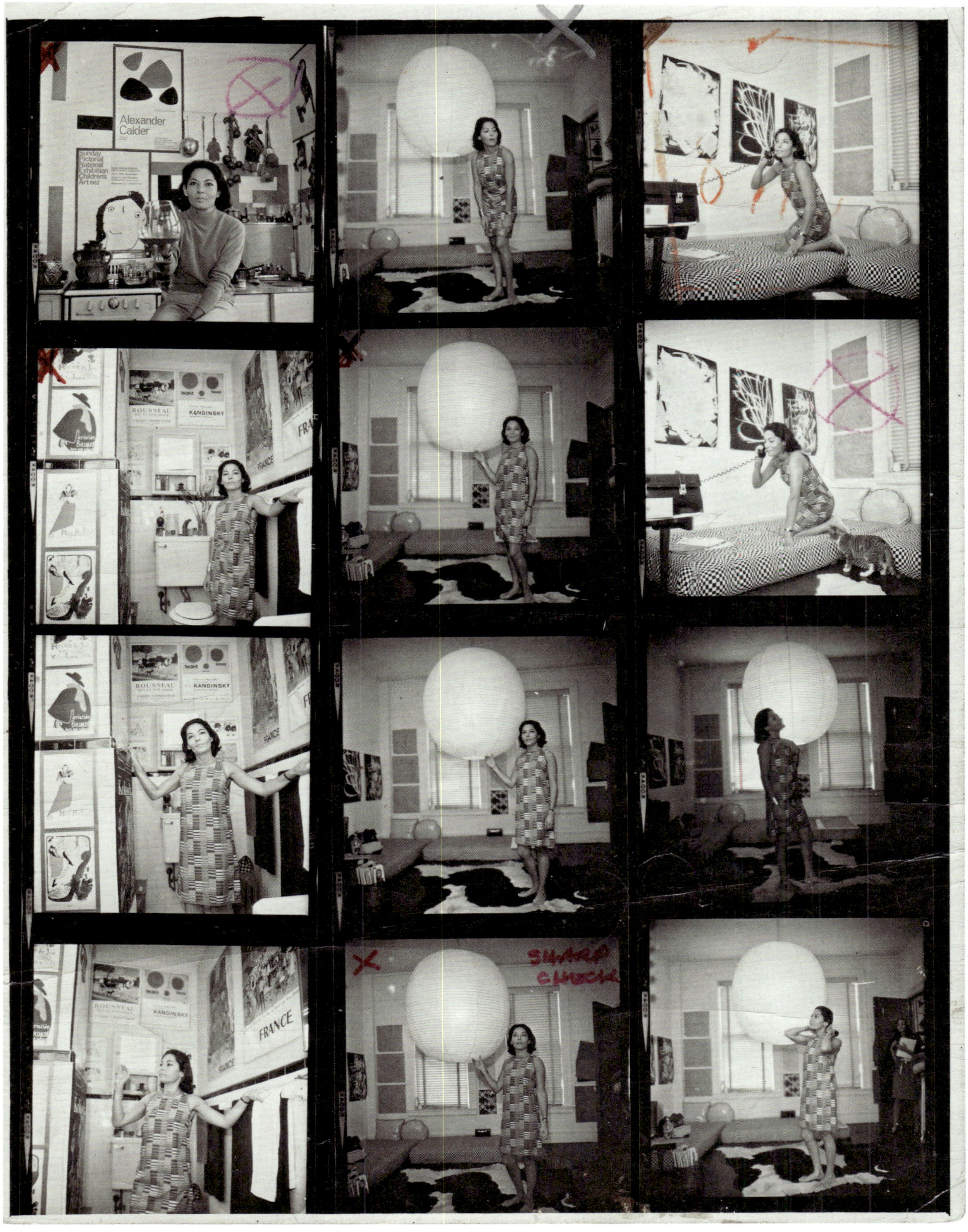
Alexander Calder
Sunday Pictorial National Exhibition Children's Art 1962
ROUSSEAU
KANDINSKY
FRANCE

There was much to be done to prepare Bettina's works for exhibition, from cleaning various materials to tracking down details, like dates of creation, to piecing together how different series were interrelated and how we could convey this through the display. Mira Van Den Neste came from Brussels to design the exhibition, and the LMCC team, led by Lili Chopra and Alice Russotti, worked tirelessly to help us realize this ambitious and challenging exhibition.

Opening night was September 12, 2019. LMCC had booked a ferry service for the opening. It was raining lightly as hundreds of people filled boats headed for the island. I coordinated with Rachel and Corinne to pick up Bettina at the hotel and make sure her family and hotel mates were all present. On a misty, cool evening we crossed New York Harbor and arrived at the island. Bettina's brother Morty, her nephew, cousins, and friends all came for this momentous celebration. Wearing her rainbow, crocheted sweater and red Wayfarer sunglasses, Bettina was incandescent, glowing from her wheelchair. The next day she told us that she slept through the night for the first time in ages.

Two weeks later, on September 28, we celebrated Bettina's ninety-second birthday in the hallway of the Chelsea Hotel, in front of her room. Corinne, Marina, and I were there with cake and flowers, along with many hotel residents, including some who had just seen Bettina's work for the first time on Governors Island. The celebration was also for the door that was opening between the wider public and her life's work. One critic wrote that the exhibit:

reflected on our individual and collective reactions to the onset of disaster ... [presenting] a small selection from Bettina's remarkable body of work. On the plinths were a set of long wooden pieces, floating like the ghostly remains of an ancient ship; on the long tables, an array of sculptural experiments in wood and marble. Each of these belonged to a larger series developed out of self-imposed constraints from which gesture and accident subtly emerged.[1]

Bettina has joined a long list of prescient female artists—including Betye Saar, Ana Mendieta, Lorraine O'Grady, Carmen Herrera, Etel Adnan, and Alina Szapocznikow—whose work has been discovered by much larger audiences at the end of their lives, or after their deaths. All are artists whose influence is unquestionable and whose resonance with current concerns is deeply moving. Only now, at the end of her life and following her death, has she been viewed as more than a symbol or a victim and restored to us as an artist.

The exhibition closed on October 31, 2019, and Bettina said: "What's next?" Having no other answer, we decided to maintain the momentum by making a catalogue for her that documented the show. But since we had unearthed so much work in the process, the catalogue swiftly turned into a book that aimed to document her works, texts, and papers. The designer, Gregor Huber—cofounder of the design collective Huber/Sterzinger and with whom I have done several books—dove in while we had no budget, deadline, or publisher. He, Marina, and I visited Bettina

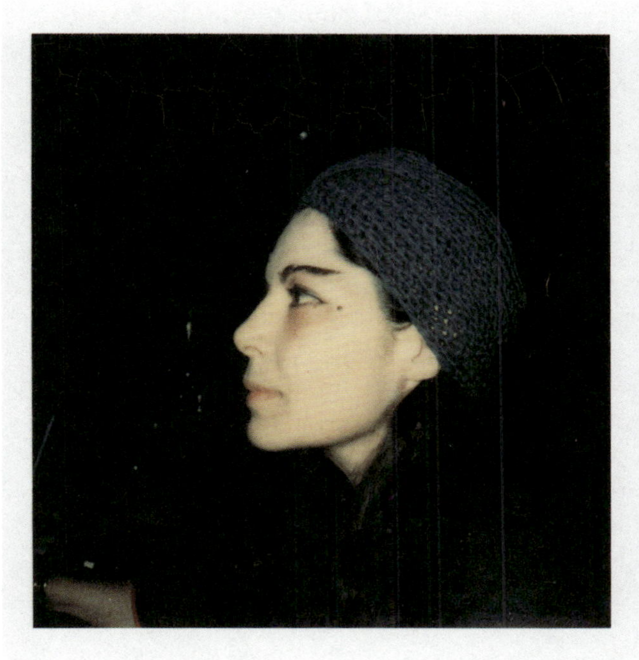

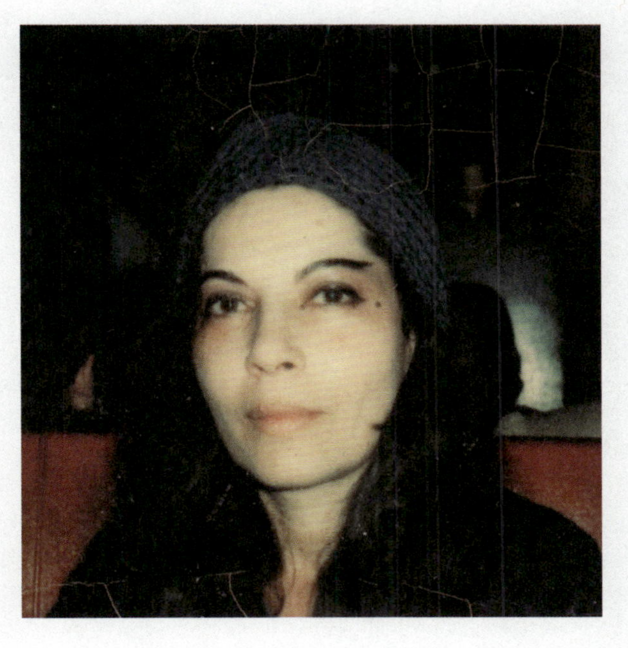

Bettina, 1970s

"A LANDMARK OF N.Y.C."

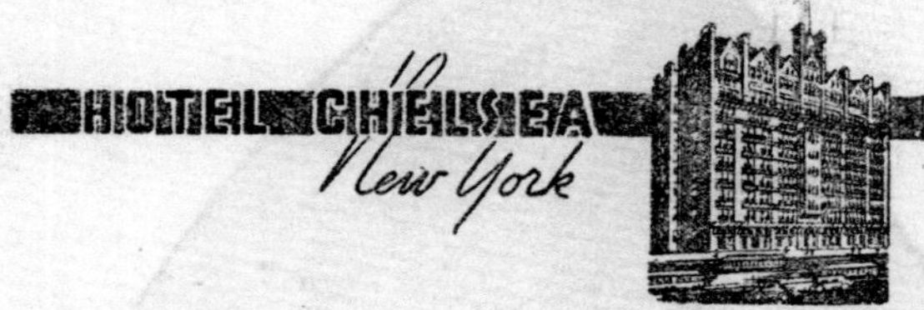

AT SEVENTH AVENUE
WEST TWENTY THIRD STREET
NEW YORK, N. Y. 10011

CABLE ADDRESS • HOCHELSEA • NEW YORK
TELEPHONE CHELSEA 3-3700

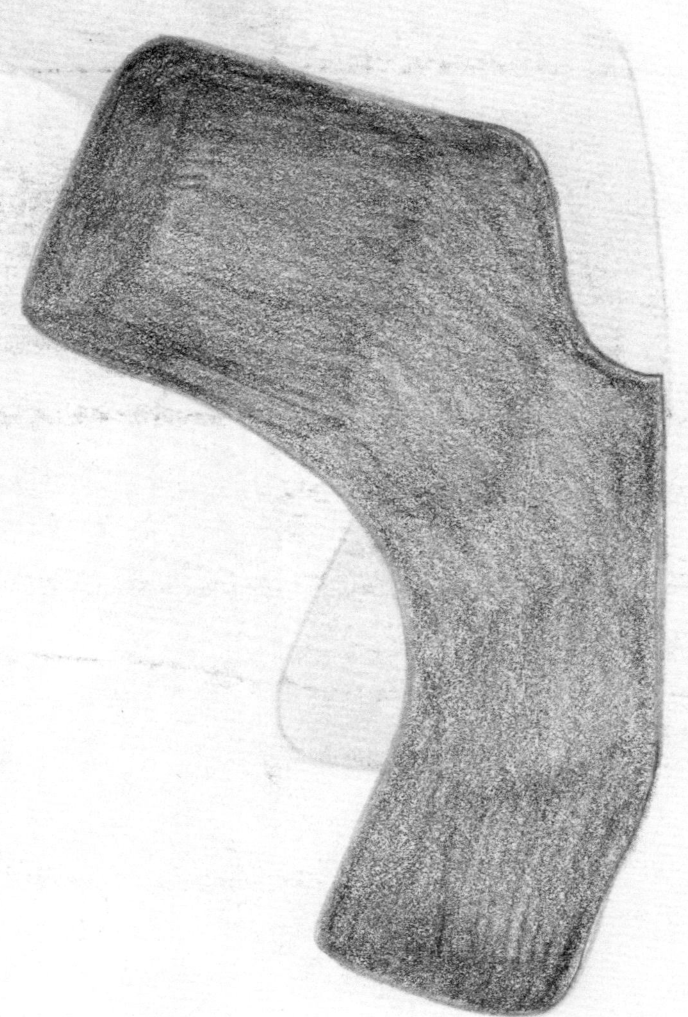

LARGE and SOUND-PROOF ROOMS

Drawing on stationary from the Chelsea Hotel, (date unknown)

on a quasi-weekly basis, bringing her favorite cake and chopped liver from the delicatessen Russ & Daughters. An ongoing conversation about things we unearthed took form. Bettina would provide wry commentary to one of us while another dug, scanned, and organized the materials in archival boxes. Every time we visited, she had prepared a small pile of work she expected us to look at. We got fractions of her biography and started taping more conversations about her experiences: the marble factory in Italy; Switzerland by convertible; collecting glass in Israel or leaves in Brooklyn. Bettina was excited by our teamwork and would summarily end the session when night fell.

Gregor's process is different from that of other graphic designers. He's rigorously intellectual and intuitive, and we were both pushing for a book that would have a punk energy and reflect Bettina's raw elegance. When we had a draft, he made three physical copies of the book on a Xerox printer: two for us, and one—with an image of one of her egg sculptures on the cover—to surprise Bettina for her birthday. In the summer of 2020, due to the COVID-19 pandemic, we couldn't visit Bettina; by the fall, she had lost her voice.

One fall day, I got a text message from Rachel: a photo with a message from Bettina written in marker on a paper towel, in capital letters:

"I NEED MY FIRST BOOK TO BE LESS COMPLETE LESS EXPENSIVE AND MORE AVAILABLE TO MORE PEOPLE. THE BOOK YOU ARE WORKING ON WILL BE VERY EXPENSIVE. TOO COMPLETE AND SHOULD BE RESERVED FOR A LATER DATE."

Well, shit. Redesign the book to be less expensive? We had been applying for publishing grants, and that same day, I got a call from France informing us we had won the LUMA Rencontres Dummy Book Award Arles 2020.

When the book was almost ready, Bettina called again, this time on FaceTime. It was hard to communicate, but what she said was clear.

"I don't want to do the book."
I said, "OK."
She said, "We have to do eight books."
I said, "OK, this will be the first one."
Silence.
She said, "You're so clever."

The story is just beginning.

1. Sukanya Garg, "Yto Barrada and Bettina Explored Responses to Disaster for Exhibition in New York," *STIR*, November 30, 2019, https://www.stirworld.com/see-features-yto-barrada-and-bettina-explored-responses-to-disaster-for-exhibition-in-new-york.

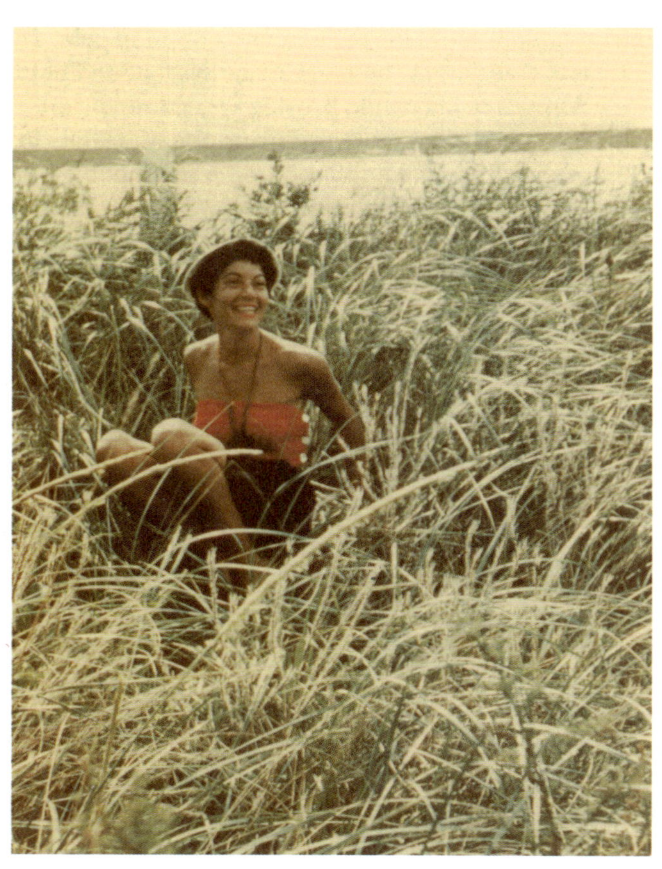

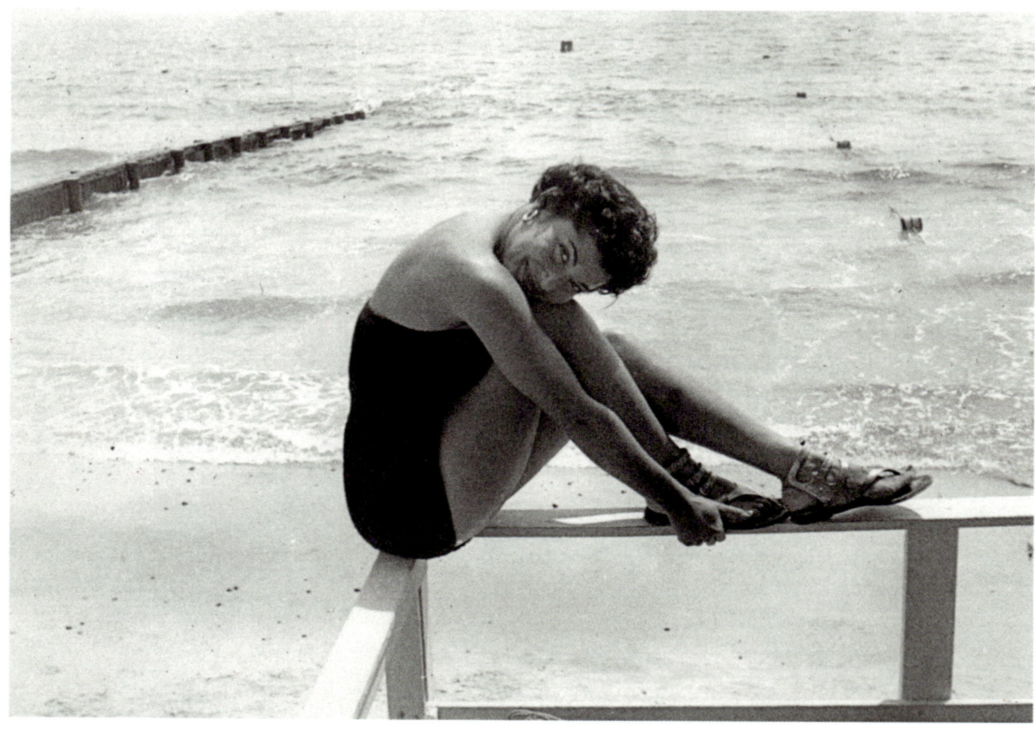

Bettina, 1950s and '60s

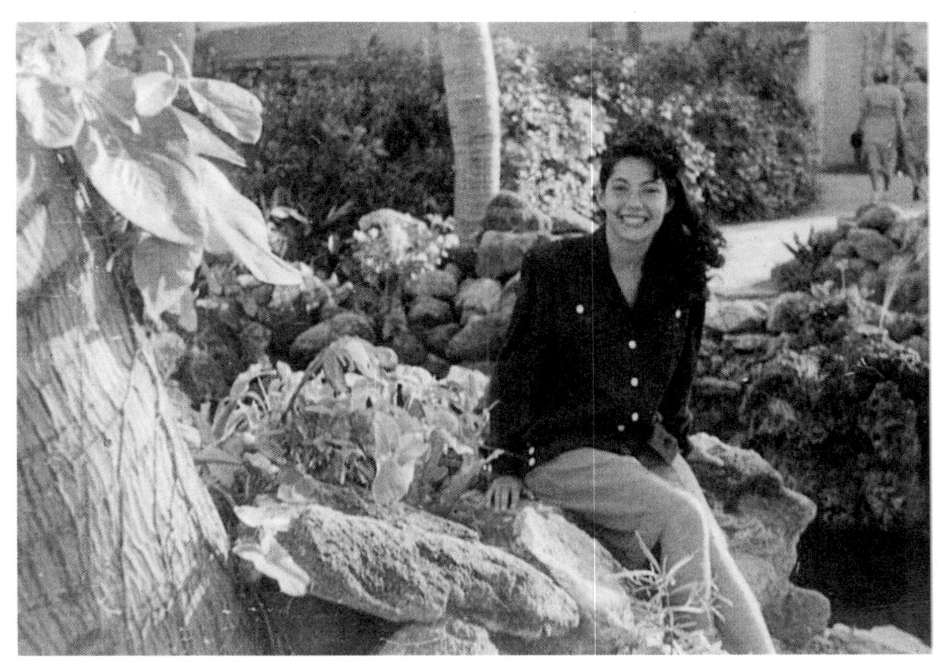

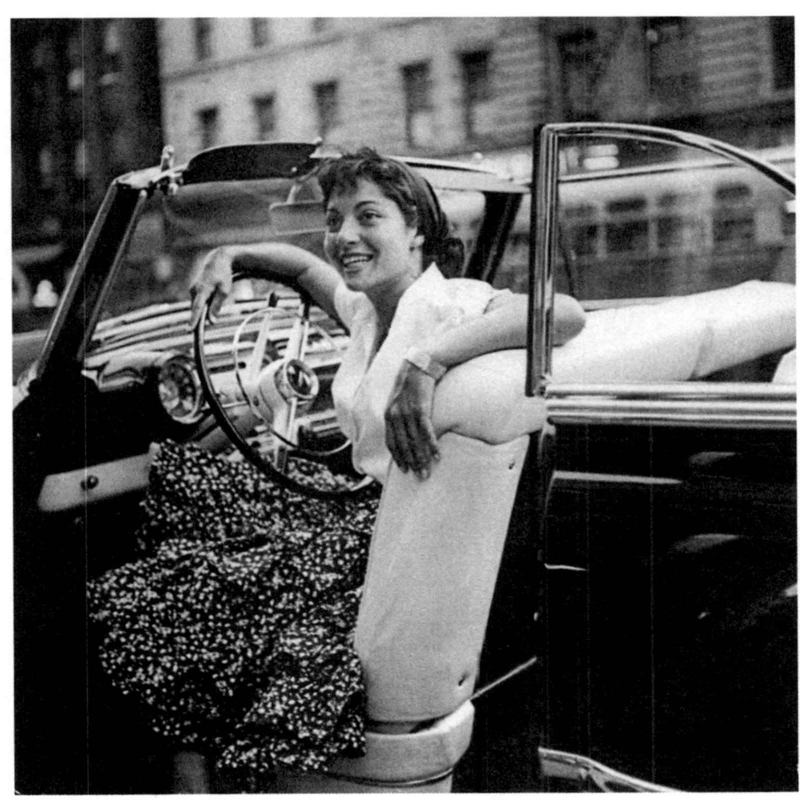

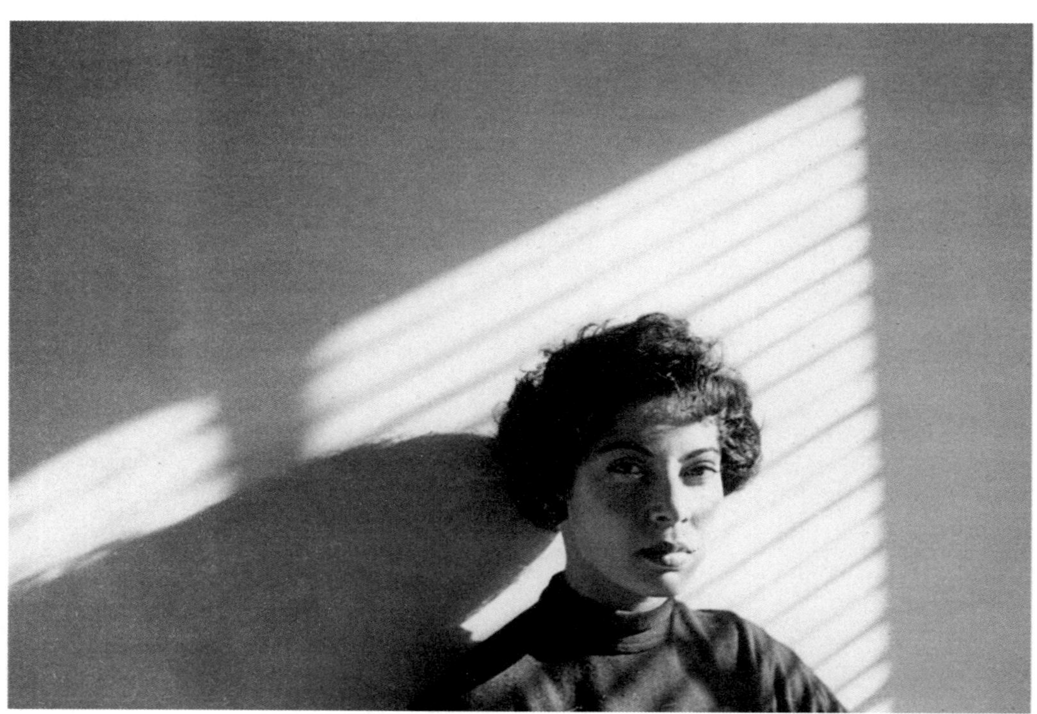

 Bettina, 1950s

Interrelated Intergenerative Interdisciplines: The Photographs and Sculptures of Bettina

Antonia Pocock

In November 1966, a month before her studio was destroyed in a fire, the artist Bettina Grossman was featured in *Home Furnishings Daily* (*HFD*) for her work in design. Bettina (who chose to go by her first name only) had recently returned to New York after eight years of designing textiles, silver, and mosaics in Europe, and she was poised to "revitalize the world of American design," according to the article.[1] Conjuring a heroine from a European New Wave film, the article describes her as "dark-haired, cat-eyed, dusty-voiced" before keenly observing that "she plays with the most intricately geometric lines like pick-up sticks. She works pattern over pattern until surface exists only in irregular repetitions."[2] A design of overlapping hexagons reproduced in the article bears out this description: seemingly random, like a scattering of pick-up sticks, the complex geometric field is the result of superimposing a variety of "constants" and "surfaces," to use Bettina's terminology.[3] Evidently paying close attention to contemporary art, Bettina told *HFD* that her earlier designs anticipated the "OPtical [*sic*] and Systematic Painting"[4] then prominent in New York galleries and museums. Bettina's designs from the '60s also foreshadow the drawings, prints, sculptures, photographs, and films she developed over the following decades, which emerge from the play between a constant and its endless variations.

Fire and Water

A photograph accompanying the *HFD* article shows Bettina perched on the windowsill of her soon-to-be scorched studio overlooking New York Harbor from Brooklyn Heights. Her previous studios—an "apartment overlooking the Seine" in Paris and a "Thames-side flat in London"—apparently offered similarly aquatic views. Bettina's predilection for water is also evident in her color photographs from Europe, published in the October/November 1965 issue of *Camera 35*. One captures a scene along the Seine in which horizontal bands of river, embankment, book stalls, and buildings evoke archaeological strata. "From across the river," Bettina wrote in a statement accompanying the image, "I was able to compose in the viewer the true proportions without perspective, which gave me a flat design surface as if I had drawn them on paper."[5] The other photograph, a close-up of a sailboat in a fishing village on the Normandy coast, similarly flattens space into pattern by focusing on the linear play of fishing nets, ropes, and riggings. Like Bettina's early design work, these initial photographs prefigure her later work. Bettina would go on to use high-contrast exposures to further abstract photographs into formal configurations that she sometimes used as the basis for sculptures. Though few of Bettina's later photographs take water as their subject, many feature rippled reflections that suggest the fluidity of river and sea. Wave-like structures also appear throughout her sculptures. Perhaps water attracted Bettina as a model of repetitive yet fluctuating forms.

Equally important to Bettina's artistic development was water's antithesis: fire. After losing all her work in a conflagration that consumed her Brooklyn studio in 1966, Bettina was forced to make a fresh start. "I had nothing, and I had to start over. And I think the thing that I started working on first were eggs," Bettina recounted.[6] As a symbol of birth and beginnings, the egg is a fitting motif for an artist who had to begin her work from scratch. Upon earning an award in 1970 to work in marble in Italy, Bettina continued to explore ovular shapes in a series of small black-and-white marble sculptures.[7] She explained her turn to sculpture as a way of making her work more tangible after the devastating destruction of the fire: "When you start with nothing, and then you go through a process of building again ... then you find out that two dimensions are not sufficient to convey the ultimate feeling. So you really have to start constructing with solid material or make it concrete."[8] Marble may have appealed to her partly for its fire-resistant properties. She also began meticulously documenting her work with photography and photocopies, perhaps to protect it from further loss. This painstaking documentation became central to her artistic process, allowing her to generate ever-new forms through iteration.

Random Constant

The suite of black-and-white marble eggs that Bettina began producing in Italy, titled *Options for an Angle: 24 Inconstants from One Constant* (1971), emerged from her theory of the "random constant."[9] As she explained, "By using absolutes I have demonstrated that everything is relative. That absolutes are merely constants that are equivocal and mediating and subject to change."[10] The constant in this series is not the egg, Bettina clarified, but the precise angle of the cut used in slicing sections from it: "I made a dozen eggs using one angle. And this one angle was consistent throughout the dozen. And I used black and white stone. And I cut through both stones at the same time using a jig, and then I relocated the white with black.... And I developed these very strange curves. Each one was different. And then I found out I could go on much further than this dozen and still they would be changing and never would I have two alike."[11] A diagram illustrating the myriad permutations that result from the intersection of a right angle and a rotated egg appears in one of the albums that documents her projects.[12] The permutations are multiplied further if two or more orthogonal cuts are made to the egg, which Bettina seems to have explored in another diagram and a set of half a dozen additional egg sculptures.[13]

Bettina's marble eggs call to mind Constantin Brancusi's egg-like marble sculpture, *The Newborn* (1915), which is similarly small, freestanding, and altered by a straight slice. Like Brancusi, Bettina also photographed her sculptures, suggesting how they may be exhibited and viewed.[14] Brancusi shot a bronze version of *The Newborn* in close-up to capture the reflection of his studio on its polished surface—a staging that establishes the work as a metaphor for the studio where artwork is born.[15] Bettina photographed her eggs in pairs that show the substitution of corresponding black and white segments. Beyond documenting and displaying the sculptures, these photographs liken the sculptures' inverted structures to the positive-negative binary of black-and-white photography itself. To take the analogy further, eggs, like photographs, are emblems of reproduction. Bettina's first foray into three-dimensional work, then, applies photographic processes of reversal and duplication to sculpture.

In Italy, Bettina also produced a collection of marble cubes with orthogonal cuts made at various intervals titled *Finite Structures / Orthogon / Random Penetration of Four Equal Constants by Eight Elements of Progressive Displacement (23 out of a possible 1,048,576)* (date unknown).[16] They are based on two-dimensional designs showing sequences of squares, partitioned by right angles, that Bettina developed in Europe in 1962 and 1963.[17] As sculptures, the cubes appear in a series of photographs that demonstrate the "progressive displacement" of black-and-white sections indicated in the title. Like Donald Judd's "stacks" and "progressions" and Sol LeWitt's orthogonal floor structures from the 1960s and '70s, Bettina's *Finite Structures* participates in "the serial attitude" theorized by Mel Bochner in *Artforum* in 1967. Bochner distinguishes "serially ordered works" from "multiple variants" based on their derivation from a "systematically predetermined process (permutation, progression, rotation, reversal)" that is "self-exhausting."[18] Bettina discussed her work in similar terms: "It doesn't require the participation of anyone else in that it, unto itself, is self-regenerating."[19]

Recognizing the application of this self-regenerating process beyond sculpture, Bettina produced a computer-programmed 16 mm film in 1975–76 based on the finite possibilities of squares cut into at right angles.[20] Moving between drawing, sculpture, photography, and film, *Finite Structures* demonstrates how Bettina's use of a "random constant" results in a necessarily fluid approach to media. Bettina described this approach in the title of one of her portfolios: *Interrelative Intergenerative Interdisciplines / Dynamics of Continuity: Theory and Experiment / Photography and Sculpture*.

Two other marble works from Bettina's 1970 visit to Italy offer a figurative counterpoint to her permutation-based eggs and cubes inscribed with right angles. In a pair of marble spheres titled *Croce / Pace* (date unknown), orthogonal cuts and the swapping of black and white sections yield a cross and a peace sign. A singular black-and-white marble piece, *The Floating Yolk: Oscillation in Rotation* (1970), resembles a hard-boiled egg cut in half. In their combination of iconic reference and geometric form, these pieces evoke Pop as well as Minimal art.

In 1970, Bettina also spent time in France where she produced a series of drawings and wood sculptures titled *French Keys* (1971–72). According to Bettina, the keys were a "figurative series" that began "on [the] paper tablecloths of Paris."[21] Elongated and jagged, they resemble the notched shafts of keys or the edges of puzzle pieces. However, they are not figurative in the sense that they represent keys. Bettina treated them like hieroglyphs or pictographic signs akin to the peace and cross symbols she represented in marble. One denotes a "fleeing figure." Another, shown as a positive "key" below a negative "key-hole" conveys the message: "Man out of His Expected Situation."[22] The keys are what Bochner refers to as "multiple variants," as opposed to a serial work, since their forms are improvised by the artist rather than determined by a mathematical system. As pseudo-pictographs, however, they form their own arbitrary system like any written language. The positive-negative relationship between key and keyhole not only offers another metaphor for photography; it also points to the binary oppositions that structure language according to Swiss linguist Ferdinand de Saussure, whose theories gained prominence in France in the 1950s and '60s.

Bettina's first *Word Work* was also composed in Paris in 1970 and, according to her records, acquired by the mayor of Zurich.[23] A list of rhyming words—*expression*, *repression*, *digression*, *suppression*, *depression*, *oppression*, *regression*, *aggression*—the work is also generated from a "random constant," that is, the last two syllables shared by all the words. Related phonetically more than semantically, the string of words is a sound poem. Rendered in tightly spaced, sans serif capital letters, it is also a visual poem. Indeed, Bettina also produced a diagram of abstract "verbal forms" derived from the *Word Works*.[24] If the keys treat pictures as words, the *Word Works* to some degree treat words as pictures.

Noumenon/Phenomenon

Bettina called her studio apartment at the Chelsea Hotel in New York, where she had resided since the early 1970s, "The Institute for Noumenological Research."[25] The opposite of a phenomenon, a noumenon is a Kantian thing-in-itself that exists beyond human perception. Like a Platonic form, the noumenon is the essence rather than the appearance of an object. Bettina's "constants" are the noumena that transcend their multiple and multimedia manifestations in her work. "[When] looking for the basic essence of something and translating it into another material," Bettina expounded, "it doesn't matter if it's a two-dimensional material or a three-dimensional material or if it is applied to industry because it is still the same one thing."[26] For Bettina, the noumenon is mystical as well as philosophical—a metaphysical or spiritual force that guided her work and may even be glimpsed in it.[27]

In *Phenomenological New York / Urban Energy Strategies, Traffic Patterns*, a body of work in photography, film, and video begun in 1972, Bettina foregrounded phenomena rather than noumena.[28] The series began with photographs of reflections in New York's glass buildings—an apt metaphor for appearances rather than essences. Bettina emphasized that these are not reflections, or at least not "straight reflections," but "distortions."[29] Indeed, her camera captured a seemingly endless stream of cars and pedestrians warped and fragmented by seams in sheet glass and revolving doors. As Bettina observed, "If you go to certain buildings at certain hours when the light is right, you will find

BETTINA ARTIST/SCULPTOR/PHOTO-DOCUMENTARIAN

A CRITICAL COMMENT BY REINHOLD HOHL ART HISTORIAN

BETTINA is an extremely serious and hard-working artist with original ideas of unforseeable consequences. Among all the aspects of contemporary life she has chosen the most disturbing one as the underlying theme of her sculptural and photographic works: the modern bondage to the concept of great numbers, and our subjection to constant change. Choices are to be made from seemingly unlimited numbers of possibilities; but the number, however large, is limited; that this is a finite world with no transcendence unless we accept the equality of all possibilities, and recognize in each and every one the mystery of the HERE AND NOW.

This drama of servitude and liberty is embodied in BETTINA's works, in their many serial forms, in their four-dimensional concerns. Projects like DEDIMENSION (of three-dimensional objects by using their two-dimensional projections) generate forms which are both full of a hidden artistic history and valid in their own right. Many of her projects explore with rare logic and insight the realm of the creation of FORM and structure and of CREATIVITY in general.

BETTINA's recent works, results of a lucid and stubborn research, are rich in multiple aspects, containing in one final formulation almost the whole span of her preceding works. Her photographic documentation dramatizes the daily urban bondage and the infinite numbers of escapes through mirage and illusion in the most formidable yet easily approachable way. She shows how every step along our way can be filled with potential revelations; how the city is transformed into an absolutely miraculous adventureland. It took the sensitivity and consummate art of BETTINA to transcend the reality and bring forth a definitive artistic creation.

If it seems sometimes that there is no alternative to the servitude of contemporary existence - here is one - in BETTINA's sculptural and photographic art.

R.HOHL author of GIACOMETTI(N.Y.ABRAMS 1972)/ consultant to BEYELER GALLERIES,
1974 BASEL

Letter by art historian Reinhold Hohl, included in Bettina's CV, 1974

fantastic surrealism created by the sun on the architecture."[30] Though the series began as still photographs, she soon realized that film would better capture the subject. "The film had to be made," Bettina explained, "[because] if I just took stills you would never see how one thing changes into another."[31] Indeed, the films emphasize change rather than a constant; shifting phenomena rather than a stable noumenon.

Bettina's undulating tabletop sculptures in wood, *Restructure / Seastructure: From Euclidean to Non-Euclidean Curve with Developable Absolute* (1973), echo the wavy reflections she photographed in glass.[32] Each of these began as an identical disc composed of eighty-six wooden strips—another "random constant"—that are glued together in staggered positions to yield various curved formations. Bettina conceived of them as models for monumental sculptures that remain unrealized. By photographing them in different positions against a solid background, however, she made them appear potentially much larger than their actual ten inches in diameter. Bettina's practice of photographing sculpture thus assumes yet another role. In addition to its documentary and metaphorical function, photography is used here as a tool of sculptural transformation, turning maquettes into monuments. In sequence, the photographs also suggest a stop-motion animation, emphasizing the implied motion in each static form. The photographic progression also highlights metamorphosis rather than constancy.

Like reflections, shadows are another exemplar of fluctuating phenomena in Bettina's work. Her "two-line limitation" in metal, a large armature in the form of a circle attached to two angles, is mounted a few inches from the wall so that it casts strong shadows. "Every time the sun changes its position," Bettina explained, "the sculpture will become multiple variations of its original self."[33] In this way, Bettina sought to include all possible permutations in a single sculpture, rather than capturing single permutations in a series of sculptures.

Photo-Text-Sculpture

In 1977, Bettina applied her "random constant" theory to street photography with *The Fifth Point of the Compass / Studies in Random Constant / New York From A to Z / Demographics on Twenty-Third Street.* From her balcony on the fifth floor of the Chelsea Hotel on Twenty-Third Street, she photographed different people doing the same things, such as carrying a package or lighting a cigarette. "I would stand there all day," Bettina recalled, waiting for certain actions or motifs to repeat themselves.[34] The resulting photographs reveal consistent patterns in lived reality. Of these patterns, Bettina exclaimed: "That's the noumenon. You find mystical things occurring when you concentrate on something. Something else will come into being and reinforce what preceded it."[35] Each photograph has an identical composition: an aerial view of a figure and their shadow at the center, set against the grid of the sidewalk flush with the picture plane. The random constant across the series, then, is not the various recurring motifs but the fixed perspective of the camera.

In an exhibition of *The Fifth Point of the Compass* at the OK Harris gallery in 1980—Bettina's first solo show in New York—color prints were mounted on cardboard in thematic groupings of fifty. As indicated in the series' full title, the themes were presented alphabetically from *Apple and Afro* to *Yo-Yo and Zebrastripe*. The OK Harris presentation included only the *R* series—*Rain / Runner / Reader / Radio / Red*—a succession of titles that evokes her *Word Works*. Bettina's series *Headlines* (date unknown), also shot from her balcony, incorporates text within the photograph itself. In these works, figures hold newspapers whose alarming headlines, such as "Help me, I'm being killed," become the focal point of the scene.

Barbara Millstein, the late curator of photography at the Brooklyn Museum, characterized *The Fifth Point of the Compass* as "anthropology as much as photography."[36] The full title of the project references the related field of demography, which also studies human populations. In its documentation of a cross section of society, the project calls to mind the ethnographic and demographic photography of August Sanders. Of course, Sanders' categories such as "woman" and "farmer" are more properly demographic than "apple" and "yo-yo." The premise and presentation of *The Fifth Point of the Compass* is more akin to Photoconceptualism from the 1960s and '70s, in which photographs follow an arbitrary linguistic directive and are often displayed in seemingly neutral grids. The absurdity of documenting every passerby with a yo-yo or a box resonates in particular with the deadpan humor of Douglas Huebler's *Variable Piece #70* (1971) that aimed to document the existence of everyone alive.

In high-contrast photocopies of the photographs from *The Fifth Point of the Compass*, Bettina foregrounded the strange silhouettes of figure-and-shadow units viewed from above. Subtitled *Photographs/Wallforms*, these photocopies suggest Bettina's intention to translate the warped figural outlines into sculptures. Indeed, while Bettina's sculptures served as subjects for her photographs, her photographs sometimes became the basis of drawings and sculptures. As the artist Robert Blackburn astutely observed of Bettina's work: "The photography, film, sculpture are as one, for the photographic medium is employed not only for documentation, but as an endless source of inspiration from which other disciplines emerge—and merge."[37]

Forty-two years after *HFD* featured Bettina as a rising designer, she was relegated by the *New York Times* to a mention as "a talented and prolific artist in the 1960s and '70s who had become a recluse over the past 30 years."[38] Though Bettina was included in several international group shows in the 1970s and early 1980s, and was given a solo exhibition by OK Harris in 1980, she never secured the support necessary to fully realize and exhibit all of her projects. As she quipped to a Swedish critic reviewing the OK Harris exhibition, "Female artists ... have an extra hard time in a world that assesses artistic quality with the same yardstick as stock-market speculators assess General Motors's or Three Mile Island's profitability."[39] In the late 2000s, renewed attention was paid to her work with films by documentary artist Sam Bassett and filmmaker

Corinne van der Borch, which focused on Bettina not only as the last holdover from the Chelsea Hotel's bohemian heyday, but also as an underappreciated artist whose work should be seen.

Still, the American abstract artist's unique oeuvre was rarely seen and largely overlooked by the art world until 2019, when a two-woman show with Yto Barrada at the Lower Manhattan Cultural Council's space on Governors Island coincided with Bettina's ninety-second birthday. Barrada and Swiss designer Gregor Huber have now collaborated to bring us this book. The self-regenerating nature of Bettina's work allows us to imagine it continuing from past to present and on to infinity. In an interview from the 1980s, Bettina asserted that the ultimate point of her projects "was to prove they were all endless; a resolution rather than a conclusion."[40]

1. Dorothy Kalins, "HFD Says Bettina Has It," *Home Furnishings Daily*, November 3, 1966, p. 7.
2. Ibid.
3. Bettina Grossman, "Interrelative Intergenerative Interdisciplines / Dynamics of Continuity: Theory and Experiment / Photography and Sculpture," undated album owned by the artist documenting her oeuvre (hereafter cited as III). Several similar patterns are reproduced in the album with the caption "Multiple Field Theory, London, 1962" and titled according to the number of "constants" and "surfaces" employed (e.g., "Two Constants. Two Surfaces" and "One Constant. Three Surfaces").
4. Kalins, "HFD Says Bettina Has It," p. 7.
5. "Bettina: A Designer Talks about Her Color Photography," *Camera 35* 9, no. 6 (October/November 1965): p. 29.
6. Bettina Grossman, interview by Juliette Elkon Hamelecourt, ca. 1980, recording, Juliette Elkon Hamelecourt papers, 1911–2000, bulk 1940s–2000, Archives of American Art, Smithsonian Institution, Washington, DC.
7. Ibid.
8. Ibid.
9. Title taken from III. An alternate title, *Two Planes: 24 Inconstants from One Constant*, appears in an accordion album devoted solely to the eggs, owned by the artist.
10. Bettina Grossman, application for a grant from the Adolph and Esther Gottlieb Foundation, n.d., Bettina archives.
11. Hamelecourt, interview with Bettina, Archives of American Art.
12. III.
13. A diagram in III shows nine rows of nine egg outlines, some of which are partitioned by four right angles. Extant egg sculptures that do not match photographs of the dozen in III and appear to have more than one orthogonal cut may possibly be from the series *Half a Dozen Eggs/Two-Line Limitation* listed in "Titles," undated typescript, Bettina archives.
14. See Roxana Marcoci, "Constantin Brancusi: The Studio as *Groupe Mobile* and the *Photos Radieuses*," in *The Original Copy: Photography of Sculpture, 1839–Today* (New York: Museum of Modern Art, 2010), pp. 96–99.
15. Teja Bach makes a similar argument, quoted in Marcoci, *Original Copy*, p. 99.
16. Title taken from "List of Slides," undated typescript, Bettina archives. A contact sheet of Bettina's photographs of the marble cubes has an alternate title on the back: *Eight Equal Elements of Diminishing Displacement.* In III the marble cubes are captioned: "Contained Possibility Structure Limitation: 281, 792, 804, 290 / Marble Constants – Volume Relocation – 1970 Italy."
17. III includes a progression of squares cut into at right angles dated 1963. Bettina recounts, "In 1962, I began experimenting with absolute forms and their relation to each other. They were redeveloped in 1967 and 8 after the fire. And in 1970 in Italy this same project was developed into cubic volumes in black and white marble." Hamelecourt, interview with Bettina, Archives of American Art.
18. Mel Bochner, "The Serial Attitude," *Artforum* 6, no. 4, December 1967, pp. 28–33.
19. Hamelecourt, interview with Bettina, Archives of American Art.
20. Ibid. and III.
21. "List of Slides," undated typescript, Bettina archives.
22. III.
23. III.
24. This diagram appears in III.
25. Corey Kilgannon, "At a Haven for Creative Souls, a Prolific Talent Is Affirmed," *New York Times*, May 11, 2008.
26. Hamelecourt, interview with Bettina, Archives of American Art.
27. "Bettina's Institute for Noumenological Research Reestablished at the Chelsea," *Hotel Chelsea Blog*, December 10, 2007, https://www.chelseahotelblog.com/living_with_legends_the_h/2007/12/bettinas-instit.html.
28. The date 1972 comes from notes on a photocopy of a photograph from the series, Bettina archives.
29. Hamelecourt, interview with Bettina, Archives of American Art.
30. Ibid.
31. *Girl with Black Balloons*, directed by Corinne van der Borch (New York: Wondertime Films, 2010), 59 min.
32. Title taken from "List of Slides," undated typescript, Bettina archives.
33. Van der Borch, *Girl with Black Balloons.*
34. Bettina Grossman, conversation with the author, February 19, 2021.
35. Van der Borch, *Girl with Black Balloons.*
36. Barbara Millstein, "Bettina: A Critical Review of Her Work," 1981, Bettina archives.
37. Robert Blackburn, "Critical Review," 1986, Bettina archives.
38. Kilgannon, "At a Haven for Creative Souls."
39. Peder Edström, "Bettina," *Foto*, April 1981, p. 83. Translation from Swedish by the author.
40. Hamelecourt, interview with Bettina, Archives of American Art.

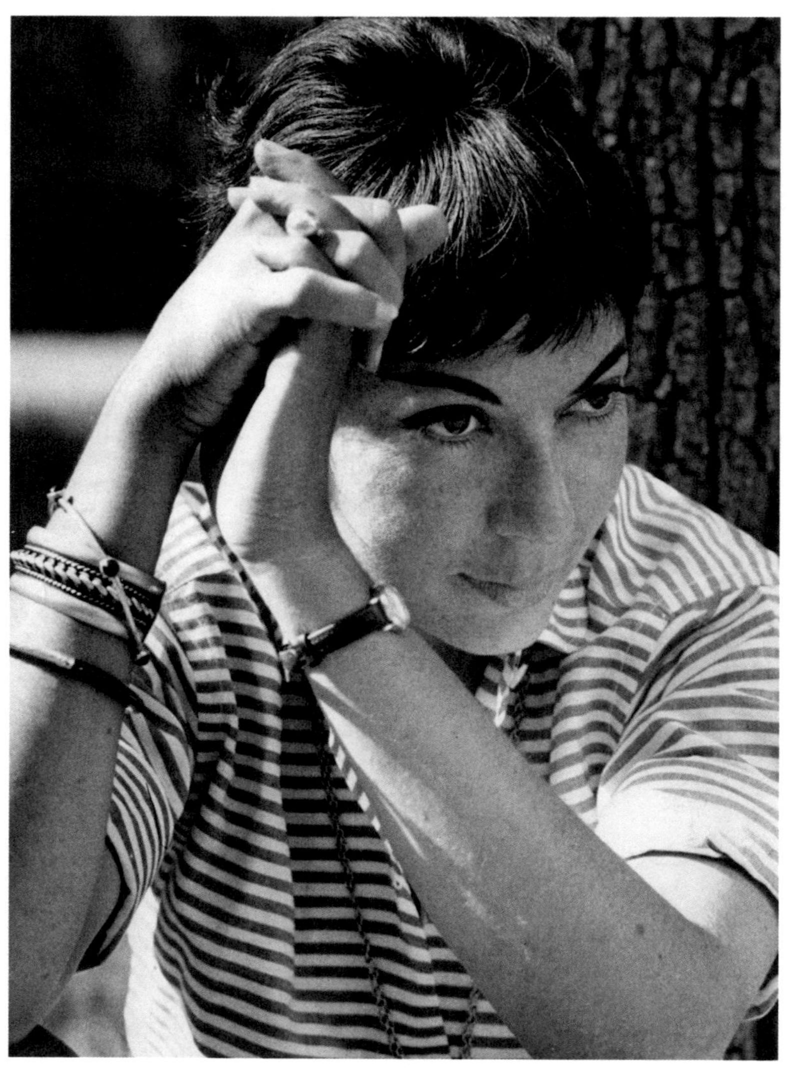

 Bettina, 1960s

Chronology

Bettina Grossman was born in New York in 1927. She attended the Girls' Commercial High School (now Prospect Heights High School) from 1942 to 1946, and upon graduation received a scholarship to Parsons School of Design, which she turned down to work in fabric design. In 1957, after working as a stylist for a textile company in New York,[1] she traveled to Europe with the intention of staying for one year but ended up staying through 1965. She designed fabric in Paris and London, silver in Stockholm, and mosaic floors in Italy. During this time, she also served as a color coordinator for Knoll Associates and developed new color combinations for the William Morris Society collection. By the mid-'60s, she had also started to work on her photography and her color photographs were featured in a 1965 issue of *Camera 35* magazine.[2] In 1966, Bettina returned to New York and established a studio in Brooklyn Heights[3], signing her work as Bettina or Bettina/Bashyi. In New York she, encountered Op art and Systemic Painting, which she declared to be "not far at all" from the work she had produced in Europe.[4] In December of 1966, a fire in her Brooklyn Heights studio destroyed her work up to that date and killed her cat. Following this devastating event Bettina returned to Europe, including travel to Italy, thanks to an award received in 1970.[5] Upon her return to New York around 1972, she moved to the Chelsea Hotel. She intended to eventually go back to Europe to work, but she was unable to raise the money to do so, and fell ill.[6]

The CV presented here details her exhibition history and key works created from 1967 through 1983. Much of this work remained unexplored and unnoted for decades, except for participation in Mail art exhibitions, and an occasional review, as in, for example, a 1981 piece in *Foto* (Sweden). In 2008 Sam Bassett made a short film entitled *Bettina*. In 2010, Corinne van der Borch released her film, *Girl with Black Balloons*, which led to Bettina's encounter with artist Yto Barrada. In 2019, Bettina exhibited alongside Barrada in *The Power of Two Suns* at the Lower Manhattan Cultural Council space at Governors Island, curated by Omar Berrada. In 2020, a selection of her sculptures was shown in *Every Boy Deserves Good Fudge*, an exhibition at the Sfeir-Semler Gallery in Hamburg, Germany, organized by Barrada; and in 2021, selected works were exhibited as part of *Artist's Choice: Yto Barrada—A Raft* at the Museum of Modern Art, New York. Bettina's work was also included in MoMA PS1's *Greater New York 2021* survey. In 2020, Barrada and the designer Gregor Huber began to produce a book of Bettina's work, a draft of which won the Luma Rencontres Dummy Book Award Arles 2020. This book was developed in collaboration with Bettina up until her death in November 2021.

1. Dorothy Kalins, "HFD Says Bettina Has It," *Home Furnishings Daily*, November 3, 1966, p. 7.
2. Kalins, "HFD Says Bettina Has It," p. 7; "Bettina: A Designer Talks about Her Color Photography," *Camera 35* 9, no. 6 (October/November 1965): p. 29; Bettina Grossman, interview by Juliette Elkon Hamelecourt, ca. 1980, recording, Juliette Elkon Hamelecourt papers, 1911–2000, bulk 1940s–2000, Archives of American Art, Smithsonian Institution, Washington, DC.
3. "Bettina: A Designer Talks about Her Color Photography," p. 26; Hamelecourt, interview with Bettina, Archives of American Art.
4. Kalins, "HFD Says Bettina Has It," p. 7.
5. Bettina Grossman, application for a National Endowment for the Arts grant, n.d., Bettina archives; Hamelecourt, interview with Bettina, Archives of American Art.
6. Hamelecourt, interview with Bettina, Archives of American Art.

BETTINA

BORN IN NEW YORK
AUTO-DIDACTIC

TEN YEARS EUROPE - research & experiment I7 countries
ALL WORKS DESTROYED BY FIRE - NEW YORK I966

EURO-ASIAN DOCUMENT - ISTANBUL I967 - theory & experiment/STUDIES IN RANDOM CONSTANT INFRASTRUCTURE / TURKISH TRANSPORT- MAN AS VEHICLE - FIXED FOCUS/BOSPHORUS BOATS ISLAMIC PATTERN/ CONTINUOUS-LINE CONSTRUCTS

VENETIAN DOCUMENT - - ITALY I967,70 - theory & experiment/STUDIES IN RANDOM CONSTANT INFRASTRUCTURE / VENETIAN TRANSPORT-BYZANTINE/GOTHIC/RENAISSANCE WINDOWS
REMAKE - originally published I966 IRONWORKS- MOSAIC PATTERN

LINEAR DOCUMENTS - NEW YORK I967-84 - SYSTEMS OF LINEAR TRANSPORT - ENGRAVINGS
RELATIVE AND EVOLUTIONARY SYSTEMS OF LOGICAL CONSTRUCTS-DRAWINGS

MARBLE SCULPTURE FELLOWSHIP - ITALY I970 - experiments in stone process

problems explored - -	FRACTIONS	divisible totalities
	PHENOMENOLOGY	oscillation
functional sculpture	FINITE STRUCTURES	auto-regeneration
architecture	PLANE/CIRCUMFERENCE	penetration
INSIDE-OUTSIDE HOUSE	SERIAL STRUCTURE	relocation
	DISPLACED ABSOLUTE	dislocation
	THE FOURTH DIMENSION	two-line limitation

INTERNATIONAL PHYSICS SUMMER SCHOOL - VARENNA,ITALY I970 - conference of mathematicians
presented FOUR-DIMENSIONAL THEORIES OF AUTO-REGENERATING CONSTANTS
resolved FINITE STRUCTURES / six to the eighth power

REBORN PARIS I970

PARISIAN DOCUMENT - I970-7I
MASTERWORKS OF THE LONDON PLANE (trees)
INTERRELATIVE STRUCTURES
INTEGREE/DESINTEGREE construct/destruct
WORDWORKS I and II concrete poetry
theory & experiment COLOR CONSTRUCT - - AUBUSSON TAPESTRY / STAINED GLASS / FOTOWORK

SCULPTURE SERIES / WOOD - NEW YORK I972-3- DIVISIBLE TOTALITIES
PROGRESSIVE ELEVATION
penetration/dislocation/relocation/auto-regeneration/limitation
RESTRUCTURE/SEASTRUCTURE -one constant
from euclidean to non-euclidean curve with developable absolute

MUSEUM OF MODERN ART - NEW YORK I97I , 2 , 3 , 4 , 5 , 6 ART LENDING SERVICE
PHOTOGRAPHY / SCULPTURE

ARTISTS FOR ENCOUNTER (drug rehabilitation project) NEW YORK I972 - SOHO GALLERY

NEW YORK PHENOMENOLOGICAL DOCUMENT - I972-77- STILLS & MOTION CAMERA
RELOCATION DYNAMICS /URBAN ENERGY STRATEGIES
THE FOURTH DIMENSION / FIXED FOCUS STUDIES
FILMWORKS - I976-77 EXPERIMENTS IN SELF-REGENERATING ENERGIES

FILMWORKS - I975- FINITE STRUCTURES - computer-generated
used in course of study TEMPLE UNIVERSITY

AUDIOWORKS - NEW YORK I966-7 THE NEW YORK SOUND
AUDIOWORKS - NEW YORK I976-8 (one constant) SELECTIVE RETENTION theory & experiment

NEW YORK SOCIO-HISTORICAL DOCUMENT -I977- THE FIFTH POINT OF THE COMPASS
23rd STREET DEMOGRAPHICS - studies in random constant / fixed focus
RAIN/RUNNER/READER/RADIO/RED - exhibited O.K.HARRIS I980 - 25,000 visitors
TIME-LAPSE I977-I984 published FOTO magazine STOCKHOLM I98I

SHANGO -shrine object sculpture series - NEW YORK I98I - NON-WAIVER/ THE CUTTING EDGE
the active essence of non-action/the passive essence of action

BETTINA II

EXHIBITIONS

I983 ABBAYE DES PREMONTRES - PONT-A-MOUSSON, FRANCE - 'CULT OBJECT'
MUSEU GALEGO DE ARTE CONTEMPORANEO - PONTEVEDRA, SPAIN - 'BIENAL DE PONTEVEDRA'
NEXUS GALLERY - PHILADELPHIA - 'RAINFALL OF THE WORLD'
CHICAGO CENTER FOR CONTEMPORARY PHOTOGRAPHY - COLUMBIA COLLEGE - 'COLOR'
SRI LANKA - 'CEYLON INTERNATIONAL'
PHOTOFACTORY - KONGSBERG, NORWAY - 'COLOR PHOTOGRAPHY'

I982 SKANDINAVISKA ENSKILDA BANKEN (SCANDINAVIAN BANK) - STOCKHOLM - acquisitions
PORDENONE, ITALY - 'SALVIAMO VENEZIA'
STOCKHOLM - 'WOMEN FOR PEACE'
AUSTRALIAN MUSEUM - 'SYDNEY INTERNATIONAL'

I98I VISUAL STUDIES WORKSHOP - ROCHESTER - 'SERIAL-IMAGE BOOKS' center for book arts
INTERNATIONAL CENTER OF PHOTOGRAPHY - 'SERIAL-IMAGE BOOKS' center for book arts
CENTRE DE DOCUMENTACIO D'ART ACTUAL - BARCELONA - 'ARTISTS BOOKS INTERNATIONAL'
INSTITUTE OF ADVANCED THINKING - BELFAST, MAINE - 'VERBAL AND VISUAL POETRY'
CENTRO PER UN LINGUAGGIO ARTISTICO UNIVERSALE - CASTEL SAN GIORGIO, ITALY - 'FANTASTIC ART INTERNATIONAL'
ARTPOOL BUDAPEST - HUNGARY - 'POSTAGESTAMP ART'
LODZ KALISKA - LODZ, POLAND - 'INTERNATIONAL COLLECTIONS'
MUSEU DE JOCS I JOGUETS - FIGUERES, SPAIN - 'ARTGAMES AND PUZZLES'
OHIO STATE UNIVERSITY - COLUMBUS - 'SELF-PORTRAIT COLLABORATIONS'
SCHOOL OF THE BOSTON MUSEUM OF FINE ARTS - MASSACHUSETTES - 'NEVER-FAIL IMAGE'

I980 MUSEUM OF THE CITY OF NEW YORK - 'NEW YORK COLLECTS' acquisitions

* O.K.HARRIS GALLERY - NEW YORK - SOLO SHOW - 'THE FIFTH POINT OF THE COMPASS'
studies in random constant- RAIN/RUNNER/READER/RADIO/RED/

CENTRE DE DOCUMENTACIO D'ART ACTUAL - BARCELONA - 'TRAMESA POSTAL INTERNATIONAL'

I979 GALERIE JOAN PRATS - BARCELONA - 'FESTA DE LA LLETRA'
APROPOS GALLERY - LUZERN, SWITZERLAND - 'RUBBERSTAMP ART'
OBERHAUSEN SHORT FILM FESTIVAL - GERMANY - 'URBAN ENERGY STRATEGIES' 3 minutes

---

I978 CARACAS SUPER 8 FILM FESTIVAL - VENEZUELA - 'URBAN ENERGY STRATEGIES' I2 minutes
AUDIOART ARCHIVE - LUZERN - 'ONE CONSTANT / SELECTIVE RETENTION' en permanence
SUN VALLEY CENTER FOR THE ARTS AND HUMANITIES - IDAHO - 'MINERAL & VEGETABLE'
NEW YORK UNIVERSITY - 'SMALL WORKS INTERNATIONAL'
PS I - NEW YORK - 'ORGANIZATION OF INDEPENDENT ARTISTS'
BOLOGNA ART FAIR - ITALY - 'ORGANIZATION OF INDEPENDENT ARTISTS'
BASEL ART FAIR - SWITZERLAND - 'ORGANIZATION OF INDEPENDENT ARTISTS'

Yto Barrada and Gregor Huber
would like to thank:

Bettina Grossman (1927–2021)
Jacques Loire - Maître Verrier (1932–2021)

This project would not have been possible without generous contributions by the following individuals:

Andrea Andersson
Anonymous
Sarah Audu
Negar Azimi
Lauren Banogon
Regine Basha
Laura Beccavin
Alice Bennahmias
Meriem Bennani
Charles Benton
Omar Berrada
Ragini Bhow
Nour Bishouty
Corinne van der Borch
River Bullock
Akvile Bukauskaite
Marina Caron
Léa Chikhani
Lili Chopra
Margherita Ciocci
Laurent Claquin
Rachel Cohen-Lunning
Stuart Comer
Tamara Corm
Andrew Cruz
Corey Escoto
Hannah Feldman
Gerald Franciosa
Giovanna Franciosa
Lucy Gallun
Aliza Green
Mordechai Grossman
Sean Gullette
Tamo Barrada Gullette
Véga Barrada Gullette
Kristina Harrison
Louis Heilbronn
Andria Hickey
Ruba Katrib
Caroline Kent
Peter Ketchum
Varun Khanna
Kelly Kivland
Margaret Kristensen
Alexis Lowry
Bruno Loire
Hervé Loire
LUMA Foundation
Laura Minnear
Maysoun Mokhtar
Noha Mokhtar
Mono No Aware
Arman Naféei
Cécile Nedelec
Deborah Needleman
Lauren Panzo
Giovanna Peppe
Cara Marie Piazza
Antonia Pocock
Francesca Pollock
Elodie Pong
George Rayson
Susan Reiner
Sarah Riggs
Alice Russotti
Paul Sado
Andrée Sfeir-Semler
Shirana Shahbazi
Ruth Shomron
Josh Siegel
Ana Siler
Montana Simone
Samantha "Slats" Slatwinski
Jana Stardelova
Frédéric Tcheng
Stacey Testa
Wendy Vanden Heuvel
Mira Van den Neste
Cyndi Vasquez
Christoph Wiesner
Cooper Winterson

Additional thanks to:

Galerie Sfeir-Semler
Pace Gallery

Published on the occasion of the exhibition, *Bettina*, presented at Les Rencontres d'Arles 2022.

This book was the winner of the 6th edition of the LUMA Rencontres Dummy Book Award Arles in 2020. Its publication was made possible by the founders of the award.

ARLES LES RENCONTRES DE LA PHOTOGRAPHIE LUMA

www.rencontres-arles.com

This publication has also received the support of *Women In Motion*, a program of Kering to shine a light on women in arts and culture, as part of its LAB.

Bettina
Photographs and works by Bettina Grossman
Texts by Yto Barrada, Ruba Katrib, and Antonia Pocock

This book was edited by Yto Barrada and Gregor Huber

Research and development: Yto Barrada and Studio

Design: Huber/Sterzinger

The Bettina Grossman archive remains largely unprocessed. When possible, individual works, series, portfolio titles, and dates have been identified according to documentation left by Bettina. Some can be identified by titles and dates that appear typed on the works themselves. In cases where information was unavailable or unconfirmed at the time of publication, no information is given.

Scans: My Own Color Lab
Photography (pp. 146-53): Ateliers Loire
Photography (pp. 229-66): Charles Benton

Atelier EXB staff:
Editor: Nathalie Chapuis
Proofreading: Marc Feustel
Production: Charlotte Debiolles
Color separation: Les Artisans du Regard, Paris
Partnerships: Yseult Chehata
Distribution: Perrine Somma

The Aperture staff for the English-language edition includes:

Creative Director: Lesley A. Martin
Associate Editor: Samantha Marlow
Senior Text Editor: Susan Ciccotti
Copy Editor: Claire Voon
Proofreader: Elena Goukassian

Additional staff of the Aperture book program includes:

Sarah Meister, Executive Director
Taia Kwinter, Publishing Manager
Emily Patten, Publishing Assistant
Kellie McLaughlin, Chief Sales and Marketing Officer
Richard Gregg, Sales Director, Books
Giada De Agostinis, Publicist

Aperture's programs are made possible, in part, by the New York State Council on the Arts with the support of the Office of the Governor and the New York State Legislature.

First Aperture edition, 2022
Printed by Printer Trento, in Italy, May 2022
in an edition of 2,500 copies
10 9 8 7 6 5 4 3 2 1

Library of Congress Control Number: 2022905415
ISBN 978-1-59711-542-1

To order Aperture books, or inquire about gift or group orders, contact:
+1 212.946.7154
orders@aperture.org

For information about Aperture trade distribution worldwide, visit:
aperture.org/distribution

aperture

548 West 28th Street, 4th Floor
New York, NY 10001
aperture.org

Aperture, a not-for-profit foundation, connects the photo community and its audiences with the most inspiring work, the sharpest ideas, and with each other—in print, in person, and online.

WHAT WE WANT :

LOGIC →	REASON →	RATIONALITY
ORDER	STRUCTURE	STABILITY
ETHICS	VALUES	MORALITY
PERCEPTION	PERSPECTIVE	OBJECTIVITY
KNOWLEDGE	EXPERIENCE	DIDACTICITY
CHALLENGE	DISCIPLINE	CAPABILITY
COURAGE	CONVICTION	CONTINUITY
PROFESSIONALISM	MERIT	EFFICACITY
COMMITMENT	MOTIVATION	PRODUCTIVITY
ALTRUISM	VISION	MAGNANIMITY
DIALOGUE	COMMUNICATION	CONGRUITY
OPTION	ALTERNATIVE	POSSIBILITY
AESTHETICS	HARMONY	CREATIVITY
VERACITY	AUTHENTICITY	INTEGRITY
RELIABILITY	ACCOUNTABILITY	CIVILITY
MATURITY	PROFUNDITY	EMPATHY
DESTINY	RELATIVITY	ETERNITY

WHAT WE GET :

REALITY